D0975151

Though built by different denominations, these
three churches on the South Dakota prairie all bear
the unequivocal stamp "Made in America." Their
architectural similarity belies the religious freedom
and diversity that thrived under their roofs.
(*Courtesy Dorothea Lange Collection, © The City of
Oakland, The Oakland Museum, 1938*)

PILGRIMS IN
THEIR
OWN LAND

500 Years of Religion in America

MARTIN E. MARTY

LITTLE, BROWN AND COMPANY
Boston   Toronto

FIRST EDITION

Jacques Maritain, from *Reflections on America*, copyright © 1958
Jacques Maritain. Used with the permission of
Charles Scribner's Sons.

For Harriet Julia

But one man loved the pilgrim soul in you, . . .
— W. B. Yeats

Library of Congress Cataloging in Publication Data

Marty, Martin E., 1928–
  Pilgrims in their own land.

  Bibliography: p.
  Includes index.
  1. United States—Church history.   2. United States—
Religion.   I. Title.
BR515.M324 1984   291'.0973   84-821
ISBN 0-316-54867-7

MV

Designed by Patricia G. Dunbar

*Published simultaneously in Canada
by Little, Brown & Company (Canada) Limited*

PRINTED IN THE UNITED STATES OF AMERICA

CONTENTS

PREFACE

HALF A THOUSAND YEARS AGO, PEOPLE FROM EUROPE (AND LATER, from Africa and Asia) entered the American hemisphere. Their explorers encountered many nomadic peoples, and their settlers jostled tribal settlements in the New World. They came to stay. Yet after almost five hundred years, the astute French observer Jacques Maritain concluded, their citizen heirs were still not truly installed. While only a few important immigrants bear the name Pilgrim in the American myth, most of the new arrivals came as pilgrims from other lands — and pilgrims they have remained in their new land.

Maritain said they have been prodded by a dream. For some, the dream meant escape from imprisonment, slavery, indebtedness, low status, or poverty. For others, it drew upon the lure of freedom from harassment and persecution, often of a religious character. Still others, tragically, were forced into slavery by their move to the New World. In almost every major case, the people made sense of their movements by reference to religious stories and symbols.

The vast American landscape immediately became — and has remained — an environment of both threat and promise. The spiritual search of the people was often designed to minimize the chaos of their milieu. They also had to make sense of the chaos of peoples around them, for this landscape beckoned — and it keeps beckoning. Never before in history have so many different religious groups had to coexist. Seldom have even several done so with so little bloodshed, even as the believers were able to hold to their faiths with integrity.

This is not a story of simple success. Newcomers may have been prodded by dreams of self-betterment. They did not always provide for others or for the justice necessary between persons and peoples. Measured by the call to justice that stamps so many of their faiths, they have failed to capture the vision or live up to it. At the same time, it should be noted that much of the most eloquent and effective calling for judgment upon their failures has come from prophets who draw words and images from the religious traditions themselves.

Where leaders of migrations imported religious views, they found it necessary to do much adapting. Where old systems weakened or visions grew dim, new ones were invented. Because of the wild diversity of the options, it is impossible to find a single ideological thread uniting the Americans in their spiritual pilgrimage. One might glance at some choices, none of which stands up to scrutiny. Thus:

Of course, the republican religion of reasonable Enlightenment-era founders left a stamp on institutions, but few citizens live or die by that religion today. Of course, most citizens recall a biblical culture, but the Bible is no official part of American creedal life. Of course, most religious institutions have been Jewish or Christian, but thousands of other kinds of institutions freely propagate their beliefs and ways. Of course, Puritan Protestantism forcefully shaped much of early America and indirectly influences it still, but millions do not recognize the ethos and many reject it. Of course, one can make a religion of pragmatism and practicality, but how do we account for the many who sacrifice themselves and live by improbable creeds?

To put the name *chaos* on chaos is the first step in ordering. Henceforth, one can follow the plot. A book called *Patterns of Anarchy* begins to order disorder. So to see the interplay of pilgrim peoples and the dreams that prod them is to begin to discern a common theme that helps describe not merely "religion in America" but "American religion." Wandering is not a new theme in religious history. Stories of pilgrimages, exiles, and exoduses are familiar in other sacred histories. Yet religion has ordinarily imparted to citizens a "settled" cast. It helps form bonds of tradition that root people within specific landscapes and near familiar people.

Some Americans tried to settle things by legally establishing religion, but establishment could not last. Many have lived in self-enclosed groups marked by ethnic and religious ties. Yet the traditional patterns keep being disrupted. No leader is secure. Representatives of rival faiths are always standing by or riding into town to provoke response from the bored and the restless. No followers have to spend their generations locked into a specific system.

America therefore helped patent freedom *for* choice as well as freedom *of* choice in religion. As such, it can be seen as the first and most modern society. Today, as freedom and choice have both expanded and many citizens follow completely personal and private quests, we might even speak of an ultramodern phase in the American pilgrimage.

While the story of American religious institutions has been told often and well, it has reached only a small portion of the public. *Pilgrims in Their Own Land* focuses instead on women and men of vision who were pathfinders, who attracted followers in search of "home" — toward spheres where they might find meaning and something to which to belong.

It is often said that Americans have amnesia: they do not know who they are, nor do they know their past. Schools teach them about past wars and statecraft but are silent about the spiritual element in their past. The United States Supreme Court has echoed the almost unanimous company of foreign observers and supports the overwhelming finding of the polls: somehow "we are a religious people." Yet few learn what this means or how we came to be such. Fearful lest the dead hand of tradition hold them, citizens ignore or reject tradition. Yet if they do not possess it, it possesses them. From the past come words, images, gestures, and choices that still inform and prod.

It is my hope that this story that concentrates on the leaders of pilgrims will reveal something about the quests of those who followed them. The story follows believers through the infinitely complex, often wondrous maze of American spiritual life. As such it may make some small contribution itself to the continuing American pilgrimage, just as it might inform people on other shores about the lives and hopes of citizens in what is still the New World.

ACKNOWLEDGMENTS

THE ORIGINAL PLOT LINE FOR THIS BOOK BEGAN TO EMERGE FROM A conversation of historians encouraged by Robert W. Lynn of the Lilly Endowment. I owe a debt to them and to him, as well as one that cannot be measured to Virginia Kassel, formerly of WNET-13 in New York, and Donald Cutler, my partner in a number of literary ventures. The Kassel-Cutler-Marty team spent many weekends over a two-year period in New York and Chicago developing the plot.

At the University of Chicago, my former dean Joseph M. Kitagawa and Dean Franklin I. Gamwell provided the climate and resources in which this book could be nurtured. Delores Smith was helpful, as she has been in the case of previous books, with generous assistance and arrangements to help make these resources available.

James P. Wind and R. Scott Appleby contributed hundreds of hours of work. To describe their title as "research assistant" and their role as one in which they were to check the references and to help assure accuracy would be woefully to understate their parts. They have become colleagues who often interrupted their own research and developing careers in order to advance work on this book. My brother Myron A. Marty, who is also a historian colleague, made valuable comments on an early draft, as did my partner "down the hall," Jerald C. Brauer. Laura Fillmore presented a complete critique; I followed many hundreds of her suggestions.

These chapters went through many drafts. Originally a team headed by Cheryl Paymaster coordinated the typing and production of the manuscript. During the past couple of years the project came into the hands of my usual co-workers in matters of this sort. This team was headed by Rehova Arthur, who, assisted by Nathelda McGee and Michelle Harewood Blair, went far beyond the call of duty and the limits of patience to help bring this forth. I thank them.

Finally, the company of students in the field of American religious history, themselves junior colleagues during my more than twenty years at the University of Chicago, have, every one of them, left creative marks on my mind and, indirectly, on this book. I hope that their intellectual pilgrimages will lead them to discoveries of a sort that will issue in another rewriting of the American religious history saga in the next generation.

PILGRIMS IN
THEIR ✍✍
OWN LAND

Americans seem to be in their own land as pilgrims, prodded by a dream. They are always on the move — available for new tasks, prepared for the possible loss of what they have. They are not *settled, installed*. . . .

This sense of becoming, this sense of the flux of time and the dominion of time over everything here below, can be interpreted, of course, in merely pragmatist terms. It can turn into a worship of becoming and change. It can develop a cast of mind which, in the intellectual field, would mean a horror of any tradition, the denial of any lasting and supra-temporal value. But such a cast of mind is but a degeneration of the inner mood of which I am speaking. In its genuine significance this American mood seems to me to be close to Christian detachment, to the Christian sense of the impermanence of earthly things. Those now with us must fade away if better ones are to appear.

— Jacques Maritain
Reflections on America

Native Americans often worshiped natural
phenomena like the sun. This 1758 drawing by Le
Page du Pratz shows the Great Sun, leader of the
Natchez people of the Lower Mississippi Valley,
being carried to the harvest festival. (*Smithsonian
Institution National Anthropological Archives, Bureau of
American Ethnology Collection*)

Chapter One

THE FIRST MIGRANTS

*I*N THIS STORY, THERE ARE AT FIRST NO ACTORS. HUMAN ORIGINS lie outside America. *Homo sapiens* emerged elsewhere, when the two American continents were isolated from the rest of the globe by impassable water barriers.

Tens of thousands of years before Columbus, geological motion turned America into a stage for human drama. Glaciers and ice caps gathered up so much seawater that at the Bering Strait the shallow ocean floor lay exposed, forming a bridge connecting Siberian Asia and Alaskan America.

We can only imagine the first crossing. For centuries Asian bands must have pushed eastward toward the new bridge, pursuing the caribou, mammoths, and other great beasts that were their game. Then, in an unnumbered year, one of those bands pushed so far toward the eastern horizon that the hunters lost sight of their camp. Snuggled in the hides torn from the kill and huddled around the fire they carried with them, they were unaware that one of the band, nameless to us, had first crossed an unmarked boundary. He had discovered America.

This wayfarer was the first in a still-continuing flow of strangers to reach North American shores. Some of them entered the American story as "*the* Pilgrims," but the first of the comers reminds us that all Americans are peregrine people. That is, they all came from foreign shores and were, at first, alien. They had to make sense of their new surroundings and neighbors, to find meaning for their lives, to discover America on their own — and themselves, while doing so.

The first settlers were chiefly Mongoloid, descendants of the Siberians, but Micronesians and other Asians may in due course also have wandered across the bridge. It is doubtful, though, that any of them came from as far away as the subcontinent — India — which later, by accident, gave all pre-Columbian Americans their ethnic name.

In the course of aeons, the ice slowly melted into seawater, covering the land bridge except for islands dotting the surface, and forming the strait that Vitus Bering explored for Russia in 1728. On a clear day one can see Alaskan land from the higher Siberian vantage points. We must assume that few in that "primitive" setting would have mastered passage from one continent to the other after the waters covered the bridge. For several millennia the descendants of the first immigrants were free to explore and disperse slowly through the continents of the Western Hemisphere. Few mariners seem to have come upon American shores or disturbed them until the southern Europeans touched in the late fifteenth century.

What were those first Asian immigrants like? Did they, like other prehistoric hunters, reckon with the spirits of their prey? Always on the move, did they ever take pains to make rock drawings of beasts, carve images, or conduct ceremonies to charm the spirits of the hunt? Silence, always silence, greets such questions. The American landscape today is marked with earthen mounds and enclosures, depressed with graves, studded with charms and ornaments — all of them mysterious testimony to the impulses of prehistoric people. But there are no writings to instruct us.

Although we cannot reconstruct the very gradual process by which it happened, we do know that the first incursion at the northwest corner of the Americas yielded a human landscape that by the year 1500 consisted of perhaps a million people in North America alone. Hundreds of distinguishable languages and dialects have been identified from the records and reports of Europeans who heard them after that year. The land that became the United States was sparsely populated in 1500 by present-day standards, and yet it was nevertheless a rich patchwork of different tribes who traded with each other and frequently declared war on each other. Their economies, their customs, their ways of life — and, of course, their religions — were astonishingly diverse.

In all these respects, not least of all religiously, they set a precedent that restless Americans have lived with ever after. Never have there been so many systems of spiritual striving existing so close together as in America. The neighbor or newcomer of a different faith or way has always represented a threat or an opportunity to those already here. The great difference between the modern pilgrims and their native American ancestors involves the pace of change. More kinds of strangers keep coming, and they disrupt established ways. Meanwhile, modern media of communication make citizens more aware than before of alternatives to their own beliefs and customs.

The Athapaskan and Algonquian peoples encountered in subarctic Canada in the centuries after 1500 were probably most reminiscent of the first Siberian immigrants. They were nomadic hunters, still living in small bands in the severe climate, moving with the seasonal migrations of the animals they hunted. They never settled anywhere very long, and so their way of life always kept its relative simplicity. They told each other stories about the spirits that roamed the wilderness and inhabited the animals. Their spiritual leaders, shamans, were gifted amateurs, not formal priests; they gained authority because they had seen and testified to visions of the spiritual world. These magical dreamers won followings as they let the wind sing marvelously through the skins of their drums.

As long as the subarctic tribes stayed in their remote forests, they were threatened little by the intrusions of exploring Europeans. By 1500, however, peoples thought to be descendants of the Athapaskans had moved south. On their way, these marauders crossed the Great Plains or migrated along the east side of the Rockies. Finally they came to remain in the American Southwest, where they disrupted the lives of more stable Pueblo tribes who were already there.

The dry climate, along with the generous accounts left by the earliest European visitors, has given us an understanding of native cultures in the Southwest that is more detailed than that of anywhere else north of the Rio Grande. Many Europeans immediately related to Pueblo tribes because these tribes had already developed calendars for rites, sacred altars, and an established priesthood. The Navaho, for example, looked to priests to help them find *hozhoni* — a sense of wholeness or union with nature.

The Zuni and Hopi of the Southwest were thoughtful ritualists.

The enemy they chose to fight was the grudging environment, not other Indians. The Hopi, "the peaceful ones," withdrew chiefly to three great Arizona mesas to avoid enemies. Planters and craftsmen, they developed religions that were devoted less to war spirits than to daily living. The priests sponsored something like seminaries to pass on their complicated rites. Deified ancestral spirits, kachinas, were believed to visit the settlements occasionally for benevolent purposes — such as to bring rain. To facilitate such visitations, the people made elaborate masks and danced to impersonate the spirits. Kachinas existed for every natural force or occasion, though probably no single spirit towered above the others. Some of the southwestern Indians believed that Sky Father and Earth Mother gave birth to humans, and that one could identify the hole where these gods emerged. They called it *Sipapu*. We call it the Grand Canyon.

The Pima and Yuma tribes who lived along the Mexican border were among those who believed in an afterlife. The Pima, for example, listened for the hoot of the owl as an early warning of death, since they believed it was the owl who carried the human soul from this world to the next.

Each tribe responded and became attached to its own specific landscape, seeing particular lakes and trees as sacred. For this reason, the faith of a settled tribe like the Pueblo was not transported as easily as that of more mobile hunting tribes.

But by 1500, there were some native religions that were clearly portable. The first European visitors to the Mississippi Valley found traces of a "Death Cult" imitative of the religious practices others found in Tenochtitlán (Mexico City). The Natchez priests of the Mississippi Valley dressed themselves in grotesque overdisplays of ritual beads and shells. To please and appease the spirits, these priests slaughtered the relatives of dead chiefs so that the whole noble family could find passage together in the next world. Fathers who wanted to become nobles sacrificed their own children at altars. The first whites who came upon the Natchez reported that a "Son of the Sun" or "Brother of the Sun" inhabited an imposing residence next to a Temple of the Sun, a building made horrendous by the heads taken from sacrificial victims and posted on spikes along the outer walls. These Death Cult people had organized themselves into rigid social classes of Suns, Nobles, Honored People, and Stinkards, each of whom knew his place. Status was most apparent at time of death. Commoners were placed in simple graves, while the bodies of noblemen were exposed on high platforms, where flies and vultures picked over their remains, or where appointed human flesh-pickers hastened the bone-cleaning process by using their long fingernails.

Also in the Mississippi Valley there flourished a Mound Culture, where villages spread out from giant earthworks; the greatest of these, Monk's Mound, still stands today east of Saint Louis at Cahokia, Illinois. The mounds were the centers of elaborate networks of villages, and the inhabitants gathered on them for rite and spectacle. Of equal religious interest were people to the east, in the Ohio Valley, who made up the cultures that are now called Adena and Hopewell. Death-obsessed people there carried on a lively commerce in religious artifacts with people thousands of miles away.

As startling as the southern Death Cults may seem, perhaps even more fascinating were the tribes of the northeastern woodlands, the Iroquois and Huron. Women were powerful in these woodland cultures. They owned the dwellings and tools; were able to divorce their husbands; passed on names and bloodlines; selected the sachems, or chiefs; shared with the men the spiritual care of children; and took part in the adult councils.

Families, huddled around smoke holes in their longhouses, heard mythic stories explaining the origins of their world. According to one Huron myth, a woman long ago fell through a slot in the sky onto the back of a turtle. Where could she and the turtle land and live? Some creature, the story continued, gathered mud from beneath the waters and shaped the Earth. Thereupon the first woman gave birth to two deities, one good and the other bad — or at least bumbling. Such woodland natives did recognize a power called *orenda* that was suggestive of a higher being, but they surrounded this force with so many haunting spirits and ghosts of the dead that its size and power seemed compromised.

Memorable among the Iroquois was the False Face Society, whose members cut stylized designs of contorted faces into tree trunks. The carvers felt they derived the power of particular spirits through the life of such trees and could effect cures through these powers. When a longhouse dweller fell ill, False Face members donned masks and made noisy processions in an effort to frighten off the evil spirits.

The same natives who were sympathetic to illness also stunned those first European observers with the cruelty of their ritual tortures. Warriors usually chose to die fighting rather than accept capture, since captors inflicted unimaginable pain. All through the night, the victors would apply fire to the captive's body until he was near death, at which point they would nurse the sufferer back until he could sing and goad his torturers once again. In the end, after they had killed the wretch, the victors ate his vital organs in order to gain his power.

Dwelling on death cultures, torture, and the games of war does not do justice to another side of peoples like the Seminoles or Creek of what is now Georgia and Alabama. Some tribes in this area and elsewhere in the Southeast displayed a love for order and a respect for rank or office that matched anything known in Europe. They picked rulers on the basis of achievement, not birthright. And the Creek took one further step to assure a healthy society. All communities face the problem of how to keep wayward members in line; executing offenders depletes the ranks and enrages surviving relatives. In Creek country, to banish offenders meant death in the swamps, or, worse, turning them into possible recruits for enemy tribes. What should the leaders do? They restored errant members to the community at the time of the seasonal Green Corn Dance, when priests lit fires to signal a new beginning in life. Men and women slept apart during the festival. Everyone danced to entertain and supplicate the ancestral ghosts and the spirits of nature. Sometimes the priests administered a nauseating herbal "Black Drink" that induced violent vomiting and symbolized a purged spirit among those who drank it. At the climax of the ceremony, anyone who had done wrong (short of murder) was free to come literally out of the bushes and have his past forgiven and forgotten. The tribal order remained stable while its members experienced a new start.

Glimpses are all we have of these earlier cultures — glimpses gained from the reports of the first Europeans on the scene, or from studying graves and paintings that reflect practices and, perhaps, beliefs. Life soon grew more complex as the Europeans brought books and bullets to America. Most of the newcomers regarded the old Indian ways as heathen, pagan, or savage. Certainly few of them were trained to see anything positive in the spiritual strivings and religious systems of the natives.

Yet one cannot pass the graves and the mounds or leave the diaries and histories without some sense of awe for the inventiveness of the earliest Americans. Like the strangers who followed them, they, too, apparently celebrated the hours and seasons, the processes of being born, maturing, and mating. They called on powers beyond themselves to influence weather and warfare. They admired courage and feared death. It was as hard for these Indians as it was for their successors to live in a merely random universe. They had to make sense of their days, to endow their joys and their sorrows with meaning.

These native Americans, then, originated some of the grand themes of what became the magnificent and puzzling story of American religion. Their descendants, pushed back to reservations, survive. So, too, do many of their time-honored ways, precedents for countless pilgrimages to follow.

Perhaps the first European attempt to depict Columbus's landing was this title page to Giuliano Dati's *Lettera* (1493). In the foreground, King Ferdinand observes three ships as they approach an island on which natives dance. (*Rare Books and Manuscripts Division, The New York Public Library, Astor, Lenox and Tilden Foundations*)

Chapter Two

A CROWNED CROSS

WHILE THE STORY OF NATIVE AMERICAN RELIGION BEGAN THOU-
sands of years before Europeans "discovered" the New World,
American religion as we know it was imported by European discoverers, having originated in the western Mediterranean lands
before 1492. In the provinces that today make up modern Spain
there coexisted and clashed three faiths: Judaism, Catholic Christianity, and Islam.

In the Western Hemisphere of 1492 there was no writing, there
were no books. The plentiful old books in the Eastern Hemisphere,
however, told stories of the calling, in sequence, of Israel, of a
Jewish teacher named Jesus, and of the prophet Muhammad. Out
of their calls came groups that today are often classified as the
People of the Book. They differed vastly in their understanding of
ancient scriptures — they even disagreed about what those scriptures were.

What they held in common, however, stood in contrast to what
they found in the Western Hemisphere. While native Americans
were engrossed in faiths that situated them in the world of nature,
the Europeans had historical faiths; they were interested in events.
The three faiths all taught profoundly skeptical views of human
existence. The thrust of European religious life was away from
simply valuing earthly life and toward founding a relationship with
an unseen God who existed within and also beyond their world.

Believers wanted to be detached in many ways from earthly life and attached to heavenly life through a process called salvation.

For the People of the Book reality encompassed several levels: heaven, earth, and perhaps a netherworld. On earth there were also divisions of sorts the Indians seldom knew: between the political and religious communities and between formal religious leaders and everyone else. Being human was quite complicated. Yet the most decisive aspect of these faiths was that they established a sense of direct address between God, who was above and beyond, and the believer. They all became religions of "the Word." God, perhaps through leaders like priests or prophets, could speak to the believer. God could tell him to engage in crusades or conquests.

Beyond this, the stories diverged. Judaism was a self-contained, seldom missionary faith. Ordinarily one became a Jew by being born to a Jewish mother. While other faiths set out to expand, Jews struggled to survive, having no domain of their own. Christianity and Islam wanted to win the whole world to their "universalistic" faiths. They must convert or subdue peoples and take over land. When the two met on the same soil there was usually trouble, for each heard a divine call to win out over the other.

The year 1492 was fateful for these faiths on the western end of the Mediterranean. Long before, in 711, Islamic "Moors" had invaded what is today Spain. They pushed Spanish Christians north and, under military control, built their cities with mosques for worship. They were never able to conquer beyond the mountains in France or Italy nor to blot out all traces or dreams of the displaced Christian. These Christians were slow to gather forces for a *Reconquista*. For centuries Muslims and Christians peacefully coexisted, but that situation could not endure.

Jews had been in Spain at least four centuries before Muslims came. Many of them sided with the Islamic invaders against the Christian Visigothic kings. These kings in the sixth century had become firm in their resolve to persecute Jews, whom they saw as rivals and traitors to the true faith. The Muslim conquerors seemed friendlier. On Spanish soil Muslims and Jews enjoyed a great burst of cultural achievement.

As military fortunes gradually changed, Christians welcomed the help and expertise of the Jews, who came to occupy a strategic political position. They were often commuters between Muslims and Christians. As a result many of these Sephardic Jews came to be powerful and prosperous, almost to the point that they often downplayed their spiritual heritage and even voluntarily converted to the other faiths. Yet a soulful nostalgia for their ancient home-lands in the East kept both Jews and Muslims from investing heav-ily in the new nationalism that took rise in the fifteenth century. Meanwhile, the preaching of crusades by growing Catholic forces inspired calls for *Reconquista*. To put their house in order for such a struggle they had to find unity, and they did so by relying not only on the sword but also on a fanatically pure and unified Catholicism.

In the century before Europeans settled the Americas, the Iberian peninsula was divided into three main areas: Portugal, Castile-León, and Aragon. Castile was larger but poorer than Aragon, and could swing into alliance with either Portugal or Aragon. Aragon needed alliance with Castile. In the 1450s both kingdoms had mon-archs named John II. The one in Aragon had a son in 1452 named Ferdinand while the Castilian fathered a daughter in 1451 christened Isabella. Since the two offspring later shared a large part in the discovery of America, it is worthwhile to glimpse their world.

Neither child had first claim to a throne. Ferdinand's older half brother was first in succession, but he died in circumstances that led the courtiers to gossip that he had been poisoned. Isabella's was a much more devious route to her throne. Her father died when she was three. Her promiscuous half brother, Henry IV — Henry the Impotent, his scoffing subjects called him — assumed the throne. When his queen, Juana, bore an heir, there was widespread agreement that Henry could not have been the father. Discontented nobles deposed Henry, whose half brother Alfonso was crowned, only to die an untimely death, possibly from murder by poison. A daughter born to Juana stood in the way of Isabella. Henry himself seemed to prefer Isabella, especially as she seemed willing to agree not to marry without his consent. After a series of maneuvers, Juana and her daughter were retired to a convent. Isabella was crowned in 1474.

Guided by astute counselors, somewhere along the way the queen decided that she ought to marry Ferdinand, whom she had never seen. She had heard that he was a handsome horseman and a practical man. But Henry still preferred that Castile should swing toward Portugal rather than Aragon. He therefore championed a Portuguese prospect so vigorously that Isabella decided he had bro-ken their covenant of having to find mutual agreement on her spouse. She leaked word that she desired an Aragonese groom.

John II of Aragon was elated, and Ferdinand himself did not cavil at the prospect of this marriage. He knew that Isabella was a fair-skinned, green-eyed, red-haired woman of the best bloodline. She was, after all, a second cousin of his own Trastamáran house. Most kings wed more conveniently and less attractively than he might in this case. All kings, he also knew, could work out personal arrangements on the side if their marriages turned out to be unhappy.

The Roman Catholic church forbade the wedding of cousins. In principle at least, the judgment of the pope who headed that church should take precedence over the wish of a king in this kind of situation. Nevertheless, in the autumn of 1469 Ferdinand rode across the Saragossan mountains to Valladolid to claim Isabella as bride. He journeyed without royal vestments, wearing a disguise to escape detection and perhaps to save money. Aragonese court fortunes were at the moment embarrassingly low, little better off now than Castile's. Then, at the moment of final decision, Isabella turned suddenly shy. Should she renege on her understanding with Henry? Should she violate Catholic law by marrying a cousin?

The archbishop of Toledo refused to let her premarital jitters ruin a useful alliance. He and the father of the groom quickly fabricated a papal license allowing Ferdinand to marry his cousin, and on it forged the signature of the pope. Isabella was satisfied, and the royal couple were wed in October. After a decade of tense moves toward consolidation, Aragon and Castile were becoming the kingdom of Spain. If a kingdom, why not an empire as well?

The royal marriage worked reasonably well. Warm mutuality, even love, developed between the couple. The queen mended the king's shirts when funds were scarce, but she was no mere doormat for his whims. Ferdinand, in turn, could be a reserved man but in his vigorous moments he was also a calculating plotter; he broke agreements as blithely as he made them. Isabella was the more winning of the two, a purposeful mother of five royal children to whom she wished to entrust much of the destiny of Catholic Europe. Ferdinand fathered at least two bastards, after the manner of kings in his day, but Isabella managed to control her destiny and keep his strayings from disrupting court life.

The consolidation of Spain coincided with a profound spiritual crisis in Catholic Christianity — a crisis of long development. The political crown always tolerated the church because it counted on its unmarried priests to be otherworldly and spiritual. Gradually, however, the church lost its self-restraining will and generated a taste for wealth. Periodic reforms tended to be centered in the life of monasteries. The church itself became a two-class system: the ascetic monasteries versus the more worldly regular clergy. A chance occasion, for example, once necessitated that the then archbishop of Toledo, Pedro González de Mendoza, introduce two of his illegitimate children to Queen Isabella. She said, "My Lord, you even sin on a grand scale."

In northern Europe the combination of nationalism, revulsion toward the worldliness of the Catholic church, and new spiritual hungers among the people would yield a historic revolt. This was the Protestant Reformation, which began about twenty-five years after the discovery of America. But in the Iberian corner of Europe there was a slightly earlier stirring in the form of a revival of mysticism, the awakening of an austere yet passionate piety along with love of doctrine. Isabella and a portion of the Spanish clergy helped establish a new style just in time for a fresh generation of missionary brothers, or "friars," to export it to the American Indian world. The Spanish Catholic renewal turned out to be of sufficient strength to keep the sects of Protestantism from taking root in Iberia.

In the candle glow of her own chapel or surrounded by icons of those who had died for their faith, the queen stayed close to the center of reformist Catholicism. Its focus fell on the form of an ancient Roman cross to which Spanish piety fixed the figure of a suffering Jesus. This "Son of God" appeased his wrathful Father — the jealous God hated human sin and the Son, as a human, was alone perfect and thus a satisfying sacrifice — and made it possible for believers to come to heaven. A complicated system of prayers and worship, notably the repeated sacrifice of Christ in the rite called the Mass, connected Isabella with this God.

The Spanish Catholic reformers to whom the queen was most attracted liked to stress the sternness of God, but they also taught that the water applied in baptism, even of infants, could bring people into His more benign presence. The friars who were soon to sail with the explorers carried such images and rites with them, to help keep the Spaniards in line and to baptize some of the Indians. On their journeys these agents of God acted confidently in the name of a whole ladder of Christian officials: the pope, archbishops or bishops, and priests like those who heard the confessions of the Christian monarchs.

Isabella never let her own piety give her simple ease. She was severe with herself, even while choosing the confessor to whom she must give account of her wrongs before God. Someone once recommended to her the prior of a convent, Fray Hernando de Talavera. She arrived majestically before him for confession and was told to kneel while the priest sat. Commoners did kneel to confess sins, but no priest dared ask this posture from a queen unless he also humbled himself.

"Reverend Father, it is customary for both to kneel."

"No," Talavera replied, "in the tribunal of God, there are no kings or queens, but only human sinners; and I, unworthy as I am, am His minister. It is right that I sit and you kneel."

Isabella acceded. "This is the confessor I have been looking for."

What do we make of such faith? It is hard to tell the story of Isabella without encountering two fierce reactions at war within oneself. On the one hand, admiration: for the clarity, firmness, and self-sacrifice that her religion inspired in her. It impelled her toward her most creative acts. On the other hand, there is revulsion — for the cocksureness, even fanaticism with which believers felt that God chartered their version of faith as being alone the pure and true one — and agony: over the way hearing the voice of God through books or priests or the soul led one to feel a mandate to torture and kill. Isabella was poised between two opposites that have often gone into vital faith. Half a millennium later the world still knows such combinations of beauty and ugliness as factors in politics and religion alike. The tendencies are compliments to the power of statecraft *and* faith, marks of their potential for danger when unchecked. Many a later pilgrim came to America fleeing such power and lived on only to try to assert it in the new landscape.

Francisco Cardinal Jiménez de Cisneros eventually became Isabella's mentor. Born into poverty, Jiménez never forgot his origins as he rose to prominence in the church. As archbishop of Toledo, he chased the fawning courtiers from his palace and stripped it of finery. When the self-indulgent pope, Alexander VI, ordered the archbishop to restore the old pomp and regalia, Jiménez obeyed, but he was sly enough to smuggle a hair shirt under his jeweled robes, his own dry bread in to splendid banquets, and for his brief hours of sleeping, a trundle under his magnificent bed. A Franciscan order of monks grumbled about Jiménez's reforms until the pope finally sent their general, Gil Delfini, to complain to Isabella. "Father," the queen asked, "have you taken leave of your senses? Do you realize to whom you are speaking?" He sneered, "To Isabella of Castile, who is dust and ashes, like me." She had him move his dust and ashes swiftly back to Rome.

When Pope Alexander VI repudiated the ecclesiastical authority for reform of the Spanish church, Isabella beat a retreat and softened her tactics — without changing her goals — until, on a happier day in 1496, the pope named Ferdinand and Isabella *los reyes católicos,* "the Catholic Sovereigns." Under their protection Jiménez pursued reform. The parish clergy had to give up their concubines and accept a higher degree of accountability for performance of their duties. So zealously did Jiménez urge monks to live up to their neglected rules that several hundred in protest took their women with them to North Africa and turned Muslim. Jiménez financed translation of the Bible and founded the University of Alcalá de Henares in order to give intellectual undergirding to reform efforts.

Reform in Spain included no hint of religious tolerance. Ironically, the more Spain recovered the spirit of otherworldly Catholicism, the less tolerance there was for the practice of other religions on the peninsula. From the perspective of a religiously more civil period in the West, it is hard for us to grasp the strength of the exclusivist feelings of fifteenth-century Muslims and Christians. They threatened each other to a degree that we do not often feel five hundred years later. Perhaps we had better look at the conflicts of capitalists and communists in the twentieth century to get a more salient comparison. An American capitalist typically believes that his ideology depends on whether the whole society maintains a particular kind of political economy. Any perceived deviation may be interpreted as a threat to the whole. The hypothetical modern citizen may very well feel, on the other hand, that his religion is grounded most of all in the self, in personal commitment, and therefore is not threatened to a similar degree if the person next door manifests a quite different religious commitment.

Spain could not tolerate such a live-and-let-live attitude. The desire to rid Iberia of Moors developed over the centuries under the patron of Spain, Santiago, or Saint James, a disciple of Jesus whose remains someone claimed to have found in Spain in the ninth century. Although the Moors subsequently were contained with respect to further advances in Europe, elsewhere in the Mediterranean world Muslims kept on the offensive. After the fall of Constantinople, the old eastern Christian capital, in 1453, they were a plausible threat from the East as well. Had there been a different military outcome in the Iberian outpost of Christendom in the 1490s, it is possible that mosques would dot the New World landscape where Christian churches now stand.

When the monarchs of the Spanish kingdom tried to exact tribute from the Moors, Sultan Muley Hacen provoked Ferdinand and Isabella by attacking the town of Zahara in 1481. For much of the next decade the outcome of hostilities was in doubt, while the Catholic sovereigns took up the language of the Crusade to rally forces. Once, when morale was sagging, a visibly pregnant Isabella rode up to cheer the troops. After at least one battle, Ferdinand prostrated himself in a cathedral, and his wife "purified" some mosques by turning them into churches. Gradually, the fortunes turned toward the Catholic side.

Christian victory was sealed on January 2, 1492, when Boabdil, the leader of the Moors, rode to surrender on the banks of the Genil. When the righteous and disdainful Ferdinand withheld the royal ring, Boabdil had to kiss the king's sleeve as he surrendered the keys to the Alhambra. Soon a silver Christian cross topped its towers at Granada. Four days later, the monarchs paraded into the city, 781 years after Islam first entered Spain.

Many Moors remained in Spain under a rather generous settlement while the cardinal Hernando de Talavera, now archbishop at Granada, set out quietly to convert them. Jiménez, however, pressed hard for a final solution to the Muslim problem and burned their books, trying also to force conversions. The Moors rebelled and were defeated again as the century turned, after which those who did not convert or feign conversion to catholicism were persecuted or expelled. In all these policies Ferdinand was relatively moderate, while Isabella followed Jiménez in his campaign to unify Spain spiritually, even if by force.

Force worked at last against the Jews, a more troubling obstacle than Muslims to Spanish unity. A coalition of royalty and mobs, more than the Catholic church, provoked attacks on Jews. That bad times were ahead became clear already in 1391 when, after centuries of relative amity, crowds rioted in Seville. They looted synagogues, burned Jewish homes, killed inhabitants, and inaugurated a century of troubles until the end came for Spanish Judaism in the fateful year, 1492. The Jews inspired envy because they excelled wherever learning and wealth abounded. Christians learned to blame them for anything that went wrong, be it a plague or an economic downturn. Catholics passed laws against intermarriage between people of the two faiths. And Christians were not above spreading perverse rumors, such as that Jews defiled holy objects or even crucified gentile children.

Despite, or because of, harassments, as many as 300,000 Spanish Jews in 1492 were conversos, presumed or real converts to Catholicism; Marranos (probably meaning "swine"), their enemies in Judaism called them. Today we call them New Christians. Some prospered in their new Catholic faith, yet many others had to deal with a sense of guilt, loneliness, and loss after their uprooting from Judaism. The situation was complicated by the fact that some Jews pretended publicly to be New Christians, while keeping up the practice of Judaism in private. There was a general suspicion, based on some fact, about the authenticity of conversions. The more prominent the Spanish Jew, the more incentive there was to convert. The best friend of Isabella, Doña Beatriz, was married to a New Christian, and the great mystic, Saint Teresa of Avila, was herself of a New Christian family. Archbishop Talavera came from a similar family, as did the royal lawyer and treasurer, Luis de Sántangel, and numerous church leaders. Given the ties of Jews to so much of Iberian life, the prudence of rooting them out seemed most questionable. Yet prudence did not rule when Ferdinand and Isabella chose to go crusading.

The Catholic sovereigns imported a device invented a couple of centuries earlier to persecute those whom Catholicism resented. Called the Inquisition, it became their tool for persecuting. Designed as it was only to root out false Christian belief, or heresy, the Inquisition was not suitable to employ against Spaniards who openly practiced Judaism, but it did create havoc among the New Christians. Isabella had declined at first when an ambassador of the pope proposed to renew the Inquisition. She wanted to believe that effective missionaries could convert Jews without force. Her reservations were overcome by assurances that the process would be temporary and free of abuse. Rome sent the queen a statement in 1478 rejoicing over her praiseworthy zeal for the faith. It then authorized a board of inquisitors "for the time being." The sovereigns stated their hope that the Inquisition would avoid unjust suspicion and persecution of faithful New Christians, but they soon lost control of the instrument, as did the pope.

What Isabella first permitted ambivalently she eventually supported with zeal. False teaching in her view contaminated Catholics and stood in the way of a pure and united Spain. She did not foresee all the inevitable abuses. Accusers kept their anonymity, supposedly to protect themselves from possible revenge. But now people could act on the basis of irrational envies and suspicions, and could destroy innocent neighbors. Few Catholic citizens stepped up to defend accused innocents lest they themselves also draw suspicion. Authorities imprisoned victims for months at a time without telling them the origin of charges against them. Sometimes even a harmless instinctive gesture remembered from the practice of

Judaism was enough to bring torture and death under the administration of the grand inquisitor, Tomás de Torquemada, himself another of Isabella's confessors and the son of a New Christian family.

Most of the accused were pronounced guilty. About one-tenth of them the church turned over to civil powers for execution. The least fortunate were the tortured. Many New Christians suffered the strappado. It lifted the accused by a rope around his wrists, which were tied behind his back. When the victim had been raised high above the ground, the torturer let him fall — almost to the ground. No one kept track of exactly how many were mistreated, but several thousand deaths blight the record of Ferdinand and Isabella.

As the Inquisition ground on out of hand, a more decisive policy was formulated for the Jews. Being a true Jew was declared "the greatest, most perilous and most contagious of crimes." Ferdinand and Isabella commanded all practicing Jews to leave their kingdoms, never to return. On March 31, 1492, soon after the fall of the Moors, the monarchs signed an order giving three months before the last Jew must be gone.

No gentile dared shelter refugees, nor could those in flight take along currency. Estimates suggest that 170,000 who refused conversion fled. Some swallowed gold for the trip; one inspector noted that women concealed it in parts of their body that "are not to be mentioned." Some lost their lives in panic while trying to scramble aboard crowded ships. Many bribed their way to Portugal, which was only partially hospitable, and that only for five years. Thence they fled to Africa, where they were easy prey for Muslims who took advantage of them.

In faraway Turkey the more judicious and generous Muslim sultan welcomed Jewish talent and sneered about Ferdinand: "Do you call this king a statesman, who impoverishes his land and enriches mine?" Other Jews dispersed through Europe and briefly, later, to Recife, a tolerant Dutch corner of Brazil, from whence the first ones came to New York. The loss of Jewish talent harmed Spain for centuries, but the Catholic sovereigns at the time overlooked the loss in order to glory in doing the will of God by creating a Spain spiritually united for mission.

The Spanish Catholic mission impelled Ferdinand and Isabella to look also to the seas. In 1474, the duke of Medina-Sidonia had entertained Isabella and Ferdinand at Sanlúcar de Barrameda, where the Guadalquivir River empties into the Gulf of Cádiz. For the first time, Isabella saw the waters that beckoned to the western seas about which she had heard so much. Portuguese explorers were already returning from those seas with word of discoveries in the Canaries, the Azores, and the Madeira Islands, and with stories of new routes of commerce and distant wealth. Learned geographers of the day insisted that adventurers could reach the Orient by sailing westward. One can only imagine what dreams possessed the mind of the young woman from Castile as she looked toward the Atlantic waters.

The western seas, for all their allure, however, never took first place in Isabella's mind. She spent her mature and declining years arranging royal marriages for her children. Only accidentally was she dragged into the Atlantic venture. On a January day in 1486, a Genoan, Cristóbal Colón, or Christopher Columbus, rode into Córdoba to seek an audience with the sovereigns. Portugal had already rebuffed him, and when he later turned to France and England, they refused to subsidize an expedition westward to reach the Indies of fabled wealth. He must succeed with Ferdinand and Isabella. Their underlings pushed him off on the royal treasurer at that time, Don Alonso de Quintanilla, but Columbus persisted and eventually saw the monarchs.

Ferdinand disliked the ambitious sailor from the first, but paid some notice when he heard Columbus mention the gold of the Indies. Isabella responded warmly to the promise that the explorer would extend Christendom and convert people of the Orient to Catholicism. For good measure Columbus, who had already convinced them that Spain would dominate trade routes to the East, added that the troops of the Catholic sovereigns could attack the flank of the Muslim Turks in the Holy Land by coming from the East.

The matter of royal sponsorship was handed over to a committee headed by Talavera. The group pondered for years and then advised against the project, but Columbus did not give up. At the most inopportune moment, in late 1491, while the Catholic sovereigns were beginning the siege of Granada, the Genoan, now garbed in brown Franciscan robes from his retreat at La Rábida monastery, histrionically arrived on the scene. The queen, preoccupied, sent him away, but was prevailed upon to reinvite the captain. Then in January of 1492, the month the Moor fell, Columbus swaggered into the court of the victors in the Alhambra. Ferdinand listened, but seethed at the demand that, if successful, the Genoan would become "Admiral of the Ocean Sea, Viceroy and

Governor" of the new lands. Columbus's persistence did stir Isabella again, but she still had to turn him down.

Years later Columbus remembered this moment as one that gave him reason for hope. Perhaps he discerned some glint in her eye, or maybe he only wrote in flattery: "In all men there was disbelief, but the Queen, my lady, God gave the spirit of understanding and great courage. . . ." At the time, however, rejected again, he bade farewell and, dejected, rode off.

The details of what happened next may belong to legend. Ten miles west of Granada, at the bridge of Los Piños, a messenger of the queen overtook Columbus with word that she had had second thoughts. An early biographer of Columbus gave New Christian Luis de Sántangel credit for turning up some funds and changing her mind. She would lose so little in case of failure and gain so much in case of success, he reasoned, that she must take risks for the service of God, the benefit of the church, and "an exaltation of the royal state of Your Highnesses and the prosperity of all these, your realms." Such language was appealingly grandiose, so on April 17, 1492, the parties signed the Capitulations of Santa Fé and Columbus began to make plans for sailing.

Columbus seemed ideal for the mission to the Indies. Bartolomé de Las Casas, an admiring biographer, claimed that in matters of the Christian religion, the Genoan was a Catholic of great devotion, and this judgment seems reasonable. There has been greater scholarly controversy over occasional conjectures that Columbus was himself a New Christian who masked his past with Catholic passion but carried along tinges of messianism from his ancestral faith. The explorer began all his writing with "Jesus and Mary, be with us on the way." He observed the fasts of the church, confessed and made communion faithfully, hated blasphemy and forbade profane swearing, and did so many other pious things in the book of Las Casas that one wonders how he had time to sail ships so masterfully.

The queen exacted three vessels from the citizens of Palos, who evidently were in debt to her. The crews included no priests. Laymen, Columbus among them, would lead shipboard worship. Among the ninety men who left the harbor at Palos on August 3, only days after the last Jews left Christian Spain, were some New Christians, including Luis de Torres, a recent convert and linguist who was to be an interpreter. As the three ships passed La Rábida, the men could hear the friars inside coincidentally ending a chant as one might at the turn of an epoch: ". . . evermore and evermore."

Weeks later, at night on October 11, a sailor thought that he saw a western light, but it disappeared before his and his captain's eyes. At 2:00 A.M. on October 12, Rodrigo de Triana, on watch on the *Pinta,* shouted, *"Tierra! Tierra!"* From the *Santa María,* now drawn alongside, Columbus shouted back the confirmation to Captain Martín Alonso Pinzón, "You *did* find land!" Later that day, Columbus's party planted on the land the flag of Catholic Castile, a green crowned cross. The party knelt on the ground to give tearful thanks to their God. Columbus named the island San Salvador, "Holy Savior." He was expecting to meet the Asians of the Indies.

Known as the Protector of the Indians, Bartolomé
de Las Casas (1474–1566) never set foot on what is
today the United States. Paradoxically, he is
remembered widely as the first great figure to speak
up for the rights of minorities in the New World,
even though he played a brief part in legitimizing
black slavery. His portrayals of Spanish cruelties in
the Americas gave rise to a "Black Legend" about
Spaniards, which the English happily exploited to
show themselves in a more favorable light.
(*Courtesy Hispanic Society of America*)

Chapter Three

THE CONQUEROR VERSUS
THE MISSIONARY

CHRISTOPHER COLUMBUS HAD PLOTTED WELL HOW TO CONFRONT the people of India. The captain was utterly unprepared, however, to understand the Taino group of Arawak people who brought him gifts. His first and lasting impression in a formal letter combined thoughts of salvation and slavery: "How easy it would be to convert these people — and to make them work for us." He reported that "they invite you to share anything that they possess, and show as much love as if their hearts went with it." With nothing more than their hand signals to go on for encouragement, he moved on, touching numerous islands, including Cuba and Haiti, but he could not learn where natives got their bits of gold or why spices were absent. The Spaniards encountered maize, or corn, and tobacco for the first time. At Christmas, after the *Santa María* ran aground, their leader left behind thirty-four men at a place he named Puerto de la Navidad. By January his two remaining ships had weathered the return trip to Spain.

The Catholic sovereigns thereupon beckoned Columbus, being eager now to outbid the Portuguese king for his continuing service. Their new admiral deposited six natives. Since they "belonged to no religion," the Spaniards saw to their Catholic baptism, the royal pair serving as godparents. Isabella refused to let them be slaves. She followed the same policy after a later voyage when she forced Columbus to release natives who had become body

25

servants: "Who authorized my Admiral to dispose of my subjects in this manner?"

In all, Columbus made three more voyages during the next decade. Almost at once the pope divided the West between the seagoing nations, Portugal and Spain. Ferdinand and Isabella took some pains to begin claiming their portion. However, when word reached the monarchs that the colony at La Navidad had been massacred, the stock of Columbus fell at court. Gold eluded him, others challenged him, and by the third voyage his Spanish rival Francisco de Bobadilla sent the admiral home in chains as an inept administrator and arbitrary leader.

After these failures Columbus rekindled old desires to lead a crusade to the holy places in Jerusalem, inspired by a reading of prophecies in the same Bible that had goaded him to the New World. Queen Isabella, meanwhile, died in 1504, weeks after his last voyage, while King Ferdinand patronized the arthritic old discoverer until Columbus died in 1506. The lands Columbus found were not the Indies, but were capriciously named America after Amerigo Vespucci.

Columbus seemed genuinely moved by three inner forces. Of course, he had, first of all, a desire for personal glory and gold. Why else lust for a title like "Admiral of the Ocean Sea"? Second, he genuinely wanted to help expand Catholic Europe into the Asia he preferred to call the Indies, and perhaps to carry on the crusade against the "infidel" Muslim. The third motive was clearly minor and late in developing: the notion that the new people he met might themselves be saved, not merely conquered, for and through the Catholic faith.

He anticipated the motives of explorers, conquerors, and settlers for a couple of centuries to come. The later florid accounts of altruism and sacrifice by and about missionaries do not do justice to the range of human impulses. Nor do the clear records of gouging the soil, raping the mines, and killing the people leave us any choice but to judge many as greedy. At the same time it is hard for moderns to understand how passionate sixteenth-century lay people could be to see themselves religiously as conquerors for Christ, for Catholicism. They had a zeal for seeing Christendom expand. Not many conquerors cared at all about the souls of natives. But at their side, often as chaplains and naggers on their voyages or as consciences in their new empires, were priests and brothers. They rarely understood native American faith and found much not to like in it. However, they often did come to care greatly for the people they set out to convert and educate. Sometimes they successfully slowed or blocked the path of the conquistadores when these exploiters were out to do their worst.

This mixture of motives makes the act of untangling Catholic ventures and keeping plots clear most difficult. Suffice it to say that most of the time the impulses were more mixed than the results. Left to themselves, the conquerors conquered and killed. Left to themselves, the missionaries converted and "civilized." But rarely were either left wholly to themselves.

Gold-hungry Spaniards who cared less than did Columbus and Isabella for saving Indian souls continued making forays into the Americas. A gifted survivor of the second Columbus voyage, Juan Ponce de León, the discoverer of Florida, was both the first known European to touch on southern mainland shores of North America and the first to be met by hostile natives. Ponce took missionaries with him, but they found the Indians resistant. So did the explorer. In 1521 a Calusa arrow mortally wounded him.

The Europeans and the natives soon learned how to bring out the worst cruelty in each other. Eight priests and four friars were in the company of Hernando de Soto when he landed in Tampa Bay in May of 1539, but he never gave the chaplains a chance to humanize his greedy venture. The rampaging captain formed chain gangs of native slaves to do his heavy work, since Spaniards had not come to the New World to labor. Little resulted from his rapine. Told of a great kingdom and a powerful ruler ahead, de Soto found only some huts on the Savannah and a frumpy queen who unloaded a few second-rate pearls on him, the only treasure he ever found. He pushed on in swamp and wilderness through Gulf Coast and lower Mississippi territories.

West of the Mississippi a despondent de Soto had his runner try to bluff a local chief with the claim that the captain was the child of the Sun. The wily chief through the translators offered befitting tribute if the son of the Sun would prove himself by drying up the great river. The chief further allowed that he as ruler visited no one. Visitors came to see him, not vice versa. He greeted with goodwill those who arrived in peace but he stepped back not a foot for anyone. De Soto's men, who were unready to face the scientific test thus posed for him, went ahead with killing while the Indians replied in kind. De Soto died of a fever in May of 1542; his forlorn troops lowered his corpse into the Mississippi to foil Indian desecraters.

On one foray, the Spanish Catholics moved among the natives

in weakness, and were met less militantly. We get a revealing glimpse of how things might have been from the *Relación* of one Alvar Núñez Cabeza de Vaca. He details the sojourn of four men during a seven-year trek from Florida to Mexico. Constantly at the mercy of the Indians, they always found ways to survive and relate to them. The party started under the command of Pánfilo de Narváez, an adventurer who was chartered by Charles V to colonize the whole Gulf territory and become its governor. On Good Friday in 1528, the gold-seeking party landed near Tampa Bay, where some Indians tried to wave them off and then disappeared. Thereupon Narváez read to the bare landscape the typical royal summons to the natives. The "Pope in Rome, the Papa or King, Lord and Superior of the Universe and Supreme Father and Governor of All Men," had given Florida to the king and queen of Spain, whose representative Narváez was. He would receive the Indians with love and charity, but they must be converted to the Holy Catholic faith. If they did not submit, he must use force to enslave them and make them obedient to the church and the yoke of Their Majesties.

Narváez came to a woeful end after finding no gold at a place called Apalachee, believed to be near Tallahassee. Most of his men died or were killed. The panicky survivors, choosing the Gulf of Mexico as an escape route, put to sea in five rickety homemade vessels; only a remnant lived to traverse the thousand miles covered during the next forty-six days. All the others were lost. The last four survivors included Cabeza de Vaca, who was the treasurer of the expedition, and a Negro, Estebán or Estebánico (a slave of one Andrés Dorantes, he had been taken captive off Morocco). Cast ashore on an island off Texas, Cabeza de Vaca and his colleagues were later enslaved by the mainland Indians. Coming not as conquerors but as sojourners, they worked their way toward freedom in Mexico, often finding ways to be needed by the Indians. When the natives took sick, the author of the *Relación* noted, they "wanted to make medicine men of us without any examination or asking for our diplomas." The Spaniards, and even the non-Christian Moor Estebán, then followed Catholic practice by making the sign of the cross and reciting the Lord's Prayer and the Ave Maria, a prayer to their patroness, the mother of Jesus. To their amazement, natives thereupon pronounced themselves healed.

Periodically during the trek, the four endured slavery and each time escaped from it. Theirs is the most sustained close-up view of the natives' life in the sixteenth century. Cabeza de Vaca dutifully noted violence in religious rites as well as the presence of homosexuality, eunuchs, trances induced by smoking, child abandonment, and even infant sacrifice. Yet he also wanted sympathetically to share the Indian point of view in the hope that in future times others would find in his writing a valuable manual of tribal usages.

Skill and luck kept the new medicine men alive. As the Christians and the Moor made the sign of the cross, word of their powers spread until villagers haggled for their services and bickered dangerously for their notice when it came time for the party to leave. The healers themselves always needed healing, as their own naked bodies blistered in the sun. Cabeza de Vaca wrote that he consoled himself by thinking always of the sufferings of Jesus and the providence of God.

The Indian grapevine spread word of the wonder workers until their miracles ironically turned into handicaps for them. In the Texas and Mexico countryside, Cabeza de Vaca wrote, "so great was their excitement and eagerness to touch us that, everyone wanting to be first, they nearly squeezed us to death." Long and curious processions snaked across the landscape until the march got out of hand and the Indians began to fall out with each other. The ordeal suddenly became an exploration of discovery: crossing one ridge in Rio Grande territory, the four became the first visitors from the Old World to see and tell about adobe dwellings and pueblos. Forty-seven years later, the next Spaniard to visit there, Antonio de Espejo, found people still using the sign of the cross.

While Cabeza de Vaca claimed to speak six Indian tongues, he knew there were more than "a thousand different ones." Exchanges had to go on largely between people who could not comprehend each other. "Had there been a language in which we could have made ourselves perfectly understood, we would have left them all Christians. All this we gave them to understand as clearly as possible." The doughty leader believed that he and his party left the land at peace everywhere as they taught by signs that in heaven was a being called God who made commands and bestowed all good.

The people of God, however, did not always bestow good. As the travelers finally came to areas where armed Spaniards had already been, they found vacant villages, the inhabitants gone "out of dread of the Christians." Seven years of wandering, however, had taught Cabeza de Vaca how to live with every kind of Indian until he came up with a formula for converting them to Catholicism: "They should be well treated, and not otherwise." Slave-seeking Spanish raiders, who in 1536 rescued the four stragglers in northern Mexico, for good measure took along a few of the Indians who had befriended them. The pattern of the *Relación* has no successors.

Catholics in what came to be called the New Spain, which centered in Mexico, now began to spread the rumor that the travelers had seen some of the legendary lost Seven Cities of Cibola with their treasures of gold and jewels. The viceroy, Don Antonio de Mendoza, in 1539 authorized a modest exploration in search of them, but failed to cajole the three weary Christian survivors of the earlier trek into leading it. Only Esteban agreed to accompany the eccentric Fray Marcos de Niza in advance of a party to be led in 1540 by Don Francisco Vásquez de Coronado.

Now was to begin a new era, in which the lust of conquerors also created openings for those who seriously took up the Catholic mission of spreading the faith among the natives. Esteban himself was soon off the scene, the Moor having unwisely welcomed tribute from the Indians and taken their women for himself. While Esteban kept luring Fray Marcos on with word of turquoise doorways in the first of the cities of Cibola, he eventually pressed too far. Vengeful Indians killed him somewhere in the area of what is today New Mexico.

The archbishop of Mexico, Juan de Zumárraga, trusted Marcos as a great religious person. Viceroy Mendoza also knew he would treat the Indians well. After Marcos first set out to teach the sign of the cross to the Pima, he reported back honestly: "There are no great cities there." But in a second report he claimed to have spied Cibola, though from a distance, of course. Did the sun reach his brain, or did his taste for the fantastic overwhelm him at this point? No one knows why he made up such a story, because Spaniards, he had to know, would certainly check it out. They remembered not his telling of the Christian message to natives but only his report of Ahacus, a very beautiful city, bigger than the city of Mexico. First tempted to enter it, Marcos admitted, he said he withdrew because he had offered his life to God. If he were killed, who then would hear of the "greatest and best of the discoveries"?

The Franciscans promoted Marcos to a new post, but the naive Mendoza made the mistake of believing him and sent Coronado off to Cibola, which turned out to be a miserable pueblo. Coronado kept hearing of more golden cities ahead at a place the natives called Quivira. He pushed on, pointlessly, all the way into the Kansas of today. At the end of his deepest probe, in the summer of 1542, he planted a cross and then turned back southwest toward the snows of mountainous New Mexico. Coronado fought many Indians along the way, and feared death after a fall from his horse when he remembered the prediction of an astrologer that thus he would die. Finally, in 1542, the adventurer gave up in defeat and departed. Development of the Central Plains by whites had to wait three more centuries.

Back north in the Kansan area called Quivira, an Andalusian known as Fray Juan de Padilla remained on the scene. An old soldier who had turned peaceful chaplain, the missionary watched with regret when Coronado placed the cross and left the scene. The Franciscan then snatched a broom and swept a little sacred space at the foot of the structure. There he also taught the natives some simple Christian gestures — how to fold their hands, how to make the signs of prayer. As he and two lay brothers rode away sadly, he fixed the spot in his mind, regretting every mile he had to put between himself and that cross.

Padilla in the months to come would transform his old military passion into a love for Indians and a dream of martyrdom. In the Spanish Catholicism of his day, people believed that to die in the name of the cross of Jesus would assure more immediate access to heaven and less punishment in purgatory. Thus Fray Juan could advance both the Indians' cause and his own by risking death. On a Sunday in the season of Lent, 1542, the friar announced to the company that the Bible and his superiors supported his efforts to teach and convert the natives. Coronado, who thought him to be out of his mind, reluctantly saw the men off. They became the first whites known to set out intentionally on a spiritual mission without weapons in North America.

Some years later stories were told of how the heart of Fray Juan de Padilla leaped when he heard that reverent Indians still swept clear the land under the cross in Quivira and how they still prayed there. He set out with flour for the bread and wine for Mass and went to teach the Indians. The Wichita, who liked him as a magician, refused to share him with their enemies the Kaw, or Kansa, people on the Kansas River. According to an admirer of Padilla's who later wrote the story, the Wichita angrily confronted the unarmed missionary. Padilla ordered his companions to retreat while he stayed on. From a distance this author, Andrés de Campo, said he saw Indians shoot and strip the saintly man and then throw rocks, killing him. The companions later sneaked back and gave the body a Christian burial.

Fray Juan thus had his wish. He became the first known European martyr on American soil. His legend grew, until two centuries later Spanish historian Matías de la Mota Padilla could tout that "at his passing many prodigies took place; the land was flooded, comets and balls of fire were seen, and the sun was hidden."

The patterns of the European forays into American Indian territory were quickly set. Columbus had proposed that the conquerors could both save and enslave the Indians. The conquistadores on his trail, though some brought along token bands of missionaries to do saving work, chose to enslave or kill those who were in their way. By accident Cabeza de Vaca had shown that there could be understanding between the two peoples if the Europeans came defenselessly. Few sane Europeans would put themselves in such a circumstance. The preachers who rode with Coronado finally took up the task of saving Indians for the Christian heaven, even if this meant martyrdom for the missionaries.

One cleric above all others, Bartolomé de Las Casas, though he never set foot on United States soil, deserves to be remembered as the most persistent representative Indians ever had in Europe. As a missionary, he tried to live up to a title briefly assigned him. He was to be "Universal Procurator and Protector of All the Indians of the Indies." God, he said, charged him forever with the office of weeping for the sorrows of these Indians, and he must suffer with and for them.

From childhood Las Casas's destiny was tied to that of the New World. His father sailed with Columbus on his second voyage and brought back an Indian slave to serve as a page for his son at the university. (This was one of the slaves that Isabella freed.) Bartolomé, who followed his father's path to the West Indian island of Hispaniola in 1502 as a planter, became a slaveholder. He helped the Spaniards conquer Cuba, and owned land and Indians as late as 1514. Meanwhile, he had also been ordained a priest; some think he was the first to take holy orders in America. Las Casas came to have a divided mind about his mission. As he told it, his conversion to the Indian cause came in 1514, when he was to preach on Ecclesiasticus, chapter 34: "The sacrifice of an offering unjustly acquired is a mockery." He was mocking God because he had taken the goods of the Indian poor. As he rode from village to village, he heard them shout, "Hungry! Hungry! Hungry!" The priest concluded that he must return to Europe to plead their cause.

King Ferdinand was unsympathetic, but Cardinal Jiménez, by then virtual ruler of Spain, backed Las Casas until the new king, Charles V, took the throne. Charles, knowing the missionary, granted Las Casas a colony on the Venezuelan coast. This attempted utopia, which he called Tierra Firma, lasted only two years. Disconsolate because he could come up with no successful scheme to replace the slave system, and disgraced in the eyes of his enemies the slaveholders, Las Casas, "as if he were already dead," he said, retired for twelve years to a Dominican monastery. He became a Dominican and set out to write *Historia de las Indias*.

The convent could not hold the restless agitator. In 1536, two years after he left it, he was in Guatemala, unsuccessfully experimenting with Indian villages. A year later Pope Paul III began a modest defense of Indian rights. Las Casas used this support to champion the interests of natives until Charles V in 1542 promulgated "New Laws for the Indies," to free the Indians from slavery.

Economics, it should be said, had as much as conscience to do with these laws. Many in Spain envied the newly rich empire-builders in America, who with their slave labor were upsetting the Spanish economy and class system. Las Casas despised the gradualism of the New Laws but he learned to live with them, while American slave-owners never did. In Peru the landholders revolted. Elsewhere they dragged their feet until it became clear that the laws were unenforceable. Las Casas cried out with his famed treatise *Brief Relation of the Destruction of the Indies,* a virtual epitaph for the Indians that he published at last in 1552. It spread the "Black Legend" with which England and other European nations tarred Spain, even though they themselves had no better record in respect to the Indians.

Through the decades Las Casas commuted between continents, unwearying in his defense of the Indians. In the mid-1540s he served briefly as a bishop at Chiapas in southern Mexico, where slaveholding communicants paid him the compliment of trying to lynch him. Other bishops were hardly friendlier. In 1545 at a Honduran ecclesiastical gathering a former friend, Alonso de Maldonado, opened the formal sessions with a cry referring to Las Casas: "Throw that lunatic out of here!" Would Charles V please dispatch this "arrogant" bishop back to the monastery in Spain? In 1547 Las Casas did return to Spain, learning on the way home that Charles V had had to revoke the New Laws two years earlier. The seventy-two-year-old Las Casas never returned to America and died twenty years later.

No well-placed European before or since so eloquently defended Indian rights. Las Casas called the Spanish conquerors wolves, lions, and tigers who tore Indians in pieces, killed them, martyred them, tormented and afflicted them. Other defenders joined the cause, including his rival, the Franciscan Toribio de Motolinía, who claimed that for half a league around the mines and along the roads in the New World one could hardly avoid walking over dead Indian bodies and bones. Governor Mendoza charged that at a certain hill Spaniards placed Indians in a row to blow them to pieces with cannon fire, to be torn apart by dogs, or to be handed to Negroes who then killed them by knife blows or rope.

Centuries before most Westerners learned to appreciate faiths other than their own, Las Casas sometimes overcompensated and spread romantic words about Indian innocence and simplicity. Even "without the light of faith" they had developed republics and lacked nothing to enjoy civil happiness. In his eye, Indians were equal to some Old World nations, superior to others, and "to none were they inferior." In his *Apologética Historia,* the old bishop wrote that he preferred Indians to Greeks and Romans, English and French, and certainly to most Spaniards.

Along the way Las Casas picked up choice enemies in Spain, notably Juan Ginés de Sepúlveda, whom he debated at Valladolid in August of 1550. Both experts used the philosopher Aristotle in their toe-to-toe contest over whether Indians were by nature doomed to be slaves. Non-Christians, said Las Casas in his opening five-hundred-page statement, had the right to be free; kings and popes must assure this. Nonsense, thundered his foe; the Law of Nature applied only to civilized people, who were to govern, not to barbarians who could be enslaved. By 1550 Europeans were well aware of the Aztec practices of human sacrifice. Sepúlveda used their example to show how savage the Indians were. Las Casas did not shrink from even that challenge. Greeks and Hebrews, Romans and earlier Europeans, he argued, all had passed through a stage in which they engaged in such sacrifice as a way to show they had a conscience — just before they realized that Jesus had sacrificed himself to God for them, making their own sacrifices unnecessary. Las Casas could not resist adding that at least such victims died for a cause, while the victims of the Spanish holocaust died pointlessly.

In the end, Las Casas turned truly radical by the Catholic standards of his day. Conversion had to be voluntary or it was not conversion. "The Indians are our brothers, and Christ has given his life for them." Case closed. Sepúlveda, on the other hand, congratulated himself with the presents that came to him from Mexico City after the debates, while Las Casas counted the crown on his side. He came finally to push his defense to the outer limits of a new humanism, where civility mattered almost more than conversion. The attempt to win the New World and convert the Indians was futile if it meant destruction: "God does not want a gain achieved with so much loss." Thus it would be a mortal sin, thought Las Casas, to toss an infant into a well in order to baptize it and save its soul, if thereby it died. What sounds like common sense to many moderns bordered on heresy when he uttered it.

Las Casas did the Indians no favor when he overadvertised their virtues; it would be unwise to misrepresent him here. A man of his own day, a day that took human slavery for granted, he made a tragic proposal back in 1516 — one that had enormous consequences. While outlining his communal system for the New World he added a fatal line: "If necessary white and black slaves can be brought from Castile." Two years later he shortened this proposal simply to "Negro slaves." Like other early protectors of the Indians, Las Casas thought them superior to black Africans, but because he was already the voice of conscience to thoughtful people in church and court, his word meant more than the word of others. In 1518 Charles V first authorized the purchase of slaves for use in the Indies. Years later Las Casas vehemently reversed his stand. In his *Historia* he, almost alone in his time, said that "the same law applies equally to the Negro as to the Indians," but by then it was too late to do much good.

In 1573, seven years after the death of Las Casas, Spain entered a new era. Distracted by European ventures, it ceased further efforts at conquest in the Indies. No longer troubled by infidel Jews and Muslims, Spain, in an age of rising nationalism, had its hands full and its ships busy against other nations of Europe. In an age of religious revolt, Spaniards found most disconcerting the challenge of Protestants from France, the Netherlands, and, most of all, England. Each of these seagoing nations wanted to share the gain of the New World and, they said, to spread the mission of their new faith among "all the Indians of the Indies." Their hour, they believed, had come.

Catholic Iberians had had the New World virtually to themselves for most of the sixteenth century — their "hour" — but such a situation could not last. It was inevitable that sooner or later other Catholic nations would challenge the papal document that divided the newly discovered hemisphere between Spain and Portugal alone. France was the first. On a gray December day in 1514, the year before he became king, impatient François d'Angoulême, pacing the floor at the castle of Blois, sputtered a first taunt in reference to Western shores: "*Non, messieurs!* God did not create those lands solely for Castilians!" However, the dashing prince at the time was too eagerly trying to win the favor of the pope to do anything about those lands. In 1516, having ascended the throne, he even packed off to Rome to declare himself a loyal "elder son of the Catholic Church." Such an elder son would not risk punishment by the pope for trespassing.

As Francis I, hungry for glory, he longed to become the Holy Roman Emperor. This would make him ruler of central and western Europe, and would further his dream of leading Catholic Europe in a new crusade to the holy places of Jerusalem. Such a campaign could unite the long-divided Christian East and West under one crown — his own. He faced formidable rivals for the office, and the electors, their pockets lined with bribes, chose instead Charles I of Spain to be Emperor Charles V. Since the base of the empire was Germany, it turned out that the same Charles could apply pressure to Francis from there and, more effectively, from Spain. When the pope, Leo X, then lined up with Charles and Henry VIII of England against France, Francis felt free to go his own way in the Atlantic.

France was wealthy, but she lacked great ships and captains. Because his was a nation of farmers and fishermen, not plotters of sea voyages, the king had to contract in 1524 with an eager Italian, Giovanni da Verrazano, to sail his *Dauphine* under French flags. Verrazano cautiously evaded the armed ships of Spain and the disasters that could await him on Carolina sandbars, and so became the first known European to sight the location of today's New York on his way up the coast to Nova Scotia. A Florentine now from Lyons, Verrazano claimed that he wanted eventually to help Christianize the "poor, tough and ignorant people" of America, so he observed them carefully. The *Report* he later filed from Dieppe contended that these gullible natives knew no creed and lived in "entire freedom." The captain had considered it a good sign when he saw Indians imitate French acts of worship, but found no trace of sacred places among them. Consequently, he decided that they knew neither religion nor law, neither First Cause nor God, and worshiped no stars, sun, planets, or sky. Their souls were empty vessels for Christians to fill.

Francis was pleased enough to learn that Verrazano had named the new lands Francesca, but where, he wondered, were the promised silks, the gold, the northwest passage to Asia? The king had no time or money for speculation during his battles with Charles V. Because the Italian merchants in Lyons who helped finance Verrazano would not back Francis's military venture, the king sent them home. Besides, rumor had it that some of these backers were toying with the dangerous new ideas of the German monk Martin Luther, who was then on the point of dividing the Christian world. Verrazano did find support for two later voyages, but on a southern swing he naively approached some Carib Indians, who ate him while his brother watched in horror as the sand turned "ruddy with the fraternal blood."

European alliances shifted suddenly, and in 1533 Pope Clement VII, choosing to favor France, gave Francis mild encouragement to venture in America. At a fete celebrating the marriage of Clement's niece Catherine de Médicis to the future French king Henry II, the pope let it be known that he considered inapplicable the grant by Pope Alexander VI of New World lands to Iberians: it did not affect territories found after 1493/94. In 1534, Francis commissioned Jacques Cartier, "a good man, fearing God," who set out on three voyages to Canada in search of a northwest passage to India.

While Cartier set out as an explorer, not a converter, his Catholic piety showed when he planted a thirty-foot-high cross on the forbidding, rocky shores of what came to be New France. Then, kneeling to show the Indians, he pointed out — one wonders how, given the language barrier — that their salvation depended only on God.

An ingenious Huron chief named Donnaccona responded with signs of his own. They added up to the idea that he resented anyone placing a cross and trying to take possession of his territory. As the French learned to translate, they somehow heard of the Huron spirit named Cudragny, but refused to think of him as a god. Only One God lived in heaven, they preached, and mortals must believe in Him. Though Cartier had brought no priests to baptize the natives, he explained that "it was absolutely necessary to be baptized or else to go to hell." The captain, almost as an afterthought, promised to bring along priests and holy oil on a future trip.

In 1542 the French made one more probe of the northern coasts. This time Jean François de la Roque, Sieur de Roberval, headed an expedition. This trip there was announced advance interest in a mission for the natives. France was showing some interest in making converts, in part to please Pope Paul III, who was less friendly than Clement VII and who demanded such conversions. But

Roberval was himself a believer in the new Protestant faith and may have probed for a place of refuge for his fellow believers. In any case, he found the natives unfriendly and, after a severe winter, returned to Europe. The French crown showed no taste for New France for another sixty years. Roberval himself was killed in 1561 at Paris in one of the riots over religion that distracted and bloodied France for decades.

As is clear from various references in this chapter — to Lyonnais merchants who were suspected of following Martin Luther, to Roberval's possible ties to the new Protestant faith, to French riots over religion — a new force was on the European scene. When Columbus "discovered" America in 1492, all of western Europe (except for pockets of Judaism) was Catholic. Popes might vie politically with emperors, and bishops might war with princes, but these were intense quarrels within a single family of faith headed by the Roman pope. Yet only one generation after the discovery of America, Europe came to be divided. Most of northern Europe defied the pope and moved into various forms of Protestantism, a different version of the Christian faith.

Since the eventual United States of America came to be regarded as a Protestant nation, the change in Europe so near the time of the country's discovery was fateful. The story of American colonization between New Spain to the south and New France to the north was webbed with the story of northern Europe's religious change. As the eastern shore of the future United States became the new landscape, it awaited the new pilgrims.

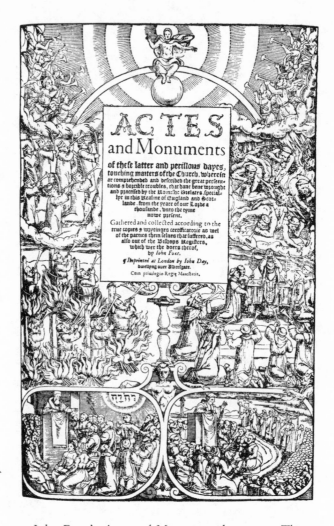

John Foxe's *Actes and Monuments*, known as *The Book of Martyrs*, was a New England best-seller. It fueled the anti-Catholic fires in many Protestant hearts during the Age of Exploration. Conflict between these Christian religions is clearly illustrated on this title page, which shows God, surrounded by angels, receiving trumpeted praise from burning Protestant martyrs while the devils look down on a Roman Catholic priest saying Mass. (*By permission of the Folger Shakespeare Library*)

Chapter Four

HOLY WARS AND
SACRED PIRACIES

THE REFORM OF CHRISTIANITY TO WHICH SPANIARDS LIKE ISA-
bella and Jiménez contributed occurred under the banner of the
papacy. Roman Catholics in many parts of Europe were discontented with immorality and laxity in the church. A generation of
prophets began to storm against excesses. They preached against
the way common people were being cheated in a system that, in
effect, led believers to act out of fear and then try to earn or buy
their way into heaven. Moved by fiery visions of God, they
scorned the moral looseness of much of the clergy and the obscene
luxury of the princes of the church, including the popes. Much of
their reform was containable inside Catholicism, though it constantly tested the borders of what was allowable.

Then, suddenly, in the second decade of the sixteenth century,
in northern Europe, the walls gave way and reform burst beyond
the bounds of papacy and priesthood. From the German monastery
where the monk Martin Luther agonized over his guilt in a search
for a gracious God, and from the new University of Wittenberg
where he taught, came angry blasts against both immoral life and
what he called immoral teaching. In Switzerland the more staid and
systematic lawyer John Calvin began to envision a further reformed church based both on grace and a strong sense of divine
providence or control in history. This Calvinist version was to
have more voice in America than did the Lutheran.

In England Henry VIII, who first was named Defender of the Faith for his attacks on Luther and then himself moved the Church of England from under papal control, made way for reforms he himself did not understand. What looked like an attempt to regularize his marital rogueries came to be an opportunity for sincere reformers to war against what they saw as Roman Catholic oppression and distortion. In England, as on the Continent, these mainline reforms were also matched by far more radical attempts to set the Christian house in order. To their advocates, Luther, Calvin, and Henry's churchmen were too conservative in what they kept by way of worship and church order. The "left wing" of the Reformation rebaptized people, demolished stained glass and organs, and overturned inherited patterns of authority.

Was there at root one single cause on which these Protestants united? They would have said that their obsession was with divine grace. They united in their attack on the way the priesthood under the bishops and pope had a monopoly on the system of grace. The Roman church, they said, made a political or financial game out of playing on people's fear of hell. In the process the biblical theme of a loving God was lost. Catholic reformers agreed with this attack in part, but wanted to make changes within the church, not by being thrown out or going into exile from it. Those who were Protestant lost patience, status, or, in some cases, limb and life. Europe was never again to be united in faith. The exploring and settlement of North America was also henceforth to reflect the battles over faith that divided Europe.

In France, this Reformation of the church centered in a party called Huguenot. Shaped less by Luther than by Calvin, a French émigré to Switzerland, it became a potent minority, attractive especially to nobles who resented both the pope and the king. Short of an Inquisition, the monarch could do little to prevent the Huguenot allegiance from spreading, so the French took to the streets to settle their disputes. Between 1562 and 1598 they fought frequent civil wars. As early as the 1560s some Huguenot losers were looking to the New World as a refuge should they have to go into exile. The first groups to sail helped transplant European styles of Catholic-Protestant holy war to America, though the collisions they inspired immediately taught colonists how futile such conflict was.

Vengeful men — Huguenots in name only, to whom faith meant little — began harassing Spain through acts of piracy as early as 1538. To the Spanish they were *corsarios luteranos,* "Lutheran pirates," who killed Catholics as they raided their galleons. In Cuba they burned churches and slaughtered priests in the name of their purses and their Lord. Responsible French Protestants had to look elsewhere than among them for New World pioneers. The Huguenot leader Admiral Gaspard de Coligny selected a redoutable Captain Jean Ribault to explore a place of Protestant refuge and then himself went off reluctantly to fight French Catholics, leaving Ribault to his own devices. In spring of 1562 Ribault built Charlesfort, on what is today the island of Port Royal, South Carolina, but the settlement lasted only two years. Protestantism lacked a toehold.

Coligny still dreamed of a place of asylum and sent Captain René de Laudonnière to America with 150 adventurers in 1564. They chose a Florida site near the mouth of the Saint Johns River and named it Fort Caroline. Just as they were on the point of accepting the offer of visiting English privateer John Hawkins to return them to Europe, in sailed Ribault with seven ships and three hundred settlers. At last the colony seemed promising. On June 30, 1564, the settlers held the first thanksgiving festival on the continent. At their reasonably cozy fort, a bell signaled daily worship. The nearby Indians now learned to distinguish between the French "good white tribe" and the Spanish "bad white tribe." Relations with these natives were friendly, though Laudonnière's stern Protestant conscience forbade sexual intercourse with them apart from marriage.

In the midst of their idyll, Spain acted. The men of King Philip II were under orders to keep their eyes on these Protestant devils. He charged Pedro Menéndez de Avilés, a veteran Indies captain, to lead an assault with ten ships and twenty-seven hundred armed Spaniards. Menéndez was eager to look for his shipwrecked son and to bring death to all heretics, just as he hoped to help save natives for Catholicism. On August 28, 1565, he founded Saint Augustine, the oldest permanent European settlement in North America. Soon he skirmished with Ribault, whose ships ran aground during a hurricane after the Frenchmen set out to attack the Catholic fort. Menéndez then sloshed overland for four foggy days and with five hundred men massacred the remaining French, who were enjoying the false security bad weather provided.

The warriors in two of the four raiding ships with Ribault bailed out and headed back to Fort Caroline by land, but Menéndez's men captured and killed these 140 heretics. Ribault soon had to abandon the other two ships, the last reminders of a planned Huguenot empire. Menéndez surrounded the Huguenots and carried on a charade following Old World rules. Would he spare the lives of captives? Outnumbered, though he did not let the French know it, he urged them to trust him. This they did, lacking the prospect of better bargains, since he promised to do what the Lord God inspired him to do. Later he boasted to the king that when the French surrendered he had his men tie their hands and take them off ten at a time to a place out of sight, where they were promptly killed. "I do this, not as to Frenchmen, but as to Lutherans." His crusade, he claimed, was just; had not these heretics played cards with decks that depicted the sacred bread and chalice of the Mass, and had they not trampled sacred objects and made fun of the saints?

While Philip II honored his warrior for the Lord, the French, including the Catholics, came alive as a nation and called for revenge. Three years later Dominique of Gourgues, whom the Inquisition had once enslaved, went looking for blood in Florida. He and some Indian allies swooped down at siesta time on drunk and dozing Spaniards and killed them. "Done, not to Spaniards, but to murderers and thieves."

The exchange was a minor incident in the history of bloodshed, a massacre matched on any number of evenings in the France of that day. As conflicts have gone through history, this was almost a toy holy war, a mixture of politics, adventurism, and religious justification. At most it was a brief, glittering if bloody reflection in the New World of a time-honored pattern from the Old World. Yet it did signal on its tiny scale the dread possibility that America might reproduce the holy wars that then plagued Europe. The pilgrimages on the new continent would then have turned into the patterns of exile that characterized so much of history as religious dissenters fled and hid from victors. Yet nothing quite like this was ever again to occur on American soil. Nothing was left of Huguenot America. When France did succeed in settling Canada after 1608, the venture excluded the Protestants.

Not all history henceforth was to be made by Protestants. There still were bits of a Catholic story to tell. Thus Menéndez lived on, freed of his concern about Lutherans. He next tried to convert Florida Indians to the Catholic faith. His priests fanned out among the tribes, but sometimes they needed his help. A chief the Spaniards called Carlos promised to convert and to bring his people along if the governor would marry his sister. Many a Spanish conqueror would have leaped at such terms for gaining a willing bedmate, but Menéndez faced scruples against being a bigamist.

Finally, he saw no way out but to have the sister baptized Doña Antónia, and to let the Christian women scrub and clothe her, after which he charmed her through supper until he could no longer evade bed. "In the morning she arose very joyful," said a chronicler of the scene. With such sacrifices by their governor as an example, Jesuit baptizers pushed all the way to Chesapeake Bay, where Indians massacred them, while Franciscans saw some success from their precarious base at Saint Augustine. Philip II, however, let the mainland mission fall into neglect after 1572 as he turned his attention to counter England, which by now was also turning its attention to America.

Before Columbus, English fishermen from Bristol may have touched on North American shores. Five years after Columbus's discovery, King Henry VII of England borrowed an Italian renamed John Cabot and sent him to subdue, occupy, and possess any places of the heathen and infidels "unknown to all Christians." Nothing permanent came of that probe. Not until England turned Protestant did it acquire the passion for New World settlement.

Henry VIII, who led England in revolt against the pope in the 1530s, was more eager to control English life than he was to change Catholicism. But he had had to turn his back on the pope in conflict over his marriages and he had dissolved the monasteries. Henry could not keep the scholars from teaching Protestant doctrines nor the people from reading the Bible in English. After 1547, during the regency of his son, Edward VI, Protestants became more bold in their break with Rome. Soon English Protestant leaders spoke as self-assuredly about their arrangements with God as did those in Spain on the Catholic side.

Historian John Foxe did as much as anyone to fire the anti-Catholic spirit that the English needed to spur them to mission and conquest. Foxe picked up Protestant ideas at Oxford University and then joined exiles on the Continent after Catholic Mary Tudor, who became queen in 1553, made life dangerous for agitators. The printing press was still quite new, and Foxe understood the propaganda value of books in an age hungry for print. He resolved to fight the pope and Queen Mary by writing *Actes and Monuments,* also known as *The Book of Martyrs,* which was full of gruesome stories about how Catholics persecuted faithful servants of Christ. The original Latin edition published in Switzerland was only 750 pages long, but in England Foxe later kept up with current events, and, by adding illustrations depicting violence, made a best-seller out of an edition that ran to 2,314 pages. Church leaders rendered the book available to the public and ministers were told to buy it for their families; pirates took it to sea for inspiration when they chased Spanish ships.

In 1558 Queen Elizabeth succeeded Mary, who by then had exiled eight hundred people and put nearly three hundred others to death. Elizabeth was for Protestantism, but first she was for England. So were members of a generation of propagandists like John Foxe. A tract by John Aylmer included the marginal note "God is English." Matthew Parker, archbishop of Canterbury, also observed that Almighty God was "so much English." Seaman John Davis carried through on the consequences: "We of England are [the] saved people," whom God sent to the heathen in the sea and the isles. The English and "none but we" must shine as the messengers of the Lord. In lines like these the English began to express the fierce pride in empire that its colonists were to import into New England.

Pirates first challenged Spain in the name of England and Protestantism. It may seem strange to link holy wars and piracy as activities of people who claimed to be doing God's will. Yet religion, a force for ennobling life and giving it meaning, can also be used to justify the ugliest of human ventures. Crusaders and conquistadores, claiming to have heard or read the word of God, find themselves righteous as they stab "infidels." Both sides in holy wars regularly feel that they are acting out a divine drama that finds God on their side. So pirates, who plundered gold that shippers had plundered from mines on Indian soil, justified their ways by seeing themselves as divine instruments against the vessels of Antichrist.

For a decade or two, many English thought it foolish to plant in America if gold was available, and stupid to dig for gold if privateers could snatch it from Spanish ships. Plunder thus became an instrument of state. Monarchs pretended to close their eyes to it while they shared the loot and then honored the pirate heroes. Just as Columbus once called for crusades against the infidel, now Elizabethans wanted to charge out against the Catholic Antichrist in the spirit of Sir Humphrey Gilbert in his pamphlet *How Her Majesty May Annoy the King of Spain*.

Piracy and religion do not make a familiar blend, but in the age of Sir Francis Drake they did. The first sea captain to survive a trip around the globe, he packed with care to make room both for expected Spanish goods and for the hefty books of his friend John

Foxe. In lonely hours during his great three-year trip that began in 1577, Drake doted on the bloody tales of Catholic treachery. When boredom threatened as his ship *Golden Hind* rolled with the gentle waves, Drake retired to his cabin and applied tints — presumably blood red most of the time — to the woodcuts in the book by Foxe showing Protestant martyrs.

Drake had nurtured his anti-Catholicism ever since childhood, but made it an obsession after the Mexican viceroy in 1568 once tricked him and his relative John Hawkins in the West Indies. They barely made off with their lives. Drake swore henceforth to become the avenging angel of God against the Catholic Antichrist. During a stop at one port he forced the Catholic vicar to look at the pictures in *The Book of Martyrs*. Drake also let his boatswain spit out "Why do you wear this? It's no good" as he bit into an image of the Virgin Mary and then tore the prayer beads from the neck of a captured Catholic. The captain further forced the hated papists to break church laws by eating meat during Holy Week, and for good measure at Guatulco he despoiled a church, destroyed an altarpiece, defaced statues, and trampled communion wafers. The Spanish captains received special orders to get this "low man," but he eluded them.

"Is the queen alive?" Drake's was a natural question when he reached home, and Elizabeth received him lavishly. He gave her stolen jewels and she knighted him. The era of such ceremonies was brief, however, because Spanish gold came in ever shorter supply and the risks of taking it became too great a threat to international peace. England came to want an empire more than it needed hit-or-miss raids. For such a realm new propagandists spelled out a Christian mission. The Reverend Richard Hakluyt mourned that after ninety long years the Iberians still possessed a monopoly in the New World. The English must spread the true message of Christ, he urged, since by 1584 not one Indian infidel was yet an English Protestant convert, while the papists had reached "millions" of them.

The two half brothers Sir Humphrey Gilbert and Sir Walter Raleigh took England toward the point of settlement. Both of them combined a Protestant identity with the new Elizabethan scientific outlook, and they seemed more ready to observe and invest in the New World than to win souls there. Gilbert was practical: if Elizabeth would send the needy and criminals to America, it would save wear and tear on the English gallows. He could handle such toughs;

he practiced for America by serving the queen during her anti-Catholic Irish wars. There he mounted the heads of his victims along the walkway of his tent to impress his evening visitors.

Gilbert in 1578 received a charter to explore heathenish lands not already possessed by other Christians. After a poorly planned start, he waited four years and ventured again in 1583. He claimed Newfoundland for the queen and turned homeward. Across some stormy waves, an observer on a companion ship saw Gilbert on the deck of his pinnace *Squirrel* calmly reading a book. Sir Humphrey waved and shouted: "We are as near to heaven by sea as by land!" At midnight the lights disappeared and Gilbert was gone; his Newfoundland project lay in neglect for three decades.

Gilbert's half brother Walter Raleigh was his match in boldness and anti-Catholicism alike. Young Raleigh remembered seeing his fiercely Protestant father snatch a cross from a church and smash it because it recalled popery. At age fourteen he was already fighting in Huguenot campaigns in France, where he recalled chasing Catholics into a cave in Languedoc. Then he let down bundles of lighted straw to kill them or choke them into surrender. Yet as a part-time skeptic Raleigh was cynical enough to observe that men on both sides commit atrocities in holy wars and mask their selfish goals with the face of religion.

Raleigh's own selfish goal was to win the favor of Elizabeth. The handsome delight of haberdashers succeeded. After he also held a minor command in Ireland, she tried to keep him close to court, where the two found poetic ways to express their respect for each other. Raleigh was eager to sail, and when he produced funds plus the know-how of astrologer John Dee and the skeptical scientist Thomas Hariot, he received letters patent to colonize. His reconnaissance party left Plymouth for Roanoke Island in today's North Carolina. It sailed without him in April 1584. When it returned the queen knighted him. He announced that he named the remote shore where he had never set foot Virginia, in her honor.

In 1585 Raleigh sent out a small fleet under his cousin Sir Richard Grenville. Sir Richard soon took the pirate route back home to England, leaving the outpost at Roanoke Island off Virginia in the hands of Sir Ralph Lane, who later did much to spread negative images of Indians upon his return to England. From Roanoke Thomas Hariot reported favorably about the natives, who he thought were on the verge of worshiping one deity and seemed likely to accept the Christian God. Lane left a hundred men behind to man the outpost, and Sir Francis Drake subsequently rescued them.

Finally Raleigh sent out a colony under the gifted John White in 1587 and then promptly neglected it in order to fight the Spanish Armada. Spain's Philip II chartered this fleet of military vessels in 1588 to back up his army in the Netherlands that was waiting to invade England. The mission was ill planned, for the 130 slow vessels with their twenty-seven thousand men aboard proved very vulnerable in Spain's effort to bring God and Catholicism back to England. The English encountered the fleet off Cornwall but could not advantageously use Her Majesty's 197 ships, which could not maneuver well enough to make the British guns effective against the massive Spanish ships. The Spanish seamen escaped, but Philip's army in the Netherlands was not ready to join them. When the British improved their tactics and the whole Armada venture turned into a fiasco, Spain retreated, with only 76 ships making it back home. The invincibility of Spain had become a myth, and England's rise was an event of epochal significance — especially for North America, a large part of which was to become part of its empire.

The little colony at Roanoke was far removed from such stirring sea battles, its settlers engrossed in the mere act of survival. There were signs that portended a future for England in Virginia. A child was born: the granddaughter of White, Virginia Dare, who was the firstborn Anglo-American. White had returned to England. No relief party was able to come back to the colonies until late summer of 1590. The new expedition reported that upon its arrival "we let our grapnel near the shore and sounded with a trumpet a call, and afterwards many familiar English tunes of songs, and called to them friendly, but no one answered." Next day the would-be rescuers found some relics, native footprints, and the word CROATOAN carved on a tree. The fate of the "Lost Colony" was never determined. Today some Croatan Indians, now called Lumbees, survive in North Carolina; observers sometimes claimed that the people had a fair appearance and that a few Elizabethan English terms lived in their speech.

Elizabethan England cared little about the mystery of the Roanoke disappearance, though philosopher-scientist Francis Bacon did chide Raleigh anonymously, calling it "the sinfullest thing in the world" to forsake a plantation, for "besides the dishonour, it is the guiltiness of blood of many commiserable persons." Raleigh himself soon joined the commiserable: he fell out of favor with the queen and spent much of his remaining time jailed in the Tower of London. When the mild king James I came to power in 1603, he wanted peace with Spain and found it advisable to restrict Raleigh, whom the Spaniards naturally despised. Yet he did not execute him until 1618.

"I have a long journey to take," said the condemned seafarer as he confessed his faith in his Savior Christ, "and must bid the company farewell." More challenging were the last words of the old pirate Drake, who had affirmed that God had many things in store, "and I know many ways to do her Majesty good services, and to make us rich." King James it was who chartered the settlements designed to make England rich and to serve the English God beyond the far western horizon.

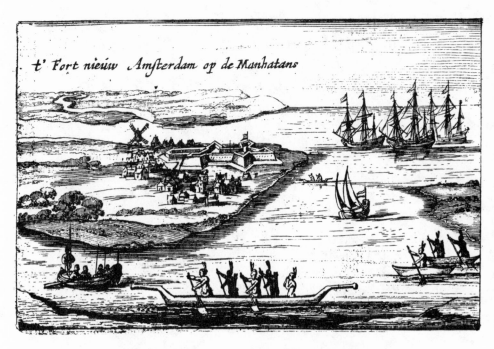

t' Fort nieuw Amsterdam op de Manhatans

New Amsterdam, today's New York City, was a
lightly populated island protected by a fort. This
early (1651) depiction of what became America's
largest city shows the fort in what is today Battery
Park as the Dutch artist believed it looked around
1627. The fort became a trading post that attracted a
religiously diverse population. (*Print Collection,
The New York Public Library, Astor,
Lenox and Tilden Foundations*)

Chapter Five

ESTABLISHING COLONIES

𝒜 PROTESTANT SETTLEMENT OF THE EASTERN SEABOARD OF NORTH America waited for a new century, the seventeenth. Because European Protestants were divided by creeds, nations, and movements, the settlements were as competitive in religion as they were in politics and commercial outlook. The Europeans established essentially three Protestant colonies in the New World: Virginia, New England, and New Netherland.

A Catholic would consider the religious ideas of the three colonies very similar, simply because all had broken with the papacy and turned to the Bible alone, rather than the Bible and the church, for religious doctrine. To the colonists themselves, however, differences between their sects were vast. The Virginians tended to be rather relaxed members of the Church of England, the official church of Henry and Elizabeth, of reformers who retained bishops and liturgies that looked like English versions of the Latin mass. The New England Puritans wanted to push reform further, to repudiate bishops and simplify worship. They were more interested in a covenant that they felt God made with them directly than they were in the idea that God worked through the official church of a nation.

Protestants from the Netherlands followed John Calvin's teachings, and had strong faith that God was the foreseeing, foreknowing plotter of human ventures. While the Dutch Reformed Church enjoyed official status in New Amsterdam and wanted to conform to the Old World's ways, the city that became New York demanded a new tolerance of the church. It was even then a town where people of many faiths found a home. From Spain and elsewhere Jews with commercial skills took refuge in New Amsterdam and were met with grudging tolerance. Inevitably, there were struggles between what the official church wanted and what it had to settle for in its diverse city in the New World.

But dwelling on the dogmatic differences between these three Protestant sects does not begin to tell the story of settlement in the New World. Formal statements of faith had very little to do with the practical arrangements of the Virginia colony, for example.

With Halley's comet as an evil omen above them in the winter skies of early 1607, three small English ships prepared to take 105 men from London to the New World. This "First Colony," later called the Virginia Company, included 59 swaggering, self-appointed gentlemen, a few artisans, and one minister of the Church of England. King James had issued a patent for them to colonize, and on May 14, 1607, they established the first permanent English settlement on American soil. Some of them wanted to help thwart Spanish expansion; some, convinced that England was overcrowded, saw their move as an investment in a plantation. Others said they were on a mission for England and God. John Donne, the poet and preacher, named theirs a "holy business"; business was chiefly on their minds, but a holy calling was at least in the background. Few of them wanted to work.

The planners back in London had first named as chaplain the veteran Richard Hakluyt, to "watch and perform the ministry and preaching of God's word in those parts." Thinking himself too old at fifty-five to migrate, he was replaced by Robert Hunt, a vicar of Heathfield who became the first English Protestant minister assigned to America.

The charter granted the settlers all the rights of Englishmen, but the investors back home burdened colonists with an unworkable form of government. Not until they opened a sealed box in Virginia did they even learn who were to be their councillors. Two names in particular spelled trouble. His enemies thought council president Edward Maria Wingfield to be a secret papist or open atheist because he carried no Bible and forbade preaching. Captain John Smith struck his foes as a pretender. To this day many are suspicious of the claims he made about his early life: how he had fought the Turks, survived slavery, was wounded in Austrian battle and honored with rank. Under a French captain he learned piracy before he caught the American fever and was evidently helped into the company by a patron. Smith almost failed to reach Virginia. En route, his rivals accused him of treason and went so far as to erect a gallows for him on their stop at the island of Nevis. He later claimed that he simply refused to mount it and in that way escaped death.

Smith arrived in chains, but his own plight soon paled as the Virginians faced up to the Indians of the Powhatan confederation. Their hostile chief, Powhatan, was head of two hundred villages and was a veteran of brief earlier encounters with Europeans on his soil. A prophet had once told him that on a third invasion by white people he would be conquered, and this was that third time. The English replied to him with cannon, and Powhatan, lacking similar arms, soon learned that he could best make his way by leaving the Virginians to their own devices, so treacherous was the colonists' life together. Meanwhile, he awaited opportunities to harass them.

The Reverend Hunt, apparently the only man who could get the squabbling settlers to talk to each other, on May 14, 1607, held the first service of Holy Communion according to the rites and doctrines of the Church of England. He later preached good doctrine and set the colonists to building a church. Service of God did little for the spirits of the men. Those who fancied themselves gentlemen refused to work, cheated on the meager supplies, and soon became dangerously dependent on trade with Indians. Illness and then death struck many, including Hunt, who was probably a typhoid carrier. Death was so frequent that the colonists buried the victims secretly. The unfriendly natives held back from attacking during the first year, and "it pleased God" and puzzled the Virginians when the natives sometimes supplied food.

Smith, eventually sworn into office, gradually emerged as a leader. During exploration of the Chickahominy River he fell into the hands of the Indians. In his precarious state he became a friend of Pocahontas, daughter of Powhatan. During what may have been an Indian rite (whether designed to adopt or execute the Englishman we cannot be sure — the event may itself have been a fiction), Smith said, she took his head into her arms and the rite ended in peace. Smith outlasted his earlier councillor rivals and became council president in September of 1608. The captain turned out to be a capable and energetic leader during the months when his men searched for a passage to Asia or turned up with fool's gold for all their prospecting efforts.

England gave little help in Indian relations. At one time Smith received bizarre orders to work on relations with natives by crowning Powhatan king in order to subject him to the English monarch. The native chief was gifted with enough combined dignity and comic-opera sense to walk through it all, but he refused to kneel when ordered to. The English wisely compromised and named him a king anyhow.

In October of 1609, because of accidental gunpowder wounds, Smith had to return to England. Luck was again with him, for after the "starving time" of the following winter, only sixty of the by-then five hundred colonists remained. A Richard Buck succeeded Hunt as minister for a brief time, until the more capable Alexander Whitaker arrived in 1611 to take care of the souls of colonists. Whitaker worked hard to establish an Indian mission at fortified little Henrico. To it some Virginians also retreated in search of a healthier climate, since it was about seventy miles up the river from Jamestown. Whitaker even championed the missions with a pamphlet he published in London two years later, "Good News from Virginia."

The Virginians generally postponed missions while they fought off starvation and civil chaos. More colonists kept arriving, until at last in May of 1611 a potent if sometimes brutal deputy governor named Thomas Dale arrived to set things on a new legal course with some "Lawes Divine, Morall and Martiall." Dale ruled for six years, and forced settlers to worship twice each Sunday under military escort, to work hard, and to fill their days with prayer. A bodkin was to be thrust through the tongue of anyone who twice spoke ill of God, and death came with the third offense. Dale showed how serious he was by executing eight offenders.

To inspire loyalty, the relenting deputy governor parceled out land to planters. To make peace with the Indians he was even ready at one time to turn bigamist. Dale wanted to marry an already wed daughter of Powhatan and requested the chief to buy back this twelve-year-old from the man who had earlier purchased and married her. Powhatan preached him an angry sermon about the evil of whites who took promises so lightly and prevented Dale from effecting his royal marriage.

While Dale and newcomer John Rolfe put Virginia on a more sound basis by exporting tobacco, Pocahontas grew up to help give the colony a good name. Virginians at one time captured her and held her hostage while they bargained for return of captives held by Powhatan. She never returned to her people. Rolfe, a man of conscience, was attracted to her and asked to marry the baptized Indian. Finally the first Anglo-Indian marriage was permitted — for the good of the country, the benefit of the plantation, and the conversion of other Indians (or so it was said). Pocahontas later became a favorite of English society; but, after giving birth to a son, she died in England and Rolfe returned to Virginia and another marriage.

White males were not alone in early Virginia. In 1619 the Company sent ninety women to delight the men and assure the future of the colony. That same year, John Rolfe entered some portentous words in his diary: "About the last of August came in a Dutch man-of-war that sold us twenty Negars [sic]." English servants were too expensive for a plantation economy; and Indians died from contact with new diseases, could not adapt to such work, or simply disappeared back into their forests. The records of early years tell little about Negro servitude in tobacco country. The English had less experience than the Iberians with blacks, though in the 1560s pirate John Hawkins began a profitable if legally ambiguous slave trade. No elaborate theories of racial inferiority were yet attached to the subject, since the English did seem to deal with the Africans who sold slaves as equals of sorts. Racism in respect to blacks was to come later. Not until 1661 did the Virginia General Assembly legalize Negro slavery. The older documents tell almost nothing about concern for the souls of these Negroes.

At Henrico, where the English built the first hospital and a "fair and handsome church," they also proposed a college in order to advance the work among the Indians, almost none of whom had joined Pocahontas in baptism. A brother of Powhatan, more vengeful than he, meanwhile had succeeded the chief, but other Indians seemed increasingly civil and the English gradually dropped their guard. They often loaned firearms to the natives and opened their homes to them. Then, on Good Friday in 1622, the Virginians sat down to Holy Day breakfasts, with Indians as guests at some tables. Suddenly, and too late, they learned why the Indians had been paying close attention to their routines. At a pre-arranged signal, along a 140-mile zone up the James River, the Indians killed 347 colonists — one-fifth of the population — including John Rolfe. Jamestown was saved because Chanco, one of the few Christian converts, tipped off a resident about the plans.

The massacre dulled the feeble impulse of Virginians to save the Indians, and so began two years of killing and conflict. By 1625, thanks to war, to an epidemic in 1624 that killed about 600, to famine, and to returns to England, Virginia claimed only 1,095 English people.

While mission to the Indians and care of Virginia Colony souls played a part in the first English settlement, the Virginians were not attracted to the New World primarily to set up the Church of England (which was not provided for by law until 1624). The bishop of London had official authority over the colonies, but he paid little attention to the plantations in those faraway swamps. And because Virginia parishes were narrow strips strung out for miles along the great rivers, the people could not form close religious communities of their own. Clerics had a difficult time ministering to the people and had to cater to the wealthy, who built their own chapels of ease on their estates. Clergy had to come from England and were under the control of the Virginia Assembly.

Thanks to an accidental arrangement, in the New World lay control over the church increased. In each parish, the people were to set aside one hundred acres of what they called glebe (land just for clerical support) and to plant it with tobacco. When tobacco prices came down, ministers went hungry. Meanwhile, well-off laymen kept clergy in virtual peonage. The ruling vestries chose merely to hire ministers as yearly appointees, and did not present them to the bishop so that they could gain the security of life tenure — their tenuous situation kept many preachers from pronouncing judgment on errant colonists.

As decades passed, the church somehow survived and earnest men of God worked to help produce a Christian way of life suited to Virginia. Late in the century, the bishop finally sent well-qualified representatives called commissaries to support and upgrade the clergy. The first of these, James Blair, helped found the College of William and Mary in 1693 to serve that end. By then, the Church of England was securely established; the cruel laws of Dale were long forgotten. Yet establishment did not mean persecution on any impressive scale; the heirs of the awful years in early Virginia began to allow varieties of religious voices to be heard in their colony.

To the north, in New England, a very different breed of English Protestants set up the colonies of Plymouth, Massachusetts Bay, Connecticut, and New Haven. They were all Puritans, reform-minded members who pushed their membership to the boundaries of the Church of England. Those who settled Plymouth, the famous "Pilgrims," went so far as to become separatists. Religion played a much larger, perhaps dominant role in these New England pilgrimages. Lovers of freedom, they came to find it — and then hurried to establish their newfound freedom by ruling out dissenters. People of the covenant, they believed that God had called them to do this work. As they read their Bibles, they saw themselves as the Israelites in God's master plan. While their policies of church establishment did not endure unchanged, the seriousness with which they set out and the depth of their convictions gave their settlements the position of most importance for later America.

Gold and the passage to India were not on the minds of New Englanders — unlike the pioneers in New Spain, New France, and, to some extent, Virginia. They did have to support themselves and, believing firmly in godly gain, came to plant a wilderness as their example to the world. These separatists who first came to little Plymouth colony were also called variously independents or congregationalists because of their attitudes toward the Church of England and their insistence that only local authorities could rule the congregation. Church of England worship, back home or in Virginia, was to them "flat idolatry."

In Elizabethan England, these exiles from the official church prayed and worshiped in homes. William Bradford and other strong lay leaders taught them to think of themselves as a biblical people, bound by their covenant with their God. No longer should English people simply inherit their established religion. They must dare to take matters into their hands and "own" the divine covenant.

King James vowed to make these deviants conform or he would "harry them out of the land or else do worse." Yet they found it difficult to find a way to flee from the profane multitude that harassed them in their gatherings at the manor house of William Brewster at Scrooby. These educated and sometimes prosperous people, knowing they had much to lose, prepared to lose it by booking a ship onto which they sneaked one night in 1607. Someone betrayed them before they could leave for Holland and religious freedom. Officers searched the men's shirts for money, "yea even the women further than became modesty." They tried to escape again a few months later, but only some husbands and fathers eluded authorities. The families of these pesky believers were then permitted to join them.

Their haven, Amsterdam, was rather tolerant, but its diversity threatened their close community, so they settled in the university town of Leyden. Brewster and their beloved Reverend John Robinson helped bind the group together, but some of their children, attracted to the worldly ways of the Dutch, tugged at those bonds until someone proposed settlement in the New World. After much travail they left John Robinson behind to keep the congregation at Leyden together while a minority followed Bradford from the goodly city where they had lived for twelve years. It was he who gave them their classic nickname: "They knew they were pilgrims" — and *the* Pilgrims they have remained.

The unseaworthy *Speedwell* and then its replacement, the *Mayflower,* took 102 people from Plymouth in England to the new Plymouth they would reach in November of 1620. Amazingly, only a minority were true "pilgrims," who called themselves saints. The others were "strangers" out to make money. The saints covered their understandable fears with attempts to read the hand of God in everything. "It pleased God" to fell a profane sailor with disease and death. "It pleased God" for them to rescue John Howland, who fell overboard in a storm. And it pleased God to bring them to the sight of Cape Cod after weeks of storms. Though they lacked any document authorizing them to stay there, they settled nearby anyhow, choosing to leave behind the "vast and furious ocean" for "the firm and stable earth."

Their land of promise was a "hideous and desolate wilderness," so they huddled offshore on the *Mayflower.* Before they settled, their factions agreed on a Mayflower Compact, which spelled out the terms of a covenanted society. By spring nearly half of them were dead, buried in graves unmarked lest Indians notice the weakness of the newcomers. Like all other newcomers, they worried about native Americans, but caught only glimpses of them and found a nearby village deserted. Not until March did they find out from a stray Indian named Samoset (who had learned some English from occasional fishermen) that about four years earlier a disease almost wiped out his people — hence the eerie silence in the surrounding woods. He also introduced the last Pawtuxet survivor, an Indian named Squanto who had been snatched off to England, where he learned language well enough to serve as a middle man with the few Indians in the area. They agreed on a treaty with Chief Massasoit that lasted half a century. A sign of the amity between the two peoples was evident when they gathered for not the first but the best remembered day of thanksgiving in North American history.

More colonists began to arrive, but no minister was among them, a sign that these radical Protestants could do without priests. Stickler John Robinson, however, would never let them baptize their children or celebrate the Lord's Supper, the Protestant counterpart to the Mass, without a minister. A clergyman, the Reverend John Lyford, finally showed up, but they found him an immoral misfit and packed him off. Yet so dedicated were these believers that the government did not have to provide legal support for the churches for the first three decades.

Back in Leyden John Robinson had given the separatists an image for community: just as people do not want their houses shaken before the foundations are settled and the parts "firmly knit," so pilgrim people must beware of novelties or oppositions that would shake the house of God "which you are and are to be." Yet novelty kept appearing relentlessly from the lips of stray Lyfordites, Baptists, and Quakers who later visited the wilderness community. So did immoralities. In 1642 the Pilgrims executed Thomas Graunger on charges of bestiality that they spelled out with Puritan precision: with a mare, a cow, two goats, diverse sheep, two calves, and a turkey. The colonists almost lost control of their emotions when Thomas Morton at Merry Mount set up drunken orgies. He encouraged coupling with Indians, set up a maypole, and sold alcohol and guns to the Indians. Bradford, now governor, had to send Captain Miles Standish to ship Morton back to England.

Bradford during his thirty years of service kept explaining the failings in his "firmly knit" community. The devil, he wrote, carried the greatest spite against the holy and pure churches of Christ and wanted to ruin them. But it was commerce and politics that worked hardest against Plymouth. The colony was doomed to be swallowed by Massachusetts and Rhode Island, which had royal charters as it did not. It became clear that America had no permanent separate room for a free and "firmly knit," exclusive community. The migrants fell out with each other; they had to endure the arrival of sects and individualists.

In his great journal, *Of Plymouth Plantation,* Bradford spelled out how New England should be remembered as if it were ancient Israel: "May not and ought not the children of these fathers rightly say: Our fathers were Englishmen which came over this great ocean, and were ready to perish in this wilderness; but they cried unto the Lord, and he heard their voice, and looked on their adversity." Out of small beginnings, he wrote, the hand of God produced greater things, and the light kindled in Plymouth would shine to the whole nation. Yet he was doleful. This poor church of his colony was left like an ancient mother grown old and forsaken of her children. "Thus she that had made many rich became herself poor."

Some of the "riches" she left became themes in American mythology: Thanksgiving Day, Plymouth Rock, pictures of Pilgrims heading for worship with guns and dogs at their side, a colony for tourists, a passion for lay leadership in religion, a love for independence, and the very name Pilgrim, which in songs sung in the "land of the Pilgrim's pride" came to stand for all the settlers, not just these few.

Only miles away and a decade later a more durable colony helped place the stamp of New England on much of America. Captain John Smith, who never could get the New World out of his system, in 1629 noted six good ships sailing from the Thames to the Charles River in Massachusetts. Accurately he reported that the people on them were of good rank, zeal, means, and quality — makers of good joint stock. Rumor had it that a jumble of sectarians were aboard, but Smith properly surmised that the sober band were good Protestants of the Reformed Church of England. This they were, though their choice of a middle way as Puritans offended both the separatists on their left and the compromising mother church on their right.

John Smith was correct when he called theirs a great company. By the end of the decade about fourteen hundred settlers were in their new Massachusetts Bay Colony and when the flow slowed twelve years later about twenty thousand were already there. These Puritans, who *did* have a royal charter, wanted unity even more than did the Pilgrims. At Plymouth, Bradford, though he feared a "mixed multitude," could feed fish on Friday to a solitary Jesuit missionary on his way through. Puritans abhorred such risks. Wanting to continue the reform of the Church of England, they dreamed of a return to the primitive simplicity and innocence of the earliest Christian church and for this they needed to be off by themselves. They preached the pure doctrine and pure life that Puritans had cherished ever since they formed under Elizabeth and chafed under James. Hard times in the textile industry and other economic concerns helped nudge some of these Puritans to look at America as a place to invest. The king hated to lose their talent, but their religious style irritated him, so he let them go.

The Massachusetts Bay Colony chose its leader well in Cambridge graduate John Winthrop, who at age eighteen was already a lusty father. He was to marry four times, outlast three wives, and start a dynasty by siring sixteen children. Winthrop cherished stability and order. Even romance followed the clock in his Puritan world; wherever they were, he and his beloved spouse Margaret thought only of each other between five and six o'clock every Monday and Friday. Their religion was equally precise and fervent; a man like Winthrop had to be able to point to a personal experience of Jesus Christ in order to become a "visible saint." The act of joining the elect and chosen people of God never distracted a Puritan from the world, but called him to work there and to invest in it, knowing that every act was part of a serious drama played against the backdrop of an invisible world.

Winthrop had no taste for leaving England, where life held promise for him. Yet he wrote Margaret that God tended to put a subtle bias into the heart of the undecided and as he read his own heart, it tilted him toward New England. As for England, "this land grows weary of her inhabitants." For the sake of all Puritan children, Winthrop decided that for a time he must part from his own, even if he had to leave Margaret temporarily behind.

On the *Arbella* in 1630 Winthrop composed "A Model of Christian Charity," which spelled out how God intended that "every man might have need of others, and from hence they might be all knit more nearly together in the bond of brotherly affection." To be knit: this was again the key to the human side of their covenant with God. They did not cross the ocean only to be divided into factions. "We are entered into a covenant with [God] for this work," and if the people broke the covenant, so would God. Therefore, the citizens must have commerce together and delight in each other if they wanted to find the God of Israel among them. Later colonies would pray to become like New England, "for we must consider that we shall be as a city upon a hill, the eyes of all people are upon us."

Winthrop ruled well. While two hundred settlers of this city of saints died during the first winter and a few headed back, nothing like the starving time of Virginia blighted Massachusetts Bay. The governor helped organize Boston as the central town and then prudentially staked out a six-hundred-acre farm on the Mystic River, where he built a small boat, the *Blessing of the Bay,* for trading purposes. He scowled at sailors or strange merchants who trespassed with ideas that differed from the Puritan vision.

This outlook also insisted that church and state were "two twinnes," linked so much that a person had to be a visible saint in the church in order to be a full citizen of the state. Religious and civil power united to support a planned economy and fair trade practices. Those who wanted freedom to see things other ways were perfectly welcome to see them — but at other places. Ministers like John Cotton kept their eyes on the biblical codes and the people who vowed to keep them, seeing to it that no one worked or played on the Sabbath or cursed and made fun of rulers on any day.

Three outside forces helped the people stay knit for a time. First, the ocean voyage kept weaklings from wanting to return to England. Colonist Edward Johnson was sure that God himself sent the storms to toss the *Arbella* and quicken fear; the story of the devouring sea became a myth; to remember it, a kind of religious rite. Second, the terror of the wilderness surrounding the Puritan garden in the promised land caused the people to confederate, and Winthrop never let them forget this. Third, there were the Indians, who, though depleted by a smallpox that the Puritans thought was an act of God, still seemed ominous. The colonists decided that the surviving Indians had a natural right to as much land as they could improve, but no more. So the settlers went through the motions of buying the land, their consciences made clear when they saw how eager the natives seemed to be to sell.

Some years later the Reverend Samuel Danforth described the Puritans as being on an "errand into the wilderness." That errand took them so far into the wilds that after seventeen years their clashes with Indians turned into war. Pequots who squatted on new land drew the ire of other Indians whose claims they thus upset, and the Puritans took the moment to ally with the aggrieved Indians against the more aggressive Pequots. Captain John Mason laid siege to an Indian fort and took it with the loss of only two men while he massacred several hundred natives in about a half hour. God, he was sure, "laughed his enemies and the enemies of his people to scorn, making them as a fiery oven."

Governor Winthrop was embarrassed that the Bay Puritans did not convert these heathens as effectively as the papists did; his own oath of office called him to a mission among them. Puritans insisted that Indians must have a conversion experience before baptism. Since the illiterate natives could not learn the Bible to prepare themselves for conversion, the New Englanders were at a disadvantage as missionaries. A few pioneers did learn Indian languages and prepared translations of the Bible. Out on the island of Martha's Vineyard, outnumbered Thomas Mayhew and his family came up with many "praying Indians" while John Eliot, the "Apostle to the Indians," displayed some converts near Cambridge in the Bay Colony in 1647. When Indians showed no interest, this was explained simply as a case of the devil holding on to his own people.

In later years Winthrop lost his gentle edge and firm hold. He hounded out dissenters, including the followers of an anti-intellectual, anti-establishmentarian prophet named Samuel Gorton who crowded the Bay Colony borders. The governor sent forty soldiers to fire on what he called the horribly and detestably blasphemous Gortonians. When in 1644 the citizens demoted Winthrop to deputy governor, he feared that they were heading toward "the meanest and worst of all forms of government," democracy. Yet he had his personal consolations, most visibly in Margaret, who came to New England and was at his side most of his years. After she died in 1647, a new wife bore him one more son in his sixtieth year. When the patriarch died on March 26, 1649, he left a smaller estate than the one he himself had inherited, but he remained a respected man in the community his vision helped knit.

Massachusetts Bay spawned offspring colonies. In 1634 the Reverend Thomas Hooker, finding Massachusetts too crowded and contentious, began to petition for the right to leave. Eventually the colony's reluctant General Court let him move dangerously close to the borders of New Netherland, where he helped found Connecticut. It became a cozy backwoods place exempt from the threats of diversity and dissension that came with life near Boston harbor. Two or three years after Hooker, businessman Theophilus Eaton and his pastor, John Davenport, also finding Boston too compromising, led their followers to the port of New Haven. We might think of its leaders as "more Puritan than the Puritans" and of New Haven as the strictest new colony of all. There John Davenport used the Bible even to set the prices and to measure the kegs of ale. In 1665 Connecticut absorbed New Haven and henceforth rivaled Massachusetts Bay for honors in the contest to produce the purest Puritanism, the most firmly knit community.

For all their commerce with England and, to some extent, with each other, the founders of the earliest American colonies wanted nothing so much as to be left alone to develop single communities for undistracted and undivided people. The American landscape denied the dream of these settlers and almost instantly beckoned or produced nonconformist people who founded Baptist Rhode Island, Catholic Maryland, and Quaker Pennsylvania. To them, not to the isolationists, belonged the American tomorrow. Mediating between these two extreme types, however, was a third, more adaptable type of Protestant community: New Netherland, with its port, New Amsterdam.

The inhabitants of the trading post called New Amsterdam were Dutch. They had come under the influence of John Calvin during the years when the Netherlands was rising to sea power. In 1602 the Dutch East India Company gave the Netherlands a taste of commercial success. English navigator Henry Hudson, who searched northern North America for a passage to India, lured the company to look westward. In 1611 Hudson's mutinous crew abandoned him and some companions in a tiny boat in the bay that bears his name. Those of his party who returned from America were convinced that the Dutch could compete for trade on American soil. As early as 1613 Dutch traders held little beachheads on Manhattan Island, where, in 1626, they set precedent by purchasing instead of taking land from the Indians. The fact that they paid with trinkets worth only sixty Dutch guilders — twenty-four dollars — obscures the more important reality that they paid at all, since they aimed only at a modest trading post. The Netherlands, which had fewer misfits in its population than did England, could spare few colonists. Holland needed the able-bodied to bring back goods from the Indies and to stay home and defend against Spain.

The Dutch, earnest enough about their Reformed faith back home, were generally casual in New Amsterdam. They displayed no desire to convert natives, had no charter with spiritual mandates, and in general made religion no more than an afterthought at their colonial outpost. Dutch governors out of habit, ambition, or lack of imagination did bluster in with various attempts to establish religious conformity. The traders, however, wisely made room for the diverse kinds of people, religious or not, who came in and out of New Netherland. So relaxed and subtle were these commercially minded people that people often overlook the fact that the Dutch laity came closer to inventing permanent patterns of religious civility in America than did any other colonists of their century.

The Dutch States General chartered the Dutch West India Company, which, seeing little opportunity to invest in trade in South America, looked on Hudson River country. Vice Admiral Piet

Heyn, by capturing a whole Spanish treasure fleet off Cuba in 1628, provided solvency for the frail company. The even-tempered Dutch, not wanting to make a policy of such risky exploits decided that uncrowded Manhattan Island in Algonquin and Iroquois country was safer and more secure. The Walloon families, exiles from the southern, Catholic part of the Netherlands, were interested in making a living, not in helping set up a Protestant refuge in the form of a Bible commonwealth. The participants were to have freedom of religion. Real estate being cheap on Manhattan Island, Director-General Peter Minuit beginning in 1626 parceled it out to the pioneers.

But the Dutch clergy could not resist taking a place at the post, and they soon caused trouble. The early dominie Jonas Michaelius, who felt that the reverent Minuit was using his office as an elder for his own ends, sized him up as a slippery fellow, liar, rogue, fornicator, profane man, and swearer — all because he did not try to police the behavior of settlers or enforce the establishment of the Dutch Reformed faith. As late as 1642, years after Minuit's departure, visitors still expressed shock when they saw the drab hut that had to serve as a church on Manhattan Island.

The Dutch lay people had plenty to gripe about as they suffered under the stray clerics who tried to make careers in the wilds. The first minister, Bastiaen Janszoon Krol, as "visitor of the sick," was a barely literate dominie who served best by quitting to become a storekeeper up the river. Michaelius, the first ordained cleric, did not arrive until April 1628, and acted as lord of a spiritual empire though only two hundred residents had arrived. He complained that newcomers forgot to bring church membership certificates along, a sure sign that they expected no church at all. In 1632 he gave up in disgust.

Dominie Everardus Bogardus, a cantankerous but more stable replacement, arrived a year later. At once he blasted Director-General Wouter Van Twiller as an incompetent drunk, which he was, and as an irreligious child of the devil, whose "goats are better than he." But after Van Twiller left, Bogardus had to contend with Willem Kieft, the new administrator — appointed, as were all of them, by the Dutch West India Company in Amsterdam. On Christmas Eve in 1645 Bogardus discoursed on Africa. There, he said, many animals interbred and created monsters. After that thought, the preacher turned to New Amsterdam and, referring to his rival Kieft, wondered where in this temperate climate such monsters as he came from. The governor replied in kind by ordering military drills, complete with gunfire and cannonades, to proceed under the church windows during worship. When they were relieved of their posts both men had to return on the same ship, the *Princess,* where they no doubt took their feud to the bottom of the sea near Swansea on its fatal passage in 1647.

Some West India Company supporters eventually reminded New Amsterdam that they had invested for the purpose of converting Indians, but the leaders did nothing in the face of such prodding. Michaelius called the natives wicked and godless, "uncivil and stupid as garden poles." Upriver at Rensselaerswyck, Dominie Johannes Megapolensis reported that when the Dutch prayed, the Indians laughed. When he preached, some of them asked what was he doing. He was admonishing Christians not to steal, to be lewd or drunk or to commit murder — and Indians ought not do these either. The natives welcomed his message to Christians but wondered aloud why it was so ineffective.

Kieft in 1639 disrupted friendly relations with Indians when he demanded that they pay tribute, a bizarre idea to people who considered the Dutch to be intruders on their soil. He ordered an attack on the Indians at Vriesendael on Staten Island in 1640, and numbers of skirmishes followed. After one of these encounters, David De Vries wrote in horror about the shrieks of dying Indians, soldiers tearing infants from the breasts of their mothers, men binding sucklings to small boards to cut and pierce them, and adults trying to escape while holding their own exposed entrails in their arms. After the settlers engaged in such savagery, Kieft piously called a day of fasting and prayer to deal with Dutch suffering under the Indians. By the time he was recalled in 1647, he had turned cooperative natives into killers.

Kieft's successor, ambitious and despotic Peter Stuyvesant, arrived in 1647, stomping on his peg leg "as if he were the Czar of Muscovy," and vowing to put the New Netherland house in order. He helped finish the church building and issued orders against drunkenness and Sabbath-breaking. When his marauding ships the *Cat* and the *Love* failed to steal enough revenues from Spanish vessels, he committed an unforgivable act on Dutch soil: he taxed beer and wine. Against all good sense he also tried to impose religion, believing that his Reformed church had the truth and should own a monopoly on religion and good order in the settlement. Stuyvesant thought it good company policy to exclude competing kinds of worship, but this was futile in the face of the variety that already existed: there were Calvinists, Catholics, "English," Puritans, Lutherans, and some Mennonite Anabaptists in New Amsterdam — and more unexpected arrivals were on the way.

Early in summer of 1654, Jews began to arrive, planning to trade. Some may have been Ashkenazim — Jews from northern, central, and eastern Europe. Most were Sephardim from Spain who had been displaced to Portugal in the time of Columbus and who then moved to the Netherlands. They lived in Brazil during a twenty-four-year period when the Dutch held control at the city of Recife. When the Portuguese regained control and turned them away, a Spanish corsair relieved them of their goods on their way to exile in New Amsterdam; so they arrived, "poor but healthy," to be slapped into jail without means to pay for their passage.

Stuyvesant desperately wanted to bar these "very repugnant" and deceitful people. Dominie Megapolensis called them godless rascals: "For as we have here Papists, Mennonites and Lutherans among the Dutch; also many Puritans or Independents, and many atheists and various other servants of Baal among the English under his government, who conceal themselves under the name of Christians; it would create a still greater confusion, if the obstinate and immovable Jews came to settle here." Nevertheless, while waiting for word from Amsterdam about what to do, Megapolensis smuggled the Jews some funds from his church.

When word reached Amsterdam, the Dutch West India Company acted. Its demand shocked Stuyvesant. New Amsterdam must be hospitable; there was land enough for all, and besides, "many of the Jewish nation are principal shareholders in the company." Stuyvesant, grousing, harassed the exiles and hampered their efforts to buy homes and cemetery plots. He and his officials asked them to build houses "close together," subtly hinting that they form a ghetto. But in 1656 an order arrived to permit Jews freedom of worship.

Stuyvesant wanted to bar not only Jews but also Lutherans from New Netherland. Peter Minuit, in the employ of Sweden in the late 1630s, helped found New Sweden, too close for comfort on the Delaware River. It was manned with four hundred Finns and Swedish deserters from the army. The Dutch did not look with favor on the Lutheran minister, Lars Lock, and called him an impious, scandalous, wild, drunken, unmannerly clown who would "prefer drinking brandy two hours to preaching one." In 1655 Stuyvesant felt ready to move on New Sweden, which he took without firing a shot.

Putting down the amiable Lutherans of New Sweden was one thing; living with Netherlandish Lutherans in New Amsterdam was another, and it drove Stuyvesant to fury. Two years after the governor first arrived, 150 Lutheran heads of families appealed for a Dutch-speaking pastor. During years of delay, Company merchants haggled with the Reformed dominies. In 1654 a council decision went against the Lutheran petitioners. The Company "absolutely" denied their request for religious freedom and asked Stuyvesant to find the most civil way to "induce them to listen and finally to join the Reformed Church and thus live in greater love and harmony among themselves." Anti-Lutheranism thus antedated anti-Semitism in the colonies.

In 1657 the Lutherans back in Amsterdam sent Johannes Ernestus Gutwasser to test the Reformed nerve and to serve the flock. The Reformed pastors considered this an invasion of their territory and two years later had him deported. In another five years Jacob Fabritius came to tend the flock. By then the English had taken over the colony and he was allowed to remain, but he was a bad bargain, a strutter who dressed like a soldier from head to foot in red, and clothed his family similarly. The Lutherans asked Amsterdam to please send them a new spiritual leader, preferably an unmarried man. Finally the congregation received a worthy one who made peace with his people but never with the Reformed faction.

The worst shock to the Dutch leadership came in August of 1657 when a flagless ship sailed into the harbor. Its master staunchly refused to doff his hat to the director-general; Stuyvesant learned to his horror that he was in the presence of insolent sectarians called Quakers. These Quakers, or Friends, were members of a new and radical English sect, free spirits unbound to Bible or established church. He suggested they go to what he called the *latrina* of New England, that sinkhole called Rhode Island, which was founded by religious mavericks who allowed in any kind of human refuse. When the ship went on to that colony it left behind, among others, two women, Dorothy Waughn and Mary Weatherhead, who quaked as they announced the coming end of the world. The nonplussed Dutch soon packed them off to jail.

The Quaker nuisance spread when another of their members, Robert Hodgson, started gathering small groups of Friends on Long Island. Authorities arrested him during open-air worship in an orchard, whereupon he preached to a crowd from the window of a justice of the peace. Stuyvesant, his patience gone, ordered an armed guard to drag Hodgson behind a cart most of the way from Long Island to a vermin-filled dungeon on Manhattan. After his trial the Quaker was chained to a wheelbarrow and twice beaten by a Negro slave until he collapsed. Day after day this treatment continued until authorities finally suspended him from a ceiling for a whipping. In the end an Englishwoman was allowed to bathe his wounds while even the sister of Stuyvesant, Anna Bogard, pleaded for banishment as a more humane policy.

Challenge came in 1658 when citizens of Vlissingen (Flushing, Long Island), wrote Stuyvesant a protest called the Flushing Remonstrance. This pioneering plea for religious freedom called diversity not a curse but a glory. The grandeur of Holland was its law of liberties that extended to Jews, Turks, and Egyptians, all sons of Adam. Government must offend no conscience by laying violent hands on believers of any sort, and citizens should look for anything of God in all of them. Stuyvesant responded by laying hands on Tobias Feake, who delivered the document, arresting and eventually banishing him. Still the Quakers resisted, while the Dutch began embarrassing attempts to banish them.

New Amsterdam, never numbering more than ten thousand settlers, lacked enough people to endure as a colony and fell with almost no struggle to the better-poised English in 1664. The good burghers and farmers did not want the delicate cups on their shelves rattled or their crops ruined merely for the sake of faraway regimes and investors, while the English, knowing they would soon possess the land, withheld their fire rather than ruin a landscape. New Amsterdam, now New York, was officially granted religious freedom, the only sane policy in the face of the human mixture that was already there. Stuyvesant later retired to his farm in the bouwerij, now New York's bowery, to the end a man bewildered by the way people in America chose to live with freedom and choice in religion.

Clearly, the lay people of Dutch New Amsterdam cared little for the church order that leaders tried to impose. No one caught them being zealous for the souls of Indians or forming a tight religious colony. In England the Puritan revolutionary Oliver Cromwell back in 1651 had mused that "the Dutch love gain more than godliness." The hodgepodge of residents in the American outpost worked out a policy to deal with diversity. They called it *oogluiking* or *conniventie,* blinking and conniving. The citizens may not all have taken the risk of something as radical as the Flushing Remonstrance, but they did expect officials to close their eyes to variety and dissent. Thus the colonists kept up a trading economy while allowing for diversity. The Dutch motto "difference makes for tolerance" capsuled their outlook. No other colony learned as rapidly as did New Amsterdam the lessons that circumstances imposed on their age.

New Sweden, on the Delaware River, today part
of New Jersey, was originally a trading post
established in the 1630s by New Netherland
dissenters but was taken over by the Dutch in 1655.
The first Lutheran minister on the continent served
there briefly. In this Swedish picture from 1702,
colonists trade with the Indians while warlike
natives engage in combat in the background. (*Rare
Books and Manuscripts Division, The New York Public
Library, Astor, Lenox and Tilden Foundations*)

Chapter Six

PILGRIMAGES OF DISSENT

ℐ COLONISTS WHO ESTABLISHED CHURCHES BY LAW SIMPLY IM-
ported thirteen-hundred-year-old European patterns and adapted
them to a new landscape. They expected all citizens to think of
themselves as members. By law the church would receive tax support. In the state the church would be privileged, for its voice
would have a part in legislation and the enforcement of behavior.
In each case only one church was to be established and privileged.
Those who dissented were free to go elsewhere. The Protestant
Reformation brought some new freedoms to Christendom, and for
the most part it did not do away with establishment or encourage
dissenters. The radicals in England or on the Continent who did
not agree with the official church were often harassed, hounded,
and persecuted. Some of them took their causes to America and
then turned around and established their own groups. Dissent in
America was sometimes homegrown. In every case, it played some
part in enlarging freedoms that later Americans took for granted.

Naturally, the really impressive outbreaks of dissent occurred
where colonists were most "knit together" by law, religion, and
custom, in New England. Two of the most notable protestors, a
man and a woman, began to make their voices heard early in the
1630s.

Over drinks of fermented honey, a gifted young minister named
Roger Williams first heard John Winthrop describe plans for the

Puritan move to New England. Williams longed to search in Massachusetts for the primitive purity lost since the days of early Christianity. In the winter of 1630 he followed Winthrop to America. Winthrop may have hosted the newcomer briefly, and the Boston church asked him to be their teaching minister. He astonished them almost at once by calling them a false church. True Puritans, he insisted, must separate from the whorish Church of England; yet Bostonians clung to it, hoping to reform it from a distance. The roots of Williams's dissent against bishops and the formal church were deep, for he had grown up near Smithfield in London, where, in the days of Queen Mary, the smoke of burned martyrs irritated Protestant nostrils. After graduating from Pembroke Hall at Cambridge, he signed the Act of Supremacy to make himself eligible for the clergy, but he soon refused to submit to bishops and attacked any Puritan who compromised with them.

Salem — a "godly" town, founded before Massachusetts Bay, and strict as Plymouth — called Williams to be minister, but he left when his church refused to become fully separatist. He returned in 1633 to reform the settlement, even to the point of enforcing biblical dress codes; the women, for example, had to wear veils to church. Because for a time his wife remained friendly with compromising types, the purist preacher felt he could not even give thanks to God with her at meals in their home. Governor Winthrop understandably feared that such fanaticism could spread to Boston and welcomed the desire of Williams to save Indian souls in the more remote wilderness.

While he was learning Indian tongues and beginning to write for the natives, Williams deplored the impure civil state alongside the impure church. At Salem he pointed to the flagpole: how dare the corrupt king of England use as part of his emblem the cross that stood for the suffering of Jesus and never for earthly power? Did people not know that it was the pope, the very Antichrist, who endorsed the cross of Saint George on this national flag? When one of Williams's impetuous church members, John Endicott, cut the cross out of the flag — a dangerous attention-getting act — Winthrop hoped England wasn't watching too closely.

Then Williams attacked the land policies. By what right did King James deed away the land that Winthrop and Boston were buying? Now Winthrop laid bare to Williams his own deepest fears: the king could destroy the colony if provoked. Williams answered that he cared for no royal authority, since it all rested on a solemn public lie. Winthrop, knowing that such talk was treasonous, tried to use reason, but Williams was obstinate. He blasted the "sin of the patents" through which so-called Christian kings took the lands of other people and then gave them away. Well, asked Winthrop, if God had not wanted the Puritans to inherit the land, why did He make room for Europeans by sending the smallpox to kill off Indians? Why did God plant his churches in New England? "If we had no right to this land, yet our God hath right to it." The conclusion satisfied Winthrop, but never Williams.

To stall off trouble from London, authorities had to joust with Williams, but the verses from the Bible that each side threw at the other convinced neither. After one court trial and numerous skirmishes, Williams was accused of subversion a second time in 1635. In the torpid courtroom that July, all parties lost their tempers and even the normally moderate pastor John Cotton sputtered that Williams had become a seditious "haberdasher of small questions." The General Court found Williams guilty of contempt — he certainly was — and exiled him with the command to "depart out of this jurisdiction within six weeks." They expected him to return to England, but Indian friends and the snows of winter in New England now looked more congenial to an apostle of freedom than did kings or bishops across the sea. Because his health was poor, the General Court gave Williams time to wait for spring, after which he wandered to wild Rhode Island, there to become the best-remembered American exile.

In the wilderness he raised his voice against what he called Puritan idolatry. For New Englanders the false image was land. It had become "as great a God with us English as Gold was with the Spaniards." Williams had fingered the vice no Puritan colonists wanted to confess. In his calm midnight thoughts, as he put it, he dwelt on the depraved appetite of his neighbors for wilderness land, that idol of New England "which the living and most high Eternal will destroy and famish."

Calm midnight thoughts soon became a luxury, since Williams had to help establish order in his new home of Rhode Island, called "Rogue's Island" because it attracted so many misfits. For a time he was a kind of Baptist and then found that name and sect too compromising, so he became a sort of seeker. As such, he must allow other seekers to come, whether they were Christians or believers in God or not, though among the people who came, the Quakers pushed even Williams to the limits of tolerance. Though he was no modern democrat, he believed for a time that in free competition the truth of God would win out. "I commend that man, whether Jew or Turk or Papist, or whoever, that steers no otherwise than his conscience dares."

To the shock of Massachusetts Bay, Williams drew a line (as they did not) between the functions of church and state, again not out of love of democracy but to keep the church pure and out of the grasp of civil meddlers. The state should only protect the seekers. All his life Williams looked for a pure paradise. To link the state to religion as Old and New England did was to make the church a "filthy dunghill and whorehouse of rotten and stinking whores and hypocrites" in most unchristian Christendom.

Williams, who came to America to be a voice for civil order, in 1643 sailed to England to seek a charter for Rhode Island. He knew that the new Puritan Parliament would be friendlier, and in Sir Harry Vane, a former Massachusetts governor now in Parliament, he had a patron who helped him gain it. Meanwhile, responsible leaders like the Newporter John Clarke, a man of Baptist convictions, worked to civilize Rhode Island. As a Baptist, he insisted on baptizing believing adults only, by immersion — a notion abhorrent to the established Congregationalists of Massachusetts Bay. Clarke therefore overstepped himself when he made an effort to take these forbidden Baptist teachings to Boston, where he and at least one follower were punished for their efforts. Acts like these inspired Clarke in 1652 to write a pamphlet called *Ill Newes from New England,* and with it to draw fire from some English Puritans against the Massachusetts zealots.

Rhode Island saw impressive diversity. Jews from Barbados came to Newport sometime before the spring of 1678, but stayed on for only about seven years. Later, other Jews found Rhode Island especially hospitable. Gortonians, Boston heretic Anne Hutchinson, and always the Quakers kept nettling Williams, but he defended their right to propagate their views. Meanwhile, in personal life he became a reasonably prosperous but crotchety landowner. Roger Williams is remembered as a premiere apostle of liberty, though some of the grounds for his work made him unusable by most later Americans with different outlooks than his. When the United States assured religious freedom around 1776, the founders paid little notice to this seeker. Even many Baptists found his regular attacks against government to be extreme. He believed that Jesus Christ would literally and soon return to earth, but went further than his fellow believers in the Second Coming when he charged that Christ's whole church had fallen away in the meantime.

*   *

Williams was the first but not the only major unsettler of the Bay colony's tightly knit order; the fathers constantly had to warn against dissent. Militia captain and historian Edward Johnson reminded his contemporaries that the colony was not set up for tolerating times; satirist Nathaniel Ward meanwhile called liberty of conscience impious ignorance, and John Cotton saw dissent as an infectious plague that needed quarantine.

These New England officials tried to use reason and scripture against the wayward. Since the Puritans believed they had the whole truth, anyone with whom they reasoned and who then refused to agree with them had to be sinning against his own conscience, and this made a criminal out of him. Or her: the second great maverick, for whom Williams was a sort of dry run, was Anne Hutchinson.

Mrs. William Hutchinson came as an insider, having followed her clerical hero John Cotton from England. She heard Cotton preach two covenants. God gave to Adam and his heirs a covenant of works to help them satisfy demands of divine law and human order. So far, so good. After Adam fell into sin God promised a new covenant of grace. Jesus Christ sealed this when he gave himself to death on the cross. The believers belonged especially to this covenant. While other Puritans delicately webbed the two, Mrs. Hutchinson thought she heard John Cotton tilting toward the covenant of grace alone at the expense of works and thus of moral seriousness guided by law. Her own hungry soul pressed this idea all the way until she excluded works. Her enemies called this heresy antinomianism. They feared lawlessness and anarchy among those who held it.

The migrating pastor Zechariah Symmes tattled that on shipboard in 1634 Anne had already disputed his preaching of truth, but in four-year-old Boston she was easy to watch. John Winthrop need only look out his window to Sentry Lane and High Street to see the Hutchinson home. At first he detected nothing unusual about Anne, the good wife of William Hutchinson and the good midwife of her neighbors, but soon he could not overlook the bustling crowds of church members who gathered at her home. She there defended the covenant of grace as she heard Cotton preach it and demolished his assistant John Wilson, who she thought lapsed back to the covenant of works. She charmed other citizens who were hungry to hear the message of grace and some merchants who enjoyed her attacks on the ministerial establishment under which they chafed. Even the young Henry Vane, soon to be governor at age twenty-three (and later to represent Roger Williams in Parliament), frequented her gatherings.

The chronicler Edward Johnson remembered her as a woman who preached the gospel better than any of his black-coated preachers who had been to the "Ninniversity." This Mrs. Hutchinson, he heard, revealed things to come, something the learned scholars failed to do. The beleaguered John Wilson and a newcomer, the Reverend Hugh Peter, both felt this kind of attack on ministry had gone far enough. Anne Hutchinson preached falsely; she also violated good practice and church order because she was a woman preaching to men. It seemed to a saddened Winthrop that the conflict in Boston was as bad as Catholic versus Protestant fighting elsewhere.

In a closed meeting in the home of John Cotton, the ministers asked why she attacked them. Because they were not able to preach a covenant of grace. Why not able? "Why, because you can preach no more than you know." She thought they had no heart experience, no direct inspiration from the Almighty. Winthrop later said her attack was dung thrown in the face of ministers. Cotton was in danger of being splattered by throwers on both sides. The case had to go to General Court.

Governor Winthrop had the mandate to act fast, but he was reluctant to banish anyone from the knit community he desired. During a twenty-four-day synod in which her case was discussed — by now ministers were differing with each other and Cotton was in danger of being drawn into the dispute — the world closed in on Mrs. Hutchinson. In the midst of the turmoil her ally and friend Mary Dyer gave birth to a repulsive "monster." Midwife Hutchinson desperately hurried to hide the creature from view, but neighbors glimpsed it and soon word spread that the devil was especially busy among Massachusetts troublemakers.

Massachusetts officials kept meticulous records of trials. Those of Anne Hutchinson are well preserved. They show that her accusers were also her judges, and that they made no pretense of trial by jury, due process, or even presenting clear charges. She wanted to know what law she had broken. They charged the Fifth Commandment because while it only demanded respect for father and mother, they interpreted it to include all other authority in church and state as well. She fired back: if parents ask a person to do wrong, must not true children of God disobey them? Winthrop cut off that line of defense: "We do not mean to discourse with those of your sex. . . ."

Scripture was decisive in Puritan trials. When the fact that she was a woman came to be an issue, Anne cited a biblical text in Titus that allowed older women to instruct the young in the faith. That point should have scored, but her accusers came back to remind her that she also spoke to men in public. No, she spoke only to people who came unbidden to her home; she quoted the apostle Paul, who praised a husband-and-wife team who instructed Apollo, a follower of Jesus. Accusers quickly pointed out to her that they had taken him privately to their home, while Mrs. Hutchinson taught sixty or eighty people at a time without the aid of her quiet husband. "I call them not, but if they come to me, I may instruct them." Where, demanded Winthrop, was there a rule for that in the Bible? Anne Hutchinson, not easily put down, reminded him that in the game of quoting Scripture she was already ahead two to nothing. When Winthrop disallowed both texts she trumped: "Must I shew my name written therein?"

The accused almost carried the day, but like many prophets, she did not know how to quit while she was ahead. Her whole career in faith pressed her toward the next moment. In front of tense townspeople she blurted out words that a Bible commonwealth had to condemn. Unprompted, she revealed that beyond the reliable Scripture she heard what to them had to be the capricious voice of the Spirit of God to her own soul. Winthrop lunged, grateful that a marvelous providence had brought things to this pass. God Himself, he was sure, led the accused to lay herself open and expose the root of all the mischief. Church and state could never survive claims that God spoke new words apart from Scripture to people.

Winthrop, pressing his advantage, called for and received the guilty verdict, so the accusers and judges now turned into sentencers. Almost all members of the General Court found Anne Hutchinson unfit for their society and decreed that she must be imprisoned first and then banished out of their liberties. Not ready to retire, Mrs. Hutchinson wanted to know why she was being banished. "Say no more," she heard, "the court knows whereof and is satisfied." Underlying all their anxieties, the Boston leaders feared that England might find them guilty of tolerating seditious libel, a crime against which they decided to pass their own laws — after the incident.

Anne Hutchinson took her time going into exile. The Reverend John Wilson took delight in reading the order that expelled her, commanding her in the name of Jesus Christ to withdraw as a leper out of the congregation. The leper walked erect, friend Mary Dyer on her arm. The natural magnet for her kind was Rhode Island, where she proved hard to live with when her neighbors there also rejected her claims that the Spirit of God spoke directly to her. Some time later the great disturber of the peace of Boston also gave birth to a "monster," no doubt a menopausal baby who seemed to the whisperers to be a sign of divine judgment. Mrs. Hutchinson's end was violent. After her husband died she moved to Long Island Sound. There, in the conflict that Governor Kieft triggered by foolish policies, Indians attacked and tomahawked her and five children to death.

The dissent that produced Maryland, in contrast to the two colonies described above, was genteel. It was the expression of a wealthy family who converted back to Catholicism when that was neither fashionable nor advisable in Protestant England. They inspired a pilgrimage to a colony of their own — a Catholic stand, as it were, surrounded by Protestant leaders. This settlement owned by Roman Catholics was to disturb its neighbors as a misfit for decades to come. The founding family was headed by George Calvert, the first Lord Baltimore. He had put money into Virginia as early as 1609, and in the 1620s tried to help found a colony in the Avalon Peninsula in Newfoundland. He was then a Protestant, who remembered as an eight-year-old hearing his elders gloat over the loss of the Spanish Armada. Evidently a sensitively religious soul, Calvert included the idea of mission to natives in his earliest colonial schemes. Inexplicably — but no doubt sincerely, given the risks — he became a Catholic in 1625, an act that led him to resign his office of privy councillor. King James I opposed religious diversity but he stood by Calvert, and it was this king who named him Baron Baltimore and kept him on the privy council. When Charles I came to the throne, Calvert resigned, but he did not lose favor.

Baltimore, desiring a place in America, first tested Jamestown. The Royalist governor, Sir John Harvey, was friendly, but the people were nervous about having a prominent papist in their midst. Intending to return, Baltimore left some of his family in Virginia and went off to explore other possibilities, but he died in 1632 before he could establish himself. On the day George Calvert died, his son Cecil, the second Baron Baltimore and also a Catholic, received a charter for an American colony — and with it more power over that land than the king had in England.

English monarchs, uneasy about the independence of joint stock companies, which established members of the colonies, favored the old feudal pattern in which a favorite of theirs simply became the proprietor of a colony. For two Indian arrows and "the fifth part of all gold and silver found," to show his fealty, Cecil Calvert became the absolute lord, sole proprietary, and viceregal governor of Maryland and far away Avalon. The charter empowered him to pass all laws and did not command him to listen to appeals; it also commended his laudable and pious zeal for the Christian religion in the territory of savages. Baltimore chose to insist that the land be purchased from the Indians, who were the prior occupants of the soil. With Catholics in short supply, he welcomed, among other English people, even the Catholic-hating Puritans. The colony would be named Maryland, after the Catholic queen Henrietta Maria, and the first settlement came to be known as Saint Marys.

Everything seemed out of the ordinary about the *Ark* and the *Dove,* the ships that brought Leonard Calvert from England to serve as his brother Cecil's first governor. To this day it is not clear how the Catholics, including the priests aboard, sneaked past the official searcher who was assigned to exact from passengers the oath of allegiance that specifically rejected the pope and Catholicism. Did the searcher at Gravesend close his eyes, or did the Catholics among the 320 passengers cross their fingers during the oath? Did they hide from view or, downwater at Cowes, did someone smuggle them aboard? The searcher, in any case, reported only 128 persons. The language of the ship's journal showed that its author was clearly a Catholic. Protestants would never note that sailing began on Saint Cecilia's day, nor ask for prayers in the name of Mary or Maryland patron Saint Ignatius. (The journal keeper was the Reverend Andrew White of the Society of Jesus.)

The Catholic's prayers were needed, especially when on a stormy night the ships, tossed in whirlpools, became separated for six weeks. Amazingly, they found each other off Barbados, then finally sighted Point Comfort in Virginia. Rumors sailed faster than the ships, for Virginians knew they were coming. The entrenched colonists hoped that Indians would repel the hated Catholics, who might want to subject the colonies to the power of Spain. The governor of Virginia, however, made things easy for the new arrivals by issuing a friendly greeting to Cecil Calvert — a gesture motivated perhaps by his desire to hold the favor of the Crown, which owed him large sums.

On the day of the Annunciation of the Most Holy Virgin in 1634, the Catholics celebrated their first Mass in the permanent English colonies. They hewed a huge cross from a tree to erect as a trophy to Christ and on bended knees sang litanies of the sacred cross. Leonard Calvert, however, was discreet and evidently did not scandalize the large number of Protestants in his company. He was more concerned not to offend Indians, so the governor and Father John Altham took a delegation to a nearby Potomac village, there to announce that Europeans came not to make war but to lead natives to heaven. Though upriver at Piscataway the Indians looked warlike, the chief gave Marylanders permission to live where they wished. The Jesuits soon boasted a chapel and a lot, while the tardy Protestants waited eight years to build their own church.

Leonard Calvert worked out a manorial system by which people paid him quitrents. In turn, he reluctantly shared power with a Maryland Assembly. In 1639, this body made history by passing laws that provided for religious tolerance. Since the king wanted such a provision, Lord Baltimore had to accept one. It ran counter to the ideas most Christians had held for well over a thousand years. Yet the policy turned out to work, and when left to themselves, the Marylanders got along well.

Problems began when Puritans came to power in the English revolution after 1642. Anti-Catholics among them tried to make life difficult for tolerant Maryland, but in 1649 the Maryland Assembly held its own and retained some of the ideas of Cecil Calvert in "An Act Concerning Religion." As if out of habit, however, the document ruled out blasphemers and Jews as legitimate inhabitants of the colony. In 1658, a Dr. Jacob Lumbrozo had good reason to test the law when a Baptist, John Fossett, deposed that Lumbrozo spoke against some biblical miracles and when Quaker Richard Preston said that Lumbrozo still looked for a Messiah. In February of that year, the physician became the only Jewish believer ever to stand trial in an American court for blasphemy. He defended himself well, and after an inconclusive trial, was somehow spared a second one. Years later, he sat on a Maryland jury, a post usually still kept for Christians. It is possible that he had secretly submitted to baptism, but also, Maryland may have winked.

Maryland acted better than its laws demanded in the Lumbrozo case, but the Act showed that citizens were sensitive even to manners in a diverse society. No Marylander, it said, was to speak reproachfully in calling anyone thereabouts heretic, schismatic, idolator, Puritan, independent, Presbyterian, popish priest, Jesuit, Jesuited papist, Lutheran, Calvinist, Anabaptist, Brownist, antinomian, Barrowist, Roundhead, or Separatist. The very catalog shows that Maryland anticipated and probably embodied as much variety as New Netherland did.

Of all parties, it was, ironically, the Jesuits who complained most in Maryland. The religious orders needed property and welcomed gifts or cheap purchases from friendly Indians, so they inevitably came to clash with Cecil Calvert, a proprietor who wanted to keep control of all land holdings. The second Lord Baltimore worried about the growing size of church properties and outlasted the Jesuits in persistent wrangles about such holdings. While Protestants stood by letting the Catholics fight each other, the Jesuits also protested when the Calverts brought in regular clergy not under Jesuit control and when the authorities required licenses in order to trade with the Indians. In response, Cecil sounded like an anticlerical Protestant as he claimed that pompous clergy made laymen into the basest slaves and the most wretched creatures upon the earth. Feeling powerless, the vested Jesuit vicar general wearily compromised: "Give us souls and he can have the rest." For all their efforts through the years, the Jesuits counted eight men lost by death and two by banishment. At one time not a single priest lived in Catholic Maryland.

The proprietary system never did work well, and the colony never became a great place for refuge. After thirty-five years only about two thousand of the twenty thousand settlers were faithful Catholics. The Reverend John Yeo of the Church of England used biased eyes when he claimed that under Catholics and Quakers Maryland was a "Sodom of uncleanness and a pest house of iniquity," but his kind undercut Maryland's tolerance. When the Glorious Revolution came to England in 1688, anti-Catholics in and around Maryland formed an "Association in Arms for the Defense of the Protestant Religion and assisting the rights of King William and Queen Mary" — probably the first ecumenical movement of any sort on the North American continent. In July of the next year, this coalition of Puritans and Church of England members, who had little else in common, seized Saint Marys under the leadership of a former Roman Catholic now turned Protestant clergyman, John Coode. In January of 1691, King William annulled the old Calvert charters. The new regime brought hard times for Catholics as the Protestants closed their church, forbade them to teach in public, and forced their children to take demeaning oaths of loyalty. In 1702 the Church of England became established in Maryland by law, but not before the little outpost of practical Catholic tolerance had left its mark of promise on the land.

North of Maryland in Pennsylvania, the only religious group more despised than Catholics by other colonists, the Society of Friends, set up a similar proprietary colony. As a Quaker, founder William Penn was also an exile from the polite society of England. He surprised his neighbors by chartering a new settlement in the form of a holy commonwealth in the heart of the American colonies.

Quakers wanted to speak out their view of divine truth, even if this brought suffering, and they saw plenty of harassment in the colonies. The tolerance of mild Virginia gave out at dockside, after the House of Burgesses in 1660 forbade ship captains from importing Quakers. In New Netherland, Governor Stuyvesant mercilessly pursued the Friends. In New England, authorities hanged four Quakers and branded, bored the tongues, or cut the ears off others. Massachusetts laws forbade people to induce others to follow false gods, and this they accused Quakers of doing. The Friends scorned authority, served in no armies, paid no taxes, took no oaths, and doffed no hats. They often reviled the clergy and riled the congregations of Puritans, denouncing all worship but their own as false. In an intolerant age, such intolerant people tested the limits of all others, except in Rhode Island, which they used as a base.

In New England, the saddest story was that of the friend of Anne Hutchinson — Mary Dyer, who, during a trip in England, became a Quaker and then resolved to test New England laws against dissenters. Authorities arrested her and entrusted her to her sensible husband, but to no avail. Twice she was shipped out to Rhode Island and twice she came back to Massachusetts. She was banished yet again, this time under threat of death. She returned anyhow, was sentenced but reprieved, and found herself expelled for the fourth time. Tireless, she came back once more and was condemned to death. Killing women was a messy business, so officials worked out a charade. They blindfolded Mrs. Dyer, roped her neck, and expected her to recant. When she did not, a son pleaded for her, so the bemused authorities took her from the scaffold. In the end, they unfortunately ran out of ruses and, in 1660, had to hang her on Boston Common. The act turned public opinion against such executions and led King Charles to prohibit hangings for her sort of crime.

While they wanted to speak out elsewhere, Quakers also desired a place of their own. A first experiment in West Jersey failed. The diplomatic Quaker William Penn, called in to make peace between quarrelsome fellow believers, became familiar with the territory and decided he wanted such rich land. Penn bore the name of his father, who was an English vice admiral and, under Puritan Oliver Cromwell, general-at-sea. In 1681 King Charles II deeded the land of Pennsylvania to the son in order to make good on old debts to his father.

The father and son had parted long before. Destined for a military post and royal favor, young Penn found trouble already at Oxford early in the 1660s when he became a dissenter. His father tried to cure him of his early overdose of religion and even shipped him off to France to learn worldliness. There he fell again into the bad company of pious Huguenots who turned the young gentleman into a religious searcher. Arrested for attending Quaker and Seeker meetings, he was excused by a judge who noted his fine dress. That day the dashing young man unbuckled his sword and never wore one again.

After the two Penns parted company, the son found solace in a happy marriage to Guli — Gulielma Maria Springett. Now a convinced Quaker, he became valuable for his connections, his legal talents, and his penchant for tract writing. The gift of Pennsylvania was the boon the Quakers needed; seldom did a utopian planner have a better chance to work out his theories. Penn had an advantage most of the others lacked: he was a practical schemer who was eager to make money by peddling real estate. Before he embarked for America on the ship *Welcome* in 1682, he had sold 875,000 acres for his "holy experiment."

Penn was met by Indians at New Castle, and soon started purchasing land from them and learning their language. The Indians at first gave the new settlers less trouble than the Quakers gave each other. The form of government Penn first chose looked illiberal to anarchic colonists. When the original plan did not work well, Penn came up with a "Plan B" that revealed considerable and unfriendly distrust of human nature. Colonists only grudgingly paid their quitrents if they paid them at all. Instead of being abrasive to non-Quakers, they were decidedly not pacific toward each other. Penn was consistent enough still to grant religious freedom, thus joining

Rhode Islanders and Marylanders in welcoming varieties of sects. He let Huguenots come and insisted that in his colony Negroes be free and educated.

For a time, the colony prospered. By 1685 Philadelphia numbered twenty-five hundred people. After two years Penn returned to England, able to boast that not one soldier had yet been seen in Pennsylvania. Yet he worried. From shipboard he wrote his deputies not to provoke the Lord to trouble their quiet land. Eloquently, he reminded Philadelphians that their city had been named before it was born, and was shaped by love and care and service for its holy mission.

Penn returned to a troubled England. James II repressed dissent like his but Penn kept up good relations during new persecutions. Then, when the Glorious Revolution occurred in 1688 and 1689, the colonizer found that he had been backing a loser and, without good reason, was charged with high treason. Queen Mary jailed him when a perjurer charged that Penn had conspired against the Crown. He spent two years alternatively clearing his name or going into hiding, during which time his beloved Guli died and his fortune dwindled. A morose Penn was almost ready to give up on his holy experiment, from which he heard nothing but bad news about his heavy-handed deputies. There was even a schism when in 1692 a purist named George Keith gathered the so-called Christian Quakers to oppose the compromisers around him.

At the worst possible moment a brigand named Babbitt raided the shore of Philadelphia from a commandeered ship. For Pennsylvanians to arrest him with force would be to deny their pacifist principles. To give him license to continue would be a threat to their property. In the crisis the Quaker government voted for property over dogma by planning for an armed force. Suddenly a man named Peter Boss spared embarrassment by surprising Babbitt and company; he boarded the boat and put the raiders to flight without using weapons. Despite Boss's success, Keith used the Quaker decision to use force as a new argument against the majority.

The Keithite ferment quieted, but Pennsylvania was never again pure. Around the turn of the century, the Crown gave up on the Quaker colony but then later restored it to Penn. The people paid little attention to the proprietor or his deputies, and he returned to the colony a dejected man in 1699. Two years later, with his second wife, he returned to England. In 1712 a stroke paralyzed Penn, though he lingered until 1718, thinking himself a failure. Yet, with Roger Williams and the Calverts, the Quaker pioneer showed that the spirit of exile and dissent could also issue in ordered government. With other experimenters, he successfully anticipated the future religiously diverse America. He made plans to welcome religious varieties, whereas elsewhere authorities suppressed or discouraged them. Like so many American visionaries, he dreamed of an innocent and simple order but allowed for complexity and pluralism along the way to it, trusting the Divine Spirit more than human laws, including those he could himself devise and try to enforce.

Few American pilgrimages have ended in
martyrdom. Yet on occasion — chiefly when
warring native Americans perceived that Christian
missionaries were favoring an enemy tribe —
priests were tortured and killed. In this 1665
composite painting (based on a drawing from 1657),
three Jesuits face death. Kneeling at left is Isaac
Jogues, who died in 1646; on the stakes are Jean de
Brébeuf and Jérôme Lalemant, both of whom
perished in 1649. (*Archives du Monastere
de L'Hotel-Dieu de Quebec*)

Chapter Seven

THE END OF THE
CATHOLIC
MISSIONARY ROAD

*F*ROM JAMESTOWN IN 1607 UNTIL THE BIRTH OF THE NATION
after 1776, Protestant peoples came to dominate the area that would
become the United States. Most of the settlers were English-speaking, though migrants from the continent of Europe who spoke
other tongues were also welcomed. Catholic Maryland was the
only partial and brief exception among the Protestant East Coast
colonies. To the south in Florida and in today's American Southwest lay the vestiges of New Spain. To the northeast in Canada
was New France. Neither Spain nor France had large enough populations to produce colonists in numbers that could match the
teeming English. When gold gave out, Spain increasingly lost interest in America; and for the fur trade in the North, France needed
few agents. Both countries kept a military presence and tried to
expand empires, but European ventures kept them too busy to be
very successful.

For all of the above reasons, the area of the United States —
unlike eastern Canada and all of the Americas south of the Rio
Grande — was for the most part lost to Catholic missionaries. But
these agents of God refused to give up. Through almost two centuries, Catholic missionaries remained restlessly on the road, pilgrims of eternity who wanted to lead native Americans to a better
country, heaven. It would be an injustice to keep an eye only on
Anglo-America without tracking some of the Catholic men with

names like Kino and Serra and Marquette — men whom their enemies call fools, the world at large calls heroes, the church calls saints.

Today it is hard for most people to understand the mentality of the missionary. There are constant debates about the morality of superimposing one's culture on someone else, of trampling on the images of other religions, of uprooting old communities. Oftentimes the missionaries' foes think of them only as exploiters and conquerors. Whether the missionaries were right or wrong, however, they can be understood only when they are seen as people who wanted to populate heaven with baptized souls and who thus acted out of love for others. They were ready to give their lives as martyrs, and thus were prompted also by love of self. Nor could they shed loyalties to France and Spain and Catholicism — thus they were also moved by love of country and church. Of such mixed motives came the missions, which we can with difficulty comprehend as with awe we trace them.

Though New Spain and New France were products of rival nations, Jesuits and other Catholic agents sometimes dreamed of overcoming national differences and joining forces to block in the eastern seaboard. British settlers on that coast claimed only a two-hundred-mile-wide strip of land from Maine to Florida after a European treaty in 1713. No one spoke more clearly of the vision of Catholic advance in that period than one of the most ardent missionaries of the era, Father Eusebio Kino.

Always an agitator for Catholic expansion, Kino chided European cartographers for drawing maps that depicted gold and spices but not the greater treasure, the innumerable souls saved by Jesus Christ. If Catholics would promote American missions until New Spain and New France linked, he foresaw that "the Catholic empire of the Catholic royal crown and of our Holy Mother, the Roman Catholic Church will be happily extended so that all the world may be one fold with one shepherd." Kino seemed to picture a kind of great Catholic pincers to squeeze out the Protestant intrusion. This, of course, was naive. France and Spain may both have been Catholic, but they were political and imperial rivals.

During a mortal illness that threatened him as a student in Austria, young Kino first resolved to dedicate his life to the pioneer Jesuit missionary to the Orient, Saint Francis Xavier, whom he vowed to follow in mission. In the world of 1663 no Jesuit trifled with a vow, so upon recovery Kino rearranged his life plans. Jesuit training demanded twelve years, some of which in Kino's case prepared him to teach mathematics. He rejected a career in Munich, preferring to use his skill, he hoped, to impress oriental rulers.

The *Spiritual Exercises* of Saint Ignatius of Loyola, written during the height of the Spanish Catholic Reformation, helped produce saints and scoundrels, nobles and cruel warriors, but especially men who swore to go without question wherever their pope or their superiors sent them. The more dangerous and demanding the assignment, the better. The discipline made of Kino a model Jesuit who had to overcome the intense jealousy he felt as his superiors kept selecting others and neglecting him for mission. Six times in eight years he pleaded that they send him and six times they turned him down. He chose college rooms whose windows looked toward the East to remind him of his destination. Finally he got word that he might possibly head there — but via the West, since he would get his final orders in Mexico. Kino feared that Mexico could be the end of the road, but it was not a worse place than Europe in which to do one's hoping, and since he was ordered to go, he went.

Work in New Spain was satisfyingly dangerous. The Jesuits had lost many men — or, as they preferred to say, gained many martyrs — in the New World. Protestants always derided the Catholic style in converting, since they thought the Jesuits made every transaction that turned pagans into Christians too easy, too magical. Yet in the American Southwest the priests, who helped build pueblos where the Indians were friendly and forts where they were not, faithfully ordered Mass, proclaimed the message of God, and claimed new ground for Spain.

The Catholics kept careful score of their conquests for Christ. In the year after the Plymouth colonists in New England met their first Indians, Jesuits in the Sinaloa and Sonora missions of northern Mexico baptized 17,000 people. On the Mexican west coast the missionaries registered a total of 86,340 converts. While Roger Williams was still learning the Narraganset language, a Father Cataño baptized 3,000 natives. In 1645 the missions claimed 300,000 baptisms in the American Southwest and Mexico. The attempt at adding-machine accuracy shows how serious the priests were about numbering the new saints bound for heaven. Whenever Navaho or Apache raiders left missions in ruin and members of other tribes dead, escaping priests could ride away serene in their knowledge that, thanks to their efforts, the population of heaven was swelling. Moderns with less sense of salvation and mission will only with difficulty understand the motivations and satisfactions of these men who made history in pursuit of their visions. A close-up of Kino will at least illustrate this mentality in action.

Getting to the Mexico mission took Kino many years. His autobiographical *Favores celestiales* painfully recorded them. He and his companion were to join a convoy of forty-four ships to Mexico at Cádiz, Spain, but as they sailed toward the rendezvous and Cádiz came into view, so did the sails of these ships, already departed and now on the far western horizon. What might have been an inconvenience of merely two hours in an age of jet aircraft was a delay of almost two-and-a-half years in the 1670s. When finally Kino boarded the *Nazareno,* a hapless captain grounded it and had to jettison baggage, leaving behind some passengers, among them Kino. For several seasons more he had to fret with the Spanish language, maps, and mathematics until his day for sailing finally came.

Superiors, as he feared, did not honor his pleas to go to the Orient and instead sent him to Lower, or Baja, California with orders to help win California by persuasion, not force of arms. Don Isidro Atondo y Antillon, who led the company, was known for his humaneness. He replaced earlier commanders who terrorized natives along the way. When Indians came into view his soldiers cowered because they knew that the death penalty awaited those who misused natives. The Jesuits in the company welcomed this policy, because it gave them occasion to show curious Indians statues of Mary and crucifixes, to teach the sign of the cross, and to build rude chapels.

Misunderstandings almost inevitably developed between whites and natives, and the days of peace soon ended. At a place called San Bruno, where the party attempted a settlement, Kino was at last ready to convert two boys. He had to watch his moves, since the Indians considered baptismal water bad medicine after a child christened by a priest subsequently died. Kino therefore held back, fearing that Indians would regard his Christian act as mere magic.

Along a fifteen-hundred-mile stretch of barren Lower California, the party started missions and then had to abandon them. Kino all along kept pleading in letters that the bishop should invest more in the work, while he himself looked for gemstones or anything of worth to support the mission. As seasons passed, the priest could account for only eleven baptized people, moribund infants all. Still he was reluctant to abandon to heathendom even the three survivors among them.

When pirate chasing stopped bringing New Spain sufficient revenues, the viceroy gave up on Lower California. Kino had to bide time in Mexico City while waiting for orders to proceed farther north, to the land of the Pimas, Pimería Alta. The priest carried with him an order from the Royal Audiencia that forbade enslavement of Indians for work in the mines. This became a difficult order to follow after silver was found in tempting abundance at a place called Los Frayles. The finding did seem a divine sign, since henceforth the missions would need no outside support.

Seventy miles from the United States border, Kino opened his permanent mission work on March 13, 1687. On a great promontory called Dolores, where he staked out a place for a mission church, the priest handed the Indians pictures and tantalized them with chapel bells. He faithfully noted that they showed great esteem for anything that touched their eternal salvation. Then at San Xavier del Bac, near Tucson, Arizona, where his mission survives, Kino taught the Indians geography by showing the map of all the lands and rivers over which Jesuits were spreading the holy faith. Kino told the natives how the Spaniards had also been heathen until Santiago, the friend of Jesus, brought the faith to their land. Now, he added, the Spaniards were to convert the rest of the world. It was he who was chosen to help those Indians.

The act of exploring consumed Kino as much as baptizing did. In his zeal, he almost lost his good sense. From a low mountain range called El Nazareno, in 1693, he once again sighted the shore of the Gulf of California. Only the lack of a boat kept him from reaching his beloved earlier site, Baja California. The sun must have confused his brain, because, far from the shores, he began the building of a boat out of sparse timbers. He slowed the project to let the timbers age. Then, just in time to save his energy and his reputation for sanity, orders came from his superior to abandon the project.

Despite such setbacks, conversion, peace missionary work, and empire claiming continued, hampered only by a shortage of Jesuits and other priests. Often the Indians resisted. In 1697, in northern New Mexico, Spain temporarily regained power after the end of a rebellion by an Indian medicine man named El Popé, who despoiled Franciscan missions during the most successful Indian revolt in continental history.

Meanwhile, to support his own work, Kino imported livestock and became the most prosperous rancher on American soil. In May of 1697 his superiors wanted to move him back to Pimería Alta.

He was reluctant to leave the Indians and the livestock, so he arranged to spend half-years at both sites, taking time for exploring routes in the interim. In one twenty-five-day period, he covered eight hundred miles. Near the juncture of the Gila and the Colorado rivers, he baptized four hundred Indians. Through the years, Kino made fifty known expeditions on horseback, riding at least eight thousand miles. In 1711 the saddle-sore wayfarer fell ill while dedicating a new chapel. When he died, they buried him in that house of God.

Favores celestiales proves that Kino saw America as an extension of Europe and Catholic domain. He dreamed of a realm that would extend all the way from Mexico to Hudson Bay, an empire whose northern reaches he thus seemed to be ceding to New France. Both Catholic Majesties, he argued, would profit from new conquests and conversions until someday a highway for the internationally minded Jesuits would connect their two realms. Kino even dreamed of a convenient land route developing northwestward, toward the Asia he still could never get out of his mind.

But the Spanish regime did not — it could not — act out the missionary dream of empire. The resources were too thin and the natives were too resistant. In Texas, even the Jesuits kept their distance from the ferocious Apache and Comanche. In the San Antonio area, Catholics reported only 5,115 Indian baptisms by 1762, a low yield on many decades of investment. For a time, the Alamo was the only surviving Spanish mission in the territory. In 1749 the Apache, who needed Spanish help against the encroaching Comanche, did bury the hatchet and a live horse as signs of peace with the Catholics. In a little spurt of faith and hope, the priests built Mission San Sabá near Menard, but few natives came, and in 1758, raiding Comanches killed the last two missionaries.

California offered a last hope. Two centuries had passed since Juan Rodríguez Cabrillo touched on it for Spain in 1542. Sir Francis Drake also probed the San Francisco Bay area during his voyage around the world. A first little Catholic mission at Monterey had represented a small beginning, but not much more happened there than the saying of a mass, and silence fell after priests abandoned California soon after 1600. More than a century later came a challenge from a wholly unexpected source, and Spain woke up once more. Suddenly Russia stirred and began to explore the Pacific, thus threatening New Spain from the west. The Danish captain Vitus Bering, sailing for Peter the Great in 1728, followed the

Canadian coast all the way down to California. Spain saw fit to send agents to occupy the land and block Russian colonies, though, as it turned out, Russia was not really positioning itself for expansion.

This last representation of New Spain came with orders to win the Indians with kindness and love. The priests, too ready to become martyrs, had to be ordered not to take great risks. One of the men of this era became the best known of all the Catholic missionaries on what later became United States soil. A delicate Franciscan from Majorca, Junípero Serra first felt called to teach. When he thought he heard God telling him to convert the pagans, "he was not deaf to this interior voice of the Lord." Not until other assigned friars lost courage did his superiors send Serra with his student and confidant Francisco Palou to the work.

The men lived as their blessed founder Saint Francis told them to, without money and never riding horseback unless they had no choice. After they landed at Veracruz, Serra refused a donkey and climbed to Mexico City on terrain that Saint Francis had never envisioned. Along the way a chigger or mosquito bit him, and for his remaining years the five-foot-two-inch friar suffered from a resultant ulcerating wound. In the Sierra Gorda in Mexico the two men spent eight years preparing for work among the Apache in Texas. Then, when their superiors showed reluctance to license their virtual suicide through such dangerous efforts, they spent nine more years at a mission called San Fernando. There they taught novices, preached to the public, led choirs, and called on the sick.

Palou preserved from these years some glimpses of the almost savage Spanish piety. One day in church during a sermon that he was preaching, Serra flung back his robe and with a chain scourged himself, to show how sinful he was. A worshiper, upon seeing this, leaped up and wrestled the chain from him. Shouting that he, not the saintly father, was the truly ungrateful sinner, he whipped himself until Serra and his friends gave him last rites and watched him die. Palou liked to tell how Serra pushed lighted tapers toward his own exposed chest to demonstrate the tortures of a soul in sin, or how he beat his breast with cross and stone until he fainted.

In 1768 orders came to the Spanish agents to move ahead into Lower California. Serra went ahead, the eager friar having packed chalices and bells, never mentioning that he knew or cared of threats from Russia (or anyone else) to New Spain. He only hoped that the two hundred soldiers and fourteen missionaries could peacefully subdue coastal Indians. Here was Serra's chance to live out a motto he chose to write in a farewell letter back at Cádiz: "Always go forward and never turn back."

In the spring of 1769, when the time came to move into Upper California, Serra offered a "Good-bye, Francisco, until we meet in Monterey." The answer came, "Good-bye, Junípero, until we meet in Eternity." Junípero had the better of that bet; they met again five years later and worked together for ten more. As they moved on, at one mission Serra consoled a brother who had almost turned mad from loneliness in an outpost where no other human could speak his language. On Pentecost, at Velicatá, after he kissed the earth in the presence of naked Indians, Serra founded his own first mission on pagan land.

Nine hundred miles from the beginning of the journey, in mid-summer of 1769, the scurvy-stricken company reached San Diego, on what is now United States soil. Here were "lands until now untrodden by Christian feet." Indians laid siege for a while, and when they relented, illness and hunger took over. The Europeans felt they could hold out no longer, though they knew help was to come in mid-March of 1770. On the day of their expectation, at three o'clock, Serra gathered strength for his last mass, a rite inter-rupted with a shout from Presidio Hill. The rescue ship, full of supplies, was in sight! The refreshed party soon moved on all the way up to Monterey. There Serra said mass under the very oak that, he calculated, had sheltered explorers and priests back in 1602. The friar erected a cross and planted a flag as he embarked on the work that led to his first converts.

Between 1769 and 1784, despite hardships and the death of some missionaries, Serra extended colonial Spain through a system of nine missions (which grew to twenty-one after his death). On a stop at Carmel during the tour of his prosperous little agricultural mission-communities, he grew weak and sensed the nearness of the end. He had confirmed 5,307 people, while his missions reckoned 6,000 baptized Indians, yet now Serra himself faced death in dread and fear. His companions read the commendation for a departing soul; he seemed relieved. Then they carried him outside for the last time, after which he died in peace within the mission.

At their peak the California missions served some 30,000 people, in buildings whose restored beauty still charms California tourists. What began as an attempt to keep Russia at a distance turned out to be a concluding futile show of Spanish power. Russia, of course, never did become a realized threat. Spain kept a couple of North American fronts into the nineteenth century, but these came to nothing. To the Jesuits and Franciscans, the only population that mattered was made up of the Indian saints who through priestly efforts were now in heaven.

What do we make of these Spanish missions in the Southwest? Tourists are drawn to them in a spirit of nostalgia for the courage they recall and the peacefulness they bring to mind. Yet there was an underside to the venture, for "Borderland America," where the Spanish worked, was an area of upheaval. Spain was used to dealing with crowded, civilized societies over which it could lord itself as conqueror. The sparsely settled lands with dispersed and mobile Indian populations puzzled the Spanish missionaries. They had to create formal societies and cultures at the expense of looser indigenous ways. The missions as islands of civilization therefore introduced new elements of conflict to a scene of conflict. The missionaries were not always aware of the dissension they sowed or of their part in the flowing of blood. They went about their ways, mixing paternalism and genuine regard for native Americans, mindful always of what they were doing to further transactions between the Christian God and the people for whom Jesus came, souls whom they should represent to the Blessed Virgin.

The French in the Northeast had similar motives, though they came across different kinds of Indian culture. Their story takes us back to 1608, when Samuel de Champlain's explorations led to the founding of New France — the northern edges of Maine and New York and extending through the upper Great Lakes. Because of political agreements around 1763, New France came to be restricted to Canada.

The French explorers weren't necessarily looking for gold, but they did seek other treasures. French fashion decreed felt hats for gentlemen. Felt demanded beaver, one of the furs that made up the New World market for which the French fought the British in four wars between 1688 and 1763. Frenchmen built forts and towns in the American interior, but they lacked the numbers needed to colonize effectively. By 1713 New France was believed to have only 25,000 European residents, no match for the 250,000 in the English colonies.

Huguenot Protestants were no longer a major political force when the French began their seventeenth-century settlements, so the New World mission was in the hands of Catholic orders alone. Champlain sincerely wanted to be friendly and win the natives, but he also played up to the advertised piety of his monarch: "The conversion of one infidel," he claimed, was "worth more than the conquest of a kingdom." He reminded French nobles that they would have to give an account to God for any souls lost to hell in America.

Even with financial support, not all religious orders were able to sustain the work, but a few intrepid Jesuits headed to the interior — "infidel" territory — after 1625. Isaac Jogues came in 1636, to serve among the Mohawk in New York. The Iroquois captured and tortured him and a companion, and after a daring escape, Governor Kieft himself arranged their safe passage to Europe. Jogues hurried back, however, only to find the Indians blaming him for having left behind religious objects that they thought were magically producing diseases and famine among them. In 1646 he was ambushed and tomahawked at a cabin door, never having gained a convert.

More successful was Father Jean de Brébeuf, who worked among Ontario Hurons for fifteen years, baptizing a thousand natives and erecting five chapels. Though he met death under Iroquois torture in 1649, his example inspired others to follow. A kind of annual almanac, the *Jesuit Relations,* spread the fame of Brébeuf and other heroes, including René Ménard, who worked in the areas of Michigan and Wisconsin. At one time he lived a thousand miles away from any other priest. The Chippewa at his mission at L'Anse, Michigan, loved to taunt him. They would abandon him on shore and row away, or throw his prayer book into the water and force him to retrieve it. Yet Ménard stayed with the work until one day he and a companion were parted in Wisconsin. No European ever saw him again; some say that he died under a Sioux tomahawk.

Father Claude Jean Allouez reached Lake Superior in 1665 and erected a hutlike chapel near Ashland, Wisconsin. From that base he baptized thousands among the Nipissing, rejoicing to report on how the Indians listened with piety and decorum to the Christian story. Like other Jesuits, he always had to hurry on, but he combined baptizing with work for tribal peace throughout Great Lakes territory until his death in 1689.

Father Jacques Marquette did for New France what Kino accomplished by way of exploration for New Spain. He came close to effecting the Jesuit bridge that could connect a single Catholic empire, a dream of missionaries unshared by French and Spanish political or commercial adventures. The two nations saw each others' advances as incursions and tried to match each other fort for fort around Louisiana. France was to lose out first.

After a brief career as a young blade in France, Marquette turned serious. He read the *Relations,* adopted Saint Francis Xavier as his model, and by 1666 was working in Canada. Superiors sent him to build on the work of Jogues and others at Sault Sainte Marie in Michigan, where two thousand people soon lined up for baptism. Marquette and his colleagues held back with the sacrament until they were sure that the docile natives would leave behind their old customs as they turned Christian.

New assignments came rapidly; soon the priest was on the French rim of Christendom beyond the station of Allouez on Lake Superior. On this icy odyssey, Marquette met several hundred displaced Hurons who, he surmised, preserved traces of Christianity carried along from their days back east. When Indian tribes ridiculed prayer, they seemed to him to be far from the Kingdom of God, but he in his turn was also disrespectful of their sacred rites.

The Illinois charmed him with their stories of a great river, but they possessed no canoes and had not traveled far along it. In his encounter with them, Marquette was enthralled to hear reports that farther south, natives wore glass beads of a kind he knew must come from Europe. Somehow the Europeans must have access to the other end of this river; was its mouth, then, in Virginia or California? Marquette hoped someday to gain a canoe so he could explore the river, minister to people along the way, and find the passage Jesuit fathers dreamed of to the South Sea or the Western Sea.

From that point, the mission of Marquette seems to belong chiefly to the history of exploration, but in his day such activity added up to serving God, Catholicism, France, the Jesuits, and his own curiosity all at once. At the beginning, the Sioux forced him to flee Chequamegon Bay. He was the last missionary to serve near Lake Superior for decades. After the setback, he withdrew to Sault Sainte Marie, there to come across a lonely Father Gabriel Druilletes, whom he helped build a little log chapel. There, as so often, the priest grumbled about the savage mind that failed to catch on when Jesuits stammered the words of Christian faith to them. Despite the grossness and superstition he found in the flock, he was glad, he said, to see that they came daily to chapel and prayed there even when he left for a fortnight. The women and children especially found him friendly and did him the honor of welcoming him to their great pumpkin feast.

The Count de Frontenac, in charge at Quebec nine years after Louis XIV made New France a province in 1663, was always eager to find new products for trade, new tribes for mission, and new ways to isolate the English. So he authorized Marquette to take a trip down the Wisconsin River in search of the great Mississippi. The Quebec-born layman Louis Jolliet was to lead the expedition. On May 17, 1673, the two paid respects to the Blessed Virgin at Saint Ignace, Michigan, and set out on their dangerous journey. In Wisconsin the Menomini tried to discourage them from continuing, but Marquette told them he must push on "because the salvation of souls was at stake, for which I would be delighted to give my life."

Early and late in the month of June the pair had a few other contacts with natives, but between June 7 and 25 the party neither saw nor heard a single sign of Indian life — no canoe, no smoke, no dwelling — until 190 miles south of Wisconsin Marquette startled himself with the sight of human footprints. He and Jolliet followed these ashore six miles to a village, where they learned that Indians of the Illinois tribe had been keeping them under surveillance. Natives stood ready with peace pipes and dancing ceremonies. An old village chief promised the French they could go in peace to all the Indian homes. To show his regard, he even offered a young boy as a hostage to Marquette, who had no particular use for one. The priest enjoyed the benediction of the old man in the name of the Great Spirit who made all men. The chief was a generous soul who evidently played up to the French as allies against the always threatening Iroquois.

Convinced that they were the first Europeans in this mosquito country, the Frenchmen claimed landmarks all along the way for Christian France until they found the mouths of the Missouri and Ohio. In one encounter they were startled to see Indians armed not with bows but guns; both sides retreated from conflict. At Arkansea, or Arkansas, the party met more warriors, who again turned out to be friendly. Finding the risks too high and fearing that uncomprehending Spaniards might overtake them and destroy all they had found during exploration, they turned around for the strenuous northbound voyage.

Only once on the whole journey, at Kaskaskia in Illinois, was the priest privileged to baptize a child, but he piously observed that such an act made the whole trip worthwhile. Marquette, weakened from the trip, stayed in Wisconsin while Jolliet set out for Canada with his maps, account books, and all records in a box. In rough waters at Montreal all but Jolliet drowned, and he lost all the reports. Unworried about the loss of records because he had been provident enough to leave duplicates at Sault Sainte Marie, Jolliet learned only much later that in a skirmish during that summer the Indians burned the mission residence there. Only the meager diary of Père Marquette remained.

The trip ruined the health of Père Marquette. When friends encountered him, they were shocked to discover how wracked by dysentery his body was. Despite his frailty, however, he prevailed on them to let him journey to Fort Kaskaskia in southern Illinois. On the way to Mud Lake, near Chicago, friends had to build him a cabin when the cold weather besieged them. When they could, his companions cut ice and thawed it for water needed in the daily mass. When spring and Holy Week came, the weakened priest instructed thousands of Indians at Kaskaskia. Then it occurred to him to wonder what sense Indians would make of it if he died while telling them that Jesus rose and conquered death. He urged his colleagues to hurry on farther with him. For weeks he lay flat in his canoe while friends retraced their way back with him to Lake Michigan.

Marquette lived up to pledges he wrote years before this passage, when he had promised never to suffer fear or anxiety. He foresaw that either of two things must happen: God would adjudge him a coward or offer him a share in the cross of Jesus.

On a May night in 1675, while friends held up a crucifix, his end came. In the formal manner of their day they recorded that he raised his glance above the cross, holding his eyes fixed upon something distant as he seemed to gaze with delight. It was important for them to say that he expired without a shudder, his face smiling and radiant, with the ease of a person falling asleep. He was not yet thirty-eight.

A fever for expansion continued to grasp New France as it did New Spain. Father Claude Dablon wanted to push to the North Sea, while the intrepid Father Louis Hennepin worked throughout the Midwest in the 1670s. Antoine de la Mothe Cadillac, who founded Detroit, helped to build up a strong central base and told missionaries to get on with their job, to instruct the natives first as "subjects to the king, and afterwards . . . Christians." In 1682 Robert Cavelier, the Sieur de La Salle, claimed the mouth of the

Mississippi. Five years later in Texas he died, perhaps at the hands of his own mutinous men. By the end of the century Pierre Lemoyne, Sieur d'Iberville, established a fort near New Orleans. Throughout the continental heartland missionaries made moves toward the Indians, but usually had to settle for being pastors to the white explorers and traders.

The French Jesuits spoke more fondly of their converts than did other missionaries. Though Brébeuf often suspected sorcery among them, he argued that the people were at least bright enough to see and to recognize something beyond their own sensory experience. In Huron country Father Jérôme Lalemant claimed that never in France did he see illiterate people who could grasp the mysteries of faith as eagerly as did these aborigines. God was finding his community among them. Were the French to die a thousand times, "the gospel must be preached here."

Time soon ran out for New France. England needed new places for its people, while France did not. Few French Canadians could read at all, so they were no intellectual match for the English colonists. Feudal land policies in Canada discouraged investors. Through the seventy-two long years of his reign, Louis XIV frittered away the chance for empire in the heart of North America. From the Treaty of Paris in 1763 until Napoleon sold Jefferson the Louisiana Purchase in 1803, the French story is one of decline, of yielding space to the new English Americans as France abandoned outposts. After King Louis XV for domestic political reasons banned Jesuits in his country, there were no Catholic elite troops to serve Indian spiritual needs in America.

By the 1760s only one Jesuit remained in the whole of the Old Northwest, and when he foresaw the papal ban, he became a "regular priest." Detroit, an important French installation, fell to the British, who assured freedom of worship to Catholics. Along the Mississippi and its tributaries only a few woebegone trading stations remained, at places named Kaskaskia and Cahokia, Saint Genevieve and Vincennes. One visitor who came across only a melancholy chapel at Vincennes, its images and sacred vessels gone, observed "the linings of the ornaments had been given to negresses decried for their evil lives; and a large crucifix . . . and the chandeliers, were found placed above a cupboard in a house whose reputation was not good." Father Pierre Gibault found very few Catholics faithful there after 1770. Those who cared stumbled forward to him on their knees, crying that he should save them from hell. Others scolded him for having come too late to save their relatives.

In 1764 a Penobscot Indian approached Massachusetts governor Sir Francis Bernard with a request that paid tribute to the French missionaries, perhaps the best friends the native Americans ever had among the Europeans. He asked for a priest who would baptize Penobscot children, perform marriages and administer the sacraments to adults, and show them all the way to heaven. Ever since Canada fell, he complained, the Indians lacked a priest. They ran wild, but he was sure a father could correct their ways. The Indian's logic targeted the Christian heart: "It is usual to help the poor; we are poor, and therefore help us in the matter of Religion." Bernard was sympathetic, but when he tried to pawn off a priest from his own Church of England, the Penobscots rejected the idea. So did the Micmac at a conference at Watertown, Massachusetts, in 1776. When Maine finally became a state, Catholics from Boston tried to resume Indian work on old foundations laid by a few stray French missionaries, but found few traces of earlier work.

Typical of the portrayals of his day, this 1742
engraving pictures George Whitefield as cross-eyed
— a feature that in no way distracted from his
allure. Known for his voice and his rhetorical gifts,
the evangelist carried the gospel to most of the
colonies, attracting enormous crowds along the
way. (*Photograph by George M. Cushing,
Massachusetts Historical Society*)

Chapter Eight

A MATTER OF CHOICE

*W*HILE THE COLONIAL PROTESTANTS WERE GENERALLY FAILURES at carrying on Indian missions, this did not mean that they lacked people to convert. Among these were some of their neighbors, people who had not practiced religion in Europe, or who, uprooted, left it behind. Other neighbors had first come on pilgrimages of faith to found colonies for God and had then let the fires grow cold. Colonial preachers never tired of referring to the good old days of the founders, when people kept to their covenant with God — in contrast to the lukewarm and lackadaisical people of their own day, the early eighteenth century. Someone had to rekindle the fires.

There was a third set of prospective converts on the hither side of the Indian line: the young. For centuries godliness was supposed to be passed on with the genes: Christians were simply children of Christian parents. But that process didn't work long in America, for many chose to fall away. Also, since the fourth century, churchliness had come with the territory. Initially, everyone on Christian soil, except ghetto Jews, was thought of as Christian. No more. The journey of so many religious groups and so many seekers to American shores meant that few could permanently claim any turf as their own alone. Believers and nonbelievers had to share space, while believers tried to win others to belief.

To effect conversion the American colonists needed new means and instruments. It is one thing to inspire a group of Christians, but it is a vastly different thing to win them for the first time to the covenant, or to get them to "own" the existing covenant with God and recognize it as their own. On the Continent and in England there were stirrings of movements like Pietism, which tried to fire up casual believers. English Puritanism long had spoken of "the heart prepared" for God and had tried to reach it and heat it with love for the divine. Yet something new arrived in both America and England in the 1730s — an Awakening or Revival movement that took many shapes, forms, expressions, and colors.

A new form of preaching pulled at the emotions, and mass meetings inspired crowd response and vibrant singing — all conjuring an atmosphere conducive to conversion. From our perspective of more than two centuries later, we may consider such efforts as "the Old Time religion." Significantly, though, in the 1730s such practices were definitely innovations and the practitioners were called, in various places, New School, New Light, or New Side. Colonists had never seen anything before like the revivalist outbreaks that swept the country in the early eighteenth century.

As with all such complex upheavals, its causes, expressions, and outcomes are hard to explain. There may be as many individual theories as there were individual observers. But our own interest in the American pilgrimage leads us to examine the Awakening from this viewpoint: how does this new movement show the colonists beginning to understand what it was to be religious in their time, their place? It is valid to note that, thanks to the new styles of the Awakening period, religion itself became more than ever before a matter of choice. Some see this increase of choice as the essence of modern faith. Faced with this new freedom, most chose their parents' faith, or the majority faith of their community, or that of their spouse. But no longer did a particular faith simply "come with the territory" as it had back in Europe. Now Americans felt spiritually stirred to take up their own pilgrimages, to be restless about the soul in their new environment. Awakeners learned to exploit or promote this restlessness.

While most historians have come to call this religious revival the Great Awakening, this name came a century after the event. Some historians question whether people in the 1730s and 1740s would have considered the term appropriate. Curiously, in this case, as in a number of later revivals, it is hard to prove that religious participation was very low before the stirrings and greatly increased thereafter. It is possible to see the period of revival as a series of generally unconnected outbreaks, each of which took on the color of its local milieu. No central person or religious organization planned or coordinated it; no single plot unfolded.

Yet *something* happened, whether or not the perpetrators and participants were aware of its historical significance. The Great Awakening can be seen as a move toward the developing of modern religion in the West. At its heart was the notion of choice: you must choose Jesus Christ, must decide to let the Spirit of God work in your heart and — note well! — you may and must choose *this* version of Christianity against *that* version. Where once a single steeple towered above the town, there soon would be a steeple and a chapel, Old First Church and competitive Separatist Second Church or Third Baptist Chapel — all vying for souls.

Most of the mainline Protestant churches of two centuries later exist because once upon a time these competitive evangelists — so named because they warmly preached the Evangel, the Good News of Jesus — had converted people to their Congregationalist, Presbyterian, Methodist, and Baptist beliefs. Those who, like the Episcopalians, shunned the movement were left behind. So influential was the Great Awakening style of "getting religion" that when Catholics reappeared in numbers in the nineteenth century, their priests and missioners had to learn the techniques of the old Protestant evangelists, to win the new migrants as they got off the boats to participate in the Catholic scheme of salvation and church.

But to get the revival off the ground, the pioneers in the 1730s had to demonstrate a need in the colonies. Never trust a revivalist preacher for a fully accurate picture of how bad the times were spiritually when he or she began work. It is too important for such prophets to show how evil were the times and the people before the rescue began. Still, there were good reasons for revivalists to look out and find falling-away from the covenant, desertion of the churches, and halfheartedness among the populace. Cotton Mather, publishing in 1701, provided a gloomy vision of need among his own fallen-away people, among the Indians, who were never the subject of English missions as they had been of Spanish and French, and among the blacks, who eventually would appropriate new-style Christianity. In Mather's veins flowed blood inherited from pioneer ministers John Cotton and Richard Mather. Their grandson, he was admitted to Harvard at age twelve and was ambitious for the Harvard presidency later in life, though he settled for being pastor of Second Church in Boston. There, as a precocious gossiper and dabbler in colonial affairs, he turned out enough books and pamphlets to amass a bibliography of at least 437 titles. His giant *Magnalia Christi Americana,* published in London in 1702, was to be the New England epic.

The first line of his book stated its purpose: Mather would write the wonders of the Christian religion "flying from the depravations of Europe, to the American strand." He was precise about the myth of the founders: "The *first* age was the *golden* Age: to return unto *that,* will make a man a Protestant, and, I may add, a Puritan." In 1701, however, he mourned the fact that the American Jerusalem in the wilderness was no longer pure, but had to include — and he named them all — antinomians, familists, Brownists, Separatists, old-style Quakers, Pelagians, Arminians, and the Roman papists, "whose religion is antichristian," and whose errors came from the devil of hell. It was clearly time for true Protestantism to reassert itself and win allegiances.

Mather more than others saw the Indian situation as a key to Puritan failure and hoped to see a revival of interest in converting them. He personally had a moderately good record with the natives, and as a mediator often took their side. In his book of instruction for the Iroquois, he mourned that Muslims, Quakers, Socinians, and papists shamed the Protestants in their zeal for winning Indians. The seal of Massachusetts Bay, Mather remembered, depicted an Indian quoting the biblical words "Come over and help us." Since few helpers of the right kind came, Mather had to console himself with mention of John Eliot, the workers on Martha's Vineyard, and a few hundred praying Indians. More aware of New France than New Spain, the New Englander sounded as if he feared a Catholic empire when he urged Protestants hurriedly to build a bulwark against the Jesuit kingdom of Antichrist.

Black American Christianity is largely a product of Awakening-style or revivalistic religion. Little had been done to win or serve blacks by 1701. If there was self-interest in his view of the Indian mission, Mather's concern about the Negro question combined humane regard for the slaves with moral disdain for the slaveholders. Though only 1,000 of the 90,000 people in New England at the turn of the century were blacks, he knew that first families like the Cabots and Browns and Faneuils had been profiting from human cargo since 1644 and that much of the New England shipping economy depended on this cruel trade. Yet here moral ambiguity appeared in his life; Mather himself owned slaves and did less than some of his farsighted contemporaries to improve their situation or that of hemmed-in free blacks.

Yet he felt there should be revival and conversion. Mather's book *The Negro Christianized* argued that blacks had souls and merited mission work; if they were barbarous, "so too were our own ancestors." In an era when religion undertook to save people for the next world, Mather also faced up to some realities in this one. He knew that many people refused to baptize Negroes because baptism conferred liberties. Then he offered his alternative: masters should insist on such huge indentures that Negroes would be in virtual slavery after baptism. The minister wanted black children to memorize lines like this one: "I must be patient and content with such a condition as God has ordered for me." Yet even such teaching did not keep Mather above suspicion, and fellow citizens were often critical when he arranged for slaves to worship at his home, even under the watchful scrutiny of church officers.

Mather was only a chronicler of the need for a revitalization. He was secondary in fame to a later and greater figure: Jonathan Edwards, a religious thinker and evangelical preacher who towered above all the others. With Edwards the Awakening, at least insofar as it was located in local churches, came to its focus and climax. No one interpreted the psychology of conversion or the meaning of revivals for community life better than he did. Edwards's story makes best sense against the background of his grandfather, Solomon Stoddard, who for fifty-seven years ministered in the Massachusetts back country along the Connecticut River. Stoddard's detractors called him "pope," so influential was he. Some of this influence grew because he had effective sons and sons-in-law also ministering in the valley.

Stoddard inherited a problem that the New England revival, but not others, set out to address. The enormously complicated issue comes under the code name the Half-Way Covenant. New England Puritanism in its Congregational churches limited membership to those whom the Congregationalists called "visible saints." These were people who were not merely baptized, following the old patterns from across the Atlantic, but who could also point to a specific experience of divine grace. This approach assured that only the elect of God would rule the colony, since church membership and the right of franchise and governing were all connected.

To make this elitist system work, there had to be a constant supply of visible saints. Whenever interest in religion declined, everything sagged. There was another problem. At first, only children of visible saints were to be baptized and thus recognized as part of the covenant. But dared people bar from baptism the little children of people who had never personally experienced the grace of God? Church leaders had to choose between demanding visible sainthood or baptizing the children of those who did not meet standards. Today such a dilemma would engross only members of a sect, but then political society was also involved.

A synod or convention back in 1662 found the majority of ministers ready to compromise. Church members who were baptized as children and grew up in agreement with the doctrine of faith, if they did not lead scandalous lives, could take on the covenant in a formal ceremony in front of church members. They could have their children baptized. But this compromise negotiated away the crucial experience of a felt conversion. Sober church leaders thought they were rescuing integrity by drawing *some* sort of line between complete believers and adults who did not meet the standard. The latter could not go to the Lord's Supper, the Protestant version of the Mass, nor could they vote on church business. The whole proposal was unsatisfying, but no one came up with a better idea than this Half-Way Covenant.

Enter Stoddard. He took advantage of the Half-Way Covenant compromise and moved uncompromisingly toward what his enemies called Stoddardeanism. Why, he asked, should one sacrament, baptism, be used to promote conversions while the other, the Lord's Supper, could not? So he threw open the gates and welcomed all baptized persons into full church membership. *Then* he went to work on them, whipping up revivals and preaching emotionally to stir conversions. Stoddard began to patent a new test in American church life. Argue with his methods? Fine: but he was prepared to lose the argument because he could simply point to statistical successes. The new means of converting worked, at least for a time.

Now enter also his grandson Jonathan Edwards, who came on the scene at Northampton in the Connecticut Valley in 1726, after Stoddardeanism had begun to run its course. Born to the clerical blue, this Yale College graduate, once a precocious child, had pored over new philosophy and old theology during his student years. Yet he also had time to survey his own searching heart, find it void of God, and agonize his way into the requisite experience of Christ's warm love.

Some think of Edwards as a cold and severe man, yet many of his writings show that he was both a participant in and an observer of things of the heart. He left a record of his attraction to Sarah

Pierrepont, the future Mrs. Edwards, whom he met when she was a thirteen-year-old and married four years later.

In his essays Edwards spoke of her as a young lady in New Haven who was "beloved of that Great Being," God. In certain seasons and in invisible ways God filled her mind with exceedingly sweet delight. Edwards rhapsodized about how she went singing, full of joy and pleasure, "and no one knows for what." When she walked alone in fields and groves, he observed, she always seemed to enjoy an invisible presence conversing with her. If his beloved thus became a proof for the existence of God, after marriage he also found in her a darker side, a melancholic tinge that served to remind them both of the terror and precariousness of human life.

An earthquake on Sunday night, October 29, 1727, however minor it was, rocked New England and shook dull believers. In those days natural disorder was always a sign that God was trying to get a message across to his creatures. Connecticut historian Benjamin Trumbull years later remembered how people trembled and thereafter momentarily filled the houses of God. But the fear passed, and so did the fervor. Edwards hoped for more lasting revival, but when Stoddard died in 1729 and the grandson took complete charge of his pulpit, he sounded like Cotton Mather when he pronounced Northamptonites "very insensible of the things of religion."

What happened next is colored by the tendency already mentioned for revivalists to paint the immediate past in darkest hues. Edwards, a master psychologist of religion, represented his town as corrupt. The youths were addicted to night walking. They frequented the tavern and engaged in unspecified lewd practices. Their corrupting mirth and the jollity of their nocturnal frolics fell far short of the standards set by God and the Puritan preacher. Then suddenly in 1733, while Edwards went about his usual business preaching the terror and mercy of God, people unaccountably began to stir. For the next two years — though some saw signs of revival as late as 1737 — people crowded the aisles and pews, converting in such numbers that ever since some observers have liked to speak of the Massachusetts Great Awakening as having "broken out" there and then.

Edwards throughout seemed to be doing little more than the droning clergy in sleepy towns did all along. He took into his high pulpit little 3⅞-by-4⅛-inch cards sewn into booklets, papers on whose reverse side were family bills and memos, evidences of busy parsonage life in years when the sacred and the mundane came so close together. Neither when he read sermons off those cards nor later when he learned to speak without using them did hearers see many gestures or feel passion. The preacher's eyes would scan the congregation until they sought out the bell rope, but whoever glimpsed the eyes in midpassage found them as discerning as his voice was penetrating. The people's emotional response was (in Edwards's favorite word about the event) "surprising," but good Puritan that he was, he had to insist that those who converted remained "sober, and orderly, and good," never losing their rationality to enthusiasm.

Edwards tried to make sense of crowd psychology as he watched converts stir in nearby towns. The young people turned serious when two of their peers succumbed to disease in nearby Pascommuck. Thereafter when he preached, "the town seemed to be full of the presence of God" and never "so full of love, nor so full of joy; and yet so full of distress as it was then." Edwards always chose his words with care, intentionally posing love or joy next to distress, for the Awakening was built on their interplay; as if the hearts of people were pierced with a dart, he wrote, their consciences stung and they feared to meet God. Then when they surrendered, God gave them a sudden bright sense of newness.

People knew each other well in the Connecticut Valley, and Edwards fittingly named names. In a day when child mortality was high and Christians believed the devil spared no infants, awakeners paid notice to the young. At age four, little Phoebe Bartlett was not too young to hide in her closet out of fear of hell until she was assured of heaven. Young Abigail Hutchinson just seven months before her death passed through three precise stages of conversion until she found repose. Some of the older people never found solace. Edwards's uncle Joseph Hawley in distress searched his soul until the devil sent a despairing thought. Hawley spent a Saturday night in insomnia and delirium and then on the morning of the Lord's Day cut his own throat. Edwards shrank back a bit when several other suicides followed, for he sensed that multitudes without his help heard an invisible voice telling them: "*Cut your own throat. Now is a good opportunity; now, NOW!*"

Terror in distress was only the first stage of rebirth. Second came an awareness of the depth of the human predicament and the justness with which God stood ready to condemn the sinner. Finally came relief through the gift of grace. While Edwards helped people move in orderly fashion through the stages, he worried about the fanatics who quickly whipped up "great noise" and disorder. Yet their more notorious method also helped spread the Awakening to nearby towns and then through much of the colony. Seldom did a majority of the citizens become part of the churches, but in curious ways the whole towns did feel their interests to be at stake. On the surface, life went on as before. Merchants haggled in New York and Philadelphia. Pioneers pushed back the frontier and the Indians who lived along it, while England and France prepared to fight over American land. Traders talked about tariffs and homemakers about tea. The people of New England towns had no reason to suspect that they were helping write a new page in American religious history.

If the people did not know their place, Edwards had the audacity to rewrite history with them as its climax. Its plot began with Adam and ended with Northampton. Well aware as Edwards was that similar revivals were breaking out on the Continent and in England, he still put the "Made in America" stamp on the doings. America in the act of being awakened suddenly came to be an instrument of the promised Second Coming of Jesus. Though the United States did not yet exist, Edwards also sounded nationalistic as he promoted the idea that nations could be born in a day when, as he put it, God would "awaken whole countries of stupid and sleeping sinners." As if they belonged in the unfolding plot of the Bible itself, Connecticut Valley villagers and other converts were to see their lives now filled with a special sense of meaning and destiny. In a strange way the all-powerful God himself depended on their will, their voluntary choice, to complete his work and end history. The Bible prophesied that such changes would occur and Edwards was sure that his followers could not "reasonably think otherwise."

If his followers found all this reasonable enough, critics at a distance tried to put it in perspective. Pious Protestant Isaac Watts in England read these startling claims from backwoods America and snorted that here Edwards's reasonings lacked force. Watts was offended by what became a constant theme in the Awakening, the suggestion that the epochal new work of God must begin and concentrate in America. The prophet Isaiah had foretold that stirrings would occur in a very remote part of the world, which, thought Edwards, could only mean in America. Though the New World was for ages under the control of Satan, it was now to be the site of "the new heavens and new earth."

Edwards spelled out this vision in *Some Thoughts Concerning the Present Revival of Religion in New England. . . .* The Old World would no longer enjoy the honor of communicating religion in its most glorious state to America, but vice versa. He insisted that the America that once supplied gold and tobacco to Europe now must send spiritual goods. God had hidden America from the world until Protestant reformers could attack the great antichristian Catholic apostasy. Now, "this utmost, meanest, youngest, and weakest part" of the world would change the rest of it. Those who opposed revivals or kept silent in their tiny Massachusetts towns therefore exposed themselves to the curse of God.

There are obvious hazards in making too much of six quaint pages in a book rarely read about an Awakening most Americans never heard of and with which they could not easily identify. To Catholics, Jews, most kinds of Protestants, and, certainly, unchurched and nonreligious Americans alike, the revival seems to be the private concern of "born-again" sects who attracted perhaps 10 percent of the citizenry. Yet more than the present church members were involved. The awakeners wanted to save souls for Jesus, but they also hoped for more. If the converted responded well, Edwards thought, Negroes and Indians would someday become divines and, thanks to the revivals, Christian books would appear in Africa and other barbarous countries. Heirs of the revivals later insisted that something of that order did occur.

Such apparent spiritual arrogance also disturbed the social fabric. Conversions divided families, churches, towns, and colonies, and Edwards knew it. During a military fracas called the War of Jenkins' Ear, fought between England and Spain, he declared that "we in New England are at this day engaged in a more important war." He pointed to two churchly figurative armies drawn up in battle array to fight about the way to find God. Leader of the opposition was Charles Chauncy. This minister at First Church in Boston, after dabbling himself with revivals for a time, dropped the efforts. By 1742, though the fever had subsided, he was charging Edwards's Northampton following with insanity.

Chauncy was a religious liberal, a man of reason who helped produce Unitarianism, but against revivalism he sounded like a biblical fundamentalist. He purveyed obsolete psychological theories as he defended the mental faculty of isolated reason at a time when new outlooks were being born. The leader of the establishment — it came to be called Old Light — saw the revival as a force of infinite evil; popery itself had not been "the mother of more and greater blasphemies and abominations." Sweet reason went out Chauncy's window as he charged that revivalists wanted to destroy all property and hold all wives and goods in common. The revival pest, he said, filled the church with confusion and the state with disorder. Edwards, in reply, insisted that the passions, which he called "the affections," could not be in true competition with human reason and will, since they were all grounded in the Great Being.

Edwards was no more than a harbinger of the new way. Far from remaining a hero, he came to grief. In a dispute made up of many petty issues, his council moved to eject him as minister; the male members of the congregation in 1750 voted 230 to 23 that he must go.

Unemployed, Edwards found two subsequent posts. For seven years after 1751 he was a virtual exile working among the Indians at Stockbridge, to whom he preached some reworked obscure sermons. From this rude congregation whose odors of bear grease put him off, Edwards took refuge during his working hours in a closet study that measured less than four by eight feet. There he wrote philosophical treatises for which scholars remember him.

To promote learning among the awakened, revivalists founded a new College of New Jersey, which later came to be called Princeton. Still well regarded beyond Northampton, Edwards followed his deceased son-in-law Aaron Burr in the presidency there. Before he finished attacking the mail that had piled on Burr's desk, Edwards chanced an inoculation as a smallpox epidemic closed in. Some pox formed in his throat and, unable to swallow, he died on March 22, 1758.

Edwards was essentially a staid stay-at-home during the revivals. He developed new psychologies to explain conversion but not new techniques for spreading it. His counterpart giant in leadership, George Whitefield, who started coming to America from England in 1738, had a patent on many of them.

George Whitefield represented the complementary mobile side of the midcentury renewals of religion. Through his travels he posed and embodied the unsettling social issue then called "itineracy." Whitefield was the mileage champion of the revival, the only foreigner to make a name for himself on the trail, the man who reminded colonials that their God was also stirring Europe at the same time. The cross-eyed Englishman had a genius for discerning the hungers of Americans in all the colonies. He whipped people into enthusiasm for God with a voice and style that led actor David Garrick enviously to assert that Whitefield could melt an audience merely by pronouncing "Mesopotamia." After Yankee printer Benjamin Franklin heard Whitefield and saw the crowds at Philadelphia, he offered to be his publisher, bewildered though Franklin was by the delight crowds showed as they heard that they were "half beasts and half devils." Yet Whitefield moved even the skeptical and penny-pinching printer to give his mite in support of a meetinghouse and a Georgia orphanage, so moved was Franklin by the moral change Whitefield inspired.

Whitefield, like many apostles of American faith, was more a finder than a seeker. Sure of himself, he compared his birth in an English inn in 1714 to that of Jesus. In the manner of converted preachers, he exaggerated the seeds of corruption sown in his youth. His claim that he was once given over to lying, filthy talking, foolish jesting, cursing, swearing, stealing, Sabbath-breaking, irreverence, and trickery seems less lurid when balanced by his parallel claim that as a boy he already liked to imitate ministers and wanted to become one. In his youth Whitefield took a turn at acting, but one day as he read plays to his sister he blurted that God had greater things in store for him.

Somehow his mother helped him reach Oxford, where he joined the Holy Club. Prominent in it were the brothers John and Charles Wesley, later the founders of a fervent movement in the Church of England that eventually became Methodism. While there Whitefield went through weeks of heavings and lying prostrate, hoping for release from some "proud hellish thought." A year passed, heightened by seven especially intense weeks before he found "joy, joy unspeakable." Six weeks later he was writing about his conversion, spreading the charge revivalists like to make: that one may go to church and say prayers but still not be a Christian without a specific experience. After a round of English preaching, he felt called to Georgia. There Governor James Oglethorpe had founded a colony attractive to philanthropists who wanted to do good to the refuse of England who could be moved there.

In the harbor of Deal there occurred a coincidence of note: the same John Wesley who had earlier beckoned Whitefield to Georgia was now returning in another ship after a disastrous experience in America. Wesley tried to discourage his friend from going. Among other things, he had had a bad experience with a young woman in Georgia. Back in England Wesley was to enjoy the experience of the warmed heart and for fifty years spread his Methodism. Whitefield, however, had a very positive reaction to America. He had to go from Georgia back to England to be ordained a priest, but he returned soon, convinced that America was "an excellent school to learn Christ."

In England, where he was barred from some churches as an enthusiast, Whitefield, like Wesley, took his crowds into the open fields. In America he continued open-air preaching to crowds of thousands. Benjamin Franklin, not believing reports of their size, painstakingly stepped-off the pavement when Whitefield preached from the Court House steps and calculated a crowd of up to thirty thousand people in Philadelphia.

This commuter between continents came to America not just to scold it — though scold it he did — but also to save it. In Fagg's Manor and New Brunswick in New Jersey, he rejoiced to see crowds of seven thousand grow pale and wring their hands as they lay on the ground crying to God. In Boston, the backyard of Charles Chauncy, Whitefield's celebrity climaxed. On a single day the preacher drew five thousand to the Common, and eight thousand to the fields. When Whitefield heard that five people had died in leaps from crowded galleries in a church on Summer Street where he was to appear, he instead preached his farewell on the Common, before thirty thousand people.

As for his disruptive significance, Whitefield undercut the establishment by attacking ministers who preached an unknown and unfelt Christ. He said he literally felt darkness at Yale and Harvard, but then turned friendlier when Yale students later asked him to preach. Chauncy remained unimpressed by what he called Whitefield's popish ranting, monstrous spirit, and raw acquaintance with the arts of divinity. Worst of all, Whitefield moved the passions of young people "to the neglect of all other business." Former Yale rector but now Church of England minister Timothy Cutler fumed against the disorders of the night that took people from labor and business to Awakening excitement: "Our presses are forever teeming with books, and our women with bastards."

The classic face-off originated in Charleston in 1738: between Whitefield, the Church of England deacon, and Alexander Garden, the commissary of the bishop of London. As a kind of churchly consular official, Garden, who possessed the social graces, first greeted Whitefield with wine and ale and cakes. The wooing was useless. Two years later the itinerant returned to attack Garden outright for allowing laxity and not promoting the preaching of grace. Garden in rage barred his colleague Whitefield from the Lord's Supper and threatened to suspend him from office if he preached publicly in any church in the province. Once upon a time such a threat would have ended the conflict, but Old World codes no longer worked. In the New World preachers felt free to encroach and poach in search of souls. Whitefield paid little attention to strictures. He ignored a church trial and a dismissal that hampered him not at all.

In the encounter with Garden, Whitefield won a battle for itineracy. Later Americans may find it difficult to understand this conflict, so taken for granted is the traveling evangelist — or the intrusive voice of the radio or television preacher — invading the territory of a settled clergy. Yet standing-order ministers then were furious because travelers undercut them and shattered their monopolies. In most colonies the law established church order, but even in Rhode Island, Pennsylvania, and Maryland, up until that point, only the unusually rude would invade the precincts of other ministers and cast doubt on their qualifications to save people. Now the ministers became insecure in the face of incursions and insults. While revivalists like Whitefield by the score competed with each other, they converged with special zest on standing-order ministers who honestly feared that competition between preachers would destroy faith, manners, and morals.

By 1742 even Yale students embarked on revivalist journeys. The legislature asked the rector to discipline them. In July of 1743 ninety ministers, though friendly to revivals, huddled at Boston to protest excesses and warn against laymen who invaded the ministerial office. "Ministers do not invade the Province of others," they argued. Connecticut ministers took complaints about the "disorderly intruding" of ministers into the parishes of others all the way to the Connecticut Assembly. That body passed an act against itinerants who came without the consent of both pastor *and* people — a sign that in some localities there may have been disagreements between the two on the subject. Constables were to escort vagrant ministers out of the colony.

Revivalist James Davenport was the worst vagabond, a man of unsettled mind and coarse habits who admitted later that for a time his wild acts showed he was "much influenced in the Affair by the false Spirit," which his foes called insanity. In what his supporters called a "heaven-daring action," the constables deported him from Connecticut, but by then more moderate travelers had begun to win sympathy. Even former Yale rector Elisha Williams argued that civil authority dared not invade church life. In 1750 the assembly repealed the law. Whitefield, who had won his point, spent two more decades on the road and on the sea — going back and forth to England thirteen times in his life — converting souls. He died while on the road at Newburyport, Massachusetts, and there he finally rests.

Later observers often called the movement the Great Awakening because it crossed the cramping boundaries of denominations. Continental Protestants who did not use the terms of revival and were generally more passive reworked their Pietism to fit the moment. They also produced conflict — sometimes with other awakeners. In 1741 Count Nikolaus Ludwig von Zinzendorf arrived to bolster revivals in a new group from Europe, the Moravians, peace-loving advocates of Christian unity who accidentally spread disunity. They contended that they were simply a movement dedicated to restoring the primitive simplicity and innocence Christianity had earlier lost. Even before Zinzendorf came they were disputing with Whitefield.

Within a week after Zinzendorf's arrival in New York, the Dutch churches united against the leader. In Pennsylvania, where Quakers taught people to despise titles, being a count was a disadvantage; so he traveled as the Reverend Thurnstein, but was found out. He took refuge on Christmas Eve at a settlement he christened Bethlehem. There he wanted to base his church and proceed to reach an America he hoped would receive him gladly. For months he "traveled and prayed and wept" in search of peace from settled ministers, but could not find it.

Zinzendorf wanted to bring Lutherans and Reformed Protestants together in his "invisible house," but for all his efforts both denominations simply stepped up aggression against him and each other. Thanks in part to his challenge, the German Lutherans in 1742 sent the Reverend Henry Melchior Mühlenberg to Pennsylvania, while the Reformed united behind their Michael Schlatter. Zinzendorf had to settle for serving his own flocks and then doing Indian missionary work.

The Pietist Lutherans under Mühlenberg had to fight similar battles over itineracy, though their enemies were not revivalists so much as self-appointed and profiteering German immigrant ministers who exploited the new climate of freedom. Missionary Mühlenberg made his motto the phrase *Ecclesia plantanda,* "the church must be planted" — in America, as it was already in Europe. The patriarch wanted a stable ministry, but he found rural Pennsylvania a tangle of paths in the lonely woods that were rarely marked with towns. Since he could not expect people to travel a hundred miles to hear a sermon, he went out to preach to them, rounding up more than forty thousand immigrant Lutherans at the height of his ministry.

Wherever the Lutheran patriarch went, he ran into the problem of disorders. Pretenders from Germany had come with more greed than ministerial credentials. They preyed on people who wanted someone to baptize their children and preach to them. While the University of Halle tried to export enough Pietist clergy, Mühlenberg complained that many independent German arrivals were fakes — "squabblers and ranglers" who, like roaming knights, traversed the land to make money. They took shillings for serving the Lord's Supper. Mühlenberg came to the point of urging lay people not to give gratuities at all, even to the licensed pastors. He wanted Governor Robert Morris to protect people from unlicensed vagabonds who, he said, "laughed at us who are regular clergymen by saying it is a free country."

Time took care of the worst fakes. When Mühlenberg learned that it was indeed a free country, he made the best of things. So long as there was a shortage of ministers, "let us not bind the hands and feet of the poor souls who are swimming in the water and thus make them drown." By then he was under attack from stricter brands of Lutherans who thought the Pietists were themselves seducers of souls or, worst of all, "secret Zinzendorfians."

The privilege enjoyed by the Church of England did not protect it during the midcentury disruptions; the Episcopal network lost more than any other during the great shift in religious styles. Before these years the church had begun to filter northward, where its leaders now consoled themselves by hoping that high-quality new recruits would come to them for ordered church life because their stomachs would turn at the sight of itinerants and fanatics. In the Episcopal church in the South, such language sounded hollow, because growth was almost never visible there. Its passive techniques simply did not work.

Until this time, Episcopalians enjoyed a near monopoly south of Maryland. Not one Roman Catholic church was in the whole region, and the Congregationalists who lorded it over New England had but one stray colony at Dorchester, South Carolina. About fifteen tiny Lutheran churches spilled south from Pennyslvania and some Moravians found refuge in North Carolina. Outside North Carolina, Quakers were truly rare in the South, and the Reformed were almost nonexistent. Yet by 1800, because of the void Episcopalians left by shunning the revivalist style and to some extent because of their clerical ties to England during the Revolution, Baptists, Methodists, and Presbyterians crowded Church of England territory.

Long after the main events of the Awakening, one and only one Episcopal minister, Devereux Jarratt, tardily took up revivalism in the style of Whitefield. Jarratt came up the hard way from a youth given to racehorses and gamecocks. In the company of periwigged people, he knew his place, and he remembered from childhood that among the people he called "simple" — his people — religion meant little. His recall of childhood illustrates something of the limited reach of colonial religion; he claimed he had never seen or heard up close anything of a religious nature, including anything about eternity. No one ever asked him to be serious about God and heaven and hell. People of the simple class did not mingle with those who attended parish church, so he knew nothing of ministers except that his people thought them inept.

For a time young Jarratt lived in a rural county, where no minister came near. Then some Presbyterians arrived; they left behind some sermons by Whitefield. These writings influenced him just at the time when he met the first person he ever knew who had experienced rebirth. Though Presbyterians tutored him, he chose the Episcopal way and in 1762 went to London for ordination. Jarratt returned to America at age thirty-one to become rector at Bath in Dinwiddie County, Virginia, for almost thirty-eight years. Though proud to be in a ministry that descended from the apostles of Jesus, he was soon attacking velvet-mouthed preachers and insipid speculators within his own communion because they preached the cant of moral virtue and not the joy of rebirth. Virtue came to follow and issue from spiritual rebirth, not to replace it or precede it.

Jarratt and his only associate, Archibald McRoberts, recorded what the other Church of England clergy thought of him. He was in their eyes an enthusiast, fanatic, visionary, dissenter, Presbyterian madman, "and what not." Shunned, he remained an Episcopalian but in 1772 turned itinerant to add a six-hundred-mile circuit to his regular charge. The Baptists were becoming strong then, so he tried to do what he could "to prevent this evil." Then McRoberts deserted him for another affiliation. Jarratt was also tempted to turn Methodist, but after 1784, when Methodists formally organized apart from the mother Church of England, he cooled. All that can be said in summary is that forty long years after the impact of Whitefield and Edwards, a small awakening followed the path of the horses of two Episcopalians and ended when they left the trail.

The battle over the revivals and their styles and teachings is most visible within a denomination not previously accounted for herein — the Presbyterians. Their crisis came between 1741 and 1758, toward the end of the renewal period. The Presbyterians were spiritual heirs of John Calvin. Most were doughty old sympathizers with the Puritans, people the English once transplanted from Scotland into Northern Ireland and who thus became the Scotch-Irish. Poverty tempered them there while they fired their anti-Catholicism and hungered for a more promising home. A few came to America as scattered refugees soon after 1670, but they first gathered when Francis Makemie arrived from Ireland in 1683. With his help they formed the first American presbytery, at Philadelphia in 1706.

From the first, the Presbyterian church in the colonies seemed ready to wear the "Made in America" stamp, since it never really had strong ties across the ocean. Ministers were first brought from New England, Wales, Ireland, Scotland, and who knew where. Yet these clergy had to be hardy, because beyond their bases at Long Island and Philadelphia, they found most coastal lands already taken. The ministers therefore served people who were settling the far frontier, where Indians were close and churches remote. Many immigrants quickly dropped from the sight of the church. Others clung to old Presbyterian creeds and, because these old-liners insisted on subscription to those official statements of doctrine, came to be called Subscriptionists. While the revivalist party, called the New Side, was generally faithful to the same codes, its adherents were more casual as they pursued the warmed heart and rebirth.

The Presbyterian awakeners were led by the Tennent clan, whose father, William, opened a rude ministerial "log college" near Philadelphia. There he trained about a score of men, including four sons, for ministry. The graduates stumped the experts by passing easily the examinations that were used to screen ministerial candidates, as they took credentials on the road. William's son Gilbert attracted critics who thought him profane: they turned furious when they heard him claim that he could look at the face of a person and see whether he (or she) would be saved or damned. On the itinerant trail, which took him as far as Boston, admirers found him able to get people to cry out "under the impression of terror and love." The people of Nottingham, Pennsylvania, invited him to preach, and he offered a scorcher that lifted him above the pack of itinerants as he spoke of "the danger of an unconverted ministry." People might be conventional believers, he noted, but unless they were reborn, he called them unconverted. He added that "success by unconverted ministers preaching is very improbable, and very seldom happens."

Two months after the Nottingham sermon, the denomination's synod met to discuss who was to be qualified as a minister. A year later, in May of 1741, the two parties of Presbyterians split. The Old Side denied full status to Log College graduates, so the revivalists decided to go over their heads, directly to the people. The New Side started the College of New Jersey at Princeton and in a variety of ways gained enough momentum to dominate when Presbyterians somehow reunited in 1758.

While the Old Side Presbyterians made some common cause with the established Church of England in the South, the New Side outflanked both of its competitors on the frontier. Migrants began trekking along the Great Philadelphia Wagon Road in the 1730s; they were people bearing names like Jackson and Davis, Calhoun and Lincoln, who made their way along the 735-mile corridor road just east of the mountains all the way to Georgia. Some of the travelers were Continentals, but most of them were prospects for Presbyterians. Back-country life in the cabins was desperately lonely, harsh, and violent. Religion there had to be either very strict in the Old Side style or very emotional, as New Side men preached it. Neither side had many worldly consolations to offer.

The early stirrings in Virginia started around 1740 fairly far east of the trail when Samuel Morris, a layman in Hanover County started gathering people in what they called "reading houses" to talk up revival. When officials became suspicious that they might be subversive, the Governor's Council at Williamsburg demanded to know what the people called themselves. No one knew a name, but since they read Martin Luther, they called themselves Lutherans, and that satisfied for a moment. Then the New Side Presbyterians entered the territory, which the Old Side claimed as its own, sending from New Brunswick a smallpox-scarred Log College man called One-Eyed Robinson. He quickly convinced the people that they were Presbyterians and then with their backing set out to tell the Church of England folk that they were not yet saved. Other itinerants hurried to the scene, among them the Reverend John Roan, whom officials chased away as an unlicensed and perfidious wretch who attacked the established clergy.

Dignity came in 1747 with Samuel Davies, a graduate of an offshoot of the Log College. He chose to save his energies for preaching charity rather than for attacking the existing church. Davies itinerated in the neighborhood of Hanover County in Virginia and insisted that he taught only "the good old doctrines of the Church of England." As he wrote the commissary in 1752, he had no ambition to Presbyterianize the colony.

Many awakeners played down sectarianism, and Davies set an example for them: "We have Lutherans, Calvinists, Arminians, Zwinglians, Churchmen, Presbyterians, Independents, Baptists. . . . To be a Christian is not enough now-a-days, but a man must also be *something* more and better, that is he must be a strenuous bigot to this or that particular church." Davies wanted to find a middle way between the wild reveries of fanatics and the droning heaviness and serene stupidity of the Old Side and the official Episcopalians, wanting "to save my country, and, which is of more consequence, to save souls."

To save my country: as the excitement of the revivals died, a new concern emerged among men like Davies. After people were reborn they must serve Christ in the political world. Davies chose to concentrate on civil liberties, a natural field for revivalists who smarted under old, restrictive laws. He served as his own lawyer, astonishing the courts with his skill, and made some progress against the continuing legal establishment of the Church of England.

After fourteen months of fund raising in England for the College of New Jersey, Davies came home to find the public weary of religious disputes and friendlier than before to dissenters, whose help they needed against the Indians and the French on the frontier. The prospect of colonial war became his new cause. To fight the Catholic French was in his eyes to fight the Antichrist. British and American troops became the agents of God to begin the grand conflict between the innocents of Christ and the whorish beast of Rome. Together they would usher in a new heaven and a new earth. Davies helped build a bridge seldom since broken, between revivalism and patriotic militancy: "The art of war becomes a part of our religion."

Patriot Patrick Henry liked to drop by to hear the recruiting sermons Davies preached, in order to learn oratory. The preacher attacked people who were lazily confident about God. "Let us use our influence to diffuse a military spirit around us." To take up arms was a duty "worthy of a man, a freeman, a Briton, and a Christian." No colonial government could lightly hem in so effective a campaigner. In fact, in 1758 his recruiting sermon led to an oversupply of volunteers and the military had to turn some away, inspired as they were by his idea that Protestant Christianity could expect no quarters from "heathen savages and French papists," whose third party were the power of hell itself.

Recruits marched off to war and the sickly minister moved to Princeton, there to become a successor to Aaron Burr and Jonathan Edwards as president. On New Year's Day, 1761, he chose to preach on the text Aaron Burr had used the year he died: "Thus saith the Lord, This year thou shalt die." The superstitious gasped, but Davies scoffed at those who saw premonitions in such events. When he caught cold several days later, he had a doctor bleed him. Twice more he preached, but his right arm became infected and at the age of thirty-seven the Presbyterian pioneer was dead as if by prophecy.

Along with the fresh accent on personal experience, the voluntary spirit, and the freedom of choice that followed itinerary, the new movements left a legacy of competition for souls. Grumpy Church of England missionary Charles Woodmason, who scoured the frontier in the years after Davies did, exemplified this. He saw a need for religion there, where 94 percent of the women whose marriages he oversaw were pregnant as brides, and where venereal disease was almost universal. "Polygamy is very Common —" he noted, "Celibacy much more — Bastardy, no Disrepute — Concubinage general."

Woodmason complained that Presbyterians liked to provide wrong directions to worshipers so that they would lose their way on the path to his church services, and contended that once they stole the key to his meetinghouse. Sometimes they poured whiskey to get his people drunk before worship. Once he went to meet his congregation, only to find that the Scottish Presbyterians had hired lawless ruffians to insult him — which they did, telling him they wanted no "Damned Black Gown Sons of Bitches" among them. When he did successfully gather worshipers, the Presbyterians hallooed and whooped like Indians. Once he counted fifty-seven dogs that they set to fighting under the windows where he held services. The clergy, bigots and hypocrites, stirred up the people, he charged. Ever after, the need to win converts and support institutions led to competition: free enterprise had come to the world of religion.

While George Washington was a rather casual churchgoer and not an orthodox Christian, he was supportive of religion. The Americans who named him the Father of His Country often made icons out of events in his life. Here an unknown Chinese artist painted on glass the death of Washington, who is being received into heaven by angels, as saints had been in Christian iconography centuries before. The artist made use of an engraving by Simon Chaudron and John J. Barrelet. (*Courtesy Henry Francis du Pont Winterthur Museum*)

Chapter Nine

THREE REVOLUTIONS

*T*HREE REVOLUTIONS FOLLOWED THE PERIOD OF REVIVALS. ONE OF them, the American Revolution, or the War of Independence, tends to crowd the Awakening and other movements of the century from the main pages of the histories. A second revolution occurred in the way people conceived of church and state, the religious and civil realms. For ages they had been somehow united and now they were, by conscious choice of church *and* state, somehow to be separated. The third was a concurrent revolution in the minds of some leaders of state and church — a revolution through which they wanted to make religion a matter of reason more than heart, something accessible to all, whether or not they believed in the Bible as a special disclosure from God.

Only one of the revolutions was a shooting war, so one should perhaps be cautious about overusing the word *revolution* and call the other two occurrences "evolutions" — the one resulting from the Enlightenment's new discoveries about reason and the mind, and the other reflecting practical adjustments to new circumstances. Yet they all represented real breaches, drastic if sometimes quiet experiments for the American people on their long pilgrimage. All three changes had profound impact on the way people perceived themselves and their religions — perceptions that are now often taken for granted. Hence it takes a bit of uncovering to recreate the sense of novelty and revolution they first brought into being.

Patriot John Adams insisted that the American Revolution occurred "in the minds and hearts of the people" a generation before the beginning of war at Lexington and Concord in 1775. To explore what he meant by that in terms of religious ideas at the time, one should look closely at the religious leaders who advanced the cause of liberty and eventual separation of the colonies from England. It is always hard to demonstrate the influence of preachers, since they deal with minorities of the community and must work through persuasion, not coercion, as political leaders do. Yet, along with journalists, poets, literary figures, and agitators, they do help form opinions. Since they ask people to consider God in their decisions, their ideas — whether effectively stated or of uncertain impact — deserve examination.

For some time historians have focused on the contributions to liberty and revolution made by a small number of New England liberal ministers. While they do not occupy the privileged status they once did, their sermons and tracts reflect important opinions of elites in their day and so our story may well begin with them. Since John Adams singled out Jonathan Mayhew of Boston as being among the first to promote the cause of independence, Mayhew is a logical contender for first place here as well.

New ideas were in the Boston air at midcentury. Harvard graduate Mayhew had a hard time finding the quorum of ministers necessary for the rites of ordination when he began his ministry in 1747. Already then, colleagues recognized that he belonged to a growing circle of New England pastors who circulated newfangled and possibly dangerous notions. Many of these notions directly opposed the Great Awakening assumptions about the miraculous way the God of the Bible turns the hearts of those who abhor him. To certify Mayhew would mean to add respectability to the ranks of troublemakers. His foes knew that Mayhew was descended from a line of honorable clerics, valiants who displayed their heroism by ministering to natives on Martha's Vineyard when other ministers were turning their backs on Indians.

While at Harvard young Mayhew preferred the company of future revolutionary leaders like James Otis and James Bowdoin to that of the noisily religious students. After some participation in the Great Awakening as a youth, he parted company with its proponents. The student found a Whitefield sermon to be "low, confused; puerile, conceited, ill-natured, enthusiastic." Mayhew busied himself instead with the liberal opinions he found in imported books of English philosophy and religion. The orthodox called these books "Deist," because their authors did not talk about a personal God as did theists; "rationalist," because they stressed reason as much as the Bible; "Enlightened," because they spread the ideas of the movement called the Enlightenment in Europe. Whatever their enemies named the ideas, Jonathan came to cherish them.

By the time Mayhew was ready to become a pastor, the ministry was beginning to lose its place of honor. In each tiny New England town the minister could still influence the people who crossed the green common to worship at the meetinghouse. But in crowded and busy Boston, too many other people of power competed for notice, and citizens enjoyed attractions beyond those that church life presented. The feuding between ministers during the revivals had robbed them of some prestige and had confused people who were looking for stability. Trade and law drew the interest of the kind of talented young men who in previous generations chose ministry for their lifework. Despite these trends, Boston-area churches still continued to skim the cream off the Harvard classes and found savvy young candidates who learned how to please God and the merchants while amounting to something themselves. Mayhew belonged in their company.

Mayhew was accused of being an Arminian — after Jacobus Arminius, a Dutch reviser of Calvinism whose ideas in a garbled form became popular in the Church of England. In its New England Congregationalist version, Arminianism held that since humans could count on a benign Providence, they did not have to puzzle over his mysterious purposes. Against the gloomy Calvinists, they taught that people had the potential for doing good on their own. While the generation of Jonathan Edwards thought such ideas poisonous, the standing-order Bostonians by 1747 began to entertain them politely. The more daring even mixed in bits of the ancient Arian heresy, which called Jesus divine but ranked him lower than his heavenly Father. They favored the "reasonable Christianity" of philosophers like John Locke and set out to minimize the miraculous character of the Bible. The liberals were dabbling with the novelties that in the next century produced Unitarianism. The last thing that the discreet samplers of these ideas set out to do was to help instigate colonial revolt against the mother country, though help it they did.

Mayhew lived up to his billing and followed up his inauguration with a short but vigorous ministry. While he kept tangling with leftover revivalists, his churchly battles were against the Church of

England over an issue that later became tangled with the issue of colonial revolt. What seems today like a minor churchly issue had consequences for the revolution to come. Episcopalians had become a presence in New England, and unlike their southern counterparts, they hungered to have a bishop in the colonies. It is hard for modern readers to picture the fury this issue roused. New Englanders, however, were brought up on John Foxe and his pictures of burning martyrs and they easily connected the persecuting Catholic bishops of those scenes with *any* bishops. Some proposed a domino theory that held that Church of England bishops would lead to new domination by other bishops or other English elements. John Adams said that it was "a fact as certain as any in the history of North America" that agitation over bishops led colonial people to think closely about the authority of Parliament.

The dispute seemed absurd. The larger southern Episcopal element was perfectly content to keep bishops three thousand miles away. It was only the few who migrated to New York and New England or those who converted there who thought a bishop would lend prestige and order to their minority cause. Jonathan Mayhew first heard rumors of plans for a bishop in 1762. In finest conspiratorial tones a correspondent insisted he could not yet tell whether the bishop would settle at Boston or elsewhere. Boston newspapers, fearing for the future but enjoying the present commotion, savored the subject. Even John Adams published anonymous essays against the "desire of dominion" in religions and in 1765 issued a cry in the *Boston Gazette* for pulpits to fight off the threatening slavery.

Mayhew led the ministerial attack with veiled sniper fire at Episcopalians for sending invaders to Congregational territory. He did not sympathize with those who claimed they needed a bishop simply to minimize inconvenience to ministerial candidates. Congregationalists *wanted* such candidates inconvenienced.

After an ambitious Episcopalian agent named East Apthorp arrived in town in 1758 with dreams of glory, everything fell into line for Mayhew. Apthorp set about erecting an impressive mansion that looked too much like the future palace of a bishop. As the building rose, Mayhew smelled a conspiracy of bishops. With more than a tinge of melodrama the West Church minister asked what other New World remained as a sanctuary for free people against such aggressors? Where could he find a Columbus to explore such a new world or pilot New Englanders to it before flames consumed them or a flood of bishops deluged them? Apthorp had to stifle his ambitions in the face of such an attack, but an Episcopal rector, Henry Caner, carried on. How, he asked, could Bostonians flatter and listen to this Jonathan Mayhew, who in his own preachings demolished the doctrines of their own Puritan forefathers? For a time, nonetheless, the Congregationalist clergy closed ranks around the suspect Mayhew against the great enemy that Caner represented.

Adams and his peers remembered Mayhew and his liberal colleagues secondly for the way they set forth ideas of revolution a generation before the War of Independence. Mayhew's remarks of 1750 in *A Discourse Concerning Unlimited Submission and Non-Resistance to the Higher Powers* may now sound safe enough, but when New Englanders first heard or read them they were shocked to hear standing-order ministers challenge kings. Mayhew defended his forays toward revolt by saying that West Church called him to preach on the whole Bible, including delicate civil subjects.

The troublesome biblical text was the claim of Paul, in Romans, chapter 13, that since God established all authorities, whoever resisted the "powers that be" resisted God and must be condemned. If American Christians were ever to revolt they had to confront such biblical texts. Since Paul presumably wrote those lines while Nero was persecuting Christians, his word must have meant that believers should obey evil rulers. Mayhew, however, slipped in some new accents that Adams admired. Rulers, he argued, had no authority from God to do mischief — a fact that meant bad rulers were ministers not of God but of Satan. Christians, he insisted, had to disobey any who went against the law of reason or the codes of religion.

Jonathan Mayhew was not in those remarks issuing the first American call for revolt against England. He was only testing some heady ideas of the English Enlightenment. He had no personal objections to the king. He also had no real taste for violence and war, though he did try to make his audience and readers a bit more elastic about the possibility when he reminded them that they already approved of the English revolutions of 1642 and 1688. So Mayhew felt temporarily emboldened to say that for a people to rise unanimously and dethrone a prince was not a criminal act but only a "reasonable way of vindicating their liberties and just rights." When provoked, it was those who did *not* resist who should receive damnation — certainly a twist on the idea Paul asserted in his text. Sixty-eight years later aged John Adams was still commending this discourse to Thomas Jefferson, remembering how as a fourteen-year-old he, Adams, "who was destined in the future course of his life to dabble in so many Revolutions in America, in Holland and in France" was first intoxicated by the ideas of Mayhew.

Eight years later, in 1758, the French and Indian War found Mayhew still at home with the British empire and its liberties. Now his sermons attacked popish and French conspiracies against what he called "our liberties, our religion, our lives, our bodies, our souls." Thus current war was a step in the final triumph of Christ over all his enemies. When Quebec fell in 1763, Mayhew jeered General Montcalm for ever having thought that freeborn Britons could tremble in the face of his Catholic relics, crosses, and paraphernalia. All the while keeping his merchant members in mind, Mayhew reminded them that just war, because it provided employment and commerce, was profitable as well as just. After New France fell, Mayhew showed that he was still not ready for separation from England. When he envisioned a mighty empire in America he hurried to add, "I do not mean an independent one." He foresaw in the great spaces mighty cities where people would profess and practice religion "in far greater purity and perfection, than since the times of the apostles." The promising new king, George III, was the sign of hope for such a realm.

Then on March 22, 1765, Parliament in the Stamp Act imposed the first direct tax on the colonies. While Parliament needed the funds, colonists raged against the act as the first mark of tyranny, which would lead the British to acts of new repression without ever granting colonists the rights of representation. John Adams decided that everyone but Episcopalians was up in arms against the new tax law. Because the legislation called for duty stamps on church documents, firebrands even foresaw the day when the Crown and the Church of England could use official means to control all religion.

On August 25, 1765, Jonathan Mayhew preached his most inflammatory sermon, using a text from Paul — "ye have been called unto liberty." Boston was tinder that Sunday, and his sermon helped ignite it. No copies of this message survived, but Mayhew later claimed that in it he asked both sides in Boston to keep cool — even as he hinted that some local people were conniving with the British. The preacher did not need to name names. The mob had already burnt in effigy Andrew Oliver and his new stamp office before doing some damage to his house. Oliver was wise enough to retreat and refuse to continue in the post. The crowds had also threatened the talented Tory lieutenant governor, Thomas Hutchinson, who escaped before the agitators could do much damage to his mansion.

The day after Mayhew preached on liberty, Bostonians did set fire to the house and destroyed it. Governor Bernard, in his report to English authorities, charged Mayhew as the fomenter of disorder, and Henry Caner wrote Archbishop Thomas Secker in London that Mayhew was busy preaching sedition. The minister of West Church had indeed used language to agitate — but then was sickened at the sight of fire and the threat of blood. Mayhew wrote Hutchinson that he would rather lose his own hand than be the encourager of such outrages. The gracious victim accepted the words as an apology, but later, in his historical writing, implied that the sermon had indeed been a fuse. Just to be on the safe side, Mayhew came forth with an antirevolutionary sermon the next Sunday.

The British decided not to put the Stamp Act into effect, and an exhilarated Mayhew preached on "The Snare Broken." Now he looked for lasting harmony between Great Britain and the colonies and twice praised the stable merchants while he condemned the rioters who used rapacious violence in the name of liberty. His old friend James Otis remembered that in his final days Mayhew spoke of a "communion of colonies"; but the outspoken liberal pastor of West Church could not carry further the cause, because he died in 1766, in his forty-fifth year. Loyalist chief justice Peter Oliver later called ministers like Mayhew and even some conservatives a "black regiment" for their support of the war effort. They were in the vanguard of the religious revolutionaries.

While the war was still a decade away when Mayhew died, the zigzags and attempts at balance in his career show that notions of independence and revolt were creating tensions in the minds of religious leadership. If much of New England's establishment came to side with and goad on the patriots of 1775, the same was not the case with the Episcopal clergy in the southern establishment. Their dilemmas help recreate for us an understanding of how religion and politics, church-craft and statecraft, spiritual and military warfare are interlocked.

The choices they made also illustrate the divisions within the clergy and the gap between Loyalist clergy and revolutionary laity. It is known that many clerics in South Carolina, the lesser-known ones in Virginia, and a scattering elsewhere stayed with the colonists. Many of the Marylanders fled as war came, and only one priest remained in Georgia and North Carolina, while outside Connecticut only five stayed with the patriot cause in all New England.

Often the best of the Episcopal clergy had the hardest lot, since many of them felt they must remain faithful to oaths they once took in support of the Crown. Some of them even foresaw a bright side for their church during the turmoil. Samuel Seabury, Jr., who one day would become a bishop, was hopeful that colonial disorder would lead serious people to turn for refuge to Episcopal order.

If New England liberals helped foment revolutionary ideas and southern Episcopalians were put on the spot and sometimes driven to take refuge, the Presbyterians of the Middle Colonies gained a reputation for being hawkish, perhaps even for helping bring on the war.

Just before the war broke out, future Yale president Ezra Stiles miscalculated when he argued that the defense of American liberties would fall "to Congregationalists to the Northward and Episcopalians to the Southward." He overlooked these middleward Presbyterians. Only the Congregationalists had more churches than they, and since theirs were at strategic crossroads in the colonies, they could not avoid taking sides in the war. This they did with zest. Only a few were visibly Loyalist.

The Presbyterians had found it easy to be patriots for many reasons. They had helped lead the protest against the possibility of Episcopal bishops in America. As Scotch-Irish they carried old grudges against England. Some of them thought John Calvin helped them choose sides because he once argued that government rested on a compact between king and people, and the English king had broken one from his side. Most of all, these recent arrivals simply chose to see a better future in a separate America than in one remote and dependent on England.

The Presbyterians in general were so vigorous in support of revolt that their foes sometimes called the war "the Presbyterian Rebellion." At Trinity Church in New York, Episcopal rector Charles Inglis, who claimed he had inquired strictly, found not a single American Presbyterian minister who did not use his pulpit and every other means to promote the Continental Congress and colonist causes. Ambrose Searle, who represented Lord Dartmouth in New York, smelled Presbyterians at the bottom of the colonial conspiracy, which he thereupon considered "at the bottom very much a religious war."

One important layman, Elias Boudinot, thought the clergy had unhappily "gone distracted" and were doing the cause of religion more harm than good. For forty years they had been protesting against the Church of England for uniting civil and churchly power but now, he moaned, because Presbyterians at last had the shadow of power in their hands, they were "running into the same extreme." Because the wartime produced extremes, however, Boudinot later declared himself for the colonies and at great inconvenience to himself served in charge of prisoners of war.

At the time when he was attacking, Boudinot pointed accusingly at the Presbyterian John Witherspoon, then president of the College of New Jersey at Princeton. He aimed well. Witherspoon, who had left a promising ministerial charge in Scotland only seven years before the war, helped turn the college into a nest of revolutionaries. He also became a signer of the Declaration of Independence. Earlier, back in Scotland, Witherspoon had battled for the rights of local churches against the national kirk; now, against the British, he used weapons perfected there. He imported the commonsense realist philosophy, which included a demand that individuals be responsible for public affairs. No stormy preacher, President Witherspoon quietly won the confidence of his colleagues. In August of 1774 John Adams and several other delegates to the Continental Congress made their way to Princeton. Adams kept careful notes: the Scottish immigrant took the party to a cupola for a view that spanned eighty miles and then hosted them to a glass of wine at his home. The topic turned to the issue of the ways British miscalculated American firmness. Witherspoon did not yet think separation from England was necessary, but the cause of justice was urgent, so he proposed that colonists find better ways to make their protests heard.

Five days later Witherspoon, though unelected, headed for Congress. There he might have looked like an intruder, but Adams saw in him a man who entered with "great Spirit into the American Cause." Five days after Lexington and Concord the next spring, Witherspoon knew that destiny was calling when a horseman rode into Princeton at dawn with news of the outbreak of war. As head of a committee of the Synod of New York and Philadelphia, he wrote a letter urging the ministers to break taboos of silence by speaking out politically. While he called them to participate in the war, he also asked them to be faithful to both the king *and* the Continental Congress, hoping that the king would finally understand complaints and not force the colonies into separation. A Tory poet, knowing where the cleric's true sympathies lay, took after him with doggerel violence: "I'd rather be a dog than Witherspoon. . . . His day will come — remember Heav'n is just."

Some of his trustees complained when in April of 1776 Witherspoon openly called for severing ties with England, but no one could stop him from propagandizing now, however much such a task went against his compromising nature. On Congress Sunday in May, 1776, he rambled for an hour to townspeople and students: "You are all my witnesses, that this is the first time of my introducing any political subject into the pulpit." Because the cause of God prospered best where people were free, listeners, he preached, had no choice but to enlarge their freedoms. Good Calvinist that he was, Witherspoon did remind listeners of their own sin and also wanted them to remember that the king and Parliament were themselves not "barbarian savages." That summer he signed the Declaration of Independence, after asking for the deletion of only two words — *Scotch and* — before the words *foreign mercenaries* on the list of enemies. He stayed on at his post at Princeton, even when it was overrun by the war, and became a leader in the postwar church.

In the South, so partisan were the Presbyterian church-folk in Mecklenburg County, North Carolina, their heirs claimed that they had already dissolved the bands to the mother country a year before the Declaration of Independence. While a convention at Charlotte did speak of independence, the boast evidently rests on legend, embroidery, and faulty reminiscence. The Loyalist governor called the Mecklenburg resolves worse than any other horrid and treasonable publications yet produced on the continent; to one of his officers the Presbyterian churches were "sedition shops."

American religions that were on the scene at the birth of the nation like to show their credentials by recalling how they acted, and Catholicism, so long on the defensive in Protestant America, is an important instance, even if it was then small. Catholics had much at stake, thanks to ancient mistrust reinforced by new hostility during the colonial wars against Catholic France. Three times between 1688 and 1748 the British and the French skirmished for control of the continent. In an astonishing reversal, the colonists suddenly became friends of their old enemy France, which now was an ally against the English.

In the 1770s few Catholics lived in the colonies. While Ezra Stiles computed 3,026,678 colonists, there may have been only about 2,500,000 and only one out of a hundred of these, 25,000 in all, were in any way Catholic. Almost all of them lived in Maryland or southern Pennsylvania. In New England John Adams claimed a Roman Catholic was as rare as a comet or an earthquake, and itinerant preachers who searched almost never found one. If half the Catholics were women in a day when public roles were closed to them, and if the population included the usual number of under-aged, aged, and infirm, only several thousand Catholics were positioned to take arms or make their voices heard. All of them were on the spot.

Clearly, then, in 1775 the Catholics were outsiders. Harvard College, ordinarily a zone of enlightenment, hosted otherwise civil people who supported the Dudleian Lecture, an annual entertainment at which the learned were to expose the idolatry of the Romish church. In a sermon in 1759 Jonathan Mayhew denounced Rome as a filthy prostitute and the mother of harlots. The pope to him was the successor of the fallen apostle Judas and grand vicar of Satan who wanted to dominate the world. Catholics, he preached, trained blind and furious zealots to butcher and scalp Protestants. Wherever the more moderate George Whitefield traveled, he talked about the horrible principles and practices of popish enemies and the locustlike swarms of monks that Catholics would send as a plague on America if they could.

Americans have usually liked to credit their founders with sweet reasonableness. Yet the same John Adams who could find no Catholics acted as if one skulked behind every bush from Braintree to Philadelphia. He once wrote Jefferson that Catholicism was Hindu and cabalistic. A letter to his wife Abigail told of how he once gathered nerve to peek in on forbidding Catholic worship in Philadelphia. The sermon he found surprisingly proper, but Adams was repelled to see poor wretches fingering their prayer beads. On other days even he worried about the images his outbursts created, and assured readers that he spoke against Catholicism not because he was melancholic or envious but only as a lover of freedom.

Patriot Samuel Adams filled his *Boston Gazette* with much less moderate comment in his effort to feed the suspicions of readers. Finding no nearby Catholics to speak of, he scourged the heirs of Puritanism when he thought he saw them decked out in "the ornaments of the whore of Babylon," the trappings of Catholicism. Even the Stamp Act was, to him, a less serious threat to liberation than popery. What on earth and in New England was he talking about? At Charlestown near Boston, Adams found not a single Catholic, yet he could fault the town only for failing to be sufficiently alert against popery. Salem and Marblehead brought him cheer because they both resisted a Romish priest who for an instant appeared on their scene to display his arts and tricks. At York even the "glaring appearance of popery" in the form of little crosses that women wore disconcerted him. To a puzzled Mohawk Indian audience he spelled out elaborate Catholic designs on Canada. Not until he came to good old Northampton did he find a "true blue Protestant town."

Anti-Catholicism was the sport of the mob as well as the device of leaders. During the annual Pope Day at Newport and Boston, crowds burned the pope in effigy. In Boston, North End and South End ruffians took the day off and spent it trying to capture a papal effigy from each other; a brawl and a jovial supper always followed. But in 1774, because Boston was too explosive to allow for factionalism, sober people devised a "Union Pope." For one day, at least, the two rival neighborhoods united against a Parliament that they somehow linked with Catholicism.

In colonies nearer some actual, breathing Catholics, enlightened public figures like Benjamin Franklin sounded much like Samuel Adams. Only George Washington was moderate. When officer Benedict Arnold ranted against Catholics, General Washington asked him to show "common prudence and a true Christian spirit." God alone judged the hearts of men, who should not violate each other's consciences. Arnold, he advised, should look with compassion on the errors of Catholicism.

After Parliament passed the Quebec Act, not even Washington could quiet the furies. Much of the act made simple good sense in England, which after the wars with France found up to 100,000 largely Catholic Canadian citizens on its hands. To withhold religious liberty was out of the question. Parliament went further, also granting Canada rights to much of the old Northwest, land on which colonists had their eyes. The *Boston Evening Post* claimed it heard that 4,000 Catholic Canadians had formed four regiments to execute a hellish plan against Boston Protestants. The *Maryland Gazette* raised the figure to 30,000. In the Suffolk County Reserves that year, citizens of Massachusetts protested the Quebec Act as dangerous to the Protestant religion and the liberties of all Americans. They then dispatched a silversmith named Paul Revere to take word of this to their representative at the Continental Congress in Philadelphia.

Though the Congress lacked legal status, it accurately reflected colonial opinion when it attacked the British for erecting a tyranny in Canada. The grant of western lands meant that "civil as well as religious prejudices" would sever them from the seaboard colonies. A new swell of Catholic immigrants must soon reduce the ancient free Protestant colonies to a state of slavery. Though still a stripling at King's College in New York, Alexander Hamilton joined in: "Does not your blood run cold?" Canada to him seemed to be under priestly tyranny as vicious as any that ever had enthralled Spain and Portugal.

But when war began in 1775, the colonists reached out for loans from Catholic France, which supplied a navy and materiel, and welcomed General Marquis de Lafayette, who became an American favorite. Thereafter continued some startling reversals. Samuel Cooper of the Brattle Street Church in Boston in 1773 had scourged anti-Christian popery in the Dudleian Lecture. But after Conrad Alexander Gerard, the minister of Louis XVI, began to pay him $1,000 a year to serve as a public-relations agent for France, Cooper ground out propaganda so friendly to France and Catholicism that he befuddled old friends and especially Catholics, who suspected a doubly subtle plot in his about-face.

When Juan de Miralles, an agent of Spain, died at Washington's headquarters in 1780, members of Congress faced a new test of daring and tolerance. All of them were expected to attend a mass for his soul. Benedict Arnold could not bring himself to attend. Humane physician Benjamin Rush also thought that his presence would violate Protestant principles. Many prominent people did attend and lived to report how different the service was from what they had been taught to expect. After the war other founders had to take back their old charges. John Adams in Europe was under greatest pressure to do so.

Anti-Catholicism did not come to an end because of prudence and politeness to France, and it returned in full force sixty years later in the face of the numerous Catholic immigrants; but during the revolutionary decades, the colonists had a chance to take a fresh look at their more prominent Catholic citizens to see how proudly they wore the "Made in America" stamp on their religious styles. Later Catholics, when suspect, always appealed to the generation of revolutionaries to show how much they belonged in the United States.

The most visible of these Catholic colonists were the Carrolls of Carrollton Manor in Maryland. At the time that Charles Carroll became the only Catholic to sign the Declaration of Independence, he was the richest man in Maryland. His distant cousin John, later the first Catholic bishop in the United States, was the pioneer

Americanizer. Such an elite family could not be typical, but the Carroll attitudes were influential.

At the beginning of the eighteenth century, the Carroll clan suffered from the Maryland penal code, imposed when it was no longer a Catholic colony. Governor John Seymour had seen to the passage of laws designed to prevent public worship and to bar Catholic newcomers. Friendly Protestant neighbors found personal ways to soften the effect of the laws, but Catholics still had to huddle privately in order to nurture their religion. Despite all the harassments, wealthy Catholics endured, and few Marylanders had reason to feel sorry for the senior Charles Carroll as his slaves harvested tobacco on his huge estate, or when he entertained in his elegant town mansion in Annapolis. Yet the Carrolls never fully relaxed, because the legislature could always hamper them. At one point the senior Carroll hurried to France to seek a land grant in French Louisiana as insurance for the day when Catholics like his son might have to flee to safer ground. Were he younger, he wrote his son, he would certainly emigrate there.

The younger Charles Carroll could not join Protestant friends at school, so his father provided tutors and saw to his education at the not fully legal Jesuit school called Bohemia Manor. He was only eleven or twelve when his parents sent him to study in France, where he gathered ideas from Montesquieu and Voltaire, noting from them how to resist tyranny. But he did not let them dislodge him of his desire to return as an American gentleman. For a time he studied in England; while he welcomed its general liberties, he saw in it no real place for Catholics. Remarkably, from his vantage in England he was among the first to use the language of national separation. When he first wrote, the world did not yet offer precedent for a colonial people taking destiny into their own hands to declare independence from a mother country. Yet on November 12, 1763, Carroll observed that America "will and must be independent"; he repeated those words eight months later.

In February of 1765 Carroll was introduced to Maryland society, where, at ease with Protestant gentry, he took care of family interests. Carroll did not choose to keep a low profile but spoke up on many issues, often against the officially established religion. Jefferson never used stronger language than Carroll did against religion supported by law. He saw that savage wars, cruel massacres, and deliberate murders followed forced religion, but they never reformed morals. Such acts, he said, only served envy and the ambition of enraged parties or satisfied the cravings of lust. Then the pious Carroll went on to show himself a modern by asking that religion be placed in a compartment away from civil life and that the unhappy differences in theology never be permitted to disrupt public affairs. He insisted that his attacks did not grow out of hatred for the Church of England but out of his hostility toward knaves and bigots of all sects and denominations who crammed religion down the throats of innocent people.

Five months before independence, John Adams, ever on the lookout for company, stood in awe of this Catholic who, he said, hazarded the largest fortune in America and his very life on the patriot cause. At the Continental Congress, after other Marylanders found ways around their old restrictions against Catholics and elected Carroll to represent them, he came to know Adams well.

Charles's distant cousin John Carroll was drawn only once from the religious into the civil sphere during the war. Early in 1776 the Continental Congress sent a small party to Canada in an effort to lure the Canadians into alliance against England. General Charles Lee suggested that for strategic reasons a Jesuit or some other member of a religious order "would be worth battalions to the party." He remembered that Charles Carroll had such a cousin, and John Adams seconded his motion to invite the priest John Carroll. Carroll was puzzled over the way Protestants who had always feared priests could now demand his services. But these were times that tried old opinions, and in emergency he shelved his reservations long enough to go on the futile mission. The only benefit of the endeavor came when old Benjamin Franklin became a friend of the young priest. Father Carroll subsequently avoided political action but publicly supported independence.

After the war, John Carroll tried to inform Rome about the American system. While he seemed to be warning the Vatican not to intrude in American public affairs, in 1784 Rome named him prefect-apostolic and later archbishop of Baltimore. From there he worked to form a Catholic church that in his eyes was linked in all the United States and loyal to Rome despite the fact that in a political light, he found it farther from Rome than was the church in Goa, South America, or China.

Thus, centuries after Ferdinand and Isabella, who were crusaders for the idea that an empire must have only one faith, the most notable priest in the United States boasted of a growing harmony among all the nation's Christians. Against the monarchs' old spirit of coercion he wanted his nation to exhibit a proof to the world that "general and equal toleration, by giving a free circulation to fair argument, is the most effectual method to bring all denominations of Christians to a unity of faith." Then he attacked Protestants who claimed monopolies on national virtues just as Catholics did back in Spain when America was founded. "The establishment of the American empire was not the work of this or that religion," he said, but the result of efforts by all citizens.

John Carroll rightly reminded others that Catholic blood had flowed freely during the war. Instances from Maryland proved his point. No Protestant would ever name a child Ignatius, after the founder of the Jesuit order. Yet forty-seven Ignatiuses were in the Saint Mary's County militia and thirty-one more were in the troops from Charles County. The Jesuits who inspired the use of that name must also have made room for young Catholics to learn the cause of revolt. Under the examples of the Carrolls, Catholics in America worked for independence and then for creating distinctions between civil and religious zones of life. For a moment, at least, old enmities against them weakened.

And the Jews? Insignificant in numbers (only about three thousand in the colonies, most of whom can be traced), they liked to tell of one of their kind, Haym Salomon, who scrambled up and over a prison wall after his friends threw a rope to him one dark night in 1778. The British had taken Salomon prisoner to use as a translator in talking to the German Hessians, whom the British paid to fight the colonists. Salomon was also useful to the patriots as a financier; during the war he served at the side of Robert Morris, the superintendent of finance. Salomon also bet on colonial victory by endorsing government notes and floating loans, until he had to use his personal funds for equipping military units. He was also generous to individual leaders like James Madison. The patriots trusted him as a member of the militant Sons of Liberty. As a Polish Jew, he belonged to a generation of Polish freedom-fighters whom Americans much admired, and he was acquainted with Thaddeus Kosciuscko and Casimir Pulaski, who joined the Americans early against England. Salomon must have been a diplomat, because he even overcame the barriers between the Sephardic Jews and the Ashkenazic people when he won the hand of the wealthy and cultured Sephardi Rachel Franks.

Salomon evidently was a practicing Jew of sorts. For instance, he kept the Jewish holidays and expected gentiles to understand why he interrupted commerce on some days when they did not. When Philadelphians built their new temple Mikveh Israel after the war, they gave trustee Salomon the honor of first opening the door; he had raised one-third of the funds for the building. Congress failed to honor all its obligations, so he was no longer in the best of financial positions, but evidently he bore no grudge. Salomon entered legend and history as the foremost Jew in the Revolution.

Because only one in a thousand of the colonists was a Jew, it would be easy to overlook their ranks, but later American Jews, when challenged, could always point to Salomon and his kind to show that they had proved themselves in a crucial passage. The several hundred Jewish families were gathered in New York, Newport, Philadelphia, and several southern cities. No rabbi trained in Europe ministered to them, though Gershom Mendes Seixas, a New Yorker who graduated from the little school started at Shearith Israel in his city, was a hazan, or reader, who acted some of the rabbinic roles. When the British occupied New York, he seized the Torah and other necessities for worship as he and his people fled to Connecticut. Later he also helped impart life to Mikveh Israel in Philadelphia.

In proportion to their numbers, Jews boasted a roll call as impressive as any religious group. At Newport, Aaron Lopez fled the British and supported the colonies. Former Bordeaux wine-merchant Benjamin Nones became a major in an outfit with enough fellow believers that it became "the Jews' Company." Mordecai Sheftall of Savannah conspired against British shippers and became a prisoner of the British, who showed their special distaste for him by almost starving him in the Negro prison and then on a prison ship.

The population records of the Jews are so good that virtually all of them from the 1780s seem traceable. They failed to leave a treasure of arguments for their political convictions to match those left by the Mayhews, Witherspoons, or Carrolls. Lacking rabbis, they also lacked theorists, but the lay members liked what they saw in the colonies, where they suffered no anti-Semitism to compare with the anti-Catholicism of the day. Whether they got their ideas of freedom and equality from the Bible and their Jewish tradition or whether they simply forged these out of their minority position is not clear. Later, during the period of constitution writing they performed one more function: as the only visible non-Christian

religious group, they fought to remove Christian clauses from constitutions and oaths, and in the process helped the nonreligious gain
full rights of citizenship.

The small Protestant sects, often pacifist or Loyalist, fared less
well. Later Americans have difficulty seeing the Loyalist point of
view, but until victory came in sight, many cautious sectarians
found few reasons to place their faith in even mild revolutionaries.
They feared that history naturally favored chaos, and they could
not know for sure that the victors would not turn repressive. Later
revolutions elsewhere make their fears look plausible.

The small German groups in Pennsylvania compared the British
liberties there to the restrictions in their old homeland and were
thankful. Ministers who took oaths to the king did not want to
break them lightly. They took literally those words in Romans 13
that forbade resistance to governments. Of course, using its logic,
they later had no difficulty lining up with Congress the moment it
replaced the Crown, because they assumed that God now permitted the new order and sanctioned it. Victorious Americans quickly
forgot or forgave these waverings, but these groups' heirs lacked
credentials to show how they helped shape America.

The Lutherans well illustrated the divided mind of pious rural
Christians and, in some instances, the shift in thinking across generations. Many an unadventuresome clergyman among them
opened his service book at worship to confront in bold black print
prayers designed for support of the king. Stolid because they had
sworn to pray such prayers, a few fled to England with Episcopalians when the war came. They acted out of a conscience that
patriots despised but at least could understand. The overwhelming
majority of Lutherans stayed to enjoy America, but a few went
into exile in Canada and in at least one case, that of the Reverend
John Schwerdfeger, a pastor pulled up stakes with most of his
congregation to live there as "empire Loyalists." Patriarch Henry
Melchior Mühlenberg was a reluctant patriot, but his own son John
Peter Gabriel left the pulpit to muster a regiment and become a
major general.

A tiny German Baptist group known as the Harmless Tunkers
(Dunkers), today's Church of the Brethren, presented two faces.
The best-known family among their fifteen hundred adults were
the Sauers, a clan of printers who suffered under the Stamp Act
and spoke out against it. Yet as Dunkers they could not in conscience support the use of force or pay disrespect to the Crown.

Christoph Sauer III was a vigorous Loyalist, though not a fighting one; he claimed that he and his father one night had to hide from rebels who wanted to tar and feather them. In December of 1777 the Americans captured him and the British exchanged him for another prisoner. Such bargaining showed that they valued him highly for the appeals he published to Germans in the colonies to support England. His father suffered even more when the revolutionaries decided that he was a traitor and plundered his estate worth ten thousand pounds. While this was an illegal act, in true Dunker fashion he stood by in silence, believing it wrong to use the courts to defend himself. He spent the next six years using his meager earnings as a bookbinder to pay off debts. When war came to Dunker communities like Ephrata in Pennsylvania, the sect won new friends by caring for the wounded. One officer accidentally spent a few days with them and came away convinced that pure love still existed. Their garments were uncouth, but they were beautiful: "Until I entered the walls of Ephrata, I had no idea of pure and practical Christianity." After the war this sect retreated further into the woods in an effort to remain a set-aside people of God.

The Moravians turned out to be less consistent pacifists. Some paid for substitutes or served in the military, while on the frontier not all could resist the idea of fighting the Indians, but their love of peace and order led them to shrink from open revolt. A colony at Lititz in Pennsylvania did break ranks to lean toward the patriots, while even their relatives at Bethlehem and Nazareth or in North Carolina gradually moved from loyalism toward the American cause. The dynamic John Ettwein loved the English but stayed on the sidelines until he could see which side God ordained to be victorious. Without much difficulty this practical man then came to terms with the colonists and, while remaining a pacifist, helped his church adapt. The Moravians won good names for themselves as hosts and nurses, but their tense neighbors often made life difficult for the peaceful believers when the war crested.

Only one Pennsylvania sect of note was of English background, the Quakers; they were in a difficult predicament. George Washington, who could tolerate Catholics, let his geniality run out short of the Quakers. He feared some were Tory and that few of the others would support the colonies, yet sometimes he was also generous even to these Friends. The more staunch Quakers disowned many in their fellowship who caught war fever, and who then acted "in the quality of a soldier." Others paid for substitutes and served as noncombatants, but those who steadfastly refused to co-operate suffered harassment and in some instances pillage and imprisonment.

The major surprises during the years of revolution came from the rather new Baptist connection of churches. We do well to pause for a moment to watch their development and observe the positions their leaders took. One of them, Isaac Backus, serves as a focus for their struggles. This view of the Baptists makes it possible also to move from our first revolution, attitudes that prepared religionists for the War of Independence, to the second, which led to religious freedom based on a kind of separation of church and state. The Baptists are also worth watching because in the revolutionary years they began their move from miniscule size toward becoming the largest Protestant cluster of churches for both whites and, later, blacks.

The Baptists would certainly have defined themselves as a group concerned first and chiefly with salvation and then with life to come. But as they minded their church business, they could not avoid taking political stands as well.

In 1740 Isaac Backus's mother, Elizabeth Tracy Backus, an heir of Josiah Winslow from *Mayflower* days and a lifelong strict church-goer, was converted for a second time. Eleven years later when she refused to pay taxes to support Congregationalism, collectors on a dark and rainy night took her to prison, where she lay for thirteen days. She never knew who sprang her, but she recalled that first she was "loosed and found Jesus in the midst of the furnace with me," until "the prison looked like a palace to me."

Her son Isaac, though baptized at an early age, claimed that he grew up "careless and secure" for seventeen years until the Great Awakening arrived in Norwich, Connecticut. But even after his conversion then, the youth did not end his story with praise for the gift of grace and the hope of heaven. He was troubled. Dare he join the Norwich church and be tainted by sharing the Lord's Supper with the half-converted? Where was the pure church in the midst of such compromises? He did join, hoping to reform the church before it deformed him.

The Backuses took part in efforts to pull the church back to the older ways and to expel those who did not meet their terms for conversion. When they failed to win, they left the Norwich church along with other New Lights. The next year they met with others as Separatists and in 1746 helped form a Separatist church, something of a halfway house compared to the consistent Baptists, who refused to baptize infants and immersed adults only after they experienced rebirth. But Baptists had been around long enough to become respectable and win tax exemption privileges — something the Backuses would not accept.

When Isaac Backus felt called to the ministry he followed the revivalist road to form a radical Separatist church. Predictably, on February 6, 1749, an officer grabbed Backus, demanding that he pay the precinct rate to support the official church, against which he was competing. A peace-loving citizen prevented the pastor's trip to jail by paying the tax, but Backus found this all very unsatisfying and took his case to the General Assembly of Connecticut. Why could not Separatists have the same exemptions as did the more compromising Baptists and other licensed dissenters? He reminded the assembly, without success, that their forefathers once had left a pleasant native land for the howling wilderness for the sake of liberty of conscience; what had come of it?

Slowly and painfully Backus came to see the radical Baptist point of view, so he reluctantly decided he must be baptized again — which he was, on an August day on which he found "special clearness" of soul. He never wavered again. The struggling New England Baptists needed his kind. They were beginning to spread their views of Christian simplicity and clearness to frontiers. After five years of wrangling, Backus formed the First Baptist Church in Middleborough, Massachusetts, his home for the next fifty years. Fortified with his little cask of rum and the Bible in his saddlebags, Backus logged 918 journeys on his twelve-hundred-mile circuit for the cause between 1747 and 1806. He kept his pencil sharp for statistics and watched churches grow in number from 119 in 1777 to 325 in 1795. He also wrote the major book on New England Baptist history; in it he estimated that by 1786 forty thousand people had deserted the official church, most of them for his Baptist denomination.

When James Manning and other Baptists founded Rhode Island College, later Brown University, they found Backus a warm supporter. He helped form the Warren Baptist Association, taking pains to show that it was an advisory body that could never become superior, infallible, or coercive. To this point his life was otherwise full of nothing but the petty disputes that entertained church people and bored everyone else. The issues of the American Revolution seemed remote from niggling debates about the age for baptism or the issue of paying church taxes, yet they were all soon to become tangled.

Baptists thought they had their eye on heavenly things but found themselves necessarily mucking in affairs of earth. Around 1769 they began to hit out at the "grievous oppressions and persecutions from the 'Standing Order'" churches and set out on a course that, before they knew it, caused them to work for independence from England, at the side of the despised standing-order people themselves.

The Massachusetts standing order had learned that it could best keep its official establishment by smuggling in some respectable dissenters. They licensed these outsiders and exempted them from paying church taxes, thus buying off their discontent. The Quakers, thoroughly settled in, bought the compromise, as did the "Old Baptists." It was the Separate Baptists who nettled the establishment. For ten years after 1761 the issue nagged the legislature. At one point the Tory lieutenant governor, Thomas Hutchinson, surprised the Separates by approaching them: they should take their case to the king. This was a trap. If they did so, they would be stressing the role of the king in colonial life, while the churches would be angrier than before with each other and in this mood could humiliate the Baptists, for whom Hutchinson had no taste. Backus and the Baptists, walking into the trap, addressed the king, who intervened, but they found the process distasteful and thereafter came back to principle.

In 1773 the grievance committee of the Separate Baptists resolved to press their case. Backus urged fellow Baptists simply to refuse to pay religious taxes; the collectors could not imprison them all. He wanted them even to withhold the certificates that proved they were exempt. The members of the Warren Association of churches only grudgingly supported some of his measures, but were in a compromising mood.

In 1774 Backus wrote Samuel Adams a letter of protest as he watched constables arrest Baptists for offenses against tax laws. The legislature again took a hard line. The temptation to come back groveling in protest to the king was strong but dangerous. Backus decided that the Continental Congress provided a better forum, so he packed off with two others to press the case for the Warren Association. The three political amateurs let themselves be seen in the company of pacifist and Loyalist Quakers in Pennsylvania, and therefore met a gruff Massachusetts delegation. John and Samuel Adams smelled Loyalist guilt by association. They sat back to hear Backus read off a dour statement about how Massachusetts authorities meddled between God and their souls, but the politicians could not understand the complaint. Backus recorded that the two Adamses called the churchly establishment in their colony "a very slender one, hardly to be called an establishment." With a mere wink between gentlemen, that kind of word once pacified protestors. No longer. The Baptists insisted that they were not discussing the size of establishment but the very existence of any at all.

John and Samuel Adams paternally reminded their visitors that in fair-minded Massachusetts the General Court would be more than eager to hear complaints and make exceptions. Then Robert Treat Paine made Backus furious: Was it worthwhile to make such a fuss "contending about paying a little money"? Backus boiled: "It is absolutely a point of conscience with me." Playing the game with certificates would mean Backus acknowledged in humans a power that belonged only to God. Adams told the dissenters that they might as well expect the solar system to change as to expect Massachusetts to give up its mild and engrained religious system. Many decades later Adams looked back on that day with no more comprehension of the Baptist mind than he had shown in 1774.

Backus and his friends returned to hostile neighbors who made them out to be Loyalists. Ezra Stiles confided to his diary his fears that the Baptists would now complain to England of persecution. Thus they would play into the hands of England, which was glad to pose the churches against each other. Yet the Warren Association surprised its enemies that December when, asking for the persecution to stop, they also announced to an obstinate Massachusetts Provincial Congress that they remained hearty friends to their colonial country.

The guns of Concord and Lexington in 1775 settled for Baptist hearts what their heads could never fully decide. Already on November 22, 1774, Backus had announced to the Provincial Congress the Baptist willingness to go beyond lawful means to revolution, as readily as would any other denomination in the land. Almost all Baptists showed that they were neither outsiders nor Loyalists, and some began to give their lives for the revolt. More than he feared Congregationalism, Backus deplored popery and slavery, which he thought would come with victory by the king. All the while he was supporting the war as just, he kept complaining about restrictions on churches like his own. In his history

Backus remembered that from his childhood until the war began he never touched on state affairs or even voted in a town meeting. Now, though he saw that both sides were sinful, freedom was with the Americans.

Support for the war did not end the Baptist battle. Massachusetts unimaginatively kept its establishment for another half century. In 1778 the liberal pastor Phillips Payson preached the election sermon against "persons of a gloomy, ghostly and mystic cast" who schemed against establishment. Backus lunged back, quoting Charles Chauncy, a mentor of Payson. Chauncy once stated against the threat of Episcopal bishops that he was "in principle against all civil establishments in religion." Where was such principle now? The Baptists were not fully consistent, nor were their heirs. Yet by the standards of their time they did advance the boundaries of liberty, attaching their revolt to the larger colonial revolution.

Victories in the War of Independence led some self-satisfied Baptists to forget the battles of Backus for the end of all church establishment. In triumph the Warren Association trumpeted that America was now reserved in the mind of Jehovah to be "the grand theatre on which the divine Redeemer will accomplish glorious things." By the time Backus left that theater in 1806, his people had moved into the South and West to race against another new group, the Methodists, for the heart of the frontier people and to win the contest against all other churches to keep government most decisively out of the affairs of religion.

American believers of all sorts had engineered one of the great shifts in Western religious history by then, but to complete the task they needed the help of men who professed a new religion, an enlightened faith for a new nation. This republican religion, as we shall see, was sometimes a political ally but also an ideological competitor. As a religion not of revelation but of reason, it also was the prime agent in the third of the age's three revolutions.

The statesmen founders of the United States helped produce at least two major religious innovations. First they set out to convince churchly citizens that religion was larger than their own sects. Many of them channeled their own religious impulses into something larger, such as the nation; thus Benjamin Franklin called for a "public religion." Others, like President Thomas Jefferson and pamphleteer Thomas Paine, completely individualized religion. Paine could say, "My own mind is my church." They then also set out, in James Madison's words, to help distinguish civil and religious life, or in the language of Jefferson, to separate church and state and thus effect the third great change in these decades. They sundered what both tribal and church-minded people had kept bound together for thousands of years. No shots were fired, but in their own way these achievements amounted to an American revolution as much as did the War of Independence.

The battling churches ceased fire against each other just long enough to unite against England, but nothing in their past portended that they could get together to help build a nation. Most of the religious groups did not know how to act in concert or tolerate each other. At a crucial moment they received help from these founding statesmen, not all of whom were themselves tolerant of either the sects or each other's opinions.

Readers of documents from the decades when America was born have to acquire a new vocabulary when they deal with philosophy and religion. A European movement called the Enlightenment began to make its way into educated circles in the colonies during the colonial wars, beginning around 1758. German, more radical French, and more mild English thinkers began to question biblical language about deity. The new vocabulary pointed toward an Age of Reason where there had been an Age of Faith. The mind mattered more than the heart, reason more than revelation, morals more than miracles, public virtue more than private salvation. The common people of America did not often find that the new movement spoke to their needs, though they were indirectly influenced by their leaders.

The pioneer in the new spiritual and intellectual pilgrimage was Benjamin Franklin, who also found time to fashion a philosophy, inspire scientific societies, serve as a diplomat, and run keys up kite strings in order to study electricity. Most Americans know him as an inventor, but seldom does he receive credit for his call for a new American religion. Franklin had long wanted to start an academy in Philadelphia where elite parents could educate their sons, a school where they could defend the English people against the "vast numbers of foreigners" who were arriving annually. These people, he thought, were ignorant of English laws, customs, and language. His academy, he insisted, would employ no "concealed papists" since these might lead the students to moral depravity.

In 1749 Franklin offered his *Proposals Relating to the Education of Youth in Philadelphia,* which defended "the Necessity of a *Publick Religion.*" He argued that such a faith would be useful to the public;

it would be advantageous in promoting a religious character among private persons and it could counter "the mischiefs of superstition," which men like Franklin found in sufficient supply in most sects. The American public religion was not, however, to be anti-Christian; it would reflect some of its origins in a specific faith. Whether in order to be diplomatic or out of habit or even conviction, Franklin added that public religion would show "the Excellency of the CHRISTIAN RELIGION above all others ancient or modern."

During the next forty years, this first expression of public religion prospered under a variety of names. To its enemies in the churches, it was infidelity, a new heathenism. To the philosophers, it was a homegrown American version of the Enlightenment, a movement that favored reason and freedom in matters of the spirit. The theologians have called its substance deism, because it focused, as did English deism, on an impersonal God. In political language it became the "religion of the Republic." Two centuries later people were to call later versions of it "civic faith," "public piety," or "civil religion."

The enlightened founders were eager to produce a universal creed that they could throw like a tent over the diverse church religions. Ironically, they lived to see the churches regard it as just one more tent next to their own, one more competitive sect they must defeat. The people who espoused public religion were of Protestant Christian background and most remained church members. They respected the Bible but they began to speak of the deity as an abstraction, not an impersonal Person, and they played down miracles. Jesus was respected as possibly the greatest human, but he was not the supernatural divine Son of God. The public religionists tore the old drama of heaven and hell from the sky and the netherworld and instead anchored religion in earthly behavior. Reason for them counted more than faith, and morals more than grace. This was the chief idea of the Enlightenment in Europe and America alike. They created the climate and language that made possible acceptance of key ideas in the Declaration of Independence, much of the Constitution and Bill of Rights, and many freedoms that the churches had not assured for each other.

Benjamin Franklin bestrode two ages in religion. He was friendly to evangelists but was unmoved by their calls for his conversion. Instead of worrying as Jonathan Edwards had about the Great Being, he belonged to the Age of Reason. Franklin carried some leftovers of Puritanism along as a young man heading from Boston to Philadelphia, and remained as purposeful as Puritans wanted him to be but far more ready for irreverent wit than were they. Franklin displayed a more generous side when he prayed that God would grant love of liberty and the rights of man among all nations, until philosophers could set foot anywhere and say, "This is my Country."

Public religion to Franklin meant not the end of sects but of sectarianism, not the end of their freedoms but the increase of their duty to produce a common morality. Wherever he saw churches agreeing, he encouraged their support of the common weal, and he opposed their spats over their peculiarities. His faith, he stated, was in the Deity and the need to do good, in immortality and rewards and punishments. Franklin found those "essentials of every religion," in all the churches. He respected them all, he said, "though with different degrees of respect as I found them more or less mix'd with other articles which without any tendency to inspire, promote or confirm morality, serv'd principally to divide us and make us unfriendly to one another."

When Franklin chided a minister for pompous and petty prayers he probed: how did the man know the Deity welcomed long flatteries that even wise men despised? He twitted his own brother about all the idle prayers that Christians spun out when New England attacked the French at Louisbourg. He calculated that believers recited forty-five million prayers on the subject within a few months and hoped that the Americans would as a result prevail: "If you do not succeed, I fear I shall have but an indifferent opinion of Presbyterian prayers in such cases, as long as I live." Yet it was this same Ben Franklin who surprised everyone at a low moment at the Constitutional Convention by asking for prayer, a proposal his colleagues diplomatically received but did not act upon.

In Christian America even Franklin could not forever evade the question of what his public religion held concerning Jesus of Nazareth, and Yale President Ezra Stiles prompted the eighty-five-year-old Franklin to spell it out. Even then his response was wily. Jesus, he agreed, *did* produce the best system of morals and religion the world had ever seen or was likely to see. Like all other Americans who compared their own time unfavorably to primitive good old days and golden ages, Franklin also claimed that through the centuries Christianity had suffered "various corrupting changes." As he expressed some doubts about the divinity of Christ, he pointedly allied himself with churchly dissenters who also doubted it, but, he told Stiles, he chose not to dogmatize on the subject and thought it needless to busy himself with it now, adding that he expected "soon an Opportunity of knowing the Truth with less trouble." He could not help but add that God showed no evident disfavor to people who did not believe in Jesus. Franklin did not oppose belief in his divinity if this helped the people take the codes of Jesus seriously. Please, Franklin concluded, do not publish that paragraph; he wanted to leave this world at peace with the sects.

Fortunately for later America, the Founding Fathers, following the example of Franklin, put their public religion to good use. While church leaders usually forayed only briefly into the public arena and then scurried back to mind their own shops, men of the Enlightenment worked to form a social fabric that assured freedom to the several churches, yet stressed common concerns of society. Franklin invested less energy than did Jefferson and Madison in separating church and state. Yet he attacked churchly establishment: when a religion was good, it would support itself. If a religion could not support itself and God did not care to come to its aid, it was a bad sign if then the members had to call on government for help.

The Father of His Country, as Americans found it important to call George Washington, treated the presidency as an excellent pulpit from which to spread public religion. Though his mild enlightened faith did not square with theirs, the churches claimed him. Washington never followed Franklin out of the church, and he took his turns as a Church of England vestryman in Virginia. Because he was noble, vague, and bland in stating his faith, he showed how it was possible for the enlightened to make public religion palatable to people in the denominations. In the new century, even revivalists conferred posthumous orthodoxy on the preeminent general and statesman. Later Americans have liked to picture their hero at Valley Forge, kneeling in prayer — a posture he was never known to assume. Washington went to church approximately monthly, but evidently not to the Lord's Supper, and he was consistently silent on the divinity of Jesus.

When Washington first became president, the churches lined up to pass resolutions of friendly greetings, which he returned in a similar spirit. In his Farewell Address, employing terms broad enough for the churches to use as advertisements for their own programs, he called religion and morality the indispensable supports of political prosperity and argued that religion was always necessary for morality. In wartime as a general, Washington had summoned chaplains from churches to serve the military, showing no preference for one denomination over another. At Mount Vernon his workmen, he said, could be Asian or African or European, Muslim or Jewish or Christians of any sect, "or they may be Atheists," if they did their job well.

When the issue of separation of church and state came up, Washington was anything but a leader in the cause. So long as Jews or Muslims did not have to pay, he was ready to let general revenues support churches in Virginia and to let die a bill for assessment of taxes for religion. This inaction angered the Baptists, who in 1789 adopted a document that called on him as their tried and trusty friend to help overcome the horrid evils of "faction, ambition, war, perfidy, fraud and persecution for conscience' sake." Washington sounded tired when he answered them weakly that the Constitution endangered the rights of no church. The program of abolishing tax support therefore fell on younger shoulders. So far as Washington was concerned, even under the existing system the churches of America were living together in a charity better "than ever they have done in any former age, or in any other nation." If so, his style of advocating public religion probably helped the cause along.

It fell to later apostles to make public religion more militant. Thomas Jefferson carried it to the new stage. He did not hide his opinions in wit as Franklin or in fuzziness as Washington had. Genuinely hurt when partisan ministers called him an infidel, Jefferson insisted in the face of their belligerence that *he* was a Christian, and they were not. When he did spin out the meaning of his faith, the third President focused, as so many Americans have, on purity and simplicity, whether in nature or the primitive Christianity that Jesus embodied. Then he found this innocence embodied in the natural American, exalting that "this whole chapter in the history of men is new."

Jefferson was well schooled to be a pioneer of enlightened faith. He started a scrapbook of snippets from John Locke and other admired mentors. The samples in the book match his later outlook. "Who are to be reputed good Christians?" The answer: "In Rome papists; in Geneva Calvinists; in north Germany, Lutherans; in London, none of the above." Orthodoxy therefore was "one thing at one time and in one place. It is something else at another time, and in another place, or even in the same place."

The adult Jefferson moved consistently toward the patriot position. In the hot summer of 1776 he was assigned the task of writing a draft of the Declaration of Independence, some of whose lines became part of the creed of the American public religion: "We hold these truths to be sacred and undeniable," he began. Then he or Franklin revised the line, possibly to make it sound more enlightened and less churchly: "We hold these truths to be self-evident." These truths insisted that all men were created equal and endowed by their Creator with certain inalienable rights, including life, liberty, and the pursuit of happiness. In early August Jefferson joined others in signing the document, therewith pledging his life, his fortune, and his sacred honor.

Jefferson, who had fifty years to live after the Declaration of 1776, spent eight of them as president. In that office he translated the old church language about a sense of mission, redirecting it to the nation. The Republic was now "the only monument of human rights, and the sole depository of the sacred fire of freedom and self-government." Just as John Winthrop thought the eyes of the world were on New England, now Jefferson expected all regions of the world to look to America for light. Later, when the new century began, he wrote his friend John Hollins that the eyes of the virtuous all over the earth were turned with anxiety on the sacred fire of liberty in America. The Americans, Jefferson thought, possessed a "chosen country." Her people were "enlightened by a benign religion, professed, indeed, and practiced in various forms," yet all of them included certain common virtues.

Benign as he sounded about that religion, he could distance himself from the social forms of it and could sound like moderns who devise faiths to suit themselves: "I am of a sect by myself as far as I know," he boasted. Jefferson, in high Enlightenment spirit, never submitted his system to the opinions of men. "If I could not go to heaven but with a party, I would not go there at all." Franklin was always discreet about attacking churches, but Jefferson felt bold enough to criticize some of them by name. The Christian doctrine of the Trinity, which confessed that there was one God in "three persons," he called gibberish; it confused the simple teachings of Jesus, and was the "Abracadabra" of mountebanks and swindlers who called themselves priests. A man of his enlightened age, Jefferson charged that priests made faith sound complex in order to filch wealth and power from people who had to depend on their expertise to find heaven. Such a policy made half the world fools and the other half hypocrites. John Calvin might be the patron of American Protestants; to Jefferson he was either an atheist or a demonist.

Jefferson showed Jesus respect just as Franklin had, insisting, in standard American style, that Jesus represented simplicity. To Jefferson, it was Paul who started adding complexity. While later priests taught lies and slander, Jefferson wanted simply to go back to Jesus and take "the diamonds from dunghills" out of historic Christianity. Despite the busyness of his White House days, Jefferson took moonlight time there to snip up the New Testament in the Greek, Latin, French, and English languages. He pasted together whatever was simple, moral, and nonmiraculous and called the result *The Life and Morals of Jesus of Nazareth*. But he did not need the Bible; as he wrote a friend, "Your own reason is the only oracle given you by heaven." People had an innate moral sense, Jefferson thought, like eyesight and hearing; this sense made them responsible for their acts.

Public religion was not just talk; it issued in action more decisive than the kind George Washington supported. This action was based on an opinion that Jefferson best articulated: religion needed neither law nor sword; "reason and free inquiry" were all that mattered. In the *Bill for Establishing Religious Freedom,* written during battles in Virginia against tax support for churches, Jefferson summarized the belief in one line: "Truth is great and will prevail if left to herself." To promote this view, he welcomed the aid of dissenters like the Baptists and Presbyterians, who conspired to put passion into his cause against Episcopalian privilege. Jefferson went further than some of them did, however, when he included nonreligion in the field of freedom. In *Notes on Virginia* he insisted that it did him no injury, neither picking his pocket nor breaking his leg, for his neighbor to say that there were twenty gods, or no God.

Revenue-supported religion, not atheism, was the issue in Virginia, which was certainly no inquisitorial power. Jefferson came along at a time when he could spur an evolution of rising expectations among people who wanted to end the last traces of churchly privilege and to assure freedom of conscience among dissenters. During two decades he helped fight one of the great revolutions in Western religion without shedding a drop of blood. Virginia still had its old glebe system, and insisted on giving privilege to Episcopalianism by licensing and restricting other sects' preachers. He and the dissenters were angered to find even a few people jailed because they refused to pay the church a tax or because they broke the codes for licensing ministers. Compared to other struggles of his life, this one turned out to be easy to win, but the action was long, and someone had to stay with it.

When the showdown came, the lines of division were confusing. Washington was generally quiet through it all, though he supported a liberal and gentle establishment of religion. Liberty-loving Patrick Henry led the opposition to disestablishment. He could not picture a society without formal and privileged religion, any more than could John Adams, and it was Henry who in 1779 introduced the General Assessment Bill that named Christianity the established faith of Virginia. Henry offered a generous plan that allowed each person to designate a church of his choice to share tax proceeds. Jefferson thought this policy unfair to those who believed in no church or no God, and the battle was on.

When in 1784 Jefferson left for a French ambassadorship, he turned the battle in the Virginia legislature over to James Madison, who was one among several who had taken it up whenever Jefferson was gone from that body in earlier years. Madison was as well prepared as Jefferson ever was, both for his role in this struggle and as a major author of the Constitution. The diffident Madison never fully elaborated his creed, but he seemed friendlier to conventional Christianity than were either Franklin or Jefferson. Baptized an Anglican in 1751 at Hanover Parish Church, he grew up in Virginia but passed up William and Mary to study at Princeton, where Presbyterian John Witherspoon influenced him. We know that Madison read theology at this time, though he made little reference to it in his later career.

While the vehemence that others brought to politics seemed generally absent in Madison, this was never true on the subject of religious liberty. During the Virginia struggles he raved against the "diabolical Hell-conceived principle of persecution" that prevailed in Virginia, and said he found the clergy, to their eternal infamy, furnishing their quota of imps. "This vexes me the most of anything whatever." In the very next county, he alleged, five or six well-meaning men were suffering for having published mild religious sentiments. Madison said he had squabbled, scolded, abused, and ridiculed long about the situation; now the time for action had come.

A study of the record elsewhere helped Madison school himself for the final battle in Virginia. In April of 1774 he wrote that he envied the freedom Pennsylvanians enjoyed while Baptists and Presbyterians in Virginia had to keep fighting for theirs. "Religious bondage" in his home colony, thanks to the clergy, shackled and ruined the mind. When the Orange County voters sent him to the Virginia Assembly, he found the forum he needed to press the case. Once there, Madison urged Patrick Henry to be more bold for rights and not to settle for something so weak as mere toleration, but he did not successfully make the point. An effort to legislate full freedom was defeated. Madison henceforth had to settle for ten years of living with an unsatisfactory compromise.

In 1784 opportunity came for him to finish the conflict Jefferson had helped start. Once again he ran head-on into Patrick Henry. Knowing he was no match for Henry in debate or as a crowd pleaser, he fought for time and even gave the Anglicans a token, temporary victory while he worked to have the vote postponed until the next session. During that crucial year he supported Henry for governor, to show there was nothing personal in the controversy — and, just by the way, to help kick off the legislature floor and upstairs the best champion of the church tax. The dissenting churches rallied to the side of Madison, who also came to see that not even all Episcopalians wanted the old policy in the new United States.

The *Memorial and Remonstrance against Religious Assessments* that Madison wrote at this point ranks in importance with the aforementioned *Bill* of Jefferson. In Madison's eyes the difference between the Inquisition and Virginia was one of degree, not of kind. While the degree was enormous, an Enlightenment purist had to be as consistent as was Baptist Backus on such a point. In this same document, Madison added a new twist when he called religion an opinion. Once upon a time religion was a gift of God, a stamp on the soul that no one could change. The Awakeners made faith a matter of choice, and now the Enlighteners turned it into only an opinion. Only reason can change opinions, argued Madison; the sword cannot. The religion of a person, since it is an opinion, "cannot follow the dictates of other men."

The Madisonians won, rather easily in the end, whereupon Madison indulged in enlightened hope that Americans had extinguished forever the desire to make laws for the human mind. The Constitution of 1787, however, offered little on this subject and even its First Amendment (ratified in 1791), which did, could not apply to state constitutions. While final victory in this field awaited the action of Massachusetts in 1833, all state establishments lived on borrowed time after 1785 and the Virginia conflict. At last the point of Roger Williams from earliest colonial days was established: government could not easily interfere to corrupt the church. And Thomas Jefferson had his way: the church could not easily invade the civil realm.

Custom, of course, can replace what the law takes away, and in the next century American Protestants were strong enough to establish their empire without the support of law. Madison knew that "parchment barriers" had limits. Something of old Calvinist teaching lived on in his view of human nature, for when he looked around for a guarantee of freedom, he remembered how once he had told Jefferson that the envy of other sects toward the Episcopalians helped the cause. Now he enlarged on that theme and made a virtue of the American necessity that came with its diversity. Public religion proposed a broad faith to blanket the Republic and then to some extent wanted the churches to survive but to keep canceling each other out. Madison decided that the best (and only) security for religious liberty lay in what he called "the multiplicity of sects." Voltaire had said that if in England only one religion were allowed, it would be despotic; if two, people would war over them; since there were thirty, people could enjoy security. In the *Federalist* papers Madison wrote that on the subject of civil and religious rights, "the degree of security . . . will depend on the number of interests and sects."

Madison did not in those lines put himself in the situation of the American searcher who might be looking for truth among the confusing choices, but he did turn out to be correct about the security the multitude of churches provided. After centuries of bloodshed in holy wars and after long struggles for legal power in early America, churches in the new nation were hardly ever again to leave dead bodies in the trail of their conflict. Voltaire was wrong, of course, about the degree to which the multitude would live in happiness and peace. Wars of words continued, and the race between the churches to occupy the land was intense, so these competing institutions undercut each other. Madison also did not anticipate the degree to which the churches learned the fact that the Enlightenment faith was itself by no means religiously neutral. Since law had never given it privilege, the denominations wanted to be sure that it had to compete in the open market of opinions.

Public religion was not only a set of phrases from Franklin about "the essentials of all religions," or some self-evident truths stated by Jefferson, or some acts for religious liberty by Madison. It looked for institutional embodiment. A few enterprising deists thought they should make churches of their movement for enlightenment and public religion, but little came of such efforts. Votes at the Schaghtivoke Polemic Society and the Calliopean Society in New York State, both of them would-be counterparts to churches, tended to run 7 to 2 or 13 to 7, no matches for the crowds revivalists drew. Clubs of Bavarian Illuminati never had a trace of the power their suspicious enemies attributed to them. At Newburgh, New York, the Society of Ancient Druids turned out to be a pathetic joke that after 1804 disappeared from view. Blind Elihu Palmer promoted a Temple of Reason and published *The Temple of Reason* but few came, few read. Masonic lodges embodied some of the teachings of public religion, but the public who were not their members did not see them doing so. The nearest the Enlightenment came to founding or finding a church was among the liberal New England Congregationalists who were on the way to becoming Unitarian. Even Jefferson sometimes allowed himself to be called a Unitarian. Yet public religion found its true home in aspects of the American legal tradition, its established church in the public schools, its creed in the Declaration, its prophecies in the most compelling lines of presidential addresses, its psalms in some American poetry, its passion in the cries by citizens at the deepest crises of American life.

As an organized movement, the advocacy of this first phase of public religion came and went with one form of the Enlightenment in a forty-year period — but they were America's most decisive forty years. The ideas of this faith were ever after infused into the minds of the people, who, when they celebrated civic piety, expressed more of this new religion than most of them ever recognized. One day Americans would resurrect some of its ideas to take up unfinished business left by a generation that promised freedom and equality but did not assure it.

For no more than church religion did public religion live up to what its creeds professed. Not until the twentieth century did the language proclaiming that "all men are created equal" apply even in the legal sense to women. And the author of the Declaration of Independence did not himself intend to include blacks under this clause or those that promised freedom.

By the time Jefferson wrote a draft of the Declaration, blacks had already fought at Lexington, Concord, and Bunker Hill. The adoption of the Constitution resulted from a compromise that overlooked the problem of human bondage. Madison had to write that in the "most enlightened period of time" the distinction of color produced "the most oppressive dominion ever exercised by man over man," yet he did less to overcome it than he did to represent the smattering of momentarily jailed dissenting preachers in Virginia. Madison even helped assure his fellow Virginians that slavery was more secure than ever. Jefferson confided that he trembled for his country when he reflected that a just God would not sleep forever, but after some trembling Jefferson kept his slaves. In fact, the presence of an enslaved African work force in place of a potentially restless and rebellious white lowest class helped provide the luxury that made the Revolution possible. For years to come, both public religion and church religion seemed powerless to overthrow "the most oppressive dominion." And, besides, there was an alluring West out there to fill, converts to gain, and a world to win. The pilgrimage moved to the frontier.

Pioneers who led lonely lives on farms and in
villages came together in huge crowds to enjoy the
sensation of "camp meetings." This distinctive
form of religious gathering, highlighted by gifted if
noisy preachers and by the singing of songs, had
some of the festive air of picnics and outings. The
business was very urgent, however: converting or
being confirmed in the faith. J. Maze Burbank
painted this typical scene. (*The Whaling Museum,
New Bedford, Mass.*)

Chapter Ten

INTO THE WEST
AND THE WORLD

A AFTER THE FIRES OF THE FIRST GREAT AWAKENING HAD DIED,
after the colonies became independent and constituted themselves
the free United States, after the founders cut the churches loose
from ties to civil power and made them voluntary, and after these
founders devised a public faith to rival church religion, then,
around 1800, these churches embarked on a new journey, hoping
to fill the American landscape with their own kinds, until their
energies finally spilled beyond the national borders into a world
they wanted to win for their faiths.

Unmindful of the native Americans they displaced or the black
slaves they misused, the evangelizers started a Soul Rush that soon
outpaced the Gold Rush. This Second Great Awakening churched
the West. Here was a textbook example of free enterprise in the
marketplace of religion, a competition in which the fittest survived.
Whenever someone discovered new nooks and crannies on the spiritual landscape, they quickly developed new movements or sects.
The message of the aggressors to the uncommitted was "Be
saved!" and to each other, "Adapt or die!"

The Quakers failed to adapt and almost died. The Unitarians,
stay-at-homes near Boston, saw the size of their movement crest
early and lose relative place. Congregationalists did move westward and for a time pioneered in the mission to the larger world.
They were, however, too halfhearted in their adjustments to the

rough frontier and lost place, as did the Episcopalians. In colonial days the Presbyterians had mastered the competitive revivalist styles; now they carried their learned ministry to the West. Even many Roman Catholics adopted revivalist styles in order to bring the church to immigrants, while Lutherans, never instinctively evangelistic, became efficient at gathering in the Germans and Scandinavians who filled the Midwest all century long.

Methodists, a relatively new sect in the national landscape, vied with the Baptists for size and outdid them for influence throughout the century, North and South. Methodism was the achievement of John Wesley, the pious evangelist who was a failure in America in the mid-1700s. But he subsequently preached for decades under open skies or in chapels of England, building up a movement that spoke directly to the intuitions of people who were ready to have their hearts warmed for Jesus.

Methodism had a hard time in America during the mid-1700s, but not because it had an unsatisfying message. Americans were ready for its fervency and democratic inclinations as well as for its highly ordered church life. The problem had political roots: Wesley and his first ambassadors to America were mostly Loyalists. As a result, Methodism became unpopular during Revolutionary times and its ministers slunk away. But by the nineteenth century, Methodism stopped looking merely like an imported reform movement and became a highly ambitious American body of people who knew first how to attract and convert the lonely and then how to place them into the close company of the like-minded. Methodists asked these new members to reform the world, beginning with themselves. The key term became Christian Perfection.

John Wesley shied away at first from borrowing the term *bishops* from the Church of England, since he did not want to cause a schism, so he simply translated the term to its synonym *superintendent*. He named Thomas Coke "superintendent for America" in September of 1784, but Americans soon started calling Coke and Francis Asbury, the second appointment, "bishops." By then both had made their apologies for the Tory Wesley; he was, they explained, naive about politics and too remote from America to have known better. Had he been a colonial citizen, Asbury insisted, Wesley certainly would have been a zealot for the American cause. In 1789 the convening Methodists wanted to let bygones be gone, so they exchanged cordial greetings with the nation's new president. Washington pledged himself to the happiness of mankind, to liberty for the United States, and to vital religion. Methodists accepted this agenda, though they tended to reverse the order of priorities for their trek across the country.

Asbury, who led the journey, was born in 1745 in England. He came into the company of the Methodists at age fourteen and two years later experienced "sanctification," the holiness that leads to perfection. Like many of his fellows, Asbury dutifully kept a diary, in which he unfolded his plan to go to America. Why? he asked himself. For honor? Not if he knew his own heart. For money? Never. He was going to live for God and to bring others to do so. Since the people God owned were the Methodists and since their standards were "the purest of any people now in the world," Asbury joined their company and entered the American competition. Before the war there were only 4,921 Methodists in America; yet at the end of his life Asbury counted 212,000 of them, mostly recent converts.

Asbury found Wesley's plans for America inadequate and asked that American preachers themselves bid him, Asbury, to lead them. They did so, and he began progressively to distance himself from his mentor. Wesley wanted to call Asbury his general assistant. No, Wesley and he were like Caesar and Pompey, said Asbury; one would bear no equal, the other no superior.

Each year Asbury tried to reach every state in order to goad his men and to supervise their work. He traveled to New York more than fifty times, to New Jersey more than sixty, and to Maryland eighty times. His *Journals* show him restless, on a pilgrimage not as a seeker but as one who has found God and now must work without peace. He called the act of traveling almost 300,000 miles on horseback his health, his life, his all. The Catholic flagellants like Junípero Serra who whipped themselves for the glory of God were not more self-punishing than Methodists like Asbury on their circuits. Yet despite all his heroics, most Americans, Methodists or not, have never heard of Asbury. In his own day it was said that he was the best-known American outside the field of politics, and that a letter from Coke once reached him addressed merely: "The Rev'd Bishop Asbury, North America." The anecdote signals the place that the converting and churching of America then held.

Asbury lived out in miniature the travails of the whole revivalist epic in his forty trips across what he called his Alps, the Appalachians. Plagued by boils, bronchitis, skin disease, blurry eyes, neuralgia, intestinal disorder, rheumatism, and ulcers, he treated himself with tartar, mustard, rose leaves, tea, and the nostrums and placebos that medicine hawkers sold on the same trails. *Journal* notices had to be brief: "My bones, my bones!" "O, my jaws and teeth." And "O, the rocks, hills, ruts and stumps!" Riding the circuit, he looked forward to sleep at the end of torturous days but usually found a place only in lofts or cabins in which men slept "three deep." One October day of no particular year, Asbury recorded words with which any one who has caught the itch can sympathize: "Poor bishop! But we must bear it for the elect's sake." No studious Unitarian cushioned in a Boston study had a chance of winning the West against such a spirit.

The new migrants who crowded the trails were the targets of the Asburian efforts. He watched up to five hundred people cross Tennessee each day on the worst road on the continent. They came from Europe, from the increasingly congested American coast, from the territories where the Great Awakening had come and gone. His fellow travelers and he were always in real and imagined danger from robbers and wolves, villains and snowslides, confidence men and swamps, seducers and burning cabins. Poverty hounded the bishop, so he borrowed and cadged like a Franciscan beggar of old. When a friend once asked for a loan of fifty dollars, Asbury commented: "He might as well have asked me for Peru." At least, he noted, the circuit riders could console themselves with hopes for something better beyond the grave.

Their bodily self-punishment found its match in spiritual self-torture. While Asbury almost belligerently spread the love of God, he often left behind signs that suggested he felt far from him and had fallen short of divine expectations. The notes were constant: "My heart is still depressed for want of more religion." On another day, "I must lament that I am not perfectly crucified with God." And again: "A cloud rested on my mind, which was occasioned by talking and jesting. I also feel at times tempted to impatience and pride of heart." When someone tried to compliment him, Asbury suspected flattery inspired by Satan. No one ever caught a glimpse of his furrowed face smiling over innocent pleasantries. A friend to thousands, he was familiar with no one.

It goes without saying that Asbury never married. Not once is there a hint of sexual lust in the welter of self-examinations and confessions in his *Journals,* and what he told a colleague is probably true: no woman ever attracted him. Unfortunately for the efficiency of the bishop's cause, women did attract other men he sent out on the long roads; it was natural that the evangelists would hunger for love and families to overcome the loneliness that dogged them on those trails. Monastic abbots, by comparison, found spiritual leadership easy, because the monks were sheltered from contact with the world. The men under Asbury, however, consistently accepted the hospitality of families, where they observed cozy life and met attractive and nubile women. Whenever one did marry it was almost inevitable that such a circuit rider would then want to stop itinerating and, in the language of their calling, "locate." These ministers lost none of their fervor for souls, but they became less mobile and more expensive to support. Because the Bible called marriage honorable, Asbury had to show grudging respect for its status before God, but this assent never helped him enjoy marriage, the "ceremony awful as death." Asbury cried that he thus lost two hundred of the best traveling men in the world and feared that "the devil and the women" would eventually get all his preachers. No note of tender regard for the wives interrupted his dour musing while he watched his circuit riders "run to their *dears* almost every night."

The love of God inspired such driven men, but competition spurred them, since they knew that the race would go to those who outwitted the others on the road. The first enemy was neither the devil nor the women but the Baptist. He took orders from no bishop and could start a local church at any crossroads at which he could attract a gathering. Yet even rival Methodists and Baptists could conspire together against Catholics, infidels, or the American Home Mission Society agents who represented the more sedate and cooperative eastern Protestant interests. A new regional spirit quickly developed, as was evident when one "plain old" Baptist asked why the easterners invaded their churches instead of heading for the heathen out yonder. If the men of the West allowed such aggression, "the people will all go to hear them preach, and won't go hear us preach, and we shall all be put down." This was the language of over-reaction, since the smooth agents were no match for the popular revivalists. Yet in Illinois in 1830 the Apple Creek Baptist Association typically declared an "unfellowship" with all societies that sent missionaries to their territory.

Asbury was too grim to enjoy the competition as if it were a game. In what he called his windmill end of the continent, the bishop complained that the earth and the army and the Baptists all plotted to swallow his own converts, each of whom were worth worlds because they were precious souls. Yet even he was genteel compared to the new generation of jousters for God. Methodist James B. Finley was firm about Presbyterians: "I loved them, but I loved Methodism more, and, as we had a shop of our own, we would not work journey-work any longer." And Peter Cartwright — a tireless circuit rider who in 1832 was to spread the word that his opponent in an Illinois legislative race, Abraham Lincoln, was an infidel — on occasion physically wrestled infidels and Baptists.

The folklore of the frontier contrasts violently with the more civil sonorities of later American interfaith services and Brotherhood Weeks. In the dreary new settlements revivalist contests also provided entertainment. One James Erwin liked to have his congregants rise to sing:

> The world, John Calvin, and Tom Paine
> May hate the Methodists in vain,
> I know the Lord will then increase,
> And fill the world with Methodists.

In the 1830s the Methodists and Baptists both spotted a new frontier menace. The Disciples of Christ, who wanted to restore the simplicity of primitive Christianity and who further divided Christians by trying to get them to unite, challenged the leaders. One critic dismissed Disciples of Christ preaching as "hog slop," noting that the hog "drinks lots of slop, but don't get fat." The Disciples of Christ baptized adults by immersion, which reminded the Methodists of the way a lady made candles by dipping wicks first in water: "When she came to light them, they would hiss and spit, and sputter and flash, and go out." In his turn the Disciples of Christ pioneer Alexander Campbell announced that if someone came to him and wanted to be saved, he would send that person to a Muslim before he would let him get into the hands of a Methodist circuit rider.

Bishop Asbury liked to chart waves of competition on the national map. Back in 1789 he decided that Calvinism already had won the eastern and northern parts of the nation before it passed its peak, and now Methodists must win the South. An alert strategist, he warned Methodists not to spend many days at conferences because while they met, Calvinist Baptists fished about and raided their territories.

The battling had to go on without many actual shots being fired. The rivals could only inflict saddle sores and ulcers, indignities and humiliations on each other as they disrupted families and towns. Gradually the voluntary churches thus came to be safety valves for society, means of draining potentially dangerous conflict into harmless channels. From a distance other citizens could express amusement or shock over debates about how much water to use in baptism without seeing in them any threat to civil security. To the leaders of the churches, however, heaven and hell were literally at stake and the American future was in the balance during their tournaments for the Lord.

Empires grew from all the efforts. Baptists almost came to own the Deep South except for tips of Florida, Louisiana, and Texas, where Catholics dominated. The Methodists moved west from Baltimore to Kansas and lorded it over the border states. Efforts by the Methodists to reinvade what Asbury himself saw as Calvinist territory in New England were momentarily costly. Some even met physical violence from anti-Methodists — yet they endured.

Ten years before Asbury had to dismount for the last time, he reviewed his life from a joyless height, the pinnacle of power where, he said, he had to sit insecure and unenvied without divine aid. Increasingly his bodily and mental powers failed him. At such a moment he hoped not to jump down, fall down, or be thrown down by ambition. "I look back upon a martyr's life of toil, and privation, and pain; and I am ready for a martyr's death." Yet even his last *Journal* entry found him still on the trail. On March 31, 1816, Asbury died, leaving countless other ministers on the road or located with their "dears" among people hungry for perfection.

Such crusades for conquest followed the trajectory of the First Great Awakening but needed a Second Great Awakening for their new momentum. Around the turn of the new century, Americans first started to recover from the spiritual slump that followed the First Awakening and the distractions of the Revolution, to find that only a very small minority of the citizens were on the rolls of church membership.

The most visible signs of a growing revivalist spirit appeared in the ministry of James McGready in Kentucky. After a year of stirring, his Muddy River church sensed fresh outbreaks in September of 1799. The next summer the congregation rejoiced to see surprising conversions marked by emotional shouting, singing, and fainting. These were more uncontrolled than the conversions that Jonathan Edwards and George Whitefield observed sixty years before. When a sacramental service at the Gasper River the following July turned into a "camp-meeting," a new form of worship evolved. Such meetings were prolonged outdoor gatherings at which people who may never before have seen any sort of large crowd became part of congregations that numbered in the thousands. Revivalists lured them with the prospect of rebirth, asked them to turn their backs to the world, and then offered them a ticket into a new, approved, churchly society. Surrounded by their wagons and tents and with fires casting giant shadows, people sang and prayed late into the night. Some fell to the ground "like men slain in battle." Penitents shrieked and the healed cried in rapture. The wicked fell in alarm or awe, "curiosity was general"; all the community had to take notice. If conversion seemed a private and individual affair, the stir created a mass movement and the revivals generated their own new classes and cultures.

After the first fevers of the Second Awakening lowered, some earthquakes and trauma induced by the War of 1812 helped bring them up again. These were not the only means of church growth; it is possible to overlook the patient pastoral work of local ministers in valleys and neighborhoods because it seems drab by contrast to the spectacles. Yet new furies were loose in this age, and people tried to explain them; the converts could see nothing but a divine cause. Itinerant James B. Finley criticized those who made conjectures or who philosophized because they did not want to acknowledge that all revivals were simply the work of God. The revivals also provided for social control. After their first apparently spontaneous outbreak, Bishop Asbury had asked for a "well-disciplined army" — he had no use for uncontrolled emotions — and with perfect timing he pleaded for "order, order, good order." Not all evangelism looked at the past and present. It had a futuristic tone as well. Francis Asbury and Thomas Coke led the new generation to see in the revivals fresh signs that the Second Coming of Jesus was on the way and that with it, as Asbury put it, "our American millennium will begin." Coke also relished the language of millennium and expected Christ to come again after enough people were converted. These new recruits were not only to be the people of the revivalists' own kind but also, according to the promises of God, the Jews and the heathen.

In the headlong rush to recruit transplanted Europeans, for some years even those whom they called heathen in their frontier front yard — the American Indians — were forgotten. Yet in due course some Christians remembered their old mandates to save the natives. They failed miserably, but the efforts of these missionaries helped open the West all the way to Oregon, across lands not even known until Thomas Jefferson sent the Lewis and Clark expedition in 1804. Such endeavors required long-range planning and huge investments. The people best equipped to make them were the Methodists, Presbyterians, and Roman Catholics.

After first failing to understand the natives and then making enemies through wars and displacements, Christians could hardly expect Indians to respond favorably when the Europeans in America turned to them in renewed mission. The Indians generally remained uncomprehending or resistant. Ministers who went to reach them as part of the millennial task complained of small, ignorant, dozing, faithless congregations and sometimes of dangerous encounters. Learning the languages of migrating tribes was always a problem; before missionaries crossed language barriers, one side or the other often blundered into hostile acts. When occasional converts did come forward, they found it difficult to leave behind tribal customs, which Protestants insisted they must do. Yet some people of conscience felt they must not write off these possible converts. Such groups headed off to pioneer all the way across the continent in Oregon territory.

In 1831 an explorer from the days of Lewis and Clark, William Walker, told how three Nez Percés and a Flathead Indian once came from the Rocky Mountains asking for a Book of Heaven from white people. To the Methodists this was clearly a sign from God. When Dr. Wilbur Fisk called for workers, Jason Lee, a new convert from the revivals, offered himself, and the Methodist Board of Missions decided to send him and his nephew Daniel to the Flatheads in the far Northwest.

On April 28, 1834, the Lees joined a caravan at Independence, Missouri, then the starting point for western treks. Theirs took them to near Salem, Oregon. As they unpacked, Daniel Lee took pains to record that "here the first blow was struck by the pioneer missionaries in Oregon, and here they began their arduous toil to elevate and save the heathen from moral degradation and ruin."

Daniel soon had to be sent to the Sandwich Islands (Hawaii) to recover from tuberculosis. Upon his return he was saddened to see that the Indians were still not responding. He brightened, however, when he saw that white newcomers to Oregon were now and then joining the Methodists. Jason Lee, cheerless and near despair for his failure to convert a single Indian, and knowing that both his Lord and the Methodist Board were observing him, consoled himself with the thought that some of the natives at least were living and dying more comfortably than before. The last thing the soul-hungry board wanted to hear in the way of returns on its investments was such a humanitarian compromise, so they urged Lee to turn from worldly projects to the direct business of saving souls. Lee had to report back to the board, a venture that either demanded a trip around South America or over the Mexican mountains. He died, defeated, in 1845. One year later his successors saw the Oregon mission finally fail. When the bookkeeper closed the ledger, he found that the Methodists had spent the then incredible sum of a quarter of a million dollars without converting a single Indian.

The Presbyterians had a policy demanding that women missionaries marry and encouraging the men to wed them. Because she was single, New Yorker Narcissa Prentiss found her application to teach turned down. Before long, however, she could fill out a new form as Mrs. Narcissa Whitman, thanks to her marriage in 1836 to Dr. Marcus Whitman. At Independence, Missouri, the Whitmans joined a couple named Spalding. After gougers took most of their funds for supplies, the four of them left on the "unheard of journey for females" overland to Oregon. To catch a wagon train, they set out on horseback and then at the mountains in Idaho had to leave their wagons; so they rode more than a thousand miles on their horses. Narcissa Whitman and Eliza Spalding then became the first white women ever to have crossed the continent. While Eliza Spalding's husband was a minister, Marcus Whitman was a physician who wanted to heal as well as convert. But the Indians called his preaching "bad talk" from the Bible, and they became more surly as more missionaries came to invade.

Times were difficult for Mrs. Whitman. She endured only one day as the appointed supervisor of the mission, and shrank from her duties after the first night when, her husband gone, an Indian frightened her. For the moment she overcame sectarian competition and took refuge with the Methodist mission until Dr. Whitman returned. He had to make reports in 1843 and came back to Oregon only to find increasing agitation among the Nez Percés and Cayuse through 1845. Two years later, when four or five thousand new settlers had arrived, the Indians became ever more threatening. Whitman with good reason decided to serve the settlers. He also had to care for Narcissa, who had seen their daughter drown and, as her own health failed, had fallen into depression.

On a November day in 1847 two Indians approached the mission house at the Waiilatpuan settlement. One was Chief Tiloukaikt, who claimed that he owned the land on which the mission stood. He was wily enough to come feigning illness, thus to get the attention of Dr. Whitman. The physician warily glanced over the shoulder of the chief and recognized Tomahas, a man neighbors called the Murderer. The Indians asked for some medicines; when the doctor turned to comply, Tomahas tomahawked him. Mrs. Whitman, observing all the action, quickly pushed some children out of range, but after gunfire broke out, she was killed along with her husband and twelve other whites in two days of fighting.

The Spaldings had to abandon their mission, but first Mrs. Spalding at least had the satisfaction of hearing a Nez Percé farewell speech. The Indian chose to pay tribute to his teacher and mourn her passing from his country. His people, he said, would now see no more light. As for the book she gave him and in which she had written, this he would carry at his bosom until he lay in the grave. Evidently biblical language had some effect: when United States troops were chasing the Cayuse, the Indians hoped to escape mass revenge by turning over Tomahas and Tiloukaikt. When a priest asked the chief why he was willing thus to be given up, he heard: "Did not you missionaries teach us that Christ died to save his people? So we die to save our people."

While the Methodists and Presbyterians diverted their last resources to serve the first white settlers, only the Catholics persisted in working specifically with the Indians. Fathers Francis Norbert Blanchet and Pierre Jean De Smet were also successful converting some whites. Thinking that Catholic doctrine would best reach Indians when rendered in pictures, Blanchet invented a "Catholic Ladder" to show the line of humanity from Adam to Christ and through the church to heaven — a visual aid that depicted Protestantism as a diversion from that straight line. (Spalding followed up with a competitive Protestant version of the ladder to set things right.)

Belgian-born De Smet, who brought experience gained among the Potawatomi at Council Bluffs, Iowa, gladly followed the call to the Flatheads of Oregon. In the spirit of Kino and Serra, the Jesuit explored hundreds of miles, until he chose to work in the Bitterroot Valley, where he served as a missionary and peacemaker. By 1844 he had staffed the post with some other Jesuits, lay brothers, and six pioneer sisters of the order of Notre Dame de Namur. Catholicism appeared ready to stay in the Northwest, when Blanchet, who was consecrated a bishop of Montreal, went to Rome to plead the cause of Oregon and Pius IX named him archbishop of Oregon City.

While De Smet saw more success in converting Indians than did his Protestant neighbors, he was most effective at raising support for other missionaries. He sailed the Atlantic nineteen times to obtain money and workers, but Oregon turned out to be a sinkhole for Catholics as much as it was for Protestants. News of the Whitman massacre frightened off Catholic migrants, while after 1849 the Gold Rush lured others to California. By 1855 the church, having lost the lands it once held to the state, was bankrupt. Blanchet turned desperate enough to seek funds in South America for the Indian work, but he finally had to content himself with ministering to the few Catholic settlers. After De Smet finally abandoned his expensive mission, none was reopened until 1866. Thereafter his Jesuit superiors, never convinced as he was of the potential in the Northwest, kept him closer to the Saint Louis base, where he operated for twenty years as the most trusted and successful peace negotiator with Indians.

No other Jesuit, no Catholic, no Christian missionary of his day displayed more zeal or stamina than did De Smet. He recorded how for years he wandered as if in the desert. In one three-year period he received not one letter, no bit of news from any quarter. For two years in the mountains he never once tasted bread, salt, coffee, tea, or sugar. For seasons at a time he went without a roof or bed and for months had no shirt on his back. Often he endured whole days and nights with nothing to eat. What more did the people back east expect of him? They wanted success of the sort that so easily met Protestant circuit riders or East Coast Catholic priests as they met the immigrant boats. The Northwest seemed a dead loss for missions. Could it serve any purpose?

When Marcus Whitman wanted more funds, he reminded his Presbyterian headquarters of the threat of De Smet, but then added one new argument. The Protestants should hold "the only spot on the Pacific Coast left where Protestants have a present hope of a foot hold." In 1852, five years after Whitman died, a special committee of the American Board of Commissioners for Foreign Missions (ABCFM) did pick up his military-sounding advice to look farther west. At last, more than three hundred fifty years after discovery, American imperialists had in effect opened the Northwest Passage. "Now we realize the great vision of Columbus, and reach the Indies by the West. The barriers of ages are broken; and the heart of China is now open to the direct influence of Protestant America."

The fact that American merchants cared about routes to Asia evokes no surprise, but why, it may be reasonably asked, should church people glory in the new access to the Indies? With almost all of the American Indians still unconverted and with much of their own continent still to conquer, why would underfinanced missionaries choose to open another front, one that included the entire globe? Clues to the answer to such questions lay in events that began forty years earlier in the very part of the country that was losing out in the westward dash by revivalists: New England. The clergy there found the rest of the world attractive just as — and in many ways, just because — they were losing their own leading position at home.

The New England leaders could never forget that God called them to be a special people. The Reverend Nathaniel Emmons reminded those who chose to hear at the turn of the century: "This is probably the last peculiar people which God means to form, and the last great empire which he means to erect" until the kingdoms of the world would turn into the kingdoms of Christ. By 1812 people like Emmons believed that their empire not only could but that it must be exported. Their bravado could not obscure the fact that the New England economy was changing, that migrants from there were moving westward through New York and that many new immigrants from Europe were moving thence into the Southwest. Ministers lost status and irritated each other as diverse populations tore apart the unity of originally close-knit old towns. Clerics who watched the old establishment crumbling found it difficult to enter an ecclesiastical free market.

The old-order clergy could still often unite around common enemies, as many did when Timothy Dwight at Yale led an assault on Thomas Jefferson and the Republican infidels. The more staid ministers formed committees to head off invasions by revivalists like Charles Grandison Finney who shocked them with their crude "new measures." Together they fought to keep the tax subsidy for churches in Connecticut and Massachusetts. But while they defended against outsiders, a new enemy came from their own clergy ranks. Jonathan Mayhew and Charles Chauncy were long dead, but their heresies had sprouted a Unitarian party that was becoming a Unitarian church. These great-grandsons of the Puritans still respected Jesus but did not favor doctrines that defined him as being uniquely divine. These descendants of the Calvinists no longer taught that God predestined sinners to damnation but preached instead that he was benevolent and they were full of potential. Their new God seemed too good to consign any sinner or unbeliever to hell, so why should missionaries try to rescue Indians or heathens from it? Some liberals, like the Salem Unitarian William Bentley, even called it a "mad scheme" for someone to leave his native land in order to spread fanatic prejudices among pagans.

When in 1805 Henry Ware, an open Unitarian, became the Hollis Professor of Divinity, Harvard fell to the heretics. The Orthodox fought back in 1808 by founding a new seminary at Andover, but found that they could not rouse the relaxed lay people who kept drifting from Puritan ways. Andover needed a cause that would once more draw together into action the last peculiar people of God.

A call to take the gospel from New England into all the world became that cause. The Catholics had been missionaries for ages. After their first two centuries of sleep, the continental Protestants also began to follow and in the 1790s New England must follow. New England began to see the use of societies for missions.

When the time came for more conservative Congregationalists to look back for a father and founder, they seized on Samuel J. Mills, Jr., who in 1808 first organized a society for missions while at Williams College. Mills and his "Brethren" favored secret codes and clandestine meetings, both at Williams and after they moved on to Andover Seminary and started a Society of Inquiry on the Subject of Missions. No one but reborn or evangelical Protestants with a passion for missions were allowed. Mills quickly recognized the allure that the word *foreign* possessed in a day when Indian missionary work had become so wearying and frightening. Overseas "the difficulties are the least."

Rejuvenated elder clergy encouraged the youth movement; the General Association of Massachusetts eagerly supported four prospects who asked for aid. Funding prospered and there began to be the first extensive bureaucracy in American religion. A network of fund-gathering agencies and promotional instruments resulted. The best device was the growing legend of Mills himself. Williams College President Edward D. Griffin liked to point to a meadow near the Hoosic River where Mills and his friends once prayed into existence what Mills named the embryo of American foreign missions. Griffin footnoted this claim by adding that the society was then formed in "the north west lower room of the east college" — a somewhat less romantic locale than the haystack in the meadow, which midcentury supporters memorialized as a sacred place. One alumnus contended that in 1812 he was present with other founders in a grove and that with them he took prayerful refuge under that haystack during a thunderstorm. There and then they vowed to send the gospel to the pagans of Asia and the disciples of Muhammad. Ill health kept Mills from overseas work, but in two sweeps around the United States he raised funds and taught Protestants to unite for causes abroad even before they settled their differences at home. Mills used his last energies to boost the American Colonization Society and died on a ship returning from a brief trip to Liberia in 1817.

The War of 1812 forced postponement of the first proposed sailings and then the uncooperative East Indian Company ordered the first arrivals in India to return home. One of the ejected was Samuel Newell. With his wife Harriet and a daughter born on shipboard, Newell fled to the Ile de France to escape the gruff Company agents, but there the islanders killed the child and his Harriet. Worse from the viewpoint of New England Congregationalists, who needed martyrs but could not tolerate heretics, three other young recruits — Luther Rice and the Adoniram Judsons — converted to Baptist ways en route to India. Later the ABCFM overcame many sectarian differences, but desertion in the pioneering group stung the sponsors and they refused to send money to the party.

The first missionary companies pushed beyond the Judsons, who worked in Burma, to Bombay and Ceylon. Everywhere, they exported bits of New England to the heathen, and they liked to name native children who boarded in missionary homes after various sponsors back home. Thus one child in Ceylon was named Jordan Lodge after a generous Massachusetts Masonic unit. Men and women from New England taught, translated, and set up clinics among Asians while they fought off the bitter loneliness, filth, and discomfort of hot climates that forced many into early furlough and killed others.

At last New England Protestants again had found something about which to get excited. Missionary couples became the new saints; children in Sunday schools enjoyed their heroics. Returning missionaries spoke to large audiences who were eager to hear how their efforts elevated the heathen. None of these returnees, however, were crowdpleasers as much as real former pagans, like the "prince" from the Sandwich Islands who showed up on a New England wharf one day, or other princes — all the strays seemed to be royal — from the Islands who were sent to a special school in New England. The sponsors were glad to hear assurances of the payoff on their efforts from the lips of foreigners who profited from their largess.

Orphan Henry Obookiah, whom a Connecticut captain picked up in the debris of tribal battles on the Sandwich Islands, became the best agent of his decade. A Yale student who found the boy crying on the college steps turned him over to President Dwight, in whose house he lived for some time. Young Samuel Mills met him, and before long the senior Samuel Mills at Torrington took over his care, until Obookiah caught on to the processes around him and experienced the new birth. Thereafter the younger Mills took the Sandwich Islander to Andover and put him to work in the cause. For the next two years Obookiah prepared to return as a missionary to his home islands. Though he died of typhus in 1818 before he could go, his best-selling *Memoirs* opened hearts and purses for years to come.

One year later the ABCFM commissioned Andover graduate Hiram Bingham, a lean and tall Vermonter, to take the gospel to the country of Obookiah. Bingham married a young woman who shared his interest and, with the Reverend Asa Thurston and some lay people, was commissioned for the Sandwich Island mission. The promoters urged that along with the gospel the party should import the Puritan virtues and moral values of New England. They should cover the Islands with fruitful fields, pleasant dwellings, and the schools and churches of Christian civilization.

Charges by detractors a century later that missionaries were mere agents of the American flag and dollar did not hold true in this case as they did so often elsewhere. Bingham and his co-workers found better company among natives than among American commercial agents. The enterprisers here resented the way missionaries imposed the dour ways of Puritan Sabbath on fun-loving people or restrained the American sailors who took rest-and-recreation leave in the island paradise. The United States consular agent in Honolulu, John C. Jones, Jr., vented both his Unitarian and fiscal furies on the brash intruders. Trade, he complained, could never flourish until the Andover crew went home. These missionaries were subversively telling the king and his chiefs that white traders cheated them. The Christian "blood suckers" of America thereby devalued American articles for sale while distracting the minds of the Hawaiian "children of Nature with the idea that they are to be eternally damned unless they think and act as [the missionaries] do."

The showdown came when the Andover people helped impose a ban on prostitution. This worked hardship on the lusty men of the U.S. Navy, who arrived on the *Dolphin* in 1826. The seamen were ready to rough up the Reverend Mr. Bingham until Lieutenant John Percival of the *Dolphin* bargained with the island chiefs to relax the ban. Encounters like these quite naturally drew notice in the United States, since now the opponents of mission in general — and among them, the Unitarians in particular — could easily be made to look as if they favored prostitution overseas. The ABCFM also exploited a similar incident at Lahaina, where English whalers for the same reasons wanted to take out after a reform-minded missionary. In due course certain naval officers and ship captains began to see value in the Andover and Board efforts, and President John Quincy Adams occasionally heard favorable reports from them.

The Unitarians in Massachusetts remained firm in their resistance. As early as 1822 one of them asked the question enemies of the mission so regularly posed: Why should a few missionaries — sent from a nation of two hundred years standing and ten thousand miles away, the existence of which was hardly known among native peoples — persuade foreigners to renounce five-thousand-year-old religions, government, laws, and manners for the sake of Christianity? The same editor on another occasion jabbed at the touchy issue of status when he charged that people were going overseas simply because they could not find jobs at home. Yet many of those who stayed "at home" continued to like what they saw. Board secretary Rufus Anderson went so far as to applaud the fact that the Sandwich Island venture was bringing church and state back together again in America. Soon it would resemble the way that "existed in the palmy days of the Israelitish nation, and in the Puritan age of New England."

The Americans kept adding other beachheads, including China, and then Africa, to which Mills and other colonizers wanted to return slaves as missionaries. Others wished to carry the crusades back to Palestine, where the faith began, and to the Jews, who, according to the Bible, must hear the gospel preached before Jesus would come again. The crusade would proceed without the sword. The United States had the best credentials to return to the Holy Land because it was the "only Christian nation, which has never persecuted the descendants of Israel." In 1819 Levi Parsons and Pliny Fisk left Andover to undertake such work but died after converting a few gentiles and no Jews in the Middle East. Only a tiny Protestant cemetery survived as evidence of their work; American evangelicals put their money not into converting Jews but educating Eastern Christians. These first Americans in the land of Jesus did, however, stir the old millennial hopes once more.

The idea of millennium: this was the goal and the goad behind so much of the mission. America, many sermons said, was the agent of God to bring in the last days of the world. Yale's Timothy Dwight dreamed of the day when in the near future the Romish cathedral, the mosque, and the pagoda should not have one stone left upon another. Such language spread quickly. When a New England–trained Sandwich Islander saw chiefs baptized in 1825, he pronounced, "It is Millennium"; and the editor of *The Missionary Herald* speculated that the new reign of Christ might begin in the final West, the Pacific Islands.

The crusades against paganism for a time did inspire otherwise laggard New England churches. The Reverend Samuel Worcester attacked American infidels who thought that paganisms were "only so many diversified forms of the true religion." It was false to say that "all nations acknowledge and worship the true God, only under different names, and with different rites." Such a dream, he said at Salem, was as "false as it is delirious." Pagan worship was barbarian or idolatrous and, in the case of Hindu phallic religion, too indecent even to be named. Agitators saw the battle in global terms. In 1830 the ABCFM warned its men in Syria that Rome and Islam were acting as a great pincers, where "the Beast and False Prophet" united against evangelicals. When these two would be overthrown, Christ must reign.

Marvelously the mission *to* America from colonial days had now become the mission *of* America to the world. The Reverend Henry T. Cheever, seeing the Sandwich Islands as a virtual colony of the United States, predicted that in a few years the heart of the Pacific would beat in twin with that of the great American Republic. They would be organized under the same laws and would pulse "with the same Anglo-Saxon blood that shall animate the united millions of all North America between the Atlantic and Pacific." This was the language of manifest destiny, whose speakers assumed that they were moral examples to the whole world.

Ironically, the missionaries were not to have the moral field to themselves. It was not enough simply to claim and to preach that the Christian message would make people better. One could open eyes and see the flaws in American life. For some the eye-opening meant a need for wholly new religious outlooks that could change the American landscape into a *new* moral order. Something was wrong with the family, the economy, social arrangements, even religious competition. Perhaps, some thought, a new revelation or a new community was needed. From such stirrings came movements like Mormonism, communitarianism, or the Shakers. Others used the religious sentiments they received from evangelical and missionary religion in efforts to change the *existing* moral order to make it more like the Kingdom of God. Some of these eventually had to take their protest outside the churches. Taken together, the two developments changed the emphasis in American religion so much that their stories deserve separate tellings.

The most ambitious American mass movement for religious purposes was the pilgrimage of Latter-day Saints to their new home in Utah. This heroic trek, which covered many hundreds of miles, took a toll of lives and tested the faith of the Saints. Around 1900 Carl Christian Anton Christensen painted a number of scenes from the trek, such as this one. (© *The Church of Jesus Christ of Latter-day Saints*)

Chapter Eleven

BEYOND EXISTING BOUNDS

THE STORY TO THIS POINT HAS SEEN AMERICANS MAKING THEIR pilgrimages within the bounds of inherited religious institutions, usually churches. New Spain and New France had permitted only the Roman Catholic church. Most of New England and the English colonies transplanted Protestant churches from the British Isles or the Continent. Religion was thought to be bounded within these churches. Dissenters flattered the older churches by imitating them, as all the groups debated who were most traditional. They despised the idea and even the word *innovation*. Only the Founding Fathers with their Enlightenment experiments significantly pushed beyond the bounds in colonial times.

Then, suddenly, in the nineteenth century, those bounds no longer could contain the religious impulses of all citizens or new immigrants. The American landscape offered so many remote places in which to try new ventures. The new century presented challenges that visionaries thought the old forms could not meet. While their visions contradicted each other, they still had much in common. They ignored or despised the existing churches and were dismissed, in turn, as heretics, pagans, atheists, or crazies. Some of them were communitarian, some radically individualistic, and some made the nation itself into a kind of church. They had in common a sense that they were pathfinders beyond the bounds of existing pilgrimages.

Between the Revolution and the Civil War there emerged a generation of uncompromising dreamers, most of whom were utopians and millennialists. With their eyes on a whole new moral order, they took their models from some perfect past or their direction from some perfect future. These leaders fearlessly denounced what was wrong in America, even if they had to tear at fabrics that were as sacred as the economy, the church, and the family. The land of America was their lure because they were sure that it had a place for the new communities each of them must gather to lead in treks to new promised colonies or kingdoms.

Millions of Americans lived in range of one or another of their woodland conclaves and took notice of these experiments. Some saw Robert Owen, for example, buy the failing German Rappist town of New Harmony, Indiana, and there launch what he called an "entire new system of society" that lasted from 1825 until 1828. In that environment his was an especially scandalous venture, because he made no secret of being a socialist and of having nothing to do with God. Owen conceived of his venture as a new moral order that did not need God or churches. He held high views of human potential and thought that a wise ordering of life in the backwoods community could reform the family, the economy, and the nations. Unfortunately his communitarians did not always cooperate, and New Harmony, like so many other socialist ventures, soon fell into disarray and failed. Owen belongs to the story of American religion chiefly as an example of the "infidelity" that churches scorned. To others fell the task of using religion positively in their visions of a spiritual life unbounded by church religion.

Each schemer devised a different ideology. Founders of the Massachusetts communities of Brook Farm and Fruitlands called these Transcendentalist ventures. In the 1840s, visionary Albert Brisbane brought an ideology called Fourierism from France to America. Before this new philosophy ran its course, he helped set up forty "Phalanxes" in its name. Eccentric religious leader Eric Janson from Sweden established Bishop Hill in Illinois. He helped the colony prosper briefly, until sexual scandal blighted it and a disgruntled member of the community assassinated him. From Germany came True Inspirationists, who established the Amana colonies in Iowa. Social planner Etienne Cabet sent a group to Texas in 1848 and himself led a colony at Nauvoo, Illinois, where he failed as leader.

In most cases, only the names survive: Economy, Bethel, Zoar, Aurora. In other instances, after the vision died the survivors regrouped without the old ideology; the Amanans in Iowa and the Oneidans in New York were among these. The culture of factories, families, and marketplace competition triumphed over them, but for decades they confronted Americans with alternative views of religion, the rights of women, patterns of education, eugenics, and the like.

Almost all the original leaders of such colonies thought the world around them was disordered and too intricate. They advertised their own myths. Most believed in natural human innocence and thought that new social arrangements would end corruption, that simpler or primitive ways of organizing life would improve the community. Yet outsiders saw these experiments themselves as being complex. The communalists often failed because their own members could not or would not live by codes that turned out to be more confusing than old churchly canons. Outsiders would not respect the hierarchies of leaders whose ranks were as formally defined as those of the Roman Catholic church. Still, a little song cherished by the celibate Shaker colonies captured the spirit of those who undertook their pilgrimages in the paths of the utopians:

> 'Tis the gift to be simple,
> 'Tis the gift to be free,
> 'Tis the gift to come down
> Where we ought to be.

The Shaker movement lasted for over two hundred years, but because they did not believe in childbearing and could not convert new members in sufficient numbers, their ranks quickly dwindled. Despite their failure, however, many Americans today still admire the directness and clarity of their expressions in song, tools, and furniture.

Few of these later admirers know that the English-born founder — "Mother Ann" Lee, as Shakers called her — had expounded an elaborate theology to support her simple vision before she came to America in 1774. God was both female and male, as were the creatures God first fashioned. Jesus Christ was the male Messiah; the Catholicism that followed him failed in its mission to bring complete purity to the world. Now the Second Coming of Christ had occurred in the female Messiah, Ann Lee. With her, women and men were equals and Eden could be restored. Ann Lee quoted Jesus, who said that "in resurrection they neither marry, nor are they given in marriage, but are as the angels of God in heaven."

The resurrection age had arrived, she announced, so her followers must live without enjoying sexual relations.

Angelic living did not turn out to be simple at all. Bad experiences in her own marriage and childbearing back in England surely influenced Ann Lee in her revelation that her disciples must avoid sexual expressions. Yet Shaker men and women lived under the same roof in large dormitory-like houses. The communalists took pains to keep men and women from any enticing bodily contacts, whether in their famous Shaker dances or in the wide hallways of their communal dormitories. At each end of the second floor of these dwellings typically were staircases, one for men and one for women. In the morning the women waited for a "second trump" before they left their beds, while the men paraded past to empty their chamber pots — items that might remind the women of male bodily functions if they saw them. Ordinarily a man could converse with a woman only when a third person was present; the sexes could not sit together in worship. Despite such severe practices, between 1830 and 1850 the Shakers attracted as many as six thousand members. After their decline, respect by others for their "gift to be simple" endured.

Like many other critics in his age, seminarian John Humphrey Noyes believed in the Second Coming of Jesus, but, like Mother Ann Lee, he believed the doctrine with a difference. While she saw herself as the female Messiah, he carefully calculated that the Second Coming had occurred seventy years after the birth of Christ. Though Americans did not know it, they were already living in the age of millennium. Noyes must set them right. If the Shakers survive in national memory for their furniture, to later citizens Oneida usually means silver craft. Yet in the years of its notoriety, the Oneida community confronted the nation with one of the best-known and most feared alternatives to family living and capitalist economy.

Vermont-born Noyes won Phi Beta Kappa honors at Dartmouth College. Six weeks after his conversion at age twenty, he headed for Andover Seminary, which in 1831 was the center both of orthodoxy and foreign-missionary concerns. The idea of perfection that was then in the air gained little hearing at Andover, but the Wesleyans believed in it, and some other revivalists preached a practical version of perfection. Noyes favored the idea and took it to extremes when he transferred to Yale and began to minister to what was called the free congregation at New Haven. There he lost some of the "outward-bound missionary zeal" instilled at Andover and decided that the quality, not the number, of believers must henceforth engage his efforts. In this respect he was similar to other utopians, who concentrated on the few in their hope to change the many by indirect influence.

Noyes picked up the clues he needed to promote perfection from the writings of Saint Paul. While he was wrestling, as Paul once had, with the problem of sin, Noyes found that he lost both his appetite and his good spirits. In due course he picked up a Bible and read the words of an angel to Mary: "The Holy Ghost shall come upon thee, and the power of the Highest shall overshadow thee: therefore also that holy thing which shall be born of thee shall be called the Son of God." The revelation came to young minister Noyes: now, in his day and in his person, such great power was again present!

On February 20, 1834, Noyes announced to the free church at New Haven that he was no longer a sinner. More than that, he could look at those around him and divide them into the camps of the sinners and the perfect. The next day a student stood up to him. Had he heard right? — did Noyes, a mortal, really not sin? No, Noyes insisted, he did not. Since language like that made him seem crazy or dangerous, friends directed him to a counselor named Charles Weld, who was himself recovering from an emotional breakdown, to see what Weld would make of it all. Noyes found Weld to be a "sick doctor." In their conversations he chose to reverse their roles. He pronounced himself "healthier but not yet wiser" than his counselor and helped guide Weld toward further mental health.

Noyes could serve as a case study in narcissism, delusion, sexual fantasy, or competition between a son and his mother. He insisted, however, that it was pure divine inspiration that led him to wander into the "vilest parts" of New York City, to see if he could raise to perfection the "abandoned men and women" who were denizens of such neighborhoods. From that experience he drew the conclusion that there could be no compromises in life, that those who wanted to be perfect must claim and spread perfectionism. This he set out to do in the summer of 1834, when he gathered some followers and published the first issue of a journal called *The Perfectionist*.

Noyes wanted to marry Abigail Merwin, the subject of his sexual fantasies and his first convert. He felt rejected by her, and poured out his feelings in a letter intended for a friend but later published as *The Battle-Axe and Weapons of War*. There Noyes told how the New Testament convinced him that people who served the will of God on earth just as in heaven should realize that "there will be no marriage. The marriage supper of the Lamb is a feast at which every dish is free to every guest." In a holy community Noyes thought that exclusiveness, jealousy, and quarreling should have no place. There was "no more reason why sexual intercourse should be restrained by law, than why eating and drinking should be — and there is as little occasion for shame in the one case as in the other." Such words, spoken in the name of Christian simplicity, outraged most Americans who heard them. But the remarkable feature of Noyes's career was not that shock was instant but that some were ready to give him a hearing at all. His career suggested to them that he was not trying to license lust or lechery but to make sexual intercourse spiritual and to overcome exclusiveness in pairing.

In 1837 when Noyes established a new journal called *Witness,* he turned his attention to his most impassioned convert, Harriet A. Holton. A year later he proposed marriage. His letters to her offered no erotic promise; there should be "no particular love of the sentimental kind between us." Noyes did have sexual feelings, but these he directed to the wife of a convert of Charles Finney, Mary Cragin. Through the next six years the unsentimental union with Harriet produced five births, four of them stillborn, a fact that led Noyes to sympathize with suffering women. As the new prophet of Christ, he felt called to correct what was wrong in present practices of sexual union.

Noyes eventually devised a two-part program. First, the men must learn perfect self-control, which he called "male continence." The males must withdraw from sexual union without ejecting semen, during the "amative" stage before the "propagative" one took over. After proper practice men could learn to do this while giving orgasmic pleasure to women. Would it work? In May of 1846, on an evening stroll, Noyes took liberties with Mary Cragin. Later, with the consent of both their spouses, the couple enjoyed "full liberty." Evidently mastery of male continence was not complete and constant; twins born to Mary Cragin in 1847 were probably sired by Noyes.

Along with male continence came "complex marriage," a practice born of science combined with scripture. On June 1, 1847, Noyes asked his followers: "Is not now the time for us to commence the testimony that the Kingdom of God has come?" Deciding that it was, they intensified their community at Putney, Vermont, where they developed what their scandalized neighbors called "free love." The practitioners saw it as a regularized form of bonding in which all the communitarians were married to each other in Christ. To no one's surprise, enemies pursued Noyes into court, charging adultery. He preferred to be a mover rather than a martyr, so he transplanted the community to Oneida in New York. To lessen community tension, Noyes now developed a ritual of "mutual criticism." A final innovation came in 1869, when he invented stirpiculture, or selective breeding, a pioneer form of eugenics in America.

Visitors for a time commented on the economic productiveness and apparent friendliness of these communalists. The families of Oneida really did seem to be learning how to overcome exclusive feelings. But Noyes had a larger mission, which he spelled out for all America. Since people no longer felt communion, the young were "shaking the pillars of the temples their fathers built." Noyes said he had no complaint about those temples; between the days of ancient Israel and the final Kingdom of Christ, no government excelled that of old Puritan New England. But now it was gone, and its successor, American democracy, had failed as a substitute. In 1837 he issued a "Declaration of '76," an act of independence from a government that tyrannized Indians and Negroes. Noyes wanted to renounce allegiance to the United States in order to live only under Jesus Christ. "My hope of the millennium begins where Dr. [Lyman] Beecher's expires — viz., AT THE OVERTHROW OF THIS NATION." Yet when Noyes foresaw a war to emancipate the slaves, he became cautious. He remained a millennialist who looked for final unity, when the church would "BE the state; and this Church-State was to be the only government over the whole world."

In the late 1870s Noyes, now in decline, began to delegate some of his powers to a committee. In 1879, when legal troubles in the United States dogged him, he moved for a time to Canada. By the time of his death in 1886, Oneida no longer practiced complex marriage or communalism. Noyes never wavered, however, in his belief that God had chosen a community to embody perfection after the manner of Christ. Other seekers of his day left behind more successful institutions, but none matched Noyes for the consistency with which he tried to display a New Testament outlook that was at odds with everything Americans around him held dear.

Among all the experimenters, one cluster shocked people in their own time but turned out to be regarded as orthodox Christians who only for a time could not be content with church life as then organized. The career of Noyes had shown how some people blended futurism with primitivism. But more orthodox believers came on the scene to argue in extravagant ways that in complex America, the path ahead lay in a return to pristinely simple Christianity. Promoters of the "primitive gospel" claimed that they wanted to start a movement, not sects, in order to overcome the sin of denominational division. Though in every case they added one more sect to the national catalog, no prophets of purity permitted the unsuccessful examples of competitors to deter them from offering the wholeness for which the American souls hungered.

More than five million Americans today belong to groups that descend from these more moderate, even orthodox, primitive movements. Their spiritual ancestors rejected names like Luther, Wesley, or Calvin or descriptions like Congregational, Presbyterian, or Episcopal. Their congregations, they said, must be only made up of Disciples of Christ; their congregations would be the Churches of Christ; they were simply Christians. The new primitives formed no withdrawn communities, but instead chose to compete on the open market with the revivalists on the frontier.

First among their founders was Marylander Barton W. Stone, who learned revivalism at a Presbyterian log college. Then he took his message to Cane Ridge, Kentucky, where the camp-meeting revivals of a Second Great Awakening erupted in 1801. Thrilled as Stone was by the conversions, he was appalled to hear ministers dispute over niceties after the revivals, so in 1803 he joined four others in signing a document in which they agreed to "bid adieu" to their old presbytery and formed a new one. An associate said that this move cleared away the rubbish of human opinions, turned the Westminster Confession, a Presbyterian creed, over to the bats and moles, and let the new Christians build on the original rock of ages. After hardly more than nine months of gestation, their movement next produced a sarcastic "Last Will and Testament." In it the founders dissolved also their own presbytery and headed back for their model to the ideal primitive church. Stone wanted his Christian union to have no "authoritative creeds, party names, and party spirits."

The sponsors of the new movement insisted that it was born in Jerusalem, but it also had Scottish roots transported by Thomas

Campbell. Wishing to escape the factionalism in Irish Protestantism, Campbell in 1807 sailed to America, where he found the most factionalized churches in history. At once he fell into dispute with fellow seceder Presbyterians at Washington, Pennsylvania, and decided to secede from them. Before long Campbell devised one of the most appealing slogans for the primitive cause: "That rule is this, that where the Scriptures speak, we speak; and where the Scriptures are silent, we are silent." By the end of 1809 Campbell successfully created innovation with a movement designed to oppose all "human innovations." His son Alexander soon migrated to join him and to give leadership to the movement.

On May 4, 1811, the Campbells and their friends organized their association into a church designed to unite all churches. A rereading of the Bible led them to discount their own baptism as infants, to be immersed, and to delay baptism for the new daughter of Alexander and his wife. This choice led the group into the natural company of Baptists and caused a breach with Presbyterianism; the first path to unity was thus necessarily blocked from the first.

The fourth founder of the movement, Walter Scott, also a Scottish Presbyterian, who arrived in Pittsburgh in 1819, linked up with the Campbells but carried their claims further. His slogan for the frontier was to be only "Jesus is the Christ." Understanding well the psychology of the common people who gathered for revivals, he entertained and educated crowds with a five-finger exercise, with which he ticked off faith, repentance, baptism, remission of sins, and the gift of the Holy Spirit — all that believers needed to be saved! Scott with such devices and with native gifts as a preacher brought in thousands to the fledgling movement.

Success in organizing and gaining numbers brought no traces of victory in the search for unity. Alexander Campbell's magazine attacked the Baptist kin of the Disciples by calling them the most "proscriptive, illiberal, and unjust" sect in the union. In Kentucky, Campbellite "Raccoon" John Smith tried to be friendly with both sides, but one day when he said "Good morning, my brother," this member of another church rebuffed him: "Don't call me brother, sir. I would rather claim kinship with the devil himself." Smith, such a prodigious baptizer that people called him "the Dipper," also savored battles. In 1828 he boasted to his wife that he had "*baptized* seven hundred sinners and *capsized* fifteen hundred Baptists." For a time the Stoneites and the Campbellites even fought each other, until their majorities united during the 1830s to form the Disciples of Christ. For a time they grew at four times the rate of the national population, from 22,000 to more than 190,000 by the Civil War.

The Disciples promised to restore "the ancient order of things," but in 1830 Alexander Campbell showed that he looked ahead as well when he named his magazine *The Millennial Harbinger*. This journal, he announced, would set out to destroy sectarianism, infidelity, and antichristian doctrine and practice. Its object was to introduce a religion *and* political order called the Millennium, the grand world that Christian Scriptures promised so long ago. The Disciples found a following among those who looked to the plow and the pew but who also dreamed that they could really begin at the beginning and discover a new kingdom beyond the sects. Yet even such dreamers carried some baggage from the Old World and did not travel light enough for everyone who then trekked west on spiritual pilgrimages.

During the years of these orthodox primitive gospel moments, and on their soil, there emerged a drastically different rival, one who at times paid the Disciples of Christ the mixed compliment of recognizing them as in some ways precursors. Campbellite leaders like Sidney Rigdon brought members of their own congregations to the new movement. Disciples of Christ renegades like Parley Pratt also transported the language of promise and empire that the Disciples of Christ first nurtured into the new Church of Jesus Christ of Latter-day Saints. As "the Mormons," they became the best-known of the innovators, and led the most ambitious communal trek in American history.

Mormon founder Joseph Smith was born in Vermont in 1805 to parents who migrated along with so many other New Englanders to the New York frontiers. The young man much later claimed that the "unusual excitement on the subject of religion" in his day wearied him. The sects pitched convert against convert, priest against priest, until there was "no small stir and division." Even his own parents took divergent paths. His father was religious but despised churches, while his mother Lucy favored worship and sampled it in church after church. In 1820 she took her children into a small Presbyterian congregation.

By now the family had migrated to Palmyra, New York, which in the five years before 1821 was torn apart by sects and disputes in the wake of revivals. Young Smith watched the triumphs of large camp meetings, the tactics of the little competing churches, spectacular baptisms, and the futile debates about them all. Since the

Smith family often earned a little money by selling baked goods to crowds, it is possible that Joseph gained a concessionaire's view of such tumults, but he was also close enough to see some of his family fall to revivalism and there are some hints that he may briefly have experimented with Methodist exhorting.

God eventually revealed to Smith a plan that carried him beyond such partial measures for salvation. The young pathfinder later wrote a number of statements about that revelation, some of which added details missing from earlier accounts; each concentrated on different aspects of it. One version, which he published in *History of the Church* in 1838, so aptly condenses his views on the subject of sectarianism that it merits a full hearing whether it accurately reflects his views of the 1820s or not. "In the midst of this war of words, and tumult of opinions, I often said to myself, what is to be done? Who of all these parties are right . . . I came to the conclusion that I must either remain in darkness and confusion or else I must do as James directs." Therewith he referred to the place in the Bible where James urged those who lacked wisdom to ask it of God. "I retired to the woods to make the attempt [and] immediately I was seized upon by some power which entirely overcame me, and had such astonishing influence over me as to bind my tongue so that I could not speak. Thick darkness gathered around me, and it seemed to me for a time as if I were doomed to sudden destruction. . . . just at this moment of great alarm, I saw a pillar of light exactly over my head, above the brightness of the sun, which descended gradually until it fell upon me."

In the light Smith saw two personages, dazzling him with their brightness as they stood in the air. One pointed to the other and said, "This is my beloved Son, hear him." What should Smith make of all this? "My object in going to inquire of the Lord was to know which of all the sects was right. . . . I was answered that I must join none of them, for they were all wrong, and the personage . . . said that all their creeds were an abomination in His sight; that those professors were all corrupt." He told his mother that Presbyterianism was not true. A Methodist preacher with whom he shared the good news of his revelation then shattered his naiveté with the unsurprising charge that such visions came from the devil. Years later Smith remembered how valuable it was to see that, though he was only then fourteen or fifteen, he could create a stir among grown-ups.

Response first came from fellow upstate New Yorkers, who were also displaced Protestants from New England. Until then most of them had enjoyed little of the wealth that the American landscape promised. They were nobodies in the society of western New York, hardly more than mere additional numbers when they converted under the revivalist efforts of existing sects. Along came Smith, who called them Saints and told them they would rule. They knew secrets that the "gentiles" around them did not possess. And while other people lived mean and purposeless lives, they were called by God to be builders of the Kingdom and its temples, to be warriors in armies for the Lord.

While other New Yorkers were trying to induce crops from hard soil or making their pennies count in country stores, Smith reported on more visions. Neither then nor later did he make a claim like John Noyes did, that he was perfect; nor was he like Mother Ann Lee a new Messiah. Even after the vision, Smith owned up to errors and temptations and admitted that he had associated with what he called jovial company. But on September 21, 1823, as he prayed alone in his quiet room, a glorious personage, he said, again appeared to him. The messenger of God, Moroni, revealed that in nearby hills lay hidden a book of golden plates and with it two stones called Urim and Thummin, through which Smith could see and translate the writings.

After Moroni twice more visited New York to renew the announcement, Smith said he found the stones and the plates of the book on nearby Hill Cumorah. The angel would not yet let him have them because it was known that Smith wanted them "to obtain riches." This announcement fit the pattern of the times, for a craze of digging for treasure afflicted the area. Joseph was well known as a digger; it was also reported that he fancied a peep stone as a means of finding wealth. In March of 1826 civil authorities charged Smith with a misdemeanor for just such activities. Then in 1827 the angel gave him permission to translate the plates.

Few moments in American history have been more controversial than those that deal with Mormon origins. Was Smith an impostor, a hallucinator, a self-deceiver, a confused young man, or a true prophet and revealer of God? One hundred fifty years after the event equal numbers of people might each choose one of the above descriptions. Those who matter most, however, are the four million devout around the world who follow his prophecy. They walk in the trail of early witnesses Oliver Cowdery, David Whitmer, Martin Harris, and eight others, including family members, who swore they saw the plates. In the face of skeptics, the Saints like to note that although the named three later broke with Smith, they were never willing to retract their original testimony.

Somehow the first circle of believers found funds to publish five thousand copies of the translated *Book of Mormon* on March 26, 1830. Its revelation was a story of America as a new land of promise, an explanation of mysteries that puzzled Europeans in America ever since Columbus. People always wondered whether the Indians were a special creation, children of the devil, or miraculously arrived migrants. *The Book of Mormon* confirmed a popular theory that these were the Ten Lost Tribes of Israel from biblical days. As for Africans in America, they were lesser parts of God's plan, a people God could save but who were second-class members of His Kingdom. Though in 1836 Smith once ordained a black elder, Negroes were ruled out of the priesthood — which is the common rank for other males — until a new revelation, announced in 1978, permitted them to be ordained. Readers of *The Book of Mormon* could trace the migrations of three groups of people to America, most notably the family of Lehi, who constantly had to fight off the feuding Nephites and Lamanites. The Lamanites conquered the Nephites, whose record keeper, Moroni, wrote the book of annals and buried it in the New York hills.

Scoffers attacked the book from the first. Even after 1833 one theory held that it was nothing more than a plagiarized version of a novel by one Solomon Spaulding, written in 1812 but somehow available to Smith. Sidney Rigdon, the Disciples of Christ minister who turned Mormon, knew the publisher of the novel and, it was claimed, helped produce *The Book of Mormon*. But though he later fell out with Smith and was rejected by the Saints, Rigdon never admitted a role in such skulduggery. Alexander Campbell dismissed this book of his rivals with a charge that while it supposedly came from the past, it debated "every error and almost every truth discussed in New York for the last ten years." All too conveniently it decided the controversies over infant baptism, the Trinity, the fall of man, church government, religious experience, republican government, and freemasonry. Others thought it was influenced by the Masonic ritual of the day.

The Mormon cause prospered on controversy. On April 6, 1830, in a home at Fayette, the believers gathered to form what they later called the Church of Jesus Christ of Latter-day Saints. The "Former-day Saints" had been exterminated not long after Christ preached his message in the New World. The new church set out to vanquish the continent where they prophesied "Zion will be built" and to which Christ would return. Orson Pratt, one of the originals, stressed the clean slate of history on which they wrote. For centuries there had been no gentile prophet from heaven to lift his voice. "No vision from the Lord. No answer. No inspired dream. No voice. No sounds from the heavens. No revelation . . ." until Joseph Smith received his.

From the beginnings the Saints were a migrant people. New converts like Brigham Young and Heber C. Kimball took their families with the Smiths and others to Kirtland, Ohio, where Rigdon and his Campbellites joined them. While the Saints built their first temple, neighbors made life miserable and the Mormons neared bankruptcy. Rather than retrench, they expanded. Kimball and seven impoverished colleagues found England ready for their message, and soon returned from there with converts and new funds. They found Kirtland nearly deserted; the company had been uprooted to Missouri, where they found little more peace.

After a fracas at a voting booth between Saints and gentiles in 1838, the Missouri governor gave his militia orders to exterminate Mormons if necessary. Smith saw no alternative but to barter for the safety of his followers; under a truce flag he yielded himself for arrest. In the mix-up the prophet was at one time on the point of being executed. The general who was assigned the dirty work, however, was seized at the last moment by a spirit of fair play and failed to carry out orders. The militia then did not move against the Mormons, who were allowed to retreat to Illinois, leaving Smith in jail at Liberty, Missouri. In the light of a calmer day, officials feared the Mormons had a legal case against them, so they helped Smith engineer an escape to Illinois.

Because the Saints gave an economic boost to the young state, Illinoisans at first greeted them congenially. Some of them even derided Missourians for the treatment they gave such fine folk. But as Mormon Nauvoo on the Mississippi River became the second-most populous city in the state, other residents began to fear the encroachments of the Saints. While in 1840 a Mission of the Twelve went back to spread conversion in England, in Illinois the threat of growth by an international force seemed ever more ominous. The imposing mansion house being built for Smith and his guests offended Illinoisans. They resented the great temple being built on the Mississippi shores to honor false gods in the heart of Christian America.

The Twelve returned to find the Illinois community in uproar.

Most controversial were whispers that Joseph Smith had gone so far in restoring ancient ways that he had reintroduced polygamy. While biblical patriarchs were allowed more wives than one, biblical America forbade the practice. Why did Smith make this move? Detractors then and now thought it was designed to satisfy the lustful desires of the lusty prophet. But leaders of such movements could easily work out less controversial and more discreet arrangements to satisfy their drives. Was the plan necessary to even out the numbers of partners? That made no sense, since Mormon men already outnumbered women. Nor did the policy promise a more rapidly growing number of Saints: the mathematics of birth came out the same whether in monogamy or polygamy.

For whatever reason, on July 12, 1843, Smith claimed a revelation that he should resume the covenant of the Old Testament and take extra wives — or be damned by God. A month later he discreetly announced it to a select few. As for Emma, the wife with whom he eloped years before: "If she will not abide with this commandment, she shall be destroyed, saith the Lord." The hurt and angry Emma agreed: "I guess I will have to submit."

Polygamy, which alienated the rest of America, split the movement. *The Book of Mormon* itself had condemned polygamy. A reorganized church, later headquartered in Independence, Missouri, blamed Smith's successor Brigham Young for inventing plural marriage. But the Saints did believe in progress and additional revelation, so *The Book of Mormon* did not need to be their final word. Evidence that Smith himself introduced the practice and the idea is now firm. Smith forced polygamy as the test of loyalty among his closest friends. Stormy John Taylor, a leader of the next generation, first thought polygamy "an appalling thing," but came to practice it. Brigham Young, an apparent Puritan of the Puritans, remembered the day he heard the command to take another wife: "For the first time in my life . . . I had desired the grave." Soon after, at a funeral, Young said, he envied the corpse. He overcame his scruples and by 1846 took thirty-five wives, eight of them widows of Joseph Smith.

Political tension, not polygamy, doomed Nauvoo. An ejected dissenter, John Cook Bennett, inspired resentment when he wrote letters and a book exposing the pretensions of the movement, but Smith was his own most troublesome enemy. In 1844 he announced that he must run for the presidency of the United States, a legal move that Illinoisans found threatening because they now feared Mormon bloc voting. When Smith ordered the printing press of some ex-members who printed an exposé destroyed, his enemies pressed a legal case against him.

As the processes of law began to work against the Mormons in June of 1844, local authorities jailed Smith so he could face treason charges. The prophet appealed to Governor Thomas Ford, but Ford refused to interfere. Though rowdies by now were threatening Smith with death, the governor showily rode out of town with the words "the people are not that cruel." Some were. On the night of June 27 a crowd of up to two hundred people stormed the jail. Smith and his three companions, armed with two guns, a cane, and a club, were no match for the raiders. One of the mob shot Smith. "O Lord, my God," someone heard Smith shout; then he fell. The Mormons were given the greatest boon a struggling movement can want, a martyr.

Not long before this, Smith had written that he and his people should seek to "secure a resting place in the mountains, or some uninhabited region, where we can enjoy the liberty of conscience guaranteed to us by the Constitution of our country." His regrouping congregation, supported by their leaders, the Twelve, unanimously rejected Sidney Rigdon and chose talented Brigham Young. After he took the presidency, Young gathered people to move into the empty West, where they would never again have to abandon their temple as they did at Kirtland and Nauvoo and where none could harass them as they did in Missouri and Illinois. Some of the Saints had heard General John C. Frémont describe the wonders of the Great Basin and the Great Salt Lake, and they were lured to these lonely places away from the trail toward Oregon.

In February of 1846 Young packed his many wives and few dollars for the Mormon trek west. Regretfully he looked back for a last time on the Nauvoo temple, dismissing the shadow that lay behind for what he called the substance of Zion that lay ahead. Mormons sang and danced to fight off the bitter cold of Iowa in winter. North of Omaha on the Missouri River, they made their winter camp. No buyer for the Nauvoo temple ever emerged, and their funds ran desperately short. So did their tempers, as the campers questioned the direction Young was giving or debated why the Smith family had stayed behind. Chief Black Elk, who welcomed Mormon trade, came to the rescue by offering squatting rights. Then, after the ambitious Mormons cut down trees to build cabins — thus depleting the groves from which Indians took game — the natives became less friendly.

So the Saints resumed their march. Each morning after the trumpets of the Lord sounded, the Saints fell into their military regimen. Toward the end, Young sent ahead an advance party of 148 Saints in 73 wagons to spy out the Salt Lake region. Late in July, on a day when Young had to lag behind with mountain fever, the party glimpsed the valley at whose northern end the waters of the Great Salt Lake glistened in the sunbeams. Five days later the recuperating leader arrived; his followers heard him say of the vista, "This is the place." Young envisioned the ark of the Lord resting there, from whence the Saints could fan in all directions to "spread abroad and possess the land."

Mormons came to boast with good reasons that they endured and transformed a desert in the land of Deseret, but it was a fertile valley that Young chose. Salt Lake City, set out with 132-foot-wide streets, began to rise; a tabernacle and a temple would dominate its cityscape. Young headed back eastward with 70 people to wave west a caravan of 1,553 people bound for the "goodly land," but his own party was unlucky: at South Pass a band of Sioux stole their animals. In plucky Mormon fashion they walked to Missouri, surviving on an occasional straggling buffalo that they could shoot without benefit of horseback.

In 1848 Young marshaled another 1,229 Saints and Kimball pulled together 662 more for the great migration. Gentiles resented the trekkers, but the Saints grew ever more sure of themselves. Spokesman Orson Pratt started contending that all governments other than that of the Saints were illegal. His brother Parley announced a new prophecy that foretold a dynasty of people who must overthrow gentile troops. Just as boldly Young asserted — as late as 1866 — that the great object of his own life was to establish the Kingdom of God upon the earth. Any prophet could say that, but the Mormons had guns to back their claims on the Promised Land.

The Saints used double vision to look at America. Up close they believed that the Declaration of Independence and the United States Constitution were divinely inspired documents, a claim that made them intense and conservative patriots. In the distance, these believers in progressive revelation thought, the American founding documents would be superseded by those of the kingdom that God through them would effect. No territorialists enjoyed red-white-and-blue celebration more than did Utahans. President Millard Fillmore and the Congress, however, paid little attention to their claim on Deseret and tried to set up Utah as if no Saints existed. Then, realizing the limits of his power, Fillmore named Young the territorial governor, a risky political act in the eyes of most gentiles.

Brigham Young returned few favors to Fillmore. No earthly ruler dared interfere with the civil life of his church and kingdom. The president in Washington pretended not to hear such bravado, but pressure was building against Mormon polygamy, and officials had to face up to it. The army held back, fearing both Mormon power and the Indians who found alliance with the Saints advisable. General George A. Custer added an explanation for the Indian preference for Latter-day Saints: these newcomers did not encroach as ruthlessly as gentiles did. The Mormons understood that "the Indians have a strong attachment for the land containing the bones of their ancestors, and dislike to leave it. Love of country is almost a religion with them." Despite its wariness, Washington finally had to prepare in 1855 to move against an empire that held sixty thousand people in its "absolute despotism."

His reputation already in jeopardy, Young further offended gentiles with what they thought was his most heartless scheme. The newest converts back east, he decreed, must come to Utah pushing handcarts. The Lord promised that such companies would be given health and strength. Young figured that the carts would be economical, the act of pushing and pulling healthful, and the ordeal a test of Mormon loyalty. Unfortunately manufacture of the carts was slow. One group of migrants embarked too late in the season to evade the blizzards and attacking Indians. As news came back from the trail, the nation called Young a murderer of the many scores who died. He wrote off their deaths. "It is the will of the Lord" was the head Mormon's conclusion.

The public also came to learn of the Danites, a Mormon association authorized to take the life of Saints who failed to keep the standards. Facing such realities in 1857, the new President, James Buchanan, felt called to bring national law to bear and thus restore order. For a while an old friend of the Mormons, Thomas L. Kane, mediated and held off an impatient government. Then, as the United States Army neared, the well-mobilized army of Young pulled a trick. At their leader's call they helped the citizens abandon Salt Lake City and move down to Provo. The government soldiers came upon an eerie, apparently dead city — sleeping for a moment but, after the strategic retreat, soon to be filled again.

At about this time, while the drama at Salt Lake was unfolding, without the knowledge of Young there occurred a disastrous incident at a place called Mountain Meadows in southern Utah. After the Gold Rush, the Saints had difficulty recognizing that commuters would insist on crossing their kingdom. Not even Utah offered the Mormons a place to hide and be permanently alone. Some Saints tried to harass those who made a highway of their territory. A migrant group unwittingly came onto the scene where trigger-ready Mormons were preparing against a United States invasion. Since their own supplies were short, the Saints refused to sell needed items to the intruders. In the midst of bad tempers, it was said that some of the Missouri wildcats in the migrating party indiscreetly bragged that they were among those who years before had attacked Mormons back in their state. By then the interloping gentiles had poisoned a spring, fed rotten meat to a native (who died of it), crippled one Indian, and shot another. In such chaos the Indians attacked.

The Mormons soon joined in the action. The Missourians held out for a while. Someone took word to Young, two hundred miles north; his word that no one should be harmed came too late to help spare lives. On September 11, 1858, the Mormon militia lured the migrants from their besieged camp with the promise of safe conduct, but then at a given signal fired on them. After the smoke lifted, 120 people were found dead; only 17 children were spared. Twenty years of litigation followed before militia leader John D. Lee paid for the massacre with his life. Most Mormons, who blamed the Indians, regretted the killing, but Heber Kimball announced that the thread between gentiles and Mormons was broken and that, world without end, the two people would never join again.

Not since the time when Spaniards and Huguenots similarly decoyed and destroyed each other in Florida three hundred years earlier had the United States seen anything so close to a holy war. The "Mormon War" was that rare exception in North American history, the moment when religious ideas helped keep communities from coexisting and carried them to deathly conflict.

The end of the Mormon War did not bring immediate statehood to Utah. So spectacular was the scandal of polygamy that P. T. Barnum, who considered Young the best show in America, could offer him $200,000 a year to appear in New York. By then the prosperous Saints were in little need of money. Young chose to retain leadership in Utah but one day even a great lion of the Lord like he must tire. At this point Young sent his favorite wife, Eliza

Snow, to reinforce the old prophecy and encourage the people: "We must occupy the land. We must keep out the Gentile. We must give him no place for the sole of his foot."

Near the end of his life, Young, fearing martyrdom, started going out in public only with armed escort. Keeping old feuds alive, he charged that President Ulysses S. Grant and the new Congresses only made a showcase of polygamy, a practice the Saints finally in 1890 repudiated as a step toward statehood, because of "priestcraft and religious jealousy and intolerance" against the Mormons. Satan, they said, always opposed the work of chosen people. In May of 1877 Young announced that he wanted to die with his people; he was "peaceful, prosperous and happy." Even then the leader of the great trek and the Latter-day kingdom never forgot the source of his inspiration. On August 28, 1877, he uttered four last words, simply: "Joseph, Joseph, Joseph, Joseph." The next day he was gone.

Most Americans rejected revivalists and never joined their churches. They refused the utopians and kept their communities at a distance. Yet many of these citizens considered themselves independently religious, and in many ways they were. They simply took individual paths for their pilgrimages, striking out on their own as no tribal people or members of historic faiths before them could ever have dreamed of doing. Taking advantage of the freedom of choice that modernity brought, they developed faiths that were satisfying to themselves, although many individualists felt that the truths they found were universal.

The public religion of the Founding Fathers gave such seekers their first outlet, though no church or state gave focus to their faith. They were more at home with Thomas Jefferson and Thomas Paine, the enlightened thinkers who called a person's mind his church and asserted that reason and nature were the only sacred oracles. But this first expression of public religion waned at the turn of the century, when church religion again prospered and the revivalist chased the individualist "infidels" off the trail. Such persons did return, however, in the decades before the Civil War, this time to be inspired not by statesmen but by literary people like Ralph Waldo Emerson and Henry David Thoreau — men who took freethinkers on pilgrimages independent of the Bible, Christianity, or church.

The individualistic wayfarers resisted ecclesiastical organizations, but some gathered for a few years around a journal called *The Dial,* or joined the experimental Brook Farm community in Massachusetts. Many were drawn to a movement called transcendentalism, without ever being able to define for others quite what the word meant. English novelist Charles Dickens "was given to understand that whatever was unintelligible would be certainly transcendental," while others said it had to do with "intuition" or "mind" or "being beyond sense experience." One critic read works of the greatest of the new pilgrims, essayist Ralph Waldo Emerson, and charged him and the movement with *Incomprehensibilityosity-ivityalityationmentnessism.* Emerson equated transcendentalism with idealism and thanked philosopher Immanuel Kant for having spelled everything out with "extraordinary profoundness and precision." Whatever the definition of transcendentalism, people of talent in the era of its prime successfully outlined new religions for themselves and added to the spiritual lore and options of the American canon.

Emerson, like so many others of his generation, had to leave church religion in order to take the solitary path. Born on May 25, 1803, the essayist was the son of a minister who held the First Church pulpit where Charles Chauncy once preached in Boston. The stolid senior Emerson felt called to help people fight off alarming attacks on their holy religion "by the Learned, the Witty, & the Wicked," never foreseeing that someday holy religionists would see his own son thus perfectly described. In 1834, three years after the senior Emerson died, the family moved to Concord, where Ralph Waldo heard his step-grandfather, Ezra Ripley, preach the virtues of mild Unitarianism to a secure flock. The shelter of Concord seemed at times warm, at others, confining. Quite naturally Emerson found his way to Harvard and decided there to become a teacher. For three years he taught, but found the classroom distasteful and the ministry alluring. After more study at Harvard, he positioned himself under the pulpit of his new hero, Unitarian pioneer William Ellery Channing, who commended books that Emerson found daring. His first shrill critic was near enough at hand: when the young man praised the values of the biblical criticism that Harvard was then importing from Germany, his aunt, Mary Moody Emerson, dismissed it all as atheism.

Waldo faced true atheism on a Florida trip he took, where he met Napoleon's nephew Achille Murat, who appeared to be a philosopher and scholar, a man of the world, and a lover of truth. Young Emerson was glad to notice that his own faith stood up indestructibly during their talks, but he also found virtues in the sublime soul of this friend who, as a "consistent atheist," disbelieved in immortality. After the encounter, Emerson resolved to develop his own "middle way" in order to occupy new ground in the world of spirit, ground untenanted before. He took his search back to Harvard and was then ordained at Second Church in Boston in 1829.

When his new bride, Ellen Louisa Tucker, died of tuberculosis, an unprepared Emerson had to face up at once to his own views of immortality. Thanks to what he had seen in Ellen, he believed the soul was immortal. He wrote in his journal that he felt both "alone in the world and strangely happy" not to see her suffer anymore. A year after her burial, acting on an impulse he could never explain, Emerson had her coffin opened and took a look at her remains. Wherever he went, he found himself still in communion with Ellen. Though he loved her yet, Emerson had to admit that, with her gone, the air was still sweet, the sun was not taken down from his firmament, and "the universe remained to us both." Such ideas, so distant from the old Puritan concepts of afterlife in heaven, became part of his transcendentalist package.

The young minister soon rejected almost every feature of the old faith, but he did share with revivalists at least the belief that religion must have feeling, must *be* feeling. Now, Unitarianism itself seemed to him cold and pale. As for the ministry, he grew restless in a calling that made men fit into a mold instead of urging them to make a world of their own; "in an altered age, we worship in the dead forms of our forefathers." In order to be a good minister, Emerson must leave the ministry.

Almost as if he were looking for a fight, Emerson made an issue of the Lord's Supper, about which he had some scruples. In his journal he posed himself with Martin Luther when the reformer defied the emperor: "Here stand I." Boston shrugged and paid less notice than Emerson hoped it would to his attack on the rite. When Second Church subsequently dismissed him, even his old friends could no longer fire themselves up to rally over such an old and drab issue. Only his Aunt Mary mourned, "I have lost him." To her, his letters seemed confusing and dark; they mingled heathenism and half a dozen modern heresies. When his brother then defended Waldo as a reformer she disagreed; he had "never loved his holy offices," so it was better that he left.

The unemployed minister visited Europe. In Italy he absorbed great art, in France, took in new philosophy, in England, made friends with writers like Thomas Carlyle and developed his casual interest in the mystical faith called Swedenborgianism. Yet Emerson would not let these enlivening influences overwhelm him, and he resolved upon his return to America never to utter any speech, poem, or book that was not entirely his own work. For a sample, in 1836 he published *Nature,* with its claim that its author was "part or parcel of God" because the "currents of the Universal being" circulated through him.

Notoriety came in 1838 when Emerson addressed students at Harvard Divinity School (then known as the Divinity College of Cambridge). Six graduating seniors and a few friends and teachers made up the meager audience, but word spread quickly from Cambridge to the larger public that this former divine was attacking the believers who he thought exaggerated the role of Jesus. The Unitarians, who had demoted Jesus from his status as fully divine, did not believe in going this far. While Grandfather Ripley and his colleagues became agitated, Aunt Mary started to think that Waldo was speaking under a malign demon. The Unitarian magazine *The Christian Examiner* fumed that the ideas Emerson voiced in such sacred halls were barely intelligible but they were utterly distasteful, being neither good divinity nor good sense.

Emerson broke with the mere conventions of church membership. While he kept giving money to the Concord church, he criticized the Reverend Barzillai Frost, its minister. Though he was the junior of Emerson by only one year, Emerson said the "young preacher" tried to be suave like all the Harvard men but was a man who could neither match the virtues of the old Puritans whom they rejected nor preach anything personally felt. Parishioner Emerson remained friendly to Frost, but, after sneering at the secondhand ideas he heard from the pulpit, stopped attending church, to the considerable spiritual discomfort of Lydia Jackson, whom Emerson had married in 1835.

As a pilgrim, the former minister seemed suddenly at a dead end, because now he found himself nostalgic not for the modern faith he had just left but for the old New England religion he could never possibly believe. Its passing left a void. "What a debt is ours to that old religion," he wrote, "which, in the childhood of most of us, still dwelt like a Sabbath morning in the country of New England." Such a faith urged "the spirit's holy errand through us." Almost mournfully, Emerson asked what would replace the piety of that earlier race. "We cannot have theirs; it glides away from us day by day."

Emerson took his thirst for new religion to the college circuit.

At Middlebury College the students heard him gladly, only to hear the host minister close the service with a prayer that God would deliver them from ever hearing "any more such transcendental nonsense." Those who listened to him at Wesleyan College were also an eager congregation, but sponsors there refused to print the lecture unless Emerson would trim his ideas to please the donors. Ministers began to preach against him, while the public lionized him, assuming that in his lectures there lurked profound ideas that they could use.

Through his early years Emerson seemed too individualistic to help shape a civic faith for the Republic. Yet in the course of the years a number of causes also led him to see the need for activity by groups of people. For a short time he paid attention to the socialist notions of Robert Owen, but then let them fade. He agreed with feminists that women must band together if they wanted more rights, but quickly limited these: "I should not wish women to wish political functions, nor, if granted, assume them." The Fugitive Slave Act of 1850 finally impelled him into political controversy, though before this he let out word that in his own usual mild way he personally favored abolition of slavery. By the time of John Brown's raid on Harpers Ferry in 1859 and the attack on Fort Sumter in 1861, he could even say that "sometimes gunpowder smells good!" To his journal he confided that he had other slaves besides Negroes to free, namely "imprisoned spirits, imprisoned thoughts . . . which, important to the republic of Man, have no watchman, or lover, or defender, but I." He was to live beyond the Civil War as the gray eminence of American letters, and died in 1882.

Emerson all along was forthright enough in his rejections. "Forget historical Christianity" was a clear enough message. Christianity as it lived on stood between the individual and nature or Truth or the Whole. The person should seek direct access, through intuition, to the One and the All. At times in his positive program Emerson sounded very much like mystics of earlier days, but he did not need or want the framework of the church or synagogue, on which most of them relied for their symbols and mythical underpinnings. Yet if he looked for the One, he could always live with the many. "Go inward and I find the ocean; I lose my individuality in its waves. God is Unity, but always works in variety. I go inward until I find Unity universal, that is before the World was; I come outward to this body a point of variety." In a way Emerson had become a church unto himself, and in another, when his pantheistic side came to full display, all the universe was his church and he communed with the All and with all. In either case, Emerson said he did not need the earthly communities called churches; many in his day followed him into what became one-person churches of their own.

Writer Henry David Thoreau, whose later influence on the American journey matched that of Emerson, left the church more abruptly and with no trace of the mild agonies that prolonged the Emersonian transit. A letter survives:

Concord, Jan. 6th 1841

Mr. Clerk

Sir

I do not wish to be considered a member of the First Parish in this town.

Henry D. Thoreau

The parish church that essayist Thoreau repudiated was the same Unitarian congregation that Emerson left behind. George Ripley, Theodore Parker, and other Unitarians were making similar moves from pulpit or pew, but Thoreau went further than they. He became the forerunner of the millions who claimed to hear not only a different but even a personal drummer, who turned soul-searching into an entirely private affair.

Thoreau first tried to make a career of teaching school and then wrote essays, which almost no one bought. He became more famous when he moved to Walden Pond, which he saw as a kind of sacred place. He made news of a sort when authorities put him in jail the night he refused to pay taxes for support of causes that he rejected. His rebellion began quietly enough in a dispute over whether or not to pay taxes for established religion. The state, he charged, had met him in behalf of the church and commanded him to pay a sum for the support of a clergyman at the church his father attended. The son could not see why the state should tax the schoolmaster to support the priest, but never vice versa. Someone came along at the crucial moment to pay that tax for him when he refused to do so.

Thoreau felt compelled to press further in his bid for freedom from church religion, so he turned nature into his church. "The foregoing generations beheld God and nature face to face; we, through their eyes." Why should not the people of his own time also enjoy an original tie to the universe?

Thoreau well knew that for every one who sympathized with a Hindu bather in a Walden Pond, there were a thousand baptizers on the Baptist trail. In the marketplace he caused no stir. Yet, a century later, people who never read a page of Barton Stone or Francis Asbury still bought Thoreau's *Week on the Concord and Merrimack Rivers*. The first publisher had to unload the unsold copies on the author. "I now have a library of nearly nine hundred volumes," he remarked, "over seven hundred of which I wrote myself." Not until *Walden* sold two thousand copies, five years later, could Thoreau point to any audience at all.

Though an individualist, Thoreau, after the Fugitive Slave Act, also entered the public arena to declare that "to act collectively is according to the spirit of our institutions." Now he called not only for noble men but "noble villages of men." While he favored nonviolence, the bloody raid by John Brown was "the best news that America has ever heard." Yet Thoreau's own abolitionist contributions were chiefly his criticisms of church religion and its support of slavery. Nothing infuriated him more than to hear claims that America was a Christian nation, while its policy toward slaves still crucified a million Christs a day. A republic that stole four million human beings and broke up their families, he thought, showed no triumphant superiority over Muslim nations.

Like so many rejectors, Thoreau carried along on his journey a mixed bag of relics from the past. Though he despised grim Puritan toiling, he could be as priggish as these ancestors ever were in matters of sex. In any balance sheet, however, Thoreau kept less than he threw away, so he needed something with which to fill the void. Through him, oriental religion began to get its first slight hearing in America. Though he sometimes called himself a mystic or transcendentalist, he liked to practice Yoga and called his Hindu-style morning bath at Walden Pond "a religious exercise, one of the best things I did." Later in the day he bathed his intellect in the Bhagavad Gita and the Chinese and Persian scriptures, reading matter entirely beyond the range of earlier New Englanders.

Finding a better way than the churches did to reform the social world was not the true mission of Thoreau. He rejected Christianity because it lived in the past with "an old book," as he called the Bible. Instead of living, the church peddled dogmas; instead of communing with nature, it recited lifeless history. He wanted to overcome, or at least to forget, historical Christianity because it chopped up truth into its many sects. Thoreau was in search of the Whole, which nature and solitude better provided. In his individualism he found a system that spoke to his soul, even if it only added to the bewildering number of spiritual options whose variety the sects merely symbolized.

There was still another way. To follow one who pursued it may seem like a diversion into frivolity, for Orestes Brownson seems through much of his life to be nothing but a sampler of all the religious options of his time. Yet the conclusion of his pilgrimage shows something of another option that began to become more plausible to Americans. They would go on long spiritual odysseys, looking fickle and flighty in their attachments — only to attach themselves, in the end, to churches that had the strongest sense of boundaries. Most notable of these was Roman Catholicism, which began to offer to some the lure that here, at least and at last, was the faith that so antedated and so assuredly would outlast the others, that it was a rock, a refuge, a place of security, a final home for the pilgrim.

Born in 1803 and raised, after his father died, by an elderly couple of relaxed Congregationalists at Royalton, Vermont, Orestes Brownson read the Bible on his own and worked through some sermons of Jonathan Edwards. No wonder he could later say, "Properly speaking, I had no childhood." Townspeople listened, amazed and amused, as he spun out theories of free will in the plan of God. Soon Brownson tried out the revivalist churches, including the Methodist and the primitive gospel "Christian" group. At age fourteen, he moved to Ballston Spa in New York, where he gave Presbyterians a chance, but nothing stirred in him. With adolescent melodramatics he declared that life was a "stream that flows out of darkness into darkness." As an "intellectual desperado" he joined the Presbyterians but soon left with a vengeance, feeling cold and dead to religion.

Brownson went west to Detroit to teach school, but the old debates about Calvinism followed him even there to the frontier. Then, during an illness, he joined Universalism, the most anti-Calvinist church in sight. For a little while he enjoyed the message of a God who loved so much that he damned no one to hell. The Universalists licensed and ordained him to preach, so he moved back east to New Hampshire with the word that he had found the permanent goal of all his strivings; he married, started a family, and busied himself editing *The Gospel Advocate*. Universalism was totally liberating — but that was the problem, because it left him free only for chaos, for every belief he wanted. How could such a system with its unprincipled God bring order to the world?

As Universalism began to lose its sway, Brownson entertained the socialist ideas of Robert Owen, who was fresh from the British Isles hoping to start communities to promote a new moral order that depended on no religion. On a trip to Utica, New York, Brownson was attracted to Frances Wright, whose radical attacks on the churches helped him break with the Universalist ministry. Then he dropped her system after Margaret Fuller and Harriet Martineau joined her in advocating the rights of women too stridently. Not able either to be alone or to give up the search, Brownson spent some time as a Freemason, and steeped himself in the lore of its symbols. It dawned on him that in the winter of his life he was still a skeptic, "lost in the wilderness of doubt." He needed a new religion that would build, he said, and not destroy; it must serve as "the agent to induce men to make the sacrifices required in the adoption of my plans."

To further his plans he became an independent minister. Then he decided that Unitarianism suited him best because it promoted charity and moral feeling; for four years he served in its churches and put his talents to work editing *The Philanthropist*. His autobiographical novel, *The Convert,* found "a believer in humanity" who "put humanity in the place of God." Unfortunately for him, not enough other Americans cared about such humanism, so the magazine failed. He clung to the pulpit work to earn money, some of which he spent on the fashionable French books whose authors promoted a faith in the Absolute in place of the old gods.

In 1836 Brownson felt ready to copy the French style and become the American inventor of a new religion of humanity. "God has appointed us to build the new church," he proclaimed in *New Views of Christianity, Society and the Church*. In *The Convert* he confessed his faith that the whole family of man could fit in the sacred enclosure of "a new religious institution, church, or organization" if only it were devoted to belief in progress. Brownson was so intoxicated with hope that he invented the Church of the Future. Almost at once he experienced what most religious innovators of his type suffered: not a single person joined his worldwide movement. Trying again, he wrote a book on Jesus, with which he hoped to start a religious revolution. No one bought it.

To this point Brownson, a specialist in sampling the cafeteria line of American options while adding his own, looked silly or even pathetic. Yet somehow he stayed in range of people who could influence him toward a more sober future. For six weeks Henry David Thoreau tutored the Brownson children. William Ellery Channing, the great Unitarian spirit, influenced him, and he became friendly with Isaac Hecker, who then called himself a transcendentalist. The two studied Catholicism for six years, but instead of joining the church, Brownson started consorting with a transcendentalist community. The experimenters there for the most part snubbed the newcomer. Ralph Waldo Emerson wanted nothing to do with him, and he, in turn, found Theodore Parker drifting too far toward infidelity. Bronson Alcott and Margaret Fuller were more kind and for a moment gave him a chance to catch their spirit, but soon they also became estranged. Only George Ripley and Isaac Hecker remained patient; "we have sympathized as few men have done," commented Ripley. The more astute Hecker discerned that Brownson, without knowing it, was really pointing himself toward Catholicism. In July of 1844 Hecker turned Catholic, to become the best-known Catholic clerical convert of the century. Brownson followed him the same year, to become the leading lay convert of his day.

Brownson, who finally found the authority his soul was seeking, never left the rock of Catholicism, but his restless spirit never quieted during his remaining thirty-two years. Somehow he found ways to alienate the Catholic left and right, the Irish hierarchy and new immigrants, liberals at one side and conservatives at another. He attacked Protestants with the old slogan that "outside the Church there is no salvation." To Brownson, Parker was now an infidel, Emerson a madman, and Protestants were non-Christian since "orthodoxy is a definite quality and one has it, or has it not." In 1873, three years before he died, after a liberal Catholic phase, Brownson wrote that his greatest mistake had always been to present Catholicism in minimal terms and make it "as little repulsive" as possible to non-Catholics. Apparently far removed from the Emersons and Thoreaus during his last decades in Catholicism, he shared their enterprising and independent spirit in religion during most of his years and showed how difficult it was to sustain the mercurial maverick spirit in or out of religious organizations.

Brownson thus broke with both Protestantism and transcendentalism, and expressed his individualism by identifying with the religion that then best represented continuity and community of civilization from beyond America. Like the transcendentalists, he was looking for the One, the Whole, the All, and found it best in the God of the Roman Catholic church and the system that devoted its faith to Him. In *The Convert,* Brownson summed up his argument: "Protestantism was a schism, a separation from the source and current of the Divine-human life which redeems and saves the world." He who had lived with schism and separations and had caused a few himself never tired of seeking to partake of the Divine-human life, which the apostles infused into the church and the world and which he found accessible through that church.

The fulfillment of his vision was denied, for rather than solve the problem of schism and separation, Brownson was forced to become a part of the "church of his choice" (to quote an American language usage invented to cover the modern situation). But if his was not a solution for everyone, it satisfied the restless soul, as much as the broken world could ever satisfy it. He had found the Truth — and woe be it to all who interrupted their odysseys short of the goal of his own, or who took other paths than his.

Emerson and Thoreau, leaders of churchless religion, chose to become sects unto themselves, while their contemporary Brownson escaped from choice by making the most extreme one in the days of his pilgrimage. If they could not find the innocence or purity they thought America had lost, they looked into various futures, as eagerly as did Disciples of Christ or Mormons in their efforts to begin again, to repudiate the warring sects. The generations saw new sects and utopian communities come and go. What would give cohesion to a republic that many feared would splinter? It was all right to be churchless, since the churches could not serve to promote common values and form a community. But to many seekers, public institutions or the Republic itself had to serve. Thus literary people spoke up once again for public religion.

Novelist Herman Melville at one stage in his life wanted the Republic itself to promote cohesion and mission. He called forth again the language of the elect, but turned it from the Puritan community to the whole nation. Melville quarreled with the Calvinist God with whom he had grown up, and ended by elevating the innocent individual, the American Adam. But for a time along his pilgrimage he idolized the Americans and their nation:

"And we Americans are the peculiar, chosen people — the Israel of our time; we bear the ark of the liberties of the world. . . . God has predestined, mankind expects, great things from our race; and great things we feel in our souls. The rest of the nations must soon be in our rear. We are the pioneers of the world; the advance-guard, sent on through the wilderness of untried things, to break a new path in the New World that is ours. In our youth is our strength; in our inexperience, our wisdom. . . . Long enough have we been skeptics with regards to ourselves, and doubted whether, indeed, the political Messiah had come. But he has come in *us*, if we would but give utterance to his promptings. And let us always remember that with ourselves, almost for the first time in the history of earth, national selfishness is unbounded philanthropy; for we cannot do a good to America, but we give alms to the world."

In those words the dream of American community came to clearest expression. But in the face of the Civil War and eventual shattered hopes, Melville could not sustain this faith in chosenness. In 1876 he wrote the long poem *Clarel* to express his disillusionment. Abraham Lincoln, who more appropriately had chosen to speak of an "almost chosen people," never had to retreat or modify his views the way Melville did.

Melville's contemporary Walt Whitman matched him in celebrating both the innocent individual and the American empire as he rejected the churches as the old bearers of vision. In "Children of Adam," Whitman, called a pagan by the church people, shared the note with which Melville ended, one of disappointed hopes.

> Inquiring, tireless, seeking that yet unfound,
> I, a child, very old, over waves, toward the house of maternity,
>   the land of migrations, look afar, . . .
> Now I face the old home again — looking over to it, joyous, as
>   after long travel, growth, and sleep;
> But where is what I started for, so long ago?
> And why is it yet unfound?

But when the poet did celebrate America, even the Civil War could not shatter him. Whitman foresaw at the fulfillment of the American saga a new union with nature and a proper use of industry, until all people of the world would come into communion.

> All these hearts, as of fretted children, shall be sooth'd,
> All affection shall be fully responded to — the secret shall be told;
> All these separations and gaps shall be taken up, and hook'd
>   and link'd together;
> The whole earth — this cold, impassive, voiceless Earth, shall be
>   completely justified; . . .
> Nature and Man shall be disjoin'd and diffused no more,
> The true Son of God shall absolutely fuse them.

For churched and churchless alike, America was itself becoming the new Beloved Community, to be bound together again after the Civil War.

Churches prospered and declined. Religious communities were invented, had their moments, and were abandoned. One or two new movements like the orthodox Disciples of Christ and the innovative Mormons became part of the permanent landscape. Emerson and Thoreau, Melville and Whitman made names for themselves with their highly individualistic visions. Yet there was, alongside the church, one other repose for the soul, one other generator of group values: the nation itself. The nation came to be a parallel path for Americans on pilgrimage. Sometimes church members were superpatriots who made a kind of religion out of their support of the nation. At other times non–church members saw the nation break the bounds of church religion and serve as a kind of church itself. In all American history, no one more success-fully turned the nation into a spiritual center than did its sixteenth president, Abraham Lincoln.

The crucial career of President Lincoln, preserver of the Union to some and Great Emancipator of slaves to others, illustrates better than that of any other person the fact that not all Americans used the church and synagogue for their spiritual journeys — that much religious striving has been personal or has used vehicles other than religious organizations for its expression. Though Lincoln fre-quently attended New York Avenue Presbyterian Church while in the White House, and while he was respectful of the churches and shaped by the biblical message that they transmitted, he kept some distance from their doings. He was the only president known never to have joined the church. Through much of his life, he therefore was haunted by charges of the pious — the same pious whose de-scendants wanted to remake him posthumously into a great churchly Christian — that the Illinoisan was really an infidel. Whatever his stance toward church religion, Lincoln stands at the spiritual center of American history and increasingly is seen as the theological thinker whose reflections are most apt and most pro-found.

Abraham Lincoln was able to do exactly what Benjamin Franklin long before hoped would happen when he spelled out the necessity of a public religion. As Franklin through his writings assumed, such a faith could draw on the points of agreement or of overlap in the religion of the churches, on what Franklin called "the essentials of every religion." These essentials, each sect would insist, were not to be used to save souls or make sad hearts glad, but they did assist the society in its search for some sort of moral consensus to support public order. This public faith — or, as Lincoln would have it, this political religion — also helped form private character — which was an element in the proposal of Franklin — and clearly helped steel the president for the crises of war. Once more recalling Franklin, the Lincoln version pointed to what the Emancipator considered the excellency of Christianity — as his use of the Bible demonstrated.

In the presidency of Abraham Lincoln, two grand themes in the moral history of the nation converged. When the Civil War came in 1861, Americans reluctantly and with arms took up at last some of the unfinished business of the Enlightenment and the Declaration of Independence. They faced up, with weapons, to what their creed demanded concerning human equality and freedom, and they dealt with the issue of slavery as their predecessors from Thomas Jefferson on did not or could not. At the same time, Lincoln turned to the question of the Union itself and began to make its survival an article of faith. He regarded the Union as mystics concentrate on the One or the All, something he could not surrender, whether with or without slavery. Never idolizing the Union or letting it escape divine judgment, he did see the nation itself as a kind of uncanonical church.

Lincoln came of the Old Scotch-Irish people who made their way west back in the years when revivalists competed with each other for the loyalty of rude migrants on the frontier. The Lincoln family, it is believed, took up with the Separate Baptists, but other revivalists kept working their district, and some of the clan also came under Methodist influence. At the time when Abraham was born, on February 12, 1809, preachers of any sort were few and far between around his birthplace at Hodgenville, Kentucky. Family members recalled however, that little Abe could give imitations of the backcountry preachers, so he must have had some contact with them.

When the Lincoln family later moved to Illinois, young Abraham felt himself "a piece of floating driftwood," unmoored between all the fighting sects. In the course of time he put together his own spiritual fare, independently garnering bits from sources as wide apart as the Bible and skeptic Thomas Paine. For reasons of his own, his sometime law partner William Herndon, never too reliable a witness on matters of this sort, even claimed that Lincoln once wrote an essay against the truth of Christianity. If so, the future president must have had nothing against the Bible, since in 1832, during a race for the state legislature, Lincoln supported free education in order that people would be able to read the Scriptures and other religious works for themselves. The position he took helped him little; he finished eighth out of thirteen candidates.

Before an audience at the Young Men's Lyceum of Springfield, Illinois, in 1838, Lincoln coined a phrase that underscored the call of Franklin. Reverence for laws must produce "the *political religion* of the nation," and this religion, Lincoln went on, should call forth unceasing sacrifice on its altar. The revivalists knew this faith would not suffice for Lincoln's trip to heaven. Methodist circuit rider Peter Cartwright therefore raised the religious issue during their contest for the U.S. Congress in 1846. Two stories, one almost certainly fictional and one based on hard evidence, indicate something of the myth that protected the independent-minded president.

In the legend, Lincoln once planted himself in a congregation and heard Cartwright single him out as Exhibit A of the unconverted type. The boisterous revivalist asked Lincoln where he was going, since all the others present indicated they did not desire to go to hell. As his devotees told it, Lincoln defended himself with dignity by saying he resented being singled out by Brother Cartwright, though he did agree that the questions the preacher raised were of great importance. "I did not feel called upon to answer as the rest did. Brother Cartwright asks me directly where I am going. I desire to reply with equal directness; I am going to Congress."

The discovery of a handbill in 1941 witnesses to the seriousness with which Lincoln had to take charges that he was irreligious. On it the candidate defended himself against claims that he was a scoffer against Christianity. While it was true that he belonged to no church, he said, he never denied the truth of the Scriptures nor spoke with intentional disrespect of religion in general or any denomination in particular. These were deliberately mild affirmations, to say the least. Lincoln also thought that no open enemy of religion or anyone who scoffed deserved public office. The reason was not because the religions were all true but because no one had the right to "insult the feelings, and injure the morals, of the community in which he may live." Lincoln won by a vote of 6,340 to

4,829. Still he felt called to write letters to voters in areas where Cartwright had been strong, charging that never in his life had the revivalist heard Lincoln utter a word that in any way indicated his opinions on religious matters.

After a period of retirement from Washington, Lincoln reentered politics through the forum of his debates in 1858 with Senator Stephen Douglas. Lincoln gained a national base that led him to the White House two years later. Subsequent speeches testify to his political religion. At Buffalo the candidate said he trusted that the Supreme Being would guide him to lead "this favored land." Then at Trenton he marvelously qualified the old notion that Americans were a chosen people with his hope that he might become the humble instrument of the Almighty and of "his almost chosen people." The idea of chosenness endowed the people with a sense of worth, while the notion of being "almost" chosen took some of the fun out of being chauvinist and exclusive.

As president — especially when war came between the North and the South, with slavery as a central, if not the central, issue — Lincoln confessed that he was often driven to his knees by the overwhelming conviction that he had nowhere else to go. But now he felt called to criticize believers who liked to claim that God was exclusively on their side in the war. The Confederate chaplains were leading religious revivals to inspire troops with the rightness of the proslavery cause. Almost to a man the Northern ministers of note connected the will of God with the fate of the North. Liberal Congregationalist Horace Bushnell at Hartford, Connecticut, despite his reputation as a gentle moderate, shouted that the Civil War was "a religion, it is God!" Every drumbeat was a hymn, said the minister; the cannon thundered God, "the electric silence, darting victory along the wires, is the unaudible greeting of God's favoring word and purpose."

Such language repelled Lincoln. According to one story, the president raised bitter questions when a clergyman told Lincoln he hoped "the Lord was on our side." In this telling, Lincoln said that he knew that the Lord was always on the side of the right; it was his only constant anxiety to find the nation on the side of the Lord. When a particularly obnoxious antislavery cleric spoke in arrogance, Lincoln could be sarcastic: "Well, gentlemen, it is not often one is favored with a delegation *direct* from the Almighty."

In September of 1862, at the low point that followed the military loss at Bull Run, Lincoln wrote some lines that came to light only after his death. "The will of God prevails. In great contests each party claims to act in accordance with the will of God. Both *may* be and one *must* be wrong. God cannot be *for,* and *against* the same thing at the same time." The will of God might very possibly differ from that of both sides. Late in 1862 came the spiritual climax of his presidency. In a speech to the Congress, Lincoln spoke of his love of the American land and people and then tried to gather the nation into a congregation: "We shall nobly save or meanly lose the last, best hope of earth."

On the following New Year's Day, Lincoln issued a proclamation emancipating the slaves, invoking the considerate judgment of mankind and the gracious favor of Almighty God as he prosecuted the rest of the war to put the seal on the slaves' freedom. Yet in April Lincoln charged that America had forgotten God. Near the end of the war, in his Second Inaugural, he reminded hearers that both the North and the South read the same Bible, prayed to the same God, and invoked His aid against the other. It may seem strange, he claimed while reviewing slavery, that any man should dare to ask a just God's assistance in wringing his bread from the sweat of other men's faces, but the North dared not in this case judge lest it be judged. Thinking of two contenders, he added: "The prayers of both could not be answered; that of neither has been answered fully. The Almighty has His own purposes." There he left the case.

The words of Lincoln condense American political religion into its classic statement. They affirm the worth of the land and its people and then go on to judge all sections, all parties, all churches. In an age of intense sectarian warfare, Lincoln used the White House as a pulpit to remind citizens with competing viewpoints that they were all too ready to be "equally certain that they represent the divine will." If God wanted to reveal that will, he asked, why did he not do so directly to the president, who wanted to know that will and had to lead the actions? Lincoln more modestly had to "study the plain, physical facts of the case, ascertain what is possible and learn what appears to be wise and right."

The end of the war in 1865 did not produce national unity. The bullet of the assassin that in April of that year took the life of Lincoln did, however, seem to many to place the most eloquent prophet of the American political religion in the front rank of martyrs for the cause. Certainly Lincoln became a pathfinder in a pilgrimage that has beckoned citizens *as* citizens ever since.

This turn–of–the–century photograph, "Class in
American History" by Frances B. Johnston, shows
the children and grandchildren of slaves studying an
American Indian. The site is Virginia's Hampton
Institute, which was founded by the American
Missionary Association as a training center for black
missionaries. (*Collection, The Museum of Modern Art,
New York; gift of Lincoln Kirstein*)

Chapter Twelve

A CENTURY OF EXCLUSION

*D*DESPITE ALL THEIR EXPERIMENTING WITH NEW COMMUNITIES, religious individualism, and turning the nation into a kind of church, Americans in the first half of the nineteenth century mostly remained conventional Protestants. Whether they attended church regularly or not, they thought of themselves as Protestants and seemed content with laws reflecting the general outlook of the majority churches. Pleased with their nation, they wanted it to be somehow homogeneous — a land of shared values and world views encouraging public virtue in the context of a believable moral system.

In their attempt to build a "Righteous Empire," the Protestants knew that they had to keep reforming the nation. And only certain kinds of people truly belonged in it. Thus, their reform efforts might help lead to the abolition of black slavery, but that did not mean that blacks were regarded as equals. Protestant struggles over who should be free and who should truly belong became religious battles. They lasted more than a century and still determine much of national life.

As for reform, the Protestants readily faced up to those personal vices that were not costly to reformers because self-improvement inconvenienced no one except the individuals involved. The voluntary associations and churches moved with passion to eradicate what one might call breaches of the simple virtues: dueling, profanity, drunkenness, whoring. But these same agencies seemed powerless to affect the controversial issues of freedom, equality, and justice, which are complex because their pursuit does inconvenience others.

A whole economy and way of life were based on slavery. For thousands of years people of most cultures, not least of all Christian, took the practice for granted and amassed scriptural texts to justify it. Otherwise humane people saw no inconsistency in their support of it, and their awakening to the light of equality was painfully slow.

The roots of abolitionism went back a full century before the Civil War and the Emancipation Proclamation of 1863. The morally conscious evangelists of the Great Awakening and the enlightened but slaveholding founders who gave the nation its language of rights did not plant the seed, but they helped prepare the soil. In the revivals individuals learned to be responsible for their own souls. As they began to see the bad effects of their own waywardness, they also could see positive results of change. The Enlightenment made claims for equality that waited to be acted upon. As long as slavery survived, how could the awakened know a true millennium, and how could the enlightened truly speak of the pursuit of happiness?

Protestant voices now and then broke the silence. Thus, the Reverend Samuel Hopkins of Newport, Rhode Island, promoted the theme of "disinterested benevolence." In the 1770s he started asking people spontaneously to serve God and do good on earth. Self-interest was the worst sin and slaveholding was the worst form of self-interest. The revivalists insisted that no person had to wait for a reformed world; rebirth at once produced a new world for each transformed person. Hopkins was among the first to say that awakening could not truly take over a heart until its owner freed slaves. As for missions, how could slaves really hear the message of freedom from masters? Hopkins positioned himself to minister to a few slaves in the Congregational churches in Newport, a city strategic in the slave trade, and promoted a rare colonial antislavery booklet, *The Selling of Joseph,* by Judge Samuel Sewall of Boston.

Such scant notices say little for the years of the revivals. From the 1720s to the 1760s, 150,000 new African slaves arrived. The subsequent period of "enlightenment" did nothing to cut into the traffic. The first important questioning of slavery issued from the despised and declining Society of Friends (the Quakers), particularly in the person of John Woolman. Some have later called this traveler and diarist a saint, and saints are not necessarily representative of their sets. Yet Quakerism did produce a climate, an ethos, in which people like Woolman could survive. The Founding Fathers generally overlooked him. Though Benjamin Franklin published Woolman's treatise *Some Considerations on the Keeping of Negroes,* and though their interests overlapped and collided in Pennsylvania, Franklin showed little sign of Woolman's influence and expressed a career-long distaste for most Quakers.

While few sects knew as much about the language of rights as did the Friends, and while they saw themselves as a humane and pacific people, they were not innocent. Prosperous Friends traded in slaves at Newport, lived off investments in them at Philadelphia, and, as Woolman was to find, owned them in the South. In 1696, before these investments were yet great, the Philadelphia Yearly Meeting only timidly chided the traders and asked owners to transmit the faith to slaves, but few listened. A religious group that could effectively weed out offensive people, the Friends found slave owners sufficiently inoffensive. By 1750 only a few local meetings had treated the issue at all; sometimes a member who raised the question was later shunned as a troublemaker by others. Benjamin Lay spoke up at his meeting and his fellow believers thought him insane. Lay ranted against "brave Gospel ministers" who kept slaves so that they could maintain themselves in idleness; he charged that Quakers in plain dress who tolerated slavery only feigned humility. For them were reserved the hottest places in hell. Few listened.

Then in 1758 the Philadelphia Yearly Meeting passed a surprising resolution to exclude slave buyers and sellers. Until that time the members devoted most of their energy to keeping their own groups unspotted from the world. Now they began also to look over their walls at humans in general need. Such acts of conscience had to be costly in religious groups. One of the innovations of the Great Awakening era was a new kind of politics between the pulpit and the pew. Religious leaders, henceforth increasingly dependent upon their ability to attract, convert, hold the loyalty, and then gain the support of people, dared never push them too far. The freedom of choice that came with the revival style permitted a slave owner who did not like to be judged by his fellow Quakers to go shopping for a church down the block. There he could affiliate and no longer face judgment. Some Quakers began to denounce slavery beyond their circle in society at large, and they drew negative response for doing so.

The thread of the antislavery story passes back through Quakerism, then, to its most remarkable member and to his book, the *Journal of John Woolman,* where one can glimpse the beginning of a turn in the New World. The Woolmans were comfortable landholders in the valley of the Rancocas River in New Jersey, where in 1720 John was born. He was a simple child who responded to both nature and his own inner stirrings. He enjoyed the stable world of his parents and was content to sit with them in the silence that ordinarily spelled their Quaker meetings. Woolman passed through the stages of conversion, evidently quite independently of any onslaughts by revivalists.

The young Friend found that he preferred shopkeeping to farming. When Woolman displayed a gift for the field of law, his employer put him to work executing legal documents. This boss owned a Negro slave, whose presence evidently was so taken for granted that in Woolman's mind she blended in invisibly. Then one day in 1742 the employer casually asked his clerk to write up a bill of sale for the woman. This was not an act perpetrated by a man who wanted to test or embarrass his worker, but an ordinary request that meant no more than if he were to ask for a bill for a bag of potatoes. Woolman automatically set out to obey, but then found that in distress he could not write. The buyer, he knew, was an elderly person, a good one, a "member of our Society," a Friend. Keeping all that in mind, he somehow was able to complete the bill of sale. Woolman became depressed, however, and told his employer that slave keeping now seemed inconsistent with the Christian religion. Witnessing in this manner quieted him, but he kept on wishing that the man would excuse him from anything that went so much against conscience.

When a second Quaker asked the young clerk to draw up a bill of sale for a slave, Woolman found he had to refuse. While many in the Society seemed at ease with the practice, he had to speak up. The owner then admitted that keeping slaves was disagreeable to him as well, that this slave was a gift to his wife from friends. When Woolman recorded his impressions, he avoided the language of the crusader. Instead, we read: "I was distressed," "I was depressed," "I was not easy." To be more free of legal duties, he concentrated on his skills as a tailor. Then, late in 1743, he did what so many Americans have done when called to a cause: he mounted horseback to spread the word as a minister of the Society of Friends.

A Quaker itinerant was among the lower forms of colonial life.

John Woolman had no power base from which to thunder, no access to the press, no slogans or grand theories to propound. He only offered his life and later his *Journal,* but somehow he was heard. On the frontier, where he welcomed the hospitality of the poor, Woolman often slept on cabin floors. But he also came into the range of power and, finding slavery a dark gloominess hanging over the land, he emboldened his words and pressed slave owners over the issue. "What . . . shall we do when God riseth up?" Eventually, he broke an ageless barrier and called the slaves his brothers, insisting that God never extended favors uniquely to one nation exclusive of others. Not since the days of Bartolomé de Las Casas, who thus identified with Indians but not with Negroes, had language this clear been sounded, or voiced with so much moral plausibility. Woolman chose not to crusade, in part because he never liked to offend sober people, but also because he admitted that he needed money and wanted friends. Without raising his voice, he would say he "had a scruple" in his mind against noisy styles of moral reform.

As early as 1746 he began writing *Some Considerations on the Keeping of Negroes,* which he tested on "overseers" at the Yearly Meeting in 1753 and then published in two parts in 1754 and 1762. His language anticipated that of the Age of Reason: "If I purchase a man who hath never forfeited his liberty, the natural right of freedom is in him." Later the tone became more urgent, as he spoke of how God held scales in which He weighed mountains. Those scales at last were turning against America, because the Parent of all mankind could not forever overlook the slaves. The day must come when He would turn the channels of power, humble the haughty, give deliverance to the oppressed, and, as the "end and event of things," bring down America if it did not change.

In 1757 Woolman made a second journey into the South, where he found slave owners tense and even hostile to him. As Quakers, these hosts at first quite naturally opened their doors to him, but he offended them by insisting that he pay for the lodging — after which he confessed that even this quiet kind of witness gave him much inward suffering. The itinerant returned with new resolves to agitate at the Philadelphia Yearly Meeting in 1758.

At almost any other time, the Yearly Meeting would have been a forgettable event for everyone except those who took part in it. With some poetic license, Quaker poet John Greenleaf Whittier, however, called 1758 "one of the most important religious convocations in the history of the Christian church." Of course, it was far less than that, but the Meeting did appoint the first committee to begin working to abolish slavery, deciding to attack first the Newport slave trade.

Woolman was on the examining team that went to the Rhode Island port to see the slave ships at close hand. His *Journal* records how his appetite failed. He grew outwardly weak, and had a feeling of the condition of the prophet Habakkuk: "When I heard, my belly trembled, my lips quivered, I trembled in myself, that I might rest in the day of trouble." His stomach was so tender that he could not even bring himself to the wharf itself, nor did he gain access to the legislature, though he prepared an essay to be presented to it. The mission merely left a few upset Quakers who had investments in the slave trade, and some informed consciences among other Friends who lived in Newport.

Instinctively, the conscience of Woolman also stirred when he thought of the native Americans, the other overlooked people. While later abolitionists looked back on him as the first effective voice raised against Negro slavery in America, in his own time it was almost as dangerous for a member of the Society of Friends in Pennsylvania to speak up for Indians as for Negroes.

As Woolman compared the lives of the transplanted Europeans that he met along nine hundred miles of coast with those of slaves and Indians, his feeling of doom kept growing. "In this lonely journey I did greatly bewail the spreading of a wrong spirit." Only calamity and desolation awaited this continent, and he felt almost powerless against the evils. At the very least, he decided that he personally could shun anything that had to do with slave trade. This commitment led him to wear only undyed clothes; he refused to use rum, sugar, or anything else that linked consumers to the ships of slave traders.

It would be nice to see Woolman's life build to a grand climax, to some clear achievement in the field of human rights. But his personal life seemed increasingly to meander and lose point. For reasons never made fully clear, Woolman boarded a ship for England in 1772; when he arrived, he began to make the rounds of Quaker meetings. The London Yearly Meeting paid him almost no attention. While visiting York, he became a victim of a smallpox outbreak, and Quakers there risked their lives to treat him. They watched him die and tenderly saw to his burial.

In the next century, when reformers began to work seriously for the emancipation of slaves and the abolition of slavery, few took direct inspiration from the *Journal of John Woolman*. To violent abolitionists, he appeared too gentle, while practical reformers found few reasons to follow the trail of his leisurely spiritual journal. To the hasty, he appeared to be too much the gradualist, while progressives never have welcomed the prophecies of doom and disaster that seers feel called to propagate. Despite the burdens of his inheritance, the *Journal* remains a classic, among the better personal documents of his century, to be remembered alongside the best work of Benjamin Franklin and Jonathan Edwards, a quiet revelation of the American soul on its sacred journey.

In Quaker circles, it is possible that his witness did create some ripple effects. The New England Yearly Meeting came to vote disciplinary acts against members who were in the slave trade. Even though the Pennsylvania Abolition Society grew up partly under Quaker influence, Benjamin Franklin, a former slaveholder and no friend of Friends, helped lead it. George Washington called the conscientious motions of Quakers malapropos, ill-judged pieces of business that occasioned a great waste of time. If such ideas were to spread, his own slaves might find them too great a temptation to resist. Patrick Henry agonized over the fact that some of his fellow citizens could be humane and mild, meek and gentle, yet still hold on to a practice as repugnant to liberty as slavery. "I will not, I cannot, justify" slavery. But, he "inconveniently" kept his own slaves and announced he could do no more than lament, which was all the best of his fellow citizens also found to do.

Woolman belongs to the long prehistory of the moral and social reform that erupted during the half-century between the Second Great Awakening and the Civil War. Those were the years in which slavery began to haunt the righteous empire of the dominating evangelical Protestants. In the South, church leaders came to defend the institution of slavery as the will of God. In the North, it seemed too plaguing for them to overthrow. The moralists simply busied themselves with the reform of attractive vices while they evaded the evil that brought injustice to millions and was to tear the nation itself apart.

The Protestants of the day liked to look out on the empire they were building and pronounce it good, though not very good. Early in the century they were able to chase the infidel from the scene, to keep Catholic Europe at a distance, and to begin to win a sizable number of people to their church rolls. Yet when they compared the United States to the millennial kingdom still to come, they found faults. Though the civil and religious spheres of life were increasingly separated, Protestants still made efforts to pass laws in their own favor, but they also found it valuable to form voluntary groups that crisscrossed lines between denominations, between clergy and laity, between men and women. Their errand of mercy could not be effective, however, without the presence of professional preachers, who could scold the people and prophesy a better world ahead.

One of the most ambitious of the Presbyterian preachers who embodied the new ministerial style was the Reverend Lyman Beecher. Like many colleagues, he promoted the ideal of "sameness," the renewed dream of an organic and tightly knit community made up of like-minded people who worshiped the same God the same way and who imparted to one another a sense of wholeness. Beecher was a master of the jeremiad, or scolding sermon; he realized the limits of his vision. From his New England parsonage in 1812 he complained that the mass of people were changing, that they were becoming another people. Too many hands, he mourned, pulled at the foundation and too few repaired the breaches. The building was tottering and might go down forever. Because American decline was a gradual process, Beecher feared that almost no one would notice it. So he felt called to drag into the public eye "the whole army of conspirators against law and order." In 1815, in an address to an earnest group with a typical name, the Charitable Society for the Education of Indigent Pious Young Men for the Ministry of the Gospel, he thought there was still time, but only a little time, to produce "a sameness of views, and feelings, and interests which would lay the foundation of our empire upon a rock."

Nothing would be more unfair to Beecher than to picture him consistently in a warning or mourning mood. He was typically manic about possibilities for the evangelical empire that America was becoming. As a self-appointed cheerleader and coach of a generation, he wrote in 1812 that "we are rather looking up with hope than desponding." His daughter Harriet Beecher Stowe remembered the glow and glory that came from the house of her father; its atmosphere was "full of moral oxygen and intellectual energy."

A catalog of the societies for mission and reform at that time suggests the moral oxygen and energy that filled the air elsewhere, too. The giants were the American Bible Society, the American Colonization Society, the American Home Mission Society, the American Sunday-School Union, and the American Tract Society, all founded in the decade after 1816. In their shadow were national, state, and local agencies devoted to female moral reform, to the suppression of vice and the promotion of good morals, to the encouragement of faithful domestics, to promoting manual labor in literary institutions, and, of course, to the promotion of temperance. Builders of the Protestant empire like Beecher constantly looked for unfilled moral crannies or niches and did so in an environment that nurtured their efforts to improve the world and to reshape it into the millennial kingdom.

The Beecher household displayed something of the talent available and the human damage to family members that accompanied the strivings. Some of the thirteen children became famous. Harriet wrote *Uncle Tom's Cabin,* the best-selling novel that spurred sentiment against slavery and helped induce the Civil War. The wife of a professor of Bible teaching, she made her name by writing moralistic fiction through a career that lasted three decades. Her brother Henry Ward was a mild abolitionist and a bold publicist who became the prince of the American pulpit in his generation. Brother Edward founded the first college in Illinois and became its president. A lifelong abolitionist, he guarded the press of Elijah P. Lovejoy when a mob came to murder the emancipation-minded publisher.

As for the father: under President Timothy Dwight at Yale young Lyman had been well trained to demolish infidels and revive religion in a day when the French Revolution and Thomas Jefferson looked like the Antichrist at worst, as threats to American morals at best. Beecher's education did not lead him into an otherworldly disdain for politics; he developed a trust in politicians and common people alike, whether or not sectarian interests moved them.

Beecher wanted his first congregants at East Hampton, Long Island, to be a sort of new Northampton, the theater in which to make memorable if improbable displays for God; but he found it hard to move people. First off, he decided to attack dueling, which was hardly a threat any longer. Though the practice was disappearing, Aaron Burr had incited Beecher by mortally wounding Alexander Hamilton in a duel in 1804, an event that caused a wide sensation and led Beecher to name it the "great national sin." Some of his ministerial colleagues objected to his meddling in such issues, but he enjoyed being able to "switch 'em, and scorch 'em, and stamp on 'em," until he had a taste of public victory.

In his bones Beecher, as an émigré from New York, had to know that churchly establishment was doomed everywhere, but in his second parish, Litchfield, Connecticut, he lobbied to keep it alive. In September of 1818, he mourned to see the state legislature vote 134 to 61 against tax-supported religion, and then in October he listened for the popular-vote count that at last overwhelmed the church's legal privilege: "They slung us out like a stone from a sling." His daughter Catharine remembered years later how her father reacted as he sat in one of the old-fashioned rush-bottom kitchen chairs, his head drooping on his breast, his arms hanging down. In that uncomfortable posture, as she vividly recalled, he spoke of the vote that day as the worst thing that ever happened to Connecticut. Only days later, however, he was preaching that the outcome was the best thing that state had ever seen. Now the Northern evangelical churches were free and voluntary, ready with their own resources.

Beecher moved to Boston in 1826, there better to support his family with its three newest children and to take up Calvinist defenses against the newest covey of heretics, the Unitarians. From Park Street Church at the edge of the Common, he fired verbal fusillades at these new infidels and then settled in at his own Hanover Church pulpit. There for six years he fought a losing battle against the liberals — all the while liberalizing his own system. With the aid of Yale professor Nathaniel William Taylor, he worked to soften the harder edges of Calvinism until their enemies grew suspicious — worried lest these moderates move into halfway houses along the road to Unitarianism (which to Calvinists was the "half-way house to infidelity").

The geography of his ministry to this point gave Beecher reasons to postpone facing the issue of slavery. When he followed the call of the New West, he could no longer evade it. The Presbyterians needed a president to head the new Lane Theological Seminary with its hundred students in the Queen City of Cincinnati. Daughter Catharine and he spied out the place, pronounced the semi-Southern city a future paradise, and prepared to make it the strategic center for western operations. In those days Beecher was suspecting a deep-laid Catholic conspiracy to outpace the Protestants in what remained of the American West. Thus preoccupied, Beecher underestimated the issue of slavery, which was now dividing the South from the North and tearing apart the Protestant network.

Cincinnati and the students at Lane wasted little time putting the newcomer to his test, chiefly through a challenge by the abolitionist Theodore Dwight Weld. Weld was a convert of Charles Grandison

Finney, a showier and more influential revivalist than his less mobile competitor Beecher. Because Weld wanted to move against slavery, he became a hero to his fellow students. Beecher had gone only so far as to list slavery, along with infidelity and Catholicism, as the enemy of God's kingdom in the West, but he knew his trustees would never support a radical seminary in that border area. His son-in-law Calvin E. Stowe later remarked that Lyman unconsciously held to a few of his old Connecticut prejudices against blacks and was too busy to correct them. Weld, whose arguments Mrs. Stowe had openly borrowed for her *Uncle Tom's Cabin,* had little else but abolition on his mind, and he converted most of his colleagues to his position as he busied them with work among blacks in Cincinnati.

President Beecher, serenely confident that his trustees and the Cincinnati clientele backed his position, found it advisable to go on the road in search of funds for his troubled seminary at the time of the confrontation. Daughter Catharine sat in for him while faculty and students wrangled through eighteen nights. Weld alone contributed eighteen hours of talk to debate. In the manner of revival meetings, the mood was alternately serious and entertaining, the outcome expectable. Beecher and the trustees chose the gradualist approach, which in Cincinnati really meant that they would do nothing, so the students voted with their bodies. Beecher grieved to see 28 of them leave on October 15, 1834, to be followed by 11 the next day and a straggler still one day later. In all, 37 of the 40 theology students were gone, and when the exodus was over, only 5 of the 60 in the literary department remained. Even prospective students made their stand against Beecher clear.

The students, "he-goat" Weld among them, converged on Oberlin Collegiate Institute in Ohio after being recruited by founder John Shippherd. There they fell under the influence of activist revivalists and reformers. Beecher then chose to put his energies into the Second Presbyterian Church, which had also called him to Cincinnati and where he spent eleven declining years of ministry until members ousted him over a petty Sunday-school matter.

As his power began to waste — a pathetic phrase for a lion like Lyman Beecher! — depression, he said, appeared, like a gray, wintry cloud over his sky. All his life he had looked back on the Founding Fathers as "a race of men as never before laid the foundations of empire," and he had looked forward to the grand millennium. Now he had to acknowledge that his own generation could not face up to the most plaguing moral issue of the day, and his leadership failed at that point.

Others of his tribe tried to keep the cheering going. Albert Barnes, a friend, spoke in the language of hope: "In the era of better things, which is about to rise in the world, our land shall be first," At Hartford, Connecticut, the preeminent liberal minister Horace Bushnell, a Congregationalist, still boasted that America was the grand experiment of Protestantism, that American destiny would still show unheard-of national greatness and moral capabilities through these people God chose in a world he reserved for his purposes. But Barnes and Bushnell no more than Beecher knew how to prevent the deepest division ever to split the nation.

The moralists were always stumped when challengers asked how Negroes would act if they were free. The critics assumed that blacks were inferior, incapable of running their own affairs. Even Christian people who cared about Negro souls — and not all of them did — often remained paternalistic and showed no faith in the possibilities of blacks. The people all failed to look around them, for during this period there developed the most powerful and durable of black institutions of the century, the freemen's churches. These churches, the spiritual creations of blacks, bring us to the main subjects of the slavery story themselves — and to Richard Allen, the patriarch of the strongest early Negro denomination, the pioneer who wanted Christian blacks to write their own story inside the otherwise white Protestant empire.

Like the other black pathfinders, he came out of slavery. Allen was born in 1760 to a slave owned by a Philadelphian who sold Richard and his family to a "kind master . . . more like a father," near Dover, Delaware. Unfortunately, this master Stokely fell upon hard times and had to sell members of the Allen family one at a time until only two others were left with Richard, who never again saw the rest of his family. In the face of boredom in the field, restless young Allen started becoming aware of alternatives to his way of life whenever circuit riders sent by Bishop Asbury galloped onto the plantation. In the course of time he experienced rebirth and began to show talent of his own as an exhorter to his companions.

John Wesley and Francis Asbury liked to teach Methodists to set goals for themselves on the road toward perfection. Allen aimed to purchase his freedom, so he agreed on terms with Stokely. Both Richard and his brother eventually met the price and became free, which meant they now had to face problems of survival in what was then a seriously depressed economy.

Allen felt called to preach. In a day when even the top missionary leader, Bishop Asbury, was dreadfully poor and other itinerants were even more deprived, clearly a black itinerant would be abjectly poor. Yet Allen wanted to travel for the cause, and for a time did so. Because Asbury's policy allowed him no access to slaves, Allen decided to strike out on his own, and he did odd jobs to support his preaching in Philadelphia. With some followers he formed a Free African Society, and after a snub during worship at Saint George's in Philadelphia, they founded their own little church, which they named Bethel. To celebrate this event, the members listened to the Reverend Daniel Coker rouse his fellows with the boast that from now on no one could make them afraid again. Words like his inspired a meeting of five fledgling congregations in 1816; they formed the first Methodist General Conference for free blacks, and chose to follow the discipline of the Methodist Episcopal church. The conferees offered prayers of thanks for their freedom from the "spiritual despotism" of the bad years and named Allen first an elder and then their bishop.

Not many years after these freedmen invented their church organization, desperate militants inspired slave revolts. They used the only language available to them, the biblical phrases they had learned on the plantations. Each became a Moses or a messiah, and each compared his efforts to the exodus of Israel, just as years before the American Puritans read the story of their own migration into the biblical account. Thus, an acquaintance of Allen, Denmark Vesey, blended African folk religion with the Christianity he had picked up. Vesey, who had bought his freedom after winning a Charleston lottery, inspired one such revolt. Vesey hoped to seize Charleston in 1822, but a conspirator alerted the authorities, who disrupted the plot. They hanged Vesey along with thirty-four other accused rebels and the South thenceforth toughened its codes against slaves. But such policies could not stifle all urges to freedom. In 1831 Nat Turner, a Virginian who also saw himself as an agent of God, gathered about seventy slave associates and with them killed fifty-one white people before they were similarly put down.

For every leader who preached the implausible hope of violent revolt, there were hundreds who took steps like those of Allen to help their fellows within the cramping bounds that the times imposed. No revolutionaries at all, the Allens were as meticulous about church order as Asbury ever was. Yet so successful were they at attracting freemen who craved a better way of life that a century later black intellectual W. E. B. Du Bois, hardly an admirer of organized religion, called the African Methodist Episcopal church "the greatest Negro organization in the world."

Bishop Allen faithfully and autocratically made the rounds and carried on oversight of the first 6,748 Methodists under his care around Philadelphia, Baltimore, and Charleston. Though he dreamed of unity, Allen saw freemen oppose each other in black denominations that were as full of conflict as were those of whites. He failed to find terms for merger with the new African Methodist Episcopal Zion church that grew up originally in New York. Though such competition frustrated him, Allen poured energies into welfare work, mutual aid, and preaching. He and his colleagues inspired members with hopes of heaven while they imparted dignity to blacks in their daily struggles.

A new lure came along in these years in the form of the American Colonization Society, which whites founded on New Year's Day in 1817. While America was as much the homeland of free Africans as it was of European immigrants, Allen and his kind expressed increasing interest in blacks' ancestral continent. Since whites permitted them no missions in the American South, they set out to convert Africa. Some envisioned that the Colonization Society, which sought to solve the slavery problem by shipping blacks back to Africa, could be an ally. Such hopes created a strain for men like Richard Allen and fellow cleric Absalom Jones, who opposed the ACS as much as they promoted African missions. Jones did what he could to keep Society vice-president Robert Finley away from the black community. Something, he thought, must be wrong with the ACS scheme if a slaveholder and colonizer like Henry Clay in Kentucky, who called free blacks pernicious, could call on ACS members to promote moral fitness by restoring liberated blacks to Africa.

Allen, to clear the air, decided to host a debate for three thousand people at Bethel. While he did not scorn colonization out of hand, he told the audience that he mistrusted the pushiness of whites who were trying to determine the destiny of his people. But he also moved on to ask why other Americans should uproot blacks from their churches and lodges and schools, only to dump them in abandoned corners of Africa. Such a stand forced him to explain why he opposed the "good men" who were colonizers. He was eloquent in *Freedom's Journal* in 1827: "This land, which we have watered with our tears and our blood, is now our mother country, and we are well satisfied to stay where wisdom abounds and the gospel is free." David Walker, another anticolonizer, dared anyone to try to budge blacks even one step. "America is more our country than it is the whites' — we have enriched it with our *blood and tears.*" The congregation at "Mother Bethel" church also reminded America that African ancestors, though brought here against their will, were the first successful cultivators of the wilds of America. Their descendants now felt entitled to share the richness of her soil, "which their blood and sweat manured."

Long before Emancipation, the pulpits of these freemen started sounding with calls for a new black Americanism. In 1837 Samuel E. Cornish defended the name of his paper, *Colored American,* by arguing that in complexion and nativity, blacks were more exclusively American then their white brethren and no one should think of them as exotics. In 1833 James Forten resorted to satire as he recalled that in the War of 1812 he personally had recruited twenty-five hundred blacks to defend Philadelphia. For seventy years he had lived in that city, yet now, he all but sneered, some ingenious gentlemen figured out he was still an African! If such folk would deposit him on an African shore, would they expect him to recognize the old hut his fathers lived in a hundred years ago? Let whites have their colonization plans; blacks, unmoved, were here to stay.

Freemen dared to speak boldly, but slave Christians had no chance to develop national leaders with well-known names like Allen and Jones. Revolts were all but impossible in the world of plantations, which were so widely spaced that no large number of blacks could get together. Swamps and dogs threatened escapees, posses were always ready to rein in those who wandered, and the worst kind of punishments were prepared for offenders. Still there developed a grapevine through which enslaved believers became aware of each other and developed their own blend out of African religion and the Christian faith that their masters dispensed to them.

Visitors from Europe or the North, occasional masters, and the children and grandchildren of slaves left precious records of what plantation religion was like. Curiously, even there sectarian disputes divided the worshipers. When Methodists and Baptists debated the different ways to baptize, slaves turned out to cheer for their own sides. In their terms they debated the very issues that divided Calvinists from Arminians. One familiar story of a Mississippi slave gravedigger in conversation with a white visitor shows a logic that remains compelling:

"Massa, may I ask you something?"
"Ask what you please."
"Can you 'splain how it happened in the fust place, that the white folks got the start of the black folks, so as to make dem slaves and do all de work?"

Not wanting to see the stranger riled, a helper of the gravedigger quickly intervened:

"Uncle Pete, it's no use talking. It's fo'ordained. The Bible tells you that. The Lord fo'ordained the Nigger to work, and the white man to boss."
"Dat's so. Dat's so. But if dat's so, then God's no fair man!"

Many white Christians tried to convince slaves that their bondage was a mark of sin because God cursed their biblical ancestor Ham, the wicked son of Noah, back in the days of the Genesis Flood. This myth, which so pleased the masters, did not find acceptance among slaves. Of course, they accepted the idea of sin and they hoped for heaven, but they also had a daily life to live and needed to make sense of it. The spirituals they sang often served a double purpose: the same songs spoke openly of hope beyond life and, in code language, about underground railroads on the way to freedom. While they could not hope for revolt, such slaves did find dignity and meaning under the whip through their persistent faith.

Like white Christians, it was up to each of the slaves to "get religion," American style. All of them were, directly or indirectly, uprooted from African tribal settings; family traditions through the generations meant little to the people who bought and sold them. Their dislodgment led them to the voluntary style of revivalist faith. For some owners, of course, religion existed less for conversion than control. Thus one Thomas Affleck advised masters to devote an hour to moral and religious instruction each Sunday in order to produce better-disciplined slaves. Former slaves remembered the different ways they spent Sunday. One named John Brown talked about life in Alabama back when Sunday was a great day. People hurried through light chores and then forgot the fields in order to get ready for the church meetings in the huge front yard. The wife of the master always started the meeting and then all would burst into singing "the old timey songs." Brown recalled by contrast that white folks on the very next plantation whipped their slaves for trying to do the same: "No praying there, and no singing."

Given their generally bad state of health and care, slaves turned both to faith and to magic for healing. Often they combined bits of African conjuring rites with Christian plantation teaching. Whether for such ceremonies or for conventional Christian messages, it was natural that they preferred to hear black preachers, gifted people who knew how to thread their way between what the owner permitted them to say and what their listeners desired to hear about Moses and Jesus. Former slave Anthony Dawson reminisced: "Mostly we had white preachers, but when we had a black preacher, that was heaven." And Litt Young from Mississippi recalled how the preacher would say, "Obey your master," when the master was there, but when she left, "he came out with straight preachin' from the Bible."

Unfortunately for the slaves who heard the message of freedom in the Bible, their masters found a license for slavery in the same book. In the early days, when Francis Asbury urged his men to oppose human bondage, Methodists resolved to stand behind any circuit riders who expelled slave-trading members from the church. Thomas Coke backed the words in the *Discipline,* which spelled out that no slave owner should be allowed at the Lord's Supper.

In the course of time, however, slavery became so webbed into the economy and custom that Methodists, in the heat of churchly competition, learned that when they pushed too hard, people simply signed up with Baptists or Presbyterians, who endorsed slavery. Rather than lose the game, Methodists compromised, beginning as early as six months after their first strong stand in 1784. Yes, they announced, they abhorred slavery, but they would use only wise and prudent means to destroy it. Mere prudence won. Revivalists who once called slavery a sin came to decide that it was wiser to be silent than to have owners block their access to the souls of slaves. This policy seemed to work, and Asbury was not ready to argue with success. By the time Allen organized his church, the Methodists already claimed 42,500 black converts. Asbury came to ask just how much personal liberty meant to an African if weighed against the salvation of his soul. After the death of Asbury, the Methodists in 1816 adopted a report that admitted they were powerless to abolish the evil.

In 1837 and 1838, the Presbyterians divided into New School and Old School factions, partly following North-versus-South lines. Slavery was only one veiled issue in the schism, but Presbyterians in the South thereafter came to support slavery with formidable biblical arguments. In 1845 the congregational Baptist church also divided on sectional lines, never to reunite. Tightly organized Methodism presents the most dramatic story of separation. Across boundaries of North and South, Methodists were supposed to be united and interconnected through their *Discipline*. Yet in the face of slavery, even their faith and order meant little. Northern Methodism produced noisy critics of slavery, quieter abolitionists, and silent fence-sitters, while Southern Methodists owned slaves and defended ownership. Each side argued on the basis of the same Bible. Usually as a result of marriage to slave owners, but sometimes because they purchased blacks, by the 1830s some Southern Methodist clergy openly admitted that they held slaves. National leaders, when pressed, tried to hold the church together by evading the issue. When the crisis came in the mid-1840s, 13 percent of the Methodists, 145,000 in all, were of African background.

In 1836 the General Conference first refused to elect a bishop because he owned slaves, an action that provoked Southerners to start setting up their own shop, including in 1840 a Southern Book Concern. When the conference met in May of that year, voting followed regional patterns. On one issue there was no one to break a 69–69 tie. The stalemate portended a short-term victory for Southerners, but they also pressed for division, grumbling that Northern Methodists were substituting social issues for the task of converting people.

When the General Conference met in 1844, America was in turmoil over anti-Catholic riots in Philadelphia and over the choice of candidates for the political campaigns that fall. Yet the press converged on the conference and especially on Bishop James Osgood Andrew, who had owned slaves gotten by inheritance and marriage. Andrew was embarrassed by the spotlight, but Southern colleagues would not permit him to resign. He decided to defend slavery as a domestic arrangement that lay beyond the scope of busybodies. As debates turned heated, visitors crammed the galleries, while the chair tried with little success to keep order. This year the Northerners were present in good numbers and won the vote: 110 against, versus 68 in favor of slaveholding bishops. On June 10 the era of Asbury and his dream of a united church ended with this beginning of secession by Southerners.

Ministers in border areas suffered most. They had to attempt ministry where people on both sides had already made up their minds about slavery. Most preachers wanted simply to lead revivals and save souls, but they were captives of clienteles on whom they had to draw for support. Some now complained of a "thirst for applause" that made many a minister timid. British visitor Harriet Martineau thought that a magic ring circled those who lived with slavery. People who thought within the circle, she said, could never think beyond it. Clergy to her seemed quiet and gentlemanly people who preached about the four seasons and the attributes of the Deity. Only once did she ever hear from the pulpit any reference to the grand truths of religion or principles of morals. While the ministers were not vicious or greedy men, they were simply guilty of the idolatry of opinion and thus were "self-exiled from the great moral questions of the time." One citizen who sidled up to her observed that to grown people, the clergy seemed to be "a sort of people between men and women."

Not all Northern leaders were timid. People like Wendell Phillips surprised audiences by blending old Calvinism and new abolitionism, though it was easier for Unitarians like Theodore Parker and Thomas Wentworth Higginson, whose liberal fellowships expected to be shocked, to be abolitionists. Some Quakers kept the antislavery witness alive, while at Oberlin, Charles Grandison Finney, and, more particularly, Theodore Dwight Weld helped produce a generation of agitators. Despite such exceptions, the burden of outcry gradually shifted to people whose religion was not confined in the churches.

The new day began when William Lloyd Garrison first published *The Liberator* in 1831. Garrison was on a pilgrimage from Baptist beginnings through the Presbyterian flock of Lyman Beecher and then beyond perfectionism to an inspiration he gained from the book that came to be a scripture to him, *Uncle Tom's Cabin*. His career typified the love-and-hate relation abolitionists expressed toward revivalist Protestantism. They often scolded the churches by quoting biblical texts on freedom, and threw Christian words about equality back at the meek preachers. Finally abolitionist William Goodell came out with a clear program: the antislavery organizations must fill a void; they had to be "united together to do what *the Church OUGHT* to do." When liberal preacher Moncure Conway saw Garrison burn a copy of the United States Constitution at a Fourth of July service, he carried the trend further. Garrison now belonged, Conway thought, in a line of prophets that included John the Baptist, Luther, Wesley, and George Fox. "That day I distinctly recognized that the anti-slavery cause was a religion." Phrasemaker Henry Ward Beecher put the best word on it all when he called the abolition movement an "uncanonical Church" of the best kind, a church that was held together not by ordination but by faith and principle.

The upheavals of the era tended to come together, one kind of revolution easily attaching itself to another. While the antislavery impulse was developing, an awakening of women began to occur, especially in the "uncanonical Church" in this time when the canonical church clearly allowed them too small a role. Religious feminism and antislavery issues began to fuse when significant numbers of women in each cause blended them. Thus suffragist Elizabeth Cady Stanton, in a letter to Lucy Stone in 1856, linked the two concerns. While the bondage of the Negro slave differed from that of women, said Stanton, it "frets and chafes her just the same. She too sighs and groans in her chains; and lives but in the hope of better things to come." To connect two of the less popular and more emotional issues of the day hurt both campaigns, but feminists had to speak.

The women's cause as it moved from early stirrings at midcentury until the constitutional amendment assuring woman suffrage in 1920 was largely in the hands of women. They had to form their own coalitions, and many of the religious resources came from women in the revivalist tradition and the missionary movement — or from beyond the circle of the churches entirely. Some of the early woman-suffrage legislation also appeared, curiously and ironically, in states and territories dedicated to conserving Puritan and traditional old-stock values. Yet the overall effect of the feminist cause was to promote the coherent idea of a coming realm of greater justice and freedom for all, including the majority gender in society and the entire human race.

In 1869, the year when the transcontinental railroads met in Utah, the threat of numerous outsiders arriving in once-remote Zion disturbed the Mormons. Many gentiles agreed that the Latter-Day Saints had good reason to be concerned about holding on to their Kingdom as a preserve. One gentile prophesied that "when the United States goes to Utah, Mormonism will disappear like a puddle with Niagara Falls turned into it." To assure that their influence would not suddenly disappear, the Mormons decided to rule out the threat of immigrants by ruling in women at the polls.

Thus they doubled their phalanx against the factionalized gentiles. A Mormon bishop boasted that when the women of Utah voted, they voted for the tried friends of the church. When in 1886 the U.S. Congress prepared to vote against permitting woman suffrage in Utah, two thousand Mormons gathered with such a show of unified force that the first line of their resolution was almost literally true: "Resolved by the women of Utah in mass meeting assembled. . . ." Nowhere else could citizens create the impression that they could gather *all* the women of a territory or state for virtually unanimous activity.

Sparsely settled Wyoming, on similar grounds even though it lacked a single, powerful church, became the first territorial jurisdiction to pass woman suffrage. Only a few settlers had arrived by 1869. Only one person per twelve square miles lived in Wyoming's expanse, but the railroads, as in Utah, threatened the values brought by the first Protestant stock. These old settlers called the transients "hell on wheels" because they were lawless men who only wanted to get rich quick in mining or ranching and then be on their way. Though transient, the newcomers often stayed long enough to vote. The way to outvote them was to double the number of people who held to the old ways. In 1868 the Wyoming Territory in its first legislature adopted woman suffrage and certified its support with more sincere interest in female equality than Utah ever showed. With the help of women, some of whom were selected as jurors, Wyoming enforced Sunday-closing laws and won other issues that Protestants used to assert themselves.

The events of 1869 were part of a long prehistory to battle lines Americans drew in the 1920s. Decades passed before anyone else followed up on these early victories for women. In the years before suffragism won, leadership came increasingly into the hands of women who could and did count little on church support. In most cases the churches excluded women from ministry, at a time when most other professions — teaching and nursing were the grand exceptions — also kept them out. Many feminists found the Bible itself to be their enemy. Some of its texts placed women in inferior positions in family and church, and these were quoted over those that showed them as judges, prophetesses, and preachers. What was good enough for Saint Paul — namely, silence on the part of women — in the church was good enough for antifeminists in the state.

During the final years of the old century, women found opportunity to attack such use of the Bible, because the new-fashioned biblical criticism helped them cast doubt on the old-fashioned uses of scriptural authority. Some of the critics argued that the antifeminism of Paul was simply a result of his cultural conditioning and not of divine revelation — part of the husk that modern-day believers must throw away in order to keep the kernel of truth. When feminists seized on such ideas, however, they created a new set of enemies in the Protestant camps where literalism about the Bible ruled. In exasperation some militants openly attacked the Bible. One of the most aggressive was Elizabeth Cady Stanton, who with more fury than political finesse published an assault called *The Woman's Bible*. When the book appeared just before the end of the century, it frightened off some supporters of feminism and almost split the movement.

Some of the early feminist leaders had come up through the churches and remembered well what they had been taught about the role of women. The Reverend Anna Howard Shaw worked to teach her colleagues how to bring out positive teachings from the Bible. In her seminary days she and a professor argued about a passage in the Book of Joel, repeated in the New Testament Book of Acts: "and your sons and your daughters shall prophesy." This the women did on Pentecost, the birthday of the church. If women were not to preach, what were those who prophesied doing? Her professor had to admit that "to prophesy" meant "to preach." Did this imply that women preached in the beginning? The professor, an enemy of women preachers in general and of Shaw in particular, barked back, "No, no, the women talked to each other." Did the men also talk only to each other then? "No, no, they preached." Anna clinched her argument: "But the two are connected by a conjunction, 'men and women,' and when the women talked they talked, and when the men talked they preached. Is that the way it was?" The professor: "We will resume."

While the rights of women to be ordained for ministry in most churches waited more decades, the civil public was free to charter more rights for them. It was at this point that efforts by leaders of the women's movement came to difficulty. They could conveniently make a foil out of all the churches, because so many conservatives in churches opposed suffrage. Yet it was precisely conservatives such as the Mormons who had blazed paths to the voting booths fifty years before. In addition, feminists received more support from clergymen than from male members of any other profession. Still, the militants attacked both public religion and evangelical faith. Harriet Martineau in 1834 began the assault, reciting the Declaration of Independence to audiences and asking where women found themselves in a document that called for governmental power to derive its just powers from the consent of the governed. How could they give consent? More telling were feminist attacks on the ministers. Elizabeth Cady Stanton, who could never forget how a Finney revival helped lead to her nervous breakdown, sounded like the old infidels when she attacked "priestcraft and superstition." Most of her colleagues were less bold but their case against canonical religion was as strong as their use of its uncanonical counterpart.

Women were major contributors to the story of American religion all along, as our tracing of the New World journey makes clear. Figures like Queen Isabella and Queen Elizabeth set the terms for a century in Europe. While the Catholic mission was a masculine enterprise, some of the liveliest colonial disturbers of the peace, Mary Dyer, Anne Hutchinson, and the founder of the Shaker sect, Mother Ann Lee, were women. If being women seemed to condemn some to marginal status, people like the black poet Phillis Wheatley and heroines of the parsonage like Sarah Pierrepont Edwards became more orthodox models. Women outnumbered men as converts in the Great Awakening, and found new paths in the missionary movement in the new century. Pathfinders like Narcissa Whitman and Eliza Spalding in Oregon became prominent on the Indian frontier. Arabella Stuart Willson, who wrote the biographies of three Mrs. Judsons, saw foreign missions give women "a sphere of activity, usefulness and distinction, not, under the present constitution of society, to be found elsewhere."

The missionary movement, usually dismissed by later progressives and radicals as demeaning, deserves special mention in the story of emancipations. When the missionary wives, wrenched from home comforts, died or were killed, they became heroines, independently of their husbands. The pious like to quote Harriet Newell, who had written before she sailed overseas to meet death: "All will be dark, everything will be dreary, and not a hope of worldly happiness will be for a moment indulged. The prime of life will be spent in an unhealthy country, a burning region, amongst people of strange language, of a returnless distance from my native land, where I shall never more behold the friends of my youth." Tones of masochism and the self-concern that moved Jesuit martyrs were in such words, but the language was also realistic.

The auxiliaries and support groups that sprouted to promote

foreign missions do not excite latter-day feminists any more than do Richard Allen's debates over church polity fire black militants, but out of such safe domestic agencies came a generation thirsty for change. Eventually unmarried women found vocational outlets as missionaries. The first of these was a black named Betsey Stockton, who taught in the Sandwich Islands from 1823 to 1825. Two years later Miss Cynthia Farrar sailed to the overseas mission from Boston, where she had earlier worked to win support for education of girls in India. Despite these pioneers, almost all women were left far short of license to be ordained for ministry, which became one symbol of the limits of their acceptance. They could be missionaries, nurses, or Sunday-school teachers, but to take the public forum was too shocking an idea for all but some Quakers.

Then, out of the circle of people converted by Charles Grandison Finney and the perfectionists, came some more women who saw no reason why the call to preach should be limited to men. In its prime "the old-time religion" permitted the newfangled to occur. But when women spoke up for religion and abolition, even some of the bolder Finney men had to learn to make adjustments.

One example is the case of Theodore Dwight Weld in his association with Angelina Grimké; the two and her sister Sarah formed a trio whose career combined moral reform with the uncanonical churches of abolition and feminism.

The fact that the Grimkés came of notable Southern Huguenot stock made their case especially poignant. Their parents, dutiful slaveholding Episcopalians at Charleston, were tolerant enough to permit their daughters to teach the Negro children. A Presbyterian evangelist converted Sarah, but left her with more feelings of guilt than of grace. After Quaker merchant Israel Norris introduced her to the *Journal of John Woolman,* she spent the years 1819 to 1823 adopting the Quaker style. Midway through that period she sailed for Philadelphia to be with Quakers and gradually came to desire the ministry. The Friends, who accepted her as a member, found her unconvincing and turned her down as a minister.

Angelina, her junior by thirteen years, followed most of Sarah's steps, beginning with a move from Episcopalianism to Presbyterianism. In 1827 she wanted to move to the fellowship of the Society of Friends. Two years later she left for Philadelphia. Neither sister ever returned to her old home, though they never found it easy to make a new one. The cautious Philadelphia Quakers with good reason mistrusted Angelina's free spirit.

Now, at ages forty-three and thirty, the sisters felt they had made nothing of their lives. They could choose to be depressed or to take up causes; the causes won. The American Anti-Slavery Society, formed at Philadelphia in 1833, virtually became Angelina's next religion. Sarah frowned at the ardent manner of her sister but slowly followed her into the society. Controversy marked their every move. When William Lloyd Garrison printed a letter from Angelina in *The Liberator,* he added a reminder that she was a sister of the famous Southern gentleman Thomas Grimké. The letter caused anguish for Angelina, who had not intended to embarrass her family, and it angered the Quakers, who always found Garrison too violent.

The response to this letter pushed its author toward the front ranks among abolitionists. In 1836, using both the Bible and the Declaration of Independence to make her case, Angelina wrote her *Appeal to the Christian Women of the Southern States.* While the author admitted that in public life men dominated, women in the households of slaveholders also had power, which she thought they should use. She received all the reaction she could want at Charleston. The post office there publicly burned the whole shipment of her books and the police warned her family never to permit her to visit the Southern city again.

Women who wrote tracts did not automatically create scandal in those days, but public platform speaking was denied them. When the New York chapter of the American Anti-Slavery Society asked the younger Miss Grimké to lecture, she pondered the invitation through the summer of 1836. An excellent tutor was at hand to prepare newcomers among the agitators: Theodore Dwight Weld of Oberlin was now coaching abolitionists in New York, and he allowed the Grimké sisters to be the only women in his class. Angelina said she found this lion of the tribe of abolition unremarkable in appearance, but his two-hour speech was a feast. Weld helped her find little circles of women on whom to practice public speaking; before long, men started attending. Weld defended the circumstance, scoffing at what he thought was a ridiculous idea, that a man must be shouldered out of a meeting for fear of a woman speaker.

By May of 1837 the sisters were ready to invade New England, where they were already so well known that Garrison could arrange an audience with former president John Quincy Adams. They carried away from him the observation that only women could abolish slavery. Ministers less courteous to them had passed codes the year before prohibiting "itinerating agents" from speaking uninvited at churches. With doors slammed on the Grimkés, both became more aggressive.

Catharine Beecher led the attack against the sisters, arguing that by speaking to mixed audiences they violated a "beneficent and immutable Divine Law." Women were not even to send petitions to Congress, but could only influence their men in the quiet of their own homes. Angelina in response insisted that women by right did have a voice in all laws that affected them in church or state. Ministers quite naturally found it impossible to stay away from such arguments. In July, Massachusetts Congregationalists attacked women speakers; thirty-nine crusaders from Andover Theological Seminary seconded the motion. But gradually some ministers were won over by the eloquence of the Grimkés, who outlined a religious case for the cause ten years before the feminist movement emerged at a convention in Seneca Falls, New York.

The Grimkés enjoyed their first public triumph when they testified before a committee of the Massachusetts legislature and a crowd of clergy, press, and abolitionists. Angelina spoke of the "blood, sweat, and tears" of her sisters in bonds. As a Southerner she had been exiled from the land of her birth by the sound of the lash and the piteous cry of the slave. Two days after the speech, she was back for more stir. A reporter on the scene felt she exhibited herself in a position unsuitable to her sex and against the doctrine of Saint Paul. Then he paid a grudging compliment anyhow: "She exhibited considerable talent for a female." He was certifying the obvious; in twenty-three weeks the sisters spoke to more than forty thousand people on a trail no women in America before them dared travel.

While New England thawed, Weld in New York chilled. He feared backlash, and warned against it in letters. Angelina Grimké answered his messages, complaining of their "scratchifications." He improved his writing and clarified his concern: "I know it will surprise and even amaze you, Angelina, when I say to you as I now do, that for a long time *you have had my whole heart.*" But he knew that Quakers dared not marry heathen and he dared not marry at all, having taken a vow not to wed until slavery was abolished. Miss Grimké: "I feel, my Theodore, that we are the two halves of one whole, a twain one, two bodies animated by one soul and that the Lord has given us to each other."

On May 14, 1838, Angelina Grimké and Theodore Weld overcame their scruples and married. After a day of retreat, they prepared to make a joint appearance in Philadelphia at a $40,000 hall that the Abolition Society had dedicated on their wedding day. Two days later mobs milled around as William Lloyd Garrison began to speak. When Angelina Weld took her turn, the crowd outside started throwing bricks through windows. She shrugged off the violence. What was a mob? What would breaking every window mean? Would such destruction be evidence that slavery was good?

Despite her display of courage or perhaps because of it, even bigger crowds gathered the next day. The manager decided to close the building in order to protect it, and he gave the key to the mayor. The mob in reaction burst in and set the torch to the structure. The crowd cheered when the roof fell in, while firemen lifted no finger or hose through it all. Having savored victory, the ruffians moved on to attack the homes of well-known abolitionists in the neighborhood. When the city quieted, Philadelphians were relieved to learn that no lives were lost, but an official investigating committee censured no rioters, choosing instead to fault the speakers for promoting doctrines repulsive to the moral sense of the majority of citizens. The morning after the fire, in a nearby schoolroom, the Grimkés were back leading a meeting of the Women's Society.

But moral appeal once again failed in the face of slavery. John Woolman had drifted off in his last year or two, his life showing no focus. Lyman Beecher, defeated for his gradualism, retreated in senility. The Grimkés, more vocal than these others, for a time frittered their energies away on spiritual fashions and fads that lured them from their journey for freedom. One postwar incident, however, also revealed some consistency in the Grimkés' commitments. In 1868, while living near Boston, they taught at a boarding school run by a founder of the Women's Christian Temperance Union. There they learned about three sons of their brother Henry and his slave mistress, and took an interest in two of them. They helped sponsor their mixed-blood nephews through school. Francis James Grimké later was graduated from Princeton Theological Seminary and became a minister in Washington and a trustee of Howard University. Archibald Henry Grimké was graduated from Harvard Law School and found a career as an editor, biographer, politician, consul, and an officer of the National Association for the Advancement of Colored People. At least this Grimké investment paid a good yield.

For all the efforts of the abolitionist Welds and Garrisons, of the quieter dissenters like Emerson and Thoreau, of the evangelical gradualists, and of black church people who spoke up for themselves, slavery was not to be abolished without the Civil War. The final story of emancipation for blacks, then, belongs more to the history of war and politics than of religion.

But even after the Civil War, the former Africans represented an enduring problem in the eyes of the white majority. Like Israelites after the exodus, the liberated slaves saw themselves free to live in the Promised Land. Their Lord had vindicated his people and honored their suffering and their struggles. Despite the economic ruin of the Southern region and the limits of their training, four million free blacks seemed ready for better days. Hope and encouragement reached them through their own peculiar institutions, the black churches, which ministered to a potent minority among them.

The Baptists had the head start. A hundred years after Emancipation, thanks to efforts that began as early as the 1740s, half the black church population would still be Baptist. On the plantations, Baptist soul-winners had no difficulty converting slaves from under the noses of slaveholders, whose more formal religions held less appeal than did revivalist faith. Around the time of the American Revolution, a "Brother Palmer" brought together a few slaves in the first Negro Baptist church, a model of the tens of thousands that followed it in the rural south and then the urban north.

The Civil War almost devastated these little Baptist houses of worship. Many congregations saw their ramshackle churches burn, victims of the marauding military or vengeful Confederate citizens. Some black Baptists became aggressive, and in heady moments after the war, a few even tried to take over church buildings from the defeated Southern whites. In a typical scare, at Selma, Alabama, the Reverend J. B. Hawthorne and his church members took up arms to defend themselves against a takeover, but the threat turned out to be only a rumor started by "white instigators."

The whites' Southern Baptist Convention at first made a few efforts to keep ties with black Baptists, and a few whites did remain in contact, but almost nothing came of the efforts. Nor were missions by Convention boards and bureaus of much use; most of these were soon abandoned, as the Negroes took their destiny into their own hands. One of the Convention missionaries looked on in dismay because "the colored race are exceedingly disposed to religious excitement" and they were alarmingly exposed, he thought, to the artifices of fanatics, demagogues, and fake preachers who wanted nothing but their pennies.

Despite all obstacles, state conventions of black Baptist churches did form. At Montgomery, Alabama, the African Christians by 1880 had already started their own Foreign Mission Convention in order to send missionaries to Africa. In 1895 at Atlanta they formed the National Baptist Convention of the U.S.A., which claimed most of the 1.8 million black Baptists. The churches they formed were the most available of all local agencies for blacks who were working their way "up from slavery." But they were loosely organized, wary of tight connections with each other, and suspicious of superiors in church life; so much of their story is lost and what survives is difficult to grasp and tell.

Vastly outnumbered but taking a more defined shape were the black Methodists. Their stories also display the struggles of blacks against blacks. Most Negroes wanted to turn from the Methodist Episcopal Church, South, because that group had defended slavery. Both the more thoughtful white members, who foresaw such drives for independence, and the most racially prejudiced ones, who wanted to bid blacks good riddance, encouraged them to set out on their own. Between 1860 and 1866 two-thirds of the black Methodists joined the two African Methodist denominations that dated back to 1816 and 1820. They resented the loss of those who joined outpost churches started by invading northern Methodists after the war. To cut off this drain, some of them founded in 1870 a southern Christian Methodist Episcopal church. Inevitably, this being America, the bodies competed, sometimes viciously.

When pioneer CME leaders set out to lure back the sheep they regarded as stolen by other Methodists, they met resistance. CME Bishop C. H. Phillips and his colleagues had to defend themselves against charges that they were sellouts, heirs of the old "Rebel Church," the "Democratic Church," or the "Old Slavery Church." This was "maliciously misrepresented, wantonly maligned, and frequently calumniated by stronger denominations."

The African Methodist Episcopal church was best poised to construct southern black church life. While the CME, starting from scratch, did grow to 120,000 members by 1880 and the AME Zion church prospered, growing from 4,600 members in 1856 to 250,000 congregants fifteen years later, the AME moved from its base of about 20,000 to 400,000 in 1880. One month after the war ended and thirty years after he had first been driven from Charleston,

Bishop Daniel A. Payne returned there to take up work again. The CME complained that Payne and his AME preachers were very hostile — that they insisted on squatters' rights as they won people and took over territories and properties, paying little notice to CME complaints that the AME ministers were "forbidding us preaching in our houses of worship, that are occupied by your congregations." Amazingly, the AME and its counterparts, while busy scrapping with each other, began to plan for missions back to Africa.

Some denominations lost out completely. By the time Presbyterians decided what to do about their own ten thousand Negro members, most of these blacks had drifted off to the competition. The strongest Presbyterian leader of the day, Robert L. Dabney of Richmond, bade them less than fond farewells. They had "deserted their true friends, and natural allies, and native land," to follow the most unmasked and unprincipled demagogues on earth, the Yankees, to the most atrocious ends. Curiously, while certain civil authorities in Virginia ruled out inferior races because they could not assimilate or amalgamate, people like Dabney feared that they could. Unless blacks disappeared into their own churches, what he called "that most repugnant thing, *amalgamation,*" would result. Congress acted against the Black Codes — the first Jim Crow laws — with the Reconstruction Act of 1867. Southerners struck back against such efforts to enforce equality. Founders of the Ku Klux Klan, whose members took oaths on the Bible, had not foreseen how much horror their hooded members could generate among blacks or how quickly rowdies could prevail in their organization. Whites and blacks alike suffered lynching in the new era of lawlessness (though not in comparable numbers).

Resentments soon turned to racism in the churches. The year after the war concluded, Southern Baptist leader Jeremiah Jeter specified why the races must stay apart. Not to do so would "degrade our noble Saxon race . . . to a race of degenerate mongrels." The old myth that Negroes descended from the cursed biblical character Ham survived the war, but such myths also received support now from scientists in northern universities. The scholars measured and weighed brains, hoping to find that the brains of blacks were smaller. They used the devices of anthropology, sociology, history, and biology trying to prove that Negroes were inferior. H. Melville Myers, who drew up the South Carolina Black Codes, reminded citizens that the Negro race was to be excluded from all civilized governments. "Doomed by a mysterious and Divine ordination," it was, he said, the lowest and most degraded form of humanity.

Church papers seized on the scholarly support to reinforce the distance between whites and blacks. In 1889 the Baptist *Christian Index* reminded Georgians that "blood will tell" and that someday cavaliers of Anglo-Norman blood would rule the South again. Northern church leaders used equally strong language about their southern counterparts. The year the war ended, Henry M. Dexter employed the *Boston Congregationalist* to charter an invasion, since "the great territorial churches of the South," corrupt and tainted, were morally unfit for reconstruction. And Lyman Abbott editorially scowled at Presbyterian seminary professor Moses Hoge and his South: "We cannot trust the cause of Christ to the Judas who betrayed it." They accompanied bad language with good works. The American Missionary Association and other voluntary groups dotted the South with agencies of reform, humanitarianism, religion, and education, until notable schools like Atlanta, Fisk, Tougaloo, and Hampton Institute took root.

While southern church folk ranted about the invasion of do-gooders, they raved about black roles in Reconstruction. Professor Hoge, finding that he could not even out of curiosity bring himself to look into the Virginia state capitol, where blacks were representatives in 1868, told his sister that he wished to escape the spectacle of beastly baboons ruling where once sages and patriots sat. Jeremiah Jeter said he was ready for the South to do without schools rather than to permit mongrelization and barbarism. Henry Holcombe Tucker, the Georgia Baptist who headed Mercer University and then the University of Georgia, summarized the creed of the 1880s: "We do not believe that 'all men are created equal,' as the Declaration of Independence declares them to be; nor that they will ever become equal in this world. . . . We think that our own race is incomparably superior to any other. . . . As to the Negro, we do not know where to place him."

The Negroes knew they had to find their own places. The most influential direction came near the end of the century from Booker T. Washington, a leader much admired in his time but often despised by militant black leaders of later decades, because they found the white world too comfortable with the apparent low ceiling he envisioned for blacks. Given the possibilities of his day, he helped his people advance. As his autobiography, *Up from Slavery,* recounted, he rose from bondage to head Tuskegee Institute, where his vocational-education policies imparted a sense of dignity and worth to the freed. At Hampton Institute the talented Washington came to see hard work as a "spiritual force," so he spread that message. In his famous Atlanta Exposition speech in 1895, Washington stressed opportunity and responsibility rather than equality: "In all things that are purely social we can be as separate as the fingers, yet one as the hand in all things essential to mutual progress." Yet even so mild a man offended many whites, not least of all on the day he lunched at the White House with President Theodore Roosevelt, who drew criticism for having invited a Negro to violate that sacred precinct.

A second familiar approach, one that like Washington's was as applicable to the unchurched majority as to the churched faithful, represented steps by which blacks found alternatives to religion as instruments of fulfillment. Any number of leaders spoke for this more secular approach, but over many decades, Dr. William E. Burghardt Du Bois came to be the most prominent and forceful critic of Washington's approach. In Du Bois's view the Tuskegee president taught a "Gospel of Work and Money," one that almost completely overshadowed "the higher aims of life." Foreseeing dangers for blacks in the American business creed, Du Bois, a great organizer of secular agencies, did pay black churches many compliments. He remembered the age of prayers, when the black man with tears and curses implored God for freedom. "At last it came — suddenly, fearfully, like a dream." Far into the next century, Du Bois lost support of many black church people when he espoused the creed of Marxism. He showed effectively that whites, more than they knew, remained Europeans spiritually, yet were loyal to America. So, he argued, the black soul remained African, and Negroes must live with a "two-ness" that led them to look with memory and hope to Africa while remaining truly American.

The third spiritual option, taken by few but rich in what it revealed about the black sense of confinement, preached "back to Africa" for the elect. This movement recovered the ideal of the American Colonization Society that decades before most blacks had rejected. By now it seemed clear to many that America was not the Promised Land. Black farmers had to settle for sharecropping. When the cotton crop failed or when prices dropped because it was too abundant, blacks almost literally starved. Jobs and relief agencies were scarce in northern cities, where anti-Negro sentiment kept growing.

In 1891 a Georgia correspondent named Jackson wrote to the fossilized American Colonization Society that in the midst of land poverty he felt homesick for Africa. Society files bulged with letters like his: "We are quite sure that the U.S. of America is not the place for the colored man." A. G. Belton wrote that in hard times Africa looked most attractive but Oklahoma was the nearest place of safety. Yet Oklahoma simply reproduced the old southern problems for Negroes.

In this cramping atmosphere the African movement found a voice in Bishop Henry McNeal Turner. Born free in South Carolina in 1834, Turner refused to work alongside slaves, so he found work as a janitor. Young clerks in the law office that he cleaned risked their jobs by teaching the attractive child to read and write. At age twenty he was ordained to be an itinerant in the Southern Methodist church, where audiences of both races responded favorably to him. The taunts of some prejudiced people unnerved him, however, so three years before the war, Turner transferred to the AME church at New Orleans. From there he moved to Baltimore for seminary studies and then served a church on Capitol Hill in Washington. In the Civil War he mustered blacks in his own churchyard, following them into the army as a chaplain, where he had to fight battles against discrimination.

Having spotted an opening in Georgia, after the war he hurried to represent the AME church there and led the Reconstruction Republicans. They elected him to office in 1867, but the legislature excluded him. "White men are not to be trusted. . . . This thing means revolution" was his response. While waiting for revolution to occur, Turner became the first postmaster of his race in Georgia, but Georgians trumped up fraud charges and removed him. He then became a customs inspector, but he found the work dreary and went back to the ministry. Through the years Turner had begun to dream of Africa as a land of promise. Soon he preached that American blacks should heed the voice of the mysterious Providence that said, "Return to the land of your Fathers."

Though his message seemed eccentric and even disturbing to many, Turner climbed in church ranks. His travels and publishing efforts brought fame, and in 1880 fame brought him a bishopric. He attracted a larger hearing for his preachments. From the beginning, he asserted, the distinctions God created had to do not with status but color, yet in modern America whites threatened a war of extermination over status. The sight and sound of the resulting anarchy and horror reached to heaven; "whoever the white race does not consort with, it will crush out." We Africans, he went on, "were born here, raised here, fought, bled and died here, and have a thousand times more right here than hundreds of thousands of those who help to snub, proscribe and persecute us, and that is one of the reasons I almost despise the land of my birth."

Since America was no longer a place of refuge, it must yield to Africa as a shelter for exiles from "the red tide of persecution." To migrate was no disgrace; if it were, why did Americans honor the Pilgrims of Plymouth for their journey so long ago? In the age of imperialism, Turner urged that Negroes must hurry to Africa before European conquerors finished carving it up and seizing it. Late arrivals there would be nothing but bootblacks and groomers of Europeans' horses in Africa. Only an elect few were called for this new pilgrimage; it was nonsense to think, the bishop added, that he was trying to get *all* colored people out of the United States. Two-thirds of them were useless anywhere. He needed no "riffraff whiteman worshippers, aimless, objectless, selfish, little-souled and would-be-white Negroes." They were scullions who only gave glory, honor, and dominion to whites. Then Turner thundered his drastic point: "God is a Negro: Even the heathen in Africa believed that they were 'created in God's image.' But American Africans," he charged, "believe that they resemble the devil and hence the contempt they have for themselves and each other!"

Though few volunteers were ready to migrate, not everyone thought Turner a crackpot. In 1891 his fellow bishops sent him to visit Africa; there he wept as he stepped on the soil and praised the wonders of the landscape. One month of life among AME missions confirmed him in his cause. Upon his return to the United States, Turner took advantage of the climate momentarily created in America by Edward Blyden, a black West Indian who now worked in Liberia. Blyden was visiting the United States to encourage Christian missions before Islam could take over Africa. At this opportune moment, Senator Matthew Butler of South Carolina proposed a bill that would authorize financial support for individual Negroes who wanted to return to Africa. Of course, the measure stood no chance of passage. After the Butler bill failed, the American Colonization Society continued to struggle on without governmental funding, and Blyden returned to Africa.

With Africa largely out of range and Oklahoma a forbidding place of escape, some blacks wanted to colonize the American North, and many were soon stranded there. Their embarrassing presence gave the black editor of the *New York Age*, T. Thomas Fortune, an excuse to attack Turner as the "agent, the hired man, the oiled advocate of a white man's corporation." The *Indianapolis*

Freeman also scolded Bishop Turner for promoting what it claimed was a money-making corporation. Turner denied any financial interest, and pointed out that if he were a vengeful person he could almost literally flood the North with disgruntled southern colored people.

Turner's denunciations of America as "the worst, the meanest country" gave him notoriety but cut further into white support for his new self-help schemes to take people back to Africa. Despite the handicaps he created, Turner's International Migration Society was able to transport 198 emigrants from the port of Savannah on the *Horsa* in 1895. Unfortunately, no one had prepared Liberia for their arrival, so the people aboard became objects of African charity until some of them could struggle back to America. Turner tried to help support the agents of his cause who remained in Africa, but Blyden came back to America to urge blacks now to lower their hopes; mass exodus to Africa would harm both continents.

Through all the troubles, Turner managed to keep some followers, and in 1896 he put on one last desperate good show in a sermon that helped send off the *Laurada*. Evidently no one had learned lessons from the fate of the smaller *Horsa*: this time scores died of fever within months after their arrival in Africa, just as many more returned with vows of revenge against promoters of the fiasco. Turner journeyed to South Africa to help build up the AME church, but his effectiveness was largely gone.

Booker T. Washington, riding a crest of popularity, taunted Turner with statistics. On January 1, 1900, at Macon, Georgia, he made the obvious point that at least one baby would be born in the Cotton Belt for every adult who might ever leave for Liberia; "back to Africa" solved nothing. "As we came to this country at the urgent solicitation and expense of the white man, we would be ungrateful to run away and leave him now." Lines like those enraged Turner, but he was powerless to muffle the applause they evoked. As his Society crumbled, whispers rose about his personal life, especially after he married his young divorced secretary. When the bishop died in 1915 Du Bois eulogized him as the "last of his clan," not for his policies but because he was one of the mighty men who by brute strength had come from the bottom to the top.

On the short range, Washington won the day, though Du Bois and his colleagues and their organizations eventually became more credible. Yet a voice like that of Turner expressed a rage and detailed a vision only dimly seen by many others. His alternative was no more — though also no less — workable and effective than the other utopias of his century. More vividly than most, it forced both his followers and his enemies to ponder the meaning of America against the background of the most drastic choice open to them: to leave and reject it.

The issue of exclusion, however, remains as a sign of the tragic flaw in American life: its inability to include in its promise of freedom *all* its people. This problem extends far beyond the Civil War and the history of blacks in America, and remains unresolved even in the twentieth century. But during Civil War times it wasn't only the African slaves who suffered discrimination: Asians, especially Chinese, were routinely excluded from society and native Americans were sequestered on reservations or faced extinction — all in the name of God and the American empire.

The Asian story can be told briefly. When nearly starved Chinese, lured by American demands for cheap labor, began to arrive in California just before the Civil War to work in mines and on railroads, Americans still had little understanding of the Orient. For over three hundred years China remained a mystery in the American imagination, from the days when discoverers looked for a passage to Cathay until missionaries went to win the heathen there. Almost as soon as the United States opened the door to a few Asians it slammed the same door to all. In 1868 Congress approved a treaty that allowed for immigration, but Californians protested when it became clear that Chinese immigrants were crowding the settlers out of jobs. After nineteen Chinese arrivals were killed in a Los Angeles riot in 1871, the governor started speaking of "an irrepressible conflict" between the civilizations of China and America. Though President Rutherford B. Hayes vetoed a bill that would begin to exclude the Chinese, he gave little hope for the future: "Our experience in dealing with weaker races — the Negroes and Indians, for example — is not encouraging."

American Christians made a few early efforts to welcome and convert the Chinese. In such a spirit a crowd gathered in San Francisco on August 28, 1850, to celebrate some new arrivals. On the plaza at Kearney Street, dignitaries resplendent in top hats, with well-dressed ladies at their sides, clustered around a platform while a hundred Chinese, "their pigtails nicely braided," ceremoniously marched forward to take seats. A pioneer in the American Chinese community, Norman As-sing, led the parade. The Reverend Albert Williams prayed for these "citizens of the celestial empire," and an array of speakers expressed hope that more Chinese would follow these in years to come.

Norman As-sing translated during a main address by the Reverend Timothy Dwight Hunt. Hunt picked up a theme as old as the one native Americans first heard from Spanish friars on this soil: "Though you come from a celestial country, there is another one above, much better, much larger than your own." He combined realism and promise: "Here and in your country, you are sometimes taken sick and suffer and even die, and are seen no more, and your fathers and mothers and brothers and sisters all die, but in the other heavenly country, all the good China boys live. They will meet there and never die!"

The translator looked quizzical for a moment; the words were not difficult but the idea made no sense. Dutifully he plunged on, reworking these words. When he finished, the previously grave "China boys" broke into laughter over the concept of an afterlife; soon irreverent miners, enjoying the Chinese enjoyment of the concept's absurdity, joined in with guffaws. Though Hunt and his colleagues almost lost control of the gathering, they recovered enough to hand out Bibles and some imported Christian literature translated into Chinese. Mayor John Geary sealed the ceremony with the word of hope that in events like these, China and America would join hands.

For the most part the newcomers stayed or were pushed off to their own Little Chinas or Chinatowns. Instead of joining hands with them, Californians passed laws to exclude them. Because these ran counter to the Fourteenth Amendment to the United States Constitution, the Court of Appeals had to strike them down, but concurring justice Stephen Field showed that, like President Hayes, he was of two minds about the Orientals: "They do not and will not assimilate with our people." In 1889 the Supreme Court finally upheld restrictions; Field decided this was the best policy for preserving American civilization. Three years later, former mayor but now Congressman Geary celebrated the laws of exclusion: "There is not room in this country," he insisted, for people like the Chinese, who could not amalgamate. By the turn of the century the number of Chinese in the United States had dwindled from a high of over 107,000 to fewer than 90,000. Outside of their crowded little Chinatowns, representatives of this quarter of the human race hadn't found a home in America.

The Indians, meanwhile, remained officially a foreign nation on soil that was originally theirs. Westbound United States settlers kept pushing them farther back; when the natives resisted, the government sent military force to subdue them. A congressional committee after the war used language that reflected the Chinese and African dealings: an "irrepressible conflict between a superior and an inferior race" resulted when they were brought into the presence of each other. President Ulysses S. Grant came forward with a humane-sounding "Peace Policy." He claimed that "a system which looks to the extinction of a race is too horrible for a nation to adopt without entailing upon itself the wrath of all Christendom." Grant called on major Christian churches to administer Indian reservations, hoping thus to appease both railroad builders who wanted to cut through the western land and idealists who were genuinely eager to serve the Indians. But President James A. Garfield thought it best "to let the Indian races sink as gently and easily as possible in oblivion, for there they will go in spite of all efforts."

The United States Army saw to it that the sinking was neither gentle nor easy. After the Gold Rush and with the Oregon and Mormon trails open, no one could hold back new settlers, many of whom killed the defending Indians as casually as they did the buffalo. Military agents often forced the Indians to go through the motions of selling their land, and when they resisted, physically removed them. After a new method for tanning buffalo hide was discovered, hunters killed millions of the animals; the Plains Indians' food supplies ran low. In desperation some holdouts like the Comanche and Cheyenne fought last-ditch actions and enjoyed occasional victories. The tribes, however, used up so much ammunition in efforts like the massacre of General George A. Custer and his troops at Little Big Horn in Montana, that after 1876 they faced extinction. Great leaders fell. The army used false promises to beguile Crazy Horse of the Oglala Sioux into surrendering and then bayoneted him in 1877, contending that he resisted imprisonment. The act of getting revenge on Sitting Bull took longer, because the chief found refuge in Canada for several years. During the years of his exile, in the setting of devastation and hopelessness, a messianic faith developed. This new and fast-spreading awakening helped give meaning to Indians' lives, but it also helped make possible their final uprooting and even death.

Wovoka, the new Messiah, was born around 1858 in southwest Nevada, in whose Walker River Valley he spent almost all his life.

The Paiute shaman Tavibo was probably his father; tribal respect for the holy man was transferred to the boy. A California-bound family that chose to settle in the valley took Wovoka in, so he adopted their name and became Jack Wilson. From Bill Wilson, who treated the Indian boy like a brother, Wovoka heard of Jesus, a medicine man who healed people without touching them. This Jesus made intoxicating drink out of water, fed thousands of people with a few small fish, and brought the dead back to life. The child marveled at how Jesus taught people peace and love and schooled them in prayer to the Great Spirit. He heard how bad people killed Jesus, but that the dead man later came back from the spirit world and showed his wounds to people. No one informed Wovoka that such wonders were no longer to occur. Was it possible that people could be dead for three days and live again, and that they could heal and teach with many signs? Could *he,* Jack Wilson, be like the wonder worker Jesus?

Wovoka could identify with the best stories of both the Indian and Christian worlds, but in his living he also had the worst of both. Neither people regarded him fully as their own. Only when he saw that some Paiute still regarded Tavibo well did he begin to make his way slowly back to them. They told him how the whites stole their land and killed their game, or broke the treaties and misused their women; with his own eyes he learned the effects of defeat and alcohol on tribesmen.

During the time Wovoka was among them, the Paiute made increasing contacts with other tribes. He learned from a Skokomish family how a once-depraved man named Squ-sacht-un in their northwestern lands had experienced rebirth. On one occasion people thought him dead, but after his corpse came back to life he declared that he had seen heaven and been with angels. Thereupon he called the people to live a pure life of discipline and prayer. Squ-sacht-un evidently borrowed bells and crucifixes from Catholics, doctrine from Presbyterians, and ritual from the Skokomish. With his first convert, Ai-yäl, he spread faith in God the Father and Jesus Christ, in heaven and hell. But Christian missionaries who would not tolerate his frenzies had him imprisoned with other leaders at the Puyallup Indian Agency in Washington State. This act only added to the lure, and among those drawn to the cult, none was more curious than Wovoka. During a healing ceremony he, too, fell unconscious for a night; his life was at the point of a decisive turn.

Wovoka faced several choices. While he could keep working for

David Wilson, his heart was no longer in it. The Paiute honored its medicine men, but he was not tempted to be one of them, even though his inheritance made him eligible. The way of Squ-sacht-un remained, and its appeal led to a bizarre turn in Wovoka's career. Recalling some old shaman tricks, he started out establishing himself as a leader.

By his twentieth year Wovoka was embarked on his career as a wonder-worker. He borrowed ideas to promote his work from the Skokomish, the Christians, and even the Mormons. He knew that to be the new Messiah he must produce a miracle. During one two-day trance the aspirant seemed to be on the point of death. Then, before the eyes of his followers, he came back to life and told how heaven had received him. Angels there had shown him the glory of the Indian way and had urged him to teach his own people that Jesus was again among them, teaching them a pure life and working miracles. His career prospered further, thanks to his recovery from scarlet fever. During its worst stage, Wovoka lingered in delirium; only his wife Mary dared minister to him. After he fell into his deepest trance, other Indians came to test him with painful tortures, but he seemed to be beyond mortal agony. Then, suddenly, he revived. During those days also "the sun died"; there was an eclipse, during which Wovoka prayed with special fervency.

"I have talked with God." Now he gave the western Indians an idea that kept their last, futile hopes alive: The earth itself would die, but Indians need not fear. In the grassy otherworld their Messiah learned that the Indian dead had already risen and were waiting in the west where the sun dies. Someday, after the earth shook, Indians would gather to see it die and come to new life. Thereafter there would be no whites, and Indians would live in paradise again. They should in the meantime put away weapons and notions of war and live at peace with whites. For five days he taught them to celebrate a new rite, which whites later named the Ghost Dance. Then he baptized converts in the Walker River and shared a sacral meal with them.

By the summer of 1889 both the prophecy and the Ghost Dance spread beyond the Rockies all the way to the Mississippi. Porcupine of the Cheyenne was one of the chiefs who became convinced by the cult; by June of 1890 he had taught so many Cheyenne to take part that the Indian Affairs officers stepped in. Because they made no sense of the peaceful ceremony, they stepped up efforts against it, being doubly suspicious of anything that led Indians to act in concert. When the officers heard that at Pine Ridge among the Sioux in South Dakota militants like Short Bull and Good Thunder were teaching the dance to resisting Indians, they felt they must act.

At this point Wovoka evidently resorted to trickery again to pass a messianic test. He was boasting that nothing could happen to his body. While crowds of the faithful constantly protected him from violence, he felt he had to make some public display of his powers. The Messiah prepared some shotgun blanks and then ordered an aide to fire them at him in front of an unknowing crowd. Wovoka fell forward, releasing some buckshot from his hand as he tumbled, as if the shot were falling off him. As he rose, Wovoka took off his shirt, hung it in the breeze, and let the same accomplice shoot at the shirt, which also thus miraculously escaped harm. Whether through such an incident or whatever, the militant Sioux took over the Ghost Dance and transformed it. They decorated shirts for the dance and contended that they would all be protected from bullets. They could thus destroy whites and go back to the old ways. An innocent rite now became dangerous, because natives believed they could safely resist armies.

The conversion of the Sioux came about under the leadership of the devout and mystical warrior Sitting Bull. The U.S. Army had long tried to lure him back from Canada with promises of peace and amnesty, but the chief rejected the appeals, preferring pitiless Canada to the beguilements of General Alfred Terry. In 1881, however, he did return; four years later he was the main attraction of Buffalo Bill's Wild West Show. Then his fortunes declined and he settled in to sulk and plot at Standing Rock reservation. On October 9, 1890, a Miniconjou named Kicking Bear came to tell him of Wovoka and the Ghost Dance. Sitting Bull was half skeptical, but he did allow his people to try the dance. It was Kicking Bear who convinced him that if the dancers wore the shirts they would be safe from the army. The fates converged: just when the Indian bureau was making its final move to stop the Ghost Dance, a most powerful chief was beginning to take it up.

"White Hair" McLaughlin and other agents, knowing that Sitting Bull through his interest was prolonging the rite, concentrated on the chief. On December 13 the military received orders to end the threat once and for all. Two days later dozens of military men circled the cabin of Sitting Bull, while more troops waited in the distance. One or more Indian policemen on the government's side crept up and surprised Sitting Bull in his sleep. Despite the quiet of the hour, swarms of Ghost Dancers appeared as if from nowhere when the two stepped out-of-doors together. Details of what followed remain confused. Evidently one of the dancers momentarily resisted arrest, a gesture that gave the impression that Sitting Bull was going to rebel. In the chaos a dancer fired at an Indian policeman. As the man fell wounded, he aimed for his attacker but hit Sitting Bull. Then Red Tomahawk, another Indian in governmental employ, shot and killed the chief.

Wovoka had taught the starving people not to resist, so no one went looking for revenge. Even the Miniconjou chief Big Foot moved peacefully as he took his people toward Wounded Knee under the orders and in the company of cavalry troops. The cavalry counted 120 men and 230 Indian children and women when they established camp on an icy December evening. The next day the army planned to disarm its captives, but for the moment simply took pains to point to ominous guns above the camp; at nightfall the troops posted guards and toasted the capture of Big Foot, who was ill.

Morning came, and with it the frightened Ghost Dancers heard orders to gather. They surrendered their guns and watched as soldiers looked for other weapons in the tents. At just that moment a medicine man threw some dust into the air, a signal that the millennium was present and that the end was near for white men. The Indians formed a circle and began the Ghost Dance. During the stir Black Coyote, who had somehow retained one of the last Indian guns, fired. It is possible that his near-deafness left him confused about orders. Whatever the reason for his act, the army now opened fire, Hotchkiss machine guns and all.

When the cloud cleared, 153 dead bodies littered the landscape; many more Indians died as they tried to make their way into the wintry hills around them. Many of the 25 dead soldiers were killed by the ammunition of the military. Most of the approximately 300 Indians were simply abandoned on the ground during the approach of a blizzard. Days later Chief Big Foot was found, his frozen features distorted in the snow. The survivors were left to thaw on the floor of the Episcopal Mission at Pine Ridge. The Ghost Shirts and the dreams of Messiah and utopia had failed. The United States government took note of the incident: it rewarded Medals of Honor for bravery to eighteen soldiers.

Wovoka became disconsolate. However his vision first came to him, he had come to believe the truth and value of his peaceful faith. Now he felt partly responsible for the tragedies and consoled himself only by remembering that in his teaching any kind of resistance went against the faith, and a few people *had* resisted at Wounded Knee. The heart went out of his revival, however, so in 1891 he withdrew into the mountains. One day he would tell his story to James Mooney, a gifted student of Indian religion from the United States Bureau of Ethnology. Thanks to this chance circumstance, Mooney passed on to the world a precious glimpse of an American religion that for a year and a half transformed the lives of Indians on the land they saw disappearing into the control of the people who excluded them.

As Jack Wilson, the discredited Wovoka lived out his days. Storekeeper Ed Dyer befriended him as the Indian made a meager living by trading in ceremonial objects. By the end of the century Wovoka could no longer find enough followers to make up a Ghost Dance circle, and few still called him "Our Father." His surviving daughter became a staunch Mormon. Yet Wovoka was no more willing to deny his belief that he had visited and talked with God than was Joseph Smith to deny his Mormon vision. In 1932 Wovoka's wife Mary died and soon thereafter he, the man who should never die, followed her. Almost forty-two years after the nightfall on the trail at Wounded Knee ended hopes of a millennial dawn, the Messiah was gone.

What today is known as pluralism, the presence of
many religions, struck Britisher Joseph Keppler of
Puck as a valid subject for satire. Here in "The
Religious Vanity Fair" (1879) the rabbi readies his
knife for circumcision, the cardinal collects money,
the Mormon practices polygamy, Henry Ward
Beecher runs his own booth, and numbers of other
religious types and figures are insulted.
(*Boston Public Library*)

Chapter Thirteen

ADAPTING TO AMERICA

♫ WHILE NATIVE AMERICANS WERE FORMALLY REGARDED AS CITIzens of a foreign country on American soil, while blacks were segregated even after slavery, and while Orientals were demeaned and rejected, other minorities, such as the Catholics and the Jews, did begin to make headway in the nineteenth century. They were like the Indians, blacks, and Asians in that their faith helped provide the symbols for their identity and their struggles. They also shared the disfavor of the old Protestant majority. As they arrived in ever greater numbers, they presented a challenge to the keepers of the old covenant, yet progressively they met the challenges presented them in turn.

One can picture what amounted to a kind of pact. In effect the America made up of earlier revivals said to its immigrants through thousands of subtle and unsubtle signals: "Well, we guess you are going to stay and we guess you are more or less welcome — but you have to change." With external pressure upon them, and deep religious memories within them, these groups began their long process of adapting to America. While there is considerable drama in the story of their harassment and stigmatization by their neighbors, another, more revealing tension developed within the groups. They began to contend over what it meant to be in America, what the new land meant for their old faith, and who among them had a better vision of both old and new.

Catholics drew most fire from their neighbors. However, Irish and Continental immigrants, clearly in America to stay, continued to clear space for themselves in the old Protestant empire. They also fought a home-front war between their own "Americanizers" and those who in the name of Roman tradition resisted adaptation. The story of these internal hostilities unfolded against the background of an anti-Catholic crusade.

The "Americanist" battles came to a head late in the century. This was the period that ended the Indian trail, that saw free blacks segregated and newly arrived Orientals shunned. Yet to make sense of the Americanizing issue, one has to retrace steps to a period half a century earlier, when much of the Catholic vision of America was shaped by response to an anti-Catholic crusade.

Between 1815 and 1845 about a million Irish people entered America, to begin the tide of new Catholic immigration. A bad potato crop in Ireland in 1845 and then a mysterious blight a year later served as virtual death sentences on the Celtic people dependent on the tuber. Within six years little Ireland lost two million people to death or emigration. Many of these "famine Irish" came penniless, victims of brutal "runners" who took advantage of them on old shores and new. Bone-tired, frightened in the new land, looking almost like skeletons, many of them had to huddle in seacoast cities after their voyages in crowded and stinking ships. At first they were often more despised than blacks and they despised the blacks, yet they set out to compete for American space and in the course of years many gained moderate prosperity. These newcoming Irish found their Catholic churches to be magnets and they became part of a new power base in the cities.

People from the continent of Europe then helped add to the Catholic influx. The victims of a German governmental *Kulturkampf,* or "battle for civilization," against Catholics joined others who wanted to avoid military service in Europe or who simply longed to take advantage of American opportunity. They arrived in great numbers, many of them to settle in the rural Midwest. The Italian population grew from fewer than 4,000 in the middle of the nineteenth century to 500,000 fifty years later. In 1800 only 50,000 Catholics lived in the United States; by 1850 theirs was the largest church in America, and in 1900 it claimed 12,000,000 members. In 1808 only Bardstown, Kentucky, had a bishop in the lands west of the Appalachians. After the Civil War most cities outside the South boasted their own bishop and cathedral. Were the old dreams of

New Spain and New France for a Catholic North America at last to be fulfilled?

Anti-Catholic memories were long and hatreds were deep. Actions based on such attitudes bonded Catholics to each other and for a time hid from view their inner tensions. Catholicism in Europe was then an embattled force, but anti-Catholics in America conveniently portrayed the church as a juggernaut poised to crush the United States. The ever alert Lyman Beecher, for instance, raised funds in the eastern states to head off Catholic gains elsewhere with his *Plea for the West,* a tract that in 1835 warned that Catholics and infidels had a head start and that "if we gain the West, all is safe; if we lose it, all is lost."

Four years later the editor of the Protestant *Home Missionary* picked up the cry for the West, where was to be fought a great battle "between truth and error, between law and anarchy — between Christianity . . . and the combined forces of Infidelity and Popery." In the nineteenth century the pope had restored the aggressive religious order of Jesuits after his earlier ban. Protestants now sometimes sounded paranoid about these capable agents of Rome. One serious report announced as an ascertained fact that Jesuits were "prowling about all parts of the United States in every possible disguise." A minister in Ohio claimed to know that "the western country swarms with them under the names of puppet show men, dancing masters, music teachers, peddlers of images and ornaments, barrel organ players, and similar practitioners." Samuel F. B. Morse, both inventor of the telegraph and the noisiest anti-Catholic around, fairly shrieked: "Up! I beseech you. Awake! To your posts! Let the tocsin sound from Maine to Louisiana. Fly to protect the vulnerable places of your Constitution and Laws. Place your guards; you will need them; and quickly too, — And first, shut your gates."

In 1829 the Catholics' bishops encouraged them to form their own parochial schools. There they could nurture the faith and keep out influences from beyond the church. Nothing the leaders planned since did so much to build American Catholicism or enrage non-Catholics. The public schools, a new invention to integrate and educate all American children, looked too much like a junior department of the Protestant religious establishment — a department that read only the "Protestant" King James Version of the Bible. By 1840 about two hundred Catholic schools, half of them west of the Alleghenies, existed, to the irritation of their neighbors.

Even institutions of charity like the Catholic hospitals founded by orders of Catholic sisters aroused hostility.

Inside the Catholic churches immigrants felt that they were minding their own business as believers. As citizens, meanwhile, they provided the muscle to build the American city and as patriots they offered loyalty to the American state. Priests learned techniques that matched those of Protestant revivalists and then gathered settlers on the frontier or among the crowded urban masses. They built great if often gloomy sanctuaries to the glory of God and for the enrichment of their group life. The church calendar set the rhythms for the week and the year: mass on Sundays and feast days, meatless seasons and Fridays, hours for confessions, last rites and burial on Christian soil, prayer for life in heaven, fund-raising events to support the schools, mutual aid in times of need. These formed a cocoon of shelter and meaning for their members, whose descendants later called the result a Catholic ghetto.

Nativist and Know-Nothing movements, which went beyond the calls of Beecher and Morse, came to disrupt the coziness. Founders of *The Protestant* back in 1830 and of the American Protestant Association twelve years later gathered the ignorant, the fearful, and those lusting for power. They organized these as "Native Americans" against people they pictured as invading foreigners. Hell-raising ruffians took advantage of a foul spiritual climate and vandalized churches. Overlooking the rather consistent American Catholic criticism of Mexico, these forces used the Mexican War in 1846 to promote the idea of a world-wide Catholic conspiracy for power. The more literate Know-Nothing agitators liked to read what European Catholics wrote in criticism of republican government, but remained deaf to what American bishops argued in support of it.

The nativist crusade deserves attention for what it shows both about how an old Protestant establishment grudgingly yielded space and about what it did to shape conflict *within* Catholicism and, to some extent, Judaism. Two illustrations from the 1830s and 1840s set the scene for the later controversies within what we might call cocoons, and what others have called the ghettos. In 1834 a trivial spat between some brickyard workmen and convent laborers disrupted the serenity of a school that Ursuline nuns had opened seven years earlier at Charlestown, in Boston. After a minor riot the bricklayers left the scene, but rumors spread that convent inmates were violating standards of moral purity. In the midst of the whispers an emotionally troubled teacher named Elizabeth Harrison left the convent in a frenzy. While the family of a student was kindly taking care of her, Elizabeth's brother and the bishop of Boston arranged for a physician to see her. Though all of this activity was innocent, two Boston newspapers reported that a "young lady at the nunnery" disappeared and was not to be found.

Bishop James Fenwick, taking alarm, tried but failed to quiet the city. Charlestown officials who visited the convent to check out the stories announced that tales by Miss Harrison of her life as a prisoner in dungeons there were grounded only in her fervid imagination. The town selectmen assured the public that nothing was amiss. Nevertheless, at nine in the evening on August 11, about fifty people staked themselves around the school and demanded to have Miss Harrison delivered to their care. Soon a thousand people came to hoot down the selectmen who arrived to defend the school. The mob broke furniture and moved against the cross. "Now for the torches!" With presence of mind the nuns spirited the girls, not all of them Catholics, to the safety of homes. Rioters set about burning the fences and storming the building, which they defiled and looted while authorities and firefighters stood by silently.

Next day the ashes cooled, and so did some heads. Responsible citizens offered rewards to those who helped bring to justice those guilty of the "base and cowardly act," while others began to raise funds to repay the Ursulines. The mob, undeterred by these humane acts, regathered and for days continued to mill. In admiration the *Boston Gazette* spoke up for Bishop Fenwick; it both tried to keep Catholics from taking revenge and denounced as a degraded human species those who attacked the convent. Ministers began to decry the rioting; among them was Lyman Beecher, who had spent the Sunday before the clash raising $4,000 after three antipopery sermons. When the chaos ended, courts acquitted all rioters except one boy, who was later pardoned. The Charlestown tumult mingled envy, class resentment, sentiment against immigrants, rebellion without a cause, and ignorance over the unfamiliar with strands of old-style anti-Catholicism.

The same mix led to loss of life at Philadelphia some years later. In 1842 Bishop Francis P. Kenrick protested that Catholic children had to endure Protestant Bible translations in public schools. A compliant school board thereupon decided to allow Catholics to read their own versions, an act that inspired nativists to flail against foreign prelates who were invading their American city. The *Native American* even called for an assault against "aliens and foreigners."

Violence followed when "Native Americans" at a mass meeting decided to invade the Irish laboring section called Kensington. In the crowd that gathered, either one of the Native Americans or a frightened hothead in the Hibernia Hose Company fired a first shot. The attackers fell back and then returned to the front. While the militia momentarily kept the peace, Kenrick calmed the Catholics, but then the nativists broke through and burned thirty houses. The *Native American,* disappointed over the quiet that followed the shock of mob action, issued threats that *"no terms whatever"* were to be extended to any who followed the bloody hand of the pope.

On the third and worst day of rioting, an outmanned militia could not keep the assaulters from burning homes, Saint Michael's Church, and its adjacent seminary. Despite pleas from the mayor, they also moved against Saint Augustine's Church. Having gotten what it wanted, the *Native American* now tardily adopted tones of horror in reaction against the "wanton and uncalled for desecration" of a Christian altar. However, the day after the Fourth of July, hearing that a committee had found eighty-seven weapons stored at Saint Philip of Neri Church, the mob turned on that building. In a confrontation two days later, only the fact that the powder was wet in two cannons saved that edifice, but rioters battered down a door and killed an Irish vigilante. Hours later seven more people were dead. Though troops arrived with barricades, cannon fire continued for several hours.

When silence came at last, fifty were wounded, thirteen were dead, and Philadelphia was unrepentant. A committee of inquiry faulted the Catholics for having stored arms in a church. Up in New York, *The American Republican,* savoring more war, asserted that "Blood will have Blood." But there Bishop John Hughes put an end to folly using the only language nativists understood. He announced that if a single Catholic church were burned in New York, the city would lie ruined like Moscow. When Hughes learned that the law could not oblige the city to repay Catholics for any ruined property, he simply stationed armed men around churches until the crisis passed. The day for bloodshed was over, and Catholics were free to face other problems of adjustment to their new land.

James Cardinal Gibbons dominated other strong Catholic prelates late in the century. A little more than a year after the Civil War, a public sign of the new day was evident when these leaders gathered in Baltimore for their Second Plenary Council. Seven archbishops and thirty-seven bishops led the great procession to the Cathedral of the Assumption, while coaches deposited other dignitaries there. The acts of the council meant less than did such images, especially since the public had become aware of a two-year-old Syllabus of Errors that Rome issued to catalog and condemn, among others, the heresies of republicanism and its freedoms. Four years later, in 1870, a new problem of public relations developed when at the Vatican Council in Rome all but one American bishop voted to declare the pope infallible in faith and morals. Since morals, they knew, took in considerable territory, non-Catholics resented this claim.

Baltimore-born James Gibbons, who spent much of his youth in Ireland, was well poised to meet the new crises. After being graduated from seminary in Maryland, he climbed quickly in the clerical ranks. One of three priests chosen to pay respects to the assassinated body of President Lincoln in Baltimore, this young man favored by bishops himself became the "boy bishop" of Richmond in 1872. Five years later, at age forty-three, be became bishop of Baltimore and served in this most prestigious Catholic post until he died in 1921.

Gibbons possessed less evident intellectual talent than did some of his colleagues. His book *The Faith of Our Fathers,* a durable best-seller, was a routine work. No charmer, the frail-appearing diplomat often impressed others as indecisive. While he capably presided over the Third Plenary Council, he was not a great administrator of his diocese, nor did he easily delegate responsibilities or train successors. Gibbons settled for small gains, regularly recouped after losses, and constantly repaired old friendships when they were tested. All the words used to describe him suggest small virtues: he was equivocal, cautious, prudent, loyal — but he had everything he needed to become the greatest official leader American Catholics have seen.

Since Roman Catholic immigrants made up a great part of the working force in the cities, their spiritual leaders were drawn into the grand public debate of the Gibbons decades: did labor have the right to organize? In Europe most laborers abandoned Catholic practice through indifference, out of resentment, or for socialism. In America, Protestants failed to hold or even to win in the first place the loyalty of urban workers as a class. Their leaders were suspicious of what was new and threatening. To them the idea of collective bargaining violated natural law and the way God arranged things. They feared that labor organizations would compete with the church for the loyalty of members. Worst of all, the fame of Karl Marx and other socialists was spreading, and Americans often feared that the radicalism of European labor movements would infest the United States. Since acts of violence during strikes were more visible than were the subtle acts of oppression that wealthy managers enacted against employees who worked six twelve-hour days weekly, most Protestant church leaders instinctively sided with order and quiet against strikers.

Catholics were of two minds regarding labor. The well-off James Roosevelt Bayley, a convert who was a predecessor of Gibbons at Baltimore, had preached that no true Catholic dared encourage the subversive and communistic "miserable associations called labor organizations." Bayley sounded like a Protestant prince of the pulpit when he avowed that God permitted poverty as "the most efficient means of practicing some of the most necessary Christian virtues of charity and almsgiving on the part of the rich and patience and resignation to His holy will on the part of the poor." To speak up for organized labor, then, did not mean adapting to an American consensus but, rather, anticipating a new way of life for workers in the United States.

In 1869 along came a secret society. The Noble and Holy Order of the Knights of Labor emerged as part of the Philadelphia Garment Cutters' Union to become the chief early labor group. Because employers usually fired organizers, the Knights had to work secretly. They used models found in Freemasonry, which was an old enemy of Catholicism. Since Catholics had recently been in a fracas with secret societies, their guns were aimed at the Knights of Labor. Because so many Catholics were laborers, membership in the Knights of Labor posed cruel issues of loyalty for them.

For a time Gibbons, who could not have avoided the conflict even if he wished to, encouraged separate Catholic brotherhoods, like the New Knights of Saint John. Meanwhile the secret Ancient Order of Hibernians, to which many laborers belonged and which at some times flirted with Catholicism and at others used hostile terms against it, asked Gibbons where the church stood in relation to their organization. The archbishop, who counseled "vigilant masterly inactivity" in such cases, cautiously studied the Hibernians. He also summoned nerve to ask a rival, Bishop Michael A. Corrigan of New York, to appoint chaplains to the Order, reminding Corrigan of the unpleasant fact that in New York alone were 50,000 Catholic Hibernians. "If we want to preserve these thousands of souls to the faith, let us show sympathy for them." Gibbons cajoled the other American archbishops into going lightly against the Hibernians, though in a meeting at his residence in 1886 they did not go so far as to endorse the Order.

In 1886 the still-threatening Knights of Labor, under Grand Master Terence V. Powderly, rose to its peak of 700,000 members. Gibbons sensed correctly, however, that the Knights would soon be declining and that condemnation would only help them survive to become an anti-Catholic force. He shared the concerns for workers that his fellow-Catholic Powderly affirmed, but found it hard to speak up when Corrigan, Bishop Bernard McQuaid of Rochester, and Archbishop Elzéar Taschereau of Quebec took the case to Rome. Taschereau came back with a condemnation of the Knights in Canada, so the enemies of Gibbons used this act in order to organize for an onslaught in the United States. Powderly, on the spot, was confused: "Between the men who *love* God and the men who don't believe in God I have had a hard time of it."

Gibbons backed Baltimore streetcar drivers in their strike in 1886 and then supported the Knights when they struck some railroads. Cincinnati's Archbishop William Elder pressed Gibbons for a clear word about his stand on the Knights, only to hear again the characteristic counsel: in matters of this sort "a masterly inactivity and a vigilant eye" best served. Gibbons was sure that the Canadian condemnation could not apply in the United States. Elder should not be so severe with the Knights that they would think the church sided with huge corporations and employers. McQuaid and Corrigan thereupon found this the moment to engage in masterly activity against Gibbons. They began to pull strings in Rome. Taschereau wanted the Vatican to declare that truth in Canada was the same as truth in the United States. In the showdown in Baltimore that October, neither faction of the archbishops won decisively.

The next January Taschereau and Gibbons had to share shipboard on the way to Rome, where both were to become cardinals. The Canadian fired first: he was going to Rome to have the Knights condemned. In Rome, however, Archbishops John J. Keane and John Ireland were helping prepare a classic Catholic defense that saw labor as "natural and just." This treatise Gibbons signed and transmitted to America: "To lose the heart of the people would be a misfortune for which the friendship of the few rich and powerful would be no compensation." Rome "should not offer to America an ecclesiastical protection for which she does not ask, and of which she believes she has no need." Gibbons tried to gain the support of American bishops; the press divided over his efforts. The *New York Times* thought the bishop was siding with brutish and lawless movements. *The Nation* accused Gibbons of "partaking freely of the labor beverage" until his head had become unclear, and the Protestant Episcopal *Churchman* curiously thought Rome was encroaching on America through the wily Baltimorean.

In June, Gibbons returned home to a generally friendly reception. By midsummer the Knights on their own had lost 200,000 members. A mild address by Gibbons failed to rally them; a year later he guessed they had only 350,000 members left. After Chicago hanged its Haymarket Square "labor anarchists" — rioters whose violent activities were used to stigmatize all labor organizations — McQuaid wrote Corrigan that the pets of His Eminence Gibbons were now "breaking to pieces and . . . getting many more kicks than kisses." But Rome refused to join in the kicking. The Vatican came out with a weak decree that did not explicitly condemn the Knights. Gibbons acted as if his grand point about labor had now been made, while the Knights disappeared as an issue and other organizations began to take its place. "You were a prophet!" cheered Archbishop Ireland to Gibbons from Rome. In 1890 Cardinal James Manning in England congratulated Gibbons: "This is surely the New World overshadowing the Old, and the Church walking with its Master among the people of Christendom." A year later Pope Leo XIII issued a papal letter, *Rerum novarum,* which openly endorsed views of the sort Gibbons was advocating. Ever after, Gibbons looked back on the crisis of 1887–89 as the time when the church kept the hearts of laborers and remained true to her own history.

If labor was a public issue, the second great struggle of the Gibbons era more directly concerned the inner life of the church and the issue of Americanizing. The English-speaking, largely Irish, Catholic majority generally sided with those Protestants who saw America as a phoenix grave of European nationalities. While religious differences should remain, they thought, in America ethnic boundaries would mean progressively less until a fused Catholic people would emerge. The German vanguard of Continental immigrants spoke up for an opposing model. United in faith with other Catholic ethnic groups in America, they feared Irish dominance and fought to keep their own sense of peoplehood, their own language and custom, their right to govern their own churches.

"Stay German — German! Do not become English." Thus King

Ludwig I of Bavaria sent off the first order of sisters from Germany in 1847. For the next seventy years, until the First World War, many Catholics in America tried to remain faithful to such charges. They turned their Cincinnati hillsides, Saint Louis neighborhoods, and Wisconsin valleys into little bits of Germany. Gibbons looked on in concern: "Is not this country chiefly indebted to Ireland for its faith?" Irish hands built more churches from Maine to California, from Canada to Mexico, and contributed "not only to the *material* but also to the *personnel* of the Church." This was a fact that Germans certainly did not need to hear reinforced.

Though a man of Irish provincial mentality, Gibbons also had a grand vision of a united American Catholic church. Under his leadership the Third Plenary Council in 1884 compromised by drawing ethnic parish lines and then looked for devices to bring Catholics together despite them. Resistance came from many fronts. In Cincinnati, one German priest feared that his people might drift toward the American way, with its "hotbed of fanaticism, intolerance and radical ultra views on matters of politics and religion." His people must stay German to fight off the American nationality, which bred "all the vagaries of spiritualism, Mormonism, free-loveism, prohibition, infidelity, and materialism."

Seeking to use Baltimore as a pattern for amity among Catholics, Gibbons wanted to be friendly to Father Peter Abbelen, a representative of Milwaukee's German-born archbishop Michael Heiss; so he wrote a letter endorsing Abbelen's complaints against Irish dominance in German churches. Abbelen, not playing fair with the diplomatic Gibbons, flaunted the document in Rome, until Keane and Ireland had to wonder aloud how their friend Gibbons could have given a recommendation to "this secret emissary of a clique of German Bishops among us." The letter was innocent enough, but some words in it gave plausibility to the charge that attempts were now being made to Americanize Germans and in that way lead them away from the church.

Gibbons, on the spot, wrote Rome that he refused absolutely to recognize any ethnic distinction in the government of the church. To do so would be self-defeating, "for if any one nationality is accorded special privileges, other nationalists will thereafter demand the same." He wrote one bishop that he wanted to ward off a "war of races" that would only vindicate charges of enemies that American Catholicism was "a religion of foreigners." Abbelen then lost his appeal to chop up the American church on national lines. The Congregation of the Propaganda in Rome turned it down.

The conflict heated again when Peter Paul Cahensly pressed the German theme. This Rhineland merchant had arrived in 1883 to promote a Saint Raphael's Society for the Care of German Catholic Emigrants. He played on fears that atheists, infidels, and Protestants would lure neglected Catholics from the faith. His society tried to show that millions of them had already drifted because their leaders showed no interest in their nationality. In 1890 the Saint Raphaelites drafted a "Lucerne Memorial" from Switzerland and the next year took it to Pope Leo. The appeal asked that wherever possible, Catholics of each nationality have in the episcopate of the country where they immigrate several bishops who are of the same origin. Bishop Ireland, now in Saint Paul, Minnesota, defensively wrote Gibbons: "We are American bishops, and an effort is made to dethrone us, and to foreignize our country in the name of religion." Bishop John Samuel Foley of Detroit pleaded with Gibbons to save the Irish from "the wicked wretch Cahensly."

Gibbons remained publicly calm as he tried to win over the German bishops in America to his side in the war against an "Americo-European conspiracy" that could lead each "greedy ecclesiastical adventurer that comes to our country" to grab an episcopal see. In a courageous sermon at Milwaukee, he shouted woes on anyone who would divide American Catholics. "Brothers we are, whatever may be our nationality." The ties of grace and faith were stronger than those of flesh and blood. "Loyalty to God's Church and to our Country! — this is our religious and political faith." The *Chicago Tribune* found these to be "wise words"; Gibbons's policy officially prevailed, while the new Europeans from the southern and eastern areas looked for ways to dig in and keep their own identities despite the official policy of the church. They found it possible to be loyal to America, to Catholicism, and to what "the old country" represented in the new.

More tests of Americanism were ahead, as Catholics fought off a minor round of nativism when midwestern populists organized the ineffective American Protective Association, which challenged those who were in "the shackles and chains of blind obedience to the Roman Catholic church." Then, when the United States declared war on Catholic Spain in 1898, there came a new test, which the church easily passed. After it was over, Gibbons counseled policies of moderation to both Presidents McKinley and Roosevelt.

More illuminating of internal strife was a richly symbolic event, the Catholic participation in the World's Columbian Exposition at

Chicago in 1893. At a Catholic congress connected with the fair, Gibbons, at the urging of Archbishop Ireland, spoke a few words, but the papal legate, Archbishop Francisco Satolli, made the headlines. Non-Catholics were not prepared to hear such words from the apostolic delegate to the United States: "Go forward, in one hand bearing the book of Christian truth and in the other the Constitution of the United States. Christian truth and American liberty will make you free, happy and prosperous."

The cheer of this Catholic sideshow was eventually dispelled after a more controversial day during the accompanying World's Parliament of Religions. For eighty years Americans had sent missionaries to rescue pagans from the religions whose leaders were now welcomed to parade their saffron robes, turbans, and other regalia in Chicago. To appear to be tolerant to Buddhist, Hindu, and Muslim visitors was a risk for Gibbons, but Bishop Keane encouraged allowing a Catholic presence alongside them at the festival. The progressive bishops decided that since Catholicism possessed all the truth, the church could display it without leading people to think that all faiths were on a par. When the parliament climaxed, ill health kept Gibbons off the stage most of the time, so Keane read a paper by him. In it the prelate did little more than praise charity and benevolence among people of separate faiths, and the day passed without crisis.

From as far away as Palermo, Italy, priests applauded Gibbons and Keane for having opened a "new era in the history of the Catholic Church." Still, the uneasy Baltimorean thought it best to report to Mariano Cardinal Rampolla in Rome that everything in Chicago was proper, that the occasion helped display Catholic truth against atheism. Rampolla sent back word that the pope was satisfied. Then, in March 1894, Protestant journalist F. Herbert Stead published a thoroughly garbled account of the parliament incident in *Review of Reviews*. Stead had heard Cardinal Gibbons publicly say that for him the attraction of Catholicism was her system of charities more than her faith and morals, her worldwide scope, or apostolic succession of bishops.

Suddenly all the old enemies of Americanization and Gibbons threatened to reemerge. Pope Leo opened 1895 with a long-promised letter to the American churches. He praised the church and the nation, but one sentence in the document seemed designed to flush every leftover nativist out of the bushes. It would be false, Leo said, for anyone to conclude that the United States had developed the most desirable status for the church, or that everywhere it would be lawful and expedient for state and church to be "as in America, dissevered and divorced." On highest authority the old secret was now out: if the pope would have his way, he would unite church and state. Gibbons and his friends, vulnerable after Stead's misreporting about Chicago, prepared to duck for cover and wait for reaction. Evidently by then they had done their task of advertising Catholic adaptation well: Americans seemed to be yawning about the papal letter. Ireland was supposed to write an article commenting on the fateful sentence for the *North American Review*. First he showed reluctance because he felt it could not be explained to Americans and later he begged off simply because the pope's letter evoked so little controversy.

Non-Catholic Americans were becoming more convinced than European Catholics that two loyalties were blending into one in American Catholicism. Fighting their own battles, some Europeans invented a heresy, called it Americanism, and then went looking for people who might hold it. In Rome those who opposed adaptation attacked Monsignor Denis J. O'Connell, rector of the North American College there, charging that he was an American-ist progressive. Soon the same parties saw to the dismissal of Keane as rector of the Catholic University of America, the Americanizers' stronghold. Papal diplomat Satolli seems to have caused the change in climate. Despite his friendly flourish at Chicago in 1893, he kept feeding Pope Leo stories biased against the American moderates. Gibbons fought back and somehow helped win a new post for Keane in Rome, where he could provide the eyes for the American-izers. In 1897 Keane reported back that Satolli and company were attacking in Americanism even policies that were "simon-pure Catholicity and disinterested devotedness to the Holy See." Satolli held the privileged spot. Keane became almost powerless.

The battle site then shifted to France, where conservative royal-ists seized on a translation of the *Life of Father Hecker* because the French progressive Abbé Felix Klein had affixed a too-enthusiastic modernizing preface. The royalists contended that this approach turned Isaac Hecker into more of a democrat than a Catholic. Though neither Hecker nor the Americanizing groups held the heresies that Klein all too eagerly found in them, the royalists con-sidered the moment strategic. They named the errors that they opposed in Americanism. Gibbons knew how to rate their fury: "I regard the attacks of Protestants as mild compared with the unprin-cipled course of these so-called Catholics." To be sure, fighting within was more disturbing than storms without the church.

Satolli lunged, hoping to settle old scores. He even charged falsely that Americans were promoting war against Spain in order to carve up the Catholic empire. Gibbons tried to prove that no set of bishops was more loyal to Rome than the Americans, but his language was futile. Pope Leo asked the biased jury of Satolli and the Jesuit cardinal Camillo Mazzella to summarize the case against Americanism. On January 22, 1899, the pope issued the meandering formal letter *Testem Benevolentiae,* which he asked Gibbons to publicize in the American church. No one had to wince, because the letter was only a very vague attack on ill-defined errors held by unnamed heretics. Corrigan and the German bishops in America, using their interpretation of the document, rejoiced in the letter, but friends of Hecker and Gibbons defended them. Gibbons himself wrote the pope that what the French called Americanism was absurd, extravagant, and unrepresented in America.

In a meeting of the American archbishops at Catholic University in October, aggressors failed to amass enough enthusiasm to look for Americanist heretics. Non-Catholics seemed to be looking away in boredom. Satolli, it is true, had won a momentary, if partial, victory. For a while Gibbons had to move cautiously. The long-range triumph, however, went to the party that set the new terms for Catholic life in a republic. In April 1902, a peace-seeking Leo wrote Gibbons a letter signed with both tears and cheers. "While the changes and the tendencies of nearly all the nations which were Catholic for many centuries gave cause for sorrow," the state of the American church "in this flourishing youthfulness" filled his heart with delight. Leo's successor, Pope Pius X, decided that the youth had matured. Four hundred sixteen years after the Catholic discovery of America, on June 29, 1908, in *Sapienti consilio,* the pope finally declared that the church in the United States was no longer under the missionary Congregation de Propaganda Fide. America was no longer missionary territory. Rome recognized what it was becoming to millions of Catholics who made pilgrimages to it and in it: their own land.

As for Judaism, its problems of adaptation to America differed in most respects from those of Catholicism. Through most of the nineteenth century anti-Jewishness in America was mild compared to anti-Catholicism, perhaps because there were so few Jews. Any one of a dozen almost invisible German Protestant sects in Pennsylvania outnumbered the Jews, who seemed by weight of numbers alone to be no threat. Given eighteen centuries of bad experience on Christian soil, however, Jews found it difficult to feel truly at ease. Leaders who urged them to prove themselves to fellow citizens and to find in America their Zion were more enthusiastic Americanizers than were the Catholics, whose extremes were reined in by Rome, which had no counterpart in Judaism.

Jewish Americanizers, on the other hand, met formidable opposition from traditionalists, Orthodox Jews who felt that to adapt spiritually to America would mean to barter away the belief and practices of an ancient people. The two parties battled over language and law, over building Zion in Jerusalem or in America, over how to be a Jew in the American environment.

The temptation simply to blend into a congenial environment was strong. To live as did other Americans without calling attention to separate ways would make passage to modernity easy for Jews. Most of them were in the North and thus strongly pro-Union, though many in the South defended slavery. Politically they presented no distinct Jewish profile. They made their livings just as did their neighbors. The historically minded element that later took the name Conservative therefore feared that in these circumstances nothing unique about Judaism would survive.

A pioneer who helped urge Jews to be both traditional *and* American was German-born Isaac Leeser. After spending his young adulthood in Richmond, he made Philadelphia his base. In 1830 he became hazan, an appointee who held leadership posts but was not a rabbi, at Congregation Mikveh Israel in that city. Since the congregation was largely Spanish-Portuguese, or Sephardic, in background, it was exceptional for them to invite this Ashkenazic brother to be their leader. Leeser refused to accept the limits of his office. He wanted to preach, as rabbis did — a desire that induced thirteen years of controversy. He won the rights he sought, but after seven more years felt called to move on from the scene of his victory.

Leeser next took to the road for seven years of circuit riding, having learned the lesson of the revivalists: religious leaders in America could take no one for granted. They had to round up worshipers and move them from apathy to enthusiasm. The hazan-turned-itinerant thus set out on a sixteen-week trip in 1851. The sojourner toured from the Great Lakes to the Gulf of Mexico, always reporting subsequently on lonely Jews, isolated congregations, absent or inept leaders. He promoted the Hebrew language and a "federal union" of congregations for the sake of identity and a common spirit. There must be a college for "travelling missionaries," rabbis who could minister in needy locales. He expected to find not a Jew between Buffalo and Chicago, yet in every village he claimed to find some. Twenty families each were known in Detroit and "Ipsylanti," and even smaller Marshall and Ralmazoo (Kalamazoo) had ten each. They lacked Jewish spiritual advisers to guide them.

Isaac Leeser seemed obsessed with the need for leadership. He founded *The Occident* to spread the Jewish word. His Jewish Publication Society, founded in 1845, soon failed, but not before he had begun to turn out books for teaching children. More important to him was his Maimonides College at Philadelphia — founded much later, in 1868, but still the first Jewish agency of higher learning in America. The little, short-lived seminary had only a half dozen faculty members and never so many students. One year it enrolled only three Philadelphians and a stray student from Dubuque, Iowa. Leeser in 1857 settled down at Beth El Emeth in Philadelphia for his final eleven years. After he was gone, Conservative Judaism languished for some decades, to be renewed at the turn of the century. Yet he had left it with an important model, an American vision as vivid as were those of John Winthrop, Jonathan Edwards, and Bishop John Carroll: "This country," said Leeser, "is emphatically the one where Israel is to prepare itself for its glorious mission of regenerating mankind."

So far as the Jewish public was concerned, however, the decades toward the end of the nineteenth century belonged less to Conservatism or to Orthodoxy than to the more visible Reform branch. This was a movement that captured wide public notice, even though it did not enlist most of the newly arriving Jews. In some ways akin to Unitarianism, early Reform set out to turn the Jewish story into a universal ethical faith. Its advocates liked to claim that "the spirit of the age" impelled them to adapt, to fuse Judaism and Americanism. Despite the individualism that goes with such a free-spirited movement, Reform boasted an organizer to match Leeser in Rabbi Isaac Mayer Wise, whom Leeser came to resent even though he knew how to work alongside him. Though to the Conservative Wise often seemed inconsistent, foolish, or wrong, the diminutive and cocky rabbi outlasted his opponents with his own vision of America as the New Zion.

Born in 1819 into a family of physicians and financiers in Bohemia, as a child Wise did not feel the restrictions or prejudices that limited many Jews there. Discouraged by his schoolmaster from reading the mystical Jewish cabala and other presumably pointless and out-of-date literature, he turned to German literary classics or the works of the Jewish Renaissance and Enlightenment. Wise surprised his family by announcing that he would be a rabbi. He drifted from place to place, gleaning what he could for his calling, learning at the Zigeuner Shul, or Gypsy Synagogue, as well as at the universities of Prague and Vienna.

In 1843 Wise became a rabbi at the fairly prosperous Radnitz synagogue, where he studied the Talmud and the codes of Jewish custom in the Shulchan Aruch, but the philosophers he met pleased him as much as did these Jewish sources. The dream of a modern Judaism pulled him toward America. He became what he later called "a naturalized American in the interior of Bohemia." Sick of home, morbidly dissatisfied with country and city, fed up with Judaism and Christianity in Europe, he read his own needs into the ancient biblical call that began Abraham's pilgrimage. "You must emigrate" became a divine command. After a grand tour of German intellectual centers that included interviews with Reform leaders, Wise and his family left Bremen in 1846 and joined the little wave of Reformists at Charleston, South Carolina. After visiting two other synagogues, they settled in at Albany, New York. Isaac Leeser, who overlooked very little in *The Occident,* took notice of this "young schoolmaster who also preaches, and is said to possess some Hebrew learning."

Albany seemed a part of an "utterly strange land," but there Wise devised his plan for *Minhag America,* or "The American Way," an approach to worship and living in the new land. Prominent rabbi Max Lilienthal admired Wise's talent but wanted him to forget the plan: "This is a land of practical men; your program is utopian." Leeser openly denounced the prayers in *Minhag America* because Wise conveniently dropped those that called for the rebuilding of the temple at Jerusalem. How dared a rabbi disbelieve the clear promises of the Hebrew Scriptures?

For eight years, while he wrestled with doubts about remaining a rabbi, or at least about serving the congregation, feisty Rabbi Wise stayed on at Albany. Rarely could he resist opportunities to set forth his own way in the face of both Leeser and the Christian missionaries, many of whom liked to make Jews their prime targets. In a typical instance, he learned from the *Albany Argus* that a "Reverend Rabbi Cohn," now a Christian, was to speak. Wise stepped out in his frock coat to hear the missionary. He sat in a seat reserved for Protestant clergy. The local host, assuming that etiquette must rule in the meeting, invited anyone to speak. This call was to be the cue for Cohn, but Wise instead jumped up first and blasted the Christian mission to Jews. To his surprise, many in the audience applauded him. Quickly he moved for adjournment. A Unitarian minister seconded the motion. The "Aye!" shouters were noisiest, and the gathering broke up in chaos.

Religious jousting in the 1850s was seldom decorous. During one Rosh Hashanah, or New Year, festival, Wise entered his synagogue to find his seat preempted. This rival, he wrote, "steps in my way, and, without saying a word, smites me with his fist so that my cap falls from my head. This was the terrible signal for an uproar the like of which I have never experienced. The people acted like furies. . . . The young people jumped down from the choir-gallery to protect me. . . . The Sheriff and his posse, who were summoned, were belabored and forced out until finally the whole assembly surged out of the house into Herkimer Street." A constable then, by prearrangement, arrested Wise for ringleading a rebellious mob. Was this to be the American way? "It was agonizing, hellish torture. This victory of orthodoxy proved its grave wherein it was buried." Wise enjoyed every moment of the conflict.

In 1853 Congregation K. K. B'nai Yeshurun of Cincinnati buoyed the rabbi with a call that was a "streak of lightning rushing through a dingy atmosphere." It beckoned him to the "broad, healthful and youthful West." First, however, Wise had to wonder whether the call itself was not a hoax or a jest. Did not the people of that Far West read the papers and know how discredited he was? Then Wise decided that Cincinnati was full of people who were not yet cast into a fixed mold. Forty years later, he still pleasurably remembered the pioneers of Reform in that Queen City as a noble band who welcomed his patriotic sermons. At last he could begin to realize his dreams through a paper, *The Israelite* (later *The American Israelite*).

To unite American Jews, Wise helped convoke a "Cleveland Conference." For it he packed all his goals into one line: he hoped for an "American Judaism, free, progressive, enlightened, united and respected." At the conference Leeser and Wise found that they had to deal with each other and also that, very tentatively, they could do so. Wise also now learned that there were reformers even to his left — "the Little-Big Men of New York," he called them — who would abandon the Talmud as the cherished exposition of Scripture. Unless they were sent to Salt Lake and their schemes were jettisoned, he thought, New York must soon be a miserable place for Judaism. Their radical position led Leeser to compensate by more firmly holding to tradition as he moved toward Americanization. Wise meanwhile held to his American plan but spoke henceforth more fondly of Jewish tradition than before. After the two men parted, Leeser accused Wise and the Reformers of violating the uniting spirit both had known in Cleveland. Wise grumbled about Leeser and his "mad dog cry of heresy at our heels" — a fanaticism he claimed would do honor to a pope preaching crusades against infidels.

As an Americanizer Wise naturally felt called to speak out regularly on issues beyond Cincinnati. In 1855 he defended Catholics against the nativists. He chose to lambast abolitionists as much as he criticized slaveholders. Nothing dared interfere with the design of Providence for this "sea-girt continent." Wise feared Southern secession. Protestant priests as reckless abolitionists had to be hypocrites, since "no power on earth can change this manifest destiny" by which America was to produce the last and highest triumphs of humanity. Why, the rabbi also asked, did Protestants of the North defend remote Negroes and rebuke distant slaveholders while having no word to say "for the white Hebrew who gave you God and a religion?"

Wise put most of his energies into the Cincinnati congregation and his vision of America. When he dedicated a two-thousand-seat, Moorish-looking synagogue, he pressed the theme of American Zion. "We do not wish to return to Palestine. . . . We are American citizens and Israelites by religion." In 1869 he attended a Philadelphia conference organized by some of the "Little Big-Men of New York" and their kind. While nothing came of the convention, its mood definitely supported liberal Judaism as a universal set of values. A year later, in the 1870 conference at Cleveland, the congregations that used *Minhag America* rallied with enough verve that Wise thought his would turn out in the end to be the liturgy of all American Israelites. Now he took to the road with the astonishing message that Reform Judaism was not just a faith for Jews but was *the* faith for moderns, the fulfillment for Americans.

In 1873 Wise saw the Union of American Hebrew Congregations (UAHC) take form. Two years later he founded his most impressive monument, Hebrew Union College in Cincinnati. The rabbi spent his last quarter-century defining American Judaism. To his left were the New York liberalizers and the radical Felix Adler, who tried to beguile Jewish recruits into the Ethical Culture movement. But Wise's durable foes were on the right. In 1883 Jews of many outlooks attended a UAHC banquet in Cincinnati. After they were seated, they found to their great shock that the menu included oysters and other seafood that openly violated the laws of kashruth, ritual purity in diet. Wise was not personally at fault for this accidental breach of practice, but he later spoke far too light-heartedly about the offense. He greatly miscalculated the sentiment of many other Jews when he announced his lack of interest in "men of purely Jewish stomachs and unadulterated tastes." Nobody, he said, had appointed them "overseers of the kitchen or task-masters of the stomach." The American Israelite "does not deal in victuals."

Despite setbacks and withdrawals, the UAHC prospered. In 1889 the Central Conference of American Rabbis formed in Detroit. The outline of Wise's program seemed complete. He could boast: "We are the religious monitors of this country, we opposed the follies and errors of sectarianism, and clinging tenaciously and firmly to the word of God as revealed to common sense, we are of incalculable benefit to the spiritual development of this country."

As readily as Gibbons and Keane and Ireland among Catholics, Wise and his colleagues had captured something of what he called "the spirit of the times." Reform Jews helped bridge the experience of people who moved from European shelter to American exposure. Hundreds of thousands of Jews took this path through the years, but it was very remote from the new millions who swarmed through New York's immigrant station Ellis Island from eastern Europe. Wise was condescending and sometimes almost cruel about them, insisting that while he could help them with food and clothing, religiously "they will come to us, we can never come to them."

Wise found the newest arrivals ungrateful for accepting his charity and then attacking his program. These new Russian immigrants he must call Jews, while the Reformers were Israelites. The "semi-Asiatic Hassidism and Medieval orthodoxy" they brought might lower the social status of all Jews; "it is high time for them to understand that they live in America." His attacks grew ever more strident. "We are Americans and they are not," he said of those who held to the "half-civilized orthodoxy which constitutes the bulk of population" in the cities of the Northeast. More, "we are Israelites of the nineteenth century and a free country, and they gnaw the dead bones of past centuries." For the honor of American Judaism and Reform defense of enlightenment, the two sets of people should not even want to have a name in common.

Almost needless to say, Wise and early Reform Jews opposed budding Zionism, the urge for a new homeland in reborn Israel. In 1882 the rabbi wrote that the idea of a Jewish return played no part in the Reform creed. Jews were not a nation among the nations but a universal people. He was well aware that pogroms in Europe inspired anew the old ideas of a Jewish homeland, but he thought they would pass as the anti-Jewish craze disappeared. "It is all a momentary furore [sic]," and when it died down no European Jew would wish to migrate to Palestine. The rabbi said he had scant patience with any man who wanted something better for Jews than the United States offered.

Wise, who died in 1900, acted in the end as if Yiddish-speaking newcomers were the only alternative to Reform in America, but the historical school in the shadow of Leeser also revived. Near the end of the century it resurfaced as Conservative Judaism. This was a movement as literate as Reform and as eager to be American, but more ready to stress the Jewish tradition. Conservatives worked hard to win the exiles from the pogroms. Sabato Morais, a successor to Leeser, even pronounced a shame on the renegade rabbis who dared, before the ark of God and from the pulpit of Jewish temples, to say that these brothers were "too low." Then he showed where his heart was as he asked whether Americans must send them back "lest America become Russianized."

After 1878 the Conservatives set out to start their own seminary and program. When Reform temples as early as 1854 added Sunday services to the traditional Friday-through-Saturday Sabbath, the historical school took a negative stand. Benjamin Szold decreed that whoever denied the unique Sabbath denied the whole Torah. "A congregation which holds Sunday services may be compared to a bigamist who still clings to his first wife and loves both his spouses." The Reform Pittsburgh Platform of 1885 helped produce a formal break between the two schools. When Rabbi Kaufman Kohler boasted that Pittsburgh represented a Jewish Declaration of Independence, his Conservative foes agreed: yes, it was "independence from Judaism."

At the end of the year 1886, the Counter-Reform started frail Jewish Theological Seminary. A year later it chartered the Jewish Publication Society. Hopes of many that the movement would win over the mélange of Orthodox congregations, however, died with the turn of the century. The Orthodox found Conservative worship too staid and genteel. This Counter-Reform movement itself was, in their eyes, too frankly Americanized. But some notable rabbis and lay leaders, including prominent New Yorkers Simon Guggenheim, Mayer Sulzberger, Jacob Schiff, and Isidor Straus came to give aid with their pledge of a half million dollars. The seminary was assured a future. In 1901 they prevailed on the gifted rabbi Solomon Schechter to come from England to head the school and do battle for Conservatism. Schechter sensed that the new theory that America could blend all nationalities was not appealing to everyone. The English newcomer discerned instead that the most marked feature in American religion was its conservative tendency, to which Judaism could minister. For him American history began with neither the native Indians nor peculiar sects. The country was a creation of the biblical Old Testment, which still exercised enormous influence as a spiritual power despite all the new destructive tendencies, "mostly of foreign make." For Schechter, America stood for "wideness of scope and for conservatism."

In their tenement cellars and sweatshops, the new immigrants heard nothing and cared nothing for the debates of these learned leaders. In the indignities of Ellis Island or their smoky garment-workers' union halls in New York, the refinements of Americanism were remote. Most of the newcoming Jews took for granted the existence of shul, or synagogue. They rejected the vehement atheism of their anarchist few. Their little synagogues, however, tended to be unorganized, separate from each other. Jews needed settlement houses, playgrounds, and union halls. They often neglected the synagogues, which for generations in Europe had nurtured their life in the small communities of the shtetl as well as in the urban ghetto.

The new immigrants found the frontier closed. They had no funds to reach it in any case. Unwelcome in commerce or industry, the masses were mechanics, artisans, tailors. Yet they too had a vision. Abraham Cahan, their most popular journalist and novelist, gave voice to their hopes: "I paced my room in a fever. America! To go to America! To reestablish the Garden of Eden in that distant land. My spirit soared. All my other plans dissolved. I was for America."

America, however, was not very much "for" these Jews. For the first time, large-scale anti-Jewish expression now emerged. Novelist Henry James returned from Europe to bemoan in language too common among elites the amazing "extent of the Hebrew Conquest" of New York. Christian missionaries tried to raid the ghettos for converts. The uprooted immigrants found it hard to transplant their faith, to live by Jewish custom and law in the harsh routine of their depressing lives. Yet from the synagogue they took the heritage of learning and now made a virtual new religion out of education. Parents saved pennies so their children could climb up in the ghetto or, better, out of it. Long had they loved learning and scrolls for their own sake and for the love of God. Now they added the themes of achievement and secular advancement until these became replacements. Charities, benevolences, philanthropies, public schools, self-help organizations, and, eventually, the Zionist program became the new network of competitors to the synagogue, on the Lower East Side of New York and in other cities.

The debates of the Wises and Leesers were not, however, beside the point. For people who never learned their names, they posed two of the main alternatives for religious Jews in the century to come. They could choose to be faithful to the ancient religious tradition and adapt their grasp of America to it. Or they could show so much confidence in the values of that tradition that they could risk its detail in an open embrace of a modernity that half-respected but only selectively preserved the past. For both sides America was still a kind of Eden or Zion. In the face of decisions between pure tradition and pure modernity, neither the Jews nor other Americans have found the choices simple.

One of the last causes that united liberal and
conservative Protestants alike was temperance. The
coalition helped legislate Prohibition but lost some
of its credibility and most of its unity by the time of
Repeal. In 1894 Milton W. Garnes mixed pastoral
imagery with an industrial symbol, the railroad, to
suggest the dire future for the drunkard.
(*Granger Collection, New York*)

Chapter Fourteen

CRISES IN THE
PROTESTANT EMPIRE

$\mathscr{W}$ WHILE TRYING TO EXCLUDE NONWHITES FROM PARTICIPATING IN American life and while forcing tests of Americanization on non-Protestant whites, the keepers of the Protestant empire themselves faced four profound tests toward the end of the nineteenth century. How they faced them helped pose issues that have troubled the heirs of old-stock Protestantism ever since.

Two of the crises were chiefly intellectual. They nagged those who trained or became ministers more than the millions who made up the congregations. Still, uncertainty and conflict among leaders had a bearing on the faith and outlook of followers. One of the crises, the theory of evolution, hit the church in two waves. First, in reaction to Charles Darwin's *Origin of Species* in 1859, most avant-garde church leaders were able to adapt mainstream scientists' own response. The American scientific community had not yet bought the theory of natural selection, which introduced a random plotlessness into the story of human and universal origins. Still, any theory of evolution posed the possibility of conflict with conservative views of human nature and the Bible.

The Bible: it became the other battleground for intellectual leaders and has divided liberal from conservative Protestants through the twentieth century. What was the nature of its authority? This question had to be asked afresh because importers were bringing in European theories that called for people to treat the Bible historically and literarily, like any other ancient document. To do so seemed to rob it of claims that it was uniquely the inspired Word of God. Since Protestantism based its authority on the uniqueness of that book, any assault on the old view — even in the hands of reverent people who thought "scientific" views would enhance faith — could undercut belief, morals, and even the foundations of Bible-based America.

The other two crises were less theological in nature and had to do more with the practice of faith and strategies for serving industrializing America. The first had to do with economic doctrines. Protestants had fused old notions of their callings, stewardship of the earth, and individualism with practical patterns of making livings. These had worked in a world of one-to-one relations. What would they mean in corporate America, where decision was often remote from the people? Huge sums of money were at stake in the new factories and railroads, and policies concerning these enterprises were in the hands of people far from workers and consumers. In response, laborers began to organize, yet organization seemed to contradict natural law, old habits, and the Word of God. How should Protestantism handle this? Should it attach itself, as some leaders did, to the semi-secular teachings of a "Social Darwinism"? That school of thought was also individualistic, but, as we shall see, it fostered a dog-eat-dog competition that compromised other Protestant teachings.

Concurrently there was the fourth crisis. Protestantism had prospered in town-and-country America, among northwest European and British immigrants who adjusted easily to the covenants of the Republic. Now, suddenly, America was becoming an increasingly urban and industrial scene. Protestants did not know how to minister to the millions of new arrivals in crowded cities or to the workers in the new factories. The Protestants realized that industrial change brought into being a new victim class of the poor and overlooked. Could the churches find in their own tradition ways to understand, motivation to serve, techniques to be effective?

Internal conflict over these four crises weakened what was left of the old Protestant empire, which already had been divided between North and South and compromised by the way white Protestants had failed to recognize or relate to black counterparts. Now the divisions came to be "conservative" versus "liberal," "traditional" versus "progressive," "resistant" versus "adaptationist" in character. The house divided was less able to define the terms to which non-Protestants had to relate. The Protestants' divisions also left the opening for new secular schools of thought and churchless ways of behavior to develop.

One might say that millions of Americans perceived these crises through billions of particulars. They heard sermons, read articles, watched smokestacks develop, saw their lives determined by men who could hire or fire them en masse, read popular magazines. It probably best serves our purpose here to attempt to understand the changes wrought in the Protestant empire by focusing on a number of prominent pilgrims or leaders of pilgrims.

Until the 1860s most believers thought that God created the world in six days and placed humans in it by instantaneous acts of creation. In this view the various species never developed beyond the form they possessed on the day God made them and presented them to Adam for naming. Stable views of the universe tied God to a younger world and smaller heavens than the scientists discovered. To the believer, however, that world was special because humans were in it and in the Bible God revealed a special concern for them. Those who look carefully should see enough grandeur in the world to be awed by it, but they must know that someday God will bring an end to that world.

Through the first half of the century, intellectuals heard about new theories of development coming out of German universities, but dismissed them simply as atheistic philosophy. When American transcendentalists talked about the development of nature by a fluid deity or divine process, it seemed to be the private language of Boston elites. Then, in 1845, there appeared an American edition of a sensational new English book, *Vestiges of the Natural History of Creation*. Robert Chambers, its anonymous author, traced the growth of the world from a "universal fire-mist" until life generated itself. Chambers, still thinking such processes came somehow from God, gave him honor, but his American critics feared that such processes made God obsolete or useless. When they called Chambers an atheist and his book a work of the devil, these early critics first tasted blood.

Fifteen years later the more important book came from the hand of a man who took fewer pains to protect himself against charges of atheism. One year after its publication in England in 1859, Charles Darwin published *The Origin of Species* in America. The American scientists could understand Darwin without waiting years for translations, as they had to do with dangerous books from Germany or France. Ministers who wanted to mount pulpits for counterattack could do so almost at once. Darwin especially tantalized them because he was a former theological student who still puzzled as did they over the question of order in the universe. The English scientist confessed, however, that as he traveled on the *Beagle* and then spent years pondering his findings, his childhood religious beliefs tended to shrivel and become impotent.

Accounts of jousts between brilliant scientists and stupid clergymen in the battle of those decades are stereotyped now. It is hard to remember that from the first many scientists opposed evolution while ministers, even conservatives, often found ways, however strained some of them seem, to harmonize Darwin and the Bible. Editor Lyman Abbott made it all too easy with his blithe assertion that "evolution is God's way of doing things." More profound thinkers in the mainstream churches found other ways to integrate the idea of development into Christian thought and vice versa. Yet the noisier critics of this view received more publicity.

In command of the scientific opposition to Darwin was Louis Agassiz, the Swiss-born expert on the ice ages who pleased citizens by choosing to stay in America when other European scientists avoided its intellectual wasteland. A Harvard professor since 1848, he opened the museum of comparative zoology there the year the Darwin classic appeared. Agassiz developed a different theory of development, one that better squared with existing religious thought.

Religious leaders in intellectual circles clung to Agassiz and shopped for other respectable defenders. More strident churchmen started attacking the integrity of anyone who questioned the literal biblical account of human origins. To these traditionalists, evolution debased humans and allowed for immoral conduct in a universe devoid of heaven and emptied of God. When views of natural selection became popular, they left wholly to chance what the doctrine of creation or Agassiz's view of evolution had related to design.

Meanwhile, there occurred a subtle and often overlooked revolution in the higher academy, the site of evolutionary inquiry. Earlier, Harvard, Yale, Princeton, and the other major schools were small colleges that cohered around some sort of religious outlook. In the 1870s they suddenly began to diversify, to allow for independent disciplines and specialities. They grew gigantic, and were matched by tax-supported state universities where raising theological questions was difficult. Administrators now displaced religion into segregated divinity schools or seminaries. No coherent philosophy provided the unity that the earlier Christian scheme had. Each succeeding year the boards of trustees included fewer ministers. Scientists and philosophers, many of whom were reacting to the confining outlooks of their childhood religion, were free to go their own way, and many did.

The evolution debate reached the larger public when noisier disciples of the scholarly Darwin left the academy and took to the lecture trail in America. First on the scene was Irish scientist John Tyndall, who just before an American trip in 1872 proposed a test to determine the validity of science and religion. Let hospital patients in one ward receive no treatment except prayer and let those in another be treated by medicine without prayer, he proposed; compare the results. Tyndall succeeded in stirring up nothing but prayer meetings for his own soul, large audiences for his daring lectures, and a proposal that Christians foul the experiment by praying for patients in both wards, should such experiments be tried. That way God would take care of both sides.

English sociologist Herbert Spencer soon after became a circuit rider for the cause as he drew crowds to hear him apply evolution to social forms. Now the idea of the "survival of the fittest" began to explain society. While Darwin did not set out to propagandize against the faith of anyone, his militant disciple Thomas Huxley itinerated in England and then in America in 1876 in praise of what he called "agnosticism." This was an attitude that claimed that no one could know enough to affirm divine order and purpose.

On more serious levels, scientists of Christian outlooks found new possibilities in the thought of the European naturalist Lamarck, who revived the idea of evolution without including the offensive notion of natural selection. For thirty years neo-Lamarckians probably outnumbered Darwinians in American science, a fact that made possible the early acceptance of evolution by so many Protestant scholars. Yet Lamarck eventually faded, as had Agassiz. Even while their help was available, it became clear that the churches were being forced to yield enough to cause a crisis of doubt about the intactness of the Christian system, a system whose parts once fit so snugly together. Some conservative Protestant leaders henceforth began to develop a siege mentality and went on forays to track down the "modernist" compromisers.

The developing camps soon found themselves fighting wars on two fronts. The second issue troubling the churches was posed not by biology or geology but by scientific history. A century earlier, during the Enlightenment, historians and literary scholars proposed to change one hypothesis about the Jewish and Christian past. They allowed that no book, not even the previously exempt Bible, was protected from historical processes. The Word of God spoke through it, to be sure, but the book was not lead-encased or hermetically sealed from the world of events. This meant that literary scholars should read and examine it just as they would Homer, Shakespeare, or any other document from the past. They would better serve the purposes of God if they were less nervous about proving the literal accuracy of every phrase and instead tried to understand the influence that shaped the Bible, how it was composed, how to account for its inner contradictions, how to discern its true meaning, and the like.

Debates about any other book concerned only scholars in their classrooms and studies, but the Bible was different. To raise questions about it created a crisis in the public forum. Most citizens, including the unchurched majority, at least paid respect to the idea that biblical laws had given birth to America and stood behind civil and moral laws. This Bible impelled both the first Spanish friars to save the New World and the New England founders to plant Bible commonwealths. The God of the Bible, they thought, pushed America into history and pulled it to its manifest destiny. Excepting a few transcendentalists and some visionaries who claimed that God spoke directly to them, almost all other reformers promoted their causes by presenting a design for America through the call that the nation go back to the Bible.

Americans were unprepared for the end-of-the-century battles over the Bible. Historic Christianity took biblical authority more or less for granted and developed few precise or binding ideas as to exactly *how* the Holy Spirit inspired the Scriptures or insured their truth. Not until the new age of science came did people have to ask what kind of scientific text or treatise the book was. Even the Protestant reformers three centuries earlier felt free to engage in some criticism of biblical detail because they so obviously luxuriated in the authoritative Word of God that they heard in the Bible. Their heirs in America had to scramble to come up with hard-and-fast theories to provide lines of defense against critics.

Before the Civil War, formal scholarship was rare. Retired ministers taught the Bible in seminaries. Each good preacher pondered and memorized much of the book and lived in its pages. Few were able to see the Bible in its historical context or to probe its literary depths. The South especially cherished the most literal readings, because on these terms it could find biblical passages in support of slavery. Revivalists often opposed a learned ministry and chose to reduce the Bible to simple slogans for saving souls. The clergy long ago had learned how to denounce challenges from infidels like Thomas Jefferson or the transcendentalists and they used distant German thought about the Bible as a bogey to frighten the wayward in America. Historian George Bancroft, himself anything but orthodox, came back from Germany reporting that theologians there treated the Bible as an old wives' tale, fit only for the nursery. No believers in America wanted such an attitude to prevail.

Despite the bleak scholarly landscape, two landmarks of thought appeared early. At Andover Seminary a strategy developed similar to that of the Lamarckians: yield on minor points in order to hold the fortress. Professor Moses Stuart, who taught at Andover, and his pupil Edward Robinson were no mossbacks. They favored archaeological research and grammatical inquiry. Of course, agreed Stuart, the Hebrew Moses could not have written all of the biblical books associated with his name — at least not the account of his own death. But what did such an acknowledgment have to do with the inspiration of the whole Bible? Nothing.

The other scholarly front was Princeton Seminary. For a century this school became such a citadel of changeless orthodoxy that Professor Charles Hodge gained support by bragging that during his long tenure there, from 1820 to 1878, not one new idea crept into or originated at Princeton. Yet Princeton did begin with a novelty — the Scottish common-sense philosophy that Archibald Alexander and his peers had imported in 1812 at the time of the founding. President Francis Patton was able to boast that "no oddities of manner, no shibboleths, no pet phrases, no theological labels, no trademark" ever colored the school. He stood too close to it: everyone else saw the stamp of "common sense" and the philosophy of Francis Bacon on the Princeton mold. The Princeton defense of the Bible was neat, logical, and durable. Of course, agreed the professors, there were errors in the book now at hand, but the original autographs of the biblical books had to be perfect and errorless, because they came from the hand and mind of a perfect and errorless God.

The Andover school lost out among biblical critics because it did not go far enough. The Princeton approach, however, survived and later became transformed into the more intellectual forms of fundamentalism. This view of an uncomplicated and inerrant Bible was appealing to a laity that wanted no doubts and no troubles about the Word of God. They cherished religion because it solved problems, not because it raised them. In this sense President Grover Cleveland was a typical layman, on whose vote Princetonians could count while the critics merely talked to each other. His response was folksy: "The Bible is good enough for me; just the old book under which I was brought up. I do not want notes or criticism, or explanations about authorship or origin, or even cross-references. I do not need or understand them, and they confuse me." Let the scholars sputter about the divine mandates to seek truth; people like Cleveland were giving their support to uncritical viewpoints.

Even more than the evolutionary crisis, the biblical struggle produced two increasingly defined political parties in the churches. At the Niagara Bible Conference in 1883 and in similar summer camps elsewhere, conservative believers took positions that squared with those of the Princeton stalwarts. They had a special reason for their literalism. By now many of them had become premillennialists, which meant that they looked for an early and sudden Second Coming of Christ. They derived this teaching from some of the more obscure and visionary books of the Bible like Ezekiel, Daniel, and Revelation. What if the apostle John did not write Revelation and what if Daniel was written centuries later than people thought? All would be destroyed. Any attack on the Bible undercut not only their literal view of the past but their faith in a specific future.

Two controversies, one in the South and one in the North, brought the camps face to face. Crawford H. Toy, in the first case, was a gentle man loved by his enemies, who felt guilty about attacking him. Professor Toy unfortunately had to test his ideas in one of the more cautious denominations, the Southern Baptist Convention. Because these Baptists loved freedom, they were expected to give reasonably free rein to each other. Because they were strongly congregational, they could not easily mobilize for common action against a heretic. Yet defense of a literally trustworthy scripture, back during the days of slavery and later, and associated mistrust of northern and foreign scholarship made any questioning of the Bible dangerous. Virginia-born Toy was the son of a druggist who was an amateur linguist. The son acquired a love of Hebrew from his father and his local minister, John A. Broadus, who himself became a scholar of note. Toy served in the Confederate Army; his comrades remembered him as an engrossed student of ancient languages. After the war he studied for two years in Berlin, where he caught the critical virus.

Though the young scholar had planned to be a missionary in

Japan, he joined the Southern Baptist Seminary faculty in 1869. While students flocked to his courses, behind his assured facade he faced up to doubts that had haunted him ever since he read works on geology as a child. The German scholars, however, taught him to "take the kernel of truth from its outer covering of myth" in the Bible. This approach helped him, but dare he teach it in the seminary? President James P. Boyce, both a friend and hero to Toy, very reluctantly spoke to the professor as word got out that some of his support for the Bible seemed shaky. Boyce was raising funds for the seminary, now newly located in Louisville. While he had no taste for pursuing a heretic, he could not afford to have his seminary mistrusted at such a time. Broadus, who became the middleman in the controversy, heard Toy say that the new views would actually aid students in their difficulties over faith. Broadus, however, found this unconvincing and suggested the professor be quiet about the ideas. Despite his promise to do so, Toy in *Sunday School Times* let slip unapproved views about Isaiah. Alert editors, especially Northern Baptists, spotted them and made their move against him.

In May 1879, the Southern Baptist Convention was to bring the matter to a head. Toy, elected a delegate, wrote a careful letter defining his position. Since he believed that his teaching did not violate the divine inspiration of the Bible, he was living up to his vows of fidelity, and he assumed that his offer to resign would be turned down. He reminded his colleagues that the Bible said nothing about how the Holy Spirit did His inspiring of the book. "Against facts, no theory can stand," Toy insisted, "and I prefer, therefore, to have no theory, but submit myself to the guidance of the actual words of Holy Scripture." For him the biblical views of science were the husk he could leave behind while keeping the saving kernel. "If our heavenly Father sends a message by the stammering tongue of a man, I will not reject the message because of its stammering."

Toy could never complain about the degree of friendliness of the Seminary Board committee that was charged to take up his letter. The committee realized it was imposing a new standard on the professor, since the Baptists had been a creedless church. They did not so much insist that Toy was wrong as that "there is a divergence in his views of inspiration from those held by our brethren in general." Reluctantly, they had to accept the resignation of their beloved and, they agreed, deeply Christian brother. Toy, who asked his friends not to rally behind him, then turned down the presidency of Furman University, a Baptist school. He saw his fiancée, a missionary in China, reject him for his unpopular views. President Boyce saw him off from Louisville for his new career at Harvard. It was said that while he embraced Toy, he swung his free arm: "Oh, Toy, I would freely give that arm to be cut off if you would be where you were five years ago, and stay there."

The Southern Baptist crisis revealed that creedless churches could be as dogmatic as creedal ones. After a second Louisville scholar, President William H. Whitsitt, ran afoul of defenders of the faith and had to resign in 1898, one of his admirers argued that the seminary could now only teach tradition, which was "truth's last year's crop of leaves." Better "no Seminary than a Seminary in which truth cannot find a home." Trustee J. A. Chambliss feared that the Baptists and the seminary would lose something if the school became a factory of theological music boxes, "all shaped and pitched alike to give forth an invariable number of invariable tunes."

Charles Briggs now brought a crisis to the northern and creedal Presbyterians. Like Toy, Briggs attended the University of Virginia, and after serving on the Union side during the Civil War, also studied at Berlin. He left for Germany in 1866 a convinced conservative and returned sure that biblical conservatism was a lost cause: "I feel a different man from what I was five months ago. The Bible is lit with a new light." Briggs, who felt liberated in his faith, was not agonized by doubts; he argued that the truth of the Bible showed through better when it did not have to depend on human theories of inspiration and nervous defenses of its truth.

In 1874 Briggs became a professor at Union Theological Seminary in New York. For a decade he carried on running debates with his Princeton-based coeditors of *The Presbyterian Review*, but he ran into real trouble when a brash Union student started feeding suspect materials from his classroom to enemies of Briggs. Briggs meanwhile was publishing some unapproved ideas. In a major address in 1891, the scholar took up controversial biblical issues at the request of the chairman of the seminary board.

For a year what came now to be "the Briggs case" passed through a maze of committees, presbyteries, seminary boards, and the General Assembly. Briggs was an abrupt man, but even had he possessed the personality of a Toy, he might well have been doomed. The local New York presbytery stood by him with votes that ran as close as 67 to 61, but conservative ministers easily gathered troops for the General Assembly battle of 1893. There votes went against him 383 to 116. The abrasive reject became an Episcopal priest in 1900; he then displayed the innate conservatism that friends at Union had long discerned. He simply could not conform to what he thought were false views of biblical authority.

Presbyterians and then other groups repeatedly had to fight the battle over the Bible. The conservatives never were patient to see whether the new scholarship might serve faith. They combined their legitimate fears with moves for political power and chose to see alternatives to their views as nothing but attacks on the Bible. The biblical critics were insensitive to the fears of the laity and naive about the way militants could exploit the fears and turn them into a political force. By the turn of the century, the church people paid little attention to attacks on the Bible by outsiders, most of whom had chosen to ignore such religious themes. The issues posed by modernity were no longer between the believer inside the camp and the infidel without, but between two kinds of believers, whose controversies further distracted from the credibility of religious organizations.

The scholarly fights over Darwin and the Bible were formal and focused. They came to a head when certain books appeared or when professors staged debates, and they came to conclusions with heresy trials of denominational votes. The third trauma of change was much more bewildering. The churches were hardly even aware that they were on the defensive as they were being forced to adjust their views of how life was organized and wealth divided in the world of the modern city, factory, and corporation. The very laymen who rejected Darwinian ideas of the survival of the fittest and natural selection in biology unwittingly but forcefully defended the same ideas in the field of economics. Though most of them avoided the name, they were Social Darwinists. They preferred to think of themselves as Christian defenders of laissez-faire free-enterprise competition. These adapters found themselves fighting on the same side as the agnostic Andrew Carnegie and other nonbelievers in a contest that saw historic Christian rationales give way to those that the new sciences supplied.

Importantly, nonchurched Americans had powerful views on religion. Some people saw Carnegie as an imitator of agnostic Thomas Huxley or a Social Darwinist like Herbert Spencer. But such tagging is hardly fair to Carnegie. He was an individualist who read the theories of the day to fashion his own independent philosophy. He never made a secret of the fact that he and his family had left their faith behind in Scotland. After the Carnegies settled near Pittsburgh in 1848, young Andrew worked in the mills for $1.20 a week. He enjoyed only about five years of schooling, and at eighteen was already the private clerk to a superintendent of the Pennsylvania Railroad; three years later he owned shares in sleeping cars. Carnegie foresaw a future in steel. During a financial panic in the 1870s, he founded his own steel firm. Never knowing financial insecurity after he began his climb toward the top, Carnegie outlined economic theories about survival by simply writing his autobiography.

Having discarded the old Calvinist faith that God favored the elect with success, Carnegie, in the spirit of his new day, looked for a scientific alternative to explain the process. It was at this point that he both read and found coincidence with the thought of Herbert Spencer. He favored an idea of Darwin's, which he applied too glibly to human affairs: the fittest survived by the process of natural selection. To test his theories, Carnegie chose the company not of other rich clubmen but of the intellectuals who debated evolution and the new "religion of humanity" at the Nineteenth Century Club. His autobiography described his odyssey away from the God of Calvin. Each stage of civilization, Carnegie thought, created its own God. As man ascended and became better, his conception of the Unknown likewise improved. "Thereafter we became less theological, but I am sure more truly religious." So much for any crisis of youth in his case. Now he spelled out his motto: "All is well since all grows better." Carnegie spent less time with the corollary, seldom asking how well things went for the less-than-fit, the unselected.

While the steel man did not organize his thought to oppose religion, he took advantage of his encounters with the pious to let them know where he stood. On a world tour the magnate was once placed at a table with some "poor girls" who were heading for China as missionaries. When one of them asked him for funds nearly twenty years later, he replied emphatically that money for foreign missions among the Chinese was misspent. "I believe that all religions are adapted to those for whom they are provided" — a summary of the evolutionary view of religion. But Carnegie could not resist going further in his criticism. While Christ never used force, Carnegie reminded the women that missionaries needed gunboats to defend themselves in China. While the erotic religious statues in India offended him and blood sacrifices in Asia appalled him, these seemed no worse than the diabolical scheme of the

Christian creeds with their angry and irresponsible God. "I decline to accept Salvation from such a fiend."

Carnegie was the most articulate in the whole generation of industrial giants named robber barons by their enemies. His philosophy was parallel to that of the others in all respects but one: most of them *did* accept salvation from the God he despised. They believed that not natural selection but Divine Providence had positioned them to struggle to the top and had smiled on their efforts by blessing them with achievements. Now they should carry that blessing one step further — into philanthropy, a field in which Carnegie pioneered without using doctrines of Christian charity. Critics of their philosophy liked to see the money these magnates passed on as tainted, but the institutions that prospered as a result of the industrialists' largess became so widespread as to be almost unavoidable.

When people asked railroad baron Cornelius Vanderbilt by what law of the universe he lived, he asked: "Law! What do I care about law? Hain't I got the power?" Vanderbilt gave surplus funds to help found the originally Methodist university that bears his name. The inventor of the reaper, Cyrus McCormick, gave funds and his name to the Presbyterian McCormick Theological Seminary in Chicago, where the McCormick family took the conservative side in the Presbyterian doctrinal battles of the day.

None of the Christians outdid John D. Rockefeller of Standard Oil for both philanthropy and expression of philosophy. He served the Baptist cause by helping found and support the University of Chicago. Sunday-school student Rockefeller, convinced that God gave him his opportunities, wrote an essay that amounted to a creed, in which he chose to talk about the American Beauty rose. He reminded that lesser buds needed to be pruned to produce the greater beauty. The Rockefeller parable for the way the fittest financiers prevailed over competitors in America might represent the opposite pole to biblical language about how the last were first in the kingdom of Jesus, but even conservative church leadership by then had changed enough not to be literal about such words from the Gospel. It was left to muckrakers outside the church to raise embarrassing questions.

Carnegie was not burdened with any philosophy he did not himself develop, though in 1882 he spent some time with Spencer during the Englishman's tour of America. Having borrowed a few terms and phrases, he struck out on his own. His independence even led him to heresy in Social Darwinist circles, since he did not absolutely oppose efforts by workmen to unite in agitation for improvements. The Social Darwinist Professor William Graham Sumner of Yale, like Darwin an ex-Episcopalian who saw his Christian faith disappear, had no use for charity. In that area Carnegie sinned on a grand scale. And while Spencer and Sumner thought social classes owed nothing to each other and that winners need make no room for losers, Carnegie openly embraced American democracy and welcomed the new immigrant, "the sectary, the refugee, the persecuted, the exile." Economically he merely exaggerated "the law of competition" to which he felt America already owed its greatness, no matter how cruel it seemed. "We accept and welcome, therefore, as conditions to which we must accommodate ourselves, great inequality of environment."

Significantly, Carnegie's essay on wealth appeared in book form as *The Gospel of Wealth,* a sign that he was not so much irreligious as religious about something new, the laws of competition that replaced Providence. In a democracy, he wrote, the rich man had a right to great wealth so long as in return he helped build initiative in others. That is why Carnegie gave libraries without endowments for books, so that local communities must fill them on their own. He and the men of his generation had induced a crisis by transforming old Calvinist views of work and wealth and posing new philosophies for Christian social prophets to criticize. The schism that occurred in that industrial shift divides American religion to this day.

While evolution, biblical criticism, and economic doctrines demanded argument, the fourth challenge, that of the modern city, called forth action. The number of Americans grew from 31 million in 1860 to 106 million in 1920. Citizens jammed into the metropolises, where the tenements and skyscrapers became the signs of change from the older rural and small-town Protestant America. While 6 million people farmed in 1860 and almost 9 million did so in 1880, the number of factory and construction workers grew from 2 million to 18 million in the same period.

After prospectors drilled the first oil well in 1859, entrepreneurs soon learned how to refine oil and put its power to work. Ten years later railroads connected the coasts, tying communities together; before long the telephone helped shrink distances between people. Labor organizations and violent strikes disturbed the peace of old-stock citizens. Moralists who long before had proposed ethics for small businessmen and shopkeepers found no word for the large and impersonal corporations nor for the new millionaire magnates whom they could envy but could not reach. The Industrial Revolution, it is said, changed all details of human life more drastically than anything since the invention of agriculture and the village aeons before. Certainly in the United States it changed the course of the mainstream and still largely Protestant culture.

The Protestant empire had relied on life in intimate town-and-country settings, where the "sameness" that Lyman Beecher had hoped for still prevailed. But church leaders were never able to cope with the maze of the metropolis, because of the diversity within it. Immigrant Catholics and Jews, who had no reason to respond to the Protestant covenants, converged on the cities, whose very growth stunned church people of village mentalities. In 1850 only six United States centers contained more than 100,000 people, but in 1900 there were forty-one such cities. Thanks to men like James Cardinal Gibbons and his priests and nuns, the Catholics did not lose out in the industrial city, but Protestants, who dealt more with middle classes, had to revise their strategies. They came up with two divergent ones, typified by the two most popular Protestant leaders of their half-century, Henry Ward Beecher and Dwight Lyman Moody.

The task of moderate, mainstream Protestant ministers like Beecher was to help their people bridge the gap between old faith and new science and learning, between old static views of work and wealth and the new evolutionary ones, and between their church life and the city and corporation. Remarkably, the preachers of this generation preserved almost all the old language about God and Christ and sometimes even of heaven and hell. Yet they subtly transformed it all with one plea in mind: people must adapt to the modern world. They assumed that a loving God was producing the good in their new world, and that Christian thought should be flexible enough to absorb strange ideas. This son of old Lyman Beecher was certainly adaptive enough. When evolution frightened the conservatives, he announced himself "a cordial Christian evolutionist." Historical scholarship of the Bible would, he thought, help people find the Scripture's essential truth. Christians should easily transform corporate life and economic competition to their purposes.

As Beecher's career prospered, listeners sensed that he was tampering wildly with the doctrines that his father had only slightly opened up. Henry's best friend, Jonathan Blanchard, later commented that the younger Beecher dealt out "the love of Christ to sinners with the indiscriminate fondness of a successful prostitute who loves everybody who does not condemn her trade." He feared that Beecher might debauch his whole ministry, but in a day when statistical and financial success was becoming ever more the test of truth, what mattered were the crowds that came to hear Beecher, not the opinions of Blanchard.

Beecher became a national figure at Plymouth Church in Brooklyn, where members idolized him and the press followed most of his moves. The crowds Beecher attracted showed that Protestantism was entering a new phase. The preacher knew just when to draw back from a too open embrace of modernizing ideas, so that he could seem daring and reassuring at once and thus minister to people who lived between the times, who wanted to be modish and modern but who needed security as well. Blanchard spotted the strategy: "When Henry Ward Beecher is about to assail some fundamental truth, held and suffered for by the Puritans, he always begins by proclaiming himself their descendant." Just as Beecher knew his people needed a sense of rootedness to become free for novelty, so they needed a hint of otherworldliness to affirm the alluring world. As he strutted the stage in Plymouth Church, Beecher affirmed that world: "There are many troubles which you can't cure by the Bible and Hymnbook, but which you can cure by a good perspiration and a breath of fresh air." Once the Puritan faith had centered in the supernatural; but Lyman Abbott saw Beecher making religion seem a natural experience, "something to be enjoyed" for everyday use.

The cities in which Beecher succeeded in gaining followings were those of the New York Jews in their sweatshops or of the Baltimore Irish Catholics in their unions. He helped his middle classes justify their ride to new status. In 1877, during labor strikes, he announced that if a man did not smoke or drink beer, he could feed a wife and six children on a dollar a day. Those who earned more than a dollar a day applauded. "Is not a dollar a day enough to buy bread with? Water costs nothing; and a man who cannot live on bread is not fit to live." Even in the most crowded eastern cities, frugal people, he promised, "can scarcely help accumulating." The idea that in almost every case no man in America suffered from poverty "unless it be his *sin*" was an idea that the prosperous applauded. Christians, the preacher thought, should not inveigh against riches but teach people how to gain them. The preacher worried when the rich fell into scandal; they might bring wealth into disrepute and laborers would then forget "the great law of subordination."

As revivalism moved to the city under the leadership of a new evangelist titan, Dwight L. Moody, Beecher at once recognized it as the great rival to the approach he and other princes of the pulpit were promoting. "Mr. Moody thinks this is a lost world, and is trying to save as many as possible from the wreck; I think Jesus Christ has come to save the world, and I am trying to help him save it."

Moody, a convert from childhood Unitarianism in hometown Northfield, Massachusetts, went to the city of Boston at age seventeen, announcing his awareness that it was a wilderness where no one cared about others. The Young Men's Christian Association did care for him, however. In the company of other lonely young men, he there enjoyed hearing the "smart men" of Boston lecture. A Sunday-school teacher pressed for his conversion until Moody could report, "I was born twice, once in '37; once again in '55." He was a shoe salesman who wanted to use his selling techniques to convert others, even though a deacon took Moody aside and told the youth that his grammar was so bad he ought to serve the Lord some other way than as a witness.

A year later, in 1856, a young Moody headed for Chicago, "the marvel of cities," where the eighty thousand citizens struck him as all being in a hurry. So was he. Soon he was renting five pews in a church and filling them with neighborhood people. Such endeavors did not prevent him from succeeding as a footwear salesman. Then, in 1857, a financial panic induced businessmen to gather for prayer at noontimes in efforts to make sense of how their business failures fit into the plan of God and how they might recover. This spontaneous revival inspired Moody to stop selling shoes and start saving souls. At a meeting one night when no ministerial student showed up to sermonize, a prosperous follower, John Farwell, challenged Moody to preach. That night he began a lifelong career as a lay preacher, the most noted of his day. "Except to go in one door and out the other," he had never been to theological school. Moody found no need to pursue scholarship or to take on intellectual challenges. A buoyant man, optimistic in style if pessimistic about the city and the world, he took campaigns to England after 1867 and attracted permanent followings there. Back in Chicago he had to rebuild all his enterprises after the fire of 1871 — so he simply raised more funds and built bigger ones than before.

While never as adaptable or compromising as Henry Beecher, Moody did not always growl or snipe at people who adjusted their outlooks to face modernity. England's Henry Drummond was noted as a mild evolutionist, yet Moody gave him a platform. George Adam Smith used the critical method to study the Bible, but Moody did not become unfriendly to him. Even some Unitarians mildly thanked him for helping save British religion. The scholarly Philip Schaff at Union Seminary in New York complimented Moody by comparing the way the evangelist stopped modern materialism and atheism in their tracks to the way Methodism blocked deism a century before. The Moody blend of charity, showmanship, evasion of intellectual difficulties, and ceaseless activity attracted the notice of the evangelical world.

The city was his consistent target. "Water runs downhill, and the highest hills in America are the great cities. If we can stir them we shall stir the whole country." Moody took his rallies from city to city; whether in stifling summer heat or on drafty winter nights, congregations found seats at a premium, no matter how great the tabernacles his devotees built for him. At Brooklyn and Philadelphia, Moody even had to chide the church people, who preempted all the seats so the unsaved could not get in. He disarmed opposition. The Roman Catholic *Tablet,* in a day rarely marked by ecumenical tenderness, considered his rallies "a thing of God, a testimony to Jesus in the midst of an age of mocking and unbelieving." When most intellectuals froze him out, Quaker poet John Greenleaf Whittier broke ranks and cheered because he thought Moody turned drunkards and gamblers into decent fathers and husbands.

Moody divided cities when he set out to conquer them. When his people sectored New York City into districts and sent teams to convert people in each, the *New York Times* complained. Moody's approach represented to the editors "a sort of guerrilla warfare" led by a crowd of sharpshooters who pushed uninvited without inquiry. The paper pressed a point that critics of mass evangelizing ever since have raised. Was it proper to "bully and insult those who are caught in their interviews"? Whatever the critics thought, such techniques worked. Moody never bothered much with etiquette, never cared if people thought he was lowering the pulpit to bring it to the people: to hit Boston, he said, he would not fire into the air from Bunker Hill. And if his means looked crude to the followers of Beecher and the glossy preachers, he still attracted the backing of Cyrus McCormick, New York banker J. Pierpont Morgan,

Philadelphia shopkeeper John Wanamaker, and New York manufacturer William Dodge. Their phalanx permitted social radicals to dismiss Moody for buying off discontent by offering heaven to the people who should face up to the evils of the social order.

"Make the meetings interesting" was the first advice Moody told ministers on his stages. He gave his partner, the singer and composer Ira Sankey, together with his melodeon, a proud place and welcomed the spectacle of huge choirs. Moody entertained crowds with his messages. To be sure, the old portrayals of hellfire survived in his sermons, but he preferred to paint the pleasures of heaven. In "after-meetings" in inquiry rooms, his workers spiritually propped up the people who converted as they heard him. With such a program he could take on all comers. While other religious leaders were bowing to each other at the World's Parliament of Religions at Chicago in 1893, he chose to snub but not directly to attack them. Instead, the evangelist besieged the fair itself after he heard to his shock that it drew the largest crowds on Sunday. He must make Jesus Christ so attractive that people would notice only him, not the fair. A flank attack worked: the Moody crowds pulled so many people from Sunday fair attendance and his criticisms created so much nervousness that management eventually caved in and closed down on the Lord's Day.

Who came to Moody's rallies? Watchful newspapermen noticed almost no Negroes there, except in a few segregated southern gatherings. Catholics were not expected to come, and Moody made little impression on the new Lutheran immigrants. Most of the rich and elite had other things to do, and the really poor were out of range. A New York editor who looked at the audience thought it seemed "able to pay its way," and in 1880, at Saint Louis, Moody admitted his appeal was "principally to the middling class." Along with most American evangelists before him and since, he found it valid to act as if he were converting people from raw paganism. Like the rest, however, he apparently drew chiefly the previously converted or the half-converted, displaced church people who reaffirmed their faith when he reclaimed them and sent them back to supportive churches.

Moody's value system kept him from reaching the working poor. Remarkably like Beecher in this respect, he connected failure with sin and success with virtue. "Whenever you find a man who follows Christ, that man you will find a successful one." Eager to avoid controversy, he urged his lieutenants not to have "anything to say about capital and labor. You don't know anything about it."

He was right. Content with the division of labor between religious and public life, the revivalist wanted President Cleveland to take care of questions of state.

Yet Moody consistently lined up with the economic conservatives. Despite the highly publicized evangelicalism of candidate William Jennings Bryan, whose religious outlook was akin to his own, Moody leaned toward William McKinley in a presidential campaign. In that stormy campaign year of 1896, Moody gave an example of both his social policy and his hunch about what class of people made up his audiences: "Send your carriages out and give poor people a drive in the park once in a while and they'll call you an angel, I'll warrant."

As years passed and party lines in Protestantism hardened, Moody became increasingly less friendly to people like Henry Drummond and George Adam Smith. He played to the anti-intellectual instincts of his crowds, delighting to tell audiences that professors of "New Theology" went up "in a balloon whizzing above the heads of the people." Revivalism had wandered far from the way of Jonathan Edwards, who appealed to both the head and the heart. Now the preeminent American evangelist dismissed intellectual ventures with "you call it metaphysics, but I don't know what it is."

No matter how firm his leadership of the conservatives, Dwight Moody did not have it in him to be mean, as many later militants of both parties became. When a liberal contended that two authors wrote the book of Isaiah, Moody, asked about his stand, shrugged off the question as later fundamentalists refused to do: "See here, it doesn't make much difference who wrote the book anyhow. God could have used half a dozen Isaiahs."

The millennial century was ending and Jesus had not returned. Moody stamped on later revivalism the enduring theme of the Second Coming. Where once evangelists wanted to convert the world to make it attractive for the return of Christ, Moody belonged to the opposite school, which thought that the worst traumas for both the church and world still lay ahead. Until the catastrophe ended the existing world and brought Jesus back, efforts to improve the world were largely futile. Asked to preach against corruption in New York in 1894, Moody told backers that soon Christ would come anyhow and there would then be no more chicanery: "There will be no men seeking office." Against the evidence of his supporters, he claimed that when Christ filled the heart, a person lost interest in gas stocks and water stocks. As it worked out, his followers capably watched out for their stocks *and* the Second Coming. They rallied to hear him preach against the "outrageous despotism" of the unions, for they had chosen the other side in labor conflicts. While Beecher accurately pictured how differently he and Moody viewed the world, Moody gave the most memorable summary of his own mission. "I have felt like working three times as hard ever since I came to understand that my Lord was coming back again. I look on this world as a wrecked vessel. God has given me a life-boat and said to me, 'Moody, save all you can.' " Finally he tired, and when he died in 1899, they buried him far from his cities, back in Northfield, "just about as near Paradise as we can get on earth."

Beecher and Moody, as noted, were the most popular leaders of urban middle-class Protestantism. Yet they and their kind were unable to minister successfully to citizens who were looking for personal healing or a new social order. But America did not lack prophets for those causes either. Our story will not be complete without the tale of the searches for these provinces, far beyond the pulpit of Beecher or the lifeboat of Moody.

The Seventh-Day Adventists combined a belief in
Sabbath observance and Christ's Second Coming
with health regimens, including vegetarianism. At a
sanitarium run by Adventists in Battle Creek,
Michigan, devotees of God and health are here
shown engaging in breathing exercises. (*Loma Linda
University Heritage Room*)

Chapter Fifteen

HEALING THE RESTLESS

A MEN LIKE HENRY WARD BEECHER AND DWIGHT L. MOODY WOULD not have gained followings had they set out only to give identity, purpose, and salvation to the people who faced change in American cities. These people also suffered psychic damage in the suddenness of change, as their letters and diaries often made clear. They turned for help to religion, which through the ages had given solace to sufferers and offered cures to the ill. Both Beecher and Moody offered remedies for the mental upsets that afflicted their contemporaries, though they were not specialists and had to yield to more adventurous physicians of the soul.

Neither the liberal nor evangelistic Protestant healers tended to all the new diseases of American citizens. People became restless and, in their own way, joined the ceaseless spiritual pilgrimage of Americans in their efforts to find more satisfying faiths and symbols — even if this meant leaving behind much of cherished but now, they thought, shopworn church religion. Late in the nineteenth century the United States saw the rise of therapies that pushed far beyond the bounds of conventional religion. This occurred in the face of fresh diagnoses of what might be ailing an outwardly prospering society — one that offered physical boons to so many who still experienced spiritual malaise or bodily affliction.

History is never neat. Americans did not first exclude the unwanted, then proceed to force adaptation on unwelcome religious groups, and only *then* begin to clear the desks and devise a new agenda that would concentrate on alleviating the crises of the Protestant empire. These were all concurrent tumults throughout the nineteenth century, though most of them came to public notice near its end.

For a clue to understanding the nineteenth century's new focus on physical malaise, one might look to a best-selling book of the 1880s, the widely approved *American Nervousness* by physician George M. Beard. Beard claimed that the climate of the nation helped produce "neurasthenia," or nervous exhaustion, because America was located in the temperate zone — the "nervous belt" of the Northern Hemisphere. People nearer the equator evidently solved their problems through heat-induced lethargy. Close to the North Pole, humans shivered themselves into a kind of alertness they needed for survival. They had no time to think their way into the functional nervous disorders that came with living where the temperatures were just right for creativity and for living with high risk. The indoor classes of all civilized countries experienced such disorders, but in each of the "brain-working households" in the northern and eastern United States, there was at least one sufferer. Beard blamed the "modern condition" for the disorders. He faulted fast means of travel, the noise of cities, and heady ideas for producing the symptoms he quaintly but appropriately called "fear of society," "fear of fears," "fear of everything." The call from a Beecher to cheer up or the offer by a Moody of a heaven someday did not overcome such fears. "The American people are rapidly becoming the most nervous, the most highly organized, in the world, if, indeed, they are not already such."

American nervousness possessed a long and honored history. Quite naturally most people who pointed to physical or mental remedies expected religion to play its part in healing. Medicine was not then a highly developed art or science, and physicians killed as readily as they cured. In such a landscape there was room for spiritual healers who made fresh if not always scientifically sound connections between bodily disorder and mental upset. The cures, like the diseases, took rise in the minds of the nervous in the "brain-working households" of the American North and East. This point is important: experiments with vegetarianism and phrenology, animal magnetism and mesmerism, mind-cure and Christian Science were not mere ventures of eccentrics at the margin of society while Episcopalism and evolutionism were the provinces of elites. The boundaries and borders between holders of all these remedies were extremely fluid.

The mania for physical cures originated not in some alchemical laboratories or latter-day coven of Salem witches, but on the respectable trail of revivalists. Angelina and Theodore Weld, who consorted with highbrows, fed their child the vegetarian Graham diet that originated in the 1830s with Presbyterian minister Sylvester Graham, an evangelist who insisted that sick souls and sick bodies went together. A loving and healing God wanted to produce not only healthy-mindedness but health in general. After the days of his fashion passed, people of medical sophistication looked back on Graham as quaint and possibly deranged, though 140 years later people in the advance guard of culture readopted some of his theories. Not all shared his cheerless view that masturbation produced insanity or that married couples wasted their precious life fluids by having sexual intercourse more than once a month. But his counsel for people to wear loose-fitting clothes, get plenty of exercise, and enjoy the open air seemed sane enough, and his more extreme preaching not only against alcohol — a standard theme in the revivalist repertory — but also against tobacco and stimulants, and for vegetable diets, looked later like genuine discoveries. Horace Mann wanted to introduce such a diet and such ideas into the public schools. Literary people at Brook Farm for a time set a Graham table, and evangelist Charles Grandison Finney force-fed Oberlin students on it until they rebelled. When, in Graham's trail, other healers came up with the pleasant medical system called homeopathy or the water cure named hydropathy, notables like poet Henry Wadsworth Longfellow became true believers.

Graham lacked a permanent institution to which to attach his remedies; his Presbyterianism had a different agenda. And he failed to associate the cures with a whole plan of salvation, a complete system of interconnecting ideas. The genius for making such connections was a woman little known to later Americans, even to those who have heard of her movement, which still is growing rapidly in over a hundred nations. She was Ellen Gould White, the virtual founder of the modern health-minded cause of Seventh-Day Adventism.

The Adventists first responded to the preaching activities of one William Miller, who was famed for having set the date for the Second Coming of Christ in 1843 and then again in 1844. When nothing special happened on earth those years, the Millerites had to live with what they called "the Great Disappointment." Many of them left the movement. Then the more persistent among them decided that the events that Miller found foreseen in his Bible did in fact occur in 1844 in heaven and thus were not visible to earthlings. The new Advent or coming of Jesus was still imminent, but no human should set a precise date for it. Ordinarily one would expect that people who looked for the world to end any day would not take great pains to cure diseases or to establish sanitariums. A number of the regathered Millerites, however, did make healing as much a part of their program as the Second Coming was, and they have prospered ever since.

Mrs. White did not introduce healing to Adventism. In 1863, when interest in such cures was generally waning, Ellen Gould White took up the prayer-centered formula of predecessors and rejoiced to find her two sons come back from near-death induced by diphtheria. By then she was a leader among those who were picking up the pieces of Adventism after the Great Disappointment.

On the evening of June 5, 1863, not long after her sons were cured, Mrs. White knelt in a circle of prayer with perhaps a dozen other Adventists in a home near Otsego, Michigan. During these prayers she suddenly began to drift off into a vision that called her and her husband to forget "the dark, gloomy side" of living. They must come out for the Lord against "intemperance in working, in eating, in drinking, and in drugging" and then lead a crusade for "God's great medicine, water, pure soft water." The same vision and successive ones also led her to attack doctors or anyone else who prescribed drugs, though her early opposition to medicine gradually changed into support for sanitariums.

Not surprisingly, most of the pioneer healers and inventors of remedies had had to face bad health in their own lives. Mrs. White was certainly no exception. Her case history began in childhood when a spiteful friend threw a rock at her and her twin in a park at Portland, Maine. The rock felled Ellen and freakishly led to a near-fatal injury. She recovered but was blighted with a facial disfigurement and suffered a weak body for years to come. These were as nothing compared to the nervousness — indeed, the panic fear — in her sick soul. What if that dark day Ellen had died unprepared to meet her God? She turned her soul to a search for salvation.

In 1846 her young life took a better turn when she married a capable Millerite preacher, James White, who was as eager as she to find means of healing and to help publish their Adventist teachings. Through the years they gained a following; they were prominent in the 1860s in forming both the Seventh-Day Adventist church and the Western Health Reform Institute at Battle Creek, Michigan. There they allied themselves with a sequence of physicians, especially, after 1875, with Dr. John Kellogg, who had ideas of his own about health care — some of which conflicted with those of the Whites. The healthy-minded Dr. Kellogg encouraged patients at Battle Creek to celebrate holidays with pantomimes and parodies and even with nonalcoholic toasts. The more stern and busy Mrs. White had no time for amusements and despised even harmless games like checkers and chess. Almost inevitably a break had to come; for a time she abandoned the prosperous sanitarium. She once called it not a cure but a curse.

A year after she left the institute, Mrs. White was back promoting the health causes that blended well in her mind with belief in the Second Coming of Jesus and support of the true Sabbath. She showed the influence of Dr. Graham when she began to prescribe bland diets to counter masturbation, the self-abuse that she was sure produced imbecility, dwarfed forms, crippled limbs, misshapen heads, and other deformities. She followed Graham in counseling married couples against frequent intercourse. The Adventists carried on crusades beyond liquor and tobacco to coffee and tea and promoted vegetarianism and water cures when such therapies were novelties. Then, when hoopskirts came into vogue, Mrs. White became notorious for promoting more healthful short skirts to be worn over long trousers, a costume that differed little from the bloomers worn by feminists and that shocked the public no less.

The good news that kept coming to Mrs. White through over two thousand visions impelled her, after her husband died, to take Adventism into all the world. From 1885 to 1887 she lived in Switzerland, and later, after some time in Norway and again in America, she carried her medical missions to Australia and New Zealand between 1891 and 1899. While she spent little energy formally directing her followers to accept the 100,000 pages of her transcribed prophesy as on a par with the Christian Scriptures, many of them did cherish her visions as if they were literally scriptural.

Like all pathfinders in America, Ellen Gould White has suffered her detractors. Some Adventist scholars have found in her visions numerous borrowings from the writings of others. Charles E. Stewart, a friend of Kellogg's, became embarrassing and even obnoxious when he discovered in her writing on Saint Paul about two hundred apparent copyings from a published work on the apostle. Later her admirers passed off the questionings simply by saying that it was possible for God to put similar ideas into two minds at different times. Nor were they greatly disturbed when Stewart pointed to her inconsistencies, to changes in her inspired teaching, and even to the fact that for some years Mrs. White evidently fudged on her prescribed vegetarian diet. Somehow her qualities of leadership helped Adventists dismiss such charges or overlook them in the interest of the greater good she worked.

Critics did not successfully sting Mrs. White with charges of profiteering. Beyond her own circle she remained hardly known, and could disappear for years into foreign medical missions without awakening curiosity among non-Adventists. Yet by the time she died in 1915, 136,000 people were in the Adventist fold, and they operated over three hundred medical-care facilities around the world. Years later, when medical scientists compared charts and graphs to find that Adventists were generally more healthy than their counterparts, even her ideas about diet and health struck many as plausible.

When the orthodox bothered to criticize Adventism, they blamed its heresies on William Miller, ordinarily letting Mrs. White escape their notice. In the field of healing, they saved their fire for a much better known and to them more threatening innovator, Mary Baker Eddy, discoverer of Christian Science. She was born in Bow, New Hampshire, in 1821, six years before and less than a hundred miles from the birthplace of Ellen White. Mary Baker probably experienced conversion at Old North Church in Concord, New Hampshire, though she learned what she called the old "relentless theology" from her father. Since her mother taught her a warmer outlook, she later traced her idea of a loving Father-Mother God to such experiences. From childhood she carried enough positive memories that she never felt called to repudiate all of the past. Like so many other pioneers, she was able to say: "I never left the Church, either in heart or in doctrine; I but began where the Church left off."

If childhood injury disfigured Ellen Gould, childhood illness did not take away from the beauty of Mary Baker, the village belle. Yet she could have sat for the portrait of the nervous American about whom Dr. Beard wrote; nervousness was her "skillful torture." She looked for cures but received no plausible help when her talented brother Albert died of what they called exhaustion. Her life momentarily took on more promise in 1843 when she married George Washington Glover and moved to Charleston. Soon after they settled in, however, his business ventures met disaster and George died after only a year of marriage, three months before their son was born.

Nine years later Mrs. Glover again married. This time she entered an unfortunate union with Dr. Daniel Patterson. The unhappy marriage did nothing to help her overcome her illness or depressed outlook, and at Groton, while he was on the road practicing dentistry, she found herself a confined and neglected semi-invalid. Mrs. Patterson took solace in sullenness, reading her Bible and, she said, absorbing the world of nature. A financial panic created additional stress on the Patterson marriage, and the Civil War disrupted it further. One day her husband wandered too near Confederate lines and was captured. He returned late in 1862, but resumed his personal trail, leaving Mrs. Patterson to find company elsewhere.

Not even zero-degree weather or icy walks could keep the wife from her regular meeting of the Good Templars one winter night at Lynn, Massachusetts. Unfortunately, she slipped and fell, and when Dr. Alvin Cushing examined her at a nearby residence, he pronounced her internal injuries critical. In a city larger than Lynn, no newspaper would even note such an incident, but because from it the victim dated a basic change in her life and a stage in the birth of Christian Science, her later followers came to speak of "the fall at Lynn" as an event of world significance.

Critics have examined the fall at Lynn and its consequences as carefully as they have the revelation to Joseph Smith, and have come to bitterly differing conclusions about the event and its meaning.

Tired of morphine and clerical advice that she found discouraging, Mrs. Patterson began telling callers that despite the seriousness of her injury, she would soon be walking again. A friend chided Mary for such foolish optimism, yet on the same evening she found Mrs. Patterson sitting up. Not many days later, when the Reverend James B. Clark came to call she even greeted the astonished minister at the door.

Detractors claimed that hers was either a feigned injury or a minor one and that her cure was a form of imposture or self-hypnosis. To Mary Baker Patterson the event was a miracle and more: it was part of a new way of knowing, a science. On a dreary

Sunday afternoon, she had turned to read her favorite Bible passages, which told how Jesus healed. While reading one of them, she suddenly felt whole. When Dr. Cushing visited and failed to grasp her view, showing little faith in its outcome, she suffered a brief relapse; but then, remarkably, after the negative thinker left her, she recovered again.

Recovery from one specific injury and comfort from a few Bible passages did not end her physical problems, so Mrs. Patterson pursued healing further. She made contact with an old friend turned new healer, Julius Dresser, and pleaded, "Now can't *you* help me?" She was asking for relief from a spinal affliction that plagued her through the years, but she also wanted him to pick up the expanding work of Dr. Phineas P. Quimby, the best known of the mental healers. After getting little encouragement from Dresser, Mrs. Patterson seemed alone and abandoned. Her dominating father had just died and her sister Abigail slammed the door on her. She had long before surrendered the care of her son, George Glover, who was estranged from her and was now somewhere out west. As for her husband, the dentist, he was of no help because he "craved the fleshpots, the gauds and baubles of sentimentalism," and always became too friendly with female patients. With their marriage breaking up, Patterson packed off without leaving her even $1.50 for her weekly lodging bill. He was to return briefly, but then permanently deserted his wife. After she found a note telling her that he had run off with a wealthy married woman, his wife published a pathetic poem, "I'm Sitting Alone." She sat little, because boardinghouse after boardinghouse evicted her. Her autobiography took care of all the migrations in one line: "I then withdrew from society about three years." Boardinghouse hosts remembered "Mrs. Glover" as a sometimes spellbinding, often crotchety, and occasionally almost violent person who grasped the grapevine of the Quimbyites and mind-healers.

She drew closer to the great Dr. Quimby. A former clock repairman but now an expert on American nervousness, Quimby learned mesmerism and hypnotism from Charles Poyen, who came from France to spread the techniques. Quimbyites believed with Dr. Mesmer that a magnetic fluid in one organism could influence that same fluid in others through a process called "animal magnetism." Disease was the disturbance of these fluids of mind, while mind itself was "spiritual matter." Quimby cured himself and taught the remedy to others after he diagnosed his own problem as neurasthenia, the fashionable new disease.

In the brain-working households of the day, Quimby was not universally dismissed as a charlatan, and many serious and some learned people were attracted to his cures. Mary Patterson's sister Abigail, however, came to want little to do with the man she called a crank and would not even permit Quimby to come to her house while Mary lived there. Though emaciated and almost destitute, Mary hoarded her funds and her vigor in order to meet Quimby at his Portland, Maine, headquarters. She felt a surge of new life when the little bearded man bent down, held her hand, and looked into her eyes. Quimby discerned in her a writing talent that he could use. She, in turn, moved into his thought world, though she later strenuously resisted the idea that she merely reworked his ideas.

During the time of her discipleship, Mrs. Patterson began to advertise the fact that Quimby had moved far beyond animal magnetism with his remedies. To the *Portland Courier* she wrote that his whole new science "must stand as firm as the rock of ages," because it was a new spiritual doctrine. The *Portland Advertiser* then threw back a derisive question: "What! P. P. Quimby compared to Jesus Christ?" In a way, yes, replied Mrs. Patterson, since both of them healed without jugglery or drugs. Quimby, she wrote, spoke "as never man before spake, and heals as never man healed since Christ," so "is not this the Christ which is in him?" Matters threatened to get out of hand, so Quimby wrote an essay that he called "A Defense Against Making Myself Equal with Christ."

After some time back with her skeptical sister, Mary was able to spend a few more months at Portland before Quimby died on January 16, 1866. The good doctor had the foresight to explain his forthcoming death: he had allowed error to get the upper hand, and therefore could not conquer an abdominal tumor. He professed faith in his theories to the very end, though his family faltered and brought in a homeopathic physician. Mrs. Patterson mourned his passing with a poem unpoetically titled "Lines on the Death of Dr. P. P. Quimby, who healed with the truth that Christ taught in contradistinction to all isms."

Her Christian Science was to go far beyond Quimbyism, as no one was more eager to insist than she was, but she also accepted other influence into her formula. She learned from an ex-Methodist, the Reverend Warren Evans, who in 1869 published *The Mental Cure*. Evans adopted some ideas from Emanuel Swedenborg, whose mystical views of the "divine influx" of Christ were then having influence in America. While Evans continued to use language he had learned as a revivalist, he added voguish new talk about "spiritual laws" as well. The key notion that attracted Mrs. Patterson held that the universe itself was a simple extension of mind. Soon she carried such ideas to the point of devising a system and then repudiated the Quimbyites because among them she "found not Christianity."

Mrs. Patterson's career as a healer advanced when with partner Richard Kennedy she began offering "Moral Science." Such remedies were not oddities; in the competition of advertised cures that filled the Lynn newspapers and were common elsewhere in nervous New England, the partners claimed that they taught others how to "HEAL THE SICK without medicine," on the basis of Mrs. Patterson's new manuscript, *The Science of Man*. She taught that God was not so much the divine Person the churches claimed he was, as much as the Principle of everything that exists; that life in conformity with this Principle brought healing.

In 1872 she and Kennedy parted after a violent scene in which he tore up their contract. She attacked him as a leftover mesmerist and animal magnetist who never had caught up to Moral Science. Free of him, for a time she moved from boardinghouse to boardinghouse, where she spent her days drafting a book to be called *Science and Health with Key to the Scriptures*. On October 30, 1875, she published it for an unprepared America. The book was unnoticed, unsold, and unreviewed until eventually transcendentalist Amos Bronson Alcott found it in him to say some kind things.

Mrs. Patterson, in Alcott's view "a very attractive woman, with a lovely face and a very good figure," next attracted a disciple who was twenty years her junior, but he was married and she rejected him. She turned her thoughts toward the kindlier Asa Gilbert Eddy. On January 1, 1877, Mrs. Patterson became Mrs. Eddy. Five years later, Asa Eddy died of heart failure; his widow blamed "malicious mesmerism" and "mesmeric poison" for his passing; she never married again.

On April 12, 1879, Mrs. Eddy and her followers formed the Church of Christ, Scientist, and added to it on January 31, 1881, the Massachusetts Metaphysical College. As years passed, a drastically revised *Science and Health* began to sell well and she became a sensation in Washington, Philadelphia, Chicago, and other cities in the "nervous belt." The conventional churches, who thought they had something to say about a Christian theme as ancient as healing, started attacking her modern Christian Science; tensions were worst in Boston. As her audiences grew, the clergy felt called to unite against her. In autumn of 1884, Professor Luther T. Townsend of the Methodist Boston University taunted her to prove her cures and promised to reward her if she was successful. Mrs. Eddy refused the "prayer gauge test" but not the other challenge.

After the Reverend Joseph Cook at Tremont Temple made fun of the "lady apostle" for promoting pantheism and blasphemy, she all but forced him to yield her some time on his popular Monday Morning Lecture platform. Cook offered her a cold shoulder and only ten minutes to speak. When she finished, a few Scientists in the crowd of two thousand clapped in their balcony seats. Though the day looked like defeat for her, the courage she showed gave her fame, and the fact that Cook had to deal with her signaled that she had arrived. The *Times* of London reported that clergy of all denominations were puzzled over how to regard the "most dangerous innovation that has threatened the Christian Church in that region for years." The *Times* added that no one knew how to check the flow of valued church members who were becoming Christian Scientists.

Cook coaxed some heretical terms out of the lady apostle. He sensed something special in her announcement that she was the "faithful messenger of the Second Coming" and heard pantheism even when she used the language of a personal God. In answer to her widely known view that the body and the physical world were illusions, he pushed common sense. *Of course* people have bodies and *of course* mortal man must suffer illness and death. Mrs. Eddy in effect asked why everyone said "of course." For Cook, the senses did not deceive. But of course they did, urged his sixty-four-year-old opponent: "It doth not yet appear what is the real personality of man."

Like the American innovators before her, Mrs. Eddy characteristically camped on primitive Christianity and claimed that on her side were Jesus, the apostles, and the prophets: "Christian Science and Christianity are one." She alone went all the way back to the Bible, she said, to discover the church as it was before the Roman Empire corrupted it. When a student asked why it was she who finally discovered the pristine truths, she compared herself to one who had been standing near a window and, she said, "because I was nearest the pane, the light fell upon me." On less modest occasions she saw herself as a revealer and considered *Science and Health* to be inspired. Her private vocabulary won followers and maddened critics, who found it impenetrable because she seemed to wrench all their old words into puzzling new contexts. It became her call to learn all her life long "the higher meaning" of her own book. She revised the work constantly, but declared the edition of 1906 to be final: it cannot be changed.

The fact that she was a woman hurt Mrs. Eddy in her battle with preachers. Though no feminist, she was vulnerable since she revealed "the Motherhood of God," since students called her "Mother," and since Boston was the site of "the Mother Church." When admirers compared her to the Virgin Mary because she gave birth to Christian Science, Mrs. Eddy drew back, having neither "the inspiration nor the aspiration to be first or second Virginmother — her duplicate, antecedent, or subsequent!" She retired "with honor" a Christmas picture that enthusiasts published in 1894, since it showed Jesus with a haloed figure who looked like her.

As she grew aged, Mrs. Eddy busied herself fighting off schism and protecting the church against power struggles after her death. With iron firmness she promoted *Manual of the Mother Church*. It was "God's Law, as much as the Ten Commandments and the Sermon on the Mount." Messages that the local churches preached all came from the Mother Church. An empire grew, though the founder herself took little interest in the shape of the many Greek Revival churches that Christian Scientists started building. Near the end she may never even have glimpsed the great Mother Church that Bostonians were building. She did not have to be on the scene, since her hand controlled everything.

The other churches never relented in their attacks on Christian Science. In 1899 the New York Methodist Episcopal Conference passed a resolution regretting the move of the Reverend Severin E. Simonson to Christian Science and recognizing his past service to Methodism. In stormed James Monroe Buckley, the fire-breathing editor of the *Christian Advocate,* who traveled all night just to oppose any showing of regard for a person infected with the bacilli of Christian Science. "Atheists cannot do as much harm, in my opinion, as can Christian Scientists." The conference thereupon rescinded the action. Seven years later, the Reverend A. Lincoln Moore summarized the whole case at Riverside Baptist Church in New York: Christian Science was "un-Christian, anti-biblical, Christless, Godless — in brief, Pagan."

Since Christian Science practitioners competed with physicians for care of patients, the medical profession was as angered by Mrs. Eddy as were the clergy. In 1899 *The Journal of the American Medical Association* called for efforts "to restrain the rabid utterances and irrational practices of such ignorant and irresponsible persons as her followers." Progressives who wanted to improve the world saw Christian Science as the enemy that distracted people from social causes. Mrs. Eddy was not surprised by the furies: "We need 'Christ and him crucified.' " But as age finally caught up with her and she became more reclusive, the fight went out of her. Admirers waited near her gate to glimpse her during drives in her coach. One day in December 1910, after one of those drives, she came home with a cough. The healer slumped in exhaustion at her desk and asked for a pencil, with which she simply wrote, "God is my life." Two days later she was gone. Her legacy was a religious movement that brought healing to hundreds of thousands. Its secret was an all-inclusive outlook on life that ennobled their days. Hers was one of the more impressive visions and achievements on the American spiritual landscape.

While as an individual Mary Baker Eddy had the genius to create a world, to give names to nervousnesses and offer remedies for them, movements like hers also depended upon a world, a climate. The environment that made room for her and in which she flourished was full of experts at the spiritual healing of mind-cure. The most durable result of these New Thought trends was the Unity School of Christianity. In 1889 two former invalids, Charles and Myrtle Fillmore, started a magazine, *Modern Thought*. Like Mrs. Eddy they made an appeal both to modern science and "practical Christianity," but they formed what they thought of as a school and not a church, a mail-order movement for self-help. Some of the early converts to Unity came from Christian Science and its less successful competitors.

The gap remained narrow between the middle-class followers in these movements and much of the intelligentsia. Many of the New Thought people sounded like the literary transcendentalists and sometimes paid respect to them. Phineas Quimby and Warren Felt Evans often echoed Ralph Waldo Emerson when he talked about Over-Soul and self-reliance. In his book *In Tune with the Infinite,* which sold 1.5 million copies after 1897, Ralph Waldo Trine seemed a parody of Ralph Waldo Emerson as he spoke of a "spirit of Infinite Life and Power . . . creating, working, ruling through the agency of great immutable laws and forces" that surrounded people on every side.

So tantalized was the great American philosopher and psychologist William James by what he called mind-cure that he included the topic in his classic *The Varieties of Religious Experience* in 1902.

The scholar apologized lest he "jar upon the nerves" of an academic audience by pointing to such contemporary vagaries, but asked for patience since he wanted to show how varied were the spiritual lives of different people. Mind-cure was to him a deliberately optimistic movement that combined elements of the four Gospels with Ralph Waldo Emerson, idealism, spiritism, mysticism, vedantism, evolutionism, and even among the isms, Hinduism. But most of all it stressed intuition. "The blind have been made to see, the halt to walk; lifelong invalids have had their health restored. The moral fruits have been no less remarkable." So successful were mind-curists, thought James, that one could even catch their spirit at second hand in popular counsels to relax and not to worry. One pictures the audience perking to hear and American readers piqued to read that mind-cure was the American people's "only decidedly original contribution to the systematic philosophy of life" — a fact that medics and clerics were beginning to have to notice.

James believed that the New Thought people were a psychic type who deserved to be studied with respect. Theologically, their doctrine of the oneness of human life with God's life squared, he thought, with some recent Christian systems. This sense of oneness, one suspects, was part of what drew the notice of James, since in his diagnosis modernity had disrupted it, offering brokenness instead of the wholeness that sensitive people must seek. He also saw in mind-cure a judgment on conventional religion, since, he said, "the ideas of Christian churches are not efficacious in the therapeutic direction to-day, whatever they may have been in earlier centuries." The belief in the power of suggestion, the counsel to "let go," and the respect for the subconscious life that mind-cure offered needed to be recovered. Whether or not the adherents were cured mattered less than that they seemed to *themselves* to have been cured. Why could not science and spiritual therapy divide labors? Science gave telegraphy, electric lighting, diagnosis, and some kinds of prevention and cure. But "religion in the shape of mind-cure gives to some of us serenity, moral poise, and happiness, and prevents certain forms of disease as well as science does, or even better in a certain class of persons." On that view, science would not succeed religion, as James must have assumed many of his readers thought it would; rather religion and science, "each verified in its own way from hour to hour and from life to life, would be co-eternal."

The scientist who could speak so expansively was himself from a brain-working family. James was born in New York in 1842 of a family with long Scottish-Irish Presbyterian roots. His father, Henry James, Sr., left Princeton Theological Seminary to desert church religion. Thereafter he devised his own amalgam, which included imported notions of mystical Swedenborgianism. While the James home always stirred with discussions of religion, Henry passed on to his children no formal creed or code or cult, a fact that made them candidates for being American moderns. Henry James, Jr., the great novelist, restlessly commuted between Europe and America. All his life long his brother William expressed a kind of homesickness for security, a drive to "feel at home" somewhere. The James children used to ask their father what was their church home, and he gave them the new kind of answer: they could "plead nothing less than the whole privilege of Christendom and that there was no communion, even that of the Catholics, even that of the Jews, even that of the Swedenborgians, from which we find ourselves excluded."

Henry James, Sr., and his son William kept religious questions alive, moving not beyond religion but beyond socially expressed faith. The idea that one could be religious without a sect or a group, a radical proposal of Thomas Paine and Thomas Jefferson, seconded by Henry David Thoreau and Ralph Waldo Emerson, was gaining wider acceptance. A younger contemporary of James, Harvard philosopher Alfred North Whitehead, went so far as to define religion in terms that the native Americans and African immigrants, to say nothing of the people of church and synagogue, could not have comprehended: religion was what one did with his solitariness. So specialized, so individualized and private had modern searching become that no two pilgrims necessarily shared the same path.

If group religion meant little to James, the religious impulse had few better defenders than he in literary and academic circles. Whenever he taught at Harvard, he attended the university's chapel, in a day when most professors had drifted away and dropped the practice. But his patent view of ordinary faith did not make him uncritical. In a preface to *The Will to Believe* he argued that what his century lacked was "criticism and caution, not faith." If he were to address the Salvation Army, a kind of Methodistic movement, or a miscellaneous popular crowd, James averred that he would not promote "the liberty of believing." No, such an audience needed "their faiths . . . broken up and ventilated, that the northwest wind of science should get into them and blow their sickliness and barbarism away." In the century when Joseph Smith and Cardinal

Gibbons knew for sure how to be saved, James wanted to help people live in a "half-wild, half-saved universe."

Himself a victim of illness and depression — at one point he had a severe breakdown — James was aware of the need for cures to American nervousness. "We are all *potentially* . . . sick men. The sanest and best of us are of one clay with lunatics and prison-inmates." To find remedies, the Harvard professor must be a path-finder, which meant he could never give people the whole forest with all its sunlit glories and its moonlit witcheries and wonders. Pathfinders, he said, only gave a direction and a place to reach, with words that were "blazes made by the axe of the human intellect on the trees of the otherwise trackless forests of human experience." James spoke for the new kind of American who, he wrote, "wants facts; he wants science; but he also wants a religion."

James wrote at the end of a century that had begun with camp meetings and revivals, where people were "born again" and found the full truth, and that had concluded with Mary Baker Eddy and the mind-cure people, who offered oneness in life. James, a victim of the chopping forces of modernity but a would-be therapist, instead talked about the "rich thicket of reality." Formally he called his approach "pluralism, which represents order as being gradually won and always in the making." This was the least satisfying of all notions to sick souls hungry for Methodist conversion, but it ministered to strenuous ones who in an age of science looked for religion. As for God, in 1904 James wrote: "I have no living sense of commerce with a God. I envy those who have, for I know the addition of such a sense would help me greatly." He could only hear a deeper voice that pointed *"thither lies the truth."*

The psychologist attacked people who engaged in "the idolatry of the '*Whole*' in order to enjoy the 'eaches,' " in order to come to terms with the fractioning of modern life. In the end James did not preach chaos or nihilism. His "multiverse" still made a universe, because everywhere connections "strung along" realities. But he refused to satisfy those who wanted the answers of firm dogma or authoritarian churches. His faith said that tragedy is only provisional and partial, that "shipwreck and dissolution are not the absolutely final things."

Is this, then, what it all came down to? A century of striving ended in religion defined by James as "what goes on in the single private man"? Smooth preachers, rousing evangelists, mind-cure therapists, and philosophers of solitariness, whatever their psychic demons, still lived in worlds of relative ease and affluence. Around them was a public, social world in which their mysticisms were luxuries; they were removed from the desperate search of others for jobs and bread. At the same time there rose a generation of religious people who had their own means of addressing the brokenness of modern life, who wanted to make it one and whole again by uniting people, in work and faith. Such activists also had a claim on the moral passions of people in one century as they looked toward another. The story of these social-welfare pioneers and religious reformers balances the one of private searches to which the healers so often exclusively directed themselves.

Jacob A. Riis was the most noted photographer of
the urban poor. His camera caught both religious
and secular social agencies in the act of serving the
victims of the industrial city. Here, at Five Points
Nursery in New York, orphans are supervised by
their caretaker in a moment of quiet and reverence.

Chapter Sixteen

THE DREAM OF ONE KINGDOM

✒ MUCH OF THE PLOT OF AMERICAN RELIGION BETWEEN 1850 AND 1950 involves the old Protestant majority interacting with the rest of the population while developing factions within. It is important to remember, though, the continuing potency of the Protestant majority through most of the period and the significant contributions it made to the national ethos. The vision and fate of the Protestants held vast consequences for the American spirit — even among those who resisted it. For whenever crises came, American Protestantism proved remarkably adaptable. There always seemed to be those who inspired a following by suggesting that things could get better, that God would use this people to bring on His Kingdom. Mainstream Protestantism during the half-century before the First World War has to be called optimistic, progressive, and, in some respects, increasingly liberal — though a massive conservative counterforce was also forming and has to be accounted for. This attitude that affected Protestantism could not help but have a bearing on the health of the whole national body.

Many were the religious pilgrims who helped Americans adapt to the challenges of modern times. When the diversity of ethnic backgrounds threatened the vision of "sameness" in the American kingdom, turn-of-the-century promoter Josiah Strong advanced the prospect of an Anglo-Saxon realm that would transform the whole world. As more and more denominations were being invented to satisfy the hungers of Americans on pilgrimage, and as vicious competitions resulted, John R. Mott dreamed and worked for a united Christianity and, in his more fantastic reaches, a concordant religious world. While Dwight L. Moody tried to rescue souls from the city before the gloomy apocalypse he foresaw, Walter Rauschenbusch tried to rescue people *in* the city as part of a venture to bring the world to a climax called the Kingdom of God.

Strong, Mott, and Rauschenbusch are not household words in our time. That these three men — a best-selling author, a Nobel Peace Prize winner, and a controversial Protestant visionary — and others like them were so well known then and are so little recognized today is perhaps the best indication that many of their dreams have died.

Their dreams may have died or at least been shaded for many reasons. Maybe their faith turned so expansive as to seem foolish when the parties for whom they spoke did not massively respond. They lacked access to millions of Americans, including the lower classes and immigrants whose causes they championed — people who would not have known how to translate or respond to what they offered. Ironically, when a great unifying force finally came along to bring these dreamers and the people for whom they spoke together, that force was an alien and abhorrent instrument: the First World War. At the same time, the war served to undercut many of their notions about human nature and progress and the rapid pace of the Kingdom of God among people. Trying to see through their eyes is one way of understanding their world, and, in part, of seeing how and why they failed to see the Kingdom come.

In 1893 the Reverend Josiah Strong wrote *The New Era, or the Coming Kingdom,* in which he crowed, "Surely, to be a Christian and an Anglo-Saxon and an American in this generation is to stand on the mountain-top of privilege." Eight years earlier Strong had earned the credentials that gave him personal privilege by publishing a book that sold more copies than any other work (excluding the Bible) in the fifty years after *Uncle Tom's Cabin.* In *Our Country: Its Possible Future and Its Present Crisis,* Strong, echoing George M. Beard, wrote that American religion and life were full of "feverish activity . . . excitements . . . restless energy . . . stress of the nervous." These were "diseases of civilization, and of modern civilization, and mainly of the nineteenth century, and of the United States." If they were contagious diseases, Strong was a carrier.

Though Strong rested momentarily on that "mountain-top of

privilege," he could not stay long because he had work to do. Under the tones of bravado he could not conceal some worries. *Our Country* portrayed perils to the new era and the coming Kingdom. The author could in no way tolerate "manyness," the pluralism that William James relished. Strong still looked for the sameness that Protestant imperialists since Lyman Beecher favored and that the Puritans still earlier used as the key to their vision of community. Any threat to the unified Anglo-Saxon empire knocked him off balance. Nothing nettled Strong more than did the hordes of diverse people whom he could not exclude from his America.

The new multitudes jammed into the cities, making these centers the most fearful jungles of the "manyness" that threatened the Anglo-Saxon empire. To illustrate the peril, Strong cited statistics. While in 1790 only one-thirtieth of the people lived in cities with more than eight thousand inhabitants, by 1880 almost one-fourth of them lived in large urban sites. While the American population in the meantime was growing twelve-fold, the urban population increased eighty-six-fold. The city was the storm center as well as the nerve center, because every serious menace to America — Mormonism excepted — lurked there. Worst of all, the combination of immigrant plus city meant Roman Catholic plus saloons. In Chicago and New York, where such immigrants congregated, Strong counted one saloon for about every 170 people. The city was not only the home of roughs, gamblers, thieves, robbers, lawless and desperate men, rioters, skeptics, and the irreligious, but was also the lair of wealthy and luxurious people who did not care for the Kingdom.

Josiah Strong talked as he did because he was raising funds for causes whose potential supporters had to feel like potential winners. His audience was made up of what he called the "conservative forces" of society, and he, a progressive, wanted them to join him in preserving the best in empire. Such folks knew they were already losing the cities. In 1890, Strong noted, there was one Protestant church for every 438 citizens nationally, but Boston, the original Puritan city set upon a hill, could claim only one for 1,778 people; and poor Chicago, which after it rose from the fire of 1871 impressed people as the metropolis of promise, forebode a bleak future by having only one Protestant church for every 3,601 citizens. The civilizing and educational institutions were weakest and corrupt government was strongest in the cities. In order to meet these perils, Strong, as an agent of the American Home Missionary Society and the American Evangelical Alliance set out to rally the troops. He made public the notion that he had arrived in "the nick of time" to unify the people of the original stock and to push back newer and alien people.

The Strong strategy in the end came down to one word: cooperate. If only the Anglo-Saxon element would get together, they could keep the American empire pure and firm. While living in the East, the former Wyoming minister never forgot what he had learned in his frontier years. The scepter of world power, he urged, had once passed westward from Persia to Great Britain and then to the American West, "there to remain, for there is no further West." But the Anglo-Saxons could not win and hold on to that West unless they cooperated. A single foe could stand off the separated and squabbling Protestant churches. This enemy was the Roman Catholic church, which with characteristic foresight was trying to win the last frontier because, "as the West is to dominate the nation, she intends to dominate the West." Like so many Protestants, Strong was especially bitter about Catholic parochial schools, because they undercut the public school, the "principal digestive organ of the body politic."

The Reverend Mr. Strong, ever alert, picked up his cue to urge cooperation from the most unlikely sources. Through the years, he acquainted himself with the problems of urban laborers and watched them unite to gain power. He was not, by the way, unsympathetic to the needs of these workers and he well understood why they were attractive targets to socialists. Yet for all his criticism of big corporations, Strong picked up from them the strategy that churches needed. Open-eyed giants of industry and finance saw the immense advantage that lay in consolidation and organization. They became the model for his full-scale attack against the competitive struggles of church people in overchurched towns. Protestant congregations did not yet appreciate the advantage of consolidation. Strong asked readers to imagine the confusion if two military leaders who were set for the defense of the same city and were supposed to fight a common enemy for twenty-five years would fail to hold a council of war or even to meet each other personally in all that time! Yet church leaders were that isolated from each other.

As Strong traveled the circuit for the Evangelical Alliance, he kept before audiences the prospect that they should form "the *collective church* of the community," just as workers and magnates organized collectives. If they would knit themselves into state organizations, Christian public opinion would utter itself quickly and emphatically, in order more easily to win dominance. Strong never got his way. He resigned in 1898 when the Alliance directors turned out to be too much the "conservative forces" in society. The determined progressive then put together a league that became the American Institute for Social Service, an ancestor of the Federal Council of Churches, which, in 1908, he also helped form.

Visionaries build on hope; they use warnings only enough to gain attention so that they can set forth their prospects for a better future. Strong was no exception. He liked to remind his readers who they were, how their glorious ancestors brought the world the two great ideas of civil liberty and a pure *spiritual* Christianity. Now God poised them to spread their way into the whole world. Unfortunately, Strong never spelled out clearly how his camp would come to dominate; he only knew that they would. His language sounded ominous and cruel: "Whether the extinction of inferior races before the advancing Anglo-Saxon seems to the reader sad or otherwise, it certainly appears probable." Look at the Dutch Boers successfully making their way in South Africa, he urged, or at the English as they moved into Africa and India. Their advances, he thought, might be God's "final and complete solution to the dark problem of heathenism among many inferior peoples."

Strong had to postpone the Kingdom's deadline, but he never lost faith in the theme of *Our Country:* that during the next ten or fifteen years the Christians of the United States would either hasten or retard the coming of Christ's Kingdom by hundreds or thousands of years. None of these were the words of an eccentric: Strong was in the mainstream of the progressive Christianity that looked so promising at the turn of the century.

Nowhere in the world and never in history had Christians been divided into so many conflicting groups as in America. Nowhere else were people on pilgrimage forced to make their religious choice from among appeals by more conflicting organizations. Nowhere else was it so easy for people to be bewildered over their personal holds on religious truth because they saw so many people up close who held to opposing truths. This situation meant that the United States was crucial in any scheme for Christian reunion. Josiah Strong did work for the "collective church." But the movement of Christian unity for its own sake or for winning a world needed its own prophet, and found it with the rise of John R. Mott to world prominence.

Mott, like Strong, lived by a simple conquering idea. When in 1946 the Methodist layman won the Nobel Peace Prize, he reviewed his long career: "My life might be summed up as an earnest and undiscourageable effort to weave together all nations, all races, and all religious communions in friendliness, in fellowship, and in cooperation." Mott died in 1955, just before jet air transport made comfortable nomads out of religious bureaucrats. More than twenty years before that, however, an admirer calculated on the basis of his diaries that Mott had already traveled 1.7 million miles, virtually all of them in a state of car sickness, train sickness, or seasickness. His discomfort no doubt qualified Mott to claim all records until then as a Christian traveler and placed him securely in the miserable tradition of his fellow Methodist circuit-riding sufferer Francis Asbury.

The turnaround that Mott and his generation effected appears especially remarkable against the background of four centuries of mere competition and outright conflict in American Christianity. Religious leaders efficiently filled every unoccupied niche and cranny on the spiritual landscape, but they could not successfully project the notion that faith could be of any help in overcoming disintegration in the modern world. Missionaries reported that would-be converts were confused by the many Christs peddled among them and were reluctant to join one church if this meant being further divided from their fellows who joined other groups.

To understand Mott's contribution, one has to look backward, at some of the coalitions Protestants experimented with earlier. In 1801 Presbyterians and Congregationalists launched the Plan of Union, which lasted until 1852; but long before its demise, imbalances within crippled it. "The Presbyterians milked Congregationalist cows, only to make Presbyterian butter and cheese," observed one wag. More effective than the Plan was the less formal network of missionary and benevolent agencies that engaged in an "errand of mercy" on Protestant soil early in the century, until the time when denominations set up their own competing agencies. The nondenominational American Bible Society, for example, was torn in 1836 over Baptist charges that the Society supported baptismal practices that were a part and a pillar of popery. The Baptists wanted to solve that problem of confusion by having the Society distribute Bible versions that translated the Greek word *baptizo* as "immerse." Of course, the other members, who poured or sprinkled water on infants and converts, would not agree to that idea, so the Baptists confused the public by organizing their own group.

They named it the American and Foreign Bible Society. The Baptists followed up with other walkouts and soon showed by their prosperity that the law of religious life in the land was Darwinian: the more uncooperative a group was, the more likely it would be successful and among the fittest, who survived. Sectional rivalries split churches of the North and South. Western frontier groups felt remote from the eastern establishments. Midcentury prophets of unity like Swiss immigrant Philip Schaff among the Reformed, or Samuel S. Schmucker among the Lutherans, were often seen as deniers of their own traditions.

In the crowded landscape of American religion, a new force had to find its own figurative nook, had to find or develop a cohort of people with discernible, if yet unnamed, needs and drives. John R. Mott came along at the right moment to discover a generation who felt the burden of "manyness," the sense that disintegrating modern life was demolishing Christian claims of truth and love. It was easy for his pioneer generation to find models for their ministry, since they could reach back — reformers in American religion almost always reached back — to the primitive simplicity of early Christianity. The New Testament pictured Jesus praying that all his followers might be one. The apostle Paul was preoccupied with the problems of divisiveness in the fellowship. While people who spread ideas of unity were usually realistic enough to speak of councils and federations more than of the disappearance of denominations through mergers, they did insist on overcoming the spirit of competition and conflict. Suddenly, weary missionaries, embarrassed students, and disappointed congregants wanted to overcome the tooth-and-fang approach to faith. People like John R. Mott had the genius to read their needs and provide a movement for them.

Though Mott was born in New York in 1865, he grew up in Postville, Iowa. During study at little Upper Iowa University, he announced that he had enjoyed the Methodist conversion that gave him credentials. Before that, he was secretive about his inner life, he said, but now he wanted to live an open, active religious life. On this promise he made good a thousand times over. Mott became active in the Young Men's Christian Association (YMCA), which provided him contacts across sectarian lines. He continued work with the YMCA when he moved for further studies to Cornell University in New York State.

In the winter of 1886, famed English cricket player J. Kynaston Studd, later lord-mayor of London, came to Cornell to promote revivals in the manner and spirit of Dwight L. Moody. Hero-hungry young Mott heard Studd and henceforth was determined to give his life to Christian student work.

He retired to his room and wrote a pained letter in which he asked his father to dispose of the family business in due course; the son no longer wished to succeed him in it. The parents complained that their son was deserting the lumber business, but he patiently explained that Dwight L. Moody had more important plans for him, that he was already ministering in jails. Moody showed confidence in the twenty-eight-year-old when he turned over to him his Northfield, Massachusetts, conference operations for a summer and went to his campaign at the 1893 World's Columbian Exposition at Chicago.

The Student Volunteer Movement, like the YMCA a pioneer for unity, called Mott to conferences and promotional work in Europe and elsewhere. Between 1895 and 1896, he circled the globe, but added enough side-trip mileage to have circled it twice. His mission took him to 144 colleges and universities in twenty-four countries, where he listened to and goaded on his contemporaries. In 1895, at the medieval Vadstena Castle in Sweden, he and several other adventurous souls founded a new World's Student Christian Federation (WSCF), the agency that took him far beyond the Anglo-Saxon sphere. At Constantinople, Mott reached out to Orthodox Christians at a time when violence against Armenians led members of the Armenian, Bulgarian, and Greek Orthodox churches to get together and to give him a hearing. In Japan, he faced Unitarian-minded students, but in their presence insisted that the Lordship of Christ must define Federation witness. The organizer knew few other limits, nor did Mott let that one keep him from making friendly gestures toward other faiths.

Along the way, Mott invented the slogan that grasped evangelical imaginations for decades; he wanted to see "the evangelization of the world in this generation." By this he did not mean that everyone would become Christian, but that there would be a Christian presence in the hearing of all people. By 1910 he had gained such a name that when the World Missionary Conference convened at Edinburgh, Scotland, he was among those who presided, and he chaired a continuation committee. From that event most people date the rise of the modern ecumenical Christian-unity movement. Rather than follow up at once on its organizational progress, through the war years he worked to keep student movements from being torn apart by World War I. As he did so, he learned that the rest of the world saw the war as the final moral crisis of Christendom itself.

Traveler Mott thought that "no movement can be adequately led from an office chair." Between his waves of seasickness, he kept a notebook full of Methodistic counsel against the perils of hurried devotions, being satisfied with small things, or "unreality." In 1914 he compared the critical battlefields he had already visited. Among these were the Muslim world, the educated classes of Japan, the literati of China, the citadels of Hinduism, and the areas of neglect in Latin America. One battlefront dwarfed them all: "Our own American and Canadian universities and colleges." The churches must reinvade these seats of learning. "If we are to go forth to attempt world conquest, we must have no untaken forts in our rear." To overthrow moral evils and unfavorable college traditions, thought earnest Mott, Christian students had to make an appeal to the heroic. John R. Mott began to reverse patterns that Josiah Strong had just finished reinforcing. For the first time, groups of American Protestants united without using Catholics as their common foil. For the first time also, these Christians coalesced without denouncing Jews, heathens, or pagans in the process.

What seems commonplace today was a radical breach with the past by Mott. He assured Catholics of a welcome in the WSCF, and long before Latin American clergy allowed such activity, he found ways to work with Catholic lay people there. In America, Eastern Orthodox Christians looked exotic, but he found them to be friendly. In Egypt, he was at home with Copts; in India, with the Syrian church; in Japan, with the Russian Orthodox. So promising a diplomat was Mott that in 1917 President Woodrow Wilson named him to a Special Diplomatic Mission of the United States to Russia. His broad contacts on this trip brought him into touch with both dissenters and the official Russian Orthodox church. Certainly never before had an American Protestant layman spoken at the behest of the high procurator to the Commission of the Holy Synod in Petrograd.

Against the usual background of American coalitions, it might seem easy to explain even the pan-Christian impulses of Mott: he must have wanted to unite all Christians against all other religions. Not at all; he even tried to teach missionaries to resist such temptations. While at Cornell, he had helped form a "Religious Association" at which Buddhists, Jews, and Ethical Culturists would feel welcome. Then he helped form a Ramabai circle in support of Pundita Ramabai, a Hindu who sought money with which to help the child widows of India. Of course the Chicago World's Parliament of Religions in 1893 attracted him. Sight of the erotic religious sculptures in India naturally repelled the Methodist tourist, but he also looked for the more congenial side of Indian faith and made a point of stopping to show interest at shrines all over the Orient. He talked to Baha'i leaders, was friendly with Muslims, and interviewed young Mohandas Gandhi.

In his great leap forward from American sectarianism, Mott learned to appreciate other religions without losing hold of his own. In typical messages, he encouraged leaders and students of other faiths to come alive, to live by their vision, and become better acquainted with Christ. Conservative Protestants attacked him, but he reassured them that the more he saw of other faiths, the more Jesus appeared as "one other than all the rest." The more he studied non-Christian systems — and he used capital letters to make the point — the more sure he was that "in Christ we have the Central Figure of the Ages . . . the Creative Energy, the World's Redeemer, the Desire of all Nations."

While Muslims or Jews could not welcome the way Mott drew close in admiration and then changed the rules of the game with a witness to Christ, they no more expected him to give up his truth than they would theirs. Against the background of Christian hatred of the heathen, they found this a refreshing change. Some American modernists went further than he, to the point that they finally abandoned the uniqueness of Christ. In 1895 the noted Boston cleric George A. Gordon spoke for this new "Gospel for Humanity." He told the American Board of Commissioners for Foreign Missions that since God had left a witness among all peoples, missionaries should not impose their message on others. Instead modern Christians should collaborate with other religions to improve the world. Then Gordon pulled rank by supporting his case with the argument that Western civilization, since it was incomparable, had much to teach the rest of the world.

These forays into friendliness led to backlash at home. The Federal Council of Churches (FCC) of 1908 became the chief battlefield, with the Baptist groups acting out the tensions. The Northern Baptist Convention joined the council in 1908, but the larger Southern Baptist Convention stayed out and thus resisted risks to its own prosperity. In the eyes of its members, people must choose between missions and unity. These Baptists did not always debate with the FCC or Mott; they settled things among themselves. Professor James B. Gambrell of Southwestern Baptist Theological Seminary, editor of *The Baptist Standard,* led the fight with his 1913 statement that Baptists were for Christian unity — so long as unity resulted from others agreeing with or becoming Baptists. The moderate Edgar Young Mullins spoke up modestly for unity, but Gambrell won the day with typical Social Darwinist calls for "denominational efficiency" and his warnings against "entangling alliances." To Gambrell the unity movement was a "seducing, undoing apostasy." The Arkansas State Convention secretary in Gambrell's spirit editorially urged: "Smite, smite, hip and thigh, the 'bastard' Union movement, dear preachers of God's Book, by calling every Baptist soul under the reach of your prophetic voice to toe the denominational line." And Gambrell attacked Mott head-on for trying to get the War Department to work only with "Judaism, Catholicism, and YMCA-ism."

By the time of American entry into World War I, the new lines of conflict were clear and hard. The Federal Council of Churches and the World's Student Christian Federation were keeping alive a vision of unity at the expense of competitive efficiency. The competitive groups, meanwhile, prospered, despite this vision of unity. Then the religious in America learned a secret few could face openly. For the first time since the Civil War, they found that they could suppress some of their differences — but only for a great cause. Once again it was a war that created the illusion of unity, a war that was both a judgment on disintegrative society and an agent of unimaginable chaos in the years to follow. Before we take up its story, however, we should observe a third, social view of the Kingdom of God. Walter Rauschenbusch was its greatest representative.

Rauschenbusch derived not from Anglo-Saxon but from Teutonic immigrant stock; he was a seventh-generation minister. His father, Karl Augustus Rauschenbusch, arrived from Germany when social protest was strong in the 1840s. In America the father revealed an independent turn of mind when he left his native Lutheranism and selected instead the small and more free German Baptist group. Young Walter was never close to his father, whom the Germans at the Baptist-affiliated Rochester Theological Seminary always considered a learned but quirky professor. The boy spent some childhood years in Europe with his mother and her other children, perhaps to escape the family tensions, connected to his father's depression and alcoholism, that plagued the home.

The first generation of Social Gospel progressives were not secular-minded worldlings. Rauschenbusch, typically, underwent the standard evangelical conversion. While he later had to admit that much in his turning "was not really true," he was always grateful, he said, for this tender and mysterious experience. Being "born again" helped him stay close to thousands who professed such an event in their lives, though he also separated from them and scolded them if they let their personal rebirth be the end of their Christian striving. He pressed for a sort of second conversion, one that carried people back to the world with the work of Jesus in mind. He felt, he said, that every Christian ought to participate in the dying of the Lord Jesus Christ in order to help redeem humanity — a thought that had to sound bizarre in the company of the socialists whose notice he courted. The concept gave him his life direction. Almost as a matter of course, he attended Rochester University and Seminary. After graduation in 1886, he thought of following his sister into foreign missionary work, but a suspicious professor sensed budding heresy in him and the Baptist boards decided not to risk his spreading it to India.

In 1886 the young minister settled for a pastorate at tiny Second German Baptist Church at Forty-Fifth Street and Tenth Avenue in New York City, on the edge of the appropriately named Hell's Kitchen area. Most of his 125 members brought home meager incomes from jobs, but they were close enough to misery to enable Rauschenbusch to see the insecurity of urban life. As he wandered among the helpless and hopeless people around his congregation for eleven years, he admitted that he had to revise most of his notions of what it meant to follow Jesus. He had difficulty learning how to use one little congregation as a base for attacking crowded and sinful New York. One thing was certain: the seminary classrooms had in no way prepared him for the kind of ministry he faced. Yet he took to it with zest, "as if I had stepped from a land of shadows into bright sunshine," he liked to say, "when I came out of the artificial circumstances of seminary life into the whirl of New York. Here things are tangible."

Every pioneer or shaper in American religious history promoted some commanding vision, some conquering idea. The first sermon theme on which he preached in New York became the consuming one for Rauschenbusch: "Your Kingdom Come." As the prayer took over his mind, he asked his congregation for two months' leave so he could read up on the theme, which hit him with the force of a new discovery. The parishioners gave him the chance he asked for, and he used it to devour the writings of British Christian Socialists. They used the idea of the Kingdom of God to face up to disintegration in modern England. It came to shake his soul and impel him back to Hell's Kitchen: "That was the brilliancy, the splendor of that conception — it touches everything with religion." The Kingdom of God as a conquering idea was the magnet that unified competing churches and, he hoped, would lead the whole world to rebirth, because it was not a cramping concept that dealt only with the institutions of the church. Instead, the Kingdom of God was "humanity organized according to the will of God."

Like Strong, Rauschenbusch insisted that he was not a despiser of his age and its achievements, but he then spent sixty-five pages in a book named *Christianity and the Social Crisis* pointing to the disintegrations of the age. He called believers back to the simple power of Jesus and primitive Christianity, but he also embraced modernity and became a prophet of adjustment to new environments. His kind of modernism, widely shared by Social Gospel leaders, alienated conservative Protestants, who either wanted simply to rescue souls out of the world or to improve the world without accepting modern ideas. Thus, while he agitated for unity, Rauschenbusch helped create a schism between progressives and conservatives. On social issues, his party claimed that the Kingdom of God embraced the social and public zones of life, while the evangelists like Moody, whom he admired only to a certain extent, accented personal change and Christian individualism. They could never create a "united and harmonious and daring religious conception of the world."

In an age called progressive, Rauschenbusch often made utopian-sounding claims, and to some he seemed a naive optimist. Yet there was a dark and haunting side to his existence and to his view of the world. Black crepe outlined his earliest memories and colored his final days. He could recall the black cloth that draped Rochester when Abraham Lincoln was killed. And on his own lapel in his last years he wore black crepe that dated from the outbreak of World War I, to mourn the conflict and its setbacks to civilization and the Kingdom of God. But instead of hanging crepe or enjoying fashionable despair, he thought that assassinations and wars only pointed to the urgency of offering humans the prospect of the Kingdom. As Rauschenbusch promoted the daring concept of a united world, he was confident that when future people wrote histories of how Christendom became more Christian, the turning-point chapter must deal with his own generation.

Once his obsession became fixed, the young minister went out looking for company. Photographer Jacob Riis, whose pictures of tenement people awakened some Americans to the constrictions of slum life, drew his attention. Like so many urban progressives, the Social Gospel minister admired Henry George, the author of *Progress and Poverty* (1877–1879). The book awakened Rauschenbusch to the idea that social change could come without the violence Marxist-socialists threatened. George advocated a single tax on land holdings as the key to all reform. The Hell's Kitchen pastor even went to hear and applaud Father Edward McGlynn when that reform-minded priest was in trouble with his superiors over his social viewpoints. Edward Bellamy also impressed him with his best-selling utopian novel, *Looking Backward.*

While the pastor carried the excitement and burdens of ministry in Hell's Kitchen, problems of health came to deter him. First he suffered eye trouble, but after 1886 more serious problems of hearing plagued him. After a case of the Russian grippe two winters later, he went back to work before he was fully recovered and as a result became nearly deaf for the rest of his life. His mother and a specially trained parishioner ministered with him, and later his wife helped bring the world to him while he became a skilled lip-reader. Yet his defenses made Rauschenbusch more shy and lonely than he already was. Since he feared that someday he must be cut off from people entirely, he sped up his work.

Despite the hearing loss, Rauschenbusch carried on a successful ministry. As his little congregation grew, he finally, in 1889, agreed to their pleas to help them build a new church. The task of fund raising was most difficult in his kind of neighborhood, but he knew how to cultivate prosperous Baptists. Though he liked to criticize the wealthy, he must have decided that John D. Rockefeller had either come by his riches honestly or could be reformed, because on occasion that magnate sloshed through the muds of the West Side as a confidant and benefactor of the socially progressive minister. And through it all, the congregation loved their pastor because he not only came to save souls in the sense that they expected but also cared about the other needs of their lives. The Kingdom of God forced Rauschenbusch to ever more basic thought, until he sounded like the primitives before him: he needed only "the basic test of the Bible and the people in the original."

The restless minister felt intellectually confined by West Side life, so in 1891 he took a study trip to Europe. There he was overjoyed to learn that the biblical scholars had rediscovered the Kingdom of God motif. Now secure in his new social impulses, Rauschenbusch returned and between 1892 and 1893 formed a little "Brotherhood of the Kingdom" with some other Baptists. Their journal, *For the Right,* enlarged on the Kingdom theme; increasingly Rauschenbusch found himself attacking competition and the amassing of wealth because they were to his mind barriers against realizing the Kingdom.

It must be said that the members of this little brotherhood never came close to solving the economic issue that perplexed them. They had no clue as to how to break the hold of monopoly wealth or disrupt an unjust class system. The capitalists knew that they needed to gain and hold power and the Marxists knew that they needed violent means to prevail. But Rauschenbusch wavered: "To hit or to endure? — usually one or the other has to be chosen." He was not capable of hitting, for religious reasons; but to endure permitted injustices to continue. The Social Gospel progressives never came up with a clear address to this issue or with any decisive program at all. Many of them retreated with Rauschenbusch to the claim that they were called to be prophets, not programmers. This meant that they influenced church people more than the other agents of social action in the world around them. The latter could go about their business pretty much the same, whether or not idealists preached the new era or the coming Kingdom.

In 1897 Rauschenbusch felt called to leave Second Baptist Church in order to teach at the Rochester Seminary. He looked back. While Dr. Beard and the Reverend Mr. Strong were looking for nervous America in brain-working houses, Rauschenbusch looked at urban hovels and concluded simply that "the people are restless." They came to their ministers, he said, as the people of Israel once asked the prophets, "Do you have a word for us?" Too often the people had to turn away in disappointment. "Is it to remain that way?"

As a teacher, Rauschenbusch targeted not the professors but the people who still sensed in him the common touch. Legend reinforced their view of his character. Thus word spread of the time a streetcar in Rochester accidentally knocked him over. The professor picked himself up, dusted himself off, and apologized to the conductor for having obstructed traffic. Then, still not satisfied with himself, Rauschenbusch went home and enclosed five dollars in a letter of apology for any inconvenience.

certain prophetic moments in which he saw or heard the prospect of the Kingdom. He cited the Hebrew prophets in support of his conquering theme, and called in as witnesses John the Baptist and, of course, Jesus, for the way they pronounced judgment on the unjust. The early Christians who "had all things in common" showed how community should look. Later in the course, Rauschenbusch pointed to the dissenters who suffered and lived so simply in the Middle Ages, followed by the radical Protestant reformers and Baptist lovers of freedom. He chose to deal with collisions and conflicts in history because these best revealed how people acted in crisis — as they must in his own day.

While the Social Gospel movement never became a majority voice in developing two-party Protestantism, it found a niche among leaders who were ready for change. In 1908 the Methodist church produced a "Social Creed" to help impel the followers of old Tory John Wesley into a world that needed transforming. In the same year Josiah Strong and his company formed the Federal Council of Churches, which became the chief agency for uniting efforts in support of social, as opposed to private, Christianity. Because the pronouncements of these leaders often stirred churchly reaction, Rauschenbusch expected fierce attacks on his second "dangerous" book, but to his astonishment "everybody was kind to it. Only a few 'damned' it." Reformist Christianity was facing a new threat: it was becoming accepted, and was to be fairly respectable for another ten years.

In competitive American Protestantism no party is allowed to surge ahead unchallenged. Enemies of the Social Gospel soon got it into focus and started firing. Evangelist Billy Sunday, an ex–baseball player who carried on in more flamboyant ways the mass ministry of Dwight L. Moody, knew that he could always outdraw the more staid prophets of the Social Gospel. Sunday looked at the social creeds and programs and blasted at them as "godless social service nonsense." In his own way he also could claim that he favored aspects of social reform, but he stuck to the old-fashioned gospel of conversion. His sermons were full of attacks on immigrants and saloon keepers, big money men and socialists, dancers and prostitutes, "shiftless" people and reformers, whom he could all jumble for condemnation in a single sentence. His Kingdom of God meant nothing but the sum of saved individual souls. He had no use for the complex "institutional churches" with which progressives faced the needs of slum dwellers. Sunday insisted that "the road into the Kingdom of God is not by the bathtub, nor the gymnasium, nor the university, but by the blood red hand of the cross of Christ." More moderate evangelists than he cooperated with the Federal Council enough to establish a small department of evangelism in 1915 in order to complement the social interest.

In 1912 Rauschenbusch published *Christianizing the Social Order* for a Protestantism that was now split widely over the issue of Christianizing. As usual in American religion, those who wanted to unify produced more division. Yet Rauschenbusch refused to slow down in order to quiet the opposition. He cited several systems in American life that looked partly Christianized: the family, the church, education, and some aspects of politics. But the Social Gospel was now up against economic life. The competitive way did not yet look Christianized to him, because it enslaved the winners and demoralized the losers. Whoever lost faith in the existence of the devil, he argued, could quickly regain it by tackling big business hard enough to make the moguls angry. God had even raised up secular socialism because the church had grown blind and slow about His purposes, but this socialism would also pass away when the church caught on to the higher and vaster idea of the Kingdom of God.

By the time the tired warrior published *A Theology for the Social Gospel* in 1917, the book looked more like a summing-up than a prospectus. At that time, the First World War consumed the energies of the churches, and conservatives employed fears of radical socialism to keep the Protestant majority away from Social Christianity. But the war itself did most to devastate the programs of progressives. Few felt the disaster more personally than did Rauschenbusch.

He was not always a pacifist. Back in 1898 he had stood with Strong on the mountaintop of Anglo-Saxon privilege and scowled down on Spain. "It is a war for which we give thanks," he gloated in the year that he named the greatest in national history. In that war Rauschenbusch somehow strained to see God busy cleansing out the dross and purifying the gold of holy humanity. God was calling America forward out of the safe isolation of its ocean walls. Manhood lay ahead; America must break camp and follow the divine pillar of fire that led the nation ahead.

Given his background as a militant, Rauschenbusch had difficulty explaining how and why he opposed American entry into World War I. Long before Germany loomed as an enemy, he lost his taste for both empire and war. His book on the social crisis back in 1912 claimed that force, apparently the shortcut to the Promised Land, always turned out to be the longest way of all. On some occasions, he accused capitalist merchants of promoting war — and death — in order to gain wealth. But he did have a problem making his point, for one simple reason: his was a German name, and he had visited Germany. Super-Americans mistrusted any German in America who was not ardent about fighting.

After 1914 Rauschenbusch risked losing friends and harming his movement when he suggested that English atrocities might match the German ones, just when it was fashionable for clerics to advertise German inhumanity alone. When others attacked him for pacifism or disloyalty, he lapsed into gloom: "I am glad I shall not live forever." Yet his old faith somehow endured and he trusted that goodwill must still be the final goal of all people. In 1918 Rauschenbusch looked back dolefully on the four years: "Since 1914 the world is full of hate, and I cannot expect to be happy again in my lifetime." So much for the image of Rauschenbusch as superficial optimist.

When America entered the war in 1917, pacifists felt new pressures against them. Rauschenbusch found it advisable to make much of the fact that his son Hilmar served on the western front in the ambulance service. No one knew quite what he meant when he explained: "We best realize some things through our children." Cornelius Woelfkin, a rabidly anti-German colleague at Rochester, pressed him ruthlessly, until Rauschenbusch could say that he felt like a swimmer in a stormy sea: he could struggle only with each impact as it arrived. Perhaps others, he thought, found it easier than he to come to fixed conclusions, because they were in more ready contact with public opinion than a remote and nearly deaf man such as himself.

Rauschenbusch began to write little testaments when cancer struck him in 1918. "I leave my love to those of my friends whose souls have never grown dark against me. I forgive the others and hate no man. For my errors and weaknesses I hope to be forgiven by my fellows." Death was welcome, since he could leave behind the handicap of deafness that blighted his last thirty years. Aware of the way his mental depression destroyed his physical health, the aged professor wrote his young secretary that "if Christian Science and the New Thought contain any truth, we ought all to be sick." One last time, in May, he remarked about the physical loneliness of life and his awareness of conservative Christian sniping, but in his sadness, he did not forget the dream of the Kingdom. On

July 25, four months before the war ended, "upheld by the comforts of God," he died.

The Social Gospel did not die with Walter Rauschenbusch, but its enemies were henceforth better organized than before to attack its survivors. To secular America, even in its prime the movement seemed to be a mere footnote to the Progressive movement in politics, but among religious forces it meant much more. The Social Gospel people felt they were recovering the primitive Christian concern for all of life as they reached for the future Kingdom of God with justice for all. To them the trend toward individual conversion that came with the revivalists was a departure from the larger Christian approach. And in the modern world, where competing and adapting forces chopped up the various aspects of life and led to disintegration, they wanted to reintegrate life and make people whole. When the sympathetic journal *The Baptist* in 1920 looked at the ruins of the movement, its editors decided that Christians and other Americans were "going back to the old ideas that made a hell of the world."

Part of that hell was war and support for its ideology. War came as no stranger to the American religious forces, which usually were more or less enthusiastic supporters of national military conflicts. But the first foreign war of the United States, the Great War that erupted in 1914, disrupted the tendencies of national life as previous wars did not. Yet just before 1914 most religious leaders genuinely opposed war and few saw reasons to partake in a remote struggle in Europe. For decades a spirit of progressive optimism had moved many of the more powerful leaders, who saw no point in settling human differences with anything so destructive as war. Yet when it came, they closed ranks and generated an ideology to support it. The majority suspected innocents for presumed lack of patriotism and punished dissenters. For a brief moment they also found that the specter and cause of war united them as no spiritual impulse of their own ever could.

Why? A surveyor of the religious people of America would have to say that the citizens were naturally patriotic. The newcomers from eastern Europe and the old-timers from England united in love of the land. Whatever hardships any knew in the rural West or the ghettos of eastern cities, they made it plain that they liked it in America, their Zion — "God's country," as many liked to call their place. Groups that had been suspect so far as patriotism was concerned because they were the pope's people, Jews with divided loyalities, or Europeans who, in America, still talked the language of the people who were now the enemy, all found an opportunity to outdo each other in supporting the war effort.

There may have been other reasons. It was hard to portray the conflict in Europe as a threat to American shores in a time when the Monroe Doctrine still served mythically to separate the hemispheres. It was less hard for the astute to see that between 1914 and 1917 American economic order had come to depend more and more on support of the Allies against Germany, and defeat by Germany could mean crash at home. Yet the common people do not show much evidence of such economic calculation. In the churches most were trained to obey "the powers that be" and to support them enthusiastically without much criticism.

Finally, it must be said that Mars as the god of war has a powerful claim on human imagination. In the world of 1917, if not yet in 1914, Mars somehow outshouted the voices of Moses and Christ, or, more ingeniously, turned their voices into supporters of the national cause. The sound of prophetic judgment was almost stilled.

Ironically, in 1914 the nation's foreign-policy leaders were both strong Presbyterian men of peace. Rarely before did leaders present better credentials for resisting war than did Secretary of State William Jennings Bryan and President Woodrow Wilson. Yet their alliance was not to last. Latent disagreements surfaced and they broke with each other. There were more ironies. Progressive politician Bryan would later be known chiefly as the greatest lay defender of conservative Protestantism in its fundamentalist form. And Wilson is known for his success at leading America into war and his failure at leading it into subsequent peace policies.

Both were dedicated moralists, more ready than other political figures in this century to fuse their private faith and their civic calling. They shared biblical belief, though Bryan increasingly became militant in defense of literal readings of the Scriptures while Wilson came to be more adaptive. Bryan held fiercely to the inherited old order of small-town Protestantism and Christian America. The more urbane Wilson thought he personally could shape a new world order. When the U.S. entry into the war ruined his image as a peacemaker, he hoped again to invest the conflict with a moral cause, to make the world safe for democracy and ready for peace ever after. Both leaders had to reverse their stands by 1917. In support of war, the differences between them collapsed into nothing.

William Jennings Bryan, partly misremembered by later Americans as a fiery, rumpled presidental candidate who turned into a senile but arrogant defender of the Bible against evolution, was a populist of sorts throughout his political career. He stood for the values of a simpler, premodern America and thus for the presumed outlook of farmers and villagers in the South and West against the schooled and moneyed interests of the North and East. Walter Lippmann, who embodied the suavity of the latter, observed that to easterners in 1914 Bryan looked irresistibly funny because they thought he moved in a world that had ceased to exist. His virtues, his habits, his ideas, were "the simple, direct, shrewd qualities of early America." The pundit saw that the progressive Bryan was more conservative than many a propertied bigot when he stood for the popular tradition while most of his enemies represented the power that was destroying it.

The "Great Commoner" had long midwestern roots. He piously liked to recall that from his Illinois parents and their Bible he learned how to conform both his public and private life to the demands of Christianity as a step to happiness in the present world and the one to come. Little wonder that a person with such a world view would evoke sneers from the people who read Lippmann, or that they would find passé his "sweetest recollections" of a life of prayer or hours in churches that sophisticates would find stifling.

The biblical outlook at Salem called on young Bryan not to gamble, dance, smoke, drink alcohol, use bad language, or countenance anyone who did. All the while he was to work hard, waste nothing, and be dutiful. Such a code led many restless adolescents to rebellion, but young Bryan attended Methodist Sunday school with his mother in the morning and a Baptist version in the afternoon with his father. When Mrs. Bryan also joined the Baptists, the piety at home doubled, but the son dared a tinge of independence by choosing the Presbyterians. Years later he was honest enough to admit that for him the problem with being a Baptist was his irrational fear of water and the need to be immersed in it if he wanted to minister among the Baptists.

Church and home were a cocoon to shelter the youth from modernity. As an adult, Bryan smugly announced that he could think of no virtue that he had to acquire on his own, because his parents taught all of them. Being "born again," then, meant turning his back on nothing, since it was a ticket to the endorsed adult world. While the children of northeastern brain-working houses boasted of their neurasthenia, he took pride in how continuous his own life always was. To hear a man of his eminence speak in the language of stability in 1916 reassured those Americans who wanted to remain untainted by Europe or the big city. While modernists told people to adapt to the new, Bryan spoke to the resisters. For him, however, biblical conservatism did *not* mean keeping religion out of politics; as late as 1920 he begged to say that "Christian men MUST take an interest in politics" — they must apply the teaching of Christ to government.

Nebraska, his chosen scene, was unpromising territory for a politically hungry Democrat, but in 1890 during the populist revolt, Bryan won a seat in Congress. From the first he made his stand clear as he cried out in Washington against banks, eastern newspapers, and legislators unlike himself who did not support the farm, the West, and Thomas Jefferson. Neatly he divided the world into two sides. The allied hosts of monopolies, great trusts, and railroad corporations — the money power — wanted laws to benefit themselves and impoverish the people. He, on the other hand, spoke for farmers, laborers, merchants, and common people who, he said, produced the wealth and carried the burdens of taxation. Bryan lost a bid for a Senate seat in 1894 and was unsuccessful in two presidential campaigns thereafter. When the Spanish-American War erupted in 1898, the Great Commoner momentarily set aside his provincial instincts and enlisted, but then showed his true colors the moment the war ended. On December 10 he resigned his commission and wrote his wife saying that the nation was now in more danger than Cuba was when he first enlisted. Now he felt free to overcome his "military lockjaw" and attack the new American imperialism. The Nebraskan was sure that moneyed interests were turning the war into a conquest for land instead of letting it remain a battle of civilization against barbarism, as they first had advertised it. Now, he thought, Americans who had just defended themselves against Cuba had better defend their country against foreign ideas and colonial impulses. Bryan announced a fight against the alien idea of expansion.

Between election campaigns Bryan became a popular lecturer on the Young Men's Christian Association circuit, where he turned out to be more consistent in his attacks on people of wealth than were Social Gospel leaders. He resigned from the board of Illinois College when the school accepted funds tainted by the hands of donor Andrew Carnegie. Walter Rauschenbusch and the University of Chicago modernists accepted gifts from John D. Rockefeller, but Bryan said that "a Christian has been too well defined to enable a man like Rockefeller to be mistaken for one." From University of Nebraska sociologist Edward A. Ross he learned the concept of "social sin" and applied it freely to the system that produced such men of wealth while others hungered.

Rarely did Bryan disappoint his supporters, who never numbered quite enough to make him president. He confused his backers when he accepted the secretaryship of state from easterner Wilson, but assured them that the president was a prophet of peace who incarnated the spirit of Christianity. For a while, Bryan restrained himself and conformed to Wilson's wishes, thus postponing an inevitable clash between titans. Now and then, religious issues intruded. Bryan grumbled when Wilson named not a Christian but Unitarian Charles W. Eliot, the president of Harvard, to be ambassador to China, though he could breathe easily when Eliot declined the post. On a more trivial but equally revealing issue, Bryan followed his temperance principles and broke protocol by serving no liquor at a reception for retiring English ambassador James Bryce. The guests professed to be content with the arrangement, having little choice but to do so after Bryan announced that he was acting on principle. If the urban press ridiculed him, Bryan received letters of support from "his" America.

In May of 1915, writer George Fitch in *Collier's* magazine wrapped up all the criticisms of Bryan as cabinet member. Fitch found that they represented a "comprehensive, wholehearted, constitutional, fundamental, temperamental, special, religious, anatomical, gastronomic, and sartorial disagreement." Somehow the secretary endured for a while, buying time by writing treaties that momentarily quieted Caribbean and Central American interests. He thought America should become a "modern good Samaritan" through generous loan programs, never seeing how subtly imperialistic his policy was since America could thus exert a controlling influence without much risk of loss.

Staying out of the European war was Bryan's consuming passion beginning in 1914. At first he thought some patchworking with treaties would quiet the zeal for conflict. In the summer of 1914, he tried some symbolism on the home front when he requisitioned War Department swords, had them melted into plowshare paperweights, and gave them to Wilson and other officials. One of his own slogans adorned a side: "Nothing is final between friends." On the obverse it said: "Diplomacy is the Art of Keeping Cool." The base was inscribed with the inevitable biblical verse from Isaiah that promised a day when swords would become plowshares.

Ambassador to France Myron T. Herrick accurately described the Bryan of 1914 as not pro-German or pro anything else except "pro-peace and pro-America"; but a shift in the climate stranded the State Department chief. He wished to survive without having to sound anti-German. When Wilson started bypassing his secretary of state as a mediator between parties in Europe, Austrian ambassador Constantin Dumba surmised why: Wilson wanted through his own efforts to find peace so he could be "the saviour of humanity, the Messiah whom future generations would laud as their benefactor." That was the role Bryan had been seeking for years, but Wilson was in a higher position to fulfill it.

After the Germans sank the British ship *Lusitania,* Wilson sent Germany a note so belligerent that in June of 1915 Bryan felt called in conscience at last to resign. He was sure that Wilson still wanted peace, but such angry notes did not befit "the greatest Christian nation." After resigning, he went home, slumped on a sofa, and poured out his grief to his wife. Little had changed from the old days; the president, he thought, did not realize that the great part of America lay west of the Alleghenies, while Wilson played up to the prowar eastern interests. Now Bryan thought he must represent the westerners against the munitions makers and other Wilsonian profiteers.

Cabinet members fought back tears when Bryan for the last time met with them. Interior Secretary Franklin K. Lane could not keep from gushing, "You are the most real Christian I know." For some time tributes arrived, proof that not everyone yet felt called openly to support England. A *Literary Digest* survey confirmed what everyone knew: that a considerable number of westerners and southerners retained their confidence in the motives and purposes of William Jennings Bryan. Someday, said the *Los Angeles Tribune,* all peoples on earth would remember Bryan as "that follower of the Prince of Peace who wrote the Sermon on the Mount into the statutes of the world."

Bryan was not the kind of man who could see his resignation as any sort of failure. To say that war must continue even for a day, he thought, was equivalent to saying that some questions could be settled only by the sword and to deny the coming of the day of peace. This was "to challenge Christian civilization — a return to savagery." Who would represent the righteous cause when America stopped setting an example? Wilson campaigned on the slogan "He kept us out of war." Bryan supported him again in 1916 and helped carry the states in which he promoted the president's cause.

The *Chicago Tribune* — friendlier now than when it had earlier wished that Bryan had been born a "German or a Jap" — considered him the most powerful individual in the United States, the man whose mood was the mood of the whole West.

Bryan made the mistake of being virtuous too long. Suddenly in 1917 the climate changed and neutrality sounded pro-German. He was still resistant when Congress declared war. "Gladly would I have given my life to save my country from war, but now that my country had gone to war, gladly will I give my life to aid it." Bryan had to make the best of what was now a "People's War" by turning it into a moral battle of democracy. Silver linings were far apart, but he looked for a few, hoping that cooperative American Christians would remain amiable after they finished with war causes and humane relief. He was also cheered to see that the war was advancing both the Prohibition and woman suffrage causes. Otherwise he seemed a loser. Yet by the mid-twenties Bryan would be back to oppose evolution in Tennessee's famed Scopes trial, an event more familiar to later generations than any of these prewar endeavors.

The case of Woodrow Wilson, the supreme moralist-statesman of American history, is even more illuminating. More than Bryan ever wanted to, Wilson embodied faith in the new order, yet his vision had to die, and when he revised it, few followed him. That vision was shaped from childhood. Wilson was born in 1856 at Staunton, Virginia, the son and grandson of Presbyterian ministers and the nephew of still another. In the name of biblical righteousness, his slaveholding father supported the Confederacy and served as a Civil War chaplain. Woodrow's oldest memory went back to the day he heard that the election of Abraham Lincoln must mean war. The four-year-old walked into his father's study and asked, "What is war?"

Five years after that war ended, the Wilson family moved to South Carolina, where Dr. Wilson taught his family and seminarians the Calvinist moral system. Woodrow learned well; his conversion experience on July 5, 1875, was the beginning of an adult lifetime of devotion. All his years he remained the kind of man who knelt to pray before retiring at night. At Davidson College Wilson combined ministerial and political studies, but, after a nervous breakdown, he dropped ideas of ministry when he moved to Princeton. After studying law at the University of Virginia and Johns Hopkins University, he published his book *Congressional Government* in 1885. Accompanied by his new wife, Ellen Axson, he took his Ph.D. and his teaching impulses to the new Quaker college for women at Bryn Mawr in Pennsylvania. Wilson chafed in that post and looked for something better. After a stint at Wesleyan College, he came in 1890 to his natural intellectual home, Princeton. Despite controversies with colleagues, deans, alumni, donors, and students, in 1902 he became president of the university.

Wilson was uneasy in his campus position. At times he sounded like Bryan and the populists or Rauschenbusch and the Social Gospel forces. In a famed speech at Pittsburgh in 1910, he attacked alumni as snobs who failed to keep their eye on the great mass of the unknown people — those who murmured from the hills and woods and the farms and factories and the mills. He criticized the churches, which served "the classes and not the masses"; they had more regard for pew rents than for souls. "What we cry out against is that a handful of conspicuous men have thrust cruel hands among the heartstrings of the masses of men upon whose blood and energy they are subsisting." While Wilson steeled himself for the expectable and abundant criticism he received, he told himself that his conscience impelled him thus to speak out. If it all just happened to sound a bit like campaign oratory, in a way it was.

In a quirk of New Jersey coalition politics, the Democratic bosses allowed Wilson to be nominated for governor and he was elected. In 1912, with the aid of Bryan, he sealed his destiny as the nation's president. During the campaign, Wilson found that his piety could be an asset in the West. He won over a huge Denver crowd with an extemporaneous paean to the Bible as the agent of American morality. Bryan applauded a man who could say that "nothing makes America great except her thought, except her ideals, except her acceptance of those standards of judgment which are written large upon these pages of revelation." Calculating supporters spread copies of that speech to more than a million readers.

In his first term, Wilson vacillated between the interests of the moderate progressives who elected him and the conservatives who could help him get his way. The foreign scene soon made demands on him. "The life of the new world grows as complex as the life of the old," he remarked as the old simplicities and innocence fell away. He knew that America had to turn complex, so he applied his moralism to the demands of modernity ("the force of America is the force of moral principle"). When war came he taught the country that "to reenter the world was now a wholesome and natural impulse." As if there had never been an Enlightenment, never a public religion that overlapped and transcended the sects, Wilson kept pressing a biblical case alone: "America was born to exemplify that devotion to the elements of righteousness which are derived from the revelations of Holy Scripture."

After Wilson watched Germany invade Belgium and push into France, he saw that the shrinking globe made pure neutrality difficult, so he pushed for arms aid to England. He knew that American banks had already loaned so much to the Allies that their defeat could bring America to economic destruction. By the time the *Lusitania* went down, the United States was irretrievably tilted toward England. For two years Wilson tried to keep up appearances of a balanced approach, and he halfheartedly supported his slogan in 1916: he *had* kept America out of war; this implied that he would continue to do so. On January 4, 1917, the reelected president still thought that "there will be no war." To take his nation, the only uncommitted great white country, into war would be a crime. On January 22, he pleaded before the Senate for "the single supreme plan of peace, the revelation of our Lord and Savior," which called men to cease hating, so that wars would end.

Through the winter, Germany kept stepping up aggression and moving toward some sort of victory, while Wilson was pushed ever closer to war. A journalist heard the president speaking in the language not of *if* but of *when;* when war came, it would "overturn the world we had known." Wilson said that he dreaded war because its spirit of ruthless brutality would infuse every fiber of national life. Then, on April 2, he asked Congress for a declaration of war, a fearful thing, but "the right is more precious than peace."

Subtly the war brutalized the Wilsonians. The Committee on Public Information, whose mission it was to stir public support, started calling the Germans "the Hun" or "Boche" and tried to instill hatred as part of the national program. But as the Americans helped reverse the trend of battle, and when he foresaw victory, Wilson decided to use his idealism in the contest for peace. After the war, the president wearily told a crony a story he had heard of a Confederate soldier who soliloquized after a long, hard march: "I love my country and I am fightin' for my country, but if this war ever ends, I'll be dad-burned if I ever love another country."

The vengeful Allies were in no spirit to make the generous peace Wilson wanted, and a hostile Congress embarrassed his efforts at home. He wanted to believe that his ideals had won the war, but his enemies knew that guns and blood had done so. Now his faith led him to delusion. Wilson believed that a great mind or moral force moving through the world would take down in disgrace every man who opposed it. He went on a pilgrimage to the Paris Peace Conference for "the greatest success or the supremest tragedy in all history." Divine Providence told him that no body of men could defeat his plan for a great world enterprise toward peace. When he arrived, the French people cheered him and French leaders despised him. In ill health he brought home a treaty that countenanced a League of Nations, but his enemies coalesced against it. Wilson took to the road, but he could not gain Senate support to match the warmth his crowds generated. If the nation did not support the plan, he knew "with absolute certainty that within another generation there will be another world war." This turned out to be his most accurate prophecy.

On September 28, 1919, a weary Wilson arrived in weak health in Washington following another nervous collapse. On October 1, he read his daily chapter from the Bible, but then fell ill. Doctors diagnosed a thrombosis that left his mind clear but his emotions and body shattered. The Senate failed to approve the treaty calling for the League of Nations. In 1920 the voters chose Warren G. Harding over James M. Cox, a Democrat who had no ties to Wilson. Wilson lived on four more years. When he died in 1924 his survivors placed his remains in the new Episcopal "National" Cathedral.

Many years before, the young Woodrow had complained to his father that God had mistreated Moses by not letting him lead the people into the promised land. "It was God's will," answered the minister, "and his work was done." Perhaps something of that Mosaic outlook kept Wilson going long after his ideals stood any chance of winning. After the president's death, someone found a paper on which Wilson had scrawled a biblical phrase — some words of hope: "The vision is yet for an appointed time, but at the end it shall speak, and not lie: though it tarry, wait for it; because it will surely come, it will not tarry."

As for the moral forces on which Bryan and Wilson counted, the churches ranked first. Almost all fell into line in uncritical support of the war. Catholicism had so little of a pacifist tradition that most histories of American peace movements do not even include it in accounts that lead up to the First World War. Only one or two priests were known pacifists and only two or three conscientious objectors appealed to their Catholic faith. Though the huge Irish population in America lost no love on Great Britain and though many Catholics were of German stock, all fell into line. Only twelve days into the war, in April of 1917, the archbishops promised that their people would, as ever, rise as one person to serve the nation. Wholeheartedly and unreservedly, they wanted to go on record in support of the declaration. At the end of the war, Cardinal Gibbons sounded like Wilson: "We have conquered because we believe that righteousness exalteth a nation."

While they were supporting the military, Catholics found each other during the war as seldom before. In August of 1917, Father John J. Burke helped invent the National Catholic War Council — the NCWC, which did more than any other agency to produce concerted Catholic action. (When peace came, its leaders, having a spare *W* on their hands, changed the organization from a "War" to a "Welfare" council and kept it as a voice of the bishops in the field of social policy.) The original NCWC helped sell war bonds and supported Catholic work among servicemen. The patriotic Catholics may have made up as much as 25 percent of the U.S. Army and 50 percent of the Navy and Marines in a day when only one in six Americans was nominally Catholic.

The historic peace churches suffered in World War I, but they were used to suffering in wartime. The Dunkers (or Brethren), the Quakers, and the Mennonites were partly protected from public scorn by their relative geographical remoteness and because some of their members served in relief agencies or other noncombatant roles. The Quakers rarely disowned young men of the flock who went off to fight in Europe. The Mennonites produced more conscientious objectors than did other sects, but, like the Brethren, usually allowed members to sell Liberty Bonds as a demonstration of patriotic support.

Ugly scenes emerged in the contest bestween the rest of the nation and a new group, the International Bible Students' Association, then often called the Russellites and later known as the Jehovah's Witnesses. Before 1914 few paid much attention to them, except for irritated people who resented their house calls, or denominations whose membership lists the Bible Students raided for recruits. To the public they were merely one more strange outfit that preached the impending end of the world. The Russellites turned out to be different, however. Dwight Moody and his premillennialists, who preached the imminent Second Coming of Jesus, sent their converts back to enjoy America and the good life — and to serve in the army. Not so the International Bible Students. Pastor Charles Taze Russell, who incorporated the association in 1884 and became its president, was very specific about the ways the biblical revelation called his followers away from contact with the world of the devil.

The Russellites lived out fully the logic of competitive sectarianism in America. They had no interest in claiming that erring churches should be tolerated. All the churches lived under the control of the devil. To spread that word, they moved out of their "kingdom halls" into streets and homes; every member was a minister who must spend generous hours each week publishing the word in print or by word of mouth. They claimed that the present age, which they called millennial, would end in 1914 and that in a forthcoming battle, called Armageddon in the Bible, Jesus would lead his own army against the armies of Satan. The witnesses dared fight in no war except that one. After their victory, 144,000 elect people — the Book of Revelation spelled out that precise number — were to gain special status in heaven, while evil people would lie in their graves and ordinary servants of Jehovah God would live on earth. World War I was the first great test of the believers' willingness to resist churches, business, government, armies, and all the other allies of Satan.

The war gave revengeful churches their chance to get back at Russellites, and they took it. Law enforcement officials and, sometimes, posses of citizens with judicial support hounded the Students. In June of 1918 a Brooklyn magistrate sentenced seven of them, including Russell's successor, Judge Joseph Rutherford, to twenty years in a federal prison. Their crime was distributing a subversive book by the late Pastor Russell. It contained lines like these: "Nowhere in the New Testament is patriotism (a narrowly minded hatred of other peoples) encouraged." The Bible, it continued, forbade murder; the wars of earthly governments were acts of murder. Almost the entire religious press endorsed the legal action against the Bible Students, and few made positive comments later when the men were set free. Thanks to the wartime notoriety, the group grew more rapidly after the war than before.

Beyond the circle of Russellites, the few individual pacifists were harassed, though they were blurry targets, ill-organized clusters of people. Some of them came from liberal Protestant backgrounds. Socialist Norman Thomas — once a Union Theological Seminary student, later an agnostic — was a leader, as were progressive reformers Jane Addams of Hull House in Chicago and A. J. Muste, who later led the Fellowship of Reconciliation. Others came from long lines of dissenters; among these was Fanny Garrison Villard, daughter of abolitionist William Lloyd Garrison. She hounded the peace societies because they asserted that war was wicked but then, when it came, said that it was sometimes justifiable. "The fear of being peace-at-any-price men makes cowards of them all."

Remembered religious themes often motivated the pacifists. Norman Thomas still saw war as being absolutely opposed to Christ's way of love and His reverence for personality. Conflict, he thought, turned people into things and brutalized everyone. His brother Evan went only so far as to say that Jesus taught great ideals and principles, but "more than that I don't care about." Some others used the coming Kingdom of God as a motif, but mere vague talk about love and brotherhood satisfied many.

While German Catholics had to fight for the right to teach the German language in their parochial schools, they enjoyed the protective coloration their militant bishops provided. With German Lutherans it was another story. They were too large a group to hide, as Mennonites and Dunkers could. Thanks to immigration they were now the fourth-largest denomination in the country. A decade before the war, Theodore Roosevelt, speaking at a Lutheran gathering in Washington, predicted that they would become one of the two or three greatest American churches. Yet large though their following was, most Lutherans, whether of German or Scandinavian background, seemed remote from other churches and were easily misrepresented.

That Lutherans should be suspect in wartime was a strange irony, for they were always an intensely loyal group. As in Revolutionary days, they took literally Saint Paul's warning that anyone who did not follow governmental authority would be damned. This meant that when war was declared, they fell into line. Nor were they pacifists. When a Kansas Mennonite professor later examined the list of 360 court-martialed objectors, he found 138 Mennonites but not one Lutheran. Among the politically naive population, suspicion fell on the German element because of the accidents of their names and language and because not all of them caught on with sufficient speed the need to change after the sinking of the *Lusitania*.

The German Lutherans established many schools, especially in the Midwest. Most of these institutions taught German in order to guarantee religious orthodoxy. In the midwestern Synodical Conference, 97 percent of the congregations employed German or some other European language in their services as late as 1900. These Missourians and members of the Wisconsin Synod were remote even from other Lutherans and were almost as incomprehensible to the rest of America as the Russellites, because of the way they repudiated other ministries, including other Lutheran ones. Nineteenth-century theologian Carl F. W. Walther taught that the Lutheran church — everyone knew he specifically meant his own — was the true visible church on earth. As a speaker at his funeral insisted, this body was "in possession of the truth — the entire, unvarnished truth." While the Missouri Synod people, who were chiefly midwesterners, often generated hearty ways of life, it was easy for them to be misunderstood by nonmembers; their ministers were forbidden to pray alongside other clerics at Liberty Bond rallies, and they put limits on their tardy cooperation in military chaplaincy. Even though these stands had nothing to do with taking sides in the war, they naturally generated suspicion.

In 1915 the German Lutherans at last and in self-defense started coming out of their political shell. Longtime conservative Republicans in the main, some of them now made heroes of William Jennings Bryan and Wisconsin's progressive senator Robert M. La Follette, who saw that Wilsonian neutrality was anti-German. Belatedly these midwesterners learned the mail and rail routes to Washington, where they testified for neutrality in Congress. Through the Social Gospel years, Missouri Synod leadership thundered against churches that meddled in the public order for the sake of moral concern. Now their own synodical president announced that "anything that touches moral issues is within the sphere of the church," and for a moment he began to attack the arms industry that linked American profiteers to English destiny.

Despite what amounted to persecution from 1914 to 1917, these Lutherans did what Lutherans almost always do. They professed sincere loyalty to "the powers that be." While no Lutheran agency later went so far as to join those Protestants who called the conflict a holy war, they did vie to outdo others in support of the Red Cross and Liberty Bonds. Many started forgetting their old scruples against military chaplaincy. The war forced the newer immigrants among them quickly to learn English. When the war ended, the National Lutheran Council rendered thanks unto Almighty God who had given a just cause such a magnificent victory.

As for the evangelists and Social Gospel churchmen, the liberals and the conservatives in the old-line Protestant churches, few kept the peace witness alive, though a large number of them quietly ministered without calling for superpatriotism. The majority, however, felt called to lead the cheers for war. Fifteen years after

Armistice, Professor Ray J. Abrams, an angry lover of peace, assembled a scrapbook called *Preachers Present Arms*. Scholars since have proved that Abrams left out many exceptions, but samples of what he properly included still evoke the spirit of the day.

To set the scene, Abrams cited philosopher John Dewey, who believed that in the decade before 1914 propaganda for peace was so successful that "the movement hardly had to be pushed." The Federal Council of Churches was in the vanguard of peace causes, yet a poll by the FCC in 1917 found no evidence of clerical disloyalty to the war effort. Abrams cited prominent clerics who spoke of a divine crusade, the holiest war in history; it was a missionary enterprise whose good soldiers of Jesus Christ would help bring in the Kingdom. Harold Bell Wright, the Disciples of Christ minister who wrote the best-selling novel *The Shepherd of the Hills*, thought a thirty-centimeter gun trained on Germans was as convincing an edict of God as the notes of a cooing dove. At the University of Chicago, liberal professor Ernest De Witt Burton claimed that since defeat of the German armies was in the interest of the German people, Americans who tried to defeat them were acting in obedience to the Golden Rule.

Protesters who wanted to publicize brutalization made much of the pamphlet *Hand-to-Hand Fighting*, which was prepared by the once peaceful YMCA to goad soldiers to battle. It advised: "Eyes. Never miss an opportunity to destroy the eyes of the enemy. In all head holds use the finger on the eyes. They are the most delicate points in the body and easy to reach." Boston Baptist Herbert S. Johnson found it important to use his own body as a visual aid when instructing his people on the use of the bayonet: "Three inches are not enough," he thought, while "seven inches are too many and twelve inches are more than too many, for while you are pulling out the bayonet you are losing the opportunity to drive it into another man five inches."

The bayonet represented problems of morals and taste, but Unitarian editor Albert C. Dieffenbach set out to convince the squeamish that Jesus would have seized the bayonet to kill "the most deadly enemy of His Father's Kingdom in a thousand years." The YMCA hurried in with a helpful booklet, *The Practice of Friendship*, which showed an interest in Christianizing *every* aspect of a righteous war. The author pictured "your lad and my lad" sick at heart on the night of his first experience with bayonet drill, "at the parting of the ways of fatalism and faith." The YMCA worker came to meet his crisis. This worker should say: "I would not enter this work till I could see Jesus himself . . . running a bayonet through an enemy's body." The writer fancied an open heaven where Jesus, wearing olive drab stained with blood and mire, could be seen through clouds of gas and smoke dismounting from his white horse. He carried a bayonet.

The second difficult task to teach a peaceful people was hatred of the Germans, against whom Americans had no previous case. Mere principle would not do; Americans must fight out of hatred to shorten the war. Abrams quoted Methodist bishop William Alfred Quayle, who contended that America fought not merely Junkers, Prussianism, nor the kaiser but the German people who were united in the "chief barbarity of history." Billy Sunday used more plain talk. "I tell you it is Bill against Woodrow, Germany against America, Hell against Heaven." All the talk about not fighting the German people was bunk. "They say that we are fighting for an ideal. Well, if we are we will have to knock the German people to get it over." Liberty Bond buyers, he pleaded, should dig deep for war against hell and its commissaries and cohorts, the "bunch of pretzel-chewing sauerkraut spawn of blood-thirsty Huns."

Newell Dwight Hillis, a successor of Henry Ward Beecher at Brooklyn's Plymouth Congregational Church, went furthest of all. As late as 1914 this former Quaker, as he lectured on a visit to Germany, lauded Kaiser Wilhelm II and bragged about his own pacifist heritage. Soon Hillis caught on to the American drift and set out with atrocity stories on the Liberty Loan circuit. One tour alone took him for 400 speeches to 162 cities. Hillis won audiences with reports of rape by Germans. Why, he asked, did German soldiers cut off breasts of female victims? Because the Huns carried syphilis and had to disfigure the girls so that other Germans who came along later to rape would not get the disease. That story was mild; really bad atrocity tales, Hillis hinted, could not be named but "only be mentioned by men to men in whispered tones." In his book this preacher reported that statesmen, generals, diplomats, and editors were, he was glad to say, now "talking about the duty of simply exterminating the German people." Hillis had heard that a group of surgeons was devising a plan to sterilize confirmed criminals and hopeless addicts; now it was considering how to sterilize ten million German soldiers and segregate the women after the war — thus cutting out the awful cancer in global society.

After the war, the liberal dean of the University of Chicago Divinity School, Shailer Mathews, surveyed the disruptions. He looked at the trauma European conflict had brought to American hopes. While the war in itself excited horror, said Mathews, from the American distance something worse happened. All the forces that progressives believed might be shaping a new world order collapsed. The dean listed the prewar ranks that had lined up against the outbreak: "socialism, international labor movements, international commerce, international science, the Roman Catholic Church, Protestant Christianity, peace societies, the mixture of populations, common culture." Yet while these powers all sought maintenance of peace, in the end, they were simply powerless.

One set of church people claimed that they were not surprised by anything that had happened. The premillennialist force expected that before Jesus came again "wars and rumors of wars" would disturb the hearts of people, just as the Bible prophesied. Of course, nineteen centuries had passed with wars and rumors of war, so retrospective prophecies like theirs were never of much help. It was one thing to repeat the literal language of biblical prophecy and another to see sons of the family march off to pointless trench warfare.

Those who were not deeply touched by that trauma came to look superficial, if not silly. Lyman Abbott, the minister and editor who embraced evolutionary thought and predicted that everything would turn out right, tried to minimize the war's evil: "The human race falls down occasionally, bruises itself, and weeps some bitter tears, but picks itself up and goes on walking, and persistently in the right direction." Thoughtful people knew that the horrors of the western front were a cancer, not a bruise, and that they exposed to view the moral collapse of Christendom.

The churches had at last found the cause around which to unite. But the war ended November 11, 1918, and the imposed cooperative spirit disappeared more quickly than it had come. The churches have had to live with the brutal irony that they — the professors of the way of unity and peace — united only for a war that, in retrospect, was hard to see as a religious crusade. On the Protestant home front the realization suddenly served to compromise the church's climactic claims of moral superiority, to obscure religious divisions (which widened more than ever after the war), and to distract reformers from the task of effecting a more just world. For the next two decades, as if in reaction against the visions of unity by people of peace and the practice of conformity by people in war, Americans retreated into mutually contradictory factions and sects. The land became a chaos of isms, in a time of tribal consciousness and lost common purpose.

A symbol of religious and social unrest during the
Great Depression of the 1930s, Father Charles E.
Coughlin was the first master of radio demagoguery
in America. He combined a sort of populism with
anti-Semitism and for a time was a political figure
with whom major politicians had to reckon.
(*Wide World Photos, 1935*)

Chapter Seventeen

A SEASON OF CONFLICTS

THE FIRST WORLD WAR WAS A TURNING POINT IN NATIONAL affairs, as the United States, the New World, once more became engaged with Europe, the Old World. In the American self-concept, the war meant a "loss of innocence." America had joined a "guilty" world and could not bring the peace or the democracy that crusading leaders had led the nation to hope it could inspire. As we have seen, the war also imposed a kind of momentary and momentous unity on a divided nation.

But the war was not the only thing on the American mind during the second and third decades of this century, and it did not represent a watershed on all issues. Through all the years when immigrants were changing to "fit in" to turn-of-the-century America, and while the old Protestant majority was preaching themes of the Kingdom and unity, divisive forces were contending in the United States. During and after the war, many of these domestic rivalries came to a climax. In the period between the two world wars, everything seemed up for grabs in the wildly contrasting boom decade of the twenties and bust decade of the thirties. Old values were challenged in the Jazz Age, the Roaring Twenties, and had to be reaffirmed as Americans dug in to survive the Great Depression of the thirties. Groups that were almost coerced into common thought and action during the First World War began once again to evidence violent disagreements — disagreements that had roots in a long past. Of all the old conflicts on Protestant soil, nothing divided society and the social programs of the churches more than Prohibition, which came to a head between 1919 and 1933. Nothing upset the theological unity of the Protestant churches more than did the fundamentalist-versus-modernist controversy that led to schisms in society and church around the climactic year 1925. Less devastating was the continuing clash between North and South more than fifty years after Reconstruction. And in the northern (and sometimes in the southern) churches of the non-fundamentalist mainstream, there was sundering between those who advocated the cause of labor, often from the political left, and those who resisted in the name of middle-class individualism.

The drama involved not only the white Protestant majority, however. Black and white Protestants, as well as Catholics and Jews, were involved in the resurgences of religiously informed racism and racial controversy that characterized the years between the two world wars. One might have thought that Emancipation and the passage of time after Reconstruction would have led blacks and whites toward social interaction and concord. Anything but that happened. One might have thought that the turn-of-the-century experience of mutual immigration would have opened America to friendliness and harmony between ethnic groups. Instead, the majority in 1924 passed exclusion acts against immigrants. And one might have thought that Jews and Christians, so long amicably coexistent in America, would have been ready to work together after World War I. Yet issues separating the Christian and Jewish communities — the latter itself divided over Zionism — found new bases of tensions. New demagogues stirred anti-Jewish sentiment as never before in America.

Such conflicts do not represent the most pleasant phases of American religious history. To tell the story faithfully, however, one must recall the enduring schisms that counterbalanced the achievements in American spiritual life.

One social policy in particular came to separate Americans, splitting them into two exclusivist camps for over a decade. Prohibition politics took on the language of religious crusades and stamped the citizens as Wets or Drys, badges each side wore proudly. Most of the old-stock population lined up with the Drys, who between 1919 and 1933 enjoyed the Eighteenth Amendment to the United States Constitution.

Like all the stories of division in the twenties, this one had a long pedigree. The moral ancestors of Prohibitionists first found their voice a century before the amendment passed. While most colonial Protestants drank alcoholic beverages, drunkenness became a social problem on the frontier and in the industrial city in a day when addiction by a father could mean virtual starvation for his family. Prophets of reform plausibly attacked the liquor interests, who positioned saloons at entrances to mines and factories where men spent their paychecks relieving the harshness and monotony of their workaday lives. When revivalists first took to the circuit, they tucked a little cask of brandy or rum under their saddles. Later they came to see the misery that intemperance caused and soon included in their moral programs the call for a pledge not to drink alcohol. Progress in the cause was difficult because production of liquor was important to the economy in an era of grain surpluses. Voluntary societies to promote temperance became as strong as any religious agencies of the period, and some of them won Roman Catholic support. For the most part, however, temperance became a Protestant preserve, a sign of last-ditch defenses of the old Protestant empire.

The temperance people found more difficulty than did the old proslavery forces in their efforts to locate biblical support for their absolutist views. The supporters of slavery had no trouble quoting Scripture to support their position. The antiliquor forces cited plenty of references against drunkenness, but they were embarrassed by the fact that the Bible also included references to the joys of wine and depicted Jesus drinking it and Paul recommending it. Some reformers reached far to overcome the problem by contriving a "two-wine" theory: they claimed that some of the biblical words for wine referred simply to unfermented grape juice. Such verbal games were unconvincing to the Wets and to many honest Drys. In that regard, one letter writer laughed at *The Christian Herald* for the support it gave to such theories; according to him, new translations of the Bible would have to rephrase passages like Ephesians 5:18 into something on the order of "And be not drunk with unfermented grape juice." The temperance groups and the Anti-Saloon League of America finally had to make their case without direct biblical support. Though this was a departure from the approved Protestant approach, there were plenty of alcohol-related social problems to cite in the attack.

Protestantism itself had come to be divided into two parties that could agree on few issues until Prohibition came along. One made Christianity into a religion chiefly of soul saving; it did not want to call on believers to express themselves as groups in the political arena. The other was more public and more political; its Social Gospel advocates worked to transform society and paid less attention to personal vices and virtues as they blasted society's sins. The two parties found almost nothing else to bring them together, but Prohibition became the grand exception.

The revivalist party found prohibiting alcohol so urgent a matter that it overcame self-imposed taboos against evangelicals asking for legislation. Billy Sunday, who was the best-known evangelist of the period, led some of the push for legislation. He drew his most enthusiastic crowds and cheers when he attacked booze as the sum of all villainies. Take drink away, bellowed Sunday, and most of the other problems that immigrants created in cities would disappear. Sunday supported the Anti-Saloon League immediately after its founding, and connected Prohibition with salvation. His backers boasted that they could show a pattern: state after state supported the Prohibition Amendment following Sunday's preaching the cause in their cities.

While the popular evangelist threatened fire and brimstone for the Wets, he lacked the skill to promote laws directly. William Jennings Bryan, the discredited former presidential candidate and secretary of state, came back into prominence to lead the cause. He was far more effective and no less colorful. To license a man to sell liquor and then fine people for getting drunk, Bryan argued, was as sensible as licensing a person to spread the itch through town and then fining people for scratching. His effort was, by his own admission, "a veritable religious crusade," and when, on January 16, 1919, the Eighteenth Amendment was ratified, Bryan exalted: "Let the world rejoice. . . . The greatest moral reform of the generation has been accomplished." The Social Gospel people were no less ardent, though they were more ready to connect the crusade with other social issues.

The language of control preceded the Volstead Act (which codified Prohibition) and reappeared whenever anyone advocated Repeal. In 1912 *The American Issue* defined party lines. Dry men were native Americans who were serious about religion; they were small-town professionals, parents of children, farmers who kept high moral standards when they moved to the city. The Wets were immigrant newcomers, supporters of the great city machines; they were infidels and heathens who violated Sabbath laws and they were snobbish eastern "society people" — classes who were above the level of dry forces as others were below them. Prohibitionists used the language of war. *The Anti-Saloon League Yearbook* was emphatic: "This battle is not a rose-water conflict. It is war — continued, relentless war." What began in pity for the victims of drink became a crusade of scorn against drinkers.

During the war against alcohol, the strange coalition of evangelists and social transformers made great progress, until finally America ratified the Eighteenth Amendment, which forbade the manufacture, sale, or transportation of intoxicating liquors. Immediately after the war, the Volstead Act was passed in order to enforce the amendment. Millions of Americans subsequently became scofflaws; a half million were arrested, though the public knew that law officers winked at most violations. The moral cause spawned bootleggers, and crime syndicates profited most.

Americans ever since its passage have tended to think of Prohibition as a victory of the rural South and small-town West over the urban North and East, but its appeal crossed lines of theology, region, farm, and city. Class interests were very much at stake, and religion reinforced them. The Prohibition coalition was made up chiefly of middle-class Americans of old stock who found a threat in the unchurched and in Catholic, Jewish, and Lutheran immigrant masses. Thus, the Prohibitionists in a way passed their own version of an exclusion act against millions who were already in America. They ruled out of the bounds of law and respectability those who did not accept their way of life.

The Central Conference of American Rabbis thought Prohibition was "born of fanaticism." As the Catholic bishops fought for rights to buy wine for sacramental purposes, they made a broader protest in the name of their people. The beer-drinking midwestern Lutherans blamed Temperance on the devil and the meddlesome followers of John Wesley. The old-stock English Protestants alone connected the Kingdom of God with the Volstead Act, and used it as an instrument of control one last time.

The Prohibition crusade was ultimately a legal failure, but all through the twenties Protestants poured energy into preventing Repeal. They made their last stand when a Catholic Wet, Alfred E. Smith of New York, became the Democratic presidential candidate in 1928. Methodist bishop James Cannon, who scowled at Smith, at Democrats, and at Wets, reached for the language of exclusion: "Governor Smith wants the Italians, the Sicilians, the Poles and the Russian Jews. That kind has given us a stomachache. We have been unable to assimilate such people into our national life." In what was not destined to be a good year for Democrats, the assimilators widened the cleavages in American life and Smith went down under an onslaught that was aided by Prohibitionist Protestants.

The Protestant press had to keep up its warfare after the election, since the defeat of Smith did not mean the end of calls for Repeal. In 1929 the Methodist periodical *The Christian Advocate* claimed that enforcing the Volstead Act was now the single most important social need in America. When Repeal came four years later, the Protestant middle class found that its approach to exclusion was failing on still one more front. The Women's Christian Temperance Union leaders had nothing left to do but to look back on the good old days. One of them remembered the time in 1915 when total abstinence sat "in regal state on the throne of empires and of kingdoms." Now, after Repeal, the enemies made temperance people all look like "a bunch of old women, as frowzy fanatics." In a sudden class reversal, the old excluders became virtually the newly excluded.

If Prohibition represented a social schism, a theological issue created a deeper and more enduring cleavage in the postwar ruins of the Protestant empire. In the 1920s two parties that had been in the making for fifty years polarized the churches. Under the opposing extremist banners of fundamentalism and modernism they produced traumas from which the Protestant churches have never recovered, forcing divisions that the denominational names no longer defined. After the mid-twenties, it did not suffice for a person to be told that others were Presbyterians or Baptists; what *kind* of members were they, and to which tribe or party in their churches did they belong? Fundamentalism and modernism in their pure forms were held by minorities. Both prevented people from discerning what in their traditions they held in common. The modernists considered fundamentalists to be Neanderthals, and fundamentalists did not think of modernists as Christian. Both fought for power in and power over the churches between the world wars.

The fundamentalists cherished doctrinal statements because these were precise and therefore could easily be used to rule out unacceptable beliefs and people. The intransigents took the well-worn issues of evolution and biblical criticism, sharpened and polished them, and brought them back for political battles in denominations. The fundamentalists were often dismissed regionally, typed as only southern or, sometimes, midwestern, concentrated in an easily dismissed "Bible Belt." Their movement had a better claim on roots in the North.

The Moodyites at the old Niagara Bible Conference, as they turned hard-line, provided much of the movement's first popular appeal, while intellectuals at Princeton Seminary helped give it substance. The clerical leaders were people like T. T. Shields, John Roach Straton, and William Bell Riley, who worked from bases in Toronto, New York City, and Minneapolis, respectively. The best-known lay representative was the aged William Jennings Bryan, but he also had colleagues in men like the two Stewart brothers in California, magnates in the Union Oil Company. The Stewarts had paid for distributing millions of copies of a tract that helped give the cause its name: *The Fundamentals,* which had begun to appear nationally after 1910.

As a national movement fundamentalism could be respectable, well mannered, and in its own way intellectual. While their arguments won no favor in the general academic community, scholars like Princeton's J. Gresham Machen came up with reasonable scholastic attacks against modernists' efforts to make the Christian faith mesh with a progressive world. The public, however, was less interested in debates on the pages of lugubrious journals that issued from Princeton or Union seminaries than in the use made of some formulas by battlers. In the public eye, then, not a scholar but tireless politician William Jennings Bryan symbolized the cause and the era. As his political fortunes declined in the twenties, Bryan's religious instincts served him well. He carried his old animus against Europe and eastern America into partisan defenses of the old-time religion. Bryan toured America with diatribes against Germanized critics who wanted to demolish faith in the Bible or who wanted to convince humans that they had descended from apes. Let the intellectuals scorn him as senile; their disdain only made him a greater hero than before in the eyes of the defenders of old ways.

The city elites that Bryan despised found it a luxury to make fun of him so long as the furor was restricted to churches. When public education became the battlefield, they fought back. To fundamentalists, Darwinian evolution was not merely an assault on the truth of the Bible; it undercut the values of the good society. His admiring wife described the split that developed as Bryan moved into the field of education: "People began to fall in line. Sides grew distinct. The public divided and stood ready to do battle." Within eight years, twenty legislatures wrestled with thirty-seven anti-evolution bills. Bryan's cause lost by only one vote when he addressed the Kentucky General Assembly in 1922, pleading that the legislators prohibit the teaching of "irreligion" in public institutions. His platform quips led sophisticates to disdain him — he would rather trust the "Rock of Ages" than to know the "age of rocks" — but these won him popular support. Curiously, Bryan made his major case against evolution through arguments over the use, not the truth, of the teaching; evolution would be harmful to people who accepted it, since the theory would cause them to have the wrong view of themselves and they would then act immorally.

While the school struggles continued, Bryan never neglected the churches. In April of 1922 he preached to the converted at the Southern Baptist Convention, though their northern counterparts had moved too far to give him a real hearing. For three years he worked to gain power in Presbyterianism, where fights were furious and outcomes uncertain. Harry Emerson Fosdick, a suave New York minister, led the modernists with his sermon "Shall the Fundamentalists Win?" which he preached in 1922. Bryan, who ran for moderator of northern Presbyterianism in order to head off people like Fosdick, made a good race but lost in the 1923 assembly. He consoled himself though, when an anti-Fosdick bill then passed, 439 to 359, since Fosdick was, as Bryan wrote in a letter, the Jesse James of the theological world. The next year the Presbyterians elected Bryan nominee Clarence Macartney, a beloved Philadelphia pastor, but their assembly did not choose to nail Fosdick with a formal condemnation. At Cleveland in 1925 moderates on both sides finally settled on the tolerant conservative Charles R. Erdman. This was too temporizing for the militant minority, who headed off to found their own organizations in order to perpetuate fundamentalism.

Frustrated by the vacillations of his denomination, Bryan chose to make the school issue his showdown battle. In 1925 Tennessee passed a bill that prohibited the teaching of evolution in public schools. The American Civil Liberties Union and Bryan both hoped for a test case, and found one when the ACLU backed teacher John Thomas Scopes. He let himself be arrested for teaching evolution at Dayton, Tennessee. Coincidentally a native of Bryan's hometown, the young man some years before had heard the Great Commoner give the commencement address for Scopes's own high-school class. Subsequently he had become no great devotee of Darwin, but he did see a principle at issue and allowed himself to become the focus of legal dispute.

The Scopes trial of 1925 was not the first signal of a new fundamentalist issue. Most of the churches had debated evolution more intelligently fifty years before. Nor was it representative of politician Bryan in his prime. Now pathetically eager for applause and suffering from diabetes, he hurried to an out-of-the-way courtroom to take on a minor legal case against lawyer Clarence Darrow in what he hoped would be a struggle of titans, but which turned out to be a freak show. While the curious crammed Dayton, so did hawkers; a carnival atmosphere developed around the steaming courtroom. First Bryan would hear Darrow defend freedom and attack antievolution; then he would put his palm leaf fan aside to state his case. His old charms were fading, but Bryan could still please a crowd — until he lost some of the true believers. He admitted that he did not believe that the six days of the Creation mentioned in the beginning of the Bible were literally twenty-four hours long. Despite his faltering on this point, most of his camp stayed with him.

Almost in regret Darrow observed the waning of the old sense of humor in his opponent. Disappointment, Darrow thought, combined with futile ambitions, had destroyed the Great Commoner. Bryan by then had the appearance of one who felt the injustice of many defeats and now welcomed the chance to get even with an alien world. He snarled at or scolded anyone who stood in the way of his dreams and, said Darrow, showed that he had reached the stage of hallucination that would impel him to commit any cruelty he believed would help his cause. If so, Bryan did not lack company among the mean-spirited on both sides in the contests of the twenties.

The trial became especially memorable because for the first time radio spread such a debate across the nation. It lacked only one ingredient — suspense; in the narrow and immediate case, Scopes was openly guilty, and a Tennessee jury would certainly find him so. Darrow saw no defeat in the verdict, confident as he was of a different outcome in higher courts. Bryan, unaware of the damage his victory brought the cause, hurried to Chattanooga to help prepare his summation for print. He returned to Dayton the following Sunday. After church and dinner that Lord's Day, he made some phone calls, took a nap, but did not wake up. Cynical and agnostic Baltimore journalist H. L. Mencken commented on the death of Bryan five days after the trial: "We killed the son-of-a-bitch!"

Fundamentalism outlived the prominent layman who loved the cause even when he served it unwisely. Not all conservatives trailed away to form their own competing Bible colleges or denominations. While each year at church conventions in the twenties partisans on both sides tried to exclude each other, in the end most of them stayed in their torn and demoralized denominations. The conservatives promoted their accents on "fundamentals," such as the inerrancy of the Bible, the Virgin Birth of Christ, belief in his literal Second Coming, and other articles of faith that they turned into touchstones. Modernist extremists faded away, while moderate liberals stretched the limits of their old creeds and confessions. During the 1930s the fundamentalists regrouped, and during the Second World War the more chastened and polished of them were to unite with more moderate conservatives to form a neo-evangelical movement. No longer was Bryan in their pantheon, though in the days of their greatest disappointments and defeats he helped keep their party alive.

If after World War I the old divisions over race and ethnicity persisted, and if wartime unity did nothing to lead Wets and Drys to compromise, so also it did not serve to overcome long-term religious divisions between the North and the South. These showed up later even in the perpetuation of denominational schisms in two of the three major interregional bodies, the Baptists and Presbyterians. Methodists spent the two interwar decades moving very tentatively toward reunion. Their struggle showed how the deep regional resentments plagued people who claimed to be one in Jesus Christ and who shared a common faith. Historians have sometimes neglected the South in this period. It deserves better. This part of the country has kept vestiges of the older Protestant empire, and these help explain the nature of sunbelt religion fifty and more years later.

Regionalism has always been one of the most effective ways for Protestants to organize and define themselves. There were Southern and Northern Baptists, Methodists and Presbyterians, Missouri and Iowa and Wisconsin Synod Lutherans, and other similar expressions of bonds between a faith and a soil or a history. These served as counterparts to the ethnic ties of Catholic peoples and the racial bond connecting Jewish faith and peoplehood. The landscape became part of the Protestant outlooks, and memories of events like the winning of the frontier for westerners or the fighting of the Civil War for southerners evoked ties that can be fairly described as tribal. Many of the cleavages that occurred between the world wars fell across the lines of regions and sections. Fifty years after Reconstruction, almost nothing had happened to bring the denominational tribes themselves together across the North-South line.

A close-up of an energetic and representative southern leader illustrates this. His enemies and admirers alike often declared Bishop Warren Akin Candler, the doughty fighter for southern ways, the most powerful Methodist since Francis Asbury. He was an old but still tireless bishop in the 1920s when he shaped up for his last battles against his northern counterparts. Candler brought such zest to his conflicts that one critic compared him to a prize-fighter who enjoyed knockout blows against an antagonist. Born to a Georgia Methodist family, he went to little Emory College, which was then east of Atlanta in a "town set apart," as Candler put it, to keep students from urban temptations. Candler, though he spent much of his life in the city, never left behind the impulse to be "set apart" and to keep the institutions he loved isolated from whatever opposed his way of life.

The Methodist leader in 1888 became president of Emory College. Fund-raising efforts reinforced his impulse to stress sectional feelings. He looked on enviously as northerners supported schools for blacks in his state, and finally complained that the most prosperous college there was for Negroes. Not that he had anything against blacks, he hastened to say — he simply questioned whether it would be good for either race if Negro colleges became superior. Rather than pout, he set out to bring in money so he could assume the existence of a Methodist school that remained free of northern influences.

For a time he continued to promote religious higher education. Before his prime the southern Methodists put their energies into Vanderbilt University at Nashville, but by 1905 it was slipping out of their control. He opposed further church support for the school when it became clear that most professors there were not to be Methodists. Candler led the protest against the trustees when they accepted a million-dollar gift from Andrew Carnegie, because the philanthropist insisted, as always, that there be no sectarian control of a school that he befriended. In 1914 the Tennessee Supreme Court sided with the trustees against Candler and the other resisting bishops. Methodists lost their fortress.

Candler, who had never forgotten little Emory College, dreamed of turning it into a true Methodist university. For this cause he had good fortune; he could rely for support on his brother, a pharmacist named Asa G. Candler. Asa also had good fortune; in 1888 he had obtained a patent for a soft-drink formula that he named Coca-Cola. While the enterprising Asa was both less sectarian and less sectional-minded than his brother the bishop, he was glad to share one million of his dollars with the southern Methodists at Emory. Asa Candler appreciated all churches, he said, but preferred the southern type for its "wholesome conservatism politically and socially." Grateful Methodists named Bishop Candler the first chancellor and took care to devise a more secure charter than the one that had lost them Vanderbilt.

While at Emory, Candler developed his thesis that southern Americans must seize the last opportunity to Christianize the schools before the schools paganized America. He began to lose interest in his own university, however, when it accepted women into the law school the year the war ended; he was also unable to compete consistently for funds with the despised northern universities. His time in education seemed to the bishop to be wasted years, so he put his energies into the other public issues that defined the parties and tribes in the twenties, thus becoming a moderating influence. His heart opposed Al Smith with every passion in 1928, but his head told him that the church as a church should not take a stand in presidential elections: "Preach Christ and Him crucified. Do not preach politics."

The interwar years gave Candler his best chance to oppose northerners and liberals, including those of Methodist stripe. In 1919 some durable Social Gospel advocates formed the grandiose Interchurch World Movement to further their efforts to transform society. When the IWM met for a convention in Atlantic City, the southern Methodists' magazine, momentarily swept up in fervor for the cause, called it the greatest modern ecclesiastical meeting. Candler, however, decried the IWM for wanting to hire thousands and spend millions for dubious ends. How dared a group that did not include the huge Southern Baptist and Lutheran groups and that failed to attract many Methodists advertise itself to society as the great cooperative movement of *the* evangelical denominations? Who, he asked, made it the umpire and adviser to the separate churchly armies of God? The northern IWM autocrats, he thought, wanted to spend their money for pageants and triumphal processions in their efforts to become dictators over the churches. Candler spoke for denominationalists who by then were beginning to resist interchurch movements and for local ministers and lay people who resented the new bureaucracies that seemed so remote from their interests. He and his cohorts did not have to wait long to see the IWM fall; it died of its own weight after a year, leaving a ten-million-dollar deficit.

Having savored life on the winning side in that issue, Candler gamely spoke up for the South in the prolonged battles to prevent Methodist reunion. The northern Methodists, who looked to him too liberal, too political, too bureaucratic, and far too condescending about the South, launched postwar efforts to create a single church. After their convention started voting almost unanimously to approve a merger, he was doubly suspicious. Anything that united northerners so much must be bad for the South. Then in 1924 Candler saw that the contagion for bigness had reached the southern bishops and convention voters. They violated his sense of landscape and tradition voting 298 to 74 to go national. One line of defense remained: the local conferences. Three-fourths of them had to approve the reunion plan. Through the conferences, Candler knew, he could come closer to the sentiments of the people than could bishops in conventions or other delegated voters.

As he fought against the merger, Candler devised a defense of denominationalism and regionalism that seemed out of fashion when he voiced it — though it resembled advocacies for tribal life in American religion fifty years later, when the models of merger and bigness and sameness again inspired reaction. Christianity, he insisted, never required mergers or unions. He could prove, and the southern Baptist and Methodist successes offered him statistical backing, that to cooperate worked better than to coalesce. For example, in the South, since the Negro and white Methodist jurisdictions remained separate, both were effective at reaching their own people. In the north, Negro bishops shared power with whites and might someday even preside over Methodist education among southern people. But they were outvoted, had less power than southern black bishops, and less fairly represented their people. Candler was able to rally forces opposed to a merger and helped stave off reunion fifteen years. By 1939, on the eve of a new world war, the spirit that contributed to this particular cleavage was finally being overcome. Methodists united to become the largest and strongest Protestant church nationally.

As for the northern mainstream churches that Methodism dominated, almost by definition they wanted to be less defined or tribal. They fell into the opposite danger of embracing much in middle-class culture that appealed to them. A new version of the gospel of success in the twenties led them and their cultural heroes to blur the line between the church and the world. Poet Edgar A. Guest taught in *American Magazine* in 1925 that "religion pays." That year the best-selling book of nonfiction was *The Man Nobody Knows* by Bruce Barton. The author saw Jesus as a backslapping executive who with twelve associates built a worldwide organization. The parables of Jesus taught business techniques. The dark side of the crucifixion story disappeared during the financial boom and Bartonism. In this spirit the *Western Recorder* took "chastened pride" in the fact that the Baptists had produced only one United States president: Warren G. Harding. The *Baptist* added that Harding "associated himself with political giants, but he was outshone by none of them." And the *Christian Herald* added its postscript: "If any man had and preached ideals for the world, President Harding was that man."

The Harding reputation fell, and in a few years so did the stock market, the hopes for "normalcy," and the religion dependent on all of them. Yet even during the decade of illusion some of the Protestants chose to take on troubling issues, including one that was unfamiliar and uncongenial to most of them: organized labor. Pro- or antilabor became as divisive as Wet or Dry, fundamentalist or modernist, North or South.

In 1924 Warren Stone, president of the Brotherhood of Locomotive Engineers was asked what labor thought of the church. "Labor," he answered, "does not think very much of the church, because the church does not think very much of labor." A minority tried to change this image through action. The first test came with the steel strike of 1919. The Interchurch World Movement advocated an end to the twelve-hour, seven-day workweek, only to be called Bolshevik for doing so. Judge Elbert H. Gary publicized the prophecy that America could not survive a cut in the twelve-hour day. The foreigners in steel work, he said, enjoyed working long; they only frittered away time when they were not at the mills. The IWM and the Federal Council of Churches had some effect on public opinion, but the complacent churches lined up largely against the laborers, whom the *Alabama Baptist* typically called a "tribe" of anarchists and Bolsheviks who had ruined their own land and now had come to destroy America.

From these years we have an especially revealing portrait of churchly attitudes. Liston Pope, a young sociologist of religion, studied the communities of Gaston County, North Carolina, after textile-mill strikes in the thirties. He culled reports of ministers, who showed they were aware that there was a world around them: they preached against syphilis, pool halls, low-flying airplanes, slot machines, and the marriage of Clark Gable and Carole Lombard. The issues of low pay, night work for women, and child labor fell outside their range of vision. Mill owners built their churches.

Nothing in the experience of these preachers prepared them to connect the needs of textile workers with the gospel. Pope heard of one mill executive who gave away more than he intended to: "We had a young fellow from an eastern seminary down here as pastor a few years ago, and the young fool went around saying that we helped pay the preachers' salaries in order to control them. That was a damn lie — and we got rid of him."

The condition of workers everywhere became desperate after the Depression began. They could not strike without losing their jobs to strikebreaking scabs. Some ministers who broke ranks and sided with them looked like traitors. In 1931 a minister writing in *The Christian Century* told of a congregation in Butte, Montana, that ejected seven prolabor ministers in a row. To show how polarized the nation was and how caught between sides such ministers were, the same writer then went on to criticize labor and its leaders for only standing by or scoffing when such clerical supporters lost their jobs.

For a decade after the Russian Revolution, the Red scare frightened off many American liberals. During the Depression, socialism and communism got some hearing in religious circles. Members of an important Protestant elite toured the Soviet Union and came back with rosy reports on conditions there. In 1931 a Unitarian *Christian Register* writer, vastly overstating the case, rejoiced to see American Protestantism finding ways to see in the Soviet approach something "true to the teachings of Jesus." In 1934 radical Kirby Page thought that the ministry had the highest percentage of Socialists of any profession in the nation. But Communists never had much use for the churches; most church leaders favored nonviolence, in a day when Marxist advocates of the class struggle called for violence. Prominent theologians like Reinhold Niebuhr might speak up for Marxian thought, but most of them refused to become members of the Communist party and soon after denounced Marxism. The majority of local pastors remained silent or supported the status quo in economic life. The white Protestant lay public seemed wary of prolabor ministers and shunned also the political left, which was more at home in seminaries or bureaucracies than in congregations. Thus a young contributor to *The Christian Century* bewailed the existence of a gap between the professors who bravely and boldly told young seminarians to preach a realistic gospel and then waved good-bye to them from bombproof dugouts as the young hopefuls went out to the congregational battle unprotected and undefended.

If the mainstream Protestants were unable to provide leadership across the lines that divided labor and management, they were even less successful across boundaries of race. The seeds of racial conflict between them had been planted by earlier ideologies. Now a population shift produced new practical bases for Americans. As Negroes moved north, old southern patterns reproduced themselves until the color line became both broadest and sharpest in religion. At the end of the Depression, an estimated 0.5 million American blacks were members of largely white Protestant denominations. But some 99 percent of these members worshiped only with other blacks, in segregated congregations, while 7.5 million other blacks were in their own separate church bodies. Such statistics are tributes to the appeal of black religion, but they are marks of failure for northern whites who first had berated southern segregationists — and then bought their patterns as the policy in their own churches.

Racial situations often aggravated denominational tensions. As if Baptists were not sufficiently divided already, race drove them further apart in 1932 at a Baptist Association banquet at Rochester, New York. The president of the Southern Baptist Convention, William Joseph McGlothlin, was to receive an honor. After he learned that the Association moderator was a Negro, Dr. James E. Rose, the southerner, unwilling to lose status among his own supporters or unable to cope with the situation himself, refused to attend or to accept the testimonial award.

Given the interwar climate in which such snubs were common, it is little wonder that many blacks began to respond to the quasi-religious "back to Africa" appeal of Marcus Garvey, a man who called himself a "Negro Zionist." Garvey's Universal Negro Improvement Association gained many admirers among American blacks during the twenties. It even led to worries among some Africans, who feared he might upset the delicate economic balances on their continent. Educated African blacks, as they heard of the Garveyites, came to resent the idea that these Americans must "save" or "regenerate" Africa.

Garvey was somehow able to gather millions of dollars in America for his Black Star steamship line between 1919 and 1922. This was a symbol of the support depressed Negroes could give to someone who offered them hope. Garvey was found guilty of fraud and after 1925 spent over two years in an Atlanta prison, from which he wrote letters to his backers: "We have gradually won our way back into the confidence of the God of Africa, and He shall speak with a voice of thunder. . . . Hold fast to the Faith." His following disbanded after Garvey was deported in 1927. As before, the African tribal spirit and call were not quite strong enough to lead any great number of Negroes away from America.

Many, therefore, went on a pilgrimage of solace and escape while staying in America. Some black religious leaders eventually gained small followings across lines of race while appealing chiefly to blacks. George Baker, who styled himself Father Divine, attracted chiefly Negro devotees who thought him to be God. In 1933 he moved headquarters to Harlem, but poor blacks continued to give great amounts of money so he could hold court for them at his "heavens," great estates like his favorite one on Long Island. The leader was a mystic, a showman, and a messiah of sorts to thousands of blacks and whites alike. It was never completely clear how he gathered enough funds to entertain his followers so lavishly, but some of his success resulted from his ability as an employment agent who helped blacks find jobs. The appeal of Father Divine in the end was to blacks and some whites who wanted contact with God and believed this leader was God in the flesh. His followers willingly did without whatever he banned: movies, makeup, tobacco; he also evidently taught celibacy and forcefully attacked racial prejudices. Believers often conquered various addictions and enjoyed better health than those around them. Whether pure charlatan or a true believer in his own system, Father Divine through the thirties and even after gave hope to people who were denied it by conventional churches. Most blacks remained faithful to the durable and conventional Baptist, Methodist, and Pentecostal churches. Yet Divine typified the extravagant cult movements at the margins of black society.

Black-white relations, which had led to segregated church life and now portended disruptions not only in Protestant America but in all the United States, were nagging and acute. But they were only part of a problem that troubled interwar America. This was a period in which older-stock Americans closed the door on immigrants and excluded kinds of people whom they had grudgingly had to welcome earlier in the century. And while Congress dealt broadly with unwanted ethnic groups, a climate developed in which Jews came to be stigmatized more than ever before in America — a situation that led to self-searching among Jews and to exploitation and demagoguery among non-Jews.

The exclusion clause of the Immigration Act of 1924 symbolized the exclusive spirit of this intolerant period. The idea of drawing a line between who really belonged in America and who did not was, of course, not peculiar to this period. Nativist Protestants had wanted to keep Catholics away before the Civil War. In 1882 Congress legislated a permanent ban (since revoked) against the entry of more Chinese. President Theodore Roosevelt followed this with an informal arrangement to exclude the Japanese after 1908. Closing the Pacific gates, however, did not stop the flow of people from across the Atlantic, and Europeans kept coming in sufficient numbers to add a half million people each year after the First World War. Many of those who arrived from southern and eastern Europe looked inferior in the eyes of northwest-European people who had settled in America centuries earlier. After the Russian Revolution of 1917, conservative Americans rejected immigrants who they thought might import communism. More moderate citizens worried about new oversupplies of labor, which affected their own employment. Determining whom to exclude from immigration was one way for the majority to show who really belonged among those already in the nation. Underlying much of the language of exclusion lay a racism that many citizens openly made use of in their attempts to define true Americanism.

The years after the war thus saw a revival of an old white southern organization, the Ku Klux Klan. The Klan also moved North. There the hooded members of this secret society did what they could to spread hatred and terror against blacks, Jews, and Catholics. Now as fifty years before, their rituals were based in religion; their symbol was a burning cross. Also in the North, the best-known industrialist of this period, Henry Ford, published the *Dearborn Independent,* filling its pages with attacks on Jews, who Ford thought belittled and besmirched everything Nordic. In self-defense Jews gave new support to the American Jewish Committee and the Anti-Defamation League of B'nai B'rith, and in 1928 linked with Christians to form the eventually effective National Conference of Christians and Jews.

Racist ideologues in the twenties veiled their hatreds in scientific language. Dr. Theodore Lothrop Stoddard, the most strenuous of these, chose to wage war against non-Nordics in the name of what he called "scientific humanism." He called for selective breeding of humans in order to head off the Bolshevik threat. On the pages of popular magazines he argued that anyone who faced the facts had to know that the immigrant masses in the great cities were not and could never be anything but aliens; they could not by nature become "good Americans."

Stoddard stopped short of making religious appeals, but Dr. Albert E. Wiggam led the company of those who combined the new science of eugenics with a version of Christian faith. According to Wiggam, a provident God gave microscopes and test tubes to humans. These instruments of divine revelation were able to help spread new commandments to establish moral codes. Had not Jesus taught that some men possessed but one talent, while others owned two and still others five? Wiggam did not believe in equality. Were he back among the first Americans — by which he meant only the Europeans who migrated to America — he would have served gladly as president of the First Eugenics Congress. Wiggam imagined Jesus crying: "A new commandment I give unto you — the biological Golden Rule, the completed Golden Rule of science. *Do unto both the born and the unborn as you would have the born and the unborn do unto you.*"

Both presidents in the period caught the racist spirit. President Warren G. Harding gave his blurb to the cause in the early 1920s: the public, he thought, should read Stoddard's *The Rising Tide of Color* and then face the facts. His successor, Calvin Coolidge, published at least one popular article in defense of Nordic purity. When Coolidge in 1924 signed the act to exclude most kinds of immigrants, he needed no more words than usual to make himself clear with an endorsement: "America must be kept American." However Coolidge and his kind conceived of racial unity, they were insistent that it become a basis for national cohesion.

Some mainstream Protestants — later to be stigmatized as WASPs (White Anglo-Saxon Protestants), who had most to lose from the new immigrations — eventually provided the most effective criticisms of such attitudes. The denominational journals spent years debating the question of immigration restriction. In both 1920 and 1921, the Presbyterian *Continent* pioneered with claims that to repress the immigrant was to violate the brotherhood of man and to stultify the church; "panicky programs" to limit newcomers were out-of-date. In such editorials the leftover language of hope for the coming Kingdom of God made postwar appearances.

The Methodist papers gave space to writers on both sides of the cleavage. In 1924 a writer in *Zion's Herald* contended that southeastern Europeans could never assimilate and become true Americans. The nation needed more producers and fewer peddlers — peddlers being the code name for low-class newcomers who lived marginally, off the wealth others produced. He did not, however, have the pages of *Zion's Herald* to himself, nor did he win the day among Methodists, whose leaders responded by rephrasing the language of the Kingdom and the dream of assimilation.

Northern Baptists, led by Charles A. Brooks of the American Baptist Home Missionary Society, went furthest in opposing restriction. Much of Brooks's interest in newcomers, it is true, came from his belief that they could someday become good Americans and good Protestants. English people of Protestant stock remained for him the normal, or model, people. Yet he made some steps at least in teaching his clientele not to rule out other kinds of people. Brooks fought against the disguised racial aspects of new literacy tests and taught Baptists to appreciate other ethnic heritages while they taught the newcomers what he considered to be the true American way.

In 1924 Congress passed the restrictive Johnson-Reed Act, which almost stopped immigration. Either the act's exclusion clause marked the crest of restrictive sentiment or it satisfied the "Nordics" enough to enable dissenters to find new security in America. One year after the enactment, northern Baptists in their periodicals cautioned that "neither the 'Nordic' nor any other group has the ear of the Almighty to the exclusion or injury of any other race." Reaction spread elsewhere. Henry Ford began to have trouble getting continued support for his anti-Jewish causes and retracted his more extreme statements and policies. The Ku Klux Klan, which reached a membership high of five million, saw a drop after 1924. Humorist Will Rogers suddenly found a warm response when he attacked "one-hundred-percent Americans."

Americans did not, however, enter a new age of amity. The partisan spirit of the interwar years exaggerated the racial and religious cleavage between Jews and gentiles. Anti-Jewish thought of the blatant sort came late to American shores. Until the 1880s Christians were harder on each other than on Jews. Then, when the great migrations came from eastern Europe, the old gentile majority dismissed Jewish immigrants along with other "foreign" elements. At last traditional charges by Christians that Jews were "Christ killers" began to be focused on fellow citizens. When the World War ended, immigration for a moment swelled the number of Jews, as persecuted people fled the Soviet Union and other parts of Europe. But the Johnson-Reed Act excluded most Jews seeking to immigrate. Before it took effect, 50,000 entered in one year. This act cut the number to only 10,000 the next year. But the grandchildren of Jews who had arrived two generations earlier were making their way out of the ghettos into many visible sectors of the gentile world.

When gentiles could not prevent Jews from coming to America, they tried to bar them from schools, clubs, and businesses run by elites. In 1922 Harvard students supported the university's president, A. Lawrence Lowell, when he advocated quotas to keep low the number of Jewish students, but they lost out to a more liberal-minded faculty. Medical schools remained restrictive through the thirties, and many Jews found that among the professions, only social-service work was readily open to them. As late as the years after World War II, Dartmouth College president E. M. Hopkins defended a Jewish quota since his prestigious-but-now-secular school was a "Christian college founded for the Christianization of its students."

As so often before and elsewhere, Jews found themselves serving as scapegoats, singled out by those who looked for conspirators whenever anything went wrong. Though many Jews had to flee the Soviet Union, the fact that many Communist leaders were Jewish led their enemies to claim that all Jews were Bolsheviks at heart and subversives by design. After the First World War populists often identified Jews with Wall Street, even though banking and finance more than most fields remained a white Protestant preserve. Tendencies like these came together in Henry Ford, who convinced himself that the *Protocols of the Elders of Zion* was authentic. This was a phony report of a Jewish conclave that allegedly met in turn-of-the-century Paris to plan world domination. Not until boycotts and lawsuits hit Ford in 1927 did he come to his senses and apologize to American Jews.

The tribal character of American life became most patent when the Ku Klux Klan entered a blatantly anti-Jewish phase. In 1924 a letter writer defended the mentality that made the Klan plausible. He told *The New Republic* that "the old Americans are getting a little panicky, and no wonder. . . . America, Americans and Americanism are being crowded out of America." The Ku Klux Klan, he thought, was fundamentally right from the standpoint of American unity and destiny. The Klan was strongest in small towns and in rural areas, where supporters could work out their hatreds of the city. Thus an Oregon Klansman complained that in the cities "the Kikes are so thick that a white man can hardly find room to walk on the sidewalk." There was room on northern country roads for the Klan to ride, terrifying the blacks and stirring hatred of Jews.

Between the two world wars, the struggling Jewish community saw synagogue growth partly as a means of building a religious identity in the face of attacks by gentiles. In the ten years after 1927, the number of congregations grew from 3,100 to 3,700. These did not penetrate the lives of most second-generation Jews; only about one-fourth of them received any Jewish education. Socialists, intellectuals, and Zionists wrote increasingly of their own alienation from worship, while many in the middle classes put their energies into fraternal and charitable fronts.

No issue did more to transform the Jewish community between the two world wars than Zionism. Solemn Jewish worship always ended with the prayer "Next year in Jerusalem!" But after hundreds of years, the phrase came to mean something so symbolic or mysterious in its messianism that literate Jews did not take it literally. Then, after the persecutions and pogroms in eastern Europe just before the twentieth century, many began to look for an escape and a fulfillment. Secular Zionists began to support and supplant the old specifically religious hopes for a return to the land of promise, Israel. Such stirrings in European Judaism could not fail to reach America.

Most American Jews were not ready for Zionism. "Back to Israel" was at first hardly more appealing for them than was "Back to Africa" to Africans in the United States. Reform Judaism in its beginnings clearly had seen America as the new Zion. Tardily, a few prominent Jews made mild statements in support of Israel. With "one-hundred-percent Americans" using Zionism to argue that Jews were secretly disloyal to America, many Jewish leaders remained openly anti-Zionist.

Then, when in 1917 the Balfour Declaration placed England morally behind the idea of a Jewish return to Israel, interest also quickened in the United States. On April 28, 1918, the American Jewish Committee gave Israel a first timid endorsement but hastily added that it was axiomatic that all American Jews would remain loyal to the United States.

Late in the First World War, the politics of the Middle East became increasingly tense for the United States. Secretary of State Robert Lansing did not want to alienate Turkey, which had much to lose should a Jewish state arise, and he also was aware that many

American Jews were anti-Zionist. Lansing surmised that many Christian sects would resent turning over the Holy Land to the race they blamed for the death of Christ. He could not know that many of those sectarians were also now "premillennialist." They surprised other Christians by seeing the hand of God in the Balfour Declaration. In the literal reading of biblical visions, favored by this group of fundamentalists, Christ would not return until Israel was restored again along the lines of biblical prophecy.

By the end of the First World War, there were a surprising 200,000 declared Zionists in America. But Zionists knew that before they could make moves they had much missionary work to do among American Jews. They faced formidable enemies among assimilated Jews like financier Henry Morgenthau or the genius behind the retail firm of Sears, Roebuck, Julius Rosenwald. To recent Yiddish-speaking immigrants such leaders sounded elitist, too reluctant to give much of their heart to Zionism. To the profound Zionists, belief was even more important than halfhearted, if generous, financial support. The great European leader Chaim Weizmann never trusted assimilated Jews, believing it too late for them to grasp the soul of Zionism.

Against the traditions of Reform to which he belonged, Rabbi Stephen S. Wise emerged as a Zionist leader who helped force the issues. In the early twenties his cause suffered setbacks, but he regrouped supporters and taught them to keep their distance from radical Zionists who might offend other Americans. Then the British backed off from some of their Balfour commitments, and in the tension and chaos, the Zionist Organization of America looked like a lost cause. From the World War I high of 200,000 active members, it dropped to 18,000 in 1922. When nativism became intense, it was inconvenient to be a Zionist, and then, when prejudice declined, Jews found fewer reasons to be one. The crash of the New York Stock Exchange in 1929 doomed the fund-raising side, while the spiritual forces remained in disarray.

Through the thirties, Jews went back to the task of defining themselves in America. In 1934 Mordecai Kaplan, standing on the soil of Conservative Judaism, published *Judaism as a Civilization*. He wanted to help secular-minded Jews feel at home with Jewish civilization and hold to their sense of separate identity. Ironically, the rivalries between Catholics and Protestants would help keep the United States Christian — so Christian that Jews dared not blur into the general population. Just as Catholics used parochial schools to remain a civilization on Protestant soil, so Jews must find ways to limit their intercourse with Christian America, even those Jews for whom the God of Israel was a problem of belief.

Voices like Kaplan's became urgent when the issue of Jewish survival itself arose. Anti-Jewish hatred was the most dramatic single feature in the program of Adolf Hitler, the new specter in Europe in the thirties. While Nazis set out to exterminate European Jews, the United States was unready to play host to more than a small number of refugees. In the end, the displaced hundreds of thousands who survived could find no place to go but Israel, even though it was not yet constituted as a nation open to their purposes. Not until after the Second World War did Jews win the commitments promised by the Balfour Declaration.

Demagoguery against the divided Jewish community knew no sects or sectarian boundaries. The rightist-minded Baptist preacher Gerald B. Winrod did not make his appeal only to Baptists when he moved on from antievolutionism in the twenties to the more popular, anti-Jewish cause in the 1930s. By 1938 he had built up a subscription list of 100,000 for his publication *The Defender*. Winrod typically saw conspiracies of international Jewry in the financial manipulations that he blamed for the Depression, and he called it all communist. Winrod, like so many others of his generation, was gifted in his use of radio for demagogic purposes. By the time the Second World War came, he had reached the limits of his appeal; having failed to win election as a Kansas senator, the pitchman ran afoul of the law in 1942 and his fame began to decline, though his anti-Jewish spirit did not.

As popular as Winrod and his Protestant cohorts were, by far the best-known Depression-era preacher against Jewish conspiracy was — one is tempted to say "happened to be" — a Catholic. Father Charles E. Coughlin operated only a few miles from the Dearborn of Henry Ford. Better than Winrod, Couglin understood the power of radio; in 1934 *Fortune* called him "just about the biggest thing that ever happened to radio." In his prime, no private citizen in America received more mail than he. Though Coughlin had a limited education in matters political or economic, he reached out from his Shrine of the Little Flower in Royal Oak, Michigan, to a national audience. While the science of audience measurement was highly inexact, it was thought that, during his years of popularity, every Sunday afternoon at least 3 or 4 million adults tuned in to hear him. Some estimated that, including Coughlin's publications and organizations, the larger ripples of his following reached 30 million people in a nation of 150 million.

Coughlin came from humble backgrounds in an Irish Catholic laboring family in Hamilton, Ontario, where he was born in 1891. He spent his youth and young adulthood in the "Catholic ghetto" as an altar boy, parochial-school student, seminarian, and priest. In 1926 Bishop Michael Gallagher assigned young Coughlin to Royal Oak. In Europe the prelate had just enjoyed rites canonizing Saint Thérèse de Lisieux as "the Little Flower of Jesus," and now he desired a shrine for her in greater Detroit. He chose enemy territory; Royal Oak was a Ku Klux Klan stronghold, but Gallagher knew that Couglin was tough enough to build in the midst of its "fiery hatred." He more than succeeded.

In order to garner more fame and following, in 1926 Coughlin talked radio station WJR into putting him on the air. His first listeners, he liked to claim, were attracted because he avoided all controversies and prejudicial subjects. Before long he dropped that approach, even though he kept remembering off-the-air how to neutralize the enemy. One day he stepped in line and led a passing Klan funeral procession. Because of such gestures, Royal Oak became safer and Catholics converged there to build homes. Coughlin dreamed of a shrine whose tower would climb to the sky — as he put it, to the bosom of the Virgin Mary.

He clung on when the Depression ended his dreams of skyscraping. Coughlin used his own church as a relief agency and, as if to thumb his nose at trend watchers, embarked on a great building project at a time when it was supposed to be financially impossible to gain support. Coughlin explained the generosity of the people: he fought off the international economic conspiracies that enslaved them, and they showed gratitude. "I knew damn well that I had the ability. . . . And what the hell, no one else seemed to be interested in doing a damn thing."

Though he never took pains to learn what socialism was, Coughlin suddenly started attacking all its forms, until his radio audience fastened on it as the all-purpose explanation for what had gone wrong. Congressional committees called him in as an expert witness on communism. He kept his friendship with Henry Ford though Ford signed a contract for tractors with the Soviet Union. Earlier Ford was to the priest an agent of the communist revolution that would reach America by 1933. When the Columbia Broadcasting System and the National Broadcasting Company censored the broadcaster or refused him air time, he devised a network of his own.

In October 1931, the radio minister attacked President Herbert Hoover for finding no remedies for the Depression. Finding him a bland target, Coughlin then moved on to attack international bankers. His supporters found this more plausible; how else could they explain their poverty in a world full of stockpiled food, with millions of acres of virgin soil — a world of banks loaded with money alongside idle factories, long breadlines, millions of jobless people, and growing discontent? As if out of nowhere, the priest conceived the idea that the government could solve the problems simply by printing and circulating more money.

Coughlin's charges and proposals might have seemed absurd, but people of power dared not alienate his following. Franklin Delano Roosevelt invited the priest to the Democratic National Convention in 1932, knowing that as a candidate he needed support. After the election Roosevelt soon broke relations. Coughlin claimed that he was himself above politics, and that he wanted only to inject Christianity into a corrupt economic system. He could never realize how his attacks on modern capitalism were playing into the hands of the hated socialists and communists. His audience never sorted out the contradictions; they needed only to believe that a conspiracy existed against them.

Coughlin lived a self-contradictory life. He attacked Wall Street but employed the firm of Paine, Webber and Company to play the market. Sworn to the ideal of poverty, he lived comfortably. While he called gold "Jewish money," he relied for speech-writing help on George LeBlanc, a gold-trader. Though avowedly nonpartisan, Coughlin helped elect Roosevelt. In 1934 the priest finally came forth with a program when he formed a million-member people's lobby, the National Union for Social Justice (NUSJ). His paper *Social Justice* came to sound increasingly Fascist as it borrowed terms from Mussolini in its call for the United States to reshape itself as a "corporative state" with "class cooperation." Coughlin cheered when Mussolini invaded Ethiopia. In the field of electoral politics, he met his greatest failure. In 1936 he supported William Lemke, who was a virtual puppet for Coughlin's Union party. When Lemke made no real showing, Coughlin moved to the political far right, where responsible Catholics found it wise to leave him alone.

One sign of the chaos of the thirties was the support Jews briefly gave Coughlin, even in the years when his talk about an international banking conspiracy none too subtly evoked anti-Jewish overtones. Rabbis Leon Fram of Detroit and Ferdinand M. Isserman of Saint Louis lent credibility to him when they supported early NUSJ events. Then, when Coughlin cited the Rothschilds and Lazard Freres, the Warburgs and Morgans, and the Kuhn, Loeb firm — notable Jews — as the hated bankers, the rabbis quickly turned on him. He made some efforts to separate what he called the good Jews from atheistic Jews, but his followers could spot no visible differences between them, and the more ardent of them started beating up on any kind of Jew. In 1938 their hero called for a Christian Front in the United States and drew just short of a call for an alliance with the Nazis, whose treatment of Jews he defended that November.

Coughlin's reputation was international. The *New York Times* Berlin correspondent thought he was the man of the hour in Germany. But he did not hold such a rank in the American Catholic church. A committee known as Catholics for Human Rights called on notables from singer Bing Crosby to Governor Alfred E. Smith to counteract the Christian Front. When the priest started quoting favorably the addresses of Josef Goebbels, the Nazi propaganda minister, they found even more to oppose. He blamed three Jews, one each from France, Russia, and England, as being responsible for drawing America toward war. Must the entire world, he asked, go to war for 600,000 Jews who were citizens not of these countries or America, but of Germany? Before the war came, he saw Antichrist riding high, wide, and handsome among American Jews. "Let's be militant and fight these people to the bitter end, cost what it may."

Then came the fall. Hitler and the Russians signed a mutual nonaggression pact that weakened Coughlin's platform. He could only say now that if capitalism had accepted Jesus Christ, neither communism nor nazism would ever have taken shape. Station after station started dropping his program in wartime, and audiences fell away. In October of 1940 he had to give up his broadcast, though *Social Justice* lived on briefly. One of the last issues still applauded the Nazi war on pornography and obscenity and attacked Roosevelt for packing Washington with Jews. Three months after America entered the war, Coughlin still claimed that Hitler justifiably persecuted Jews.

Postwar evidence showed that Coughlin had some formal ties to Axis propaganda organizations, though he denied that and did not need them for his homegrown program. Washington found a back-door way to silence him by encouraging Archbishop Edward Mooney to order the priest to pastoral duties alone, and Coughlin obeyed. In his old age Coughlin insisted, "If I had to do it all over again, I would do it the same way." In the Depression, he gave a voice to the silent, the hurt, the oppressed. In a cloven society, he provided a huge cluster of religious people with simple explanations for what went wrong.

While Coughlin crusaded on his own, a representative kind of Catholic social thinker emerged in the person of Monsignor John A. Ryan. Nothing better illustrated the confusion of the years than some lines devotees found in the writings of Ryan from the worst years: "I would like to inform you that Father Charles E. Coughlin is a messenger of God donated to the American people for the purpose of rectifying the outrageous mistakes they have made in the past." Ryan later rectified his own outrageous mistake and in the name of progressive papal teachings led the fight on the anti-Jewish priest. Ryan became the director of the Social Action Department of the National Catholic Welfare Conference, from which post he worked for liberal programs in Depression years and projected the image of a Catholicism concerned about social justice.

Telling the story of so many domestic conflicts within two decades of American history may give a misimpression. Many citizens did find ways to get along with others and used religious symbols and motives to seal their bonds. Many lived ordinary lives rather remote from the calls to be Wet or Dry, fundamentalist or modernist, to idolize South or North, to support labor and the left or to oppose labor and be conservative. Many stood above or lived far from areas where whites snubbed blacks, majorities excluded minorities, or Christians stigmatized and blamed Jews for Depression troubles. The conflicts draw our eyes. It is easy to overlook the quietly faithful people who lived in harmony with each other.

During the years before the war, there was, however, one more major clash, particularly in Protestantism — between pacifists and those who prepared to face the threat of Nazi and Fascist causes. If during World War I church leadership sounded hawkish, the voice of the dove was heard thereafter. In 1934 the peace-minded *Christian Century* claimed twenty million Protestants openly in the peace camp. The schism between camps came as Mussolini and Hitler represented overseas but encroaching totalitarian threats. The towering Protestant thinker of the day, Reinhold Niebuhr, switched sides in the course of the thirties. Talking the language of "Christian realism," he urged military preparedness. He led those who asked only that *if* war came, realism would prevent Americans this time from turning it into a "holy war."

When war came, after Pearl Harbor in December 1941, the American majority closed ranks. Again, a people suffered, as innocent Japanese-Americans were herded into domestic-style concentration camps on no good or just basis. Freeing them, it must be said, did not become a major item on non-Japanese-American agendas. Religious and nonreligious America alike slowly came to be aware that Hitler was exterminating Jews, yet the religious voices made few efforts to welcome refugee Jews from Europe.

There was a war to prosecute and win, a nation to defend. The churches produced a few pacifists. This time there were even a couple of hundred Roman Catholic conscientious objectors. But pacifism was a minority vote. The religious leaders worked to stimulate national loyalty without encouraging idolatry. World War II was an uprooting and enlarging experience of mobilization, travel, and, beyond suffering, victory. When the military people finally came home, with Depression and war behind them, they helped create a climate in which America could address old and new problems in new ways.

Jesuit Father John Courtney Murray endured attacks
by members of his own order to become American
Catholicism's most notable commentator on the
public order. Of enormous influence in interfaith
affairs after midcentury, he was responsible for
much of the Second Vatican Council's Declaration
on Religious Liberty and is remembered as both a
loyal Catholic and a public philosopher. (*Alfred
Eisenstaedt,* Life *magazine © 1955 Time, Inc.*)

Chapter Eighteen

THE AMERICAN WAYS OF LIFE

◈ THE NATION'S SPIRITUAL OUTLINES WERE HARD TO DEFINE around 1945. Few postwar Americans pictured a forthcoming revival of interest in religion. Now and then a social thinker would look back to Henry C. Link's 1937 book *The Return to Religion* as a harbinger of renewal. Certainly the blend of religion and patriotism during World War II helped produce a climate open to faith. It was regularly said that "there are no atheists in foxholes." Still, it was more common to speak of America as simply a secular society in which religious institutions had a secure but boxed-in space.

Ten years later, however, all but a few mass communicators and social analysts who then kept their eyes on the subject agreed: during the Eisenhower era, which began in 1952, there was a revival of religion, or at least of an interest in religion. The returning military people were eager to set down roots, and religion provided some of these. Many Americans, remembering the Sunday-school or parochial or Sabbath-school foundations of their childhood Depression-era years, now helped support adult religious institutions. Mass higher education made possible the entrance of more people into the middle class and permitted a move to the suburbs. There, especially where single-family homes and large families predominated, people adopted styles of living congenial to support of church and synagogue.

The external indicators were easy to read. Never before in American history had citizens been spending proportionately as much per year on church building. Never had there been a higher percentage of people on church or synagogue rolls. Attendance and monetary giving reached new peaks. Celebrity religionists like Bishop Fulton J. Sheen and evangelist Billy Graham were familiar figures on the new mass medium, television. Religion produced best-selling books. Even theologians like German émigré Paul Tillich, the native-born Reinhold Niebuhr, and popularizers like rabbi Joshua Loth Liebman, who wrote *Peace of Mind,* helped place religious ideas on the public mind. At the pinnacle of it all was the new and newly baptized president, Dwight D. Eisenhower. In his era of good feelings combined with the chill of the cold war, Eisenhower used the White House, Teddy Roosevelt's "bully pulpit," to promote a generalized and nationalistic religion. Ike was friendly enough to the churches, but as a priest of this national faith, he found it more important to see the nation itself as a kind of shrine or instrument of God. In such an era, to exaggerate conflict between races, peoples, religions, and churches would be to violate the search for consensus.

Still, to the spiritual and political left of Eisenhower were people who said that friendliness to churches could not pay off. The symbol systems of traditional churches were obsolete. Such institutions themselves were exclusivistic and competitive. How could sects generate the common values a democracy needed, especially in the face of a needed crusade against atheistic communism? Such promotion of common values need not represent secularism, as many church people charged. Instead it could support the "public religion" of Benjamin Franklin, the "political religion" of Abraham Lincoln, the embracing religious support for republicanism. Suddenly, in the name of a desired consensus, Americans found themselves debating what was the best basis for their common life.

Here again we shall explore the national debate not through many small details or abstract references but by examining the lives of major contenders. On the secular front, John Dewey, now a very aged prophet, had already stated his case for a common faith in 1934; still the dominant figure in public education and philosophy, he was the leader most invoked by younger disciples. The fifties was a period when people spoke in terms of counterforces to Dewey's broad, secular "common faith." These forces were giant pools reduced to "Protestantism, Catholicism, and Judaism." Well-known and articulate figures who addressed pluralism included people like Billy Graham, Father John Courtney Murray,

Reinhold Niebuhr, Will Herberg, and Francis Cardinal Spellman. No individual could embody all that the communities behind them cared about, yet such leaders had large followings and broad outlooks, so they can help bring the issue and story into focus. First, however, there was Eisenhower.

Not since Woodrow Wilson had there been a president who felt so much at home with public piety as he. The Republican National Committee took note of his status in 1955, when it combined partisan rhetoric with reasonably accurate reportage. The president was "in every sense of the word . . . not only the political leader, but the spiritual leader of our times." A public weary of depression and war and division settled down with the assurances of their leader.

The new president's family lines included Jehovah's Witnesses and River Brethren, sects that offered little to a general of the army or a commander in chief. As president he insisted that recognition of the Supreme Being was the first and most basic expression of Americanism. "Without God, there could be no American form of government, nor an American way of life." He applied the language of the religious crusades first to World War II, then to his campaign against corruption in Washington, and, finally, to his assault against godless communism abroad.

Back in 1948 Eisenhower had announced: "I am the most intensely religious man I know" — and then hastened to add that this did not mean that he adhered to any sect: "I believe in democracy." The foremost evangelist of the day, Billy Graham, reported that the overwhelming majority of the American people felt a little more secure realizing that they had at the head of their government a leader who believed in prayer.

While Eisenhower was congenial to a faith like Billy Graham's, he was also giving public expression to a faith that lacked the particular flavor of church religion. While he would have resisted the notion that he was playing into the hands of secularism, his approach had to be broad. Thus it fit in with those who, outside the churches — especially through schools and public institutions — wanted to promote a national consensus apart from church auspices.

In order to make sense of the postwar American search, one must reach back to an exceptional statement — a statement that warred against the dominant prewar spirit of chaos when it was made. In 1934 John Dewey set forth his religious views in *A Common Faith*.

It was a slight volume, out of a catalog of Dewey publications so long that merely to list them takes 153 pages. Even though its author was the towering educational philosopher of the century, his view of "common faith" could not reverse the drift of the thirties; its kind of thinking had greater influence after the war, during the search for cohesion.

Like so many other publicists for public religion, Dewey had been brought up in the confines of sectarian religion. He knew the importance of symbols and values, even as he grew uncomfortable with and, finally, had to leave behind the demands of church religion. So it was that through him and his kind mid-twentieth-century democratic faith was still being shaped by negations of mid-nineteenth-century church life.

John Dewey was not born into the thought world of the eighteenth-century Enlightenment but into that of nineteenth-century evangelicalism in 1859. When it came time for her son to join the local church, Lucinda Rich Dewey gave the eleven-year-old a note she drafted to take with him: "I think I love Christ and want to obey him. . . ." The child chafed under such mothering and was always embarrassed when in the company of others she would ask him whether he was "right with Jesus." Years later he remembered such sessions and transported their recall into his counsel, when he argued that religious feeling is always unhealthy when it is constantly being watched, analyzed, and pulled out at the roots for observation.

While the University of Vermont, to which he moved on, had fewer than a hundred students, and though it demanded daily chapel attendance, Dewey found it an escape from confinement. Teachers there, he said, helped him overcome what he called the inward laceration that the old New England world caused when it divided people from the world, when it split the soul from body and nature from God — while religion ought all along to be promoting wholeness and harmony. For five or ten more years, through his graduate-school years at Johns Hopkins and his teaching at the University of Michigan, he still attended the Students' Christian Association and a liberal Congregational church. He could employ some of the old symbols, but he was transforming them beyond recognition, toward his "common faith." Thus, in a lecture in 1892 he set forth ideas that hardly changed when he spoke at Yale in 1934 or in his old age in the 1950s. In that lecture, "Christianity and Democracy," he said that the only religious sphere that mattered had become the commonwealth, the Republic, the public arena. Democracy itself was "the means by which the revelation of truth is carried on."

In 1894, when he joined the faculty of the new University of Chicago, Dewey found it convenient to stop attending church, and for ten years there, and then through decades at Teachers College at Columbia University in New York, he made the laboratory school and the public philosophy his virtual church.

When he produced *A Common Faith* in the 1930s, Dewey drew together his views of a lifetime on this subject. The first and last lines of the book were forceful, even belligerent. A war was going on between religions of supernature and of nature, between religions bottled up in separate institutions and a religiousness that was as broad as the Republic. Now was the time to make the public, or common, faith "explicit and militant." In this book Dewey recalled, however briefly, his own long struggle with specialized religious belief on his way to the general view that the word *God* should mean nothing more, or nothing less, than the idea that the whole self could be harmonized with the universe. In his mind, *non*religiousness was the attitude of people in the churches who cut humans off from nature and set up the crude boundaries of creeds. He did not want to abolish churches, but he expected them to transform themselves so they could support chiefly the common values. That teacher who took most seriously the socializing process was the "prophet of the true God and the usherer in of the kingdom of God." Schools that produced "state consciousness" did for moderns what the forefathers did when they called for people to "get religion."

While Dewey refused to argue with religious leaders — it took years for Reinhold Niebuhr to draw him out, though they worked a few blocks apart — the churches for half a century found "progressive education" or "Deweyism" to be a convenient foil. They feared the privileged position that educators held. In 1944 British visitor D. W. Brogan with characteristic aptness called the public school the "formally unestablished national church," and so the churchly critics saw it. To many a Catholic, Dewey was simply the newest infidel. To conservatives he and all who would make a religion of democracy were secularists: enemies of true faith. So a controversy developed as to who best understood the American past, who best guarded its present, and who should set the terms for its future. Protestantism was in the most privileged spot, though it was constantly losing relative place. Still, there was enough power that a popular voice could become a national figure. One did.

At the side of the Protestant majority was the huge and growing Catholic population. Theirs was the largest single church in America. The baby boom was helping it grow, the new patterns in higher education and federally supported home purchasing made possible entrance of more into middle-class zones of influence. The old defensiveness declined progressively with the crumbling ghetto walls. Catholicism was more free than it had been in three and a half centuries to help set the terms for North American life. But the fallen walls only revealed that there were many Catholicisms existing behind them. Leaders struggled to find an appropriate way to support the faith and the society. Just as Billy Graham and Reinhold Niebuhr represented different schools of thought about Protestantism in the Republic, so did men like Cardinal Francis Spellman, the popular leader, and John Courtney Murray, the thinker, stand for differing Catholic interpretations of the Republic.

Spellman rose to unmatched clerical power from childhood in a small Massachusetts town, where his father was a grocer. He concluded his studies at the North American College in Rome (where elite priests prepared), all the while making friends with people who were then or would become Vatican officials. There he acquired political savvy; he came back to learn the ins and outs of Boston while peddling the Catholic diocesan newspaper, *The Pilot,* in parishes. Thus he gained a power base in the chancery office, which soon made him a candidate for an invitation to come back to Rome.

By the time Benito Mussolini had risen to power, Spellman was among those who stood by with advice for Pope Pius XI on how to prosper in the new era. When Spellman became a favorite of Pius XII, the young American seemed on the way to becoming a world statesman, but then was sent back to Boston and comparatively unpromising posts. Never confined by such positions, and thanks to his Vatican friendships, Spellman climbed in the American ranks. At home with people of power, he was a friend of President Franklin D. Roosevelt through the war years. The year the European war began he was named archbishop of New York. In the era when radio and the press converged on New York and when mass communicators listened there to hear what was going on in religion, he became the natural spokesman for Catholic causes. When America entered the Second World War, he was named military vicar for Catholics.

Spellman more than anyone else invented the midcentury Catholic version of Christian America. His predecessors had to spend time showing how Catholicism was at home with the Republic, but he virtually made an icon out of the national flag. The white of Old Glory stood for "the basic righteousness of our national purpose." His naive but popular poems sometimes equated the mission of America and the Virgin Mary. Because America had escaped communism and now fought it off, he could sing:

> And these United States, united still
> In opposition, stand before the world,
> Above all passing pettiness and sloth,
> In one unflinching purpose — righteousness.

When World War II was first approaching, Spellman proudly insisted that Americans envied none, wronged none, and coveted nothing. They generously spread charities in a distressful world with a goodwill that other nations never reciprocated. When American soldiers later died for the cause, he saw their blood mingling reverently with that of Christ as they brought "salvation and peace to their fellowmen." Using language of the kind that Lincoln once cautioned against, Spellman declared that the entire American struggle grew out of a motive of charity to the neighbor, that every drop of blood fell in what was ultimately God's cause. In the 1950s he found it particularly easy to support America in the Korean War, because this time no communists were among American allies, as they had been back during World War II. Now the Reds were where they belonged, on the other side of enemy lines.

Domestically, Spellman lorded it over the American church. Since the Vatican consulted him when making appointments, the people of power in the American church increasingly took on his image. He tried to help dictate which movies Americans should see and which books they should read. Only once did he overreach, when he pressed for federal aid to parochial schools; then many non-Catholics fought back. Most notable of these was the widow of his friend President Roosevelt. Because she wrote columns criticizing aid to Catholic schools, he charged Eleanor Roosevelt with discrimination "unworthy of an American mother" and wrote, "I shall not again publicly acknowledge you." By this time, not all the language of interfaith violence was coming from Protestants against Catholics.

This face-off left Spellman more controversial than before, more vulnerable to attack by forces who previously had feared him. He had to pay a call on Mrs. Roosevelt to quiet the opposition against his strident attack on her. A new spirit was coming to American Catholicism; when a fresh generation of leaders rose with Pope John XXIII, Spellman made peace with them and lived on rather quietly until 1967, having elaborated his consistent vision.

The direction from which the new religious energies came surprised most observers. The most popular Protestant voice after the Second World War had a southern accent, held to most of the old fundamentalist verities, and recalled an America that sophisticates thought had died away after the Scopes trial of 1925. Yet for decades his kind of conservative Protestantism had been regathering energies, changing its tone, and readying itself for a new assault. It came in the person of evangelist Billy Graham, who amazingly combined the ability to speak for the most particular kind of Protestant faith and to make himself generally accepted beyond the confines of any sect in America.

Graham addressed himself both to the personal problems of Americans who did not know who they were but who wanted to be saved and to an America that did not know what it was but wanted a mission. During the fifties the question of personal identity began to become fashionable and even urgent in America. In the early years of his prominence Graham liked to tell of the night when he was conversing with a Yale student who suddenly asked, "Who am I?" Other students, not catching the depth of the question, laughed, but Graham did not. He called it one of the most profound questions ever asked. Sometimes it came in broad terms: Where did I come from? Why am I here? Where am I going? Such questions, he said, plagued every thoughtful person. But Graham also knew the question had to do as well with the social environment.

At first Graham was easy to dismiss. To most Americans, crowds for evangelists were like fossils from the nineteenth century. Only the Bible Belt could serve as their habitat. Militant fundamentalist Bob Jones, Sr., knew he was stigmatized in the liberal world because those who held to the "old-time religion" were supposed to have greasy noses, dirty fingernails, baggy pants, unshined shoes, and uncombed hair. Graham makes sense only against the background of a changed and newly powerful conservative Protestantism.

Three months before Pearl Harbor, in 1941, a tiny cluster of fundamentalist churches met in New York to form the "militantly pro-Gospel and anti-modernist" American Council of Christian Churches (ACCC). Presbyterian protester Carl McIntire was to lead this council in attack against the Federal Council of Churches (FCC) and the presumed communists in the churches. Soon the ACCC made headlines as it fought FCC monopolies on apportioning military chaplaincies and assigning network time for radio. But McIntire miscalculated the American mood; his guns were too noisy, his charges too sweeping, his goals too negative in the eyes of others.

One month after the ACCC people got together, milder counterparts met at the Moody Bible Institute in Chicago. They preferred to call themselves "Neo-Evangelical," and then "Evangelical," thus camping on a name once simply equated with Protestantism. They did not disagree with fundamentalist doctrine, but found the name tainted and the style abhorrent. The people who therefore formed the National Association of Evangelicals under the urbane Boston minister Harold John Ockenga insisted that theirs would be no "dog-in-the manger, reactionary, negative, or destructive type of organization." They later claimed that half of the American Protestants were really sympathetic with their gospel and their war against liberalism. Evangelicals knew what the problem of fundamentalist manners was, and spelled it out when they said they would never resort to bigotry, intolerance, misrepresentation, hate, jealousy, false judgment, and hypocrisy — all of which had made fundamentalists look like barbarians to the rest of America.

The modernism the evangelicals set out to fight was as much a fossil as the older fundamentalism appeared to be. Most church members in the liberal churches were always "evangelical" and had always enjoyed the traditional experiences and teachings of Protestantism. They never had the problems and did not need the solutions that the professors and scholars came up with early in the century. As a matter of fact, even the elites now were favoring what they called "Neo-orthodoxy," a more traditional approach to faith and one that itself criticized liberalism. The problem now, according to internal critics of the mainstream churches, was a too smug and easy adaptation to prosperous society during the religious revival. Still, the evangelicals found the mainline leaders untrustworthy to lead Christian America. To conservatives, the new World Council of Churches, formed in Amsterdam in 1948, and the new National Council of Churches, formed in 1950, sold out too much to the modern world.

The neo-evangelicals, who attacked social liberalism, attracted people of wealth. J. Howard Pew, the chairman of the Sun Oil Company and a member of a Presbyterian church that held membership in the ecumenical councils, grew impatient with council ventures and turned his back on them. Pew and his colleagues instinctively shared the old faith. In the competitive business world, they took refuge in religion that resisted change. They liked the way evangelists insisted that faith had to do only with private, never public, life. Such an outlook seemed neutral, but it clearly supported laissez-faire capitalism, while the Third World, which included churches from both — or all — sides in the cold war, asked the church "to reject the ideologies of both communism and laissez-faire capitalism." To Pew, capitalism was not a false alternative but an element in Christian America.

As they fought for radio time, the evangelicals tried to correct the misconception that Protestantism was of one mind; no, there were "two distinct kinds of Protestants in America." Most citizens ignored such infighting. Disputes between such groups and the mainstream Protestants concerned the Republic no more than would a feud between fraternal orders like the Odd Fellows and the Knights of Pythias. Yet the rightist Protestants were not content to be dismissed. Social analyst Albert Rasmussen sized them up in the early 1960s as people displaced from the soil to the city, dominated by vast organizations, and feeling that they had no control over their own destiny. They were, he said, uprooted people who looked for a new "sense of belongingness and a new elite of the saved in which they could enroll themselves." And they were finding belonging, in part because they had found a leader who helped them when they asked that student's question: Who am I?

In earlier revivals, personalities like Jonathan Edwards and George Whitefield, Francis Asbury and Charles Grandison Finney, Dwight L. Moody and Billy Sunday gave voice to people who were ready to "get religion." Once more, in Graham, a new leader came from old rural-revivalist roots. As he traveled, he was surprised to find that the liberalism against which he had been warned — a real, old-fashioned, dyed-in-the-wool modernism — had almost disappeared. He wanted to take his movement "into the camps of the devil," but he needed to find new camps or other devils. He found his voice in the huge tents and halls favored by mass evangelists. The churched and semichurched people who came to sing the old hymns and hear his Bible-preaching came from many denominations, and Graham tried to cooperate with most churches.

After successes at the Charlottes and Altoonas of the trail, he knew, as did Moody and Sunday before him, that the big cities must be his test. In 1949 Graham took on pagan Los Angeles. There, in a "Canvas Cathedral," the thirty-one-year-old revivalist embarked on the biggest effort of his career to date. Nightly he filled the tent with messages of judgment on the nation. Only because God's people prayed did God spare the ravages and destruction of war in America. Now God was giving America a "desperate choice" between revival and judgment. Graham told Los Angeles that the communists had targeted their city of wickedness, sin, crime, and immorality. "Fifth Columnists, called Communists, are more rampant in Los Angeles than any other city in America. We need a revival."

Newspaper magnate William Randolph Hearst kept his eye on the evangelist and the crowds and sent a two-word message to his reporters and editors: "Puff Graham!" Sinful Los Angeles and the pagan media of America did not in any way block the preacher's idea of Christian America after all. *Time* and *Life* and *Newsweek* reported on Graham's successes. Reporters conscientiously passed on word of his predictions that in a year or two Jesus would start the millennium; this meant that nothing in the culture was worth saving. Then, evidently awakening no apparent sense of contradiction in his audience, Graham would urge them the next night to preserve "our present culture." At one rally he told Los Angeles that the city, the nation, and Europe were fearful because they knew that inevitably the atom bomb would soon drop. Almost in the same breath, he then called America back to its old moral code and the Ten Commandments so that the nation would long endure. Taking the long view, he stopped calling his missions "campaigns" and named them "crusades," because a crusade was a continuing thing, he said; it went on and on.

The political world began to pay attention to his power. Harry S. Truman invited Graham to the White House, but there the evangelist made two mistakes. He let the press photograph him kneeling in prayer on the White House lawn and he quoted the presidential conversation. Truman had taste for neither kind of foolishness, and Graham learned his lesson well. He golfed and prayed with the next four presidents, but was more discreet thereafter and sometimes played down his relations with them. He did encourage Richard M. Nixon to run for the office and was one of Nixon's longest and most insistent defenders in the Watergate years, but after they were over, the evangelist said he had learned once again not to misuse his access to power.

Celebrities regularly lined his platform and people of so many backgrounds shared his prayers that he picked up a nettling foe he never could shake: the fundamentalists. Some of his mentors scorned Graham for having sold out to popularity, liberalism, and compromise. Graham shared fundamentalist beliefs in an errorless Bible, the Virgin Birth of Jesus, His death and resurrection, and the Second Coming. But he packaged these so attractively that Hollywood stars and athletes who cared little for the fine points of doctrine followed him, thus helping him teach the evangelicals to embrace worldly American culture in the name of the simplest values of the past. Clearly Graham had distanced himself from the prejudiced people with whom his earliest enemies connected him.

In his appeal for a Christian America, Graham mellowed through the years. In the 1970s he came to preach in communist nations and said relatively nice things about life there. He also spoke up for nuclear disarmament. Without naming John Dewey and his school of thought, Graham blamed many of America's failings on progressive and secular schools, and after 1963 he favored a constitutional amendment to authorize prayer in the public schools. Graham outlasted the Eisenhower revival and, after some eclipse in the 1960s, came back to lead popular evangelicalism again in the next decade. A congenial public found it could enjoy the soothing ministries of both Catholic Fulton J. Sheen and Protestant Billy Graham, as if there had never been a war between the faiths.

Graham was consistent with his predecessors. A nation "under God," as Abraham Lincoln had called it, would keep its covenant with the God of Abraham, Isaac, and Jacob, the Father of Jesus Christ — the God who was the agent of American prosperity through faithful communities that stretched back at least to Puritan times. The Republic needed no help from secularists like the Deweyites, who made a religion out of democracy. Yet Graham represented only one burgeoning faction in American Protestantism. To his critics he seemed too uncritical of America. He lacked a prophetic sense and did not apply the "Protestant principle" of judgment to his own causes. Where was his sense of irony to deal with the gap between the ideals of the pious and the reality of their actions in a world that had no room for perfection? To counter Graham there was a veteran ironist, the twentieth century's most influential native-born theologian, Reinhold Niebuhr. He had a much different view of national purpose and consensus.

Born in a Wright City, Missouri, parsonage in 1892, Niebuhr grew to be, in his own words, "a kind of circuit rider" in the colleges and political circles. With his brother Helmut Richard Niebuhr, an equally gifted theologian, Reinhold set the tone for realist Protestant thought for a third of a century. Reinhold served a pastorate in Bethel Evangelical Church in Detroit in the twenties. His eleven years there were as decisive in his thought as the Hell's Kitchen times were for Rauschenbusch. In Detroit, as Niebuhr later put it, he had cut his eyeteeth fighting Henry Ford over the issue of labor organization. He also became friendly with rabbis and Catholic bishops, who helped him overcome many of his old prejudices. And in Detroit he learned to stay close to the lay members of the churches, the religious power base.

After he published his first successful book, in 1927, Union Theological Seminary in New York invited him to teach. He there invented the field of applied Christianity. The seminary location in Morningside Heights, near Columbia University, gave him new exposure to politics and, eventually, through the mass media, to the whole nation. Niebuhr was at home in socialist circles; some would have been ready to type him as an ordinary liberal who was adjusting to modernity until his book *Moral Man and Immoral Society* surprised old-fashioned liberals. It talked darkly of Original Sin, of human impotence and flawed idealism. During the Depression Niebuhr also flirted with Marxian ideas but broke openly with them because he did not believe in their utopian pretensions or the violent class struggle.

In his own attempt to define America, Niebuhr long argued against the school of John Dewey, since Dewey himself was reluctant to be drawn into the debate. To Niebuhr, Dewey seemed shallow and naive, utterly lacking in a tragic sense. Finally, in 1942, but without naming his antagonist, Dewey replied in *Partisan Review;* he rejected the "base and degrading" view of human nature that was then in vogue. Niebuhr's expertise in political matters found him supporters among influentials like Secretary of State Dean Acheson, historian Arthur Schlesinger, Jr., foreign-policy experts George Kennan and Hans Morgenthau, and others.

He took seriously the neo-evangelical leadership in general and

Billy Graham in particular. When the Protestant Council of New York voted to support the Graham Crusade, Niebuhr grumbled. In retrospect his words seem reserved, but when Graham rode high few others dared risk criticizing him. To Niebuhr, the new religiosity looked like self-worship. Graham seemed to overlook true problems of the age; to Niebuhr, the evangelist seemed to miss the point of biblical thought and political realism when he preached that if enough people made decisions for Christ, all would be well. All would *not* be well. It was precisely the "born again" people who often were doing badly, thought Niebuhr, in the areas of race relations, social justice, and world peace. Graham in his effort to produce a Christian America overlooked the biblical concern for the pride of nations. When *Life* magazine published these views during the 1957 New York Crusade, Niebuhr received so many vitriolic letters in support of Graham that he had to wonder in print why conversion did not change people for the better. And when in 1958 Niebuhr affirmed God's covenant with Israel and wanted evangelists to call off their mission to the Jews, their attacks against him grew even more intense.

Three times at book length Niebuhr looked at the whole shape of American history, most notably in *The Irony of American History,* which appeared in 1952. He compared America once again to the chosen people of Israel; unlike most churchly predecessors, but like Abraham Lincoln, he saw America as anything but virtuous and innocent. From the beginning, Americans experienced special temptations to success and power and forgot that they were creatures. God laughed at the pretensions of such nations. He showed mercy to peoples not when enough individuals expressed decisions for Christ at rallies but when nations overcame pretense and vanity. This, "Christian America" was not likely to do.

In Niebuhr's reading, the conflict with communism laid bare all the old American illusions. While Americans blasted communist materialism, they scanted their own idolatry of things, their worship of their own prosperity. They were blind to the fact that theirs was a paradise of domestic security "suspended in a hell of global insecurity." We Americans, he went on, "find it almost as difficult as the communists to believe that anyone could think ill of us, since we are persuaded as they that our society is so essentially virtuous that only malice could prompt criticism of any of our actions." Billy Graham and Fulton Sheen could also criticize the sins of Americans, but during the crusade against communism, it was dangerous to do as Niebuhr when he compared American faults to those of Russia.

Niebuhr was not a mere critic; he was a specifically Christian critic who hoped that faith could lead the nation to examine itself. The villains of the era were not just communists or pornographers or modernists; all were guilty. To claim that Americans were pure in a struggle between a God-fearing and a godless civilization, as Eisenhower and Graham suggested, only furthered illusions. In fact the communists were dangerous not because they were godless but because their cause and doctrine made up a "god." Americans too readily claimed God for whatever they fervently desired; even a Christian civilization or people had to learn that God appeared only at the point at which people saw the gap or contradiction between what they wanted and what God had in mind. During the Eisenhower years, the people were not ready for that message. Not until American goals faded late in the 1960s, especially with the Vietnamese War, did such realism make its point.

In contrast to Spellman was the more critical John Courtney Murray — the Catholic counterpart to Reinhold Niebuhr as a theologian of the public order, a debater with secularizers about the nature of national consensus and the role of the churches. Murray was a New Yorker, born in 1904 to a Catholic lawyer from Scotland and his Irish-American wife. Murray joined the Society of Jesus and returned from Rome with a doctorate in 1937. The priest spent the last thirty years of his life teaching at the Jesuit flagship school Woodstock in Maryland.

While Murray was a formidable debater against non-Catholics, he spent much of his energy winning his way among stubborn Catholics who defended life in the old Catholic ghetto. His chief antagonists were Father Joseph C. Fenton, who edited the potent *American Ecclesiastical Review,* and a Catholic University professor, Father Francis J. Connell. The two defended the church against outsiders and kept their eye open for deviations within it. Young Murray must have looked acceptable enough in the beginning, because in 1941 the Jesuits named him the editor of their journal *Theological Studies.* Obediently if unwillingly, he stayed at his post during the war, when superiors would not let him be a military chaplain.

At the end of the war, Murray was a Catholic delegate to a meeting with heads of the Federal Council of Churches. Not until then did he realize how nervous Protestants were about Catholic views of religious freedom. Meanwhile, Protestants in attendance began to learn that they were wrong in thinking that Catholics were all of one mind on the subjects of religious freedom and civil life; clearly Fathers Fenton and Connell were far removed in viewpoint from the young man who was making reflection on this subject his lifework. Meanwhile, Murray was learning that conversation across lines of faith was no threat to Catholics, as the senior priests had contended it was.

In 1949 he argued that the peril for the future was not Protestantism or a Catholic America; these were chimeras. The real peril was secularism. Watch out, he warned, for new nativist attempts to make a religion out of "our Holy Mother the State," efforts that made old Catholic-Protestant battles look beside-the-point.

Soon Rome itself started undercutting Murray. Someone in the Vatican tried to prevent him from speaking at Notre Dame University, lest his "liberal" influence spread. More and more, however, courageous Catholics began siding with Father Murray's views of religious freedom. In the midst of the tumult, the Jesuit Saint Louis University honored him with the Doctor of Laws degree. Murray seemed at last to be winning his way when suddenly Father Vincent McCormick, the Jesuit representative in Rome, let him know that censors had just banned Murray's forthcoming journal article. McCormick's word was gentle and he quoted the censors in scholarly Latin, but Murray read him right and thanked the Roman for his delicate way of saying, "You're through!" No, McCormick responded, Murray was not finished, but he should let questions of church and state relations rest for a while.

Father Murray felt hopeless. He cleared his room of all books on religious freedom and canceled a book contract on the subject. He turned down a University of Chicago invitation to lecture on the theme, since he was taking measures to close the door on ten years of his life. Meanwhile, President Eisenhower named Murray a consultant to the Atomic Energy Commission, and Robert Maynard Hutchins asked him to discuss the definition of America at a meeting of the Fund for the Republic. Out of these talks came a major assignment, before a small but influential audience that took notice and spread word of Murray's clear and fresh voice. He could never go into hiding again, no matter what his priestly enemies asked of him.

On a May evening in 1958, at the World Affairs Center in New

York, Murray startled his audience when he accused them of being conspirators. For a moment he eased up, and they grew somewhat more relaxed as he reminded them, with a half-smile, that to conspire simply and literally means to "breathe together" — something Americans did in four sets of people. These were the familiar religious trio of Protestant, Catholic, and Jew — plus a fourth conspiracy, which the priest called secularism, humanism, or secular humanism. He treated it as a fourth religious faith in America. John Courtney Murray considered that what the conspirators fought over was worthwhile. The American people no longer knew what America was or who they were. He was concerned enough to call their loss of identity an insanity; the complete loss of identity was hell itself.

The Eisenhower era, during which Murray was speaking, was supposed to be a new era of good feelings and interfaith charm. These four conspiracies were supposed to look genteel enough to the Jesuit, but their facades never fooled him. He knew that the conspiracies represented social power, occupied ground, conflicting interests; the conspirators possessed the means to fight for their stakes. Murray attacked the Protestants who understood only power, not law, and who imposed their will and way on minorities. Such people he called barbarians in the civil city, not because they wore bearskins or carried a club, but because under their Brooks Brothers suits and academic robes were children of the wilderness who did not care about American identity and consensus, or, if they cared, wanted to downgrade or eliminate those in other conspiracies.

In debates in the Republic, sooner or later people had to fight over philosophy or theology. This, thought Murray, was difficult. Jews and Catholics and Protestants inherited different histories, lived with separate world-views, and held to conflicting interests. The problem was their inevitable and cherished religious pluralism — the diversity of faiths. The Jesuit thought that in final analysis religious pluralism was against the will of God. That far Fenton and Connell would applaud him, while many anti-Catholics could find their worst fears confirmed. But in the same sentence, Murray affirmed that pluralism *was* the human condition, it was in the script of history, it would not go away. Americans had to live with it and do better with pluralism than they did back in the days of the Know-Nothings and the Ku Klux Klan. "We face a crisis that is new in history," said the priest. The war of words must end, giving way to civilized argument — Murray did not expect or seek full consensus — something that he hardly dared expect to happen. Yet America had no hope at all if it did not turn civil.

Murray's audience and readers had no difficulty getting into focus three of the conspiracies, but many were puzzled over the fourth one. Secularism, or secular humanism, was cool godlessness that traced back to the Enlightenment, when American public religion was spawned. Murray argued that the secularist was and must be at war with the others because his ancestors and he always felt called to oppose churches whenever they claimed any authority higher than individual reason or the state. Here he spoke as if Dewey and the Deweyites were sitting for the portrait. "In secularist theory there can be only one society, one law, one power, and one faith, a civic faith that is the 'unifying' bond of the community, whereby it withstands the assaults of assorted pluralism." This fourth conspiracy had to oppose the "divisive forces" of religion whenever it represented more than a "purely private matter." Religion in general — Eisenhower style — did not disturb secularists. They were at war when religion was a visible, corporate, organized community — what Murray called a Thing.

Henceforth Murray remained a public figure. Before the Democrats in 1960 nominated Senator John F. Kennedy to be the first major Catholic presidential candidate since Alfred E. Smith in 1928, Kennedy asked Murray to serve as a consultant. The new pope, John XXIII, was also creating a new, friendlier spirit in Rome, and the visibility of candidate Kennedy enabled American Catholics to speak up as never before about matters of the Republic and religion.

Murray decided not to wait. He put together articles that became his primer of pluralism, a book he called *We Hold These Truths*. Murray, like Niebuhr, was a favorite of the Luce magazines, and this book merited for him a *Time* cover. Fenton now grew more envious and angry: the book, he thought, was careless, liberal, opposed to papal teaching. This antagonist had a new chance to influence Rome against Murray's open views of religious freedom after Pope John called the Vatican Council. Fenton was going to be an adviser to conservative cardinal Alfredo Ottaviani. Papal legate to America Egidio Vagnozzi, an associate of Ottaviani, took pains pointedly to "disinvite" Murray to Rome, so the priest languished at Woodstock. American prelates played safe during the first council session in 1962, but it was clear that the questions Murray raised were now urgent around the world, and that the council had to take them up. Could it do so without having the foremost expert on the scene? Vagnozzi hoped so. He silenced Murray at Catholic University in 1963, but this act only inspired more Catholics to speak up for change.

Before the second annual session, the American bishops realized that they needed more schooling and dared not neglect the scholar who had most to teach them. Francis Cardinal Spellman, whom Murray always thought of as backward-looking, had the foresight to surprise everyone and invite Murray — a gesture for which the Jesuit remained genuinely grateful. The bishops went further. They asked Murray to prepare their brief for a conceivably epochal "Declaration on Religious Freedom" that was up for debate in 1963.

There were struggles through the 1963 and 1964 meetings. Between sessions Joseph Cardinal Ritter of Saint Louis garnered fresh support. Murray, meanwhile, in good humor tried to convert fence sitters, citing an old folk-ballad about a Negro boy treed by a bear; "O Lord," went his prayer, "if you can't help me, for heaven's sake, don't help the bear." If you cannot in conscience come out for religious freedom, Murray pleaded with such bishops, for conscience' sake don't come out against it. Finally on September 15, 1965, the second day of the last session, "Religious Freedom" came up for voting. Bishop Robert E. Tracy later recalled some gossip he heard at that time: one bishop had said of the document and its defenses, "The voices are the voices of United States bishops; but the thoughts are the thoughts of John Courtney Murray." A test vote showed great support for the document. In the midst of the last debate, Pope Paul VI made an unprecedented trip to the United States, a sign of favor to the nation whose Catholic leaders in the main pushed for the declaration. When voting day finally came, 8 bishops cast invalid ballots, 70 voted against, and 2,308 approved the document. Murray had basically rewritten over 350 years of Catholic doctrine in America — and this only 10 years after he had been silenced for acting as if he were opposed to Catholic teaching. He delighted in the victory for religious freedom but was just as happy to see tucked into the document an acknowledgment that Catholic doctrine in a way can develop, had developed.

Murray wanted to move on to other work. He had only begun to outline a Catholic approach to American identity, to the problems of pluralism and consensus, to defining America spiritually. He had more work to do on "the fourth conspiracy," on secular humanism. The priest felt that the document on religious freedom did no more than bring Catholicism abreast of developments that had happened long before in the secular world. Meanwhile, the four competing conspiracies that Murray helped turn momentarily more civil toward each other had begun to move away from the dreams of consensus. America was again, or was still, a fragmented society; its citizens, as individuals or in groups, asked as urgently as before, "Who am I?" but found surprisingly diverse ways to begin to answer themselves in the 1960s. They had to do so without the help of the two masters of public theology. Reinhold Niebuhr lay silent and ill. Murray was slowed by heart attacks. The latter, surveying the world and the church, said: "There is no doubt that we are all in trouble, but I courageously hope that it is a good kind of trouble." On August 16, 1967, he died in a New York City taxicab.

Murray had named four "conspiracies," and one of them, Judaism, has yet to be mentioned in this context. Judaism was also prospering in the 1950s. The full impact of the Nazi Holocaust had not yet reached the thinking of the Jewish community, even though millions of Jews had lost relatives or friends in the concentration camps. They had not yet connected the Holocaust with the meaning of Jewish faith in God and peoplehood. Nor had they reorganized American Jewish life around the reality of Israel, though support after the state was formed in 1948 came to be the biggest single unifying issue. The Holocaust was remembered with horror and Israel was celebrated with joy. Yet both seemed remote, and many books of Jewish orientation did not do more than mention them.

Instead Jews reflected on the meaning of their ways in America. Racial change — as blacks and Hispanics moved into northern cities and the suburbs lured Jews away — meant the decline of the Jewish ghetto as a power base. Now Jews competed and coexisted in suburbs and in other new communities, where old traditions were hard to keep. They enjoyed a new spirit of tolerance. People of the mid-fifties did not speak much of threats to Jewish survival. (The Six-Day War of 1967 was still a dozen years away.) Instead they talked about Jewish identity. They wanted to know what it was to be in one of three clusters of religionists inside an America whose way of life itself was often regarded as religious.

While many commentators discussed the theme, one of them wrote a classic study that very aptly depicted the times, and the place of religion and Judaism within them. He was Will Herberg, who in 1955 wrote *Protestant-Catholic-Jew,* the most influential account of postwar American faith by a member of any religious group.

Will Herberg's family was from Russia. Like so many of the latecomers in America, his parents found little for themselves in the New York Orthodox synagogues. Will remembered his home environment as being atheistic. As a young man he easily fit into a climate that provided a good hearing for the thought of Karl Marx. Like many other drifting intellectuals in those Depression days, Herberg not only found Marxism to his liking but even joined the Communist party. As both a Jew and a Communist he found Hitlerism repulsive, so when Hitler and Stalin signed their pact, he rejected communism. To him, as to a generation of activists, communism became "a god that failed," so he went off searching further.

At the most crucial moment in his life, he said, he came to read the work of Protestant theorist Reinhold Niebuhr. With his Marxism shattered, Herberg felt "deprived of the commitment and understanding that alone made life liveable." He was ready for conversion, and the Christian thinker converted him — to Judaism! Though by then Herberg had only met the theologian in print, Niebuhr helped Herberg see his whole being, not merely his thinking, shift to its new center in Judaism.

Soon Herberg joined Niebuhr in efforts to use biblical prophetic language in order to judge the civic faith of Americans. His wanderings left some other Jews confused. The Zionists found him insufficiently committed to their cause. The Orthodox found him un-Orthodox; he was a practicing Conservative Jew, and they thought him too divorced from the tradition to interpret its ways, too friendly to non-Jews to keep the faith pure. Herberg was too religious for the secular Jewish intellectuals, and when, in the 1960s, he started writing for the conservative *National Review* of William F. Buckley, Jr., liberal Jews wrote him off. Since Jesuits also helped shape his thought, one wag introduced him as "Professor Will Herberg, also known as Reinhold Niebuhr, S.J." He became ever more steeped in Jewish thought, but taught at a Methodist school, Drew University in New Jersey. Despite the difficulty some Jews had keeping Herberg in focus, countless others of his faith who were thoroughly exposed to American life but who found his Jewish existentialism and social thought to their liking identified with him and his means of asking "Who am I?"

Protestant-Catholic-Jew was an almost desperate attempt to help

Americans move past the conflicts of the interwar period without falling into John Dewey's "state consciousness" and supporting a single civic faith. Though he was a Jew, Herberg worried less about a possible Christian America than about a nation that idolized "The American Way of Life." In his vision, America was neither a melting pot that fused all faiths nor a mere cafeteria line with hundreds of true religious choices. Instead it tended to generate a single "American Way of Life religion." It then provided three means of holding this — through the handles of the faiths mentioned in his book title. During the years of the midcentury revival, should someone ask a typical American, "What are you?" Herberg noted he or she would not likely say "Methodist" or "American" or "Italian-American" — as people in earlier generations might have done — but simply Protestant, Catholic, or Jew. Herberg thought they needed an identity or social location that was more defined than the one America gave. But it must be larger than any that a single sect or ethnic group made available. In the new suburbs, both denominationalism and ethnicity were played down, but never membership in those three faiths.

Almost at once critics in particular groups faulted Herberg for leaving them out. Three million Eastern Orthodox Christians, it was said, were overlooked in his reckoning. Some Anglicans and Lutherans protested that they were not simply to be clumped with Protestants. He looked too much at mainline Protestants and neglected conservative evangelicals. Herberg underestimated the marginal religious groups, bodies like Jehovah's Witnesses and Mormons that stood off militantly from Protestantism. Ethnic differences survived more than the leaders in the fifties had noticed. Most of all, Herberg did not pay attention to the huge differences in outlook and situation between black and white Protestants. Nor did the world he described long last; it emerged only during the Second World War and changed considerably after the Eisenhower revival. Yet, for the moment, Herberg's was a generally satisfying description.

Why was the question of identity so urgent? Herberg answered that except for the Indians, people came to America from elsewhere and needed help to rebuild their lives on new soil. Languages imported by immigrants from other continents did not survive one generation. While ghettos temporarily protected Catholics, Jews, and blacks, America broke down these walls in an age of mobility, intermarriage, and mass communications. The grandchildren of immigrants were too often lost in their own land. But, citing a

"Law" framed by historian Marcus Lee Hansen, Herberg pointed out that "what the son wished to forget, the grandson wishes to remember." The figurative third generation could not easily or en masse recover lost languages and customs, but they could retrieve the general religious ethos of their ancestors.

During this generation of retrieval, Herberg listed the signs of revival around him. The "village atheist" was disappearing. In 1953 church membership, at 59.5 percent of the population, reached an all-time high. President Eisenhower surprised the public when he pointed out that that percentage had multiplied more than three times within a hundred years. Catholics alone were opening four new churches each week. Religious books were best-sellers. Opinion surveys showed that the public regarded religion highly, and even the intellectuals were less hostile than before. Over 95 percent of the people told the polls that they believed in God, and most of them claimed belief in prayer, the Bible, heaven, the church. Herberg did, however, find complacent America ridding itself of the fear of hell. Only 5 percent had any fear of going there.

The Jewish thinker worried about people like John Dewey, who touted "the religions of democracy" and "democracy as a religion." He seemed less concerned than they about the possible "fragmentation" in spiritual life. His was a season of interfaith and ecumenical activity, the halcyon day of councils and mergers. Catholics and Protestants had not begun to make doctrinal peace, but they were allied against secularism and atheistic materialism. Jews were coming back to the often deserted synagogue, which now prospered in the suburbs. Secular Judaism was on the defensive. Lest he sound as complacent as he thought America was, Herberg did voice some worries. One of these concerned Jews. They had arrived and were at home with the American way of life. But they also remained perplexed and restless: Was this all there was to Judaism after all? Had it no higher purpose or destiny?

Momentarily it seemed as if five centuries of religious battling were ended during the revival, but Herberg sensed conflict and tension under the surface. Each group felt itself beleaguered. Protestantism represented a "strong majority group with a growing minority consciousness," because it was adjusting only with difficulty to the idea that it no longer was identical with Americanism. Catholicism was now secure but sounded insecure. Jews had come forward with the strongest set of defensive "anti-defamation" activities at the moment when consensus should have made these unnecessary.

Herberg also expressed his special theological concern. From the viewpoint of biblical prophecy, American Way of Life religion was idolatry. Civic religion always meant making an idol out of the society or culture it reflected and supported. Such faith was a religion of ego and of humans, not of God; a religion of *my* national tribe and not of the whole human family, of *my* thirst for self-identification and not service of others. The "unknown God" of the nation was faith itself; no one, Herberg thought, stated this more clearly or with a larger following than President Eisenhower. As a person of faith, Herberg could only hope that God would turn the follies of this religion into an instrument of His redemptive purpose.

No monk in American history has had more
influence than the Trappist Thomas Merton. His
gifted pen and his eloquence in behalf of social
causes made him known far beyond Catholicism,
and he helped introduce Buddhist and Hindu
contemplative styles among some Americans who
might have resisted them had they not had such
confidence in Merton. (*Edward Rice,*
Pictorial Parade)

Chapter Nineteen

ALWAYS A HORIZON

$\mathscr{F}$ FOR THE TWO DECADES AFTER WORLD WAR II, AMERICANS, SHOW-
ing a revived interest in religion, gave signs of wanting to work for
a consensus in national life. They supported interfaith projects,
especially between Christians and Jews. Never before had Christians drawn nearer each other than in this era of new councils and
federations. The nation did not turn out to be as godlessly secular
as prophets of modernity predicted it would be or as simply materialistic as the prophets of God often charged. Will Herberg's picture
of an America in which people found identity as Protestants, Catholics, and Jews, all in support of a common American way of life
seemed plausible. John Courtney Murray's suggestion that nonreligious humanism was also a kind of religiousness added richness,
not conflict, to the picture. Meanwhile, Reinhold Niebuhr taught
citizens to have an ironic view of their nation, its history, its religious ideals.

Niebuhr's irony is most helpful for understanding what happened next. The consensus did *not* arrive, or, if it did, did not hold
the way midcentury observers expected it to. The later 1960s saw
Americans in conflict as seldom before: men versus women, young
people versus their elders, leftists versus right-wingers, hawks
versus doves, blacks versus whites, homosexuals versus straights,
hippies versus squares, Eastern religionists versus conventional
congregants, countercultural Aquarians against nostalgic upholders

of the olden ways — these all conspired to show how diverse and restless, how unsettled Americans were.

We have been looking at Americans on a constant pilgrimage; they are not a "settled" people. That observation may seem commonplace, almost banal — hardly enough to hold together the story of five hundred years of religion. Yet if we contrast the situation to most of world religion, its drama stands out. Most Eastern religions — Buddhist, Hindu, Taoist, and the like — seek timelessness and constancy or even escape from history. Islam prides itself on consistent "submission" — Islam *means* submission — to the will of Allah unchangingly revealed in the Koran.

As for Europe, the antecedents of American spiritual restlessness were present in Judaism and majority Christianity. Only a near-sighted historian would fail to see cultural change and religious novelty in two millennia of European religion. Yet the fact that religion was almost everywhere officially established and privileged to hold a monopoly from the time missionaries or conquerors arrived until the recent past meant that there was little choice for most citizens but to go along with the culture. When the Protestant Reformation came to Europe, it simply changed the doctrines and personnel at the head of most establishments, leaving dissenters and radicals at the margin.

Rabbi Solomon Schechter may have been right in 1903 when he said that Americans were conservative in religion. They have, in the main, imported and lived with inherited Judaism and Christianity, tempered by Enlightenment ideals. Yet several things happened in the twentieth-century context to change the circumstance. For one thing, the American land was vast, so people were lured always to find new places and try new things. There was always a horizon, a frontier, a wilderness, a new city, a new suburb. The mix of peoples was awesomely complex. One never got settled before a new set of neighbors came in to challenge old ways. How to welcome newcomers? How should immigrants adapt? Americans also offered visions of great futures, futures often denied those who dreamed. Yet they could always look forward to the Kingdom, the Millennium, Utopia, or a new plan. Some entrepreneur or innovator would soon come up with such a vision for others to follow.

America's has been a story of the dialogue with the land, with new peoples, with pathfinders of vision — pioneers who conspired to prevent Americans from becoming spiritually "settled," even within traditions. G. K. Chesterton once said that if you want a white fence post, you have to stay busy. You cannot let it alone; it will not stay white. Weather, dogs, weeds, corrosion, and decay will conspire to yellow and gray it. Conservatives are very busy people. The choice to stay with a tradition is a strenuous one. Edmund Burke wrote that if it is not necessary to change, it is necessary not to change. That involves a willful act, a spiritual decision. So even those Americans who have been *apparently* settled in environment and tradition have not been actually settled, as our story into the present generation has made clear. And the present generation seems busiest, most restless, of all.

In 1958 Jacques Maritain, the prominent French Catholic philosopher who taught at a number of American universities, offered mature reflections on America during what others saw as the age of consensus. The guest chose to highlight the American pilgrimage: "Americans seem to be in their own land as pilgrims, prodded by a dream. They are always on the move . . . , not *settled, installed.*" While he warned that their sense of becoming could turn into a worship of change or a horror of tradition, Maritain also saw in it a spiritual feeling about "the impermanence of earthly things" and thought that it belied the Americans' reputation for materialism and gave depth to their strivings.

The decades since the Frenchman wrote have seen ever more pilgrims, more proddings by their dreams, more restless movement on the American road. While many pilgrims found new routes, almost none of the earlier paths were abandoned. A new generation showed interest in the oldest native American ways, in the inherited roots of Afro-Americans, and in the ancient ethnic and tribal bonds of Judaism and Christianity.

Sixteen years after Maritain reflected on the dream, economist Robert Heilbroner dealt with the American nightmare in *An Inquiry into the Human Prospect.* Threats of drastic world population growth, final nuclear war, and environmental dangers led Heilbroner to picture future reversals of long trends. The new society could not sustain unrestrained producing and consuming; people in the future would not be able to pursue scientific knowledge, delight in intellectual heresy, or enjoy ordering their lives entirely as they pleased. He spelled out as prophecy what sounded like a report on religion in his day. On the horizon in postindustrial society, Heilbroner thought, were preindustrial instincts for "the exploration of inner states of experience rather than the outer world of fact and material accomplishment. Tradition and ritual, the pillars of life in virtually all societies other than those of an industrial character," he foresaw, "would probably once again assert their ancient claims as the guide to and solace for life." And the struggle for material individual achievement was "likely to give way to the acceptance of communally organized and ordained roles."

In the short range, some details of that prophecy did not seem to be fulfilled. After a few years of revolt in the late 1960s, young Americans settled down again toward relentless pursuit of mainstream culture's benefits, including material achievements in an ever more hazardous economy. What Heilbroner called "social morale" was hard to generate while citizens consumed energy resources as hungrily as ever and looked out for personal interests. But they also balanced these drives with more attention to "inner states of experience . . . tradition and ritual . . . [and] acceptance of communally organized and ordained roles" than the prophets of the early 1960s ever envisioned. Whatever the long-term outcome of the prophecy, for two decades, at least, Americans surprised themselves and their visitors by the inward turn their spiritual journey took.

As we have found throughout this story, a view of an individual pilgrim may serve better than talk about pilgrimage. No American was a better pathfinder for his compatriots than the Catholic monk Thomas Merton, who died in 1968. His influence lived on far beyond Catholicism, and his life for a generation prefigured many of the courses that people in postindustrial societies were expected to take — though, to be sure, his monastic journey was more strenuous than were most. Merton continued the American pilgrimage, seemed "prodded by a dream" and, though he lived in a monastery, was never settled, never installed.

The son of an expatriate American and a roving New Zealand artist, Merton was born in the little Pyrenees town of Prades in 1915. Though his mother had casual Quaker ties, they provided few spiritual roots and never much security as the father's career faltered. One day young Thomas received a note from his mother in the hospital; from it he deduced that she was dying of cancer. This letter provided the shattering experience that seems so often to set a gifted child on a startling course. "I took the note out under the maple tree in the back yard, and worked over it, until I had made it all out, and had gathered what it all really meant. And a tremendous weight of sadness and depression settled on me. It was not the grief of a child, with pangs of sorrow and many tears. It had something of the heavy perplexity and gloom of adult grief, and was therefore all the more of a burden." Merton thus learned early the transiency of life. Both in his later forms of escape as well as in his responsibilities, he never was free of the burden, and he became a pilgrim of the eternal.

In 1931 his father died in England. Grandparents took over young Tom's nurture; by the age of eighteen, he had lived in Bermuda, on Long Island, in England, and in Italy, but he never found a spiritual home. Anglicanism, a "class religion," appealed only briefly. He lost what little faith he ever knew, and filled the void by reading modern literature until the poetry of the Jesuit Gerard Manley Hopkins began to lead him toward faith.

In Italy his religious interests had quickened, but they led to no deep movement of will, no conversion, "nothing to shake the iron tyranny of moral corruption" that held his "whole nature in fetters." This language sounded like that of Jonathan Edwards and the old evangelicals, but he took a different course than they. A first stirring occurred in his room one night. The sense of his father's presence was there with him. "The whole thing passed in a flash. . . . my soul desired escape and liberation and freedom . . . with an intensity and an urgency unlike anything I had ever known before." He reflected: "I think for the first time in my whole life I really began to pray . . . to the God that I had never known to reach down towards me out of His darkness and to help me to get free of the thousand terrible things that held my will in their slavery." He had begun his spiritual odyssey, but, as was the case with so many who turned before him, this mild conversion did not endure.

In both England and America Merton dabbled without satisfaction in a number of churches and went on to a disastrous career as a student, until his appointed guardian finally despaired of him. In 1934 Merton came to the United States to stay. That was a good year for a sensitive searcher to read Karl Marx, and Merton did so until he fancied himself a Marxist. At Columbia University, however, the Young Communist League seemed too rigid and violent for him, so he came back to his first loves, literature and poetry. Merton wrote for *The Jester,* raised hell, studied some, drank, caroused, grew, browsed, and experimented with "Blake, Thomas Aquinas, Augustine, Eckhart, Coomaraswamy, Traherne, Hopkins, Maritain, and the sacraments of the Catholic Church."

While teetering toward Catholicism, Merton, anticipating a theme of his own later life, stepped out ahead of his generation by looking to Eastern religion a quarter of a century before it became voguish to do so. A Hindu monk named Bramachari, who had represented his monastery at the Chicago world's fair of 1933, lingered on to take a doctorate at the University of Chicago, after which he spread his word around the country. Merton, ripe for that word, soon felt compelled not to turn Eastward spiritually but to look for monastic and mystical revivals in the West. He wrote a master's thesis on the Christian mystic and poet William Blake, and then, in 1938, asked Catholic chaplain George B. Ford for tutelage. Not long after, he was baptized.

After a sleepless night one year later, Merton announced that he wanted to take his pilgrimage to the monastery. Though the Franciscans turned down his application, he chose to live by their rule in any case while he taught at one of their colleges. Then, when World War II came, the young professor, registered as a noncombatant objector, took the more drastic step of applying for admission to the Trappists, the strictest order of monks. To his surprise and relief, they accepted him. When Merton, now a budding writer, looked at the war around him and the barrenness within him, he gave voice to what so many wandering Americans felt: "The sense of exile bleeds inside me like a hemorrhage. Always the same wound, whether a sense of sin or of holiness, or of one's own insufficiency, or of spiritual dryness." To heal that wound, he turned himself over to the Trappists, knowing he "would have to give up *everything* — including, could it be, being a writer?"

Three days after Pearl Harbor, in 1941, the doors of Our Lady of Gethsemani monastery south of Louisville, Kentucky, closed on Merton. On a visit to the abbey the previous Holy Week, he had written: "This is the center of America. I had wondered what was holding the country together, what was keeping the universe from falling apart. It is places like this monastery — not only this one: there must be others. This is the only real city in America — and it is by itself, in the wilderness. It is an axle around which the whole country blindly turns."

While his Trappist superiors swore Merton to their usual discipline of silence, they did allow him to write. Despite twenty-seven years of self-doubts and attacks by other monks, he wrote nearly fifty books and hundreds of articles. For a time he taught novice monks in the community, but as early as 1947 he began to appeal for a hermitage to pursue solitude. Not until 1965 did officials of his order permit him to move into a lonely hut near the abbey buildings. By then national fame had come to him for his autobiography, *The Seven Storey Mountain,* and other books that a generation of searchers used to serve as models for their own spiritual journeys.

Never did "Father M. Louis" — Merton was ordained in 1949 — forget Bramachari's advice to read the mystical literature of the West, but at the time of his ordination he also began to correspond with a Hindu, who opened the lore of the East for him. Though the Trappist first found nothing in Eastern theology that seemed absent in the Catholic mystics, oriental religions gradually enlarged his repertory of spiritual choices. Ten years later he approached Zen teacher D. T. Suzuki with a book he had written on the Desert Fathers of the early church. Would Suzuki help him move from there in his search for a universal, all-embracing vision of life? Merton in this encounter learned that he was unable and unwilling to convert to Zen, nor could he fuse faiths; yet he set out to learn from the East in order to deepen what he already was.

After the mid-sixties, just before many dissenters in church and society turned radical in protest against racial injustices and the expanding war in Vietnam, Merton anticipated them with his own decisive turn. His isolation contributed to the rigor of his dour outlook. While his abbot had permitted Merton to move to the chill cement-block hut, he refused permission to finish the building. For two years it lacked a kitchen, a toilet, a chapel. Quite naturally the monk suffered ill health there, but he wrote on with fresh passion. His superiors censored him as never before, yet he somehow managed to publish more fiery work than ever. He raged against the war in Vietnam, where he saw no moral base for the American side. In his hermitage, frustrated and angered by what he pictured going on around him, Merton imagined the day when white Americans would build concentration camps for the final solution to the Negro problem. "We are all living in a myth dream which is essentially racist and we do not realize it." And Americans, he thought, were also out of touch with the poor of the world and the "primitives." He pointed to the spiritual chaos: "We are out of contact with our own depths. It is our own primitive self which has become alien, hostile and strange."

Intimates who spoke to Merton in 1968 sensed such restlessness that some deduced he might turn against the vows he had made so long before. Merton squelched such notions: "Keep telling everyone that I am a monk of Gethsemani and intend to remain one all my days." But he did set up a trust for his papers, gave prescriptions for his own burial, and wrote farewell letters to three women friends. Then he departed for Bangkok, Calcutta, Darjeeling, and Dharmsala — a twentieth-century jet-age spiritual sojourner. In December he was at Bangkok, speaking on Marxist and monastic perspectives. In a talk on the tenth of that month, Merton made some comments questioning whether celibacy would continue to be a necessary aid for attaining higher spirituality. Expecting to meet audience response later, at the conference of monks scheduled for that afternoon, he went to his room to rest. Someone heard a cry from it. Merton evidently had come out of the shower with wet feet, touched an electric fan that had an exposed and defective cord, and was electrocuted. Loving friends took him back to Gethsemani, "the center of America," and there laid him to rest.

In *The Seven Storey Mountain* Merton already had foreseen his death and had advised others: "Do not ask when it will be or where it will be or how it will be: . . . It does not matter." On this side of death, the pilgrim must always be on the journey, seeking and probing, seldom at rest — even within a hermitage, where the world of external fact still pressed in on him. Yet as Merton set out for Asia, he spoke for many who would search in his trail, about the "matter of growth, deepening, and of an ever greater surrender to the creative action of love and grace in our hearts. Never was it more necessary for us to respond to that action." And then the politically minded monk summed up in half a line words that spoke for countless travelers outside the monastery, words familiar to readers of Maritain and Heilbroner: "Our real journey in life is interior. . . ."

Why bring up Merton as a model or representative of anything? Never mind that a list of his writings is as long as a short book, a sign that he had a following through publishers. Never mind that the list of writings about him has grown to book length and is an industry. No, he was, after all, a Trappist monk. There never were many of them, and quite a few of the few of his generation have left the monastery. Catholicism speaks for only fifty million, not all, Americans, and the monastic voice is a minority even there. Few Americans have time for the intense spiritual journey to which Merton's call took him. Yet, after listing all the reasons to see him as eccentric, there are also good reasons to post him as a pathfinder at the most recent turn in the road. Often the person of radical vision sees early what others do not see as yet, but learn to see through his or her eyes. Often the person of radical commitment makes footprints into which the more timid can fit their own feet.

In a way, Merton can serve for this purpose for some readers, though others may have their own pathfinders or examplars.

Few Americans followed the precise path of Merton and the monks. The sixties and seventies remained years of public action, of attempts to change the exterior world. But through it all, sensitive citizens, young and old, combined the life of action with the interior journey. Heilbroner was right: curiously, many of them turned not to future utopias but to images of primitive and simpler paths to find their way past the complexities of modernity. They wanted to go back: to nature, to the primitives, to the American Indians, to Catholic authority, to Africa, to the Bible, to the old family album of old-time religion, to the experience of being born again, and even back spiritually to the Asian continent from which the pilgrimage to America began tens of thousands of years before.

This modern Asia, however, had little in common with prehistoric Siberia, so many who looked for roots began to pay new attention to the old American Indian ways. By the later 1960s the natives spoke for themselves as never before. The Indian ways — attractive as they became to young people in the "counterculture" and to romantics in the environmental movement — were a matter of survival to native Americans themselves. Modern-day Indians could not withdraw into private spirituality, for they had to engage in public action.

Ernie Peters, a South Dakota Sioux who blended anger with soul, spoke for the activists. "Before everything we do, we pray. You can't do anything without thanking the Creator for it, and when you are done you give thanks again. You own nothing. You don't even possess your body; it belongs to mother earth. All you possess is your spirit. But the simplest form of energy is there: the energy of the human soul. Spirituality is what [our movement] is all about." Land and tribe and spirit: these were the constant American Indian themes. Despite attempts to deprive them of the last of their land, the natives survived centuries of injustice to live on, often demoralized, fearful that city life would disperse them, or that their young would all be lured from the old ways. A new generation of leaders tried to promote morale; among them was Vine Deloria, Jr., whose book titles proclaimed: *God is Red; We Talk, You Listen; Custer Died for Your Sins.* Deloria reminded Americans of European descent that tribal people still regarded the landscape as sacred. He also combined militancy with the journey inward; with his colleagues, he tried to teach other Americans that protest was itself spiritual.

Pat Bellanger, a leader of AIM, the American Indian Movement, justified activities like the Indian takeovers of a Roman Catholic center in Wisconsin, of Alcatraz Island in San Francisco Bay, and of the Bureau of Indian Affairs in Washington; he also defended the 1973 siege at Wounded Knee, South Dakota, where his people's story had almost ended eighty years before. To Bellanger, these actions emerged from "a core, a very hard religious core." Eddie Benton Banai, his AIM counterpart in Minnesota, insisted that "spiritualism is the tradition of the tie that binds us down to our ancestors." At the South Dakota mission begun in the nineteenth century by "the angel of the West," abbot and bishop Martin Marty, South Dakota Indian Margaret Fischer formed the "Face the Enemy Survival School." There she battled industrial and Christian ways that, she said, confused the Indian young. And later, militant Fred Zephier spoke for AIM in classic Indian language: "All we're asking for is land, to have our own laws, be free. . . ."

On rare occasions, at least, Indians made their point to Congress and those citizens who cared. A climax of such activity — an event no doubt overlooked by the general public, but still revelatory — occurred in the matter of Blue Lake, which is almost hidden on the slopes of Mount Wheeler, the highest peak in New Mexico. This wondrously pure lake, whose colors range on different days from azure to sapphire to indigo, greets the weary climber who reaches it (at the 11,288-foot level) with a splendor that makes the Indian concept of its sacredness easy to grasp. The Taos Indians long resented intruding fishermen who littered its shores with beer cans and cigarette butts. They had once felt secure that their Blue Lake shrine would stay out of reach of trespassers. After many centuries, they still shared the ancestral regard for their lake as the font of their life and health, the site for their rites, the abode of their spirits after death, the point of their beginnings and endings, the simple center of their existence.

In 1906, however, the United States government made the Blue Lake area part of the Carson National Forest; forty-eight thousand acres seemed too vast a holding for a mere fourteen hundred natives. The Indians, knowing that already nine million acres of New Mexico were protected by the government, protested the move, as they had World War I measures that opened these lands for grazing by the flocks and herds of others. The Pueblos persisted in making day-long ascents to the lake for ceremonies that governmental officials regarded as somehow savage and subversive. In 1922 government officials even assaulted the Taos council chamber, charging that the natives were animal-like, their annual ceremonies too pagan to be allowed in America. Pueblo sullenness was well grounded.

Only one or two whites were ever permitted to observe the Blue Lake rituals, to see Indians don robes, light fire, and lose themselves in dances. All night long "they moved like the masses of smoke, like wind made visible, like masses of clouds heaving over this sacred mountain." They called up the spirits of the wild, trying to merge with nature and to realize their wholeness and unity as a people. In their dance they drew near to their ancestors and the spirits of the sacred lake and mountain. Observer John Collier gasped. "Forces of the wild and of the universe had heard the call and had taken the proffered dominion, . . . endowing a disinherited race with an eagle's wings."

Two worlds conflicted when Indians pressed their claims on Blue Lake. Government leaders wondered why Indians could not settle for shrines built by hands; why could they not make religion a portion of their day and week? An adopted son of the Taos Pueblo, John Yaple, complained that "even some people in the Forest Service say there are no shrines up there. They're looking for man-made structures. But every source of water is a shrine — no need for a building around it. The Indians don't think they can improve on the work of God." In 1965 the Taos poor turned down offers of "mighty dollars. We want the land," came back the word, "where we can worship freely." The counterarguments they heard from Washington sounded plausible enough: other Indians, for example, regarded the Grand Canyon and the Tetons as sacred. Nine-tenths of the United States fell into someone's claim. How could the nation satisfy such demands at this late date? Opponents of pro-Taos measures argued that Indians were themselves not pure: they overgrazed the slopes and, for a price, smuggled in visiting fishermen to Blue Lake.

Despite all odds, the Indians eventually picked up important friends. The Roman Catholic archbishop of Santa Fe and leaders of the National Council of Churches supported them. Kim Agnew, the daughter of the vice-president of the United States, drew attention to the lake by taking a horseback trip there. Liberal senator Robert F. Kennedy and conservative senator Barry Goldwater teamed for the cause, as did two succeeding secretaries of the interior. An aide of President Richard Nixon, Len Garment, stepped forward in defense of the natives' "sacred tabernacle" and argued that "a spiritual vision cannot be compensated by money." On July 8, 1970, President Richard Nixon called the Blue Lake issue one of "unique and critical importance" and asked Congress to make a symbolic move to show governmental responsiveness to Indian grievances. In December of that year, after the United States Senate voted to end sixty-four-year-old claims on Blue Lake, Nixon signed the bill into law. But what was a climactic symbol became only a token; Blue Lake was the highwater mark of Indian success. For the public was concentrating on the action and spirituality of the much larger and more dispersed black minority.

After three and a half centuries, the African peoples in America, to use their own most evocative metaphor, had known many a Moses but still seemed a pilgrim people. Brought in slavery to a land they one day freely adopted, they were still seeking a promised land. After 1954, when the Supreme Court in *Brown v. Board of Education* insisted on equal educational opportunity for all citizens by striking down the "separate but equal" approach, black assertiveness for rights increased. In the 1960s the movement found its voice and gained hearing. The Reverend Albert B. Cleage of Detroit spoke of the recent "religiocification" of this movement, though religion long had played a major part in black struggles for freedom. Most of the twentieth-century black leaders, like their predecessors, were "reverends" — agents of the churches, which remained the strongest institutions blacks possessed. Now as before, ever since slaveholders and evangelists first taught it to them, the language of their calls for freedom sounded biblical. They saw their own story in the exodus of Israel from slavery and in the story of a suffering Jesus who triumphed.

Black leaders contended that the African world view was different from that of the American majority. While blacks used the same Bible and gathered in Baptist and Methodist denominations as did whites, many preserved some of their "Africanity." This meant that they criticized aspects of modernity because it chopped up the different aspects of their existence. They were opposed to complexity in religion, as in the rest of life.

When Albert B. Cleage mounted the pulpit of his Shrine of the Black Madonna on any Sunday in the 1960s, he invoked the biblical language of liberation. "If we were to describe the black man's life in America today, we could certainly call ourselves shepherds in the wilderness, propertyless, wandering nomads, going from place to place, dependent upon chance, upon circumstances, without a real place to call home." Cleage scolded blacks who were content with their bondage as if he were speaking for God to them as Israel: "I am sending you back into the wilderness because you lack the courage to do the things necessary to enter into the promised land." Now the basic task, he thought, was to form a black "nation within a nation." If it was too soon for Cleage's congregation to enter the promised land, they at least could help prepare their children to do so. The Reverend J. Deotis Roberts seconded the idea that the "search for the new land" was now urgent. He did not call for a move back to Africa, but supported W. E. B. Du Bois's idea of "two-ness." Blacks would always look to Africa as really foreign, too remote in place and time to allow for return. They must remain Americans — but, as blacks, Americans with a difference.

By the time Cleage and Roberts gained an audience for "black theology," the man certain to be forever remembered as the prophet of the black resurgence had already risen and fallen. He was the Reverend Martin Luther King, Jr., who drew much, much less on African roots than on his black-Baptist commitment. He was, however, also as ready as Thomas Merton to look for light from the East. In his case, a mentor was Mohandas K. Gandhi, the Hindu teacher of nonviolent social change.

At seminary King had read Walter Rauschenbusch and had absorbed the Social Gospel. He recalled learning that "the gospel deals with the whole man, not only his soul but his body." His professors, however, told him that Social Gospel progressivism was out of touch with hard realities and injected him with a dose of Reinhold Niebuhr's "Christian realism." King fused the two motifs, just as he blended faith in Jesus with lessons from Gandhi.

While at Boston, King married Coretta Scott, a promising singer who became a reluctant but effective co-worker, and then took up a pastorate at the Dexter Avenue Baptist Church, near the capitol in Montgomery, Alabama. At first King began quietly. But on Thursday, December 1, 1955, a footsore black woman, Rosa Parks, refused to give up her seat on a public bus, was arrested, and became the inspiration for a 382-day boycott of city buses. This action changed Montgomery, as well as Alabama, the United States, and the world that kept its eye on the largest racial minority in America. During the boycott, King won the backing of other churches for his program of "persuasion, not coercion" to fight racial injustice. This policy, because it depended upon nonviolence, forced King to help his people become, as he told them, *very* strong. He himself had to be especially strong, for he faced a sequence of arrests on trumped-up charges — charges based on laws that were not compatible with the Bill of Rights and that violated conscience and a "higher law." King's home was bombed, his life threatened.

The minister soon took his cause to the nation. At New York's Cathedral of Saint John the Divine, he preached that the decree of the Supreme Court had "opened the Red Sea and the forces of justice are moving to the other side." In August of 1956, as a national figure, he pressed legal claims of blacks before the Democratic party's platform committee. As he met with presidents, King was marked as a friend of communism by his tireless foe, Federal Bureau of Investigation Director J. Edgar Hoover, who was secretly investigating his private life. In 1960 President Eisenhower and Vice-President Nixon chose to be silent in the face of what appeared to be his patently unjust arrest and imprisonment, but Democratic presidential candidate John F. Kennedy and his brother Robert, who would become attorney general, phoned Coretta to comfort her and called a judge to urge him to grant bail. Dwight Eisenhower was later to say that these two phone calls had swung the black vote and the election to Kennedy.

In 1963, while imprisoned in a Birmingham, Alabama, jail, King wrote a letter that was first published in *The Christian Century*. It became a classic appeal for rights denied blacks after 340 years. "There are *just* laws and there are unjust laws," the letter said. With Saint Augustine, King reasoned that a truly unjust law was no law at all. As he argued his case, the minister called attention to the burgeoning and potentially violent Black Muslim movement, which loomed as a threat should white Americans continue to deny rights. "It is made up of people who have lost faith in America, who have absolutely repudiated Christianity, and who have concluded that the white man is an incurable 'devil,' " added King. The Negro church offered the best hope for nonviolent change.

While the prison letter circulated, the public became familiar with pictures of police dogs and fire hoses that law officers used on black youths in Birmingham, along with images of Governor George Wallace blocking the doors of the University of Alabama to black students on June 11, 1963. The next night a King associate, Medgar Evers, was assassinated in front of his Mississippi home. On August 28 two hundred thousand protestors gathered for a "March on Washington," where, at the Lincoln Memorial, King prodded them with his dream of racial equality. In December 1964, the thirty-five-year-old minister received the Nobel Peace Prize.

On a Sunday night in March 1965, television portrayals of police brutalities against demonstrators at Selma, Alabama, occasioned a march by national religious leaders in support of the King movement. Days later President Lyndon B. Johnson himself took to television to plead the cause. In the months that followed, Congress passed more civil rights legislation than ever before or since, but the moment of triumph was short. The Vietnam War, now being stepped up, divided America. Anarchic and frustrated blacks in Los Angeles, Detroit, Newark, and elsewhere rioted and burned their own ghettos. "Black Power!" replaced "We shall overcome" as a slogan, and separation increasingly took the place of integration as the new racial ideal.

King met failure in his efforts to tackle the problem of segregated housing in the North, particularly in Chicago. In the spring of 1968, he traveled to Memphis to support a garbage workers' strike. By then the preacher was speaking foreboding language: "Like anybody, I would like to live a long life. Longevity has its place. But I'm not concerned about that now. I just want to do God's will. And He's allowed me to go to the mountain. And I've looked over, and I've seen the promised land." On April 4, the day after he uttered the words, King was murdered on a motel balcony; ne'er-do-well James Earl Ray was arrested, pleaded guilty, and was sentenced to life imprisonment. King's body rests under a stone in Atlanta; on it is inscribed a phrase from a favorite Negro spiritual: "Free at last."

While J. Edgar Hoover for some years had been doing what he could to fire hatred of King among whites, other blacks had become King's attackers. The Reverend Adam Clayton Powell, a congressman from Harlem, called him "Martin Loser King" and discredited his nonviolent approach. Playwright LeRoi Jones named nonviolence a "white missionary syndrome." Another newcomer, Floyd McKissick, pronounced nonviolence dead at the hands of whites. At a press conference one day after King died, an emerging black leader of brief fame, Stokely Carmichael, saw the death of King as a declaration of war on blacks, for King was the last teacher of love, compassion, and mercy for whites. Blacks gained some civil rights and a minority of them found new economic and social advantage. But the number of black unemployed youths and the size of ghettos both grew. Cities remained segregated, and so did most churches. Yet King had introduced a new spirit to America by invoking the old biblical themes of promise and the dreams of concord.

In retrospect, the King approach looks moderate and, located in its black-Baptist context, rather conventional. During his prime, non-Christian ideology also gained its largest following among blacks, chiefly through the Nation of Islam, or Black Muslim, movement, which King noted as a threat in his letter from the Birmingham jail. In the course of those years, Elijah Muhammad, the prophet of the Nation, and his devotee and later rival, Malcolm X, offered an alternative. They demanded separation of races and insisted on space in America for separate existence. *The Autobiography of Malcolm X* became a modern classic of revolt literature; the media soon posed him over against King.

Malcolm X looked back in bitterness on what "good Christians" had done to him. They burned his childhood home in Michigan, had his father thrown under a streetcar, and gave him countless other reasons to repudiate them. He told a Swedish television interviewer in 1964 that his family lived in total poverty after his mother was sent to a mental hospital and the children were dispersed to foster homes. Later, as "Detroit Red," Malcolm became a Harlem hustler, a street man ready with a gun. Arrested and imprisoned, he later reformed himself as a member of "the Lost-Found Nation of Islam," in which Chicagoan Elijah Muhammad popularized the ideas of a mysterious Detroit peddler named Wallace C. Fard, who had disappeared in the thirties. The new leader fused an unorthodox reading of the Islamic scriptures with revelations of his own to build a puritanical Black Muslim society; on it he imposed military discipline.

In 1960 at the Boston University School of Theology, where King had earned his doctorate, Malcolm X spelled out his anti-Christianism. "The colonization of the dark people in the rest of the world was done by Christian powers. The number one problem that most people face in the world today is how to get freedom from Christians." To Muslims, the Christian was a white man, a slavemaster. In prison Malcolm X learned to regard blacks as a nation within a nation. He came to look for ways to escape the horror of slavemaster religion and addiction to alcohol and drugs.

For a time the young man was content with the vision of Elijah Muhammad; he agreed that "America is the place where Allah will make himself felt." He learned the details of prophecy: while white history was only six thousand years old, the Nation of Islam founder learned from Allah that blacks were "sixty-six trillion years" old as a people. While most members in both races smiled at such a myth, the smile shrouded a fear, for few could yet foresee limits to the Black Muslim rise. For centuries whites had wanted blacks to be separate, but now they trembled to hear Black Muslims agree with them too emphatically through calls for "some good earth, right here in America, where we can go off to ourselves." When asked how such dreams of place would work out, Malcolm X liked to answer, "those who say don't know, and those who know aren't saying." But if America could help subsidize Israel, he asked, why could not the local black in fairness have a piece of land, along with technical help and money?

Elijah Muhammad came to consider Malcolm X a hazard. Though in person the disciple could be gentle, he used hate as an instrument against Christians like Martin Luther King. When a jet plane full of art patrons from Atlanta crashed in France, Malcolm called it a "very beautiful thing," an answer to prayer: "We call on our God, and He gets rid of 120 of them at one whop." Was this kind of gloating over a crash different, he asked, than when Americans thanked God after they dropped a bomb on Hiroshima that killed a hundred thousand Japanese? "You did it in the name of God; . . . we rely on God."

After the killing of popular president John F. Kennedy in 1963, Malcolm X finally overstepped by rejoicing over "the chickens coming home to roost." Elijah Muhammad silenced the firebrand for ninety days and began to freeze him out, until Malcolm was reduced to pleading for audiences and had to protect himself with bodyguards and guns. In 1964 he parted with the Black Muslims to form Muslim Mosque, Incorporated, still holding the dream of "complete separation, with our people going back home, to our own African homeland." Yet he also sounded somewhat more moderate; he compared himself to Billy Graham as a shaper of a people. Just as Graham did not organize his own church, so Malcolm X would ask blacks not to follow him but to join any black nationalist organization.

After a hajj, or pilgrimage to Mecca, Malcolm finally identified with Orthodox Islam. He joined the Sunni Muslim sect and became El-Hajj Malik El-Shabazz. While some Africans thought of him as a national leader, Elijah Muhammad threatened chastisement for this "chief hypocrite." Malcolm X might have been relieved to hear his former leader ask that the hypocrite be allowed to survive as an example to others, but he also took what steps he could to take away reasons for the Nation of Islam to help Allah along in any threatened chastisement. He muted his violent words: "Even I prefer ballots to bullets." While whites had once been devils, now he could speak in praise of three who gave their lives in Mississippi for black causes.

In 1964 Muhammad stepped up attacks on this "international hobo," announcing that "the die is set, and Malcolm shall not escape. . . . Such a man as Malcolm is worthy of death." After the firebombing of his home, the beleaguered younger leader made his most moderate speech at Detroit. "I am not a racist," he pleaded; he wanted voluntary separation, not forced segregation.

After the gesture of peace, he returned to the turmoil of his headquarters in New York, there to prepare for a meeting on the following Sunday at the Audubon Ballroom. On that announced afternoon, while his helpers set up their guard, a warm-up man readied the assembled crowd: "I present . . . one who would give his life for you." Malcolm strode onto the sunlit stage, smiled, and, in words preserved on tape, said "*As-salaam alaikum*"; the audience responded with its greeting, "*Wa-alaikum salaam.*" Then a disturbance erupted; two men in the rear started to fight. When the people turned their heads to see this staged distraction, a man with a double-barreled sawed-off shotgun moved forward and blasted point-blank at Malcolm's chest. He was dead on arrival at a medical center across the street.

Though eventually three men were convicted of conspiracy and the killing, suspicious blacks blamed the government, not a "tong war," for his death. White enemies clucked about more chickens having come home to roost, but Malcolm X entered the black pantheon. Radical Eldridge Cleaver — who later, in exile, professed to have become a born-again Christian — for a time even argued that "black history began with Malcolm X." Albert Cleage praised Malcolm for having taught pride in the blood and soil of blackness. His followers continued to read his spiritual history, with its appeal for land. "Land is the basis of freedom, justice and equality. . . . A revolutionary wants land so he can set up his own nation, an independent nation." All the while they knew, as did he, that unless and until Allah intervened, there could be no separate land. For now, there must be only a story and, in the midst of violence, a rebirth of dignity and pride and measured hope.

More than a decade after the deaths of Martin Luther King and Malcolm X, there were still calls for black religion and black theology. When the Nation of Islam declined in influence as Wallace Muhammad, the son of the founder, came to terms with whites, Orthodox Islam made headway among American blacks. "Africanity" and African spiritual influences now seemed less exotic and threatening to whites, and less promising to blacks, who used their search for African roots to locate themselves in white America. The conventional black Baptist and Methodist churches survived as centers of power. And a young lieutenant of King's, Jesse Jackson, typically attracted a reassured audience of whites as he evangelized fellow blacks with calls for personal achievement. His appeal for pride in one's people and person, his injunction to young people to make good use of their time, to work hard and learn and earn well, showed how built in to American life were patterns made familiar hundreds of years earlier when John Calvin, John Winthrop, and John Wesley set forth the terms of a covenant often called "the Protestant Ethic." This covenant also belonged to the dream of America.

Alongside "red" and "black" citizens, "brown" Americans also fused militancy with spiritual stirrings in the 1960s and 1970s. The rebirth of peoplehood was especially visible among Mexican-Americans, who came to be called Chicanos. Their roots went back to a third set of agents in the early American drama, since they blended the blood of the Central American Indians and the Spanish invaders. Most whites saw the Chicano eruption as merely economic and political, because it first became public when grape pickers struck against growers at Delano, California, in September 1965. But at once there rose people who spoke for the spiritual side of *La Causa*. Thus Armando B. Rendon in *Chicano Manifesto* pointed to parallels between black and brown calls for identity and cultural separateness. In Denver in 1969 Chicano young people also drew on non-Christian heritages to elaborate their "Spiritual Plan of Aztlan." They wrote: "In the spirit of a new people . . . *we, the* Chicano, inhabitants and civilizers of the northern land of Aztlan, from whence came our forefathers, reclaiming the land of their birth and consecrating the determination of our people of the sun, *declare* that the call of our blood is our power, our responsibility." In the eyes of Rendon, Anglo-American society was nothing but "a bastard issued from the promiscuous concubinage of several hundreds of ethnic and racial people who have cast their cultural identities into the American melting pot."

To be sure, the *Manifesto* and Aztlan concepts came from elites who were no better known or more heeded by the majority of their people than were Vine Deloria among the native Americans or Malcolm X among most blacks. Yet these gifted articulators did give voice to what was more muffled among their kin; they represented a new stage in the question America ceaselessly posed for its people. "The Mexican American," wrote Rendon in 1966, "must answer . . . Who am I? and, Who are We? This is to pose then, not merely a dilemma of self-identity, but of self-in-group identity." The Latinos complained that they heard little of their heritage in the public schools; they learned only of the disgraceful slaughter of whites at the Alamo, while their own image was that of "dirty, stinking winos." Yet in 1969, around the time of their new awakening, 9.2 million Americans, almost one citizen in twenty, were of Spanish descent — half of them Mexican, half of them Spanish-speaking, and four-fifths of them urban, despite their image as a rural people.

Catholicism played a very ambiguous part in the Latino search for identity. Many of the people were anticlerical, unwilling to deal with the Catholic church, unable to move with ease into Protestantism. A National Council of Churches leader, Dr. Jorge Lara-Braud, estimated that among the Spanish-speaking people in America, only 15 percent were Roman Catholic, 5 percent were Protestant, and the rest remained unaffiliated. Rendon taunted the Catholics: "It was the Indians who built the missions; it was the Chicanos who labored and sacrificed to build the churches of the Southwest," yet the churches trespassed on land and lives and too often failed to support the striking farm workers and other liberators. Latinos must take over the church, he thought, or they must leave it. Meanwhile, official Catholicism began to make efforts to attract more Latino nuns and priests and to appoint more Latino bishops to lead their own people and to carry on missions among them.

The Chicano leader who emerged as head of the United Farm Workers, Arizona-born Cesar Chavez, came to be seen as a deeply spiritual man, a true heir of his especially devout mother. Having survived the hardships of migrant workers — he attended about thirty schools — Chavez grew up seeing Whites Only signs that excluded him from favored places in California much as blacks were excluded all over the South. After a stint with the U.S. Navy, he returned to the land and then, after marrying another strong Catholic, Helen Fabela, moved to the section of San Jose called Sal

Si Puedes: "Get out if you can." While drifting from job to job, Chavez became acquainted with Father Donald McDonnell and social worker Fred Ross, who together tutored him in the ways of leadership and put him in touch with community organizers. In 1965 Chavez helped start *La Causa,* which organized strikes to unionize farm workers. At all turns, Catholic clerics and laity were at his side as mentors, allies, and supporters; with him they followed and taught the nonviolent philosophies of Gandhi and Martin Luther King, Jr. King identified his own work with that of Chavez, and in the depth of a crisis once wired an endorsement to Chavez: "The plight of your people and ours is so grave that we all desperately need the inspiring example and effective leadership you have given."

Beginning in March 1966, representatives of the Catholic church began to lend even more formal support to the strikes; some bishops asked Congress to help the farm workers. Meanwhile, the workers, in a pattern that matched the 1966 Indian "Longest Walk" and the black civil rights marches through the South, planned a long trek up the California agricultural valley for *La Causa.* By Easter they reached the capital at Sacramento, there to celebrate with Catholic mass and Protestant services the spiritual thrust of their movement. All the while their rival, the International Brotherhood of Teamsters, with vast resources and determination, worked to subvert the United Farm Workers. Chavez and his people had to feud against the growers and fend off the Teamsters, who could buy off workers and then sell them out by signing sweetheart contracts with employers; all the while, apathy born of decades of despair plagued the people.

Chavez had little to draw upon but his own charisma and faith, the weapons of nonviolence, and help from distant people who saw in the Teamster efforts one more means to exploit the poor. Often demoralized, Chavez experienced his own low point in 1968 when some of his worker allies turned to violence. He decided to do penance to express his sorrow and undertook a fast out of a love he professed for them. During the fast, at the climax of Chavez's journey, Catholics celebrated daily masses. In the chill of March, Senator Robert F. Kennedy joined the weakened leader and five thousand worshipers at such a mass. Someone there read Chavez's speech for him: "The strongest act of manliness is to sacrifice ourselves for others in a totally nonviolent struggle for justice. To be a man is to suffer for others. God help us be men." Days later, his friend King was murdered, and only months after that, Kennedy was gone — both victims of the sort of violence Chavez worked to prevent. In place of violent tactics, he advocated boycotts and other legal remedies. He endured, outlasting schisms in the movement, attacks by militants to his left and by Teamsters or growers to his right. In spring of 1970 — before the longest Farm Workers' strike in history ended (though the feud with the Teamsters was not over) — the National Catholic Bishops concluded that no matter what charges anyone had made against Chavez, he was "a good and sincere advocate of social justice." *La Causa* had begun to teach a *people* pride.

To some, the Indian marches on Washington, the black movement for power and justice, and the Chicano or other Hispanic pushes for identity and a place may have looked merely political. So the press often portrayed them. Or religion may have seemed to be accidental, epiphenomenal, barnacled on the *real* thing, which was simply power politics. Yet to see these movements as such is to miss their inner dynamism. Their leaders evidently were genuine when they employed some of the primal religious symbols of their groups. They gained special followings because of these appeals. To picture religion as something "pure" and apart from daily doings is a modern heresy far removed from the historical record. In the past the bonding between ritual and practice, between mundane activity and the sacred, was close.

The spiritual journey of the recent decades has also taken many Westerners to the East, even if physically they have stayed at home. American pilgrims have turned to the lore and religious outlooks inspired by Hinduism, Buddhism, and other oriental faiths. These religions had had a hold among the significant Asian population in America, but had little reach beyond small minorities until the late 1960s, when interest burgeoned. The East and the occult became options for significant numbers of modern Americans.

Most visibly, if not most durably, the youth of the "counterculture" rejected the inherited Western faiths, which they thought were in disgusting alliance with the "establishment" — the "power structure" — that they wanted to see overthrown. Nor were they content for the moment with the world of exterior achievement; their real journey was inward. Some headed for the hills of California or Colorado, where they started isolated communes and sought the simple life. Others tried "mind-expanding" drugs in the quest for "instant Nirvana." If they stayed on campus for a time, they crowded courses on Eastern religion or the occult. Their more staid elders crowded theaters to see films on exorcism, the casting out of demons, or tuned in late-night television to watch the Beautiful People confess faith in astrology. At the neighborhood YMCA, they could come into contact with a yogi; for a time their children in public schools might even learn "Transcendental Meditation," a technique of uncertain Hindu origin. The counterculture eventually became a large subculture and, after the initial shocks, took on respectable guise.

These eruptions were not wholly new. More than a hundred years before, New England transcendentalists like Emerson and Thoreau urged Americans to "forget historical Christianity" with all its complexity and to "simplify, simplify." Thoreau enjoyed his Hindu baths and readings. The New Englanders read Asian scriptures and promoted what to some was "Yankee Hindooism." Spiritualism won a following, when Americans began to enjoy seances as a means of being in contact with the spirit world. In the 1870s the mysterious Madame Blavatsky visited from Europe and Asia, to establish Theosophy as a modern version of an ancient wisdom that had nothing to do with biblical faith. Some of the New Thought movements at the turn of the century in "nervous America" were also congenial to occult and Eastern ways.

A landmark event greater than all these together was the World's Parliament of Religions in Chicago in 1893. While Protestant leaders, Cardinal Gibbons, Reform Jews, and Christian Scientists lined up there, the scene stealer was Swami Vivekananda, the disciple of a Hindu yogi named Ramakrishna. Before the end of the century, this Eastern sage, who wore an ocher turban and a saffron silk robe, charmed Americans on two tours as he established Vedantic centers. More recently, during the Depression, various British expatriate authors, among them Gerald Heard and Aldous Huxley, taught "the perennial philosophy" to Hollywood and points east.

These old faiths, new to most Americans, reached only the elites for some decades, but those who met up with them recognized how different they were from traditional American faith. The God of Vedanta, called Brahma, was not considered a personal being. The Vedas, the Indian philosophical scriptures, differed from the Jewish and Christian scriptures, with their accent on how God acted in history. Christian monks had long promoted diet and discipline, but Vedanta introduced Yoga, an especially intense and vivid pattern of physical and spiritual nurture, whose literature outsold Christian works on the airport newsstands. Western faith pointed back to the creation and ahead to a climax of history, but the perennial philosophy talked about cycles of life and repetitions, as it called people away from busy and compulsive ways.

The Eastern movements in America remained small; by 1970 the Theosophical Society listed only 5,436 members, though it must be said that in this and other cases, many thousands more read theosophical texts. Spiritualism, a movement that ministered more to shifting clienteles than to stable congregations, kept no statistics, but indirectly it influenced thousands if not millions, though its institutions remained all but invisible to most Americans. Anthroposophical societies, the Rosicrucian order, Gnostic movements like the short-lived "I Am," all had their followings, but none were serious challengers to Western faiths — until the late 1960s.

Among the late starters, Zen Buddhism, perhaps the most strenuous of all, had the head start. Back in the days of the World's Parliament of Religions, abbot Soyen Shaku of the Engaku Monastery in Kamakura, Japan, was its agent. In the late 1950s, thanks to the remarkable D. T. Suzuki and the San Francisco beat poets, there was some stir about how Zen might become an alternative to Western messianic and activist religion. To Christians and Jews, it looked like a religion without God. To people of reason, it posed itself as nonlogical; its search for ineffable experience and a "sense of the Beyond" looked absurd. Zen promoted absolute freedom, "even from God," said Suzuki. "It is not that Zen wants to be morbidly unholy and godless but that it knows the incompleteness of a name."

The name and fame of Zen spread thanks also to Alan Watts, a convert from skepticism to Anglicanism, who became a circuit rider for the Eastern outlook, especially in the 1960s. Tirelessly he traveled to college campuses and produced a stream of books that began back with *The Spirit of Zen* in 1936 and crested with *The Way of Zen* in 1957. To purists, his seemed a rather showy pose, but to disciples he offered the simplicity that Western faith left behind. Followers desired to find harmony with ultimate Oneness — an attractive option in the face of American complexity. And if Zen was too forbidding, there was Nichiren Shoshu, whose devotees professed to follow Nichiren (1222–1282), a visionary Buddhist. Modern practitioners of this school found company in a fast-spreading "Value Creation Society," or Soka Gakkai, which was founded in Japan in 1930 and spread in America after 1960.

Alongside these durable Eastern faiths was gentle Baha'i, which followed the teachings of Baha'u'llah. This Persian prophet faced the issue of complexity in religion by envisioning one faith that could include all others in its embrace. His son Abdu'l Baha, who died in 1921, spread this promise in America. Unlike the Far Eastern faiths, Baha'i did conceive of a personal God. It appealed to idealists who wearied of interfaith rivalry, since it saw Jesus, Moses, Muhammad, Krishna, Buddha, Zoroaster, and Baha'u'llah as more or less equal messengers of one God for one world. Baha'i's mildly puritanical disciplines attracted quite a number of world-weary Americans.

To catalog and cite the explosion of all these groups would make a different kind of story from the one we must consider. Many belong to the prehistory of the inward journey that resumed in the late 1960s. Some of them were stable or declining by 1965. Already by the end of the 1950s a prophet might reasonably have predicted their demise. After Russia lofted Sputnik in 1958, Americans were impelled to support technology and science — to favor mastery of the external world — as never before. The New Utopians, as Professor Robert Boguslaw called them, devoted themselves to computers and gathered in think tanks, where they could confidently script godless futures. A Commission on the Year 2000 began projecting futures that excluded exotic religions. The adjectives came fast and furiously when Herman Kahn and Anthony J. Wiener, both of them central in the "2000" cause, projected their "basic, long-term, multifold," and "surprise-free" trend for the future of the West: the world would be "Increasingly Sensate (empirical, this-Worldly, secular, humanistic, pragmatic, utilitarian, contractual, epicurean or hedonistic, and the like)." Technology was the strongest and most believed in missionary force.

Christian prophets briefly rallied to support the new secularity. For a few seasons some of them even proclaimed "the death of God." They had proper cultural instincts, for they saw that secular worldliness was an enveloping outlook for a problem-solving people. But these prophets overlooked the passional side of humans. They underestimated the search for meaning in an apparently random and certainly confusing universe. The secular outlook bred suspicion very soon after Kahn and Wiener prophesied a great future for it. In society, nothing seemed to work. The world of external fact lost many attractions. When the new faiths erupted, the Kahn-Wiener scenario was one more dream deferred or nightmare dismissed. Almost all of the new gurus beckoned seekers to follow them into new simplicity, hardly noticing that by their very presence each of these competitors was making choice even more confusing.

Historian Theodore Roszak chronicled the new spiritualism. His 1969 account *The Making of a Counter Culture* spoke with enthusiasm of an "invasion of centaurs," of young barbarians who burst in upon civilized life. Though the counterculture diminished after the Vietnam War ended, some of the cultural invaders stayed on. When competition for jobs once again engrossed the young, a few who adopted professions continued to moonlight as mystics or occultists after living practically in the workaday world.

Roszak was aware of what later observers also noted: that the new barbarians of the counterculture were a small minority of citizens. Most of them were young, white, and well-off. They were warring against the culture of their parents, against what he called "modernizing, up-dating, rationalizing, planning." They did not differ from the dreamers of the American past, because, in a sense, the new seekers also looked for a Holy City, a New Jerusalem; in familiar language, they wanted to "proclaim a new heaven and a new earth." But the newly religious young did not pursue schemes advocated by militants for a takeover of society through violent revolution. They instead talked chiefly about inwardness. Psychiatrist R. D. Laing spoke for them when he said they sought "not . . . theories so much as the experience that is the source of the theory." Historian Roszak was glad that a new spirit was coming to "dismal and spiritless" America, that mysticism and magic were no longer dirty words. America was coming to look like "the cultic hothouse of the Hellenistic period, where every manner of mystery and fakery, ritual and rite," was intermingled with marvelous indiscrimination.

Most of the new religious communities formed where collegians could gather, in cities or near campuses, and in some cases in rural communes. They clustered in the West, particularly in California. In 1970 a California professor, Jacob Needleman, put his stamp on the movement; his book *The New Religions* chronicled the panoply of faiths that were spreading in the congenial climate in his state. In Needleman's view, the Californians were better poised than other Americans to reject five-century-old religions imported from Europe. This was true, he suggested, because the West Coast represented the geographical end of the American pilgrimage and because under its skies, among its diverse people, the cosmic dimension of human life seemed more accessible. Even the prosperity of the nation's most populous state played into the trend: "In all the world there is no other place where the 'attainment' of satisfaction occurs on such a scale." The thousand strange cults, sects, and fads that flourished there, he thought, "may be seen as part of this fever of satisfying the desires and allaying fears" that came with affluence. Sociologist Robert N. Bellah, also a Californian, watched the restless and rootless — misfits and outcasts from elsewhere — make their homes in his state. "Wholly different visions, oriental or utopian, have frequently had an appeal to northern Californians." But in an age of mass media, before long the "invasion from the East," as Needleman called it, spread to many other areas.

Most of the new expressions dated from between about 1965 and 1971. Thus the Krishna Consciousness movement, whose *hare krishna*–chanting devotees became familiar figures in many cities, was founded by A. C. Bhaktivedanta in New York in 1965. A year later he and a few disciples migrated to San Francisco, from where their movement rapidly spread. The members of this movement aggressively spread their word, as they pinned flowers on strangers' lapels and then tried to sell them magazines and books. While at first the devotees wore robes and, especially in the case of males, shaved off most of their hair, in the course of time they wore the protective coloration of wigs and simple street clothes. Disciples had to leave behind all ties to the complex world, to possessions, to old religions, and, ordinarily, to their families. Strenuous personal discipline that dictated the rules of diet and even sexual life were intended to help them in their search for the transcendent. As with so many similar groups, one of the major features of appeal was the substitute family Krishna Consciousness offered.

Taking the opposite course was the movement called Transcendental Meditation. In 1966 the Maharishi Mahesh Yogi organized the Students' International Meditation Society in America. In the course of the next two years, his smiling face, high-pitched giggle, and reassuring outlook made him a familiar figure on late-night television. Musical groups then popular, among them the Beatles and the Rolling Stones, made up his advance guard. Serious students of Yoga protested his "instant Nirvana," but the technique of transcendental meditation, progressively distanced from its religious ties, became quite popular. To critics, it seemed so marketable that they could call it the "fast-food industry" version of new religiosity. Though in 1968 the maharishi returned to India expressing disappointment that he had not fully changed the world, he returned before long, content to see TM penetrate middle-class culture. For a time TM was taught in some public schools, but the courts ruled that it remained religious and thus was out of bounds. The movement's university in Iowa did receive accreditation.

Slightly later, Guru Maharaj Ji arrived. His followers at one time claimed to number eighty thousand, mainly young people. The adolescent guru formed his Divine Light Mission on August 8, 1971, after the counterculture had begun to disappear and the occult explosion was beginning to be an echo. Jeanne Messer, a scholar among his disciples, praised the teenage guru when he was in his prime. "He only said of other religions that he had come not to start a new church but to make perfect Christians, Buddhists, or Moslems." She acknowledged that many of his devotees were people who had seriously been seeking God on other paths, whether as devout Jews and Christians or as followers of other teachers from the East.

For a time the mass media paid considerable attention to Guru Maharaj Ji. He succeeded in attracting some former radicals from the political scene, among them Rennie Davis, one of the "Chicago Seven" who were tried for violent disruption of the 1968 Democratic National Convention in Chicago. If the Divine Light Mission was a base of rebounding or reaction, it also offered "belonging" to the young through its coeducational households, or ashrams. Yet the movement did not long prosper; Messer had had good reason to be guarded about its future. The "Millennium 73" festival, a test of the guru's popularity, was a failure. Family squabbles and public scoldings by the mother of Maharaj Ji led to further decline. "Perhaps," mused Messer, most members "will simply return to old business from their present involvement and pursue no further the questions raised by the wave of self-realization efforts."

Momentarily, the new religions had to make room for movements designed to shock the American majority. Thus between 1966 and 1968 Anton Szandor LaVey made headlines with his Church of Satan. LaVey intended to overturn every major Christian or "Middle American" virtue in order to promote their opposites: indulgence, vengeance, and the simple gratification of impulses. But his attempts soon were greeted almost with good humor. He failed to attract the young, and could do little more than offend fundamentalists. One of his problems was obvious: Satanism was already available to people who saw no reason to join a formal movement. Certain rock music stars more effectively aped presumably Satanic ways, and free sexuality was available to people who needed no church to license it. In the end, in the eyes of some analysts, the Church of Satan looked weirdly like a Protestant sect, devoted as it was to hard work, long study, and grim purpose in spreading its gospel.

A society as rich and diverse as that of the United States had room for almost every conceivable kind of religious expression. Satanism, witchcraft, and extreme occultist groups could gain small followings for years to come. Their presence may have revealed nothing more than that their marketers had lively imaginations, that they knew how to locate sensation seekers and extravagant searchers for meaning. After more than a decade of talk about the new religions, it was clear that the map of American religion had not greatly changed. Nowhere outside the San Francisco Bay area were the cults strong enough to alter the power relations between religious groups. Thus Hare Krishna societies seldom crowded and never could displace Methodist or Baptist forces, nor did Satanism undercut Catholic centers of influence. Given their survival through several years, most of them looked increasingly like conventional organized religion.

California sociologist Charles Y. Glock, an expert who monitored the cults up close in *The New Religious Consciousness,* was probably correct when he decided that the new religions were not initiators of basic change in American life: they were visible signs of what was already under way. Citizens were disenchanted with what they already had and were open to alternatives. The religious world, on one side, pictured God in control, while, on the other, technological society proclaimed that humans were in mastery. The new cultists shunned both approaches. The old world-views, thought Glock, still held together enough that no single alternative vision could break them up. It did not seem likely to him that, short of life under a dictatorship, Americans would soon again converge on one world view, one outlook. Citizens had to grope among the competitors in the search for meaning or give up the quest entirely. Glock came close to seeing the searchers as completely isolated from each other. Each wanted wholeness, simplicity, acceptance. By forming or giving support to new religious groups, they only added to the problem of bewildering choice for those who came after them.

Obviously, not all the new religions were gentle and fluid. During the counterculture the "flower children" and hippies advertised their openness and freedom. But the strongest survivors in the 1970s tended to be rigid and disciplined, as if they were parodies of conventional religion. Best known of these was the Unification church, which blended Korean Christianity, Korean religion, and new themes that came from the mind of its well-off founder, the Reverend Sun Myung Moon. Moon promoted puritanical and ascetic styles of living for his followers, who came to be known as Moonies, but not for himself. He lived extravagantly on a New York estate; his church undertook capitalistic ventures and made a program of old-style anticommunism; Moon was among the first public supporters of President Richard M. Nixon at the time of the Watergate scandal. Moon's book *The Divine Principle* was an intricate mixture of arcane philosophy and hints that a new age was coming. The author announced that a sort of new Messiah was soon to come, who would carry revelation beyond Judaism and Christianity, and that His coming would make Korea a focus of spirituality. Critics accused Moon of being an agent of right-wing Korean government and his followers of "brainwashing" new converts. Meanwhile, the Unification church organized a seminary and held major conferences that were designed to promote its credibility in mainstream America. No established church set forth more clear-cut lines of authority or sharper boundaries than the Reverend Moon's. The invasion of centaurs seemed over.

Those who remembered how Mormons, Christian Scientists, and Jehovah's Witnesses survived from among hundreds of past religious experiments had reason to be cautious about predicting the futures of the new groups. Some of them adapted and survived; Transcendental Meditation and Yoga did so by stripping away most of their overt religious elements. Others left a significant deposit in the mainline churches, chiefly by helping conventional religions place a premium again on meditation, mysticism, and the inward journey. Few won a large place under the sun, at least outside California. As Glock observed, the battle had never been easy: "The old world views simply had too much going for them."

Martin Luther King, Jr., a Baptist minister, is the
first private citizen to be remembered with a
national holiday of his own. Drawing on deep
spiritual roots, King led the civil-rights movement
that climaxed in the 1960s. His speeches and
sermons rallied citizens of all races through an
appeal to conscience; he called for people to work
for peace and justice. (© *Bob Henriques/*
Magnum Photos)

Chapter Twenty

NEW PATHS FOR
OLD PILGRIMAGES

𝒯 TO BRING THE STORY UP TO DATE BY REFERENCE TO MYSTICS, native Americans, blacks, Hispanics, and devotees of Eastern religion may seem to be a diversion from the plot. There is no reason, however, to lose interest in the spiritual searches of people in the historic Western faiths that overwhelmingly still dominate in America. Each, coming complete with old world-views, made room in the late seventies and early eighties for a great deal of innovating. Since they represent well over a hundred million Americans, it is impossible to do more than plant some signposts indicating where changes are occurring. The purpose is chiefly to illustrate the presence of pilgrimage among restless people in traditions that are still not settled.

Alongside the other American minorities, Jews came to question the civility and conformism many found in the consensus that was forged in the 1950s and in the ecumenical friendliness of the early 1960s. Whether seen as a racial or a religious group, Jews had worked as hard as others to find and assert their identity in the United States. In the 1950s many were still content to see themselves as Will Herberg saw them — as supporters of an American Way of Life religion in its generalized Jewish version. Moves to the suburbs dispersed formerly intact Jewish communities, while the affluent society tended to lure upwardly mobile Jews away from tradition. Were they on the verge of blending into a nondescript

461

American whole? Was the Jewish issue of "twoness" vis-à-vis Israel and its heritage and the American Zion at last to be resolved as they lost distinctiveness? Many Jews were deserting their synagogues and, after the baby boom of the fifties, religious education of the young became a less attractive feature than earlier. Intermarriage contributed to a loss of Jewish loyalties.

The question of beleaguered Israel suddenly brought Jewish militancy and spirituality to a new fusion. As other bases of Jewish identity continued to dwindle, Israel grew in importance. Once upon a time, Zionism had been the faith of the Jewish few and a luxury for the rest. In the sixties, most American Jews found reason to express loyalty to Israel in its hours of need. Christian support for Zionism also grew. Fundamentalist Protestants saw the birth of Israel as a sign of the imminent Second Coming of Jesus and lent the state support. Liberal papers once critical of Zionism, among them *The Christian Century,* became increasingly friendly to the new nation. Despite the Suez crisis in 1956, between 1948 to 1967 Israel came to look ever more secure.

Then came the Six-Day War, which turned out to be a major dividing point in Jewish history. Until then, some politically radical Jewish youths on campuses, attracted as they were to anything that looked anti-Western, professed to see Israel as an extension of the North Atlantic Treaty Organization and thus of the imperial West in its Middle East intrusion. The Arabs looked like blacks and embodied, in the eyes of Jewish radicals, Third World victimage. Suddenly now, in 1967, it occurred to such Jewish young people that support for Israel was a necessity, not a luxury, if Judaism itself was to survive. The Israeli victory also led Jews to delight in what was happening to transform the image of the Jew as victimizer of Arabs to that of their victim.

In one respect the Jewish journey differed from that of more economically oppressed people in America. Despite anti-Jewish eruptions through the decades, most of the Jews shared in national prosperity. Accent on Judaism, therefore, did not mean rejection of many values of white gentiles, the way, say, native American or Black Muslim outlooks did. Thus Professor Jacob Neusner at Brown University argued that Jews could stress their own peoplehood without hating others. "One can attempt to transform a group which finds its definition by contrast to the 'outside world' into a group which is constituted on affirmative inward social experience." And so it was. The synagogues did not fill again, but Israel received new support. The year before the 1967 war, American Jews raised $64-million in cash and invested $76-million in bonds to support Israel; in 1967 these figures rose to $242- and $190-million, respectively.

Israel progressively became the spiritual center of the American Jewish experience. Canadian theologian Emil Fackenheim, who survived the Nazi Holocaust, spoke for many: Jews "are commanded to survive as Jews, lest the Jewish people perish. . . . They are forbidden to despair of the God of Israel, lest Judaism perish. . . . A Jew may not respond to Hitler's attempt to destroy Judaism by himself cooperating in its destruction."

Henceforth Jews became more aggressive in stating the case of Israel. Leaders chided Catholic and Protestant counterparts if they were slow to come to the support of Israel in 1967 or during the more threatening Yom Kippur War of 1973. Some suggested that a half-century of interfaith conversation had been futile and should now be broken off. Despite frustrations, however, most Jews did not retreat from civility. Only a few joined the stormy Jewish Defense League, which threatened to become a violent representative of Israeli and Jewish causes, ready to take the law into its own hands against American Nazis and other abhorrent groups.

Along with its new assertiveness, Judaism experienced a spiritual recovery, an "inward journey" of the sort that became so common in the 1970s. Pioneering Jews in America, especially those who sided with Isaac Mayer Wise and his heirs in Reform Judaism, were legatees of the Enlightenment. They ignored or seemed embarrassed by the mystical lore of medieval Judaism. Their faith was to be respectful of their heritage but thoroughly modern in outlook. Through the seventies, the arcane cabala looked hopelessly antiquated and beside the point. Jewish messianism of the sixteenth and seventeenth centuries seemed to be little more than foolishness born of despair after the expulsion from Spain, no more "true" or helpful than Indian messianism of the Ghost Dance era. Least promising was Hasidism, the fervent, boisterous, and often joyful heritage of eighteenth-century teachers in Europe.

While young Jews became vulnerable to conversion by all kinds of groups that offered journeys to the interior — from "Jews for Jesus" to the Eastern cults and the modern therapies — a significant minority now turned at least temporarily to the cabala, messianism, and Hasidism. Some found Orthodoxy attractive and formed communities where they could follow its prescriptions. In Conservative and Reform Judaism, revisions of prayer books usually favored tradition and, far from presenting Judaism as simply a form of rationalism, paid due respect to a formerly almost inaccessible and incomprehensible Jewish mysticism. By the 1980s visitors to a campus Hillel group would be more likely to find devotees of such mysticism than they would heirs of the Enlightenment. In every case, they would see strong supporters of Israel as a political and spiritual force for Jewish survival and hope.

A renewed sense of peoplehood also marked much of Roman Catholicism, far beyond the Hispanic people, among whom religious participation was very low. During the decade after the Second Vatican Council, many Catholics repudiated both the old idea of assimilation, which was current in the era of James Cardinal Gibbons, and of consensus, during which leaders as diverse as Francis Cardinal Spellman and Father John Courtney Murray stated the case for Catholicism in America. Now ethnic diversity was valued again. The national subgroups that had always been part of Catholicism were often overlooked by anti-Catholics who wanted to see Catholicism as a monolith and by social analysts — as well as by the dominant Irish hierarchy.

The revival of peoplehood occurred during the decades when the question "Who am I?" became intense for many groups. While the Catholic church remained officially one after the Council, it divided between left and right in thought and action, until its image became far too blurry for it to help provide an identity as it had back in the days of Will Herberg and *Protestant-Catholic-Jew*. Uprooted Catholic intellectuals began to retrieve a sense of pride in selective elements in their ethnic past, while the broader Catholic population took delight in affirming ties to the old European ways after having long been told to suppress them. A book by Nathan Glazer and Daniel Patrick Moynihan, *Beyond the Melting Pot,* signaled the new mood in 1962. It is possible that reaction to new assertions by blacks, Indians, Jews, and others in part encouraged Catholic peoples to relocate and take pride in their own roots.

Ethnic Catholicism did not set out to test Catholic dogma, to divide the church officially. Instead it tried to reestablish the "feel" of various Catholic cultures, the tone of life preserved in everything from languages through menus to marriage customs. To the surprise of scholars, these Catholics all along had been marrying outside their own groups far less frequently than was commonly supposed. Behavior patterns nurtured in the separate national communities often did more to establish ways of life than did the rules dispensed by the church.

Whatever power the sense of peoplehood played in the lives of the faithful, it was clear that national origins still helped define Catholicism. The *Official Catholic Directory* found 10 million Italians at the head of the list of peoples, followed by more than 8 million Irish, 7 million Germans, 5 million Poles and French-Canadians, and 3 million eastern Europeans and Spanish-speaking groups. They each came to be reckoned with as political forces; thus in the 1976 presidential election, it became very important for Southern Baptist candidate Jimmy Carter to win the support of these "ethnics," particularly in the urban, industrial Northeast. In Carter's administration Monsignor Geno Baroni was appointed as liaison to ethnic groups, a sign of their arrival on new terms.

The inward journey that Thomas Merton exemplified in Catholicism did not parallel the ethnic recovery. Here again, however, the blurring of Catholic identity played a part in the renewed search. The Council helped shatter the old image of Catholic unity. Gone was the Latin Mass, one old bond; gone also were many rules that commanded uniform participation. Now Catholics were free to eat meat on Friday; they were not necessarily expected to use the rosary as before for prayer, or to make pilgrimages or attend specified devotions. Priests and nuns often changed from religious garb to street clothes. For an American to be told that someone was a Roman Catholic did little to certify his or her membership in a group; there were fewer distinguishing badges than before.

In the midst of this chaos some Catholics turned to the *Cursillo* movement, a "little course" of faith and piety that came from Spanish soil. Here was an intense religious experience that stamped its participants as somehow special. Then, in 1966, at Duquesne University in Pittsburgh, a number of academic people professed that they had received the gift of the Holy Spirit, were "baptized in the Spirit." Among their signs was the ability to enjoy glossolalia, a form of unrepressed speech that was called "speaking in tongues." Some of them also favored healing and prophecy. A year later a more significant group formed at the University of Notre Dame and then at the University of Michigan. The new devotees adopted a form of what Protestants called Pentecostalism, or what most of them preferred to call "charismatic life," after the *charismata,* or gifts of the Spirit.

What began among intellectuals spread among suburban parishes and in living rooms. The charismatic movement was short on social action to change the world, and seemed to some to be a reaction to the activism of the decade past. But it was long on ecumenism, as Catholics prayed and sang freely at the side of non-Catholic Pentecostals. In the course of time, they generated their own heroines and heroes — among them, Maria von Trapp, whose life was fictionalized in the film *Sound of Music,* and the peripatetic Belgian cardinal Leon Joseph Suenens, who gave a kind of official seal of approval to the movement. Catholic Pentecostals came almost to be a people of their own. Though content with orthodoxy and rarely testing its limits, they wanted to fill a spiritual void and to share in more ecstatic forms of speech. Each summer they gathered for exuberant festivals at Notre Dame, in Kansas City, or, in one instance, in Rome. They took care to stay in the good graces of the official church even while they at least implicitly judged it for its spiritual apathy where it did not follow their charismatic path. Though the movement soon fragmented and perhaps crested, it had spread a broad influence. To its advocates, Pentecostal Christianity was the mark of a whole new age; to its detractors, it was a sign of spiritual arrogance or a diversion from the more serious life of the church.

In the course of the years, many Catholics resumed the search that Thomas Merton prefigured for their time. Some of the young flirted with Eastern religion and were drawn to occult sects. Others, however, began to explore again the spirituality of mystics like Julian of Norwich or Teresa of Avila from the Catholic centuries. The search for saints in the modern world received support in 1976 when the Vatican named an American woman, Elizabeth Seton, the first native-born saint in the United States. Publishers in the seventies and after scrambled to make available the spiritual classics of the West. In parishes where they had once been unfashionable, prayer cells flourished, as Catholicism, in the midst of modernity, looked for new spiritual horizons.

What everyone called "post-Vatican II Catholicism" was infinitely more diverse in appearance than what had gone before. The old idea that there existed a monolithic church that took signals from Rome and disrupted the Republic was buried. Traces of anti-Catholicism here and there inspired a Catholic-defense organization or two. Yet polls showed Americans eager to be tolerant of each other; Catholics were ready to enjoy non-Catholic neighbors. Catholics and Protestants united for worship everywhere but at the Eucharist, the Lord's Supper. They had common study groups, prayer cells, action movements. In 1982 Catholics and Protestants jointly celebrated the eight-hundredth anniversary of Saint Francis's birth and in 1983 they again united, to show respect for Martin Luther on the occasion of his five-hundredth birthday.

Catholic theology was no longer a single expression of official Thomism. Creative men and women worked with a variety of theologies and with diverse degrees of loyalty to the old ways — though usually while claiming a hold on the earliest Catholic traditions. The church did not shun social action. The bishops were only the most visible representatives in efforts to outlaw abortion. By 1983 they had become equally controversial and visible at the head of the movement to outlaw nuclear weapons. All these moves were made with ease, not by people on the outside or at the margins of the mainstream but as one set of contenders in a free society. It was a set of contenders ample enough — one might say "catholic" enough — to allow voices on left and right when it came to most issues.

Old world-views can also take on new casts among apparently conservative groups, as they have in Protestantism. California sociologist Robert Wuthnow once observed that during the so-called religion revival of the 1950s, "virtually all religious indicators, except perhaps theologically conservative beliefs" demonstrated some growth. After the late 1960s, however, theologically conservative belief surprised all but those who held it — and even some of them — by finding new prosperity. The general public was first alerted to it by the mass media, who reported a movement of "Jesus freaks" among the new religions. From California the phenomenon spread to campus areas across the country. In instance after instance, as if playing back a single record, converts told how they had been "born again." They had been on drugs, had lost meaning and purpose, belonged to no one. Then they experienced Jesus, thanks to efforts of friends who converted them. As converts, they cleared their own young minds of everything except Jesus. "One Way!" became their slogan; one finger raised to the cross was their symbol.

The Jesus movement drew publicity in 1967 to The Living Room, a youth refuge in the Haight-Ashbury area of San Francisco. News magazines also featured baptisms of the bikini-clad in the Pacific. Meanwhile, at Hollywood's First Presbyterian Church, the Salt Company Coffee House reached stray young people in the counterculture. In Seattle, Linda Meissner organized a coffeehouse called The Catacombs and helped start a newspaper aimed at the new converts. At this stage, the Jesus movement seemed to be only a group of overcaffeined youth with ink stains on their fingertips. But soon musicians began to sanitize the lyrics of rock music, and Jesus advocates picked up support from singers Pat Boone, Johnny Cash, Anita Bryant, among other celebrities in the Christian world. The Jesus people shared food, clothing, and the necessities of life. Few of the new sensationalists expressed hopes for the social change that their older brothers and sisters had demonstrated for only a few years before. In a best-selling book, *The Late Great Planet Earth,* author Hal Lindsey appealed to millions with his picture of a world soon to end. Since Jesus was to come again soon, efforts to improve the earth were of little point to him or his followers.

The radical Jesus people acted much like their non-Christian counterparts. They formed communes, exerted fierce discipline, and created "families." The Children of God, a group of severe biblical literalists, insisted that Jesus wanted adherents to repudiate their biological families and the churches. Parents tried to retrieve their children with the aid of self-proclaimed "deprogrammers," just as others "kidnapped" their sons and daughters from the "mind control" of the Unification church and the Krishna Consciousness sect. Church leaders resented Children of God hymns:

> O Lord, have mercy on me.
> I hate that damned old sound
> Of the church bells ringing
> And the people coming from miles around.

Though the Jesus movement appealed to collegians, it attacked education. In the name of Jesus, one young elder charged that "education is all just shit." The leaders censored the reading matter that reached their followers, and built a spiritual cocoon around them.

In 1971 the Religion News Writers Association named the Jesus movement the news event of the year in religion. But as suddenly as it came, the fervor disappeared — to be replaced by durable Jesus movements in the conservative denominations. In 1971 a Southern Baptist Convention press, for example, published William S. Cannon's *The Jesus Revolution.* Cannon contended that this revolution was the result of a meeting by troubled youth with an awesome, all-powerful, supernatural Jesus — whom the churches had been worshiping all along. The "Straight People," particularly teenagers, were now ready for harvest by the church. Cannon was right. By the middle of the decade, the only Jesus movement that mattered much was made up of middle-class young people. Young Life, Campus Crusade, the Navigators, the Inter-Varsity Fellowship, and various denominational groups attracted the young. Anything but an Eastern "new religious consciousness" prevailed among them.

Alongside this Jesus movement, another fresh flowering reached middle-class religion in the form of the Pentecostal movement. Its advocates did not think of themselves as part of the new religions, since they — like so many before them — claimed only to be restoring practices neglected since the early days of Christianity. Back then, people healed; they prophesied and interpreted prophecy; they yielded themselves to the Holy Spirit, and thus could utter the sounds of unrepressed speech, which they called speaking in tongues. Could people do so now?

As so often, one can make sense of a new outbreak only by reference to what had gone before — to movements with long roots overlooked for decades. This modern Pentecostal expression began around the turn of the century on the soil of Wesleyan and "Holiness" movements. Protestants sometimes dated it from the last New Year's Eve of the old nineteenth century and New Year's morning of the new twentieth, when a Miss Agnes Ozman spoke in tongues at a Topeka, Kansas, meeting. Five years later such sounds again erupted under black revivalist William T. Seymour at an Azusa Street meeting in Los Angeles. The movement spread among Americans in the southeastern mountains and among displaced blacks. It became the fastest-growing form of Protestantism in the Caribbean world, Latin America, and Africa. Soon it appeared to be a "third force," alongside Catholicism and Protestantism. Through sixty years it turned progressively respectable, forming denominations, publishing houses, and Sunday schools.

In the face of scorn by others, Pentecostalists enjoyed what dissenters in America always could exploit: visibility, sympathy vote, and the sense that their high standards of membership gave people special reasons to join them. Americans did join them. The Church of God of Cleveland, Tennessee, had the fastest growth rate among white churches after midcentury, while more than two million people joined the black Church of God in Christ. After World War II "tongues moved uptown," as one leader put it, in the Pentecostals' drive for conventionality. In 1951, in a Los Angeles cafeteria, some of them formed the Full-Gospel Business Men's Fellowship International, which twenty years later sponsored international jet flights for its members — one of many signs that the movement was no longer restricted to the hollows of Tennessee or the black ghettos.

On a spring Sunday in 1960, the Reverend Dennis Bennett startled his Episcopal congregation at Van Nuys, California, with word that he and numerous members were "baptized in the spirit" and speaking in tongues. His assistant in the chancel reacted by taking off his vestments and marching down the aisle as a gesture of resignation. The media took to the story with zest, reporting further on how Bennett then resigned to take up a ministry in Seattle, Washington. Soon Lutheran suburbanites in the Twin Cities of Minnesota, Yale Divinity School students, and people in prayer cells elsewhere called themselves "charismatic." In the middle-class churches, the movement often turned out to be abrasive, as its members tended to stand apart from others who had not yet had "the experience." To insiders it meant a new sense of belonging to a group, a new awareness of God, and a new step on the inward journey.

Both the Jesus movement and Pentecostalism shared space with the boom in conservative Protestantism called neo-evangelicalism and then evangelicalism. After a decade of spiritual prosperity, late in the 1970s these heirs of revivalism and fundamentalism claimed the loyalty of about every third church member in America, while the Gallup Poll concluded that one-third of the adult population had had a "born again" experience, a "new birth" of religious conversion.

While the rise of evangelicalism in its newest phase dated from the Billy Graham revivals of the 1950s, it was the election of Southern Baptist Jimmy Carter to the presidency in 1976 that gave visibility and status to the movement comparable to that which came to Catholicism with the election in 1960 of John F. Kennedy. *Newsweek* magazine called 1976 "The Year of Evangelicals," and one year later *Time* made a cover story of the evangelical empire. Miss America contestants, professional athletes, country-and-western music stars, politicians, and other celebrities made public their experience of being born again. By 1978 an enthusiastic observer and participant, Richard Quebedeaux, could write: "*Now,* of course, evangelicalism, in its Protestant, Catholic, and charismatic forms, is really the mainline brand of American Christianity." Significantly, he stated this in a book called *The Worldly Evangelicals,* wherein he argued plausibly that evangelicals, heady with success and affluence, were now as materialistic as any Americans, and that they reinforced their enjoyment of the world with appeals to the name of Jesus.

Like any American movement that numbered forty million people or so, evangelicalism displayed great internal varieties. One wing was aggressive and standoffish. Thus, the Campus Crusade organization started a Christian embassy in Washington, D.C., in order "to get Christians into office." Christians in this case meant only the born-again kind. Others promoted *Christian Yellow Pages,* which encouraged evangelicals to deal only with their own kind in the marketplace. In theology, the hard-liners engaged in what editor Harold Lindsell called "the Battle for the Bible"; only those who believed that the original manuscripts of the Bible did not and could not contain errors of geography, history, or science were considered true evangelicals. Hard-core fundamentalism also prospered during this phase of conservative revivals.

At the same time, evangelicals showed a new expansive spirit. President Carter acknowledged the influence of Reinhold Niebuhr and other thinkers who were once shunned by the born-again Christians. Because of the evangelicals' generally favorable attitude toward Israel, these reborn conservatives opened conversations with Jews. Formerly anti-Catholic, many of them found new points of contact with evangelical and charismatic Catholics after Vatican II. Because so many black Baptists and Methodists were of revivalist traditions, the evangelical movement had an interracial cast. Worldwide gatherings led the politically conservative group to have more positive views of Third World unrest. On the home front, a number of "young evangelical" movements even began to promote pacifism, simpler life-styles, and intense criticism of the American way of life.

The statistics used to measure religion pointed clearly to evangelical prosperity. People from this camp started extensive and expensive television networks, and in 1978 began to beam their messages around the world off a satellite. The Christian Booksellers' Association promoted million-sellers. Thousands came to hear the born-again witness of former Richard Nixon aide Charles Colson, former Black Panther radical Eldridge Cleaver, or the sister of the president, Ruth Carter Stapleton.

While the very theme of born-again Christianity appealed chiefly to internal and often emotional experience, it was quite natural for forces numbering in the millions to acquire and assert political power. Evangelical leaders protested all through the sixties against mainline and liberal denominations, the National Council of

Churches, and the World Council of Churches, for "meddling" in politics, particularly on the subjects of racial change and protest against the Vietnam War. Religion was to be a private affair, a matter of soul-saving and not world-changing.

The new prosperity of evangelical, fundamentalist, and Pentecostal religions propagated by television personalities and best-selling authors, coupled with the new political interests, led to the formation of a rather formal set of organizations often called the New Christian Right. This came to an early crest, after almost invisible behind-the-scenes development, in the election year of 1980. Suddenly the media converged on figures like Virginia evangelist and television personality Jerry Falwell. His "Moral Majority," in coalition with groups like Religious Round Table and the Christian Voice, teamed with nonreligious rightist movements. Using the latest techniques of mail-order solicitation and television production, they inspired voter registration among people who would help their causes.

Some observers saw conservative Christian support for Ronald Reagan as a significant factor in his election. At the same time, it helped tilt the electorate against certain liberal senators. The traditionalist Christians pressured for action on abortion, favoring a constitutional amendment forbidding it. Others advocated an amendment to the Constitution that would authorize prayer in public schools. They united against pornographic expression. Most of them were for huge defense expenditures. Sometimes they strayed into marginally religious issues like opposition to the Panama Canal treaty or the retention of the Department of Education, which they saw as the root of evils in public education.

Suddenly in the 1980s Americans were treated to a lively debate over values in education, the media, and politics. The Moral Majority and related groups never spoke for as many Americans as they claimed. When analysts observed the limits of such organizations' power, politicians and the media paid less attention to them. By the elections of 1982, some observers were cautiously predicting that the New Christian Right would henceforth merely take its place among the pressure groups of America. Its leaders had bet on some political figures who disgraced themselves in scandals or overplayed their hands in Congress and tried the patience of moderates.

More sympathetic observers saw in the Christian Right's moves something similar to what had gone on in other interest groups and causes. Like feminists, homosexuals, the aged, and various racial groups, the religious conservatives had seen that no one would take care of their story and tell it positively unless they did. The textbooks were changed for others: why, they asked, could these not be changed to include the story of creation over against evolution, their view of America as a biblical, not a secular, humanistic nation? That they moved so far with these nostalgic appeals as they did in a short time showed the extent of such hungers. That their power came to be limited showed that they, with other groups, had to settle for their place under the American sun, not for a monopoly or even necessarily a predominance in it.

In many respects evangelicalism fit the pattern of all the movements of the 1970s. On one hand, it tended to give people a sense of belonging, of peoplehood: they acquired an identity. On the other, it put a high premium on what Robert Heilbroner called "inner states of experience," and was emotionally satisfying to people who could not do much to change the world of external fact around them. Evangelical leaders portrayed themselves as being in opposition to "the spirit of the times," though in many respects their success-minded movement played up to it. Whatever the fate of organized religion in America, the Protestant born-again movement was likely to keep at least its one-third share among the Christian majority for some time to come.

All these movements advanced at the apparent expense of what suddenly came to be called "mainline" Protestantism, the heir of colonial establishments and nineteenth-century northern revivalism. Descendants of the old Episcopal, Presbyterian, and Congregational churches shared in the revival of the 1950s, but experienced relative decline ever after. The northern Baptists, Disciples of Christ, and Methodists could not keep up with population growth, and the Lutherans struggled to hold their own. Many churches had particular difficulty luring and holding young people. In an age that encouraged exclusiveness to promote identity, the mainline was not particular enough about boundaries and offered less sense of belonging than did rigid groups. In a period of new fanaticisms, it tried to stay civil and nonaggressive. In a time when personal experience received the highest premium, the older established churches remained somewhat staid and diffident about promoting "peak experiences" and getting people to talk about them.

Yet the standard religious groups, Protestant and Catholic, retained great vitalities. Up to 100 million citizens remained members, an astounding figure in a day when escape from organized religion was painless. They responded to the trends of the time, having turned somewhat more traditional and ritualist themselves. Without abandoning the movement toward church unity, the members resisted its bureaucratic forms and paid more attention than before to the particular soil of their own denominations. Thousands of local congregations remained vital. Being open-ended, they remained more vulnerable to forces around them than did strict groups, but having survived great cultural changes after the Second World War, they seemed ready for more.

In the 1960s it was the mainline churches that were on center stage. Their white denominational leadership, clerical and lay, gave support to the civil rights struggle, and it was they who offered most visible religious resistance to the Vietnam War. Such involvements were costly, since many of their members or potential converts did not welcome the stands they took. A decade later, having lost some power and not having found clear new issues, many of them backed away from making constant pronouncements on every kind of issue or sending demonstrators out into the streets. Most of them did keep their commitment to the idea that the Kingdom of God or the Lordship of Christ called them somehow to change the world, but local congregations more frequently became agencies for such change.

Through the centuries after 1607 in Virginia, the weathered Protestant groups have naturally dominated in the story of the American pilgrimage. What has occurred among them since the 1960s has in many respects been a continuation of old plots. No theologians in the camp have replaced the Niebuhrs or Paul Tillich. No great ecumenical schemes have supplanted the World or the National Council of Churches. No new patterns of social action have come to succeed those that were vivid during the civil rights and Vietnam protest years of the 1960s. The mainline temporarily has not been producing celebrities to vie with evangelical personalities, leaders of cults, or some of the Catholic leadership.

This does not mean that there has been only stagnation. One of the most vital signs on the mainline front was the effort to break from two-thousand-year-old patterns of male dominance in religion. Our story of the American pilgrimage has seen women at every turn. But women leaders were forced to the margin: in dissent, in pioneering new religions. Now the mainline made room for women in their time of self-assertion. While many evangelicals — there were major exceptions — gained popular followings by teaching female submission and submissiveness, the mainline groups risked advocating the rights of women. Much energy went into the call for the ordination of women. While a number of Pentecostal churches had pioneered in this respect, it was the more exposed denominations that made increasing room for women in the ministry. Efforts to change were costly. When the Episcopalians voted to ordain women in 1976 and began to do so a year later, a small schism resulted and much tension remained between factions in the majority who stayed. Yet the movement for enlarged roles for women seemed unstoppable. It was destined to show up in a reworking of the language of worship (God would not always be "He"), as in every other aspect of church life.

Any view of late modern American religion is bound to give an impression of competition and chaos. Tribes, racial and ethnic groups, peoples, movements, cults, sects, and denominations kept fighting for space in greater numbers than ever before. The Darwinian "survival of the fittest" seemed to be the first law of church life, as competitors worked to take advantage of every new device and technique that might assure group survival and prosperity. Choices became almost infinite. German sociologist Thomas Luckmann has spoken of "the invisible religion" as the final outcome of modernity, and such religion may in the end be the strongest force in American life. This style thrived in the world of high-rise apartments, long weekends, and airport newsstands; it was made up of clienteles and not congregations, of consumers more than converts, of do-it-yourself experimenters more than people who felt called to be judged by a living God. The journey of the new American individualists is likely to be characterized by ever more paths, by ever more bewildering choices between options.

Some prophets still worried, however, about national cohesion and social morale. Faced by sectarian confusion and the new private style, Robert N. Bellah in 1967 joined the long stream of people who had advocated something like a "civil religion." Looking back on the heady days of John F. Kennedy, when there seemed to be some coherence among Americans who were "prodded by a dream," Bellah pleaded with his fellow citizens to reach for the depths of the American experience in the religion of Thomas Jefferson and Abraham Lincoln, so that transcendent justice could play its part in civil life. Bellah was friendly to the churches, but he also urged that the traditions and rites of the American public inheritance should provide means for people to pass values on to future generations. No sooner was the ink on his essay dry, however, than the nation fragmented as seldom before — during the years of civil rights dissent, protest against the Vietnam War, and loss of faith in the moral fabric of the Republic during the Watergate scandal.

The public faith, like organized religion in America, had seen previous revivals and declines. Like organized religion, it was the subject of voluntary choice, so its fate depended to a large extent on the needs and will of citizens. When they pursued symbols of national cohesion and purpose it prospered. But some prophets came to foretell a time when the American system itself would change, when its voluntary faiths could no longer sustain social morale. Robert Heilbroner spoke for those prophets who pictured a future day of compulsory "statist" religion. In its epoch the American experiment would end and freedom of choice and freedom for choice would disappear.

Between the foreseeable chaos of total individualism and this specter of a totalist social faith, most American seekers continued to make their way. They clustered as before in their "tribes" and denominations and movements. Those who looked for identity, meaning, and belonging in life on these terms faced the issue as old as the United States itself: How could they assure a healthy *communitas communitatum,* a larger community made up of healthily interactive subcommunities? To what extent should they devote themselves to their particular and often sectarian belief systems, and how and when should they converge on the claims of the commonweal, the symbols of the Republic?

This narrative has been written as if the spiritual pilgrimage will continue; that premise is not sure. Europeans settled America in the era of the Renaissance, a time when human learning was expected by many to replace the concern for divinity. Yet their New World descendants carried on religious mission. Then Americans founded the United States in the era of their own Enlightenment. In this period leaders encouraged religion both public and private. The age of science flourished as Americans took to technology with passion, but they have also shown regard for the limits of science and kept alive the questions of supernature. To their critics, the generally prosperous Americans looked materialistic, yet never before and nowhere else in history did a people favor so many spiritual options as did they. For five hundred years prophets of both despair and hope foresaw a coming secular age, yet the majority of Americans found reasons to convince themselves that they were a religious people in a nation "under God."

Their long pilgrimage may end one day. In some undated future, Americans may wander across a horizon whose detail few can picture, there and then to stop their search. The last of their dying gods and dwindling groups may go. But it is more likely that the people's passion to make sense of things and to find company with others who share their visions will prevail into indefinite tomorrows. Citizens will no doubt continue to express their hunger for wholeness in a fragmented society, will look for simplicity in an ever more complex world, will find appropriate paths for their sojourns in a world of mazes — unless and until, one day, America itself no longer exists and its pilgrims disappear. Or, beyond that time — until one day consuming fire comes, or a new ice age descends; until nothing survives except remains of the trails on which people once undertook their journey; until the story ends as it began, and at last there are no human actors.

But if the actors remain, and remain somehow free, their dreams will prod them on to more restless pilgrimages.

SUGGESTED READING

A BOOK OF THIS SORT NECESSARILY DRAWS UPON THE WORK OF COUNT-less historians, living and dead, whose researches are issued in monographs too numerous to cite. Many years of a scholar's career may have gone into a specialized study whose findings are reflected in two or three lines here. Through thirty years of study and teaching, one accumulates in files, class notes, and the recesses of personal memory innumerable insights, theses, and data. To engage in archaeological digging through these notes and memories to acknowledge all indebtedness would be impossible. To publish even partial results would alter the size, scope, intention, and genre of this work. I hope I have done justice to some of these historians while expending part of my own vocation on specific studies that might also be of aid to others in their generalizing moments. I also hope that colleagues will see in this book an effort to enlarge the cohort of readers in the field in which we pursue our mutual labors.

The reading list that follows does permit explicit recognition of some resources. I have compiled the following as suggestions for further reading. Many of these books include excellent bibliographies. In addition to these works, I recommend that readers become acquainted with Sydney E. Ahlstrom, *A Religious History of the American People* (New Haven: Yale University Press, 1972; Garden City, N.Y.: Doubleday, 1975), the most expansive and successful attempt to tell the story of American religion. Its bibliographies are well organized and will be of special help.

I. THE FIRST MIGRANTS

Ake Hultkrantz in *The Religions of the American Indians* (Berkeley: University of California Press, 1979) and in *Belief and Worship in Native North America* (Syracuse: Syracuse University Press, 1981) expertly outlines meanings of native American religions. Walter Krickeberg, Hermann Trimborn, Werner Muller, and Otto Zerries offer specialties in *Pre-Columbian American Religions* (New York: Holt, Rinehart & Winston, 1969). Highly speculative and controversial is the work of Peter Farb, *Man's Rise to Civilization,* 2d ed. (New York: Dutton, 1978), a lively spinning-out of cultural-evolutionary themes. For a convenient summary, see Alvin M. Josephy, Jr., *The Indian Heritage of America* (New York: Knopf, 1968; there have been other printings by other publishers). It has won a following as a popular work because of its respect for Indian religion.

2. A CROWNED CROSS

Yitzhak Baer, *A History of the Jews in Christian Spain,* (Philadelphia: Jewish Publication Society of America, two volumes 1961, 1966), and W. Montgomery Watt, *A History of Islamic Spain* (Edinburgh: Edinburgh University Press), depict the backgrounds of non-Catholic Spain. Also see John H. Elliott, *Imperial Spain, 1469–1716* (New York: St. Martin, 1963). The favored biography of Columbus remains Samuel Eliot Morison, *Admiral of the Ocean Sea: A Life of Christopher Columbus,* 2 vols. (Boston: Little, Brown, 1942). We lack a good modern biography of Isabella, but William Thomas Walsh, *Isabella of Spain: The Last Crusader* (New York: Robert M. McBride, 1930), includes helpful accents. I cannot resist pointing to a young person's history: Melveena McKendrick, *Ferdinand and Isabella* (New York: American Heritage Horizon Caravel Books, 1968), for which John H. Elliott was a consultant and which is admirably illustrated.

3. THE CONQUEROR VERSUS THE MISSIONARY

There have been a number of editions of Cabeza de Vaca's *Relación,* including *The Narrative of Alvar Núñez Cabeza de Vaca,* translated by Fanny Bandelier (Barre, Mass.: Imprint Society, 1972), but one can get the flavor from a faithful tracing of it in John Upton Terrell, *Journey into Darkness: Cabeza de Vaca's Expedition Across North America, 1528–36* (London: Jarrolds, 1964). A. Grove Day, *Coronado's Quest: The Discovery of the Southwestern States* (Berkeley: University of California Press, 1942) has been a standard work on its subject. While there are eccentric features to

Henry Raup Wagner and Helen Rand Parish's biography *The Life and Writings of Bartolemé de Las Casas* (Albuquerque: University of New Mexico Press, 1967), the book presents useful information. A scholarly industry has grown up around Las Casas; it is well introduced in Juan Friede and Benjamin Keen, eds., *Bartolomé de Las Casas in History: Toward an Understanding of the Man and His Work* (De Kalb: Northern Illinois University Press, 1971).

4. HOLY WARS AND SACRED PIRACIES

For an introduction to the complex story of Florida, see the first three chapters and the bibliographies in Michael V. Gannon, *The Cross in the Sand: The Early Catholic Church in Florida 1513–1870* (Gainesville: University of Florida Press, 1965). J. H. Elliott, *The Old World and the New: 1492–1650* (London: Cambridge University Press, 1970), surveys many themes of intercontinental contact. Readers will find delight in Samuel Eliot Morison, *The European Discovery of America: The Northern Voyages* (New York: Oxford University Press, 1971), which also throws light on French adventures reported on in chapter 3. They will profit as much from Morison's comparable volume subtitled *The Southern Voyages* (1974), which offers background to some material in chapter 2. On John Foxe, see J. F. Mozley, *John Foxe and His Book* (London: SPCK, 1940). I have profited from biographies such as Robert Lacey's *Sir Walter Raleigh* (London: Weidenfeld & Nicolson, 1973) and *Sir Francis Drake* (London: Martin Secker & Warburg, 1972), as will readers with tastes for high-sea adventures.

5. ESTABLISHING COLONIES

For background on the English, see A. L. Rowse, *The Elizabethans and America* (New York: Harper & Bros., 1959). On Virginia, readers will find useful Warren M. Billings, ed., *The Old Dominion in the Seventeenth Century: A Documentary History of Virginia, 1609–1689* (Chapel Hill: University of North Carolina Press, 1975); and an entertaining volume is Philip L. Barbour, *The Three Worlds of Captain John Smith* (Boston: Houghton Mifflin, 1964).

The literature on New England is overwhelmingly plentiful, and one must select. Illustrated and salted with documents on Plymouth is the short book by Leonard W. Cowie, *The Pilgrim Fathers* (New York: Putnam, 1972). One would do well to seek out reprints of portions or the whole of William Bradford's classic *Of Plymouth Plantation*, though none have been in print recently. Anything pertinent by Perry Miller will inform students of the Puritan world, including two volumes coedited by him and Thomas H. Johnson: *The Puritans* (New York: Harper & Row, 1963), a source book; or, for dense and condensed treatments of main theological themes, *Errand into the Wilderness* (Cambridge: Harvard University Press, 1956). Readers will also profit from Edmund S. Morgan, *Visible Saints: The History of a Puritan Idea* (New York: New York University Press, 1963), or his remarkable biography *The Puritan Dilemma: The Story of John Winthrop* (Boston: Little, Brown, 1958).

On New Netherland religion, George L. Smith, *Religion and Trade in New Netherland: Dutch Origins and American Development* (Ithaca, N.Y.: Cornell University Press, 1973) stands out, while a general version is told by Henri and Barbara van der Zee in *A Sweet and Alien Land: The Story of Dutch New York* (New York: Viking, 1978).

6. PILGRIMAGES OF DISSENT

Edmund S. Morgan, *Roger Williams: The Church and the State* (New York: Harcourt, Brace & World, 1967) is one of the better studies of its subject, while Emery Battis, *Saints and Sectaries: Anne Hutchinson and the Antinomian Controversy in the Massachusetts Bay Colony* (Chapel Hill: University of North Carolina Press, 1962) fleshes out the story of Mrs. Hutchinson. Early Maryland history has been neglected, but see Matthew P. Andrews, *The Founding of Maryland: Province and State* (Baltimore: Williams & Wilkins, 1933). On Penn and Pennsylvania, see Edwin B. Bronner, *William Penn's "Holy Experiment": The Founding of Pennsylvania 1681–1701* (Philadelphia: Temple University Press, 1962).

7. THE END OF THE CATHOLIC MISSIONARY ROAD

A general survey of Catholic missions in colonial America appears in John Tracy Ellis, *Catholics in Colonial America* (Baltimore: Helicon, 1965). For lives of three major figures in this chapter, see Herbert E. Bolton, *Rim of Christendom: A Biography of Eusebio Francisco Kino, Pacific Coast Pioneer* (New York: Macmillan, 1936); Maynard J. Geiger, *The Life and Times of Fray Juníperro Serra* (Richmond: William Byrd Press, 1959); and Joseph P. Donnelly, *Jacques Marquette, 1637–1675* (Chicago: Loyola University Press, 1968).

8. A MATTER OF CHOICE

The literature on the Great Awakening is mountainous; a good selection of documents and a bibliography appear in Alan Heimert and Perry Miller, eds., *The Great Awakening* (Indianapolis: Bobbs-Merrill, 1967). Richard F. Lovelace has made his subject accessible in *The American Pietism of Cotton Mather: Origins of American Evangelicalism* (Grand Rapids, Mich.: Eerdmans, 1979). No figure in American religion has inspired more attention than Jonathan Edwards, and Yale University Press is publishing his works. A nontechnical, old-fashioned biography that is still worth reading is Ola Elizabeth Winslow, *Jonathan Edwards 1703–1758* (New York: Macmillan, 1940). See also Clarence H. Faust and Thomas H. Johnson, eds., *Jonathan Edwards: Representative Selections* (New York: Hill & Wang, 1962). Stuart C. Henry, *George Whitefield: Wayfaring Witness* (Nashville: Abingdon, 1957), is a modest introduction to Whitefield. For a localized story, see C. C. Goen, *Revivalism and Separatism in New England 1740–1800* (New Haven: Yale University Press, 1962). A section of E. Clifford Nelson, ed., *The Lutherans in North America* (Philadelphia: Fortress, 1975), describes the world of Mühlenberg, whose journals are also available from the same publisher. See also George William Pilcher, *Samuel Davies: Apostle of Dissent in Colonial Virginia* (Knoxville: University of Tennessee Press, 1971).

9. THREE REVOLUTIONS

Charles W. Akers, *Called unto Liberty: A Life of Jonathan Mayhew 1720–1766* (Cambridge: Harvard University Press, 1964), opens the issue of prerevolutionary-era ideology, which is well developed in Bernard Bailyn, *The Ideological Origins of the American Revolution* (Cambridge: Harvard University Press, 1967). A pioneer study of clerical attitudes remains useful: Alice M. Baldwin, *The New England Clergy and the American Revolution* (New York: Frederick Ungar, 1928). Giving more accent to backwoods revivalist preachers is the long and not always easy to follow Alan Heimert, *Religion and the American Mind: From the Great Awakening to the Revolution* (Cambridge: Harvard University Press, 1966). More succinct and in its own way more sophisticated about the evangelical clergy is Nathan O. Hatch, *The Sacred Cause of Liberty: Republican Thought and the Millennium in Revolutionary New England* (New Haven: Yale University Press, 1977). A beginning on Witherspoon is Martha Lou Lemmon Stohlmann, *John Witherspoon: Parson, Politician, Patriot* (Philadelphia: Westminster, 1976).

The best story of anti-Catholicism in this period is by Sister Mary Augustine Ray, *American Opinion of Roman Catholicism in the Eighteenth Century* (New York: Columbia University Press, 1936). Thomas O'Brien Hanley has written *Charles Carroll of Carrollton: The Making of a Revolutionary Gentleman* (Washington, D.C.: Catholic University Press, 1970); see also Charles H. Metzger, *Catholics and the American Revolution: A Study in Religious Climate* (Chicago: Loyola University Press, 1962).

The standard work on colonial Judaism is Jacob Rader Marcus, *Early American Jewry* (Philadelphia: Jewish Publication Society of America, 5721/1961). The peace churches receive attention in Peter Brock, *Pacifism in the United States: From the Colonial Era to the First World War* (Princeton, N.J.: Princeton University Press, 1968). On the Baptists, see William C. McLoughlin, *Isaac Backus and the American Pietistic Tradition* (Boston: Little, Brown, 1967).

The best book on the Enlightenment is Henry F. May, *The Enlightenment in America* (New York: Oxford University Press, 1976); on the religion of the Republic, see Sidney E. Mead's writings, notably *The Lively Experiment: The Shaping of Christianity in America* (New York: Harper & Row, 1963). On four founders: Paul W. Conner, *Poor Richard's Politics: Benjamin Franklin and His New American Order* (New York: Oxford University Press, 1965); Paul F. Boller, Jr., *George Washington and Religion* (Dallas: Southern Methodist University Press, 1963); Robert M. Healey, *Jefferson on Religion in Public Education* (New Haven: Yale University Press, 1962); Ralph Ketcham, *James Madison: A Biography* (New York: Macmillan, 1971).

10. INTO THE WEST AND THE WORLD

To catch the flavor of the Second Great Awakening in the West, see John B. Boles, *The Great Revival 1787–1815* (Lexington: University of Kentucky Press, 1972). L. C. Rudolph, *Francis Asbury* (Nashville: Abingdon, 1966), follows the circuit rider's trail. The Indian mission is the subject of Robert F. Berkhofer, Jr., *Salvation and the Savage: An Analysis of Protestant Missions and American Indian Response, 1787–1862* (Lexington: University of Kentucky Press, 1965). A popular, not a scholarly, story of the Oregon venture is Cecil P. Dryden, *Give All to Oregon!: Missionary Pioneers of the Far West* (New York: Hastings House, 1968).

On New England losses before the mission, see John A. Andrews III, *Rebuilding the Christian Commonwealth: New England Congregationalists and Foreign Missions, 1800–1830* (Lexington: University of Kentucky Press, 1976). I have also made use of a harder-to-find dissertation published by Harvard University Press (Cambridge, 1969): Clifton Jackson Phillips, *Protestant America and the Pagan World: The First Half Century of the American Board of Commissioners for Foreign Missions, 1810–1860.*

11. BEYOND EXISTING BOUNDS

For the story of the Shakers, see Edward Deming Andrews, *The People Called Shakers: A Search for the Perfect Society* (New York: Dover, 1963), and for biographical details of Noyes, do not overlook Robert David Thomas, *The Man Who Would Be Perfect: John Humphrey Noyes and the Utopian Impulse* (Philadelphia: University of Pennsylvania Press, 1977). A standard history of the Disciples of Christ is Lester G. McAllister and William E. Tucker, *Journey in Faith: A History of the Christian Church (Disciples of Christ)* (Saint Louis: Bethany, 1975). Donna Hill, *Joseph Smith: The First Mormon* (Garden City, N.Y.: Doubleday, 1977), is an acceptable-to-insiders biography of Smith, most of whose biographies by non-Mormons are controversial among Mormons. See also the flawed but engaging account by Stanley P. Hirshson, *The Lion of the Lord: A Biography of Brigham Young* (New York: Knopf, 1969).

For lives of Emerson, see Ralph L. Rusk, *The Life of Ralph Waldo Emerson* (New York: Scribner, 1949), and Gay Wilson Allen, *Waldo Emerson* (New York: Viking, 1981). A study of the religion of Thoreau is William J. Wolf, *Thoreau: Mystic, Prophet, Ecologist* (Philadelphia: United Church Press, 1974). Wolf also wrote *The Almost Chosen People: A Study of the Religion of Abraham Lincoln* (Garden City, N.Y.: Doubleday, 1959). For those who wish to pursue the Brownson trail, see Thomas R. Ryan, *Orestes A. Brownson: A Definitive Biography* (Huntington, Ind.: Our Sunday Visitor, 1976).

12. A CENTURY OF EXCLUSION

Janet Whitney, *John Woolman: American Quaker* (Boston: Little, Brown, 1942), remains a worthwhile biographical source. See Stuart C. Henry, *Unvanquished Puritan: A Portrait of Lyman Beecher* (Grand Rapids, Mich.: Eerdmans, 1973), for the life of that cleric. Carol V. R. George, *Segregated Sabbaths: Richard Allen and the Rise of Independent Black Churches, 1760–1840* (New York: Oxford University Press, 1973), is an excellent treatment of Allen's life. On slave religion, see Eugene D. Genovese, *Roll, Jordan, Roll: The World the Slaves Made* (New York: Pantheon, 1974), and Albert J. Raboteau, *Slave Religion: The "Invisible Institution" in the Antebellum South* (New York: Oxford University Press, 1978). Gerda Lerner, *The Grimké Sisters from South Carolina: Rebels against Slavery* (Boston: Houghton Mifflin, 1967), is an important treatment.

For southern white Protestant attitudes, H. Shelton Smith, *In His Image, But . . . : Racism in Southern Religion, 1780–1910* (New Haven: Yale University Press, 1972), is valuable. Booker T. Washington, *Up from Slavery* (New York: Dell, 1965), represents Washington's own outlook; W. E. Burghardt Du Bois, *The Souls of Black Folk: Essays and Sketches* (Greenwich, Conn.: Fawcett, 1961), is a reprint of a vintage book on turn-of-the-century black affairs. Edwin S. Redkey, *Black Exodus: Black Nationalist and Back-to-Africa Movements, 1890–1910* (New Haven: Yale University Press, 1969), includes the story of Henry M. Turner. The story of the Chinese in San Francisco is from Corinne K. Hoexter, *From Canton to California: The Epic of Chinese Immigration* (New York: Four Winds, 1976). Paul Bailey, *Wovoka, The Indian Messiah* (Los Angeles: Western Lore Press, 1957), is an updating of James Mooney's classic account of Wovoka.

13. ADAPTING TO AMERICA

The standard account of nativism is Ray Allen Billington, *The Protestant Crusade, 1800–1860: A Study of the Origins of American Nativism* (Chicago: Quadrangle, 1964), but see also John Higham, *Strangers in the Land: Patterns of American Nativism, 1860–1925* (New York: Atheneum, 1975).

There are several major laudatory biographies of James Cardinal Gibbons, including John Tracy Ellis, *The Life of James Cardinal Gibbons: Archbishop of Baltimore, 1834–1921,* 2 vols. (Milwaukee: Bruce, 1952). More of the Catholic story is unfolded in: Robert D. Cross, *The Emergence of Liberal Catholicism in America* (Chicago: Quadrangle, 1968); Thomas T. McAvoy, *The Americanist Heresy in Roman Catholicism, 1895–1900* (Notre Dame, Ind.: University of Notre Dame Press, 1963); and Dorothy Dohen, *Nationalism and American Catholicism* (New York: Sheed & Ward, 1967).

For the story of secular adaptation chiefly among New York Jews from Eastern Europe, see Irving Howe, *World of Our Fathers* (New York: Simon & Schuster, 1976). James G. Heller, *Isaac M. Wise: His Life, Work, and Thought* (New York: Union of American Hebrew Congregations, 1965), gives the flavor of the rabbi, while Moshe Davis, *The Emergence of Conservative Judaism: The Historical School in 19th Century America* (New York: Burning Bush Press, 1963), accounts for the background of Conservatism.

14. CRISES IN THE PROTESTANT EMPIRE

Essays in Thomas F. Glick, ed., *The Comparative Reception of Darwinism* (Austin: University of Texas Press, 1972), introduce some of the major themes of evolution. Jerry Wayne Brown, *The Rise of Biblical Criticism in America, 1800–1870* (Middletown, Conn.: Wesleyan University Press, 1969), covers the early years of the biblical critical controversy, which has been undertreated by historians in its subsequent phases. One can gain a sense of the ethos among liberals of the period from a fine book by William F. Hutchison, *The Modernist Impulse in American Protestantism* (Cambridge: Harvard University Press, 1976). On the new economic doctrines, see Richard Hofstadter, *Social Darwinism in American Thought* (Boston: Beacon, 1955). William G. McLoughlin, *The Meaning of Henry Ward Beecher: An Essay on the Shifting Values of Mid-Victorian America* (New York: Knopf, 1970) — one of numerous biographical treatments of Beecher — sets this clergyman into his times. On Moody, see James F. Findlay, Jr., *Dwight L. Moody: American Evangelist, 1837–1899* (Chicago: University of Chicago Press, 1969).

15. HEALING THE RESTLESS

The standard biography of the founder of modern Adventism accents healing; see Ronald L. Numbers, *Prophets of Health: A Study of Ellen G. White* (New York: Harper & Row, 1976). The approved biography of Mrs. Eddy by a church insider can serve most readers' purposes: Robert Peel, *Mary Baker Eddy,* 3 vols. (with differing subtitles; New York: Holt, Rinehart & Winston, 1966, 1971). See also Stephen Gottschalk, *The Emergence of Christian Science in American Religious Life* (Berkeley: University of California Press, 1973).

There are many editions of William James, *The Varieties of Religious Experience,* including the one I edited (Baltimore: Penguin, 1982). Still of interest is Ralph Barton Perry, *The Thought and Character of William James,* 2 vols. (brief version; New York: Harper Torchbooks, 1964). For the New Thought tradition, see Donald Meyer: *The Positive Thinkers: A Study of the American Quest for Health, Wealth, and Personal Power from Mary Baker Eddy to Norman Vincent Peale* (Garden City, N.Y.: Doubleday, 1965).

16. THE DREAM OF ONE KINGDOM

Josiah Strong, *Our Country* (Cambridge: Harvard University Press, Belknap Press, 1963) is fairly accessible. C. Howard Hopkins, *John R. Mott, 1865–1955: A Biography* (Grand Rapids, Mich.: Eerdmans, 1979) is a comprehensive treatment of its subject. We lack a critical biography of Walter Rauschenbusch; but see the admiring life by his student Dores Robinson Sharpe, *Walter Rauschenbusch* (New York: Macmillan, 1942). The literature on Bryan amply covers his religious sentiments; typically, note Paolo E. Coletta, *William Jennings Bryan,* 3 vols. (Lincoln: University of Nebraska Press, 1964, 1969).

Arthur Walworth, *Woodrow Wilson* (Boston: Houghton Mifflin, 1965) covers some of my themes; for the background, note John M. Mulder, *Woodrow Wilson: The Years of Preparation* (Princeton, N.J.: Princeton University Press, 1978). A slanted review of churchly support of war is Ray H. Abrams, *Preachers Present Arms: The Role of American Churches and Clergy . . .* (Scottdale, Penn.: Herald Press, 1969). The view of woman suffrage reflected in this narrative is corroborated in Alan P. Grimes, *The Puritan Ethic and Woman Suffrage* (New York: Oxford University Press, 1967).

17. A SEASON OF CONFLICTS

On Prohibition, see Joseph R. Gusfield, *Symbolic Crusade: Status Politics and the American Temperance Movement* (Urbana: University of Illinois Press, 1963). The best account of the rise of fundamentalism is George M. Marsden, *Fundamentalism and American Culture: The Shaping of Twentieth-Century Evangelicalism* (New York: Oxford University Press, 1980). Alfred M. Pierce, *Giant Against the Sky: The Life of Bishop Warren Akin Candler* (Nashville, Tenn.: Abingdon-Cokesbury, 1948), is a useful biography. The life of mainstream churches, especially in relation to labor and political ideology, is well detailed in Robert Moats Miller, *American Protestantism and Social Issues, 1919–1939* (Chapel Hill: University of North Carolina Press, 1961). See also Liston Pope, *Millhands and Preachers: A Study of Gastonia* (New Haven: Yale University Press, 1942).

On black religious life, see Elton C. Fax, *Garvey: The Story of a Pioneer Black Nationalist* (New York: Dodd, Mead, 1972), and Arthur H. Fauset,

Black Gods of the Metropolis: Negro Religious Cults of the Urban North (Philadelphia: University of Pennsylvania Press, 1971). A fine collection of essays is Hart M. Nelson, Raytha L. Yokely, and Anne K. Nelsen, eds., *The Black Church in America* (New York: Basic, 1971). On racism, see Thomas F. Gossett, *Race: The History of an Idea in America* (Dallas: Southern Methodist University Press, 1963); and on immigration, there is Lawrence B. Davis, *Immigrants, Baptists, and the Protestant Mind in America* (Urbana: University of Illinois Press, 1973).

The story of Zionism is elaborated in Melvin I. Urofsky, *American Zionism from Herzl to the Holocaust* (Garden City, N.Y.; Doubleday, 1975). Sheldon Marcus, *Father Coughlin: The Tumultuous Life of the Priest of the Little Flower* (Boston: Little, Brown, 1973), should be balanced with David J. O'Brien, *American Catholics and Social Reform: The New Deal Years* (New York: Oxford University Press, 1968). Robert Moats Miller's *American Protestantism*, cited above, tells more of the controversy over pacifism, as does Charles Chatfield, *For Peace and Justice: Pacifism in America, 1914–1941* (Knoxville: University of Tennessee Press, 1971).

18. THE AMERICAN WAYS OF LIFE

John Dewey, *A Common Faith* (New Haven: Yale University Press, 1934), introduces the theme of a single religion of democracy. For a biography, see George Dykhuizen, *The Life and Mind of John Dewey* (Carbondale: Southern Illinois University Press, 1973). The contemporary book that described Eisenhower's religion is William Lee Miller, *Piety along the Potomac: Notes on Politics and Morals in the Fifties* (Boston: Houghton Mifflin, 1964). A not-always-friendly biography of Billy Graham (it does account for his mid-fifties views of America, and therefore I cite it) is William G. McLoughlin, Jr., *Billy Graham: Revivalist in a Secular Age* (New York: Ronald, 1960).

Readers may wish to explore Reinhold Niebuhr's *The Irony of American History* (New York: Scribner, 1961). An appreciation of Spellman is Robert I. Gannon, *The Cardinal Spellman Story* (Garden City, N.Y.: Doubleday, 1962). See John Courtney Murray, *We Hold These Truths: Catholic Reflections on the American Proposition* (New York: Sheed & Ward, 1960), for Murray's views; and for his life, see Donald E. Pelotte, *John Courtney Murray: Theologian in Conflict* (New York: Paulist Press, 1975). Finally, for a description of religious trends in the times, there is Will Herberg, *Protestant-Catholic-Jew: An Essay in American Religious Sociology* (Garden City, N.Y.: Doubleday, 1955).

19. ALWAYS A HORIZON

The Maritain theme comes from Jacques Maritain, *Reflections on America* (New York: Scribner, 1958). The Merton literature is enormous; for his own rather romanticized account of his conversion, see Thomas Merton,

The Seven Storey Mountain (New York: Harcourt, Brace, Jovanovich, 1948, 1976). The Blue Lake story is based on Dabney Otis Collings, "Battle for Blue Lake — The Taos Indians Finally Regain Their Sacred Land," *The American West* 8, no. 5 (Sept. 1971): 32–37. A militant phrasing of Indian lore is Vine Deloria, Jr., *God Is Red* (New York: Grosset & Dunlap, 1973); more quiet are Joseph Epes Brown, *The Spiritual Legacy of the American Indian* (New York: Crossroad, 1982), and Ake Hultkrantz, *Belief and Worship in Native North America* (Syracuse, N.Y.: Syracuse University Press, 1981).

David L. Lewis, *King: A Biography* (Urbana: University of Illinois Press, 1978), and Peter Goldman, *The Death and Life of Malcolm X* (New York: Harper & Row, 1973), focus on these two leaders. James J. Gardiner and J. Deotis Roberts, Sr., edited a helpful work: *Quest for a Black Theology* (Philadelphia: Pilgrim, 1971). Glimpses of the Hispanic experience are in James Mencarelli and Steve Severin, *Protest: Red, Black, Brown Experience in America* (Grand Rapids, Mich.: Eerdmans, 1975).

For angles of vision on the Eastern or New Religions, see: Jacob Needleman, *The New Religions* (Garden City, N.Y.: Doubleday, 1970); Robert S. Ellwood, Jr., *Alternative Altars: Unconventional and Eastern Spirituality in America* (Chicago: University of Chicago Press, 1979); and Theodore Roszak, *The Making of a Counter Culture: Reflections on the Technocratic Society and Its Youthful Opposition* (Garden City, N.Y.: Doubleday, 1969).

20. NEW PATHS FOR OLD PILGRIMAGES

On Judaism, Jacob Neusner, *American Judaism: Adventure in Modernity* (Englewood Cliffs, N.J.: Prentice-Hall, 1972), and Nathan Glazer, *American Judaism,* 2d ed. (Chicago: University of Chicago Press, 1972), will be of aid. On Catholicism, the final chapters of James Hennesey, *American Catholics: A History of the Roman Catholic Community in the United States* (New York: Oxford University Press, 1981), present the issues, and their footnotes introduce readers to further readings.

Richard Quebedeaux, *The New Charismatics: The Origins, Development, and Significance of Neo-Pentecostalism* (Garden City, N.Y.: Doubleday, 1976), provides some of the flavor of the charismatic movement. The literature on the new evangelicalism is introduced in David F. Wells and John D. Woodbridge, eds., *The Evangelicals: What They Believe, Who They Are, How They are Changing* (Nashville, Tenn.: Abingdon, 1975). A "map" of mainline, civil, and other religious phenomena referred to here, appears (along with references that give access to more literature) in Martin E. Marty, *A Nation of Behavers* (Chicago: University of Chicago Press, 1976).

INDEX

Italicized page numbers indicate illustrations.

Mideast policy, 394, 462; and mysticism, 463.
See also Jews
Judaism as a Civilization (Kaplan), 395

kachinas, 6
Kahn, Herman, 453
Kane, Thomas L., 206
Kant, Immanuel, 209
Kaplan, Mordecai, 395–396; *Judaism as a Civilization*, 395
Keane, John J., 279, 281–284
Kellogg, John, 323
Kennan, George, 415
Kennedy, John F., 420, 442, 470, 475
Kennedy, Robert F., 439, 442, 449
Kenrick, Francis P., 275
Keppler, Joseph: "The Religious Vanity Fair," 270
Kicking Bear, 266
Kieft, Willem, 67–68, 82, 100
Kimball, Heber C., 202, 207
King, Coretta Scott, 441, 442
King, Martin Luther, Jr., 441–444, 445, 446, 449, 460
Kingdom of God, 187, 474
Kino, Eusebio, 92–96, 179; *Favores celestiales*, 94, 96
Klein, Felix, 284
Knights of Labor, 278–279
Knights of Pythias, 411
Know-Nothings, 274
Kohler, Kaufman, 292
Kosciuscko, Thaddeus, 146
Krishna Consciousness, 455, 468
Ku Klux Klan, 256, 390, 392–393, 395, 397
Kulturkampf, 272

labor movement in America, 277, 278, 310, 317, 447, 448–450
La Causa, 447, 449, 450
Lafayette, Marquis de, 143
Laing, R. D., 454
Lalemant, Jérôme, *90,* 104
Lamanites, 201
Lamarck, Chevalier de, 301, 303
Lane, Sir Ralph, 48
Lansing, Robert, 394, 395
La Salle, Sieur de, 103–104
Las Casas, Bartolomé de, 22, *24,* 32–35; *Brief Relation of the Destruction of the Indies,* 33; *Historia de las Indias,* 33, 35; *Apologética Historia,* 34
Late Great Planet Earth (Lindsey), *The,* 468
Latter-day Saints. *See* Church of Jesus Christ of Latter-day Saints
Laudonnière, René de, 43
LaVey, Anton Szandor, 456
Lay, Benjamin, 229
League of Nations, 364
LeBlanc, George, 398
Lee, Ann ("Mother Ann"), 191–192, 200, 249
Lee, Daniel, 177
Lee, Jason, 177–178
Lee, John D., 207
Leeser, Isaac, 286–290, 292
Lemke, William, 398
Lemoyne, Pierre (Sieur d'Iberville), 104
Leo X (pope), 36
Leo XIII (pope), 280, 282–285; *Rerum novarum,* 280; *Testem Benovelentiae,* 285
Lettera (Dati), *10*
Lewis and Clark expedition, 176–177
Liberator, 245, 251
Liebman, Joshua Loth, 404; *Peace of Mind,* 404
Life and Morals of Jesus of Nazareth (Jefferson), *The,* 161
Life of Father Hecker, 284

Lilienthal, Max, 288
Lincoln, Abraham, 174, 219, 220–224, 277, 414, 416, 475
Lindsell, Harold, 471
Lindsey, Hal: *The Late Great Planet Earth,* 468
Link, Henry C.: *The Return to Religion,* 403
Lippmann, Walter, 357
Living Room, The, 467
Locke, John, 133, 159
Lodge, Jordan, 183
Log College Presbyterianism, 125–126
Longfellow, Henry Wadsworth, 321
Lopez, Aaron, 147
Louis XIV (king of France), 102, 104
Louis XV (king of France), 104
Louis XVI (king of France), 143
Louisiana Purchase, 104
Lovejoy, Elijah P., 235
Lowell, A. Lawrence, 393
Loyola, Saint Ignatius of, 93, 146
Lucerne Memorial, 282
Luckmann, Thomas, 475
Luther, Martin, 37–38, 41, 210; attacked by Henry VIII, 42; influence of, in Virginia, 125; 500th birthday of, 467
Lutheranism, 41, 69–70, 85–86, 125, 367–368; in colonial America, 74, 148; in Midwest, 170; after World War II, 382
Lyford, John, 61

Macartney, Clarence, 380
McCormick, Cyrus, 309, 314
McCormick, Vincent, 418
McDonnell, Donald, 449
McGlynn, Edward, 350
McGready, James, 175
Machen, J. Gresham, 379
McIntire, Carl, 411
McKinley, William, 282, 316
McLaughlin, "White Hair," 267
McQuaid, Bernard, 279, 280
McRoberts, Archibald, 123
Madison, James, 146, 155, 158, 162–166; *Memorial and Remonstrance against Religious Assessment,* 163; *Federalist* papers, 164
Magnalia Christi Americana (C. Mather), 110
Maharaj Ji, 456
Maharishi Mahesh Yogi, 455
Maimonides College, 287
Makemie, Francis, 124
Making of a Counter Culture (Roszak), *The,* 454
Malcolm X, 444–448; *Autobiography,* 444
Maldonado, Alonso de, 33
manifest destiny, 302
Mann, Horace, 321
Manning, James, 151, 280
Man Nobody Knows (Barton), *The,* 385–386
Manual of the Mother Church (M. B. Eddy), 330
Maritain, Jacques, 431, 436
Marquette, Jacques, 92, 100–103
Martineau, Harriet, 216, 245, 248
Marty, Martin (abbot and bishop), 438
Marx, Karl, 278, 378, 433
Mary (mother of Jesus), 28, 99, 102
Mary I (Mary Tudor; queen of England), 45, 46, 76, 88
Maryland colony, 66, 82–86
Mason, John, 64
Masons (Freemasons), 165, 216, 278
Massachusetts Bay colony, 58, 62–65, 76, 78–79, 86
Massasoit, 60
Mather, Cotton, 109, 110; *Magnalia Christi Americana,* 110; *The Negro Christianized,* 111
Mather, Richard, 109
Mathews, Shailer, 370–371
Mayflower (ship), 60, 150